Black Hills/
White Justice

'Black Hills White Justice'

▼▼▼▼▼▼▼

THE SIOUX NATION VERSUS THE UNITED STATES, 1775 TO THE PRESENT

▼

Edward Lazarus

HarperCollins*Publishers*

FIRST EDITION

Designed by Patricia G. Dunbar

Library of Congress Cataloging-in-Publication Data

Lazarus, Edward.
    Black Hills/white justice : the Sioux nation versus the United States : 1775 to the present / Edward Lazarus. — 1st ed.
       p.   cm.
    Includes bibliographical references (p.   ) and index.
    ISBN 0-06-016557-X
    1. Dakota Indians—Government relations. 2. Dakota Indians—Claims. 3. Dakota Indians—Land tenure. 4. Land tenure—Black Hills (S.D. and Wyo.) I. Title.
E99.D1L37   1991
978.3'9004975—dc20   90-56383

91 92 93 94 95 CC/RRD 10 9 8 7 6 5 4 3 2 1

To My
Mother and Father

▼ ▼ ▼ ▼ ▼

CONTENTS

Photographs appear following page 232.

▼ ▼ ▼ ▼ ▼

Maps

▼ ▼ ▼ ▼ ▼

PREFACE

I CANNOT REMEMBER how old I was when I first heard about the Black Hills claim, but I know that my legal education started early. By the time I turned ten, the Great Sioux Case, as my brother and I used to call it, had become a topic eagerly awaited at the family dinner table. Later, when I was in high school, I would sit in the back row at the Court of Claims whenever the case was called for oral argument.

Four generations of Sioux children have grown up with the Black Hills claim. So did I. My father was Sioux counsel in the claim from before I was born until I had nearly graduated from college, more than twenty-three years in all.

I alert the reader to this special relationship to my subject because my father's role in the Black Hills litigation is today a source of anger and resentment for many Sioux. Part of this book tells how that happened. I do not claim to have written this section without passion. I do claim to have written it honestly—as years of research and a lifetime of memory compelled me to write it.

About my father and about every other aspect of the claim, I have done my very best to cleave fact from myth and to give those facts voice.

ACKNOWLEDGMENTS

I WROTE THIS BOOK, on and off, over the course of nine years. During that time I accumulated more debts of gratitude and received more support and assistance from both individuals and institutions than I can even recall, much less acknowledge. To certain people and places, however, I owe special thanks.

For the first two years of my writing, the Library of Congress furnished me with an office, virtually infinite resources, and an intellectual home. Later, the Yale Law School, which granted me a research fellowship, served the same indispensable functions. The staffs of the National Archives, the I.D. Weeks Library at the University of South Dakota, Vermillion, the Nebraska Historical Society, and the United States Department of Justice all helped me to locate the primary source material from which this book is mainly composed.

I would never have had the courage, at the age of twenty-two, to start this project had it not been for the encouragement and counsel of my college mentor, Professor Donald Kagan. Emily Buss, Victoria Nuland, Robert Kagan, Jonathan Schwartz, and my brother, Andrew, all read significant parts of the manuscript and offered many insightful suggestions. Ted Solotaroff, my wise, discerning, persuasive, yet gentle editor at HarperCollins, improved this book at every turn. Wendy Wolf, who took over from Ted on his retirement, did a wonderful job guiding the project (and me) to publication. My copy editor Janet Byrne, saved me from many errors, large and small. Attorneys Chris Goff and Joe Onek ably guided me through some legal thickets. My agents, Glen Hartley and Lynn Chu, in addition to offering welcome friendship and support, handled my business affairs brilliantly. Debbie Rizzo typed and retyped countless illegible drafts of many chapters.

Anthony Weller read and commented on every page of this book, in some cases two or three times over. From the outset, he tutored me in his craft of writing and, with enormous care and affection, helped me make that craft my own. For his countless constructive criticisms, for his sustaining friendship, I am inexpressibly grateful.

I could never have finished this project without the love and encouragement of my family. And about my father's role in the writing of this book, I cannot say enough. He fielded thousands of questions on a thousand different days. He never complained when I refused to show him the manuscript. He let me write his story as I independently perceived it. All this was a gift of faith and love that I shall remember for the rest of my life.

▼ ▼ ▼ ▼ ▼

INTRODUCTION

WHEN HELEN PETERSON was a young girl growing up in the far southwest corner of the Pine Ridge Sioux Reservation, her grandmother would tell her stories about the distant Black Hills and the ancient days when the Hills and all the land around them belonged to the Sioux. She would tell how the white men came from the east and took the Hills because they were filled with gold—more gold than any other place on earth—and how from that time forth the white men lived off the richness of the Hills while the Indians grew poorer. And she would tell Helen that for as long as she could remember the Indians had tried to get something for the lands that the United States had taken, but that they were still waiting. Someday, the old woman would say, someday the government would pay for the Hills it had stolen.

Every child on the eight Sioux reservations scattered across the Dakotas knew the long story of defeat and desolation as the white man conquered the plains and all the peoples on them. That history was their heritage. Helen's great grandmother, a fullblood Cheyenne (friendly neighbors of the Sioux), had been camped with Chief Black Kettle's band along the Washita River on the day in 1868 that George Armstrong Custer's 7th Cavalry attacked, establishing the boy general as a hero of the Indian wars. Helen's grandmother had joined the messianic Ghost Dance religion that had swept through Sioux country in the late 1880s until the U.S. Army slaughtered Big Foot's band of believers at Wounded Knee, ending the Indians' last hope that their lives would return to the way they had been before the whites swarmed over their land.

Helen came of age in the 1920s, a full generation after the last battle between the Sioux and the United States. Her world was formed by the conquest. Helen's father was white; so were many of her childhood neighbors. She grew up amid farms, churches, log cabins, and corrals, where fifty years before had stood only open prairie and millions of buffalo.

Helen attended the local day school that the whites had established to prepare Indians for life in their world. In school, she learned nothing of her ancestral traditions, all of which the government had outlawed or otherwise proscribed. For Helen, as for all Indian children in Sioux country, mixed blood or full, the white world penetrated virtually every aspect of personal and communal life. Their names, language, occupations, laws, religious beliefs, and social structures all, to some degree, reflected a forced accommodation to the culture that had replaced their vanished nomadic life.

The Sioux lived at the jarring intersection of two worlds: the tribal world of a people stripped bare of land and livelihood; and the world of their conquerors, a people by turns hostile and paternal, who assigned to itself a destiny more noble than mere hegemony, but whose lust for expansion often superseded its claims to higher moral standing.

Helen would spend her life with a foot planted in both worlds. At different times, she worked for Indian groups promoting tribal unity and autonomy as well as for the Bureau of Indian Affairs, which in the mid-1930s began hiring natives for positions of authority. Helen's career shaping Indian policy began in the summer of 1953. After graduation from Chadron State Teachers College, and several years of public service in Colorado, Helen moved to Washington, D.C., to serve as Executive Director for the National Congress of American Indians, the leading pan-Indian political organization.

Helen's exposure to the institutions of white government soon qualified her as one of only a few Indians upon whom tribal leaders could rely to interpret the often inscrutable ways of a still alien legal and political system. Eventually, in the fall of 1956, Helen's own tribe, the Sioux, asked her to evaluate the competence of its lawyer, Ralph Case, who since 1921 had handled every one of its extensive legal claims against the United States.

In the 1920s, Case had filed twenty-four separate lawsuits against the government demanding compensation for the taking of Sioux treaty lands, for the misappropriation of tribal funds, and for the decades of relentless mistreatment that had followed the tribe's confinement to diminished reservations. By 1956, he and his roughly 40,000 clients had lost irretrievably every claim but one. The last, by far the most important of all, was the famous Black Hills claim, which had kept alive in the memories of three generations of Sioux the spiritual and physical richness of their lost plains empire. At one time, the Sioux had asked for almost $1 billion in retroactive payment for the taking of the densely wooded slopes, lush plateaus, and sharp granite spires of their cherished Hills.

The Black Hills claim was the largest in the history of the United States, but in the Court of Claims and then in the Indian Claims Commission, and yet again in the Court of Claims, the Sioux had lost and were on the verge of ending up with nothing. In November 1956, the Court of Claims had affirmed an Indian Claims Commission decision which two years earlier had declared that the U.S. had paid the Sioux in full for the seizure of the Black Hills in February 1877. According to the court, seventy years of government benefit payments to the dependent tribe balanced out the wrongs of conquest. Case prepared to appeal the claim to the Supreme Court, and, undaunted, he confidently predicted success. But even the untutored Sioux recognized the danger of this step. Should the Supreme Court refuse to hear the claim, or should it find against the Sioux, as had every court in which Case had appeared, the Indians would have exhausted their last recourse.

Case had survived as Sioux counsel, despite his dismal record, largely through the strength of friendship. Long years of familiarity, and a shared history of hope for and disappointment over the course of the tribe's legal claims, had elevated Case from lawyer to tribal wise man and confidant. Many Sioux, though, had started to question the adequacy of Case's representation, especially after the Indian Claims Commission ruled against them in 1954.

With the Supreme Court's filing deadline about to pass, thirty years of trust, blindly given, succumbed to the widespread fear of finally and unreviewably losing the claim that the Sioux for so long had hoped would make them rich again. On the Pine Ridge Reservation, members of the tribal council called upon Helen Peterson to confirm their intuition, too often suppressed or ignored, that Case had failed them. That confirmation quickly came and Sioux leaders rushed east to Washington to prevent Case from filing an appeal and to salvage their last chance that the United States might one day hold itself accountable for the history of its westward expansion.

They convened in a small conference room at the Bureau of Indian Affairs: Ralph Case and Helen Peterson; Bob Burnette, the outspoken chairman of the Rosebud Sioux Tribe; J. Dan Howard, chairman of the Standing Rock Sioux; and a few other Sioux leaders, in addition to several bureau officials.

Looking across at Case's lined and jowly face as she prepared to ask for his resignation, Helen's mind drifted back to her grandmother's stories. The sadness and the passion with which the old woman had tended the Black Hills flame was alive in the conference room. That flame had burned for as long as the Sioux had been in the Hills, through all the years when cruelty, good intentions, and misunderstanding mixed as the whites pushed across the plains, and through all the years when a dispossessed people sought justice for the taking of their land.

This book tells that Black Hills history. It tells of an aboriginal people's movement to a new homeland on the great plains, and of how a burgeoning nation from the east conquered that people and took its land; it tells of a great legal battle—fought mainly by white men in the white man's courts—as the conquered sued the conqueror over the sins of empire. And it tells of an impoverished people seeking to reclaim their heritage through the sometimes tender conscience of the nation that robbed them of their way of life.

The story begins many years before Helen Peterson's grandmother was even born, in the spring of 1775—a fateful year not only for the Sioux but for the upstart colonists who would become their masters.

▼▼▼▼▼

Maps

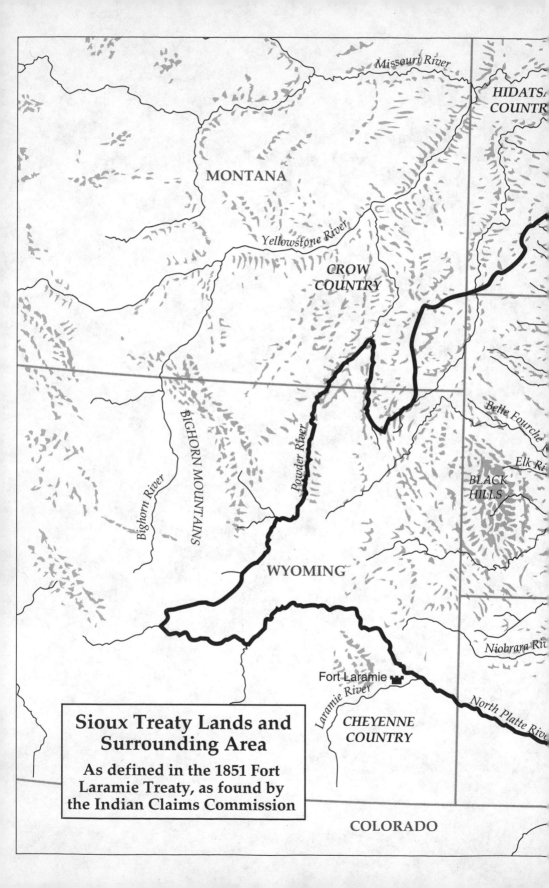

Sioux Treaty Lands and Surrounding Area

As defined in the 1851 Fort Laramie Treaty, as found by the Indian Claims Commission

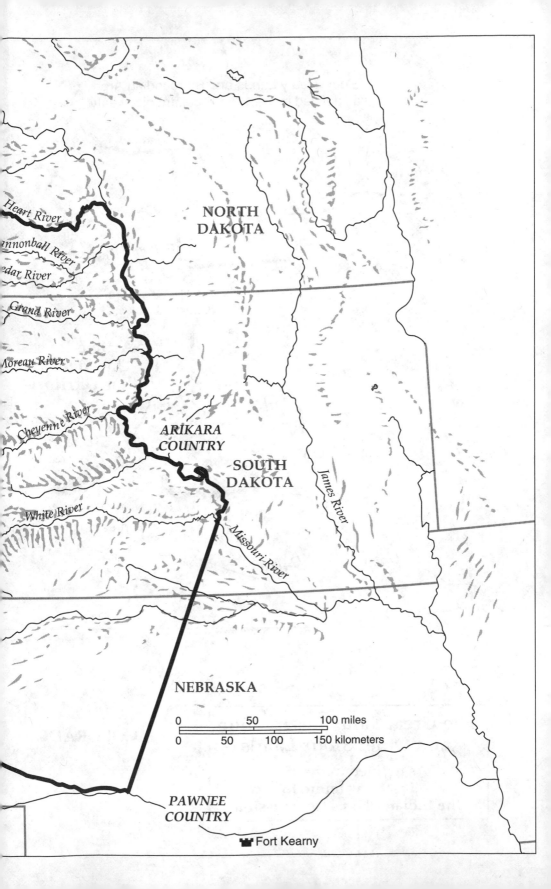

Heart River

NORTH
DAKOTA

annonball River

edar River

Grand River

Moreau River

Cheyenne River

ARIKARA
COUNTRY

SOUTH
DAKOTA

James River

White River

Missouri River

NEBRASKA

0   50   100 miles
0   50   100   150 kilometers

PAWNEE
COUNTRY

Fort Kearny

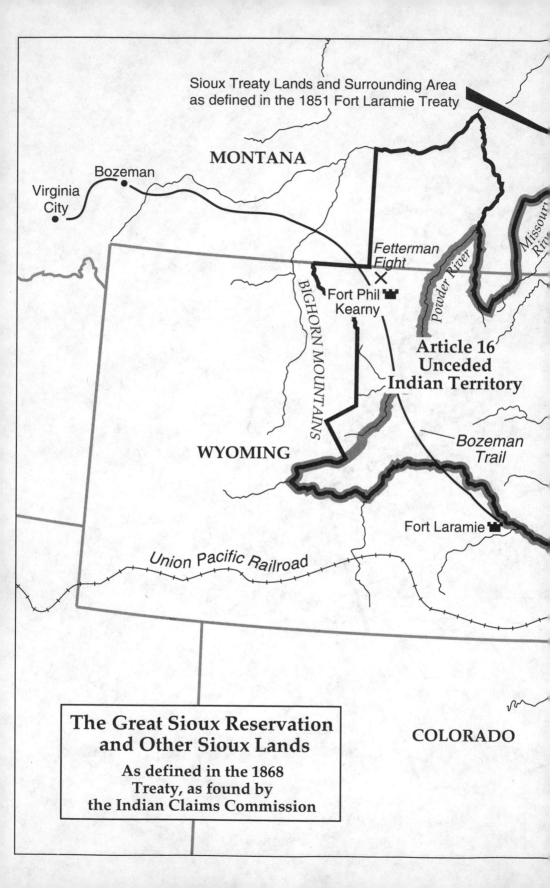

Sioux Treaty Lands and Surrounding Area
as defined in the 1851 Fort Laramie Treaty

MONTANA

Virginia
City

Bozeman

Missouri River

Fetterman
Fight

Fort Phil
Kearny

Powder River

Article 16
Unceded
Indian Territory

BIGHORN MOUNTAINS

WYOMING

Bozeman
Trail

Fort Laramie

Union Pacific Railroad

The Great Sioux Reservation and Other Sioux Lands

As defined in the 1868 Treaty, as found by the Indian Claims Commission

COLORADO

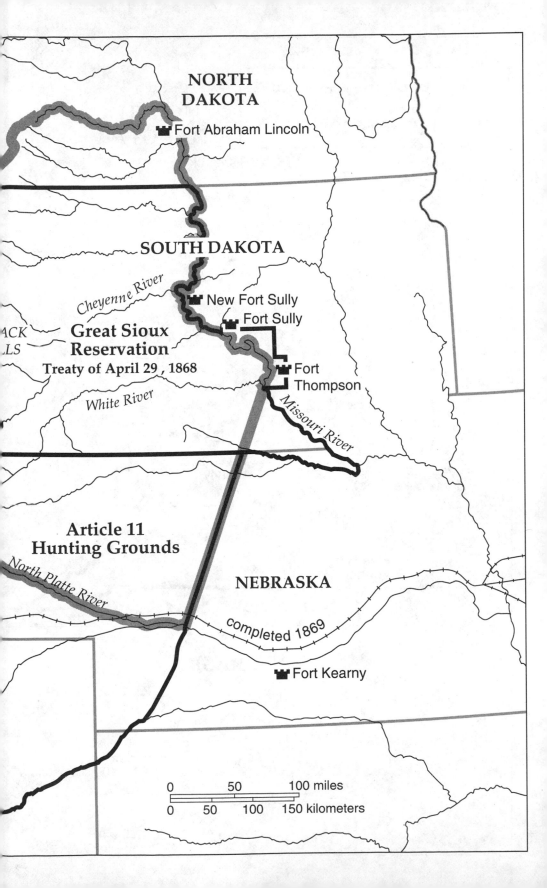

Sioux Lands as defined in the Act of February 28, 1877

NORTH DAKOTA

• Bismarck

Standing Rock Agency ■

SOUTH DAKOTA

Cheyenne River

Deadwood •

Lead (Homestake Mine)

Cheyenne Agency ■

Missouri River

White River

Rosebud Agency ■

Pine Ridge Agency ■

NEBRASKA

0   50 miles

0   50   100 kilometers

Platte River

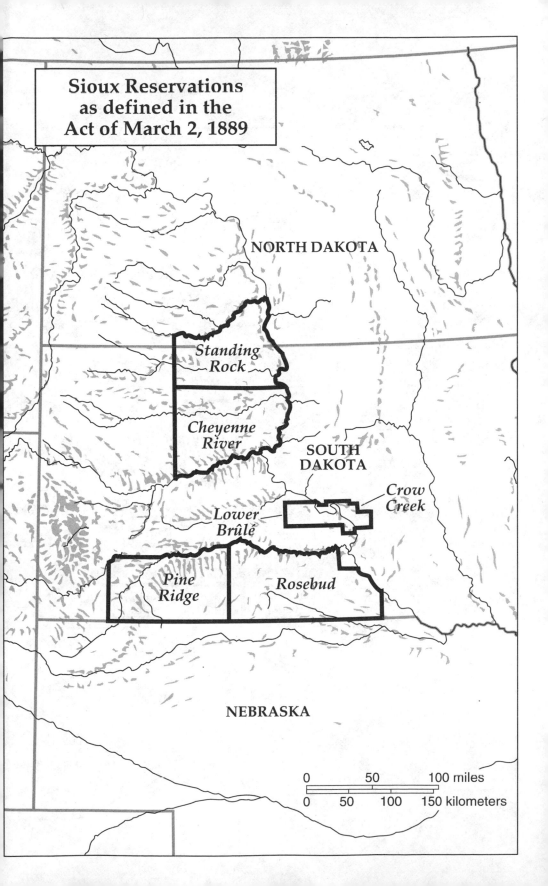

Sioux Reservations as defined in the Act of March 2, 1889

NORTH DAKOTA

Standing Rock

Cheyenne River

SOUTH DAKOTA

Crow Creek

Lower Brûlé

Pine Ridge

Rosebud

NEBRASKA

0   50   100 miles

0   50   100   150 kilometers

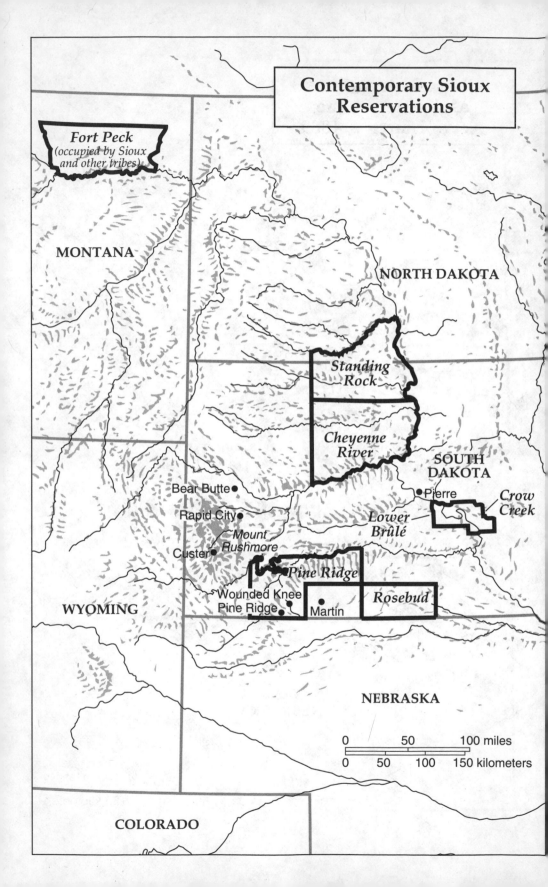

Contemporary Sioux Reservations

Fort Peck
(occupied by Sioux and other tribes)

MONTANA

NORTH DAKOTA

Standing Rock

Cheyenne River

SOUTH DAKOTA

Bear Butte •

Rapid City •

Mount Rushmore

Custer •

WYOMING

• Pierre

Crow Creek

Lower Brûlé

Pine Ridge

Wounded Knee
Pine Ridge •

Rosebud

• Martin

NEBRASKA

| 0 | 50 | 100 miles |

| 0 | 50 | 100 | 150 kilometers |

COLORADO

Black Hills/
White Justice

O N E

▼ ▼ ▼ ▼ ▼

THE VILEST MISCREANTS OF
THE SAVAGE RACE

WHEN A MINUTEMAN fired "the shot heard round the world,"
Standing Bull did not hear it. His ears were tuned not to the
crack of British muskets but to the drumming hoofs of buffalo on
the move or the calls of spotted eagles riding hot drafts above the
sun-bleached plain. Standing Bull and his followers had traveled
further west than any Sioux before. They had crossed the muddy-
watered Missouri and a hundred creek bottoms, dry in summer,
that severed the rolling alkali prairie into deep-hued crested
buttes. They had crossed lands that for a thousand years were
home to Kiowa, Hidatsas, and Mandan rivals but remained virgin
to Sioux eyes. In the vanguard of their tribe's westward migration,
Standing Bull and his people were part of their own revolution—
one of home and culture—as the Sioux spread out across the plains.

In the west, Standing Bull discovered a paradise. Surrounded on
every side by hundreds of miles of dry grass fields, virtually tree-
less and barren, he and his band gazed for the first time upon the
cool, dark, wooded slopes of the *Paha Sapa,* the Black Hills, as they
rose precipitously four thousand feet above the buffalo grass ocean.
Created in the Pleistocene upheaval that brought forth the Rock-
ies, the Hills formed a remote ridge of granite and limestone—one
hundred ten miles by forty—soaring over the surrounding landscape, basking in their peculiar isolation, and commanding a vast
arc of the plain below.

No doubt, the drama of these mysterious and ancient peaks set
against the cobalt blue of the boundless summer sky was not lost
on the Sioux. Nor was their value. Standing Bull could see the

steep canyons that might shelter Sioux families from the arctic blasts of the prairie winter. He could imagine the abundant game hidden within the dense pine forests that covered every slope, the fresh mountain streams cascading down from sharp crags, the long straight tree trunks for making lodge poles. And he could marvel at the sheer beauty of the sweeping dark heights.

Standing Bull's party belonged to the Teton group of Sioux, westernmost and largest of the groups that comprised the tribe's *Oceti Sakowin,* the Seven Council Fires. The Teton, in turn, were divided into seven bands: the Oglala, Brûlé, Hunkpapa, Miniconjous, Sans Arc, Two Kettle, and Blackfeet. Far to the east of the Teton lived their relatives, the four Santee groups: the Sisseton, Wahpeton, Wahpekute, and Mdewakanton. In between camped the two remaining groups, the Yankton and Yanktonai. The Teton, Santee, and Yankton called themselves Lakota, Dakota, and Nakota respectively, a reflection of their distinct dialects. Together they formed the "alliance of friends." Their eastern rivals had another name for them, the *nadoueissiw,* or snakes, which the French shortened to the name Sioux.*

Once, all the Sioux bands had lived in the woodlands spread about the headwaters of the Mississippi, but by 1775 only the Santee ever ranged among the forests. Many years earlier, the Sioux had begun their steady move west, prodded by the musket fire of their hereditary enemy, the Chippewa. The Chippewa, east of the Sioux and closer to European settlements, had beaten the Sioux in the race to the white man's guns and pressed their advantage. The Sioux did not surrender their woodland homes easily. Time and again they battled the Chippewa; but time and again they lost.

The more adventurous among the Teton early saw in their forced exile an opportunity to explore the vast prairies which lay west of their lost homes in what is now Minnesota. They migrated towards the Missouri and the buffalo, which, in herds many millions strong, turned the grasslands black with their numbers. Standing Bull could trace his lineage to these intrepid explorers. Emerging from the woods onto the limitless plains, they began the revolution that he continued and expanded. Over time, the Teton

---

*This book deals mainly with the history of the Teton Sioux who today occupy the Pine Ridge, Rosebud, Cheyenne River, Standing Rock, Crow Creek, and Lower Brûlé reservations in South and North Dakota as well as the Ft. Peck reservation in Montana. For convenience, I sometimes use the term Teton— denoting the familiar Sioux of Red Cloud, Sitting Bull, and Crazy Horse— interchangeably with the more general term Sioux.

had replaced a diet of wild rice, fish, and timber game with one composed almost exclusively of buffalo meat and the abundant chokecherries which grew wild along the prairie's chalky buttes. And they had exchanged their canoes for dogs and their homes of poles, earth, and bark for something portable, a tipi made from animal hides. Gradually, they abandoned the settled woodland life to become nomads following the great bison migrations north and south with the seasons.

By the time Standing Bull reached the Black Hills, this adaptation to plains culture was well advanced. The Sioux had started to exploit the pintos, the wild ponies which roved the west—descendants of the sixteen mounts that the Spaniard Cortés brought to the horseless New World. By the eighteenth century, these ponies, rarely more than fourteen hands high but remarkable for their agility and endurance, numbered in the millions. The pintos gave the Sioux undreamed-of mobility and speed, and rapidly became indispensable to their hunting, warring, and roaming. Before long, horse thieving from other tribes emerged as an honored vocation, and a man's stature within his band might be measured by the size of his pony herd or the number of ponies he had given away. The horse became so valuable that the Sioux term for the animal, *sunka wakan*, connotes something supernatural.

The Teton masterfully exploited the resources of their new environment. As the American artist George Catlin observed when he met the Teton in the 1840s, "There are no parts of the great plains more abundantly stocked with buffaloes and wild horses nor any people so bold in destroying the one for food and appropriating the other to their use." Assured of their subsistence, armed with an ever-increasing number of guns obtained from French traders to the east, and mounted on swift ponies, the Sioux learned the arts of plains survival and of empire building as well. Year by year, the Teton enlarged their new homeland through force of arms and superior numbers. And they thrived on the warfare necessary to preserve and expand their dominion. Aggressive and independent by nature, tall, strong, and lithe, the Sioux ranged far and wide across the prairies in search of fresh game and the camps of their rivals.

When the Americans fought at Concord Bridge, the Sioux could lay claim to lands many times the size of the largest colony, a territory that included large portions of what would become Minnesota, Iowa, North Dakota, Nebraska, and almost all of South Dakota. Nor did they confine themselves to these boundaries.

Sioux raiders ventured as far north as Canada and as far south as Texas—anywhere the bison roamed.

Teton life followed the seasons. During the long winter of the northern plains, where a first snow might fall as early as September, scattered Sioux *tiyospaye* (extended family groups) would settle along wooded creek bottoms: sheltered, with a water supply, and bark from the cottonwood trees to feed the horses. Here they would stay until late spring, hunkered down against the prairie winds, passing the short days with games of chance and tall stories. Then, when the prairie grass grew tall and the buffalo fat enough to warrant a hunt, the dispersed clans would emerge from their winter hideaways and gather into great camps for the fighting, hunting, feasting, and rites of worship of the clear, hot summer days.

A Sioux summer camp might spread over several acres, splashing the vibrant colors of blankets, robes, and tipis across an otherwise tawny plain. The camps were a frenzy of activity. "Warriors, women, and children swarmed like bees," the Harvard chronicler Francis Parkman observed when he visited a camp along the Platte River. "Hundreds of dogs, of all sizes and colors, ran restlessly about . . . the wide shallow stream was alive with boys, girls, and young squaws, splashing, screaming and laughing in the water."

With so many mouths to feed and so much food to store for the next winter, the Sioux meticulously tracked the buffalo herds and carefully supervised the hunt. Members of the *Akicita,* the camp police, patroled the camp circle, making certain that no one disturbed the herd, diminishing the collective kill. The hunt itself, with the warriors racing pell-mell about the herds, was glorious work for the men. For the women it entailed arduous days of skinning and preserving the carcasses, making pemmican, the tribe's winter staple, from dried buffalo meat and wild berries, and fending off the ubiquitous camp dogs. Even in midsummer, amid thousands of buffalo, the Sioux generally extracted everything they could use from their downed prey. The meat, fat, bones, intestines, blood, hide, horns, hair, even the buffalo dung served some critical function in the daily routine of survival. In Sioux hands, bones became needles or shields; fat became tallow; hoofs became glue; dung became fuel. A good buffalo hide could patch a tattered home or be bartered for guns or cooking pots with one of the French or British traders who ventured across the Missouri. Each morsel of dried meat meant that much less deprivation during the coming winter.

When not hunting or lounging and feasting around the camp,

Sioux braves vied for membership in the warrior societies—the Kit Foxes, Brave Hearts, or Crow Owners—and spent their days on forays against Kiowa, Crow, or Pawnee camps. These raids rarely amounted to a full-fledged battle. More often they provided a stage for individual warriors to prove their courage by charging recklessly at the enemy and chancing the highest act of valor: to "count coup" by literally touching one of the enemy with a bow, lance, or quirt.

Summer was also a time of special religious observance, of sacred dances, purifying sweats, and the ceremonies of the pipe—rites of renewal and restoration which brought the Teton into harmony with the sacred circles, the overwhelming unity, of the natural world. Sioux boys embarked on vision quests, *hanble ceyapi*, the "crying for a vision," venturing into the wilderness naked and without food. Alone, the vision seeker held himself alert for the appearance of a guardian spirit, ready to receive the power of the *wakan*, the animating force of the universe. And the tribe gathered for the Sun Dance, most hallowed of all Sioux dances. There, with friends and relatives looking on from beneath a specially constructed arbor, the sundancers would suspend themselves from braided thongs which ran from the top of a sacred pole to skewers that pierced the muscles of their breasts. Gazing at the hypnotic plains sun, wreaths of sage crowning their heads, these supplicants would dance, sometimes for hours, while the shrill tweet of eagle-bone whistles pierced the windless air. In the end, the dancers would offer their flesh to the Great Spirit, regaining their freedom by ripping through the skin of their chests. The ensuing scars were a badge of honor.

Standing Bull grew up in this changing culture, one that would continue to evolve with his discovery of the Black Hills. The next Sioux generation secured the Hills, expelling the Kiowa in 1814. A few years later they pushed this border even further west, taking the Powder River country (eastern Wyoming and part of Montana) from the Crow. These new acquisitions altered more than just invisible boundaries. They created a vast homeland for a people that cherished the land, lived off the land, and considered everything on or in the land in some way sacred.

Within this empire, the newly acquired Black Hills assumed a special meaning. They were a source of fresh mountain streams, scarce lodgepoles for the tipis, and the medicine plants that healed the tribe. The Hills were a holy place, a place for vision quests, home to *Wakan Tanka*, the Great Spirit, the sum of all that was powerful, sacred, and full of mystery.

There, so Lakota legend has it, on a track surrounding the Hills, the two-legged animals raced against the four-legged to determine which would be dominant on earth. There, so legend has it, the thunder-being told a chief named Red Thunder that the Hills were the heart of the earth where someday the Sioux would return and live.

As an old Teton chief remembered:

of all our domain, we loved, perhaps, the Black Hills the most. The [Teton] named these hills the Sapa, or Black Hills, on account of their color. The slopes and peaks were so heavily wooded with dark pines that from a distance the mountains actually looked black. In the wooden recesses were numberless springs of pure water and numerous small lakes. There were wood and game in abundance and shelter from the storms of the plains. It was the favorite winter hunt of the [Teton] and buffalo as well. According to a tribal legend these hills were a reclining female figure from whose breasts flowed life-giving forces and to them the [Teton] went as a child to its mother's arms.

When the first white Americans came west, they found the Sioux in this homeland, spending the winters near these Hills, hunting on the undisturbed plain and feared by every enemy. To those Americans, like Parkman, who met the Sioux at the height of their power, they seemed untouched, beyond the long reach of the western world. "The Sioux are thorough savages," Parkman remarked, "neither their manners nor their ideas have been the slightest degree modified by contact with white civilization."

But Parkman was wrong. Even by the early 1800s, when the Sioux still had not seen more than a few dozen white men, the influence of their distant and unknown world already was keenly felt. White man's guns in the hands of the Chippewa already had uprooted the Sioux from their previous habitat. White man's horses had revolutionized plains life and advanced Sioux dominion over their new home. And white man's diseases, somehow sparing the Sioux, had ravaged their foes along the Missouri—the Arikara, Omaha, and Mandan—abetting Sioux hegemony. Now, armed themselves, the Sioux used their guns to rout their rivals and increase the kill in the summer hunts.

Long before Parkman ventured west, the European world, in the form of the fur trade, had cast an outstretched arm into tribal life. Every fall the "mountain men," intrepid pioneers of the western wilderness, emissaries from the white world, semiliterate in European and native tongues, appeared at the great forks along the

Missouri River (at the James River to the south and at the Yellow-stone to the north), bearing guns and knives and cooking pots to barter for beaver skins and other hides. Most of the traders joined the tribe for the winter and took a squaw for a wife; many fathered children. In spring they left with their pelts and hides, and returned down the Missouri to the mysterious world from which they'd come. In their wake, Sioux camps overflowed with modern conveniences: iron kettles, cooking utensils, steel knives and needles, sugar and coffee, luxuries that eased the rigors of nomadic life.

The Teton's first official contact with the fledgling American republic occurred in late August 1804, when Merriwether Lewis and William Clark's expedition reached Sioux country. The Sioux gave the explorers a rather rough welcome. Having treated the explorers to feasts, dancing, and a smoke of the sacred pipe, the Tetons feigned dissatisfaction with the gifts that the Americans distributed and threatened to detain the two captains unless they handed over more goods. Lewis and Clark scrounged up a bit more tobacco while their crew readied their guns. Only a hasty council with Chief Black Buffalo brought about a peaceful resolution to the squabble.

Despite this contretemps, Lewis and Clark sought to impress the Sioux with the importance of their mission: to announce to Indian occupants that the United States had acquired sovereignty over the Louisiana Territory, including all of the lands under Sioux control. To remind the Sioux of their new sovereign's identity, Lewis and Clark distributed national medals (a tradition among French and British traders) and wrapped a newborn baby in an American flag, symbolically conferring American citizenship on the Sioux infant. Such friendly acts neither tempered Lewis's opinion of the Tetons, "the vilest miscreants of the savage race," nor brought home to the Sioux the full portent of the explorers' visit. They could not fathom that a man named Thomas Jefferson had bought the entire Sioux domain, and much more, for three million dollars, or that (under the white man's "doctrine of discovery") their homeland was previously owned by Napoleon. The Sioux knew who controlled every bluff and creekbed from the Platte River to the Yellowstone—and it was neither a president nor an emperor.

Nonetheless, Lewis and Clark's expedition presaged the opening of the upper Missouri region to American commerce. With the founding of the Missouri and American fur companies in 1808, America's private industry began competing seriously with British trade interests in the upper Missouri; and after the War of 1812

English-backed traders started withdrawing from the area. Indeed, in the decade following the Treaty of Ghent, U.S. trading companies established a lucrative monopoly throughout the upper Missouri. The Astor family, owners of the American Fur Company, amassed one of the nation's great fortunes from their annual profits of up to half a million dollars during the 1820s.

To protect the nation's burgeoning interest in the region, the government in 1825 organized the Yellowstone expedition under General Henry Atkinson and Major Benjamin O'Fallon, intending to awe the Missouri Indians with American military strength and to conclude a series of agreements with the Sioux, Crow, Mandan, Ponca, and others, that would ratify America's acquired claim to the upper Missouri.

The Atkinson–O'Fallon mission met with various Teton bands in late June and early July and concluded three separate treaties. Echoing Lewis and Clark, the agreements emphasized the overall supremacy of the United States over Sioux country. And they went further. The United States reserved the right to regulate all trade and intercourse with the Sioux, and limited trading privileges with the Indians to authorized citizens of the U.S. The Sioux, moreover, were to apprehend and turn over to the government any trespassing foreign traders, and all criminals, white or red, for prosecution.

In return, the United States pledged to protect the Indians and their property and to prosecute wrongdoers. Most important, the United States agreed to "receive [the Sioux] into their friendship" and to confer upon the Sioux "such benefits and acts of kindness as may be convenient" in the eyes of the President.

General Atkinson and his retinue, 475 strong, were still lingering in Teton country when July Fourth arrived and the Americans resolved to show the Sioux some old-fashioned patriotism. The soldiers concocted a fireworks display from howitzer shells, and reportedly dazzled the Indians with how white men could set fire to the night sky. A young lieutenant, William Harney, read aloud the Declaration of Independence. Jefferson's prose, to the extent that it bore translation, must have baffled the Sioux. But this incongruous scene along the riverbank—of Sioux families who knew only the freedom of the wilderness listening to odd talk of tyranny and self-determination—befitted the occasion. These were alien cultures, now contiguous, bound together in a peace, their first, rife with ignorance and misunderstanding. Like the Enlightenment principles set forth in the Declaration, most of the concepts solemnly sworn to in the just-signed treaty lay far beyond the ken of the Teton. How incomprehensible the idea of sovereignty must have seemed to a people who knew nothing of kings or nation-states; how foreign the idea of trade regulation to a people who never coined money, who wrote no laws.

Still, both parties could share with conviction Chief Wabasha's hope that "this peace will last a long time." From the government's perspective, the treaty with the Sioux, in addition to securing U.S. economic interests, advanced the nation's sincere, if often unrealized, intention to maintain good relations with native tribes. As codified in the first great act of Congress, the Northwest Ordinance of 1787, and as perhaps was natural for a nation whose forebears' survival had depended on the goodwill of Indian confederacies in the east, the United States had pledged to itself that

> The utmost good faith shall always be observed towards the Indians; their land and property shall never be taken from them without their consent; and in their property, rights and liberty, they never shall be invaded or disturbed, unless in just and lawful wars authorized by Congress; but laws founded in justice and humanity shall from time to time be made, for preventing wrongs being done to them, and for preserving peace and friendship with them.

Although in its first half-century the United States had often honored this noble directive only in the breach, the nation's avowed recognition of Indian rights distinguished it in principle from previous settlers of the New World and other lands whose prevailing method of expansion consisted of the wholesale slaughter of aboriginal peoples. That distinction alone, affirmed in the newly signed treaty (and in the treatymaking process generally), provided a measure of satisfaction to a nation self-consciously aspiring to establish a beneficent and moral dominion.

The Sioux, for their part, had abundant reasons to want tranquil relations with the whites. In the generation since Lewis and Clark's visit, the Teton had tripled in size to 10,000 members, testimony to the prosperous life they were enjoying. The Indians could credit their contact with the whites for much of this prosperity. The introduction of firearms, cooking utensils, and a host of other items had drastically reduced the workload of their hunting culture and brought relative leisure to their nomadic existence. To an ever-increasing degree, the tools of western civilization were becoming everyday necessities of Sioux life.

Sioux prosperity, however, was not without its perils. The trade in fur and hides was, as Missouri Senator Thomas Hart Benton noted, a Pandora's box, "irresistibly attractive to the Indians, but filled with evil." The foremost part of this evil was the introduction to Sioux country of alcohol, *mini wakan,* as the Sioux called it, "the water that makes men foolish." The Indians craved the traders' brew—usually well-watered, loaded with molasses, pepper, tobacco juice, even gunpowder—but they had no tolerance for it. Many a drunken Indian lost the fruits of his winter hunt when a sober frontiersman tricked him out of his goods. Nor was poverty the only result. Alcohol made the Indians violent, so violent that many traders added sedatives to their drinks. These drugs were not always available and drunken homicide became commonplace in the Indian camps. Other Sioux simply passed out on the way home and froze to death on the prairie tundra.

The government, so concerned with regulating commerce with the tribes, proved powerless to stop the liquor traffic because whiskey and the lucrative fur trade went hand in hand. Rival companies bribed the Indians to get their business, and liquor, for which many Sioux developed an insatiable thirst, became the most common currency.

Alcoholism was only one of numerous illnesses that the traders brought to the plains. Cholera, smallpox, and venereal disease infected the defenseless Indians. In the winter count, their ideographic calendar, the Teton portrayed 1818 as "the year many died of cramps," their descriptive definition of cholera. The Sioux could consider themselves fortunate. In one year alone, smallpox wiped out all but 31 of 1,500 Mandans, as the illness spread from family to family, unrestrained by the acquired resistance of the white man.

Still, despite the disease and the debauchery, for the Sioux the greatest potential problem associated with the trade did not weaken, dissipate, or kill. The most pernicious evil was what on the surface seemed so good to the Teton—the invaluable tools which they accrued through the fur trade, the new and easier way of life that white technology made possible. Although the trade benefited white and Indian alike, the Sioux gradually became beholden to a foreign and potentially hostile culture for the instruments of their survival. The fur trade returned nothing to the Sioux that could not easily be taken away; many of the tools the Indians already owned had to be repaired regularly by whites, or else discarded.

Years before, Lewis and Clark had warned that the Tetons "must ever remain the pirates of the Missouri, until such measures are pursued by our government, as will make them feel a dependence on its will for their supply of merchandise." In the years after the Atkinson–O'Fallon treaty, that proposed dependence developed into fact. The United States came to possess an awesome lever for manipulating the Sioux, made more powerful because the tribe had yet to realize the danger.

In the short term, however, the prospect of both prosperity and independence remained alive for the Teton because the United States showed no interest in homesteading the vast lands of the Sioux domain. In the generation after Lewis and Clark's expedition, a number of American explorers had traversed the great plains searching for valuable land and resources. But they had all agreed with Major Stephen Long, one of the earliest "pathfinders," that the territory was "entirely unfit for civilization," a "Great American Desert" in the middle of the continent.

Convinced that the land could not sustain an agricultural society, in 1825 the United States designated the entire area as a Permanent Indian Country and reserved it for the sole use and occupancy of the aboriginal race. The government established a fixed frontier along the western borders of Louisiana, Arkansas, Missouri, Iowa, and Minnesota. It removed the remnants of many eastern tribes, like the Cherokee, Creek, and Chickasaw, to the west of this line, solemnly promising them a secure and undisturbed new home "for as long as the grass shall grow and the water run."

For the eastern Indians, this removal blazed a "Trail of Tears," as the government uprooted thousands of families from their ancestral homes and sent them on a forced march to new reservations carved from the barren rangelands of what is now Oklahoma. For the Teton, the declaration of the closed frontier merely preserved the status quo. In the late 1830s, smallpox once again cut a swath of death across the northern plains. Liquor continued to flow freely. In 1841, a young brave named Red Cloud, who had watched his father die from alcohol, killed Chief Bull Bear in a drunken brawl. Occasionally, a few young braves would run off a trader's stock or fire a few shots. But, generally, the plains up to this time were peaceable, at least between Indians and whites.

In 1842, the first of the pioneer wagon trains rolled across Sioux land. Eighteen wagons strong, it had started in Independence, Missouri, and headed northwest until it reached the Platte River. Then, for hundreds of miles, the pioneers snaked along the south bank of that broad stream, across Kansas, Nebraska, and Wyoming, piercing the very heart of buffalo country and the southern hunting grounds of the Teton Sioux. The hundred settlers driving the train were bound for Oregon and the fertile soil of the Willamette valley. They were the vanguard of a land-hungry nation on the way to the new agricultural Zion in the far northwest.

At first, their wheels barely displaced the prairie grass, but the path these settlers cut did not fade away. Each year the wagon trains grew longer; each year the trail became wider. Wooden wheels carved an indelible scar in the sandy plains soil, especially when summer storms turned the ground into sticky gumbo. The transients left other marks as well. The trail was littered with broken-down carriages, discarded belongings, sun-bleached bones of devoured game, and small crosses marking frontier graves. What began as shallow ruts became the Oregon Trail, or "Holy Road," as the Indians called it—the first of the great highways west.

The buffalo recognized the trail easily from its stench of rotting carcasses and human refuse. They quickly learned to give it a wide berth and find new grazing far away from the despoiled prairie along the Platte. But the Oregon Trail did more than move the buffalo: it destroyed the hunting pattern of the Sioux, forcing them to follow the herds to the fringes of their domain and to expose themselves to the raids of their enemies. The Teton had no trouble attributing blame for their predicament, but they grew frustrated, arguing among themselves about what to do with the white intruders. The Sioux threatened; they robbed; they shot up caravans; but they could not stop the emigrants. Instead, Teton raids terrified and angered the settlers, and provoked Washington into sending out the military to intimidate the angry Indians into leaving the wagon trains alone.

Colonel S. W. Kearny arrived at the Laramie fork of the Platte River on June 15, 1845, with five companies of dragoons. His meeting with the Sioux went amicably enough. The Indians vented their rage and Kearny responded with words of peace, but a warning to stop molesting the emigrants. To add some weight to his admonition, Kearny paraded his troops before the Indians, who watched in bewilderment as the American sabers sparkled in the sun and the boom of their artillery shattered the stillness of the plains. Above their heads, two flags flew: the stars and stripes and a blue flag with diagonal lines, nine stars, and two hands clasped in friendship—the "Sioux flag," or so the Teton were told. The whites had designed it on their behalf, most likely to symbolize the strength of the Sioux nation and the respect that the United States Government accorded it. But the Sioux flag was less a symbol of the tribe's power than of the power of the whites, who felt free to foist new emblems on the peoples of the plains and were now marching steadily across their land.

The Mormons came west in 1847, carving a new path across the prairie, north of the Platte. Then a lucky prospector struck gold in a remote spot called Sutter's Mill in California, and the steady march of pioneers turned into a wild stampede. Ninety thousand settlers headed for California in the great migration of 1849, and almost every one crossed that Great American Desert, the permanent Indian territory and home of the Sioux. The 'forty-niners not only scattered the buffalo, as their Oregon-bound predecessors had, they plowed right through the center of the summer range—grasslands that fed some 15 million bison. On the way, prospective miners killed recklessly, plundering the land of its game.

The buffalo fled north and south, never to return to the middle prairies. By year's end, most of the Indians would wish they had run too. The 'forty-niners carried cholera with them to the plains and it devastated the already ravaged tribes. The Teton, though they again escaped the worst of the epidemic, concluded that the whites had come to exterminate them with the sickness. Only the Indians' fear of infection spared the emigrants a rich harvest of retribution.

As it was, enough settlers fell prey to Indian attack that the army decided to garrison strategic points along the Platte roads. To this end, the government purchased the American Fur Company's trading post at the Laramie fork of the Platte River and renamed the old post Fort Laramie. The vast prairies and the swift Indian horsemen, however, did not lend themselves easily to military control; and certainly a small regiment at Laramie could not contain the whole Sioux nation. The Superintendent of Indian Affairs for the upper Missouri, Thomas Harvey, had advised his superiors as early as 1845 that paying reparations to the plains tribes would be good policy, greatly enhancing the safety of the transient whites. He and the other government agents in Indian country predicted widespread bloodshed unless something were done soon to placate the natives.

By midcentury, the government could no longer ignore the conflict between the nation's westward expansion and a policy of peaceful, if distant, relations with the still unconquered tribes that roamed the plains. With the settlement of Oregon and California, the annexation of Texas and the end of the Mexican-American War, the United States found its sovereignty stretched all the way to the Pacific Ocean. At a minimum, the nation had developed a pressing interest in establishing safe and reliable passage between the settled Missouri River frontier and the booming settlements strung along the west coast from Baja to northern Oregon. Providing safe passage was impossible unless the government somehow segregated the plains tribes from the overland routes west. In other words, the Permanent Indian Territory had ceased to be a convenient and otherwise useless wilderness in which the natives could be left to roam and hunt and raid at will.

Realizing that it lacked the resources to police the trails adequately, the United States decided to try to negotiate a settlement to the plains crisis. As an immediate measure to secure the safety of the emigrant trails, in 1850 Congress appropriated an unprecedented $100,000 "for holding treaties with the wild tribes of the prairies," and the Commissioner of Indian Affairs, the highest bureaucrat in the Indian service, instructed his agents on the plains to make arrangements for a grand council to meet at Laramie in September 1851.

Ten years after the movement west began, government runners raced up the Missouri and the Platte, spread west along the Powder and the Yellowstone, and trekked across the Big Horn mountains, bringing word to the Sioux, Crow, Shoshone, Arapahoe, and other tribes that the Great White Father wanted to talk peace at Laramie, and that he would give them food and blankets and even guns if they would come.

The tribes flocked to Laramie from every corner of the plains, driven by apprehension and drawn by the promises of food and gifts and peace. When the government treaty commissioners arrived, they discovered thousands of Indians crowded around the fort, more Indians from more tribes than ever had assembled in a single spot. Many of them had no choice. The summer hunts had been a disaster and the alternative to peace was a winter of starvation.

Thomas Fitzpatrick and David Dawson Mitchell, former traders whom the government appointed as its principal negotiators, were astonished at the remarkable attendance of the tribes and that the Sioux, Cheyenne, Crow, Arikara, Shoshone, and a host of others, peoples divided by hereditary enmities, could gather peacefully in a single campground. But they had; and for eighteen days these ancient rivals feasted and visited like old friends and met in solemn council with their new adversary, the white man. They even waited calmly until the very last day for the presents and provisions that the government had promised to deliver as soon as they arrived, though, with so many Indians assembled, many went hungry during the council's course.

Before the tribes finally dispersed, they signed a treaty to bring peace and prosperity to every man, white or red, who ventured onto the plains. First and foremost, the Indians and the United States pledged themselves "to a lasting peace between all the nations assembled." The Indians, for their part, recognized the right of the government to construct roads and military posts within their territory and bound themselves to make restitution for all wrongs committed thereafter against citizens of the United States. They also promised to keep the peace among themselves, and approved boundary lines for the land of each tribe as carefully set forth in the treaty.

In return, the United States agreed to protect the Indians from marauding frontiersman and, most important, to compensate the Indians for the disruption of their lives by paying the tribes fifty thousand dollars each year for fifty years. The Indians accepted the wagon train of gifts which the whites distributed at the council as full payment for past grievances.

In signing a treaty with the western tribes establishing tribal domains and guaranteeing the borders of Indian country, the United States affirmed formally that Indians possessed personal and property rights, including rights in their lands, and (as Chief Justice John Marshall had written in the 1830 Supreme Court case *Worcester* v. *Georgia*) that Indian tribes were "distinct, independent, political communities" who retained at least limited rights of self-government. At a minimum, these recognized tribal rights established a legal benchmark against which the government's actions might be measured in the future, and distinguished Indians from the country's other racial minority, the blacks, to whom the law accorded essentially no rights at all.

The commissioners congratulated themselves on a job well done. "Viewing the treaty with all its provisions," reported Superintendent Mitchell, "I am clearly of the opinion that it is the best that could have been made for both parties."

The Sioux were less certain. Even as they left Laramie, swearing one last time to eternal peace and friendship with whites and other Indians, they must have sensed that they would not, indeed could not, abide by the treaty. Certainly, the Sioux eagerly awaited the wealth of presents they would receive; in their ideographic calender they marked 1851 as the Year of the Great Giveaway. And although it would only reinforce their reliance on the whites, the Sioux relished the thought of a sizable fifty-year annuity. But they surely recognized that the Laramie treaty, like every agreement that had come before, clearly was incompatible with the Sioux way. The treaty outlawed many essential aspects of plains life, the raiding, horse thieving, and warring that brought honor and authority to both a man and his tribe. Moreover, although the agreement recognized Sioux dominion over sixty million acres of land— from the Missouri in the east to beyond the Black Hills and from the Platte River north to the Heart River—it gave the Powder River country, Sioux land since 1822, back to the hated Crow and designated Sioux hunting grounds south of the Platte as belonging to the Kiowa.

What were these unearthly boundaries across the wide prairie that robbed the Teton of their cherished victories? At the peace talks, the Teton had opposed the treaty's definition of their territory. "These lands once belonged to the Kiowas and the Crows," Chief Black Hawk had complained, "but we whipped these nations out of them, and in this we did what the white men do when they want the lands of the Indians." The government had placated the Sioux with assurances that the treaty boundaries were only guidelines and that, technically, no tribe surrendered its rights to lands claimed outside its own specified borders. The Sioux, though, could hardly understand or revere such legal niceties. They soon returned to war, attacking the Crow near the Big Horn Mountains. The other tribes returned to warring too.

The 1851 treaty's insensitivity to plains culture was mostly deliberate. As in the past, lack of understanding led the treaty commissioners to appoint or have elected all-powerful chiefs for each tribe, even though the Indians, who governed themselves less centrally, would not accept their authority, and the nominees themselves often feared for their lives once named to office. In devising most of the treaty provisions, however, the Indian bureau purposefully disregarded what it knew about Indian cultures in order to further its own grand scheme for peaceful coexistence with the western tribes. Although that plan provided little room for the natives' way of life, its architects believed that the Laramie treaty would inaugurate a new, practical, and compassionate approach to the mounting crisis with the plains tribes.

In his final report recommending the treaty to the United States Senate for ratification, Superintendent Mitchell explained the revamped strategy and the way in which the treaty incorporated its ideas. Mitchell proceeded from the basic assumption, uniformly held from before Jefferson's time, that without the active assistance of white civilization, the Indians were doomed to extinction. Even

as early as 1851, the government predicated its policy on the belief
that the buffalo would soon be killed off and that the Indians' only
chance for survival required that they abandon their hunting culture and adopt the habits of a farming society. A liberal, democratic, Christian nation, the United States could not stand idly by
as the first Americans perished. "Humanity calls loudly for some
interposition," Mitchell declared, "to save, if possible, some portion of these ill-fated tribes."

At the Laramie conference, that interposition took the form of
the fifty-year annuity, the definition of tribal lands and the extensive missionary work performed by Father De Smet, a Catholic
priest who would reside among the Sioux until his death a quarter-
century later. Specifically, the treaty commissioners reserved the
right to give the promised annuity to the Indians in the form of
domesticated cattle, farming tools, seeds, and grains. If in the short
term these payments were to buy a right of way west, in the long
term they were meant to ease and expedite the difficult but inevitable process of civilizing the savages. By the same principle, the
treaty's delineation of specific tribal domains was calculated to
foster a European respect for property rights among the natives.
Fifty years, the Indian Bureau believed, would be time enough to
change the basis of Indian life and "solve the great problem of
whether or not the Indian can be made a civilized man."

The value of the treaty to the whites, however, did not rest solely
on these philanthropic grounds. As Mitchell took great pains explaining to the Senate in his report, the treaty would prove exceed-
ingly pragmatic and economical. Fifty thousand dollars was a
small amount to pay, Mitchell argued, "to save the country from
the ruinous and useless expense of a war against the prairie tribes,
which would cost many millions." It was downright cheap, considering the government distributed the money to more than fifty
thousand Indians.

The Senate did not agree. It reduced the length of the annuity
to ten years, with five additional years to be added at presidential
discretion. With that niggardly action, the senators dashed any
hope for even a first step towards a comprehensive settlement with
the Indians. The government had secured the Holy Road west, and
when the price of that security ran too high, it simply chose not
to pay the full freight. As for civilizing the plains tribes—the
fifty-year experiment envisioned in the treaty—the necessity of
that undertaking seemed terribly remote back in Washington, two
thousand miles from the changing western landscape. The prairies
were still the Great American Desert, as far as most of the senators

were concerned; with the proper restrictions, the Indians could still have that land for their own. If the passing whites slaughtered the buffalo and deprived the tribesmen of their subsistence, the government would compensate them at least for the next decade. In the absence of a more immediate crisis, few politicians thought beyond that.

The Sioux had no idea that the United States had amended the treaty unilaterally. They kept on living the same life that they had been leading for the last century. They threw away the farming tools.

The Laramie treaty failed even before it became law. One party had revised its terms; the other party ignored them. Oddly enough, the agreement did succeed in fashioning an uneasy truce between the Indians and the emigrants. But it was the sort of truce that solved nothing—bought "for cracker and molasses," an army general said. If for a few years the emigrants moved west across the plains in relative peace, the Sioux and American empires were nonetheless already headed for collision. Government annuities could no more wean the Sioux from their buffalo culture than well-intentioned treaties could halt the spread of pioneers into the heart of Indian country. In the seventy-five years since Standing Bull first reached the Black Hills, two empires, once a world apart, had become cohabitants of a continent of ever-shrinking wilderness. One empire thrived on that change; both could not.

T W O

▼ ▼ ▼ ▼

A GENERATION OF CONQUEST

IN AUGUST 1854, at a spot roughly three miles from where the Laramie treaty was signed, a Mormon wagon train snaking its way along the Platte passed within sight of a large camp of the Brûlé band of Teton Sioux. As had by now become almost customary, a few warriors rode over to scout the caravan and to cajole the settlers into parting with some coffee, sugar, or other amenity. This time a hungry Sioux brave, High Forehead, spotted a lame ox trailing behind the wagons, and he shot it for dinner.

The ox's Mormon owner rushed to Fort Laramie, where he demanded that the soldiers obtain compensation from the Sioux. Meanwhile, Chief Conquering Bear, in whose camp High Forehead had taken refuge, hurried to the fort to settle up for the killing. In accordance with the Laramie treaty, to which Conquering Bear had affixed his mark as a chief of the Brûlé, he offered the Mormon compensation for the cow: $10 or a horse from his personal pony herd. Emboldened by the fort's bigoted lieutenant, John Grattan, the Mormon demanded $25—an exorbitant sum for an animal practically dead before High Forehead shot it and with no chance at all of completing the arduous journey across the plains.

Negotiations broke down and Conquering Bear returned to his camp. Lieutenant Grattan, however, had no intention of letting the matter rest. A belligerent Irishman fresh from West Point, he often complained to his outpost companions that what they really needed to break the monotony of frontier duty was to "crack it to the Sioux." Now he had a pretext. Taking along the fort's drunken

21

interpreter, and reportedly nipping at the bottle himself, Grattan rounded up twenty-nine volunteers to arrest High Forehead for killing the cow. "When I give the order," he instructed his men, "you can fire as you damned please."

As Grattan approached the Indian camp, aiming his artillery at the Sioux tipis, his mixed-blood interpreter started shouting threats of all sorts—that he would cut out Sioux hearts and that the whites would give the Sioux a new set of ears, the better to hear their orders. Conquering Bear and several warriors rode out to parley. A long conference ensued, with the chief commuting back and forth between the soldiers and his camp where High Forehead refused to give himself up. Although the Laramie treaty did not authorize the army to arrest alleged Sioux wrongdoers (the treaty provided for the payment of restitution instead), Grattan insisted that High Forehead surrender. And Grattan soon lost patience. He ordered his troops to fire. Caught in the first volley, Conquering Bear fell, mortally wounded.

Enraged at the murder of their leader, several hundred Sioux warriors, who had watched the parley from a nearby bluff, surrounded and took their revenge upon the badly outnumbered troop. Within minutes, Grattan, the interpreter, and all of the soldiers but one were dead—and the last man, Pvt. John Cuddy, died of his wounds a few days later. By that time the Indians had slaughtered the patrons at the local trading post, plundered the American Fur Company depot, and started robbing and burning mail coaches and wagon trains along the Platte.

With the blood of American soldiers now shed for the first time upon the plains, the government hastily prepared to strike back. That Grattan had disregarded the 1851 treaty and incited the Sioux to violence was meaningless in light of the tribe's subsequent rampage. The army was smarting; terrified pioneers were clamoring for protection. For the government, the pressing issue was not to assess the wisdom or legality of Grattan's conduct but rather to reestablish safe passage along the Holy Road and to impress upon the Sioux that, despite their initial victory, they could neither match the power of the white man's armies nor attack the settlers with impunity. As the army inspector investigating the Grattan fight observed, "the time has now fully arrived for teaching these barbarians . . . how to appreciate and respect the power, the justice, the generosity and the magnanimity of the United States."

Three years after the great conference at Laramie, the era of fragile but essentially peaceful and symbiotic relations between the plains tribes and the burgeoning nation that had surrounded them was at an end. For the next generation, the map of the west would be drawn and redrawn, time and again, as the tendrils of emigration spread through the western expanse and the American people spread over the land. The pattern had repeated itself at every stage of the European conquest of America, from the first rallying of Powahatan's tribesmen to repel the invasion of Virginia, to King Philip's rebellion against the Massachusetts Puritans and Chief Tecumseh's vain efforts to stem the advance of the Appalachian pioneers. In only a century and a half, the whites had spread inland from the coast to the eastern mountains and the central woodlands. At each juncture, a precarious friendship and distant coexistence had succumbed to the pressures inherent in American growth and expansion. At each juncture, the Indians belatedly organized to defend their homelands, only to be pushed aside and overwhelmed by the power and numbers of the whites. Now the whites had arrived at the edges of the great plains. Another generation of conquest began.

In August 1855, the army high command dispatched Colonel William Harney (the former lieutenant who had read the Declaration of Independence to the Sioux back in 1845) and a platoon of 1,300 men to discipline the Sioux and secure the Platte road. On September 3, Harney's army attacked Little Thunder's camp at Ash Hollow just off the Platte River in what is now Nebraska. Although Little Thunder had taken no part in the Grattan fight or the subsequent depredations, Harney ignored the Indians' attempts to surrender. His mission was to strike terror into the Sioux. With 1,300 troops well armed against a few hundred Sioux, many of them women and children, the encounter was a massacre. Harney counted eighty-six dead Teton, some warriors, many not. Harney placed the survivors in chains and took them back to Laramie.

For the Sioux, the fight at Ash Hollow was an unprecedented disaster. Despite the incessant raiding of tribal enemies, the Sioux had always considered eight or ten casualties a calamitous loss, and in their entire history had never witnessed, or even contemplated, the loss of a whole camp. News of Little Thunder's fate whipped through Sioux country, spreading north and west from the Platte at the speed of a fast horse. As winter set in, the confused and frightened Sioux fled to the sanctuary of the Black Hills.

The following spring, Harney sent word that he was proposing a new peace treaty, one he hoped would prove more enduring than the agreement signed at Laramie. He agreed to release his prisoners of war, to resume annuity payments, and to protect the Sioux from "impositions" by the whites. In return, he expected the Indians to surrender the warriors who had been terrorizing the emigrants, to return the property they had stolen, and to stop harassing the traffic along the Platte Road. The Sioux agreed to and complied with Harney's terms, but the Harney treaty never became law. The Senate, preoccupied with slavery and the impending sectional crisis, failed to ratify it.

The government did not tell the Sioux that the Senate had rendered the new agreement meaningless, but experience soon informed them that the whites had no intention of fulfilling Harney's commitments. Harney had promised the Teton that, except for already established roads, the government would prohibit all travel across their lands. Regardless, within a month, Lieutenant G. K. Warren, Harney's topographical engineer, set out to explore the area surrounding the Black Hills. The Sioux, led by Bear's Rib, a chief of the Miniconjous band of the Teton, were tracking a buffalo herd when they stumbled on the expedition. Bear's Rib confronted Warren, threatening to annihilate his command if it disturbed the nearby herd. The Sioux surmised the expedition's purpose—"to ascertain if [the land] was of value to the whites and to discover roads through it and places for military posts." But the Teton had already surrendered all of the land that they could spare, and Bear's Rib cautioned Warren that "these Black Hills must be left wholly to themselves."

Now vigilant to the danger of white expansion, in the summer of 1857 the Teton met in a grand council of all their bands, the only meeting of its kind for which any record exists. At least 5,000 and perhaps as many as 7,500 Sioux gathered at the base of Bear Butte, a stark volcanic outcrop at the northeast end of the Black Hills. Among them were the emerging Sioux leaders who would marshal the tribe in defense of its homeland: Red Cloud, in his thirties, once disfavored for killing Chief Bull Bear in a drunken melee, now recognized as a warrior of peerless courage and skill; Crazy Horse, a loner, just sixteen, witness to both the Grattan and Harney fights, who had pledged to his father he would battle the whites for the rest of his life; Sitting Bull, singer, healer, a distinguished leader of the Strong Heart warrior society, already known for his resonant speeches against accommodation with the whites.

There, along the banks of the Belle Fourche River, the assembled Teton bands—Oglala, Miniconjous, Sans Arc, Blackfeet, Two Kettles, and Hunkpapa—rejoicing in their numbers, "solemnly pledged to each other not to permit further encroachment from the whites." (Only Spotted Tail and his Brûlé band of Teton were missing. They stayed to the south, near the Platte, and went to war against the Pawnee, while trying to keep peace with Harney's soldiers.)

Back in Washington, agents of the Indian Bureau sought an administrative solution to the plains crisis. Thomas Twiss, the government representative for the upper Platte region, outlined the theoretical basis for a whole new civilizing program based on isolating the natives from the emigrant trails and educating them in the ways of white society. Others made less grandiose proposals, such as prohibiting the trade in buffalo hides, which was rapidly depleting the already shrunken herds, or policing "the lawless conduct" of many of the emigrants.

The ideas were noble, some even well considered. But they were neither intended nor able to stop America's expansion west, and nothing less would alleviate the prospect of a full-scale plains war. The Indian Bureau knew that with every wave of unrestricted settlers flowing west across the middle prairies, some would discover new regions for exploration or settlement; and a self-confident, aggressive nation would find new reasons for setting aside old treaties, moving old boundaries, and squeezing the tribes onto ever-smaller portions of the western expanse.

Surveying the prospective battlefield, Lt. Warren recognized this. "There are so many inevitable causes at work to produce a war with the Dakotas," he concluded his 1857 report, "that I consider the greatest fruits of [my] exploration to be the knowledge of the proper routes by which to invade their country and conquer them."

These "inevitable causes" grew more powerful and more numerous. In 1859, the discovery of gold in Colorado spawned a second generation of fortune hunters. In contrast to the 'forty-niners, they did not just cross the prairies; they started to settle the nation's vast undeveloped middle. Racing to Pike's Peak, 80,000 emigrants moved into the mountain region of the Permanent Indian Territory between 1858 and 1862, most of them traversing Sioux country with predictable results. The plains tribes developed a superstition that the buffalo would never return to a place where they had previously scented a white man.

The United States started to buy the long-spurned prairies, piece by piece, dismembering the Permanent Indian country which only a generation before had been declared the immemorial home of the western tribes. Late in 1858, the government purchased an enormous tract (roughly 15 million acres) east and north of the Missouri from the Teton's eastern relatives, the Yankton. Many Yankton themselves opposed the sale, a deal consummated by the signatures of thirteen self-appointed chiefs. But the dissatisfaction among the Yankton was nothing compared to the fury of other Sioux groups, specifically the Teton and Yanktonai. These Indians flatly denied that the Yankton had any right to sell this land; it did not belong to them. Rather, according to the western Sioux bands, the land belonged to the Yanktonais, who had lent it to their Yankton cousins when they lost their own homeland further east as the frontier moved west. The Yankton had been treacherous to sell it, the government dishonorable to buy it.

Bear's Rib had warned the United States against this swindle when he confronted Warren in the Black Hills a year before the sale, and he repeated his protest in the spring of 1859. Bear's Rib's plea was not merely for the Yankton land, it was for all the Sioux domain and for a way of life that everyone, white or red, could plainly see crumbling before the weight of America's inexorable push west:

> My Brother [Captain W. F. Raynolds at Fort Pierre]: To whom does this land belong?
>
> I believe it belongs to me. Look at me and at the ground. Which do you think is the oldest? The ground; and on it I was born. . . . The Yankton below us are a poor people. I do not know where their land is. I pity them. The lower Yanktons did own a piece of land I know, but they sold it long ago. I don't know where they got any more. Since I have been born, I do not know who own two, three, four, more pieces of land. . . . These Yanktons, we took pity on them. They had no land. We lent them what they grow corn on. We gave them a thousand horses to keep that land for us, but I never told them to steal it and go sell it. . . . The white men want my land and if I should give it to them where should I stay. I have no place else to go. . . . All of this country on each side of the river belongs to me. I know that from the Mississippi to this river the country all belongs to us, and that we have traveled from the Yellowstone to the Platte. All of this, as I have said, is ours. If you were to ask me for it I would not give it to you for I like it, and I hope you will listen to me."

Bear's Rib's hope was in vain. The government consummated the fraudulent sale and the land thus acquired became Dakota Territory, U.S.A.

The encroachments continued. In 1861, Montana became the latest El Dorado, with gold rumored to be so plentiful and so easily procured that one needed only a pick, shovel, and pan to garner a fortune. The new gold strike diverted part of the wide human stream running east-west along the Platte to run north through the Powder River country toward the Montana diggings and the new town of Helena. At first this northward fork, made famous as the Bozeman Trail, was traveled sparingly, only a few armed parties risking the uncharted shortcut. Still, the prospectors who took the Bozeman Trail invaded the still pristine rangelands of the great northern bison herd, the "meat pack" of the western Sioux. The survival of the Sioux as a nomadic people depended on this land and its game. The Teton recognized a familiar pattern: first a trickle, then a flood. For once, they decided, the waters must be turned back.

After the broken promises of the Laramie treaty and General Harney, after the gold discoveries in California, Colorado, and Montana, and after states and territories sprang up where for centuries only Indians had roamed, a full-scale confrontation between the Sioux and the United States became inevitable. The Sioux recognized as much. They split into factions, one hostile to the whites, absolutely committed to the buffalo way, and determined to fight for their land and culture; the other fearful of the whites, accustomed to living off their handouts, and anxious to appease them. For the whites, or at least for the government, tensions along the frontier remained a peripheral concern. With the Civil War threatening the nation's survival as a single union, the government stripped bare the frontier of military forces and averted its eyes from the persistent clashes along the emigrant trails.

The Sioux wars started in 1862 among the "semicivilized" Santee in Minnesota, who already had experienced a generation of uneasy commingling with the whites. These demoralized Indians, resentful of what they perceived to be inequitable treaties and the undoubtedly sharp practices of the government agents who controlled their lives, clashed periodically with nervous and sometimes belligerent pioneers. In the spring of 1862, the occasional violence and the tribe's brooding unhappiness with reservation life gave way to a massacre. Decades of Santee frustration converted a relatively minor confrontation with their traders into a wild campaign of murder. They terrorized the whole Minnesota frontier, killing as many as 750 settlers.

Anguished and frightened whites called for justice and revenge. The army hastily organized a counterforce. It quickly routed the poorly equipped Santee, taking most of the tribe prisoner. The militia commander in Minnesota, General Henry Sibley, a prominent politician in the state, moved swiftly to punish the tribe. He convened a court-martial and in short order condemned 303 Santee to the gallows, whether or not the individual defendants actually had participated in the rampage.

Sibley sent his orders for execution to President Lincoln, expecting executive sanction for the findings of his kangaroo court. But when the death sentences reached the White House, Lincoln viewed them skeptically. The President remembered something about Indian fighting from his own days as a soldier in the Black Hawk War of 1832 (the last Indian war fought east of the Mississippi), and he understood the difference between justice and just "hangin' injuns." Lincoln reviewed the case file of each condemned man and commuted all but forty of the sentences. In the end, thirty-eight Sioux were hanged before a large crowd in Mankato, Minnesota; it was the largest execution in the country's history.

While the President reviewed the courts-martial, fighting along the Minnesota frontier spread westward as the army under General Alfred Sully chased after the remnants of the battered Santee, who, by 1863, had fled into Teton country. Faced with the invasion of their territory by hostile government troops (who recognized little distinction between Santee and other Sioux), the western Sioux joined their eastern kin in battle. They did so in part to protect themselves and the Santee, but also to frustrate the government's ulterior motive in pursuing the campaign west of the Missouri River. Prospectors in Montana had discovered a huge lode at the "Last Chance Gulch," about ninety miles north of Virginia City. By the time of Sully's campaign, nine-tenths of the Santee were either dead or in prison. The real reason for taking the war west into Teton country was to clear a safe path through the Powder River country to the new mining districts in Montana.

Sully's army forced battle upon the Teton, who were quick to accept the challenge. Most of the Sioux already were hostile to the government, and those who were not found themselves under irresistible pressure to fight. Bear's Rib, who had sought accommodation with the whites, was murdered by his more militant tribesmen. By the end of 1863, William Dole, Commissioner of Indian Affairs, was lamenting that the Union "had upon [its] hands, in addition to the great rebellion, an Indian War of no mean proportion."

But the two wars were very different. While the Union and

Confederate armies squared off in the monumental pitched battles of Gettysburg and Antietam and Sherman's army laid siege to Atlanta, across the plains, especially along the Platte, fast-riding Sioux shot up wagon trains, mangled telegraph wires, and burned trading posts and trail stations. On the other side, army tactics consisted largely of surprising camps, putting the Indians to flight, shooting their captured ponies, and burning their food and clothing stored for the winter. Indian fighting knew little of honor or heroics. Sioux scalps sold for $200 in Yankton, the capital of the Dakota Territory, and Sully himself ordered a pair of Teton skulls mounted on poles to adorn the city. There were no eulogies like Gettysburg's, no mercy as at Appomattox.

Indian hating spread like a prairie fire. "Receive no overtures of peace or submission from the Indians," one of Sully's fellow generals, Patrick Connor, instructed his troops, "but attack and kill every male Indian over twelve years of age." All through the region, newspaper editors clamored to let the local boys clean up the Indian trouble. At Sand Creek, Colorado, the local boys did. Egged on by their commander, Colonel John Chivington (a former Methodist preacher who, in the name of God, justified killing Indian babies because "nits make lice"), a group of local volunteers butchered hundreds of Black Kettle's peaceful Cheyenne band. Black Kettle had moved his camp to Sand Creek because the government had promised him a safe haven there. Instead, at dawn on November 27, Chivington descended upon them with a force of six hundred Indian haters rustled up off the streets of Denver. They spent the better part of the day tracking down and beating to death women and children who had managed to escape the initial onslaught, then mutilated the corpses—beyond recognition.

The public and press from Idaho to Arizona applauded Chivington's tactics. In Denver, a few days afterwards, a theatrical troup displayed a collection of Cheyenne scalps including the pubic hair of Cheyenne women. In the east, however, where virtually all Indians had long since been killed or banished west, no audiences gawked vicariously. To most easterners, generations removed from the sometimes savage subjugation of tribes like the Iroquois or Seminoles whose remnants still hung on in small pockets strung from New York to Florida, the brutality of the western Indian campaigns, Sand Creek in particular, was appalling. Congress initiated three separate investigations to comb through the moral wreckage at Sand Creek, and their findings—children murdered in cold blood, pregnant women sliced open—provided a wealth of

damning evidence for an emerging coalition working to revamp
government Indian policy.

With the Civil War drawing to a close, the formidable alliance
of humanitarians and evangelical religious reformers who had
kept the cause of abolition at the forefront of the nation's political
agenda for the last generation turned its attention from emancipation to the problem of Indian assimilation. At reform conferences
throughout the east, and in the myriad journals that had served as
the scriptures of the abolitionist movement, the new Indian reformers started intrepidly upon a second crusade: the creation of
an Indian policy worthy of their vision for post-Civil War America—a nation divinely inspired, purged of injustice and inequality.
To men like Bishop Whipple, the Minnesota missionary who had
asked Lincoln to spare the 300 Santee sentenced to death after the
1862 uprising, or Edward Everett, the Harvard professor who
preceded Lincoln in commemorating the dead of Gettysburg, or
Alfred Love, Quaker convert and radical pacifist who founded the
Peace Union, the mission for the country was not simply to make
the frontier part of America but to make its inhabitants good
Americans, hardworking and God-loving. As the abolitionist poet
John Greenleaf Whittier put it: "the more we do in the true spirit
of the Gospel for others [the negroes and the Indians] the more we
shall really do for ourselves."

To these reformers, solving the Indian problem was more than
just another political cause. It was a matter of spiritual redemption
for a nation already partially cleansed of sin by the elimination of
slavery. The red race belonged to the universal brotherhood of
man and, like the negro race, needed to be raised to a level consistent with that status. The reformers had elevated the slaves (or so
they intended) through the twin power of freedom and law. They
proposed to elevate the Indian through the civilizing influences of
education, Christianity, and an honest day's labor in the fields.

For the next half-century these men and their likeminded
successors influenced and often controlled the country's Indian
policy. In 1865, with the government still largely occupied with
the problem of the South, the reformers were just beginning to
turn their attention to the Indian problem. Joining the railroads,
the territorial governments, the army, and others, these
humanitarians (or Friends of the Indian, as they called themselves)
became yet another group demanding attention on matters of
western policy.

Congress resolved its Indian business for 1865 in a single day.
In one enormous Joint Resolution, the legislature attempted to

satisfy, or at least placate, all its various Indian-related constituencies. Among other items, Congress authorized a special committee to "inquire into the condition of the Indian tribes and their treatment by the civil and military authorities of the United States." Congress also appropriated money to build two roads from the Platte River to the Montana gold district, and allocated $20,000 for a commission to make peace with the Sioux. The humanitarians received the policy review they demanded; the frontiersmen benefitted from the prospective new highways to the land of plenty; and the inhabitants of the Dakota Territory (organized in 1861) could anticipate a respite from the incessant fighting that had scared away settlement and given the whole area a bad name. Apparently, Congress simply wished away the fact that the construction of roads to the Montana gold fields and the successful conclusion of a peace treaty with the Sioux were flatly incompatible aims.

The governor of the Dakota Territory, Newton Edmunds, took charge of the peace initiative. He had been lobbying for a treaty conference since 1863, emphasizing that the annual campaigns against the Sioux were not only cruel but useless and wasteful as well. Edmunds pointed out that the United States, with its cumbersome infantry, was still a long way from whipping the mercurial Teton bands; and maintaining an active army on the northern plains was costing the U.S. Treasury $2 million every month, or about $150,000 for every Indian it managed to kill.

Edmunds, a New Hampshire native who had a hand in nearly every Dakota enterprise from the local parish to the Yankton Bank he helped to found, realized that the future of his territory depended on a tranquil frontier. The success of the Dakota Territory was far from assured. Its land was doubly suspect, less arable than the rich farmlands to the east and ominously marked on the map as part of the Great American Desert. Confronted with the unprecedented challenge of inhabiting a semiarid region, Dakotans needed a new peace treaty at once to attract new settlers and, no less critically, to generate lucrative government contracts for the fulfillment of Indian annuities. Indian business was just the sort of reliable industry that would supplement the territory's farm income and improve the odds in the region's struggle for economic self-sufficiency.

Self-interest, then, caused Edmunds and other forward-looking Dakota frontiersmen to join the eastern humanitarians in support of a peace policy. Moral considerations motivated one group; the possibility of exploiting the Indians animated the other. Together, they resorted to the same formula for treatymaking that had succeeded at Laramie: entice the Sioux into signing a peace with promises of annuity payments. Annuities would delight the starving Indians, Edmunds felt sure, and, of course, would provide a profitable industry for Dakota businesses.

The military commander for the upper Missouri, General John Pope, however, had no stomach either for Edmunds's economic plans or the new peace policy in general. "The Indians now in hostility need some exhibition of force, and some punishment before they will be peaceful," he raged in a letter to James Harlan, Secretary of the Interior; "the treaty of peace which Governor Edmunds proposes to make . . . is, I presume, such a treaty as it has been the practice of the Indian Department to make heretofore . . . paying Indians for outrages committed upon innocent women and children."

Pope refused to let Edmunds negotiate with any of the Sioux, touching off a heated and frequently vicious battle between the Departments of War and Interior for control of Indian policy. During the next decade, each would frustrate the other's policies and trade endless accusations and recriminations. The bureaucratic struggle mirrored the mood of the nation at large as it vacillated between militant and peaceful approaches to settling the west. As public sentiment shifted with reports of Indian attacks, military savagery, or Indian Bureau corruption, so did the respective power of the Departments of War and Interior.

In 1865, drained by four years of civil war, the country had little heart for opening a new and potentially costly military campaign. Congress gave an initial mandate to the Interior Department and its peacemaker designate, Edmunds. Certain that three years of warfare must have reduced the Sioux to near starvation, Edmunds sent word to the Sioux camps to "make peace, eat lots of food."

The treaty council convened on September 25, at old Fort Sully along the banks of the Missouri. Edmunds proved right about one thing: the Indians were starving. A new band appeared in the attendance rolls, 600 strong—the "eat anything" band. The years of fighting, and scattering before army onslaughts, had kept the Sioux from their seasonal hunts and interrupted friendly trade, depriving them of their accustomed access to guns, ammunition, and other resources of white culture. For the first time, the Sioux felt the sharp pinch of their dependence on the whites. Particularly among the more eastern of the Teton bands, many had suffered enough and longed for peace.

Several thousand Sioux met the agents of the Great White Father. By the 28th of October, Edmunds claimed to have concluded treaties with nine different Sioux bands: seven Teton bands (the Miniconjous, Lower Brûlé, Two Kettle, Sans Arc, Hunkpapa, Blackfeet, and Oglala) as well as the upper and lower bands of the Yanktonai. Edmunds expedited matters with his none too subtle persuasion: "As soon as you sign," he kept reminding the destitute Sioux, "we will distribute the goods."

All the 1865 agreements read similarly. The Indians pledged to keep peace with the whites and among themselves and "to withdraw from the routes overland already established and hereafter to be established through your country." In exchange, the nine bands would receive a collective annuity of $76,900 each year for twenty years.

Edmunds and his fellow commissioners reported that the chiefs who signed the treaties represented 10,300 Sioux—an exaggerated and misleading figure. Edmunds knew well that almost none of the nearby 20,000 hostile Sioux, at that moment camped far west of the Missouri in the Black Hills and Powder River country, had any connection whatsoever with the new agreements. Trying a bit of political legerdemain to disguise his limited progress, Edmunds had executed treaties with the few thousand relatively peaceful Missouri River Sioux (of various bands), the Indians who already had begun to give up their former habits and adopt white ways— the ones scorned by the hostiles as "hangers-around-the-fort" and "Laramie Loafers."

Regardless, Edmunds held up these treaties as though he had concluded them with virtually the whole Sioux nation. In 1865, the "friendlies" were desperate, and, for a price, they were willing to sign away the rights of their fellow tribesmen, permitting roads where they themselves never roamed. Edmunds could not plead ignorance to this sham. Only two months earlier, the ascendant Oglala leader, Red Cloud, had accosted the government's road-surveying party on its way to Montana. The Sioux stripped the surveyors of their clothes and gear before releasing them naked in the wilderness. These Sioux had made no peace; they would countenance no road.

With the 1851 Laramie treaty annuities due to expire at year's end (having been extended five years by Lincoln) and the government more anxious than ever to open a safe route through the Powder River valley, the peace commissioners decided to renew negotiations the next year in hope of getting the real parties of interest, Red Cloud and Spotted Tail (leader of the hostile Brûlé), to sign. Spotted Tail, for one, was ready to give peace a try. As a warrior in Conquering Bear's camp, he had been one of the first Sioux to take to the warpath after Lieutenant Grattan murdered his chief. Later, as required by Harney, Spotted Tail had surrendered for killing Grattan's contingent and for marauding along the Platte. Imprisoned for a year at Fort Leavenworth before receiving a Presidential pardon, Spotted Tail became so impressed with the overwhelming power of white civilization he felt that his tribe's only recourse was a policy of peace and accommodation with the whites. The time in Kansas, where he observed the Otoes, Omahas, and other tribes who long since had given up the hunting way, gave him hope that such a policy might succeed. When Sully's army invaded his country, Spotted Tail returned to battle only very reluctantly, and in 1866, when the hardships of fighting and flight killed his daughter, the chief decided to lay down his arms forever.

The chief brought the body of his dead child to Fort Laramie, where Colonel Henry Maynadier, sensing an opportunity to bring Spotted Tail to terms, personally escorted the grieving father into the post. Maynadier was honored and deeply moved that the renowned Spotted Tail trusted him with his daughter's remains. "The Great Spirit had taken her," Maynadier wrote of his efforts to comfort the chief, "and he never did anything except for some good purpose." Everything would be prepared for her funeral at sunset, so that "as the sun went down, it might remind [Spotted Tail] of the darkness left in his lodge when his beloved daughter was taken away; but, as the sun would surely rise, so she would rise and someday we would all meet in the land of the Great Spirit." Maynadier spoke of the peace and friendship which the Great Father offered, informing Spotted Tail that the treaty commission would soon arrive to settle their differences once and for all.

Tears fell from Spotted Tail's eyes and for a while he sat speechless. Then he grasped the Colonel's hand and said:

> This must be a dream for me to be in such a fine room and surrounded by such as you. Have I been asleep during the last four years of hardship and trial and am dreaming that all is to be well again, or is this real? Yes, I see that it is; the beautiful day, the sky blue, without a cloud, the wind calm and still to suit the errand I come on and remind me that you offer me peace. We think we have been much wronged and are entitled to compensation for the damage and distress caused by making so many roads through our country, and driving off and destroying the buffalo and game. My heart

is very sad, and I cannot talk on business; I will wait and see the counsellors the Great White Father will send.

"The scene was one of the most impressive I ever saw," Maynadier continued in his report, ". . . and satisfied some who had never before seemed to believe it, that an Indian had a human heart to work on and was not a wild animal." It augured well for peace. Spotted Tail "would never have confided the remnants of his child to the care of anyone but those with whom he intended to be friends always."

With Spotted Tail apparently amenable to peace, the government turned its attention to Red Cloud, who was also on his way to Laramie. Irascible, haughty, and ambitious, Red Cloud had alienated many of his own people after he killed Bull Bear, a drunken Oglala chief, back in 1841, but his superb talents as a warrior gradually won him considerable power and prestige. By 1866, as a relatively young man of about forty, he already had begun to figure prominently in the Oglala councils, giving voice to the spirit of resistance to white encroachment. Red Cloud had counted eighty coup, eighty feats of valor and courage, and he had no intention of voluntarily giving up his warrior ways to live indolently around a white man's fort while his children learned white ways. Nonetheless, the treaty commissioners hoped that the poverty of his people would move Red Cloud to do what the U.S. Army apparently could not—make peace. That he was coming in to talk was remarkable in itself, so remarkable that in the spring of 1866 "a lasting peace" became the optimistic watchwords along the Dakota frontier.

E. B. Taylor, the government's new principal negotiator, arrived at Laramie May 30, and since Spotted Tail, Red Cloud, Red Leaf, Man-Afraid-of-His-Horses, and almost all of the other prominent hostiles were already assembled, the talks commenced a few days later. Taylor had learned the art of peacemaking by watching Newton Edmunds at Fort Sully the year before. He understood the importance of obfuscation and employed it liberally when he reported to Washington that "the general feeling of all these tribes is very conciliatory and friendly." Despite the supposedly congenial atmosphere, Taylor adjourned the negotiation for another week, ostensibly to wait for the arrival of more Indians, but actually because the Sioux had once again balked at the proposed Powder River (Bozeman) road.

While Taylor cajoled the recalcitrant tribesmen, General William Tecumseh Sherman, conqueror of the Confederate South, now in command of the Missouri District, went about organizing protection for the Bozeman Trail, the congressionally authorized and Sioux-contested route to Montana. Sherman dispatched Colonel Henry Carrington and a battalion of infantry to afford "the best possible protection to . . . the region of Montana and the routes thereto." Carrington marched for Fort Laramie (where the Bozeman road began), intent on constructing and garrisoning two forts in the midst of the Powder River hunting grounds regardless of what happened at the Laramie treaty conference.

On June 13 the peace council reconvened and Taylor explained the treaty to the Teton, dwelling at length on the $70,000 long-term annuity promise while obscuring the Indians' quid pro quo acquiescence to the Bozeman Trail. Taylor said nothing at all about the forts that would be built. His talk was all about making payments and selling guns to the Indians and leaving them at peace in their hunting grounds. Just at this moment, however, Carrington's battalion marched into the fort on its way to protect the still-contested trail. The Sioux were quick to perceive both Taylor's deceit and the two-facedness of congressional policy, which during a single day authorized both a peace mission and the garrisoning of the very road that had sparked the war in the first place.

Red Cloud swept up his blanket, pointed to Carrington's just-arrived troop, and denounced the peace. "The Great Father sends us presents and wants us to sell him the road," he shouted as he walked out of the council, "but White Chief goes with soldiers to steal the road before the Indians say Yes or No."

"Red Cloud promised it might be a long war," one eyewitness recalled, "but as [the Sioux] were defending their last hunting grounds they must in the end be successful." Red Cloud broke camp, making for the Powder River, where he rallied his followers:

> Hear ye Dakotas. . . . Yet before the ashes of the council fire are cold, the Great Father is building his forts among us. You have heard the sound of the white soldiers' axe upon the Little Piney. His presence here is an insult and a threat. It is an insult to the spirits of our ancestors. Are we to give up their sacred grounds to be plowed for corn? Dakotas, I am for war.

Spotted Tail stayed at Laramie and, along with a few lesser chiefs, signed the treaty. To these Sioux, it no longer mattered what price they paid for peace. Their struggle already had ended and they had lost, not on the battlefield, but on their hunting grounds, where the buffalo no longer grazed, or at the army posts, where a debauched but easy life weaned them from their habits. They were casualties in a war between two cultures, first made desperate and weary by a long and steady assault on their way of life, then broken by their consequent dependence on government annuity payments for survival.

Not all were so tenacious as Spotted Tail, who would dedicate his life to saving his people through shrewd bargaining. Many would live in squalor around the forts, ridiculed and derided by their fellow tribesmen, who viewed them as lackeys of the whites. Whatever their motives, every Sioux who signed the treaty gave notice that, even if he wouldn't yet walk the white man's road, neither would he take up arms again for the old Sioux way.

While the "friendlies" who signed the treaty were being branded cowards by their warring tribesmen, Commissioner Taylor, like Edmunds before him, trumpeted the success of his negotiations. On June 29, he telegraphed the commissioner of Indian Affairs to announce his new agreement. "Satisfactory treaty concluded with the Sioux," he reported, "large representation. Most cordial feeling prevails." When word leaked out that something was amiss, that most of the Teton had returned to the warpath, Taylor had a ready answer; he confessed that "a band of about 300 warriors" headed by Red Cloud "was refusing to obey the will of the tribe."

Colonel Carrington (a "dress parade" soldier with almost no Indian fighting experience) and his complement of raw recruits were left to discover the enormity of Taylor's purposeful deceit.

THREE

▼ ▼ ▼ ▼ ▼

A VICTOR'S PEACE

O N A BLUSTERY FIRST DAY of winter, December 21, 1866, a small
band of Teton horsemen attacked a supply train venturing
out from Fort Philip Kearny, one of Colonel Carrington's newly
erected posts along the Bozeman Trail. The attack, led by the
intrepid young Oglala warrior Crazy Horse, followed a familiar
pattern for the garrison, one the soldiers had seen dozens of times
during the arduous fall months of building and occupation. The
Indians swooped down on the wagons, firing their rifles and arrows as much to harass as to kill, then circled out of range before
reinforcements from Phil Kearny could strike back.

The Sioux forays exasperated Carrington's troops, accustomed
to seeking the offensive, and were particularly galling because
these attackers were savages picking off soldiers and riding away
with impunity. The officers at the fort thought they could rout the
Sioux, if given a chance, but they chafed under Carrington's le-
thargic, sit-in-the-fort attitude. Most shared the sentiments of
Lieutenant Colonel William Fetterman, Carrington's second-in-
command, who often bragged to his comrades that "with eighty
men [he] could ride through the whole Sioux Nation."

On the twenty-first, when the sound of gunfire reached the fort,
Fetterman got his chance. Carrington placed precisely eighty men
at Fetterman's disposal, ordered him to relieve the beleaguered
supply train, and to pursue the Sioux raiders as far as, but no
farther than, Lodge Trail Ridge. The impetuous Fetterman,
though, rushed out of the fort eager to fulfill his boast, regardless
of restraining orders. Goaded on by Crazy Horse, who charged

forward alone, taunted the soldiers, and then retreated just out of range, Fetterman chased the Teton over the ridge, out of sight of the fort.

In less than twenty minutes, Red Cloud's warriors, hidden in ambush, administered the worst defeat yet suffered by the U.S. Army at the hands of the western tribes. "There were lots of bullets and lots of arrows—like locusts," Black Elk, a Sioux shaman, recalled. Not one of Fetterman's command survived, and their eighty-one bodies, methodically mutilated, lay strewn about the field. Carrington described the carnage: "Eyes torn out and laid on rocks; noses cut off; ears cut off; chins hewn off; teeth chopped out . . . private parts severed and indecently placed on the person. . . ." The frost-covered field was a mirror image of Sand Creek, though this time it was the whites who lay mutilated on the prairie grass.

"Portuguese" Phillips, one of the most daring scouts on the plains, rode all night through a blizzard to carry the tragic news down the Bozeman Trail from Fort Phil Kearny to military headquarters at Laramie. The army high command reacted first with disbelief and then genocidal rage to Phillips's report of Fetterman's last charge. "I do not understand how the massacre of Colonel Fetterman's party could have been so complete," Sherman wired General Grant in Washington. "We must act with vindictive earnestness against the Sioux even to their extermination, men, women and children. Nothing less will reach the root of the case." Sherman spent the rest of the winter planning a spring offensive, a campaign to be waged "until at least ten Indians are dead for every white life lost."

The Fetterman Massacre, the whites called it; the Battle of the Hundred Slain was the Sioux name. Whatever the label, the meticulous and brutal ambush exploded the myth of plains peace and with it the nation's comfortable delusion that the Indian problem, if not settled, was at least under control.

Across the frontier, where fear and bigotry relegated Indians to subhuman status, editors condemned what they viewed as the Indian Bureau's pampering of the tribes and proposed their own final solution. "It's high time the sickly sentimentalism about humane treatment and conciliatory measures should be consigned to novel writers," sizzled one Montana paper. Others, like the *Kansas Daily Tribune,* were more blunt: "There can be no permanent, lasting peace on the frontier till these devils are exterminated."

The annihilation of Fetterman's command provoked a very different response east of the Missouri, where voluntary associations devoted to philanthropy, religion, education, and reform had continued to proliferate, swelling the chorus of Indian defenders. The surprising Sioux victory, like a stroke of divine retribution reminding the nation of its moral failings, plunged these reformers into a gloomy mood of reflection and self-reproach rather than anger. Certain that the country's persistent disregard for Indian treaty rights had been the root cause of the Fetterman disaster, the humanitarians responded to the cries for extermination with urgent pleas for peace. The Indians' day of reckoning had arrived, they believed. As one reformer wrote, the tidal wave of advancing settlers would "soon crush them out from the face of the earth, unless the humanity and Christian philanthropy of our enlightened statesmen shall interfere and rescue them." In journal articles, editorials, and in a specially commissioned congressional report, the humanitarians called for a new peace commission to meet with the plains tribes and arrange for permanent reservations away from the main channels of emigration. There the Indians would receive livestock, agricultural tools, education, and religious indoctrination—the time-honored implements for civilizing Indians that had nowhere succeeded before.

In Washington the Interior Department, still wrangling with the military for jurisdiction over the tribes, was glad to receive and to amplify the humanitarians' appeals. The Indian Bureau seized upon the Fetterman issue to discredit the army's treatment of the Indians. Specifically, Commissioner of Indian Affairs Lewis Bogy, a Confederate sympathizer who despised the army that had defeated the South, suggested preposterously that the Sioux who annihilated Fetterman's command, far from being hostile, actually were part of a peace delegation seeking supplies at Fort Phil Kearny for their starving families. The army's antagonism had rendered these poor souls desperate and forced them to resort to a battle stratagem that in the end had proven all too successful. Bogy was "satisfied that the recent troubles at Forts Laramie and Phil Kearny grew out of injudicious military interference" in the Interior Department's handling of Indian affairs.

In Bogy's opinion, and in the view of almost all the humanitarian groups, to turn the Indians over to the military would result in an Indian war of monstrous proportions and, ultimately, would be tantamount to a policy of genocide. As a precaution, the commissioner asked Congress for a special appropriation to collect Indian memorabilia just in case the natives should "pass away."

The proposal reflected common expectation. Though not advocates of extermination, many people in and out of the army (including the military administrators of Sioux country, General Sherman and his protégé General Philip Sheridan) agreed with Colonel John Gibbon, a veteran frontier officer, that "philanthropists and visionary speculators may theorize as they please about protecting the Indian . . . and preserving him as a race. It cannot be done. Whenever the two [cultures] come in contact . . . the weaker must give way and disappear. To deny this is to deny the evidence of our own senses, and to shut our eyes to the facts of history." The theory was essentially social-Darwinist: The Indians were a vanishing species and no amount of good will could or would change nature's law.

The experience of many tribes already had confirmed the observation of the Frenchman Alexis de Tocqueville, who, decades earlier, had written "that the European is to the other races of men what man in general is to the rest of animate nature. When he cannot bend them to his use or make them indirectly serve his well-being, he destroys them and makes them vanish little by little before him." Although the flood tide of emigration was advancing once again after the end of the Civil War, the Sioux were neither bending nor serving, and they would long recall the dark spirit of that Winter of the Hundred Slain when the white men swirled around their homeland and "everyone was saying that . . . they were going to take our country and rub us all out and that we should all have to die fighting."

If a war began, the Sioux could expect no quarter from their lead adversary, General Sherman. As commander in the west, Sherman was responsible for the safety of the emigrants and for the lines of travel and communication to fledgling settlements. A brilliant, if eccentric, military man, Sherman had demonstrated his ruthless efficiency as an officer during his famous march to the sea at the end of the Civil War. "It is a terrible thing to consume and destroy the sustenance of thousands of people," he wrote in his diary about his army's plundering of the Georgia countryside. But if "terror and grief and even want shall help to paralyze [the] husbands and fathers who are fighting us . . . it is mercy in the end." Scorched earth had proven an effective tactic then, and Sherman intended to be no less brutal to the Indians in protecting the settlers than he had been to the Confederate farmers. Tribal rights did not especially concern Sherman and, although he might recognize that the settlers themselves stirred up much of the Indian trouble, it made no difference in the performance of his duty that those he zealously sought to protect had frequently violated "some old treaty."

Bringing the Sioux to battle, though, would be no easy task. Sherman still lacked the military resources to patrol his vast western command, and without considerable reinforcements from the east, he could not possibly mount a sustained campaign against a swiftly mobile foe. To compound Sherman's problems, Americans had grown apprehensive after the Civil War about their army, a painful reminder of five fratricidal years, and Congress had insisted on sharp reductions in its size. Several critics of the army suggested that it deliberately provoked Indian wars to justify larger enlistments and provide young officers with a chance for promotion and glory. Under the circumstances, Sherman's reinforcements might be a long time coming.

And Sherman knew that even if he could muster extra troops, he would still have to overcome the Interior Department's opposition to disciplining the tribes. On prior occasions when the army finally prepared itself to strike a retaliatory blow against the hostiles, the Indian Bureau had stayed the sword while peace negotiations were pursued. Nothing irked a military man like Sherman more than to have his orders countermanded by a bureaucracy, particularly one so rife with fraud and graft that its agents, lining their pockets with annuity monies, fueled hostilities by starving the Indians into robbing settlers. Transferring jurisdiction over the tribes to the War Department, Sherman believed, was the only workable solution to the corruption and self-defeating division of authority plaguing Indian policy. It was also the only way his army would take the field any time soon.

Sherman was not especially patient, but while Congress pondered the transfer issue, he did take solace in a revolutionary change that promised to solve his major problems in fighting the Sioux. With amazing speed, the Union Pacific Railroad, the harbinger of empire, advanced across the central plains, shortening the great distances which wrought havoc with military logistics. Sherman saw the iron rails as his new Mississippi (the river by which he and Grant had beaten the South), capable of moving his army at a pace even the fleet Sioux ponies could not match.

Sherman was further encouraged as he watched the buffalo herds dwindle. The end of the buffalo, better than any military campaign, would solve the Indian problem permanently. The general gleefully welcomed the avid sportsmen who came west to sample the "wild delights of the chase" and the less courageous thrillseekers who shot out of train windows as the cars plodded through a herd. Eastern manufacturers had discovered that buffalo hides not only made fine leather products but also could be put to a variety of industrial uses. Professional buffalo hunters scoured the plains to supply the new markets, armed with suicide capsules in case they were captured by the natives.

For its part, the Interior Department did not idle as the fate of the western tribes daily grew more precarious. One observer described the Indians as willful children with a powerful but henpecked father and a weak and indulgent mother. In the mother's role, the Interior Department spent the winter after the Fetterman ambush mapping out a new childcare program for the Sioux—the reservation theory. The theory's premises, reflecting its reformer origins, were simple: a policy of extermination was unconscionable; the occupation of Indian country imposed upon the government the duty to protect the imperiled tribes; and the only way to save the Indians from extinction was "to consolidate them as rapidly as can peacefully be done, on large reservations, from which all whites except Government employees would be excluded." This arrangement was to be a sort of protective custody until the natives were sufficiently trained "in the high arts of western civilization" to assume responsibility for their own support and receive the full rights of United States citizenship.

As noted earlier, that goal was not new. Since the founding fathers, and even before, the government had attempted to remove the wild Indian "from his condition of savage barbarity" and turn him into an American yeoman farmer. In the east, that policy had failed to save the tribes from near extinction. Now, over a half-century later, another band of recalcitrant tribesmen were to be moved out of harm's way while they learned to farm, not to hunt; to settle, not to roam; to worship Jesus, not the waters, earth, and sky.

The driving force behind the reservation policy, however, was no different from that of the army's program. Its principal effect was to expedite the settlement of the American west, and to that end the plan was eminently practical. Segregating the Indians would remove them from the main thoroughfares across the plains and, as reservation proponents habitually pointed out, would save the already empty national treasury the huge expense of an Indian war. Bogy's replacement as Commissioner of Indian Affairs, Nathaniel Taylor (a Methodist minister who turned to religion after his sister was killed by lightning), estimated that under the reservation system, peace could be had for the price of two days' Indian fighting. It was much cheaper to feed the Indians than to fight them, cheaper to kill a culture than a people.

Thus as spring 1867 approached, Congress faced a stark choice in Indian policy: to pursue an aggressive military campaign to punish the tribes or to follow the Interior Department and attempt to save the tribes by corralling them until they could be broken of their doomed culture. The special commission appointed by Congress to investigate the Fetterman incident argued vigorously for the latter. The commission concluded that the government had wrongfully established the Powder River Road, that peace with the Sioux was impossible unless the road was abandoned, that the cost of military operations to defend the road was prohibitive, and, accordingly, that the road should be closed. The commission, with notable condescension, exonerated the Sioux for killing Fetterman's command: "They admit their inferiority to us in all respects and seem now to have gone to war for the purpose of averting the death and destruction of their race."

More generally, the commission denounced past policy, condemning it for having "drive[n] an independent and lordly race into the condition of dependents and beggars" and for "convert[ing] generous, grateful and noble spirits into craven, bitter and degenerate souls." The noble savage was dead and America his executioner. The reformers now sought his resurrection—as a civilized man. "This Nation cannot . . . avoid its moral obligation to these people," it declared, "and its Christian duty to save them from destruction and elevate them from their degraded, barbarous state. . . . This evil can only be remedied by the selection of some country that shall be set apart for and devoted exclusively to the use and benefit of the Indians."

On the Senate floor, the commission report widened the rift between east and west which, with peace between north and south, had become an increasingly prevalent feature of the nation's politics. Senators from west of the Mississippi, where their constituents feared for their homes and lives, mocked the prospect of civilizing the barbarous plains tribes and railed against the reservations as a senseless obstacle to frontier expansion. Less partisan and passionate critics questioned whether isolating the Indian would facilitate his ultimate absorption into American culture. "We did not take the negro and put him on a reservation," Senator Samuel Pomeroy from Kansas observed. And they questioned how this new peace, unlike so many before, would resist the adventurism of aggressive pioneers.

The eastern response reverberated with the bass tones of a Sunday preacher, ripe with moral expostulations condemning the country's faithlessness to the Indian. However bleak the lessons of history, the Indian would be civilized and his right to the land secured. But convenience, again, made the humanitarian argument compelling. The reservation system, which would clear the lines of travel across the plains and guarantee uninterrupted construction of the transcontinental railroads, was ideally suited to a nation that yearned for expansion with honor. The trains would run; the wagons would roll; a prairie of red souls would be saved. For squeamish imperialists building an empire, this convergence of philanthropy, practicality, and thrift proved irresistible.

On July 20, 1867, both houses of Congress passed a bill authorizing a new commission to make peace with the plains tribes. As a concession to the westerners, the act carried an amendment authorizing the Secretary of War "to conquer a peace" if negotiations failed. Even Senator John Henderson, Missouri unionist and sponsor of the peace proposal, had to agree: "If nothing else but extermination will do, we cannot permit the Indian to stand in the way of civilization and his termination must come."

The act of July 20 created a commission to establish peace in the west, removing "if possible" the causes of war, while safeguarding the frontier settlements and the rights-of-way for the transcontinental railroads. Moreover, Congress directed the commission to establish reservations for the plains Indians with sufficient arable land for them to become self-sufficient farmers. Congress named to the commission Senator Henderson, Commissioner of Indian Affairs Taylor, John Sanborn, and Samuel Tappan. It also empowered the President to appoint three military men: General Sherman, the old Indian war veteran Harney, and Alfred Terry, a younger officer who had been named to head the Dakota military district.

Since Sanborn, a member of the special commission investigating the Fetterman fight, and Tappan, renowned for his critical examination of Sand Creek, generally shared Taylor and Henderson's sympathetic outlook towards the Indians, the delegation had a decidedly peace-oriented and antimilitary majority. The western press was quick to pick up on its bias, denigrating the peace mission as "[t]he most senseless and ridiculous piece of business we have ever heard of." Though a member himself, Sherman saw the commission's chief function as "killing time" and ordered his subordinates to continue planning an aggressive campaign to commence upon its inevitable failure.

The peace mission did begin inauspiciously. In September, the commission met with nine bands of Sioux at North Platte, Nebraska, but very few of the hostiles from Powder River attended, and even the so-called friendlies were surprisingly intractable.

The spot for the assembly, the end point of the Union Pacific Railroad, could not have been more symbolic. Here old and new stared each other down: The white men alighted from a gleaming railroad car to clear a further path for modernity and the Sioux gathered once again from scattered camps to stop them.

Commissioner Taylor—Princeton graduate, Union man, Methodist preacher, and gentleman farmer—addressed the Indians first. "We are sent here to inquire of you and find out what the trouble is between the white men and you. . . . My friends, speak freely and tell the truth. . . . Whatever is wrong we will make right. . . . War is bad and peace is good. . . . We ought to bury the tomahawk, smoke the pipe of peace and henceforth live in friendship forever like brothers of one family."

Spotted Tail told him plainly what was wrong. "We object to the Powder River road. The country which we live in is cut up by the white men, who drive away all the game. That is the cause of our troubles."

"Tell our Great Father to quit that [Powder River] road," Big Mouth, head of the Laramie Loafers, echoed.

"Tell our Great Father to stop that road and then we could have peace forever," promised Pawnee Killer.

The others agreed. The meeting adjourned.

The following morning, General Sherman, tall and gaunt, chewing as always on a pulverized cigar stump, answered the Indians on the commission's behalf. "The United States cannot abandon its road across your country," he informed the Sioux, "but it will pay for any damage done by the Bozeman Trail. . . . You must learn to live like white men and we will help you for as long as you need—just as we helped the Cherokee, Creeks, and Choctaws. We will set aside land for you, land for farming, housing and cattle-raising and we will teach your children to read and write."

Then Sherman showed the mailed fist.

"The railroads are coming," he warned them, "and you cannot stop [them] any more than you can stop the sun or the moon. You must decide; you must submit. This is not a peace commission only; it is also a war commission. Without peace, the Great Father who, out of love for you, withheld his soldiers, will let loose his young men and you will be swept away. . . . do the best you can for yourselves," he concluded, "we shall be here again in November."

With that, the commission departed for Kansas, where it successfully arranged a peace with the southern plains tribes. When

the commissioners returned in November, not even the peaceful
Sioux chiefs showed up to meet them, much less Red Cloud. Apparently unimpressed by Sherman's highhandedness, Red Cloud
had sent a message from his war camp in the Powder River Valley.
"If the Great Father kept white men out of my country, then peace
would last forever. The Great Spirit has raised me in this land and
has raised you in another land. What I have said I mean. I mean
to keep this land."

To press home the point, he and Crazy Horse, and Rain-in-the-
Face, and Gall, and Young-Man-Afraid-of-His-Horses, and Little
Big Man, and the seven-foot Touch-the-Clouds, and all the Sioux
who followed them continued their Bozeman Trail raids. Peace
was no closer than when the commissioners had started. They
resigned themselves to another conference in the spring as the long
plains winter settled in.

Neither the reformers in Washington nor the peace-anxious
majority on the commission intended to let their hopes and plans
dissipate in the interim. Every month the Indian bureau sent runners to the frozen prairie with messages for Red Cloud, who stead-
fastly maintained his position that he would make peace as soon
as the white soldiers left his country. Meanwhile, the peace commission drafted its annual report, which again made obvious what,
in the view of the humanitarian majority, was cause and remedy
for the continuing Indian war.

"Have we been uniformly unjust," the commission asked
rhetorically. "We answer unhesitatingly yes . . . when the progress
of our settlements reaches the Indians' home, the only question
considered is 'how best to get his land.' "

The report, written by the pious Taylor, recommended replacing a policy of armed force with "the hitherto untried policy in
connection with Indians, of endeavoring to conquer by kindness."
Foremost, the commission suggested closing the Powder River
Road. Abandoning the road, the commission argued, would have
no practical effect since the Indians had prevented travel on it for
the last two years and in any case the extension of the railroad west
of the Big Horn Mountains had opened up a shorter route to the
Montana gold district. Nearly everyone in the government outside
of the military and some die hard exterminationists agreed that the
Bozeman Trail had become obsolete and the forts defensible only
at excessive cost.

Though humiliating to the army, and a bitter pill for Sherman,
the peace commission returned to Sioux country in April carrying
a draft treaty which yielded everything Red Cloud demanded. For

the only time in U.S. history the country had fought a war, then decided to negotiate a peace on the enemies' terms.

Although Indian Bureau agents spent the better part of two months trying to coax various Sioux bands to another peace parley, only Spotted Tail and Iron Shell's Brûlé bands and a smattering of Oglala met with the commission when it reached Laramie at the month's end. To have come so far, offering so much, only to find the same docile bunch that had signed the old treaties of 1865 and 1866 was an embarrassing snub, but the commission forged ahead nonetheless, explaining the treaty to those present.

> If peace is made we do not want the Powder River road, nor the forts on it, but shall within these months abandon the road and withdraw the troops from that country. . . . We therefore propose that you will now make a treaty by which you can and will abide. By this treaty you will agree to remain at peace with the whites. By this treaty we shall agree to protect you from the inroads of our people and keep them out of a portion of your land described in the treaty. We shall agree to furnish you supplies and clothing and other useful articles while you continue to roam and hunt. We shall agree to furnish cattle, horses, cows and implements to work the ground to each of your people as at any time settle down and build a home and wish to live like the whites. Under this treaty you can roam and hunt while the game lasts; and when the game is gone you will have a home and means of supporting yourselves and your children. But you must understand that if peace is not now made, all efforts on our part to make it are at an end.

Article 2 of the treaty specified the Indians' new home—the Great Sioux Reservation, as it became known—setting aside all of present-day South Dakota west of the Missouri River, including the reputedly gold-laden Black Hills, "for the absolute and undisturbed use and occupancy of the Sioux." To the north and west of this permanent reservation, the treaty (in Article 16) also designated the contested Powder River country, "north of the North Platte River and east of the summits of the Big Horn Mountains," as "unceded Indian territory," where no white man could set foot without Indian consent. And to the south and west of the Great Sioux Reservation, where white settlement already had penetrated, Article 11 of the treaty granted the Sioux hunting rights along the Republican River and above the Platte River in Nebraska and Wyoming for "so long as the buffalo may range thereon in such numbers as to justify the chase."

The treaty further promised that all Sioux who moved within

the Great Sioux Reservation would be fed for the next four years while they adjusted to farming. And it promised schools and mills and doctors and blacksmiths and "boss farmers" (as the Indians referred to them) and teachers and an agent to administer the programs and settle disputes. And it promised to end the repeated trick of convincing a few superannuated chiefs to sign away treaty rights. Article 12 of the treaty specified that no future land sales would be valid unless the government collected the ratifying signatures of three-fourths of all adult Sioux males.

In return the United States asked for peace and also that the Sioux make their permanent homes within the boundaries of the Great Sioux Reservation. Article 11, in addition to delineating Sioux hunting grounds along the Republican River, also limited Sioux rights to any lands outside the reservation, including those newly defined hunting grounds and the "unceded Indian territory" described in Article 16. Specifically, the treaty required the Sioux to "relinquish all right to occupy permanently" any of these lands. Article 11 also obligated the Sioux to withdraw their opposition to the railroads being built on the plains, to cease molesting the emigrants and wagon trains, and to refrain from taking white captives. Article 4, moreover, stipulated that the government would distribute Sioux provisions and annuities not in the western part of their reservation, near their hunting grounds, where many of the Teton bands were accustomed to trading with the whites, but at new "agencies" that the government would establish along the Missouri River as centers for reorienting Sioux life.

On April 29, Iron Shell, a chief of the Brûlé, "touched the pen" on behalf of his people. His words upon signing said more about history than perhaps he knew. "I will always sign any treaty you ask me to do, but you have always made away with them—broken them."

This first ratification encouraged the commissioners, but they realized that a few Brûlé did not constitute the Sioux nation, nor could Iron Shell substitute for Red Cloud. The commission sent a special agent north to the Powder River to inform Red Cloud that the forts would be dismantled and to invite him to sign the peace. The Oglala chief wasted no words: "When we see the soldiers move away and the forts abandoned, then I will come down and talk."

The government already had issued those orders, but the whole summer passed before the last troops departed Fort Phil Kearny, allowing Red Cloud's torch-bearing warriors to swoop down upon the empty posts and burn them to ashes. Even then, Red Cloud stayed north, laying in his buffalo meat for the winter. He kept the peacemakers waiting until November 1868, during which time they collected signatures from other chiefs until finally, out of patience, they left for home, leaving the treaty with Major William Dye, the commandant at Laramie.

When Red Cloud finally arrived on the fourth, his intentions were still not clear. The chief showed no inclination to negotiate and obvious disdain for the low-level white officials who confronted him. For some minutes, Red Cloud refused to shake hands with them, though in the end he allowed a few officers to squeeze his fingertips. Later, when Major Dye started to explain the provisions of the treaty (in particular those pertaining to settling on the reservation and farming), Red Cloud interrupted, saying that he had already heard from others all he cared to know, that he felt pleased with his present home, still abounding with game, and that he saw no reason to abandon the chase for reservation farming. In fact, Red Cloud stated, his principal purpose in coming to Laramie was not to make promises he did not know if the Sioux could keep, but to hear news, to trade, and to procure weapons with which to fight the Crow. Only after Major Dye told him that he could expect no ammunition until he signed the peace did Red Cloud seem willing to consider it.

The next morning Red Cloud did sign. Afterwards, he launched into a long speech about his plans and expectations for the coming months. The Oglalas would spend the winter along the Powder River among the buffalo, Red Cloud announced, where they would make war on the Crow. They did not want to know how to farm, and while the game lasted, they did not care to learn. The Oglalas wanted to trade, and now that Red Cloud had agreed to the peace, he expected his old friends at Laramie to resume the barter that war had suspended four years before. The fighting had impoverished his people, Red Cloud admitted, but his camp was filled with hides to make them rich again.

As Red Cloud spoke, his words revealed that the peace he had signed, however well defined its terms, was not the same peace the government had drafted. To Red Cloud and the Sioux the treaty was not the first step along the white man's road or even the last step along the old Sioux way. The Sioux had saved their way of life on the frozen ridge where they slaughtered Fetterman and his men. They had no intention of abandoning that life with the peace. To them, the 1868 agreement was a peace made on the victor's terms—Sioux terms. Over the last year, they had clearly made known the price of peace. The road must be closed. They must keep their land. They must roam and hunt. On every point the Sioux had won. They failed to realize, though—or chose to disregard—that their victory resulted not from their own strength but from the government's decision, driven by conscience and temporary self-interest, to let them win.

The United States did not for a moment consider itself defeated. On the contrary, that the nation could swallow its pride and enter into a magnanimous peace reflected how small a threat it considered the Sioux. To an ever-increasing degree, the government regarded the plains tribes as it had long since regarded the eastern Indians—as wards of the nation, to be pitied and protected.

While the Sioux celebrated their Powder River triumph, the Indian experts in Washington were recommending to Congress that the United States abolish the archaic treaty system which vested impotent tribes with a degree of independent sovereign status. The United States should assume full responsibility as guardian for the plains Indians, they asserted, and determine for the natives their own best interests. The Indians would have to assimilate or perish, the dominant theory held, and it was for the government to determine which it would be.

If to the government the most important conditions of the treaty were those anticipating eventual Sioux settlement within the strict confines of the permanent reservation, these same conditions were the least important to the Sioux. "Now we want to live as our fathers have lived," Spotted Tail told the peace commission. "There is plenty of game in our country at present and we cannot go farming until all that is gone. When that time comes I will let my Grandfather know it."

Other Sioux were even more resolute. Crazy Horse and Sitting Bull rejected the treaty altogether, staying with their bands in the Powder River Valley. "Now you tell us to work for a living," Crazy Horse, the hero of the Fetterman fight, intoned, "but the Great Spirit did not make us to work but to live by hunting. You white men can work if you want to. We do not interfere with you, and again you say, why do you not become civilized? We do not want your civilization. We would live as our fathers lived, and their fathers before them." With the whites gone from their country, they thought the old life would last forever.

Sioux pride was at its zenith, yet despite the peace commissioners' extended visit with the tribe, these whites grasped not at all the Indians' commitment to their own way of life. The Sioux believed fiercely in their special creation, that the Great Spirit had made the whites to farm and build cities and the Indians to hunt and live in harmony with the natural world. Part of that harmony was not scarring their mother earth with a plow's deep furrows. Farming was more than just foreign to the Sioux, it was repugnant. Taking up the plow meant renouncing the culture, as surely as cutting off the ceremonial braid or giving up the breechclout for pants—other innovations foisted on them by the whites. Even among the assimilationists who accepted the transition, the men relegated farming to the women. Working a field lay beneath the dignity of a trained hunter and warrior, even if he no longer hunted or fought.

With the same blind faith that led the Indian Bureau to conclude that the natives envied white culture, the government confidently anticipated the rapid and complete assimilation of the Sioux— perhaps within a generation. The peace commission had built this optimism into the terms of the treaty, limiting the food annuity to four years and ending the rest of the education program after twenty. In four years, the Sioux would become self-sufficient agriculturalists; after twenty, they would become pure white beneath the skin. The reformers could perceive no value in the plains culture: why should the Sioux hesitate to forsake it?

But they did. The government would need more than a peace treaty to transform the Sioux into yeoman farmers and turn a few meager garden plots into subsistence for an Indian nation. And it would need far more than the reformers' pious hopes to impress its will upon an ascendant, tenacious people.

General Sherman, among others, realized that moral suasion alone would not bring the Sioux to the reservation. "To labor with their own hands or even to remain in one place militates with all the hereditary pride of the Indian," he observed, "and *force* must be used to accomplish this result." In short, though the Interior Department had arranged the peace, the military would have to administer it.

Sherman had never surrendered in the bureaucratic battle over the Indians. He pressed hard for a clear-cut policy of "peace within the reservation and war without." He objected to the treaty stipulations granting the Sioux off-reservation hunting rights (both Articles 11 and 16), which obscured boundaries and delayed the inevitable. It would be better, he wrote Sheridan, "to invite all the sportsmen of England and America this fall for a Great Buffalo Hunt and make a grand sweep of them all." That would make farmers of the Sioux.

Even Sherman, though, thought the peace would work to the Indians' eventual benefit. "The Peace Commission," he reported to Congress in 1868, "has assigned them a reservation which if held for fifty years will make their descendants rich." The future of the Sioux depended on the accuracy of that assessment: first, that the land was valuable and, second, that the Sioux could keep it for fifty years. The history of American expansion suggested the two premises were mutually exclusive; and if either one proved illusory, the Indians would be at the government's mercy. With or without Sherman's Great Hunt, the buffalo were vanishing and with their passing the Sioux, however haughty, would be left to discover that, although they had won the war, in the end they could not win the peace.

JUSTICE AND GENEROSITY

E VEN BEFORE RED CLOUD signed the 1868 treaty, Spotted Tail and
the Brûlé who made peace in April had already found that
their supposed triumph looked more like defeat. Instead of hunting, they were begging. Instead of roaming, they were stuck along
the Missouri near the mouth of the White River, fastened umbili-
cally to the rations and annuities that the government distributed
at the agency it had established there.

Although the treaty allowed the Brûlé to hunt in their traditional places in the south near the Republican River, several murders there by Cheyenne and Arapaho young bloods had prompted
the military to revoke that privilege. The army announced that it
would consider hostile all Sioux around the Republican and treat
them accordingly. In violation of the treaty, the army confined the
Brûlé to the permanent reservation, demonstrating once again that
government assurances counted for nothing whenever there was
trouble on the plains.

Sherman's moment had arrived. The marauding southern
tribesmen, having terrorized the settlements along the Kansas-
Pacific Railroad without apparent provocation, provided him with
the bloody shirt he needed to promote a more militant Indian
policy. For once, the nation responded. Even the usually critical
New York Times supported Sherman's euphemistic call for "more
vigorous measures." Sherman ordered George Armstrong Custer
and the 7th Cavalry to attack those remnants of Little Thunder's
Cheyenne who had survived Sand Creek, and the army routed
Little Thunder's camp along the Washita River, killing a dozen

warriors and ninety women, children, and old men.

About the same time, on October 7, the peace commission met for a final time in Chicago. Sherman and his subordinate generals, enjoying a rare moment of public confidence, won over John Sanborn and turned the tables on the peace party delegates. By the end of the three-day meeting, the commissioners not only had adopted a series of recommendations in striking contradiction to the prevailing peace policy, they also renounced many of the provisions of the treaty they had just negotiated. They proposed to terminate the practice of dealing with Indian tribes as independent nations and to return them to the jurisdiction of the War Department. Moreover, despite treaty assurances that the Sioux might roam and hunt at will in the Article 16 "unceded Indian territory" and use their Article 11 Republican River hunting grounds for as long as sufficient buffalo remained to justify the chase, the commission advocated removing the Indians to the permanent reservation as soon as possible, and denying them the right to roam and hunt anywhere beyond its borders. General Grant, the Republican nominee for President, who attended the meeting, remarked darkly that the pioneers had to be protected "even if the extermination of every Indian tribe was necessary to secure such a result."

The Brûlé, the more southern and peaceful of the Teton, knew that they could not challenge the reinforced plains army and that they were not welcome among the wilder and more powerful northern bands around the Powder River. They had no alternative but to follow government orders and march east to the Missouri, where the buffalo had vanished long before, and where (under Article 4 of the 1868 treaty) the government proposed to feed them until they became farmers. It was a march backward in time to return to the once-rich lands that had beckoned their forefathers west. But the land was no longer inviting bison country, unfenced virgin prairie, unfurrowed and uncrowded. Now, it was the place of the "fire canoes" belching smoke, of whiskey-runners and black-garbed preachers, a place to pollute Indian souls and bodies.

Old General Harney, "White Whiskers," as the Sioux dubbed him, was waiting for the Indians on the Missouri at the mouth of Whetstone Creek, where he had already plowed several hundred acres for their benefit. Spotted Tail wouldn't go near the place. He had observed that his people adopted the white man's vices much more readily than his putative virtues. Fearing the enterprising Dakotans who wanted to run liquor into his camp, Spotted Tail kept his followers thirty miles up the White River, a safe distance from both the alcohol and the farming.

Only Swift Bear and his small "Corn Band" continued to the agency at Whetstone. Harney had procured enormous farm machines for them, but Swift Bear's group could barely manage their hand hoes. Their government rations, not their meager crops, fended off starvation.

At first Harney operated under a provisional budget, since the Senate (preoccupied with President Andrew Johnson's impeachment) did not officially proclaim the 1868 treaty until February 24, 1869. As a slap at the Interior Department, Congress assigned responsibility for the distribution of rations and annuities to General Sherman, but as of March 4, when it adjourned, the legislature had not made any appropriation for the fulfillment of the treaty. The Sioux suffered without the blankets, clothes, knives, kettles, and other goods they had been promised, and they suffered from their new diet—too short on meat, too long on flour (which they did not know how to use), and altogether lacking in quality. Spotted Tail kept his people quiet, but as his Whetstone agent DeWitt Poole concluded in his annual report to the bureau, "an agent can do little to regain their confidence in the face of treaty obligations so lately unfulfilled."

To the north and west, Red Cloud was wrestling with his own peacetime problems. He and his fellow Oglala chiefs, Red Leaf and Man-Afraid-of-His-Horses, adamantly refused to move to the Missouri, away from their gamelands. Red Cloud spent the winter near the Powder, periodically sending emissaries down to Laramie in a concerted effort to get his trading privileges restored. It was a hard winter. The game was scarce up north this year, and the government, hoping to force Red Cloud away from the overland travel routes and onto the reservation, continued its embargo at the fort. In the spring, with his people half-starved, Red Cloud literally had to beg the Laramie commander to let them trade. He relented for only six days.

By this time perhaps 40 percent (roughly 10,000) of the Teton and Yanktonai Sioux had gathered on the reservation around the Missouri River forts Sully, Rice, and Thompson and the newly established Sioux agencies at Grand River, Whetstone, and Crow Creek. Of that number, the government considered about half to be "peaceful," which was still a far cry from being self-supporting, much less Christian farmers. The vast majority of Sioux remained either impervious to white ways or as intransigent as their impoverished and starved condition would allow. They bore the suffering to keep their freedom—the freedom they thought the treaty had secured.

With the inauguration of Ulysses S. Grant on March 4, 1869, the Sioux gained a formidable new adversary. Although as a young soldier stationed out west Grant had witnessed firsthand the cruel effects of the nation's Indian policy, he understood even more clearly the demands of the country's westward expansion. To the Indians who would sit quietly on their reservations, Grant offered peace; but to those, like the Sioux, who would not, he threatened war. "All Indians disposed to peace will find the new policy a peace policy," he proclaimed upon his election. "Those who do not accept this policy will find the new administration ready for a sharp and severe war."

This new Great Father soon made plain that what he meant by peace was more precisely assimilation. At the heart of his program lay two aims: first, to end the corrupt practices of the Indian Bureau and to deal with the Indians honestly; and, second, to reduce the natives to wardship status and treat them like children in need of discipline, care, and instruction. Grant created a new arm of the government, the Board of Indian Commissioners, made up of ten eminent philanthropists, to act as both watchdog and adviser for the Indian Bureau. Moreover, after Congress rejected his plan to appoint army officers as reservation agents, Grant implemented the novel idea of inviting the interested religious denominations to select the agents from their own ranks.

Most significant, Grant nominated Ely S. Parker, a Seneca Indian, to be his commissioner of Indian Affairs. As Grant's aide-de-camp during the Civil War and the scribe of the Appomattox surrender document, the elegant, articulate, and highly educated Parker embodied all of the reformers' highest aspirations for the Indian race. Although he was a grand sachem of the Iroquois, in the view of the eastern humanitarians, Parker had become as white as any red man could be. He believed firmly that the Indians had much more to lose than to gain by resisting the dominant culture. "Unless they fall in with the current of destiny as it rolls and surges around them," Parker wrote about the western tribes, "they must succumb and be annihilated by its overwhelming force." And he wrote with a convert's passion about the Indians' need for philanthropic teaching and the importance of concentrating the tribes on reservations where the government could "more economically press and carry out its plans for their improvement and civilization." At Appomattox, just after the surrender, General Lee had turned to Parker and commented upon his heritage: "I'm glad to see one real American here." Parker could not agree. "We are all Americans," he responded.

To this man of two cultures, Grant assigned the difficult task of administering his "peace policy" and, more immediately, of bringing the Sioux within the strict bounds of their reservation. In the eyes of the Grant administration, the controlling provisions of the 1868 treaty were those locating the Sioux agencies "at some place along the Missouri River" and describing the attendant program for civilizing them there. For the Sioux, those sections were still just meaningless phrases. They focused on hunting rights and the unceded Indian territory. It had taken a century of domination over the eastern tribes to produce one Ely Parker. The nineteenth-century assimilationists, including Parker himself, meant to accelerate the process.

With peace, the war of guns and powder became a battle for cultural survival. Eighteen sixty-nine passed and both sides held firm. Red Cloud remained outside the reservation and the government kept Laramie closed. Spotted Tail stayed a safe distance from Whetstone. Unable to hunt, he waited for his annuity goods, which, due to the late shipping, had yet to arrive by year's end.

In January of 1870, the military attacked a band of Piegan Indians (a branch of the Blackfeet tribe), killing an unusually high proportion of women and children in a camp that many considered to be friendly, under circumstances that plainly invited the label "massacre." Once again the army's cruel blundering played into the hands of the peace-oriented reformers, who parlayed the public uproar over the Piegan incident into a reaffirmation of their more conciliatory approach to the western tribes.

The Indian Bureau grabbed at the chance to reassert itself and to ease tensions with the increasingly restless Sioux. In late April, Commissioner Parker called for a summit with Red Cloud and Spotted Tail in Washington, where Parker hoped at once to win their trust and pressure them into settlement. For easterners, it would be their first look at the two chiefs who, as both victims and villains, had so often graced the front pages of the national press. For the Sioux leaders, it was a leap into darkness, a trip to test not merely their talents as diplomats but their mettle in the face of a world that even the most vivid Indian imagination could not conceive.

Spotted Tail and three lesser chiefs departed Whetstone on May 17 for the weeklong trip east, and Red Cloud, with an entourage of thirty, departed from Laramie nine days later. Little is known of their respective journeys, of what the chiefs thought as they passed through Omaha and Chicago—thriving cities with old Indian names—of how it felt to ride an iron horse, so long the harbinger of suffering and death, or whether the rippling fields of corn and wheat softened their hearts to farming. Whether white America attracted or repelled, the force of its sheer numbers, its people in villages and towns with so many miles to be traveled in between, must have stunned them. In fact, that was no small part of the government's purpose in bringing the Sioux east. As much as anything, the government wanted to overawe the Sioux chiefs, to break their resistance with a display of the indomitable size and power of the United States.

As soon as the chiefs had recuperated from their trip, Indian Bureau guides whisked them off to the Capitol. The Sioux hesitated upon entering in fear that the walls would collapse. Once inside, they exhibited no interest in the democratic process even (or perhaps especially) after their guides told them that Congress was at that very moment debating a bill to promote their welfare. The National Armory was the next stop on their whirlwind tour. There the Sioux saw more guns in one building than they had seen in their whole lives. To press home the point, the government fired its huge new fifteen-inch Rodman coastal defense gun, but, though the chiefs watched attentively as the shell ricocheted four or five miles down the Potomac, they displayed no fear; such a heavy weapon was too unwieldy to be used against them. When the military loosed a few rounds from the arsenal's regular cannon, the Indians showed their familiarity with these guns: they stopped up their ears before every shot. No doubt, Red Cloud and Spotted Tail had seen enough of white soldiers before they came to Washington, but they trekked politely to the Navy Yard for a full-dress marine parade. Only the ironclad docked at the wharf fazed them. They knew that iron could not float.

After a weekend's respite (except for an unplanned trip to a bawdy revue), on Monday evening the Indian Bureau hosts tried a different sort of bedazzlement, introducing the "savage visitors" to President Grant at a White House reception in their honor. Dressed in their finest buckskin attire, bathed in the glow of crystal chandeliers, the chiefs and their entourage ran the gauntlet of official Washington, returning curious gaze with curious gaze.

The Sioux soon found themselves shepherded into the state dining room, where they were treated to a lavish buffet of white man's delicacies. Spotted Tail maintained his sense of humor amid the glitter. Munching on strawberries and ice cream, he noted wryly that the whites ate much better food than they sent out to the Sioux. When someone suggested that he should start farming, the chief remarked that he would gladly "if you will always treat me like this and let me live in a big house."

As negotiations commenced the next morning, the government, in the person of Secretary of the Interior Jacob Cox, quickly discovered that, despite their imposing welcome, the Sioux remained undaunted.

"A man must expect some trouble in his life and should face it in a manly way, not by complaining," Cox scolded Spotted Tail upon hearing the chief's numerous grievances.

"Tell him," Spotted Tail replied with a smile to his interpreter, "that if he had had as many hardships in his life as I have had in mine, he would have cut his throat long ago."

Red Cloud did not joke. "Look at me," he implored his listeners, "I was raised on this land where the sun rises, now I come from where the sun sets."

> Whose voice was first sounded on this land? The red people who had but bows and arrows. The Great Father says he is good and kind to us. . . . I came here to tell my Great Father what I do not like in my country. . . . The men the Great Father sends to us have no sense. What he has done in my country I did not want; I did not ask for it; white people going through my country. Father, have you or any of your friends here got children? Do you want to raise them? Look at me, I come here with all these young men. All of them have children and want to raise them.
>
> The white children had surrounded me and left me nothing but an island. When we first had this land we were strong, now we are melting like snow on a hillside while you are growing like spring grass. . . .
>
> Tell the Great Father to move Fort Fetterman away and we will have no more troubles. I have two mountains in that country [the Black Hills and Big Horn Mountains]. I want the Great Father to make no roads through them.
>
> I have told these things three times now. I have come to tell them a fourth time.
>
> I don't want my reservation on the Missouri. . . . Here are some people from the Missouri now. Our children are dying off like sheep. The country does not suit them. . . .

In its entirety, Red Cloud's speech was an oral history of his people, a tale of broken treaties, swindles, liquor, roads and railroads, poverty and war bitterly recalled. The point of the Chief's appeal was simple: he wished that history had been different and hoped that the future would break with the past.

But the Great Father was unmoved. He refused to abandon Fort Fetterman, asserting that it protected the Indians as well as the whites. As for trading at Laramie and settling along the Missouri, Grant instructed Secretary Cox to review the treaty for the chiefs.

Red Cloud listened carefully as the Secretary read the agreement, including Article 4, by which the Sioux agreed to receive their goods at agencies located along the Missouri. Then, in one of the most curious statements in the history of government relations with the Sioux, Red Cloud flatly denied any knowledge of the treaty Cox had read. "This is the first time I have heard of such a treaty," he declared, "I have never heard of it and I do not mean to follow it." The other Sioux nodded their assent. Bear in the Grass explained further: "I tell nothing but what is true when I say these words of the treaty were never explained. It was merely said that the treaty was for peace and friendship among the whites. When we took hold of the pen they said they would take the troops away so we could raise our children."

What really had happened at Laramie on November 6, 1868, when Red Cloud made peace, will never be known with certainty. Perhaps when he interrupted Major Dye's reading of the treaty, Red Cloud precluded any explanation of the terms that limited Sioux freedom. Perhaps in the interest of securing Red Cloud's assent, Major Dye obscured the treaty's meaning. Whatever the truth, the Sioux had always viewed the treaty in light of their victory over Fetterman and the government's retreat from the Bozeman forts. Every Sioux knew the story of Crazy Horse's ruse outside Fort Phil Kearny; every Sioux remembered the terrible battle when they killed all the white soldiers. Now, a year and a half later, Red Cloud would not let that triumph be turned into defeat. "It is all lies," the chief insisted. Then, he and the others walked out.

It took all of Parker's energy and ingenuity to convene another session. Some of Red Cloud's followers had begun to contemplate suicide rather than return to their people as party to such a dishonorable peace. Nor could the government let them go; the fate of the much heralded peace policy largely depended on Red Cloud's goodwill. The government arranged a compromise, a "reinterpretation" of the treaty which dropped the requirement of moving to the Missouri. Both Red Cloud and Spotted Tail could receive their goods in the western part of the reservation at new agencies whose precise location would be selected later.

Red Cloud had won an important point and, if not satisfied entirely, he was at least placated. The government, for its part, had salvaged the peace and with it the prospect of bringing Red Cloud and his bands under the civilizing influence of a government agency, even if located west of the Missouri.

The reformers were ecstatic. They spirited off their noble savage hero in order to bring him to New York to deliver a speech before the Cooper Union, one of their largest and most vital philanthropic organizations.

Red Cloud did not disappoint them. "We want to keep the peace," he told the tumultuous humanitarian audience.

> Will you help us? In 1868, men came out and brought papers. We could not read them and they did not tell us truly what was in them. We thought the treaty was to remove the forts and for us to cease from fighting. But they wanted to send us traders on the Missouri. We did not want to go to the Missouri, but wanted traders where we were. When I reached Washington, the Great Father explained to me what the treaty really was, and showed me that the interpreters had deceived me. All I want is right and just. I have not altogether succeeded.

The Cooper Union crowd cheered virtually every sentence of the speech, which, reflecting common feeling, the *New York Tribune* hailed as a "remarkable triumph . . . one of the most striking incidents in the history of the aboriginal race." If Red Cloud had failed in part with his Great Father, he had succeeded completely in capturing the hearts of the influential humanitarians. He left New York as the most famous member of his race and with many powerful new friends in the East—unwitting allies in his continuing struggle to preserve the peace on his own terms.

Red Cloud received a mixed welcome back in Sioux country. His government agent greeted the chief enthusiastically, assuming that the trip east had achieved its desired effect of intimidating the chief into a more peaceful and accommodating frame of mind. The hostile Powder River bands, increasingly linked with the name of the Hunkpapa leader Sitting Bull, were inclined to agree. "The white people have put bad medicine over Red Cloud's eyes to make him see anything and everything they please," they believed. A number of Red Cloud's own followers, particularly among the young warriors, deserted the renowned chief's camp and joined the nontreaty bands.

Both his agent and the hostile Sioux underestimated Red Cloud's tenacity. When the government tried to push him into an agency at Raw Hide Buttes he refused, insisting that the buttes were too near the Black Hills to allow white men around. Red Cloud held out for an agency along the Platte, about thirty miles from Laramie, and wheedled the government into temporary agreement. Though his influence was eroding among his own people, it had never waxed stronger with the whites. His followers could hunt in the north or eat at the agencies; they could roam along the Powder or settle by the Platte. Only their own wills and the scarce buffalo would dictate which it would be.

Spotted Tail, too, used his exalted position with the reformers to extract concessions and reclaim treaty rights from the government. He moved his agency away from Whetstone two hundred miles west along the White River and then successfully demanded a permit to hunt along the Republican River to the south.

Neither of the two new agencies was well suited for farming. The agents concentrated more on maintaining control over the still untamed tribesmen than on pursuing agricultural instruction. Instead, the government did its best to civilize the Sioux in other ways. To fulfill the clothing annuity due Spotted Tail's Brûlé in 1870, the Indian Bureau sent out 1,500 pairs of trousers, 1,500 dresscoats, 700 greatcoats and a large shipment of felt hats. The Bureau included only 800 blankets, the principal attire of both Sioux men and women, and most of these were of unsuitable colors. With characteristic lack of consideration, the Washington bureaucrats, having scrounged the hats and clothing from army surplus, had left on the brass army buttons. Enraged, the Brûlé tore off the buttons and refashioned the other articles into more traditional Sioux clothing.

The peace program did make halting progress, particularly at the Missouri River agencies, Crow Creek and Lower Brûlé. Among the more peaceful bands, an increasing number of Sioux adopted white fashions and the one approved vocation. Each year, a few more donned pants, cut their hair, converted to Christianity, and started farming. Even the most pliant bands, though, made little headway towards self-reliance. Tilling that Dakota ground was a fruitless task. The more fields the Sioux planted, the greater the harvest for grasshoppers to eat or drought to wither. Even experienced white farmers lost their crops to the harsh Dakota conditions. They moved away. The Sioux could not. Every year one disaster or another wiped out the Sioux crop. Every season the agents who would turn them to the soil sent excuses back to Washington. A few agents warned that the land was wrong for farming and recommended that the Sioux raise stock instead. A chorus of dogmatists drowned them out; cattle ranching, it sounded in unison, too closely resembled the Indians' savage ways.

From the Powder River country, Sitting Bull and his following, several thousand strong, looked down at all this with open cynicism and contempt. Though they had refused to sign it, these bands were enjoying the peace, following the buffalo, or, in the leanest times, sampling the government rations at the Milk River agency which the government had established to court Sitting Bull. Rumors that Sitting Bull would make peace surfaced often in the reports of eager and naïve agents, and the government made periodic efforts to secure that result. Agent J. W. Daniels even convinced Red Cloud to send Sitting Bull a personal message advising him to leave the warpath. But Red Cloud's words were more an expression of his own fears and resignation than a compelling argument for his fellow chief. "I shall not go to war any more with the whites," he dictated, ". . . you must carry on the war yourselves. I am alone. . . . Listen to me and save your country. . . . Be friends to [our Great Father] and he will provide for you. Your old people and children will not starve. Take his hand and hold it fast."

Red Cloud's appeal failed. Once, in 1872, Sitting Bull suggested that he would come in to talk "when the snow flies," but he had no intention of making peace and the belief that he would was mere delusion. Sitting Bull derived his power from his unmitigated opposition to the whites. If he did not lead the hostiles, Black Moon would; if not Black Moon, then Gall, Crazy Horse, or Rain-in-the-Face. A large part of the Sioux nation wanted nothing to do with the Indian Bureau. They stood behind Sitting Bull's taunt: "Look at me and see if I am poor, or my people either. . . . You are fools to make yourselves slaves to a piece of fat bacon, some hard-tack, and a little sugar and coffee."

Except for the "loafer" bands, the agency Indians agreed. They spent as much time as possible away from the agencies, living the old life. But the vanishing of the buffalo precluded any full return. The hunts of the early 1870s had been the most destructive of all, obliterating close to a million buffalo each year as professional hunters spread out from the advancing railroad lines and pushed into the last untouched rangelands. The buffalo vanished like smoke before a wind; and without government rations, many Sioux would starve. Red Cloud surmised as much and bitterly counseled his people about growing rich again according to white ways. "You must begin anew and put away the wisdom of your fathers," he told them sarcastically. "You must lay up food and forget the hungry. When your house is built and your storeroom filled, then look around for a neighbor you can take advantage of and seize all that he has."

In just a few years, the agencies had become a permanent fixture in Sioux life, though they were grossly inadequate for the complex role the peace policy assigned them. The most basic functions of care and administration were bogged down in fraud, incompetency, and inadequate funding. Beef contractors stole back delivered but unbranded herds; grain contractors loaded the weights and measures. The government agents were either corrupt themselves or too incompetent to stop the incessant graft between congressional appropriation and final delivery to the Indians. The fleecing of the Indian bureau, both from within and without, was so widespread and successful that critics alleged an "Indian Ring" operated at the highest levels of government, profiteering at the natives' expense.

By the admission of its own agents, the government's efforts to fulfill its treaty promises lay in a shambles. "The condition of the agency could hardly be worse than I found it," lamented the Sioux agent at Cheyenne River in 1871.

> The engine, saw, and grist mills, shingle-machine, etc., were down and scattered in different directions, more or less broken and sadly abused. The mowing machine was worn out and has proved worthless. . . . The wagons were more or less broken and out of repair. Much of the harness was worn, cut, and [had] pieces missing. Tools of various kinds scanty and nearly worn out. No horses fit for use; no mules; and but four yoke of thin oxen. . . .
>
> The buildings are few in number, of the roughest and cheapest description, faulty in construction and in bad condition. They are inconvenient, uncomfortable and un-sightly. They harbor thousands of vermin, the ravages of which upon the subsistence stores are immense.

The agent mentioned no school because here, as elsewhere, the government had yet, three years into the peace, to build one.

Despite the lack of facilities and the obvious breaches of promise, the reformers, like persistent alchemists, toiled patiently to make white men from red. Their pet formula of the early 1870s was to break the Indian's communal spirit by diminishing the power of the Sioux chiefs, forcing common tribesmen towards greater self-reliance. This tinkering had to be stopped every time the Sioux became unruly, because the agents invariably had to call on the chiefs to exercise their authority. The first years at the agencies actually increased the influence of some chiefs, like Spotted Tail, whom the agents felt compelled to befriend. Indeed, the material benefits of being head chief in the eyes of the whites fostered jealousies and even violence among rival claimants. In 1869 Spotted Tail killed his most serious adversary, Big Mouth, who, emboldened by liquor, had precipitated a shootout.

Reformer policies worked no better on a national scale. In its first two years, President Grant's peace program compiled a long record of failure. While Red Cloud and Spotted Tail checked the administration at every turn and Sitting Bull mocked the peace, Commissioner Parker resigned under a hail of accusations assailing his judgment and honor. Already, the Board of Indian Commissioners had lost its two most influential members as a result of political squabbling with the Indian Bureau.

The church-sponsored agents whom President Grant had invited to administer the reservations—intended saviors of policy as well as of red souls—had proven less competent and scarcely more honest than their lay predecessors. The many denominations involved in the new system spent more time quibbling over the exclusivity of their jurisdiction at individual agencies than helping Indians. Denominations left out of the peace program self-servingly demanded greater religious freedom for the tribes. The Indians, these churchmen argued, should "have the right to choose whatever Christian belief they wish, without interference from the Government."

Still, the reformers remained confident, consoling themselves that however disheartening their present setbacks, they were certain victors in the war of cultural attrition simmering on the reservations. The new commissioner of Indian Affairs, Francis Walker, openly advocated what had already become de facto policy—that the United States should temporize on the Indian question, biding its time until the Indians' last power vanished and they sank into utter helplessness. "In complete dependence lay the basis for reform," he urged, echoing Lewis and Clark. Nothing less would convince the tribes "that if they are to eat, they must work." And, more generally, if they were to survive, they must submit.

Walker espoused this principle with specific reference to the Sioux, whose food annuity guaranteed in the 1868 Treaty expired during his tenure in 1872. For now, while the Sioux retained the power to resist, the government should coddle them. "There can be no question of national dignity . . . in the treatment of savages by a civilized power," Walker wrote in 1871. "With wild men as with wild beasts," he advised, "the question whether in a given situation one shall fight, coax, or run is a question merely of what is easiest and safest." Accordingly, while reservation life reduced Indians to, as Walker put it, "the condition of supplicants for charity," the government should continue to provide the Sioux with rations at an annual cost of $1.25 million. Even at this price, the commissioner noted, the peace policy cost far less than a military campaign and it achieved the same result, "allowing our railways and settlements to progress without practical obstruction." Like so much of Indian policy in the past, Walker's policy of patience rested on the time-tested foundation of economy.

Not all the nation, though, wanted to wait while the power of the Sioux gradually dissipated. From the outset, many westerners had objected to prohibiting settlement on large tracts of potentially valuable land. During the winter of 1869–70, citizens in Wyoming, intent on resisting the treaty and occupying Wyoming territory reserved for the exclusive use of the Indians, had organized the Big Horn Exploration and Mining Association. Only the government's forceful intervention prevented a clash with the Powder River bands—who, unfettered by treaty conditions, occasionally strayed from the unceded Indian territory and harassed the mining camp in the Sweetwater Valley.

Dakota frontiersmen, meanwhile, urged with increasing force that the Black Hills section of the Great Sioux Reservation be opened for mining and settlement. As early as 1861, prominent Dakotans, bent on investigating the alluring rumors about Black Hills gold and on exploiting their more apparent abundance of timber, incorporated the Black Hills Mining and Exploration Association. Several times during the 1860s, the military had to restrain armed parties from marching headlong into Sioux country; and although Dakotans had so far observed the 1868 treaty, in 1872 they began an energetic campaign to amend its provisions to restrict the Sioux to the eastern part of their reservation and open the Hills for mining, lumbering, and eventual settlement.

On March 16, the territorial delegate to Congress, Moses Armstrong, himself a founding member of the Black Hills Mining and Exploration Association, pleaded Dakota's case before the Secretary of the Interior, the commissioner of Indian Affairs, and the United States geologist, Fredrick Hayden. Dr. Hayden, who had sneaked into the Hills three times during the 1850s and 1860s, could barely control his enthusiasm for acquiring them and eagerly recounted his encouraging findings about their mineral wealth. Nonetheless, the Secretary of the Interior, citing the 1868 treaty, scotched the Dakotans' plan, though he expressed "no objection" to negotiating with the Sioux for mineral and timber rights.

The Grant administration soon made clear, however, that although it had twice resisted intense territorial pressure for change, upholding the 1868 treaty was not a matter of rigid principle. When the project in question involved a national priority—in particular, the completion of the Northern Pacific Railroad—the government proved considerably less rigid. In 1870 and 1871, the rails had crossed the rich grass plains of Minnesota and eastern Dakota all the way to the Missouri. The Sioux sensed the approach of a new "fire horse." They watched the railroad survey teams with mounting apprehension as the white men worked far ahead of the tracks near the upper regions of Sioux land.

Fear soon turned to violence along the undefined border. The government allowed the railroad to continue its route along the south bank of the Yellowstone River, knowing full well that the Sioux considered this their land and would fight construction of the railroad and its inevitable consequence—the annihilation of the northern bison. Article 16 of the 1868 treaty had not specified the northern limit of the "unceded Indian territory," but no plausible interpretation, based upon either legislative history or the longstanding occupation by the Sioux, could justify a line south of the Yellowstone. The government admitted as much, sending a commission up to the Powder River country to seek a right-of-way from the hostiles. The negotiating process never even progressed to the talking stage, but the government did not change the railroad's course. It built a fort and brought in the 7th Cavalry to defend the line. During the next two years, the Sioux got their first look at General George Armstrong Custer in a host of skirmishes out beyond the creeping railhead.

This latest invasion of Sioux land had a violent effect at the agencies, too. At the Red Cloud agency, recently relocated to another spot along the White River, someone shot the clerk, mistaking him for the new agent, J. J. Saville. Later, when Saville tried to conduct a census, three hundred warriors "arrested" him and would have put him on trial had not the older chiefs at the agency intervened. A band of young braves, angered by the sight of the stars and stripes on their ground, hacked a newly erected flagpole to bits. Thefts and murders brought soldiers back to the reservation as the agents struggled to control the irate Sioux.

The army girded itself for confrontation, establishing posts near Red Cloud's and Spotted Tail's agencies, while reinforcing the numerous forts ringing Sioux country. General Sherman warned

General Phil Sheridan, now the commander of the Missouri District, that the Sioux regarded the upcoming struggle "as their last ditch stand." Sheridan agreed, remarking that the new railroad would "bring the Indian problem to a final solution." Commissioner Walker himself spelled out the army's fatal prescription for the Sioux: "Columns moving north from the Union Pacific and south from the Northern Pacific would crush the Sioux . . . as between the upper and nether millstone."

By 1873, the railroad problem had spread, poisoning general relations with the Sioux. The hit-and-run battles with the Powder River bands and the violent disturbances at the agencies underscored what even many reformers now viewed as the utter failure of the peace program among the Sioux. As blood from both sides stained the peace treaty, temporizing gave way to temper. The latest commissioner of Indian Affairs issued recommendations for stationing troops at the agencies and forcibly corralling the Sioux onto the permanent reservation. Sheridan fumed at the roving Sioux bands "coolly boast[ing] of their atrocities," and advised the Secretary of War to abrogate the right of the Sioux to roam and hunt. Sheridan had again suspended hunting along the Republican after some Brûlé (in the summer of 1873) attacked and massacred a band of the Pawnee, their hereditary enemies.

Sherman struck a somewhat calmer though not friendlier note. He urged Sheridan "to let things take their natural course until the mass of Indians commit some act that will warrant a general war." But he looked with great favor at another of Sheridan's ideas—that the government build a fort at the base of the Black Hills. Damn the treaty; a fort "would secure a strong foothold in the heart of Sioux country and thereby exercise a controlling influence over these warlike people."

Late in 1873, the Northern Pacific went bankrupt, a victim of nationwide depression. But if the country's financial woes had defused the immediate crisis, many other issues were now hanging fire. With banking houses collapsing, stock market values tumbling almost to nothing, farm prices plummeting, and a grasshopper plague blanketing the midwest with insect carcasses often two feet deep, the pressure mounted to open reserved Indian lands, whether for farms or mining, and the vision of Black Hills gold shimmered ever brighter. From the government's perspective, five years of peace had produced negligible progress towards civilizing the Sioux, a tribe now forcefully obstructing national policy while living off $1.25 million in gratuitous rations. To a government gripped by financial panic, that money became an increasingly grudging kindness.

From Nebraska, Wyoming, Colorado, and Dakota the cry sounded to confine the Sioux to the reservation, buy back their hunting rights, and break the hostiles. Like lenient parents disdained for sparing the rod, the reformers, too, looked to sterner measures as a necessary prerequisite for civilizing the still wild tribe. With the Sioux militantly resisting the best efforts of the reformers and with the prospect of a new gold bonanza lurking in the unexplored regions of the Sioux domain, the policy of peace lost its firm foundation in both thrift and humanity.

"Nothing in the history of the United States," Commissioner Walker had written with assurance in 1873, "justifies the belief that either Congress or the country will be wanting in justice and generosity in dealing with the necessities of a people impoverished that we might be rich." But an impatient democratic nation, hungering for land and gold, a nation of cultural imperialists, could create self-serving and self-flattering definitions of justice and generosity. How just and how generous remain issues to this day.

FIVE

▼ ▼ ▼ ▼ ▼

SELL OR STARVE

A WAGON TRAIN four rows across and a score deep rolled out of Fort Abraham Lincoln (just east of what is now Bismarck, North Dakota) on July 1, 1874. The team drivers passing the fort's gate listened for a moment to the distant strains of "Garry Owen," the 7th Cavalry's regimental song, then turned their attention to the lone rider already at the crest of the first hill. Even at a distance, they could see the long hemp-colored locks flowing from beneath his felt hat to the shoulders of his fringed buckskin shirt: the stuff of legend. Brevet Major General Custer, perched high on a bay steed amid forty snapping hounds, watched exultantly as 1,000 men, 110 wagons, a 16-piece band, and 100 Arikara scouts followed his trail. He had come far since graduating from West Point in 1861, thirty-fourth in a class of thirty-four. This day, Custer was beginning a new chapter in his book of glory. He was blazing a path to the Black Hills, a region, he had written, "as yet unseen by human eyes except those of the Indians."

Custer owed this latest assignment to General Sheridan, who wanted to fortify the Hills to prevent hostile Teton bands from taking refuge there. Sheridan harbored no illusions about the lull in hostilities which the financial panic had brought to his command. Sooner or later, the railroad crews would return to work and the Sioux problem, now three decades old, would surface once again. Sooner or later, the army would have to whip the hostiles.

Sheridan intended to be prepared when the time came. He ordered a reconnaissance of the entire Black Hills region and selected as commander his protégé from the Civil War and victor

71

over Black Kettle at the Battle of the Washita. But Custer was not the man for routine exploration. A master of the demerit at West Point, derided by one former commanding officer as "cold-blooded, untruthful and unprincipled," disorderly in dress, once punished for insubordination, Custer rose luminously through the ranks by force of will and deed. In the Civil War his cavalry had checked the Confederates at Gettysburg, routed Jeb Stuart in the Wilderness Campaign, and chased Lee across the South towards the Courthouse at Appomattox. Custer was dashing and courageous, reckless with his own life and those of his men. He was also endowed with a flair for self-promotion which created and embittered enemies while buoying the expectations of friends.

From the outset, he held a broad view of his Black Hills mission. With transparent deviousness, Custer asked his superiors whether "the services of a geologist could be had with the expedition." To the hordes of would-be goldseekers who flooded the streets of every ramshackle town lining the Missouri, his message could have been no plainer. Custer was asking to look for paydirt, and the government, by paying professional miners to accompany the expedition, became a willing accomplice in his search. As Custer left the fort, with a pack of reporters and an official photographer in tow, he carried with him the heady hope of his nation for a new bonanza of private fortunes and national wealth.

The Black Hills was fitting country for such a momentous expedition. More than any other area of the American west, its secrets had eluded the white man. The land itself, beautiful yet hauntingly strange, spawned rumors and speculation. An ancient geological upheaval, pushing up the rocky strata over four thousand feet, had created this inland paradise towering above the desolate sea of prairie grass. Time had worn the mountains down into concentric rings of schist and limestone; and inside the first ring of hogback ridges, mountain streams carved from soft red shale a slender elliptical valley which the Indians called their "race track." The odd geology, trapping the thunderheads, imbued the Hills with a climate all their own, far more hospitable than that of the surrounding arid plains.

Few white men had penetrated the Hills before Custer. First were the Venderaye brothers, searching for a route to the Pacific and stopping at the "Mountain of the Horse Indians," later known as Bear Butte, at the northeast tip of the Hills, on August 11, 1742. Twenty-five years later, Jonathan Carver claimed to be the Hills' next white explorer. Searching for the mythical straits of Anian, he purported to have seen the incredible "Shining Mountains"—

perhaps a reference to the silver veneer the shale gave to the Hills. Lewis and Clark skirted the region, but they employed a guide who had wintered in the Hills and had mapped their location. Even at that early date, the Hills were reputed to be goldbearing, as the French lieutenant governor of Louisiana carefully noted.

With the rise of the fur trade, the mountain men, trappers, and traders who made their homes in the wilderness sometimes worked in and around the Hills. The explorer Jedediah Smith crossed all the way through the Hills in 1823, a feat not to be repeated by a white man for over fifty years.

In 1852, thirty prospectors ventured into the heart of the Hills. Eight turned back after sighting Indians; the others disappeared. In 1855 the Sioux caught a mixed-blood trapper, Hercule Levasseur, in the Hills. They cut off his hands and chopped out his tongue. Presumably, no better fate met Ezra Kind, who just managed to scrawl a last message to the outside world on a piece of stone:

> Came to the Hills in 1833 seven of us DeLacompt, Ezra Kind, G. W. Wood, T. Brown, R. Kent, Wm. King, Indian Crow. All died but me Ezra Kind. Killed by Ind. beyond the high hill got our gold in 1834. Got all the gold we could carry our ponys got by Indians I have lost my gun and nothing to eat and Indians hunting me.

Enough of Kind's kind survived to stir the rumor mill periodically, not only about the existence of gold but also about terrifying lightning storms, inexplicable booming noises, and a host of Indian superstitions regarding their *Paha Sapa*.

Those who wanted to dispossess the natives of their land seized with particular vigor upon the legends that related the Indians' fear of the Hills; but whatever beliefs the Indians cherished about the land were based on veneration, not terror. The Indians did not value gold; the Hills themselves were their treasure and they guarded them vigilantly. At the Great Council held in their midst during the summer of 1857, the Sioux resolved to execute any tribesman who revealed the existence of gold in the Hills to the whites. And they took their vow seriously; even alcohol, one frontiersman lamented, could not loosen Sioux tongues about the Hills.

In the 1860s and early 1870s, several major civilian expeditions were outfitted for a venture into the Black Hills, but the government always dissuaded the organizers. Before Custer, the army had sent several survey parties into the Hills. In the late 1850s, G. K. Warren and William Reynolds both filed extensive reports on their strategic and economic value, the latter concluding, despite hallowed treaty assurances to the contrary, "that at no distant date" the area was "destined to afford homes to a thriving [white] population." When Reynolds wrote, the government had already confirmed Sioux title to the land in the Laramie treaty of 1851, and it reiterated that commitment in the 1868 treaty. The army, nonetheless, perceived no bad faith underlying its incursions into the Hills.

And the high command saw nothing improper about Custer's venture, either. "I am unable to see that any great offense is given to the Indians by the expedition to the Black Hills," wrote General Terry, the commander of the Dakota District. "From the earliest times the Government has exercised the right of sending exploring parties of a military character into unceded territory, and this expedition is nothing more."

Terry's rationale rang hollow. The Black Hills were not unceded territory. As the United States agreed in 1868, the Hills were part of the permanent Sioux Reservation—land that belonged to the Sioux forever unless three-quarters of the adult male Sioux agreed to the contrary. Moreover, the expressed purpose of Custer's expedition, to build a fort in their midst, was contrary to both the spirit and letter of the 1868 treaty. In any case, everyone outside the army thought the expedition's real purpose concerned what might be extracted from the ground, not built on top of it. It was no accident that President Grant's son, Custer's brother Tom, John Brown, Jr., and the grandson of Samuel Morse all volunteered for the trip, giving it the appearance of a national flight of fancy. Custer's expedition was something more than a military fact-finding mission, and most of the country knew as much and was glad of it.

The Sioux interpreted the treaty more exactly than General Terry and they became increasingly agitated at the prospect of yet another illegal invasion of their country. Custer anticipated active Sioux resistance. The general dragged three Gatling guns along with him, confident that this light artillery, 1,000 men, and his own genius would overwhelm any opposition from the savages. Much to Custer's surprise, the expedition encountered very few Indians in the Hills. Custer did stumble upon one large Sioux encampment already deserted, which frightened some of the junior officers, but merely elicited the casual boast from Custer that his 7th Cavalry would whip all the Indians in the northwest.

All told, the expedition spent about as much time picnicking as standing watch. Without a hint of Indian trouble, Custer had ample time to appreciate the exquisite beauty of the Black Hills themselves and their near-perfect resources for white settlement. The general's dispatches overflowed with superlatives about the timber, the fresh water, the grasses, the soil, the foliage, the climate, even the flavor of the wild berries which his soldiers freely foraged. "No portion of the United States," he exclaimed in one particularly glowing sentence, "can boast of a richer or better pasturage, purer water, the natural temperature of which in midsummer, as it flows freely from the earth, is but twelve degrees above the freezing point, and of greater advantages generally to the farmer or stockman than are to be found in the Black Hills."

Custer's companions agreed. "One of the most beautiful spots on God's green earth," the reporter for the *Bismarck Tribune* informed his readers. "No wonder the Indians regard this as the home of the Great Spirit and guard it with jealous care." The expedition's botanist was beside himself: "It is hardly possible to exaggerate in describing this flowery richness," he declared. "Some said they would give a hundred dollars just to have their wives see the floral richness for even one Hour."

Custer was ebullient. He scored a hunting coup en route, killing an adult grizzly bear; and he had climbed Harney Peak, 7,300 feet, the tallest in the Hills. The men's spirits were high. They introduced baseball to Sioux country, taking time out for a quick game and a champagne party in the evening to toast the winners.

Still, despite the Edenlike setting, the wild currants and raspberries, the fifty-two varieties of wildflowers in bloom, the carnival atmosphere, and the substantial progress in charting and assessing unknown terrain, the trip could not be considered a complete success until July 27. On that day, the expedition struck gold.

The discovery, forty or fifty pinhead-size particles mostly obtained from one panful of earth, was modest by any objective standard—hard digging to turn a profit. Regardless, Custer summoned "Lonesome" Charley Reynolds, his chief scout, and scrawled the note that would proclaim his find to a nation holding its collective breath. The expedition had "found gold in the roots of the grass," Custer penned, and had done so "at an expense of but little time or labor." Reynolds rode off, hiding during daylight and galloping through the night across hostile Sioux country until he reached Laramie and the telegraph lines that would send the invitation nationwide to another bonanza gold rush.

By the time Custer returned to Fort Abraham Lincoln on August 30, the men along the Missouri were already packing their gear for the trip west to the Black Hills El Dorado. From Bismarck to Omaha, frontier towns began competing to capture the lucrative business of outfitting prospective miners. Sioux City, Yankton, and Bismarck all claimed to be the nearest and safest point from which to start for the Hills, the place where every man with expense money and a dream belonged. With soaring unemployment, bank failures, and the grasshopper blight plaguing the Midwest, veterans of the 'forty-niner era, never without an attentive audience, worked overtime embellishing old apocrypha about fortunes gained and squandered. Every western newspaper from the one-page rags to the big-city tabloids tried to outdo its rivals in promoting and exaggerating the Black Hills find.

Custer, who knew better than anyone that his gold find had, in fact, been unspectacular, deliberately stoked the fires. "The reports are not exaggerated in the least," he lied to the *Bismarck Tribune*. "The prospects are even better than represented." Of course, the Black Hills were still Indian country, he reminded his readers, and the army had a solemn duty to keep the whites out. But Custer promised to "recommend the extinguishment of Indian title at the earliest moment."

For people in the west, that seemed the only sensible solution. "We owe the Indians justice and fair play," the *Chicago Inter-Ocean* concluded, "but we owe it to civilization that such a garden of mineral wealth be brought into occupation and use." The *Bismark Tribune* was more militant:

> Humanitarians may weep for poor Lo, and tell the wrongs he has suffered, but he is passing away. Their prayers, their entreaties, can not change the law of nature. . . . The American people need the country the Indians now occupy; many of our people are out of employment; the masses need some new excitement. . . . An Indian war would do no harm, for it must come, sooner or later.

For all practical purposes, the gold strike negated the treaty in the eyes of the frontiersmen, and they were certain from experience that one way or another the government would soon acquire this latest paradise from its undeserving owners.

Back east, however, considerable doubt persisted about the accuracy of Custer's mineral assessment, particularly after Rev. Samuel Hinman, an Episcopal missionary, made his own investigation of the Hills and found them "bleak" and "sterile" with "no evidence" of mineral wealth. To annex the Hills, Hinman preached, would be "an unwarranted use of our great power to impose upon the simple and the weak." Morality aside, the government wanted to know definitively about the gold and was not comforted when Dr.

Newton Winchill, Custer's chief geologist, admitted that he had no personal knowledge of a gold strike. Fred Grant, the President's son, further undermined Custer's extravagant claims, publicly corroborating Winchill's story.

While the Grant administration laid plans for a new scientific exploration of the Hills in the spring, it took swift action to avoid a confrontation with the Sioux. Much to the consternation of the gold-crazed frontiersmen, the government spent the final months of 1874 closing the border it had itself ordered Custer to cross in July. On September 3, the army warned that it would "burn the wagons and destroy the outfit and arrest the leaders" of any group venturing to the Hills. With winter already chilling the plains air, making travel and excavation more difficult, the military threat cooled the ardor of many a would-be miner. Most sat out the long winter dreaming up ways to elude the army patrols come spring and wondering why their own government was so keen on protecting the rights of savages.

However strict the government's vigilance, however sincere its effort to fulfill its treaty obligations to the Sioux, by the first thaw of spring the number of miners already residing in the Hills clearly showed that the military cordon had been too little, too late. At least one large party of miners prospected in the Hills during the winter, and, before the spring, several hundred miners, defying both the army and the Sioux, set up camp along French Creek near where Custer had made his find.

Not more than seven months after Custer's invasion, the Grant administration reached the conclusion, long thought inevitable by the miners, that as a matter of practical and political necessity the Hills had to be acquired. The scientific expedition scheduled for late spring assumed a new task: to determine the overall value of the Hills as the basis for a financial settlement with the Sioux. Even before calculating an appropriate price, the government brought Red Cloud and Spotted Tail back to Washington to test the waters for purchasing the Hills as well as to strike an immediate deal for terminating Sioux hunting rights south of the Great Sioux Reservation along the Platte and Republican rivers in Nebraska as provided in Article 11 of the 1868 treaty.

The Sioux arrived in Washington incensed that white men infested their Hills "like maggots" and disgruntled about the administration of their agencies. Despite the chiefs' anger, the Indian Bureau believed that six years of feeding the Sioux "had taken the fight out of them" and that a few thinly disguised threats would frighten the Indians into selling their rights and lands.

President Grant established the tone for the Sioux visit, warning the chiefs that there would "be trouble in keeping white people from going [into the Black Hills] for gold" and "it is possible that strong efforts might not be made to keep them out" if the Indians refused to sell. The Secretary of the Interior followed suit, reminding the Sioux that the United States was in no way required to continue food rations at the agencies. He hinted that the Indians might want to give up their land altogether and move to the Indian Territory (now Oklahoma), where the Cherokee and other originally southeastern tribes had ended their corpse-strewn march along the Trail of Tears. Spotted Tail wondered why his Great Father did not put his red children on wheels so he could move them about at will.

The Sioux refused to be cowed. They wanted to keep their land, including the Black Hills, and told the President so in stark terms. Red Cloud and Spotted Tail did agree in principle to sell the tribe's Article 11 hunting rights along the Republican and Platte rivers (where game was scarce and settlement thick) for $25,000, with the promise of an equal amount later. By the time (June 1875) the chiefs actually signed the agreement back in Sioux country, the second installment had vanished from among its terms.

While the Sioux had been in Washington rebuffing their Great Father's entreaties, events out in the Hills were rapidly steering the Indians on a collision course with the United States. In June, the expedition, directed by geologist William Jenney, began sending back its widely publicized dispatches from the Hills. Black Hills gold, Jenney confirmed, was more than Custer myth. Although Jenney found only moderate prospects, he identified a gold field 800 square miles in area surrounded by enough farmland to support a large mining population. The hundreds of newspapers following the Black Hills story dispensed with Jenney's reserved tone. The Black Hills would pay off the national debt, the press declared, at that time a sum of over two billion dollars. "If there is gold in the Hills," the *New York Herald* had published the previous fall, "no army on earth can keep the adventurous men of the west out."

To date, the policing efforts of the U.S. government had proven woefully inadequate. Jenney reported meeting hundreds of miners working the Hills and estimated that as many as 1,500 whites had moved into the forbidden valleys of the Sioux reservation. Notably, the commander of Jenney's military escort, Colonel Richard Dodge, took no action at all against the scores of trespassers he encountered—despite standing orders from Generals Sherman,

Sheridan, and Terry that whites should be expelled from the Hills. In practice, regardless of the army's dire threats, the penalty for being caught sneaking into the Hills rarely exceeded expulsion. No wagons were burned, no outfits destroyed, no leaders arrested. As one persistent prospector wrote about his brushes with the army, "I have been captured and sent out of the Hills four times. . . . I guess I can stand it as long as they can."

The army was not "standing it" very well at all. The Hills were difficult and dangerous to patrol; one company sent to flush out miners during the winter lost many of its men in a sudden blizzard. The army's greater problem by far, however, was that its officers and men empathized with the miners and were reluctant to take the harsh punitive measures that might discourage the gold rush. A number of soldiers deserted Fort Abraham Lincoln to try their hands at prospecting; and General George Crook, the crack Indian fighter assigned to guard the Hills, could not bring himself to arrest anyone. Crook met with a large contingent of Black Hills miners during the summer and actually encouraged them to stake out formal claims before he politely requested that they depart. The reasons for the general's leniency became clear in his annual report. "I respectfully submit that [the miners'] side of the story should be heard," he pleaded, "as the settlers who develop the mines and open the frontiers are the nation's wards no less than their more fortunate fellows, the Indians."

In all likelihood, as popular wisdom decreed, nothing could stop the gold rush, but the truth of that maxim lay not in a lack of men, arms, or ammunition. What the country lacked, what perhaps any democratic country subject to the pressures of popular opinion would have lacked, was the will and self-discipline to curb its own people. Although not everyone shared Crook's view that the impoverished Sioux were more fortunate than the prospectors along French Creek, general sentiment in Washington and everywhere else aligned with the President's view that strict observance of Sioux treaty rights was now "at variance . . . with sound public policy."

Just two weeks after the Sioux delegation left Washington, in August 1875, a congressionally authorized commission, chaired by Senator William Allison (a close friend of the President), left the east for Sioux country carrying a mandate to buy or lease the Hills. The government still hoped to be "just" to the Sioux, provided that justice culminated in procuring the Hills. The Secretary of the Interior instructed the commissioners to bear in mind that they were negotiating with "an ignorant and almost helpless people" and that they must "secure the best interests of both parties, so far as practicable."

By this time, the United States had dropped all pretense of dealing with Indian tribes, even the unconquered Sioux, as anything more than the nation's wards incapable of speaking for themselves. A recent law made certain of it. In 1871, the House of Representatives, jealous of the Senate's exclusive jurisdiction over Indian treaties (under the Constitution, only the Senate ratifies treaties), had forced the abolition of the treaty system. Henceforth, Congress declared "no Indian nation or tribe . . . shall be acknowledged or recognized as an independent nation, tribe, or power with whom the United States may contract by treaty." Instead, the United States would enter into "agreements" with the tribes in the same manner as it enacted all domestic legislation—through the vote of both houses of Congress and signature by the President.

While the new law changed the political rituals associated with treatymaking more than the negotiating process itself, it marked a watershed in the country's attitude toward the original occupants of its land. The act ending the treaty system codified what disease and warfare and the attrition of the bison had already accomplished. After 1871, the mighty tribes who had once held the fate of a fledgling republic in their hands lost the last vestige of full sovereignty and became the orphans of an imperial democracy.

The United States now shouldered full responsibility for protecting the interests of the Indians, interests which more often than not would conflict with those of its enfranchised white majority. In negotiating for the Black Hills, the United States intended to sit on both sides of the negotiating table—its own side and the side of its wards—and do the impossible: be an effective advocate against itself. When it came to securing "the best interests of both parties so far as pracaticable," as Congress had charged the Allison commission, so far as practicable was certain to be the essential clause.

Senator Allison and his commission arrived in Sioux country on September 4, 1875, and spent the rest of the month dickering with the Indians. From the moment of the commissioners' arrival, and at every opportunity thereafter, the Sioux demonstrated that in their own eyes, despite the rations and the clothing and their shrinking domain, they remained their own masters with their own voices that still knew well the word "no." The warrior societies, many thousands strong, paraded their defiance. Each in turn swarmed around the conference grounds, galloping their horses and firing their guns in the air.

As many as 20,000 Sioux came to meet this latest commission at the first full assembly on the twentieth. As the commissioners, agency employees, and interpreters watched uneasily from beneath the broad awning of a tent, the chiefs came forward, sat before them in a semicircle, and signaled that they were ready to listen.

The commissioners had previously agreed among themselves that they would first propose to lease the Hills, in the belief that a leasing arrangement would avoid the "inconvenient" need to secure the treaty-required consent of three-fourths of the adult Sioux male population. "We have come to ask you if you are willing to give our people the right to mine in the Black Hills as long as gold or other minerals are found for a fair and just sum," Senator Allison began. "If you are so willing, we will make a bargain with you for these rights." He advised the Indians to come to terms. "You should bow to the wishes of the Government which supports you," he told the Sioux. "Gold is useless to you and there will be fighting unless you give it up."

At first, Allison's speech confused the Sioux. They did not immediately understand the concept of a lease, although Spotted Tail soon figured out that what the senator proposed was some sort of loan. The chief thought the idea preposterous. Perhaps, he asked Allison, the senator would offer him a team of mules on such terms.

The meeting adjourned. It reconvened on the twenty-third and almost ended in violence. The Powder River bands, deliberately absent before, delivered their response to the proposed Black Hills sale. As thousands of Sioux gathered again to meet with the Great Father's councilors, Little Big Man, close friend to Crazy Horse, naked save for a breechclout and eagle-feather war bonnet, raced onto the meeting ground at the head of 300 hostile warriors. Stripped and painted for battle, they pranced forward on their war ponies, moving swiftly towards the commissioners, chanting:

> *Black Hills is my land and I love it*
> *And whoever interferes*
> *Will hear this gun.*

"I will kill the first chief who speaks for selling the Black Hills!" Little Big Man shouted, waving his Winchester as he drew close. The Indians from the agencies channeled the warriors away from Allison and the other whites. After some jostling, Little Big Man withdrew. He had delivered the hostiles' message, the words of Crazy Horse: "One does not sell the land the people walk on."

Whatever the agency Sioux might decide, Sitting Bull, Crazy Horse, and their people would fight to save the Hills, the seat and emblem of their culture.

Most of the Sioux, though, could not afford the luxury of outright refusal, however much they wished it possible. No longer self-supporting, they were trapped between ways of life, an old one loved, but to which they could never return, and a new one which seemed strange and unnatural but was perhaps the only way to survive. For some, even among the reservation Sioux, no price could buy the Hills; but for many others, Red Cloud and Spotted Tail among them, selling the Hills held out the hope of renewed stability in a land that constantly shifted and shrank beneath their feet.

"As long as we live on this earth, we expect pay . . . ," Spotted Tail informed the commissioners. "The amount must be so large that the interest will support us. . . . If even only two Indians remain, as long as they live they will want to be fed, as they are now."

Red Cloud elaborated:

> There have been six nations raised and I am the seventh, and I want seven generations ahead to be fed. . . .
>
> These Hills out here to the northwest we look upon as the head chief of the land. My intention was that my children depend on these for the future. . . . I think that the Black Hills are worth more than all the wild beasts and all the tame beasts in the possession of the white people. I know it well, and you can see it plain enough, that God Almighty placed these Hills here for my wealth, but now you want to take them from me and make me poor, so I ask so much that I won't be poor.

What Red Cloud and many agency Sioux asked for their "house of gold" was $70 million. The figure itself, perhaps suggested by a missionary or interpreter, was irrelevant to the Sioux; they did not reckon in millions. What it represented—food, clothing and shelter in perpetuity, security in a frightening world—meant everything.

At Spotted Tail's request, on the twenty-ninth, the government submitted a formal written proposal to the collected bands. The commission offered an alternative: the government would either lease the Hills at $400,000 per year or buy them for $6 million in fifteen equal installments. The Sioux rejected both options and negotiations broke off. From the Indian perspective, the govern-

ment had not offered anything that they either wanted or did not
have. Broken down into installments, translated into farming tools
and livestock, whether under lease or through sale, giving up the
Hills would only have brought more pressure to assimilate, and
the same bad food they were already receiving for free. The white
men might say gold was useless to the Sioux, but it was not worthless.

Senator Allison dutifully reported to Washington that the Sioux
would not sell except for a price that the nation could not even
consider. From the moment of his report, whatever remained of
the longstanding economic rationale for peaceful relations with
the Sioux vanished entirely, and the policy itself was reduced to
nothing more than a patina that glossed the administration's rhetoric. "The occupation of the Black Hills by white men now seems
inevitable," Commissioner of Indian Affairs Edward Smith reported after Allison's return, "but no reason exists for making this
inevitability an occasion for wrong or lasting injury to the Sioux."

"Wrong and lasting injury" apparently did not include starving
the Sioux into relinquishing the Hills. Secretary of the Interior
Chandler pressed Congress to cut off food if the Indians refused
to give in, noting that the Sioux would die without their rations.
Commissioner Smith advised Congress to expropriate the Hills
unilaterally; the United States, he reasoned, should receive some
consideration for the $1.25 million in gratuitous rations it pro-
vided the Sioux each year.

The Grant administration did not wait for congressional action.
On November 3, 1875, at a meeting with his top Indian Bureau
advisers and Generals Crook and Sheridan, the President, who had
made the "moral view" of the Indian problem a hallmark of his
administration, took his own unilateral action to clear the way for
white occupation of the Hills. Although the law still prohibited
non-Indians from entering the Great Sioux Reservation, Grant
secretly ordered that "no further resistance shall be made to miners going into [the Black Hills]." Although the administration
stuck to a pretense of observing its responsibility under the 1868
treaty of safeguarding the borders of Sioux country, as General
Sherman wrote to a subordinate, if miners wanted to invade the
Black Hills, "I understand that the President and the Interior
Dept. will wink at it."

Sherman commented at the time that such a blatant violation of
the treaty would probably "bring collision and trouble in the
spring." Once the miners flooded unimpeded into the Hills, the
government—complicit in their trespass—would have to do some-

thing to protect its citizens. Thus, having committed himself to opening up the Hills, Grant either had to acquire the land at what he considered an exorbitant price or send the army into the Sioux reservation to enforce the de facto occupation.

The army was hankering for the latter. General Sherman summarized the military view: "Inasmuch as the Sioux have not lived at peace, I think Congress has the perfect right to abrogate the whole treaty or any part of it." With the price tag for the Black Hills running as high as $70 million, the Indian Bureau and the rest of the executive branch were finally coming around to the army's way of thinking.

For years, Indian affairs experts had been looking for a way to tame the hostile Powder River bands who so delighted in disrupting the civilizing programs at the agencies, raiding mining camps, stealing cattle, disrupting negotiations for the Black Hills, and, in general, defying the whites at every turn. Gentle persuasion had not worked. The Black Hills controversy seemed the perfect opportunity to try a new approach.

On November 9, just six days after the White House policy meeting, Special Agent E. C. Watkins from the Indian Bureau issued a scathing report on the condition of the hostile Sioux who "laugh at the futile efforts that have thus far been made to subjugate them, and scorn the idea of white civilization." Watkins recommended a winter campaign, the sooner the better, to "whip them into subjection." The government "owes it to civilization and the common sense of humanity," Watkins wrote, to administer the punishment which the hostiles "richly merit."

The government manufactured a crisis. On December 3, the Secretary of the Interior instructed the commissioner of Indian Affairs to deliver an ultimatum to the Sioux bands in the Yellowstone and Powder River valleys. Unless they abandoned their hunting grounds in the unceded Indian territory and returned to the permanent reservation by January 31, 1876, the government would declare them hostile and treat them accordingly. In other words, notwithstanding their treaty right to winter where they were, if the Sioux in the Powder River country refused to come in to the agencies, the government would have a pretext not only for punishing the hostiles but for seizing the Hills, either in the course of the fighting or as part of a new peace settlement.

As all the top military officers knew, even if the hostiles had wanted to comply, they could not. The severity of the winter made it physically impossible for the bands in the hunting grounds, encumbered by women, children, and possessions, to reach the reservation before the deadline. Even a number of the government messengers dispatched to warn the Sioux failed to make it back to the agencies by January 31. The Sioux, deeply ensconced in their winter camps, shrank from exposing themselves to the arduous and unwarranted return journey. "It was very cold," a young Oglala warrior recalled, "and many of our people and ponies would have died in the snow. We were in our own country and doing no harm." In fact, most of the off-reservation Sioux were part of relatively peaceful bands out hunting with the prior permission of their agents, as they were entitled to do under the 1868 treaty and as they had been forced to do by another year of insufficient government rations and a Dakota drought. Had the Sioux somehow managed to return to their agencies, they would have starved, since the agencies had nearly run out of rations.

The government agents on the reservation could not understand their superiors' provocative order any more than could the Sioux. As Commissioner Smith himself observed, the Sioux had been more peaceful in 1875 than in any year for more than a decade. According to the government's own figures, in the fall of that year, no more than 500 warriors remained who could fairly be characterized as hostile. Several agents confidently expected that most of these hostiles would come in as soon as it grew warm enough. They recommended an extension of time.

In his State of the Union message at the end of 1875, President Grant told the Congress and the country that in the next year it would be increasingly difficult to protect Sioux treaty rights, and that the legislature would have "to adopt some measures to relieve the embarrassment" of the Black Hills predicament. Of course, Grant had already taken those measures. He had opened the Hills and then set the stage for a military solution to the Sioux problem, putting to an end two decades of vacillation over what to do with the most powerful and vexing tribe still roaming the west.

On February 1, the Secretary of the Interior promptly notified the Secretary of War that his order had not been complied with and that the Sioux were being turned over to the army for appropriate action.

By the time the government started its military preparations for the late winter campaign, fifteen thousand miners had begun prospecting in the Black Hills. After Grant removed the army patrols, the miners flooded in, reshaping sacred Sioux ground into a home for frontier boomtowns. Deadwood and Custer City grew up overnight and became home to legendary frontier figures like Wild Bill

Hickok and Calamity Jane. Butch Cassidy and the Hole-in-the-Wall gang robbed their first bank in Belle Fourche, just north of the Hills.

Cheyenne, Wyoming, emerged as one of the primary staging grounds for Black Hills expeditions. The town was "wild with excitement concerning the Indian war which all the frontiersmen felt was approaching and the settlement of the Black Hills, in which gold of unheard-of sums was said to be hidden. No story was too wild, too absurd to be swallowed with eagerness . . . even the stagedrivers, bootblacks and bellboys could talk of nothing but Black Hills."

"My dear wife, Mary," one typical miner wrote home from Cheyenne, "I wish you to know that I am leaving here today for Black Hills or death. Mary, there is at present a great war between the white men and the injuns. If they will leave me my scalp I will be satisfied. I will lose my life or find out what there is in the Black Hills or die. You bet."

Insurance companies were spontaneously generated to write policies for the goldseekers, who were by no means defenseless before the onslaughts of the Indians. In Custer City, the citizens marked the start of the centennial year by organizing their own 200-man militia—the "Custer Minutemen." The Sioux had a name for their "Freedom Trail," Custer's now well traveled route to the Hills: the "Thieves Road." Indian fighters and gunslingers of all descriptions flocked to the Hills and were well rewarded. Sioux scalps commanded as much as $300 in the Hills when, as was common, they were sold at auction. One Indian hunter, Texas Jack, received a citation from the Board of Health on the theory that killing Indians was conducive to the health of the community.

In the meantime, the army's preparation for the winter campaign moved ahead swiftly and by March 1, General Crook was ready to move his troops into the Dakota wilderness in search of the off-reservation Sioux, all of whom were now considered hostile. A novice at plains warfare, having earned his fame as an Indian fighter tracking the Apaches in Arizona, Crook soon discovered how merciless the plains winter could be, and why the Sioux had been so reluctant to leave their winter camps. Several weeks of marching through deep snow in subzero temperatures aged the expedition's first lieutenant "more than any five years of [his] life" and produced only one minor battle. In March 1876, a small contingent overran a Cheyenne village, mistaking it for Crazy Horse's. The army captured six hundred Indian ponies in the first charge, but the Cheyenne stole them back before morning.

In all, the shortlived winter campaign accomplished nothing except to drive the northern Cheyenne into the arms of the hostile Sioux, swelling the ranks of those whom the army planned to attack that spring.

The Cheyenne were not alone in joining Sitting Bull and Crazy Horse. By early spring, the Sioux were streaming out of the agencies in unprecedented numbers on their way to the Powder River for the spring hunt. The agencies had run out of rations in February; many of the Sioux had no choice but to fend for themselves, which for most meant uniting with the hostiles. A great camp gathered along the banks of the Rosebud, 15,000 or more Sioux slowly making their way northward in search of game and fresh grass. Thousands of warriors were there, anxious to prove their courage in defense of the homeland, inspired by Sitting Bull, for whom "the only thing that smelled good in those days was gunpowder." The government still believed what Commissioner Smith had reported the previous fall, that "it is not probable that as many as 500 Indian warriors will ever again be mustered in one place for a fight." The Sioux could count at least seven times that number by the end of April.

Early in June, the Sioux on the Rosebud held their annual Sun Dance. Virgins selected the sacred tree; elders carried it to the dance circle. Sitting Bull offered his flesh to the Great Spirit, gouging fifty small strips from each of his arms. His blood streaming, the chief danced for eighteen hours without rest or food, staring at the sun and the moon by turns. He fell into a trance and saw a vision: white soldiers falling into his camp, while a voice boomed in his head that these white men were a gift from the Great Spirit, *Wakan Tanka*. The soldiers were dead and had no ears because white men never listened.

Not far away, in the third week in June, General Crook and Crazy Horse met in battle by the banks of the Rosebud. One of three units assigned to encircle and destroy the hostile Sioux, Crook's command tried to push them north and west to where Custer and General John Gibbon lay waiting. After six hours of intense fighting, Crook claimed the field, but the victory belonged to Crazy Horse. The Sioux had badly mauled Crook's forces, and though the general camped for the night on the battlefield, the following morning he retreated to his supply base, where he remained during the critical juncture of the spring campaign.

The Sioux moved west after the fight to the Valley of the Greasy Grass along Little Big Horn River, where scouts had found antelope and good pasturage for the horses. Sitting Bull did not think that the battle with Crook had fulfilled his prophecy. He waited on the Little Big Horn for *Wakan Tanka*'s gift.

General Custer's 7th Cavalry attacked the Sioux and Cheyenne camp from the southeast on the afternoon of June 25. Major Marcus Reno, second in command, led his 112 men at a swift gallop into the south end of the Indian village. "Move forward at as rapid a gait as prudent and . . . charge afterwards and the whole outfit will support [you]," Custer had ordered Reno. Within a few minutes, Reno was looking around desperately for that support. Instead of running (as was their custom), the Sioux stood their ground, and after repeated charges began infiltrating the thin skirmish line Reno had formed. The soldiers were tired from a long ride, "sway[ing] to and fro . . . like the limbs of cypresses in a strong wind," Sitting Bull would recall. A well-aimed shot struck Reno's Arikara scout Bloody Knife in the head and splattered the Indian's brains onto the major's face. Reno lost nerve. With no help from Custer in sight, he called for a retreat, and Reno's men dashed across the Little Big Horn seeking shelter among some bluffs on the far bank. In the forty-five minutes from charge to flight, Reno lost nearly half his command. Those who survived asked themselves the obvious question: where was Custer?

The bare outline of an answer would not be known for another day; more than that will never be known for certain. After splitting with Reno, the boy general veered north and rode along the bluffs that paralleled the east bank. From this high vantage, Custer probably saw for the first time the immense size of the Indian encampment and the huge pony herd that had prompted many of his paid Crow scouts to flee in panic. He doffed his felt hat and waved it above his head to rally the troops, then sent his trumpeter, Giovanni Martini, to find Captain Benteen, in charge of the ammunition train, and deliver this note: "Come on. Big Village. Be Quick. Bring packs. Hurry." Martini rode off.

The battle was short and fierce, no more than twenty minutes. The Indians came charging across the river from their camp, supplemented by warriors freed to fight by Reno's retreat, and rallied by Crazy Horse, who was everywhere yelling: "*Ho-ka hey!* It is a good day to fight! It is a good day to die! Strong hearts, brave hearts to the front! Weak hearts and cowards to the rear." Only one government horse, Comanche, survived the Sioux and Cheyenne onslaught; every other living thing lay dead about the bluffs. Surrounded by two brothers and a nephew, Custer fell at the north end of the battleground on a small ridge—perhaps the site of a heroic "last stand," perhaps not. Nearby lay the corpse of Mark

Kellogg, the doting *New York Herald* reporter whom Custer had secretly brought along with the expedition to record his exploits.

Two hundred and sixty-nine members of the 7th Cavalry, the proudest and most heralded outfit in the west, died in the battle. For the second time in a decade, the Sioux had annihilated an army command.

The nation learned of the "Custer Massacre" just after the Fourth of July centennial celebration. At large expositions held across the country, the American people had marveled at their own industry and ingenuity—Edison's electric light, Bell's telephone, Corliss' 700-ton steam engine—and basked in the bright light of pride and self-congratulation. What would have been terrible news at any time became a national tragedy of enormous proportion. Not since Lincoln's assassination, and some said not even then, had there been such an outpouring of public grief. Though Custer was no favorite of the defeated south, even from the cradle of the Confederacy, the Richmond *Whig* joined the national eulogy. "The North alone shall not mourn this gallant soldier," the paper insisted. "He belongs to all the Saxon race; and when he carried his bold dragoons into the thickest of the last ambuscade, where his sun of life forever set, we behold in him the true spirit of that living chivalry which cannot die, but shall live forever to illustrate the pride, the glory, and the grandeur of our imperishable race."

Grief soon gave way to rage and rage to calls for revenge. In every city, in every state, in every region of the nation, volunteers sprung up like desert flowers after a rain vying for the honor of tracking down the murderous Sioux. Sioux City offered a thousand ready men. Salt Lake promised twelve hundred. In the little town of Custer's birth, New Rumley, Ohio, first-graders swore oaths to kill Sitting Bull on sight.

Custer had predicted a few months earlier, "It will take another Phil Kearny massacre to bring Congress up to a generous support for the army." And he was right. The Little Big Horn was not a Fetterman's fight prompting a national self-examination. Terry was already regrouping his forces and collecting additional troops to continue the campaign against the hostiles. Nebraska Senator Algernon Paddock introduced a bill calling for the extermination of the Indians. A more sober President quietly expanded the army's jurisdiction to include not only the hostile Sioux but also the many thousands who had stayed at their agencies, away from the fighting. Already half-starved for lack of rations, these friendly

Sioux became the nation's prisoners of war and convenient targets for its wrath.

In August, Congress attached a punitive rider to the Indian Appropriations Act, cutting off food and rations to the agency Sioux until they agreed to cede the Black Hills, to give up their other rights outside the permanent reservation, and to grant rights of way through the remainder of their land. President Grant appointed yet another commission to visit the agencies. This time there was to be no negotiation. The commission would deliver the nation's ultimatum, which, in its simplest terms, gave the Sioux the choice to die in battle, to die from starvation, or to surrender everything they held of value.

With the irony that so often characterized government relations with the Indians, this "sell or starve" commission comprised some of the most prominent friends of the Indian. George Manypenny, a former commissioner of Indian Affairs and a staunch advocate of Grant's peace policy, chaired the commission. Bishop Whipple was another member, and Reverend Hinman, the man who had declared the Black Hills worthless, was the official interpreter. These men did not sanction the government's war against the Sioux. "I know of no instance in history where a great nation has so shamefully violated its oath," Bishop Whipple told the *New York Times,* in reference to the war for the Black Hills. Rather, the men of the commission sincerely believed that by taking the most valuable land the Sioux possessed they were pursuing the only course that would save the Sioux from annihilation. To the commissioners, the most important clause in their instructions was not the one expropriating Sioux land but the one authorizing them to devise yet another program to save the Sioux from extinction and lead them to civilization.

On September 7, at the Red Cloud agency, Bishop Whipple convened the first treaty conference with an invocation. Red Cloud could not help but wonder to what god the bishop was praying. Was this the same God, the chief asked, that the whites had deceived twice before when they made treaties in His name and then broke them? The bishop tried to quell Red Cloud's skepticism. "I do not know of a single instance," Bishop Whipple declared, "when the friends of the Indians have provided for them as careful protection as is promised in this [new] treaty." The Great Father's heart is "full of tenderness for his red children," the bishop continued soothingly, "and he has selected this commission. . . . That instead of growing smaller and smaller until the last Indian looks upon his own grave, they might become as the white people have become, a great and powerful people."

The Sioux, knowing what it was like to be great and powerful and knowing why they were no longer, balked at the terms of the proposed agreement. Under Article 1, the Sioux would forfeit not only their cherished Black Hills (7.3 million acres of the Great Sioux Reservation) but all their rights in the unceded Indian territory established by Article 16 of the 1868 treaty. In return, the Sioux would receive a mere 900,000 acres of additional grazing land on the north side of the reservation. Manypenny's proposal also required them to accept three more roads across their reservation and to return to the hated Missouri for their annuities. Article 4 threatened even worse. It authorized the appointment of a Sioux delegation to "visit the Indian Territory" (present-day Oklahoma) in the hope that the tribe eventually might be enticed or coerced into abandoning its treaty lands entirely for better farmland to the south.

As for the Manypenny commission's plan to save the Sioux (codified in Article 5 of the proposed agreement), that amounted to little more than a reiteration of the largely unfulfilled promises already contained in the 1868 treaty regarding education, farming, land allotments, carpenters, and blacksmiths. The government also agreed to provide the Indians with life-sustaining rations until they became self-supporting. Even this last, most basic, necessity, though, had qualifications attached to its distribution.

All the Sioux chiefs spoke out against the treaty and said they wanted to keep their land, and that their people would die along the Missouri. "This war did not spring up on our land," Spotted Tail complained when the commission reached his agency towards the end of August, "this war was brought upon us by the children of the Great Father who came to take our land from us without a price, and who, in our land, do a great many evil things. . . . This war has come from robbery—from the stealing of our land."

Many chiefs rose to give fine speeches, recounting past promises and pleading against moving to the Indian Territory, away from the lands of their grandfathers; but they were speeches full of grievance and fear, not defiance. "Your words are like a man knocking me in the head with a stick," Standing Elk said. "What you have spoken has put great fear upon us. Whatever we do, wherever we go, we are expected to say yes! yes! yes! yes!—and when we don't agree at once to what you ask of us in council you always say, You won't get anything to eat! You won't get anything to eat!"

The commission kept a stone face. If the Sioux did not sign, the rations would be cut off and the army would return to the agencies. In the end, the agency chiefs, even Red Cloud and Spotted Tail, heeding the naked threats of the commissioners and clutching every reassurance about the future, succumbed to the inevitable. They signed.

Forty years later, aged Sioux would remember the moment of capitulation. "Behind the Commissioners, next to the wall, there was a line of Army officers," Joseph Black Spotted Horse recalled. "At the door there was a company of soldiers with guns with bayonets. Further back towards the fort, all the cannon were turned toward us. I think this was done to scare us." The Sioux never forgot the threats. They never forgot the liquor and the bribes of $20 that the whites offered them to touch the pen. They never forgot the speeches of their chiefs. But they remembered nothing about—or perhaps never knew—the actual words on the paper: the precise terms of what they had signed. Some even mis-remembered that the treaty only allowed the whites to lease the Hills for a time. Written in a language the Sioux could not read, perhaps garbled or glossed over by translators, the treaty terms, to the extent they were ever understood, had faded from their minds even as the reason for signing remained vivid. The Sioux remembered that they had to sign, or die.

The commissioners did not bother trying to collect the signatures of three-fourths of the adult male Sioux, and only 10 percent ratified the new agreement. No one knows how many Sioux would have signed had the commissioners tried to meet the requirement of the 1868 treaty. In the aftermath of Custer's last stand, neither the commissioners nor the country cared a whit about technicalities. The commission returned to Washington "full of gratitude to God" for the success of its labors, which had dispossessed the Sioux of the Black Hills, over seven million acres of their finest and most valued land, and curtailed their use of the unceded Indian territory, perhaps forty million acres more. The commissioners still hoped to remake the Sioux according to approved white standards, but now they had taken most of the land that was good enough for farming, indeed most of the land that was good for anything at all.

The commissioners concluded their final report with a condemnation of the government's earlier treatment of the Sioux. "Our country must forever bear the disgrace and suffer the retribution of its wrongdoing," they intoned. "Our children will tell the story in hushed tones, and wonder how their fathers dare so to trample on justice and trifle with God."

On December 22, 1876, President Grant forwarded the Many-penny agreement to Congress for official ratification, and on February 28, 1877, Congress made it law. One hundred and two years after Standing Bull first beheld the *Paha Sapa* as the Sioux empire waxed, the Black Hills were gone and the empire fallen. Force had won the Hills originally; force had taken them away.

Out on the plains during the fall and winter of 1876, the U.S. Army was teaching the Sioux a lesson in reprisal and defeat. On October 22, Red Cloud's and Red Leaf's bands woke to find themselves surrounded by government troops. Although no one had accused them of any crime, and although the agreement the chiefs had just signed promised to secure their persons and property, the soldiers searched the camps and confiscated all the guns and horses. At Standing Rock and Cheyenne River, the army repeated the disarming and dismounting. In all, the army seized very few quality weapons, but over 4,000 horses—which, like the land already taken, were more than property to the Sioux; Sioux society could not function without those ponies. Adding insult to injury, the Government turned over hundreds of the Sioux horses to General Crook's paid Crow scouts, the hereditary enemies of the Sioux. The government marched the rest to St. Paul, where it sold for a pittance the small fraction that survived the trek and were not stolen by the herdsmen.

Up in the Powder River country, the army was getting its revenge. Through the short fall and the long winter, Crook, Terry, and General Nelson Miles chased Sitting Bull, Crazy Horse, and the other hostile leaders, tracking them across the deep snow, burning their camps, destroying their food stores and shooting down the stragglers. Outnumbered and outgunned, by February they had run out of food, ammunition, and places to hide. Sitting Bull took the remnants of his band to Canada. Crazy Horse, Big Foot, and Touch-the-Clouds, the last holdouts from reservation life, began to turn themselves in at the agencies.

Crazy Horse, the greatest of Sioux warriors, the last except Sitting Bull to surrender, arrived at Fort Robinson near the Red Cloud agency on May 6, 1877, at the head of his 1,000-member band. The post commander, Lieutenant William Clark, rode out a few miles to escort the Sioux chief to the fort. When they met, Crazy Horse dismounted and sat on the ground, saying that this was the best time to smoke the pipe of peace. He extended his left hand to the young lieutenant: "Friend," he said, "I shake with this hand because my heart is on this side. I want this peace to last forever." Crazy Horse took off his war bonnet; he would need it no more. The war was over.

Behind Crazy Horse rode Little Big Man, He Dog, Bad Road, and Little Hawk. Recognized for their exploits in battle, they too left their warrior trappings with the whites. Some who witnessed the surrender caught the glint of silver at Little Hawk's neck. The shimmering came from a peace medal stamped with the image of President James Monroe given to Little Hawk's father at a conference on the North Platte in 1817. After sixty years's wear, the symbol of friendship had become a mere decoration.

The Sioux had received countless tokens of friendship like Little Hawk's, countless words of peace in the intervening years. Meanwhile, a whole world had vanished. Gone were the 20 million buffalo; gone were the trackless plains. In their place stood gold mines, sod shanties, roads and railroads, and the crowds they carried. Less than two thousand Sioux warriors had died in battle, but the rest had lost health, happiness, freedom, and a way of life. The taking of the sacred Black Hills and the bountiful Powder River country, the forced movement onto the reservation, left the Sioux spiritually and economically bereft. Theirs became a hunting culture without game, a religion of celebration with remembrances only of tragedy, and a society of nomads cowering in desolate corners of the vast plains.

In the fall, the Sioux began the long journey back to the Missouri on the eastern border of the reservation, where the government could feed them at the lowest cost. (The Congress had decided against sending them to the Indian Territory, apparently because the railroads wanted that land opened for development.) Crazy Horse watched disconsolately as the bands moved east. He talked of going back to the Powder. Unsure of Crazy Horse's intentions, a jittery government ordered his arrest. In a brief stuggle outside the guardhouse of Fort Robinson, one hundred miles south of the spot near the Black Hills where he had been born, Crazy Horse died before his thirtieth birthday, impaled by a soldier's bayonet while Little Big Man, his childhood friend turned reservation policeman, pinioned his arms. Embodiment of resistance, a man who had signed no treaty, posed for no photograph, farmed no land, and never considered himself anything but free, was gone.

Before leaving office, President Grant reflected upon his eight years of guardianship over the Sioux, noting: "The question might be asked why the Government has not enforced obedience to the terms of the [1868] treaty." Grant found the answer in "the avarice of the white man such that an effort to remove the miners would only [have resulted] in the desertion of the bulk of the troops sent to remove them."

Sherman, too, mused about the devastation wrought upon the natives. "If our Indian policy has failed," the general advised, "we should look for the cause . . . in the nature of things, rather than in a systematic desire to do wrong." Thus, two of the principal actors in the Sioux drama exculpated themselves from the tragic resolution.

Neither Grant and Sherman nor the country as a whole were so blameless. The problem they faced was beyond human wisdom to solve: how to commit a great wrong—depriving the Sioux of their patrimony—without inflicting pain and injury upon the tribe. But if it was inevitable that the United States would take the Indians' land, the manner in which it did so was not. Did the government have to send Custer into the Black Hills? Did the government have to end negotiations after the Sioux rejected Allison's $6 million offer for the Hills? Did the government exhaust every reasonable alternative to war before precipitously moving troops into Sioux country? Did the government provide a workable future for the Sioux in return for their land? If our Indian policy has failed— Sherman should have written—we should look for the cause not in a systematic desire to do wrong, but in a consistent inability to do right.

SIX

THE WHITE MAN'S ROAD

IN 1878, ONLY ONE YEAR after their forced march east to the Missouri River, the Sioux moved one last time. With Crazy Horse dead, Sitting Bull in exile, and miners dredging the Black Hills for gold, the Indians spent the winter crying out for relief from months of exposure, starvation, and countless deaths. In desperation, a group of Oglala and Brûlé leaders traveled to Washington, where their entreaties softened the heart of the new Great Father, Rutherford B. Hayes. In the spring he let these Sioux return once more to the western part of their diminished reservation, where the government would establish new agencies on their behalf. Spotted Tail led his 4,000 Brûlé one hundred miles up the White River to Rosebud Creek; Red Cloud and 7,000 Oglala continued an equal distance further, finally settling at a spot just north of the Nebraska border in the far southwest corner of Sioux country.

This was familiar territory to the Teton, not far from where their agencies had been for most of the previous decade. To a casual observer it might have seemed that little had changed on the Sioux reservation as a result of the recent war except its western boundary. But the Sioux realized that even if they had begged back the right to live in their old surroundings, their new agencies would feel nothing at all like home. The days were over when restless bands could strike out for the Powder and live off the buffalo or when the Sioux could pit the reformers against the military to get their way. The days were over when the Sioux could acclimate themselves to white culture at their own pace, if at all.

Even the names of the new Sioux agencies would be different. The Indian Bureau stopped the custom of calling the Oglala and Brûlé sites after Red Cloud and Spotted Tail—a symbolic change to mark what the government intended to be the very real demise of the old chiefs. The Indian Bureau chose the name Rosebud for the permanent home of Spotted Tail's Sioux and Pine Ridge for the permanent home of Red Cloud's Sioux, but few pine trees graced the ridges of the sunburnt brown valley that surrounded the new agency. Those that did grow clustered along a few chalky ravines, a living reminder of the sandy alkaline soil that had foiled government reform policies in the past. What the new name reflected—all the better for being ill-suited—was not the surrounding landscape but the nation's resurgent determination to break down the old Sioux life and remake the beaten warriors into civilized ploughmen.

Having lost their lands and their freedom, the Sioux found themselves caught in the nativist storm that swept the country in the later decades of the nineteenth century. Protestant America had begun to retrench after years of an open society that welcomed freedmen and immigrants alike but undermined its cherished notion of a unified caucasian nation. The United States slammed shut the Golden Door, adopting the Chinese Exclusionary Act in 1882, and it disowned the progressive legislation of Reconstruction, abandoning blacks to Jim Crow rule and barring another distinctive element from the general mixture of American society.

But the Indian, admired for his nobility and his unyielding independent spirit, stood above the Asian and the African in the racial hierarchy. Christian Anglo-Saxon society would not barricade or railroad him out. American would not merely civilize the savage, it would assimilate him into its midst. With characteristic evangelical fervor, the nation focused its considerable missionary power on the one race it still considered worthy of salvation. With an American God, American education, American laws, American homesteads, and, in the end, American citizenship, the Indian would finally become truly human. Nativism would engulf the native; the last Indian would vanish either because they had become white or because they had died.

Mark Twain wryly captured the nation's new attitude towards the natives. "The time has come when blood-curdling cruelty has become unnecessary," he wrote. "Inflict soap and a spelling book on every Indian that ravages the plains and let them die." The reformers' policy was more comprehensive than that, but Twain captured their idea of cultural extinction in a nutshell. With the

Sioux now squarely under the government's thumb, the country at last had a clear opportunity to make its policy work. For the next two decades, the United States did everything in its power to undermine or eliminate tribal practices that might impede the radical reorientation of Sioux society and replace them with American institutions that would promote assimilation.

The Sioux did not remain oblivious to the zeal of their guardians, and they sensed their virtual impotence to resist the changes inherent in the new reservation life. The Sioux knew that white soldiers were posted ominously just across the border of Sioux land. They knew that simulating the thrill of the hunt by chasing down beef cattle at the agency was a far cry from tracking the buffalo. One by one the Sioux were surrendering the fundamental customs of their culture. No longer did they raid their tribal enemies, stealing horses and counting coup, garnering the honors that earned a man his stature within the tribe. The war societies withered, then wholly died away. The long hours of recounting exploits and mourning defeats were now filled with ragged, distant stories that only grew more tattered as the days passed.

In 1882, a small band of buffalo wandered onto a corner of the reservation near the Standing Rock agency and the whole camp raced out madly to join the kill. It was the first hunt in several years, and the last. The old life soon became a memory many Sioux, resentful and mistrustful, labored to keep fresh in their minds. And even the wisest could not imagine what the government had planned.

The Indian Bureau concentrated its first reform efforts on the most formidable barrier to any civilizing program, the Indians' native leadership—"those relics of barbarism"—the old chiefs. An Indian "cannot serve his chief and the agent at the same time," Pine Ridge Agent Valentine McGillycuddy concluded, as he initiated his effort to deprive the chiefs of their accustomed power. McGillycuddy "deposed" Red Cloud as head chief and stopped the traditional practice of permitting Sioux leaders to distribute government rations to their followers. "Every man his own chief," the agent declared, as he encouraged each family head to pick up his own handouts.

Many a family man, no longer dependent on his chief for sustenance, gradually grew more independent and also more susceptible to government pressure pushing him away from the old chief's camp circle and onto fresh farmland. Gradually, too, the title of chief began to mean less and less as more and more Sioux claimed it. Though the path to chieftainship had vanished with the past, the number of Sioux chiefs at Pine Ridge swelled from 12 in 1878 to 63 only two years later.

With these pretenders came factions and with these factions violence. The Sioux split between the "progressives" who, in varying degrees, accepted the assimilation programs and cooperated with the agents, and the "non-progressives" who resisted every change from the old life and held out the vague hope that someday it would return. These groups were close cognates to the friendlies and the hostiles of bygone days, but now they shared a cramped homeland. Sometimes it seemed they had come to hate each other as, together, they had once hated the Crow.

The government encouraged this split among the Sioux. It recruited actively among the progressives in search of respected headmen who might rival the old chiefs for influence. However powerful the agents, they still needed Indian help, chiefs of one sort or another, to keep order on the reservation and to advance government initiatives. They promoted young warriors like American Horse, Young-Man-Afraid-of-His-Horses, Gall, and John Grass: strong leaders, veterans of the Powder River campaigns, but not truly chiefs. These Indians were not assimilationists, but they acknowledged that in their new world the Sioux had no choice but to keep the peace and learn white ways. And they had the standing to lead the break with the past. The agents relied heavily on these progressives as they struggled to control the thousands of cooped-up and frustrated warriors who were experiencing agency life for the first time and who more than once brought the reservation to the brink of another war.

The rivalries in their own ranks left the Sioux confused and vulnerable, even if the persuasive efforts of the "progressive chiefs" prevented a general bloodletting. Ambitious and resentful Indians schemed against their leaders, currying favor with the agents and doing what at other times would have been unthinkable. In August 1881, one such plotter, Crow Dog, shot down Spotted Tail in the middle of a dusty road, killing the tribe's finest statesman. Spotted Tail's death plunged the Rosebud agency into chaos because no comparable leader emerged to fill his place.

More significantly, Spotted Tail's passing marked the beginning of the end for a unique generation of Sioux: those who had lived in the days before the whites had come and had survived the awful battles both on the free prairies and on the reservations to preserve their way of life. The Sioux were losing the last leaders whom they had chosen for reasons of their own. As Spotted Tail lay dying, his people's power of political choice already had passed substantially into the hands of their conquerors. To this day, the Sioux have never found another Spotted Tail nor overcome the crippling divisiveness that caused his death.

Crow Dog was arrested and put on trial for murder, but went free. The Supreme Court ruled that the United States lacked jurisdiction over crimes between Indians committed on reservation land. A shocked Congress, cutting away another great chunk of Indian autonomy, swiftly enacted legislation extending the nation's federal court jurisdiction to major crimes, such as murder or armed robbery, committed on tribal land.

And the government went a long way to assert its control over minor crimes, too. The Indian Bureau established Indian police forces and Indian courts on the reservations, putting the progressives in charge, and creating another apparatus for circumventing the traditional tribal leaders while schooling the natives in the ways of the white man's law. "We owe it to [the Indians]," one reform group (the Board of Indian Commissioners) concluded, "to teach them the majesty of civilized law, and to extend to them its protection against the lawless among themselves."

Yet, while the reformers lamented Spotted Tail's murder, they were not the least discouraged by the resulting anarchy in Sioux politics or made more cautious in experimenting with cultural annihilation. The United States must not recoil from the "sacrifice of a few chieftains' feathers, a few worthless bits of parchment, the cohesion of the tribal relation and the traditions of their race," admonished Phillip Gannet, one of the leading humanitarians; "let us shed the few tears necessary, embalm these relics of the past and have done with them."

The reformers had compiled a long list of Indian customs earmarked for eradication. In 1882, the Commissioner of Indian Affairs proclaimed a list of Indian offenses, in effect proscribing just about every Sioux tradition or ritual he could identify. "Rooting out paganism" to make way for civilization, the government outlawed holding feasts or dances, having more than one wife, acquiring a wife by leaving property at her father's door, and distributing personal property in the "giveaway" ceremony. The government struck at the heart of the Indians' spiritual strength, forbidding the healing and religious practices of the medicine men and banning the Sun Dance. The shamans could and did take their work underground, but the Sun Dance, the core of Sioux religious expression, could not survive in secret. With the conclusion of the last dance in the summer of 1883, the Sioux lost their medium for appealing to the spiritual power of nature and a critical source of personal and tribal inspiration.

To fill the void left by the suppression of their own religion, and at the urging of dozens of Catholic, Episcopal, and Presbyterian missionaries who ran schools and churches on the reservation, increasing numbers of Sioux adopted Christianity, which for so many years had made only halting progress among them. Many of the tenets and symbols of Christian faith were readily recognizable to the Sioux. They had always believed in a life after death and they already appreciated such values as asceticism and charity. But what the Sioux valued most of all, especially at first, was the opportunity to seek the strength of the God of their conquerors, the God whose power they no longer could deny.

"In war with the white people I found their *Wakan Tanka* the superior," an early convert, George Sword, explained. "I joined the church and am a deacon in it and shall be until I die," he said. Yet he and most other Sioux did not replace one religion with another. "I still have my *Wasicun* [the ceremonial bundle of a shaman] and I am afraid to offend it," he admitted, "because the spirit of an Oglala may go to the spirit land of the Lakota." Jesus took his place in the pantheon of the Sioux.

The Indians' partial adoption of the white man's religion was perhaps the longest of the grudging steps the Sioux took in the first decade of assimilation policy. The Sioux exhibited far more intense suspicion and active hostility towards the keystone of the government's assimilation effort—its education program. Ever since the government assumed responsibility for schooling Sioux children under the 1868 treaty, they had avoided attending, and the government had made that truancy all but inevitable. For more than a decade the Indian Bureau was glaringly delinquent in fulfilling what was not only a written obligation but avowed reform policy as well. Promised schools went unconstructed; teachers were too few and incompetent; school supplies scarce and the curriculum irrelevant to the Indians' needs.

The act of 1877 carried forward the government's commitment to build and staff one schoolhouse for every thirty Sioux children who could be compelled to enroll. In keeping with the renascent reform spirit, the Indian Bureau vowed to be more faithful and innovative in meeting this requirement, so crucial in any attempt to make the Sioux civilized and self-supporting.

In 1879, Captain Richard Pratt arrived in Sioux country to enlist Sioux children for his Carlisle Indian Industrial School, the first and most famous of what would become a whole system of off-reservation boarding schools for Indian students. Eighty-four Sioux children from Pine Ridge and Rosebud, about two-thirds boys and mainly from prominent families, returned east with the stern captain. Neither parent nor pupil foresaw the short hair, the starched shirts and squeaky boots, the Christian names, or the other trappings of the assimilationist regimen to which Pratt harnessed his charges. When Spotted Tail witnessed firsthand the thorough anti-Indian indoctrination of Carlisle's operation, he withdrew his nine children in a rage. For several years after, most Sioux refused to trust their children to the "kill the Indian, save the man" philosophy of off-reservation education.

When enrollment at the distant boarding schools did pick up again in the mid-1880s, the schools at best achieved only qualified success. The complete severance from home and family succeeded in isolating the Indian students from their culture and instilling in them a heavy dose of white values, but it did not give them much of a future. As one Carlisle-educated Sioux leader observed, "most girls [found] their life's work in city kitchens and most boys who [did] not drift back to the reservation lost their identity in a shop." In any case, the reservation reclaimed most of its offspring, though few found themselves welcome. To the extent government indoctrination had succeeded, the returned graduates were misfits back home, estranged from their families and former friends. Because the reservation offered little opportunity to apply a basic grammar school education, most did not even get the consolation of using their skills and training. Many "went back to the blanket" in search of acceptance.

The day and boarding schools on the reservation suffered from very different failings. Fiscal limitations precluded anything close to adequate conditions for learning. One hundred sixty-seven dollars was the annual allotment per student in 1885 to cover food, shelter, clothing, and instruction at reservation boarding schools, many of which consisted of buildings that had been or should have been condemned. Under pressure to augment enrollment, school officials forced unfit and unwell students into the dorms and classrooms. Not surprisingly, scrofula, tuberculosis, and a swarm of other infections as well as behavior problems followed them in. Water and fuel scarcity often compelled students to haul supplies more than a mile in the dead of winter to keep the schools going. Even then classes were often cancelled because room temperatures had not risen above zero.

When the schools were open, the Sioux attended reluctantly when they attended at all. "There are camps at this agency where the mere mention of a prospective school operates like a red flag on a bull," a Rosebud agent reported. This reflexive hostility often stemmed from incidents like the one that occurred on the first day at school on Pine Ridge. A nervous crowd gathered around the shuttered schoolhouse to catch a glimpse of their children. An untimely breeze parted the blinds, and the parents saw one matron pinioning a boy while another chopped off his ceremonial braid. Head shaving and even shackling with a ball and chain were common punishments for Indian pupils who ran away or spoke in their native tongue. Suppressing the Sioux language rated high among both the Indian Bureau's educational priorities and the reasons Sioux parents kept children at home.

Yet despite the draconian discipline and the abysmal conditions, gradually the schools took hold in Sioux country. Each year more Sioux children began reading and writing, learned trade skills, and immersed themselves in as white an environment as the government administrators could design. They did so for one compelling reason: under the act of 1877, the government provided rations to only those children between the ages of six and fourteen who attended school. Most Sioux families, never far from starvation, chose survival over the more abstract attachment to their cultural heritage.

The reformers did not always find the treaty provisions so convenient to their purposes, especially their efforts to change the Sioux from hunters into farmers. The act of 1877 required that the United States provide the Sioux with specified amounts of beef, flour, corn, coffee, sugar, and beans "until the Indians are able to support themselves." The government thought of these rations merely as a stopgap measure, just enough food for just long enough to tide the Indians over until they could subsist on their own. But the Sioux, who never seemed to receive their full complement of anything, viewed their rations very differently. As the only tangible benefit they had obtained for their Black Hills, the Sioux looked upon their guaranteed food supply not as a bridge to self-reliance but as a well-merited substitute for it. "The white man can work if he wants to," Red Cloud informed his agent, "but the Great Spirit did not make us to work. The white man owes us a living for the lands he has taken from us."

As had happened many times in the past, each side imbued the letter of the law with its own peculiar spirit. What seemed an act of benevolence to one seemed a payment of tribute to the other. Once again, mutual and colossal misunderstanding made inevitable the unmet expectations and heartfelt grievances that had too often led to tragedy. The government worked doggedly to wean the Sioux from the dole while the Indians never stopped depending on what literally and symbolically was all that remained of their most cherished land. "They promised to feed us till the very last dog died," an old Sioux recalled about the last paper his people had signed. That promise was their final blanket of security and the Sioux hugged it close as government agents tugged at the corners.

It took more than thirty years and several new acts of Congress for the agents to convince most of the Sioux to establish homesteads away from the agencies, even though the government provided a new house for anyone who took an allotment. In any case, dispersing the Indian onto individual plots did not alter their attitude toward farming. Since an Indian living on fertile land lost his rations unless he worked, the Sioux would farm just diligently enough to keep the agents from hounding them—which was not nearly hard enough to make it on their own.

Had the Sioux wanted to farm, the result would probably have been no different. Corralling the Sioux onto their reservation had not made the Dakota soil more fertile or the climate more temperate. The crops they did plant—mainly corn—burned up under the relentless plains sun or vanished in a windstorm or fed the grasshoppers for another season. In 1887, Charles McChesney at Cheyenne River stated point-blank what agent reports had hinted at for twenty years: "The drawbacks to successful agriculture are so great as not to be overcome with any reasonable amount of labor."

The reformers had worked themselves into a paradox. On the one hand, they could not allow the Sioux to become permanent pensioners; on the other hand, they refused to consider any alternative to farming as a means of raising the Indians to self-sufficiency. The apparent solution was to encourage the Sioux to raise stock—the one occupation for which the Indians showed considerable aptitude and enthusiasm and which nature did not preclude.

But the east coast reformers who controlled Indian policy were blindly determined to break up tribal land masses such as the Sioux reservation and to settle every Indian on his own 160-acre plot. The ownership of private property would inculcate the Christian values of hard work and thrift in every savage breast; and it would liberate the individual Indian from the bondage of the tribe and expose him to his white neighbors, making him even more susceptible to salvation. That was theory—conceived in Washington two thousand miles from the plains desolation—and the theorists, blinded by their moral certitude, denied the Sioux any realistic chance to create a viable economy on the reservation and denied themselves any hope of ending the primitive welfare system that frustrated their program at every turn.

A great deal changed on the Sioux reservation in the 1880s. Many Sioux put on different clothes; many moved into houses; many sent their children to school; many recognized new leaders; many adopted a new god. None hunted; none went to war.

Yet a great deal did not change. Despite the army and the Indian Bureau, despite the congressional legislation and departmental edicts, the Indians remained essentially Indian and the nation continued to treat them as such. The government still did not abide by its commitments to them. Rations were always short and often inedible. In lieu of the promised "suit of good substantial woolen clothing," each Sioux received a suit of ten-ounce canvas which the government's own employees described as "devoid of appearance, warmth or durability." The government-issue blankets, replacements for the buffalo robes that had protected the Sioux during the fierce Dakota winters, were grossly insufficient to keep the Indians warm, made of "wool shoddy apparently mixed with a cheap adulterant." Shoes, tools, and other useful materials showed the same dreadful standard.

The government representatives who were assigned the monumental task of implementing the civilizing program continued for the most part to be political appointees with little or no experience in Indian affairs. A state governor blithely admitted that for party workers fit for nothing else, he found jobs in the Indian service. One inspector reported finding an "abandoned woman" in charge of one Indian school, a lunatic in charge of another. Mismanagement was another burden the Sioux had to bear.

Half frozen, always near starvation—without the right to practice their religion, move about freely, assemble peacefully, choose their own leaders, or be let alone—the Sioux sank into despair. As complete dependents on a nation that had so often broken its word, they had to wonder whether soon they too would go the way of the buffalo.

"There is a time appointed for all things," Spotted Tail had reflected. "Think for a moment how many multitudes of animal tribes we ourselves have destroyed; look upon the snow that appears today—tomorrow it is water. Listen to the dirge of the dry leaves that were green and vigorous but a few moons before! We are part of that life and it seems our time has come."

Some Sioux refused to resign themselves either to death or accommodation and spoke out against the whites. Sitting Bull returned from his Canadian exile in 1881 to reassume his position as spiritual leader of the non-progressives. Ironically, when the Northern Pacific Railroad celebrated the completion of its transcontinental track two years later, the famous medicine man delivered the welcoming address for the company he and his people had fought against for most of a decade. One witness claimed that Sitting Bull's speech, delivered in his native tongue, was really a diatribe against the whites altered by the government interpreter. Perhaps Sitting Bull did rail against his conquerors. If so, it was a hopeless gesture. Few understood him, fewer cared. The whites sent Sitting Bull on a nationwide tour with Buffalo Bill's Wild West Show. As a circus novelty, the "Conqueror of Custer" amused American audiences and further impressed on the popular imagination the image of the Sioux as the archetypally defiant (though now subdued) noble savage.

While Sitting Bull acted out the past on stage, his people lived the present waiting for the next assault on what little they still possessed. They did not wait long. More treaty commissioners were sniffing around Sioux country looking for more land.

Dakota Territory was bursting. During the 1870s the population of southeastern Dakota increased from 10,000 people to over 81,000. By 1885 that number had grown again threefold, as Norwegians, Germans, Russians, Swedes, Danes, and other immigrants moved west to try farming and ranching on the prairies of their adopted homeland. In the years 1878 to 1887, more than 24 million acres of Dakota land were parceled out to homesteaders. In the peak year, 1883, Dakota land filings in the southeast section alone, east of the Missouri and south of the 48th parallel, accounted for 23 percent of the entire national market.

In the western part of the Territory, the recently acquired Black Hills, the growth was as impressive. Over 16,000 fortune hunters had flocked to the Hills by 1880, and, more important, they were beginning to produce commercial returns for the government's landtaking efforts on their behalf. In 1877, a wealthy California investor named George Hearst bought out the claim of the Manuel brothers near the town of Lead for $66,000 and incorporated the Homestake Mining Company. After two years of pulverizing from his giant 80-stamp mill, Hearst had extracted $120,000 worth of bullion from the land that over the next century would yield more gold than any other mine in the western hemisphere.

Between the eastern and western portions of the Dakota Territory sat 43,000 square miles of undeveloped and underpopulated prairie, land where skilled and enterprising white farmers and stockmen wanted to test their mettle. This 150-mile-wide strip was all that remained of the Great Sioux Reservation. Yet whites of virtually every political inclination agreed it was still too much for its present owners. At Yankton, the territorial capital, local politicians, greasing the wheels for a run at statehood, weren't keen to enter the Union bifurcated by the once feared, now contemptible Sioux. In 1882 the Dakota delegate to Congress, Richard Pettigrew, convinced the legislature to appropriate $5,000 for a commission to sound out the Indians about the possibility of relinquishing roughly half again of their attenuated homeland. No sooner was the bill signed into law than the Secretary of the Interior, Henry Teller, a westerner in thorough sympathy with the Dakota settlers, appointed a three-man delegation to meet with the Sioux. As chairman, he named that old hand at Indian dealings, Newton Edmunds—the savvy territorial politician who had masterminded the abortive treaties of 1865.

Under the proposed agreement, the Great Sioux Reservation would be divided into six smaller reservations, in aggregate about 14,000 square miles smaller than the original. In return for the ceded land, the Sioux were to receive 1,000 bulls and 25,000 cows—a herd for cattle raising, though only to tide the Sioux over until they successfully adapted to farming. As they traveled from agency to agency, the Edmunds commissioners explained how the new, smaller reservations would be further divided into allotments, thereby finally securing the Indians' inviolable title to their lands. The Sioux could not figure out how this latest agreement differed from the last three times the United States had promised them secure title and, initially, the Sioux chiefs withheld their consent. Nonetheless, with the usual combination of threats, cajoling, and outright deception, Edmunds eventually changed their minds.

Many of the chiefs became so confused under the cascade of speeches that they had no idea what they were signing away. Others know all too well, but had been intimidated by the threats to cut off rations or to move the Sioux down to the Indian Territory as had almost happened before. After touching the pen, a band chief at Pine Ridge named Yellow Hair stepped forward to show the commissioners a ball of dirt he was holding. "We have given up nearly all our land," he told them, "and you had better take the balance now, and here I hand it to you."

Three hundred eighty-nine chiefs and headmen signed the 1882 agreement and, like Manypenny before him, Edmunds did not bother with the necessary three-fourths majority. He ferried the treaty back to Washington, alleging that the Sioux had sold their land and pushing hard for quick congressional ratification. The Indian rights groups in the east, however, though they welcomed a new land cession, had grown more punctilious since 1877 about meeting treaty requirements. With the Sioux already protesting that Edmunds had tricked them, Congress sent the commission back to Sioux country for more signatures. Some precocious six-year-old Indian children found themselves counted as "adult Sioux males," but the commission still could not muster enough names.

Congress rejected the 1882 agreement. In the absence of a compelling national emergency—as had apparently existed during the Black Hills crisis—the reformers in Washington could not justify a blatant violation of Sioux treaty rights. That did not suggest that the reformers wanted the Sioux to keep their land, only that they would find a legal means for dispossessing them. The friends of the Indian never had interpreted the nation's guardianship over the tribes to mean that the tribes could impede American expansion. It was an offense against nature, against progress, and against Christian civilization that 25,000 Sioux should possess so many millions of acres and, worse yet, let them lie fallow. The Sioux occupied more than twice enough land to provide a homestead for every tribal family. What the Sioux did not realize as they celebrated the death of Edmunds's swindle was that the alliance between the land boomers and the eastern reformers made it certain that eventually much of the Great Sioux Reservation would join the millions of acres the Sioux had once owned.

In 1887, Congress enacted and the President signed the General Allotment Act, the brainchild of the country's foremost reformer, Massachusetts Senator Henry Dawes. The act was the first attempt at near-universal application of the principle of allotment in severalty. Once a tribe consented to application of the act on its reservation, each head of an Indian family, upon applying for a patent, would receive 160 acres of land; single adults, orphans, and minors would receive specified lesser amounts. The government would then hold these patents in trust for twenty-five years, after which the Indian owner, having been granted American citizenship and supposedly having learned to handle his own affairs, would be free to use or to dispose of his lands at will. The government would purchase the leftover ("surplus") lands of each tribe (at bargain prices) and then sell them to homesteaders.

Sponsors of the new legislation hailed it as the Indians' emancipation proclamation, compared it favorably with Magna Carta, and congratulated themselves for having taken a giant step towards investing each Indian with land of his own, saving the 200,000 aborigines who had survived the trials of disease, defeat, and destitution. Westerners joined in the celebration as well, because the act ultimately would open millions of acres of "surplus" Indian lands to white settlement. ("A mighty pulverizing engine to break up the tribal mass," President Theodore Roosevelt later called it). The few critics characterized the act as "a bill to despoil the natives of their lands and to make them vagabonds on the face of the earth."

"If this were done in the name of greed," one congressman protested, "it would be bad enough; but to do it in the name of humanity, and under the cloak of an ardent desire to promote the Indians' welfare by making him more like ourselves, whether he will or will not, is infinitely worse." Time would make prophets of the naysayers. During the next forty-seven years, while the Dawes Act remained the fulcrum of American policy, 60 million acres of land (roughly 40 percent of all Indian landholdings) passed into white hands, having been declared surplus to Indian needs. As the act took effect in 1887, no tribe seemed to have a greater overabundance than the Sioux.

In fact, the Sioux held so much more land than they would need for allotment that the government decided to negotiate immediately to divide up what remained of the Great Sioux Reservation after 1877 and purchase 9 million acres of surplus prairie. Allotment itself could follow later. Not a year after the signing of the Dawes Act, another commission, this one headed by the dour educator Captain Pratt, made the long trek to Dakota bearing an agreement that differed little in substance from the one Edmunds had presented six years earlier.

The new proposal divided Sioux country into six separate reservations, each corresponding to an existing agency: four along the Missouri River (Standing Rock, Cheyenne River, Crow Creek, and Lower Brûlé) and two to the southwest at Pine Ridge and Rosebud, where Red Cloud and Spotted Tail, respectively, had settled down. For the 9 million acres that the government intended to siphon off as part of this division, the Sioux would receive 50¢ an acre, plus the 1,000 bulls and 25,000 cows, extended education benefits, and a few added incentives for those who voluntarily selected allotments.

Though Pratt employed the now commonplace methods of intimidation, the Sioux, even the progressives, held firm. The commission spent an entire month explaining and menacing by turns, but with Edmunds's visit still rankling, the Indians had made a pact among themselves to turn stone faces to the commissioners. On these few occasions when they did address themselves to the proposed sale, they limited their remarks to a litany of past grievances and broken promises. Returning east, Pratt recommended that his threats become reality: that the United States should once again ignore the 1868 treaty and take the land without consent.

The government decided instead to be more generous. After consulting with a large delegation of Sioux chiefs in Washington, Congress authorized a new proposal for 1889, with some significant concessions to the Indians. Rather than paying 50¢ an acre for land it could resell at more than $3.00, the government agreed to give the Sioux $1.25 an acre for land homesteaded by whites in the first three years, 75¢ an acre for the subsequent two years, and 50¢ only for the land that remained unclaimed after five years.

The new treaty (technically an agreement, since Congress had abolished the treaty system in 1871) also stipulated, in contrast to previous proposals, that the United States would bear the administrative costs of the program and that this land cession in no way presaged a forced allotment of remaining tribal lands. A majority of adult males at each of the separate reservations would have to approve allotment before the Dawes Act could be applied, and even then, family heads would receive 320 acres—twice the established quota. In a further amendment calculated at snaring Red Cloud's endorsement, the government agreed to pay $40 a head to the individuals from Red Cloud's and Red Leaf's bands for the ponies that the army had confiscated in 1876.

Again three distinguished commissioners, this time led by General George Crook, went to meet with the Sioux. Though he as much as anyone evoked bitter memories of the Black Hills war, Crook had earned a reputation for honesty among the Sioux, and, in the atmosphere of distrust that pervaded every conference, that was an invaluable quality. Crook had no need to exaggerate the Indians' predicament. One way or another the government was determined to acquire the Sioux land, and the general made that clear from the outset:

> Last year when you refused to accept the bill Congress came very near opening this reservation anyhow. It is certain that you will never get any better terms than are offered in this bill, and the chances are that you will not get so good. And it strikes me that instead of your complaining of the past, you had better provide for the future. . . . It strikes me that you are in the position of a person who had his effects in the bed of a dry stream when there was a flood

coming down, and instead of finding fault in the Creator for sending it down, you should try and save what you can.

The Sioux had heard before the advice "It's better to light a single
candle than to curse the darkness," and they resolved to be more
careful this time in their experiments with fire.

In the sixty-four years since the Sioux had concluded their first
treaty with the United States in 1825, if there remained one constant in their world, it was that they never understood either the
terms or the import of what they had signed. This treaty, rife with
the foreign concepts of acreage, graduated prices, trust funds, and
property rights, twelve pages of closely typed fine print (well over
an hour in translation into a language that lacked the corresponding vocabulary), was essentially unfathomable, like every other
they had signed.

The Sioux labored to understand it. They searched its clauses for
hidden meanings and deceptions. They asked for their own copies.
They asked for their own stenographers. They asked for countless
explanations. In the end they still could not grasp what Crook's
treaty auguered, and in their speeches they retreated onto ground
they knew well—the past. At Standing Rock, Pine Ridge, and
Rosebud, the three largest and most trouble-filled agencies, the
great chiefs mustered their eloquence to talk down this latest assault
on their land. Sitting Bull gave their thoughts their best voice:

> Friends and Relatives: Our minds are again disturbed by the Great
> Father's representatives, the Indian Agent, the squaw men, the
> mixed-bloods, the interpreters, and the favorite ration chiefs. What
> is it they want of us at this time? They want us to give up another
> chunk of our tribal land. This is not the first time or the last time.
> They will try to gain possession of the last piece of ground we
> possess. They are again telling us what they intend to do if we agree
> to their wishes. Have we ever set a price on our land and received
> such a value? No, we never did. What we got under former treaties
> was promises of all sorts. . . . We are dying off in expectation of
> getting things promised us. . . .
>
> Therefore, I do not wish to consider any proposition to cede any
> portion of our tribal holdings to the Great Father. If I agree to
> dispose of any part of our land to the white people I would feel
> guilty of taking food away from our children's mouths, and I do not
> wish to be that mean. There are things they tell us that sound good
> to hear, but when they have accomplished their purpose they will
> go home and will not try to fulfill our agreements with them.

Poetry and truth invested power in the old chief's words, but Crook had his own instruments of persuasion and he orchestrated them brilliantly. For two days he feasted the Indians on beef until they were content and pliable. At the same time he tried to relieve the Indians' apprehension. The Sioux worried that the new treaty would cancel their various benefits from the 1868 treaty or the Black Hills agreement. Crook explained that the old agreements and the new one would all run side by side until the old treaties died. Most of all, the Sioux wanted assurances about the quantity of their rations, which the non-progressives insisted would be cut once they gave up their land. Crook promised that was wrong.

Next, Crook turned to the progressives, singling out the most influential leaders, keeping them up all night, offering them bribes, working them over until one or another at each agency agreed to speak for the treaty. John Grass did Crook's bidding at Standing Rock. American Horse, who had ridden with Crazy Horse at the Fetterman fight, spoke on Crook's behalf at Pine Ridge. He held the floor for more than two days, reviewing past and present, predicting the future, struggling to make some sense for himself and his people out of the chaos of Sioux life. As the third day drew to a close, as he feared that his tribesmen would reject the better future promised in the new treaty, American Horse ended in despair: "You were sitting there with your eyes shut and your ears plugged up refusing to hear or see," he chastised his audience. "I will sign this bill knowing that I have done what is best for my people."

American Horse touched the pen to the treaty and at every agency the same scene was being enacted. Once a few Sioux signed, for fear of being excluded from the agreement's benefits or from faith in its faintly understood terms, the Sioux rushed forward to sign the death warrant of their "Great" reservation. Sitting Bull did not sign; neither did Red Cloud, nor most of the old chiefs; but after more than a decade of reservation life, they could no longer hold the majority. Slightly more than the three-fourths Crook required—4,463 Sioux of the 5,678 eligible—formed their X's on his paper.

Crook left behind a Sioux reservation more bitterly divided than ever. Progressive and non-progressive traded accusations of cowardice and betrayal. Indian children absorbed their parents' hatreds and broke into fist fights along factional lines. The government stepped in to settle the argument. Looking to cut its budget for Indian affairs, Congress reduced the Sioux appropriation for fiscal 1890 by 10 percent ($100,000), leaving the Indian Bureau no choice but to cut rations. With the government commissioners only two weeks departed, the agent at Rosebud announced an annual beef reduction of two million pounds, the agent at Pine Ridge a reduction of one million pounds.

The Sioux who had signed Crook's agreement became the objects of derision, dupes to have trusted the whites. For the non-progressives it was too bitter a time, too important a deception to gain satisfaction from I-told-you-so's. "They made us many promises," an old Sioux recalled in resignation, "more than I can remember, but they never kept but one; they promised to take our land and they took it."

Winter descended on the Sioux. Their crops had failed again, in part because they had been at the agencies meeting with Crook. Many of their cattle had frozen to death in the terrible snows of the year before. Once more their clothing and other annuities arrived months late, well into winter, delayed by a miserly Congress. Measles, whopping cough, and influenza epidemics swept across the reservation. Disease aided by hunger killed forty-five Sioux a month at Pine Ridge alone. Grief and hopelessness overwhelmed the camps. "The people said their children were all dying from the face of the earth and they might as well all be killed at once."

And then word came from the south, word of an Indian prophet, and hope was reborn. His English name was Jack Wilson, but to the Indians he was Wovoka, a Paiute, and he preached a new religion, essentially Christian, distinctively Indian, which filled the crushed Sioux with joy. A new world was coming from the west, a regenerated world to arrive in the spring of 1891. This new world would roll back the teeming swarms of white men and push them back across the ocean. In the cleansed land left behind, only Indians would live, all the Indians who had ever lived—friends and ancestors, past and present, at home once more with the buffalo, eternally happy.

Eleven Sioux went to Utah in the winter of 1889 to see the rumored messiah. In the spring they came back to Sioux country convinced of the miracles they had beheld and preaching the doctrine of Wovoka. They carried his word among the people and began his special form of worship, the Ghost Dance—a rite in which the participant fell into trances and, for a moment, glimpsed the coming paradise. For those who clung desperately to the old life, Wovoka's vision answered a prayer. "There was no hope on earth and God seemed to have forgotten us," remembered Red Cloud. "Some Sioux said they saw the Son of God; others did not see Him. . . . The people did not know; they did not care. They snatched at the hope. They screamed like crazy men to Him for mercy. They caught at the promise they had heard He had made."

The Ghost Dance spread from agency to agency, taking its strongest hold at the least progressive, Pine Ridge and Standing Rock. And in Sioux country, the religion gained a new and dangerous gloss. Interpreted in the light of bitterness and deception, Wovoka's pacific teachings assumed a unique militancy as some Sioux came to believe that their ceremonial Ghost Shirts were impervious to white bullets. They took up arms in a gesture of defiance born of immunity. Everywhere the Sioux were dancing, defying the agents, chasing off the Indian police as resentment flamed into frenzy. Ironies abounded. American flags fluttered above the Ghost Dance prayer trees; Sunday, the white man's medicine day, became the Ghost Dance sabbath; Carlisle graduates used their white-taught skills to disseminate the religion more rapidly, communicating in English with celebrants on other reservations. The old chiefs seized the moment to reassert their waning authority, embracing the new faith and exhorting their kinsmen to abandon the "black road" of the whites.

The calmer and more experienced heads among the agents counseled patience, allowing time and the coming of winter to cool Sioux passions. Nonetheless, the white settlers near the reservation, with their own visions of the past, began to panic at the prospect of a Sioux rampage. They called for government protection. At Pine Ridge, the weak and incompetent recent patronage appointee, D. F. Royer, lost control of his agency and started the telegraph wires singing with his pleas for federal troops.

In mid-November the army returned to the reservation, concentrating most of its 3,000 men in the especially turbulent Pine Ridge area. The Sioux dancers fled north, taking refuge from the soldiers in the eroded hills and canyons of the Dakota badlands, while the military presence enforced an uneasy calm at the agencies.

The high command decided to use the comparative peace to arrest the "bad influences" on the reservation. At dawn on December 15, Agent James McGlaughlin's Standing Rock Indian Police surrounded Sitting Bull's house and took the medicine man into custody. A crowd gathered, pushing the policemen against the walls of the cabin. As Sitting Bull stepped into the crowded doorway, his son Crow Foot taunted him for going along so peacefully. Sitting Bull paused; he called on his people to rescue him. One of the faithful shot a police lieutenant. Another policeman, Red Tomahawk, put his gun to Sitting Bull's head and fired, killing him instantly. Six Indian policemen and eight other Indians, including Crow Foot, fell in the vicious close-quarter melee that followed. One way of Indian life against another, Sioux warrior against Sioux policeman, shot it out in Sitting Bull's camp. The old Sioux way lost its greatest prophet; the new way lost a few converts who would easily be replaced.

Big Foot, a chief from Cheyenne River, was next on the army's list of supposed troublemakers. On the night of December 28, 1890, Custer's old outfit, the 7th Cavalry (still with many officers who had fought under Major Reno at the Little Big Horn), caught up with Big Foot's band. Colonel George Forsyth surrounded the 340 Indians with a cordon of 470 troops and a battery of four Hotchkiss guns. Just west of Wounded Knee Creek, Big Foot, near death from pneumonia, hoisted a white flag in the center of his camp and bedded down for the night. Come morning the Sioux would surrender their guns—many of them for the second time.

Early in the morning the disarming began, with nerves raw on both sides. When the warriors weren't forthcoming with their weapons, the troops began ransacking the camp, breaking up furniture and bullying the squaws. The Indians grew nervous at the shouts of their women and children. A medicine man, Yellow Bird, started blowing shrill tweets on his eagle-bone whistle—encouraging the young men to resist, reminding them that their ghost dance shirts would resist white bullets. A Sioux brave lifted his blanket, produced a gun, and shot a soldier.

The 7th Cavalry opened fire, killing half the hundred men in the first volley. The Hotchkiss guns obliterated the Indian camp where the army had segregated the women and children. Those who survived the artillery fled into nearby ravines only to be tracked down and butchered by soldiers beyond control. Nearly three hundred virtually disarmed and utterly helpless Sioux, two-thirds women and children, died at Wounded Knee. (So did sixty soldiers, mostly from their overeager comrades' bullets.) A blizzard came on suddenly in the night, as though to hide the carnage. For two days it snowed before a burial party and Dr. Charles Eastman, the Pine Ridge doctor and a Santee Sioux himself, could come out to collect the corpses and look for the few chance survivors. Dr. Eastman recorded the scene:

> Finally three miles from the scene of the massacre we found the body of a woman completely covered with a blanket of snow, and from this point on we found them scattered along as they had been relentlessly hunted down and slaughtered while fleeing for their

lives. . . . When we reached the spot where the Indian camp had stood, among the fragments of burned tents and other belongings we saw the frozen bodies lying close together or piled one upon another. I counted eighty bodies of men who had been in the council and who were almost as helpless as the women and the babes when the deadly fire began. . . .

All this was a severe ordeal for one who had but lately put his faith in the Christian love and lofty ideals of the white man.

The frozen bodies were gathered up and buried without cere-mony in a mass grave. They lived on in Sioux memories; as Black Elk said: "When I look back now from this high hill of my old age, I can still see the butchered women and children lying heaped and scattered along the crooked gulch as when I saw them with my eyes still young. And I can see that something else died in the bloody mud and was buried in the blizzard. A people's dream died there. It was a beautiful dream."

So the year 1890 ended. The white man's road loomed ever broader and even more rugged before the Sioux. The Ghost Dance fervor melted away; the plains wars, a half-century old, finally ended. Congress authorized money to restore the Sioux beef ration and fulfill the promises of the Crook commission. America's pol-icy, well articulated by Senator Dawes, however, remained un-changed: "We may cry out against the violation of treaties, denounce flagrant disregard of inalienable rights and the inhu-manity of our treatment of the defenseless . . . but the fact remains. . . . Without doubt these Indians are somehow to be absorbed into and become a part of the 50,000,000 of our people. There does not seem to be any other way to deal with them."

It was an admission of sorts: for all the fine speeches and noble sentiments, for all the goodwill organizations and professional philanthropists, and as much as they principally directed Indian policy, the effect of that policy was virtually indistinguishable from the intent of the Indians' most crassly or viciously motivated enemies.

Having assumed responsibility for the interests of a land-rich alien minority whose way of life it had just extinguished, the U.S. Government—both out of folly and on behalf of its enfranchised white majority—abused its trust. Endemic land hunger, a lack of vision and needless cruelties wrought by congressional stinginess, bad administration, and military blundering had paved a straight track to Wounded Knee. American idealists, however sincere, had shown once again that they could neither fashion an evenhanded compromise with rational self-interest nor translate their benevolence into wise and effective policy. The Sioux became the latest victims of the reformers' grand social experiment that in a perfect world would have taken generations to succeed, if indeed success were possible. The reformers had no truck with gradualism, and theirs was anything but a perfect world. Little had changed since Tocqueville observed about America's treatment of the Indians, "It is impossible to kill men with more respect for the laws of humanity."

The Sioux were not quite dead. With little skill or education and as few cultural supports as possible, on poor lands that by law would continue to shrink in size, they left the old life behind them. The Sioux had a history of adaptation. When the Chippewa had expelled them from their woodland homes a century earlier, the Sioux had assumed a foreign culture, the plains culture, and made it their own. This time there were neither unclaimed prairies nor plentiful buffalo to effect the second transition—which would prove a thousand times more difficult than the first. As a people, the Indians' hope for the future rested on their ability to inspire the conscience of their conquerors. That alone had secured them the right to live, own some small parcel of land, and enter into citizenship—and distinguished them from the many aboriginal peoples throughout the world whose conquerors cared not at all whether native tribes vanished from the earth.

The greatest weapon the Sioux possessed had never been their formidable skill as warriors but the way they reminded Americans of the yawning gulf between their high ideals and their political actions. This talent not only survived the old life, it became ever more potent the further the Sioux declined and the less alien they became. Another group of Sioux chiefs visited Washington soon after Wounded Knee. They did not wear buckskins or warbonnets. They wore cheap, ill-fitting suits with funny-shaped ties and battered cowboy hats over their shortened hair. However modified their appearance, however far they had gone along the white man's road, like their fathers and forefathers, they recounted the undeniable wrongs and asked the guilt-pricking questions their guardians wanted to forget. Young-Man-Afraid, son of one of the great chiefs of the 1850s and 1860s, friend to Crazy Horse, now progressive chief, reminded Interior Secretary John Noble:

> The troubles spring from seed. The seed was sown long ago by the
> white man not attending truthfully to his treaties after a majority

of our people had voted for them. When the white man speaks, the
Government and the army see that we obey. When the red man
speaks it goes in one ear and out the other. . . .

Why was not the late treaty fixed promptly by the Great Council?
Why were our rations cut down a million pounds? Why have not
our winter annuities come? Why was the Sioux nation called to
account for dancing a religious dance? Why are our agents always
being changed? Why was Agent Gallagher discharged when he
wrote that our crops had failed, and our rations must not be cut
down? . . . And why does not the blame for what followed belong
to the white men?

Young-Man-Afraid and every other Sioux, progressive or non-
progressive, shared this active sense of grievance, a history of in-
flicted tragedy that, even as the "dream died," was already becoming a bond of identity that no reform program could destroy. No
longer could the Sioux hope to resuscitate the past, but they would
not forget the promises made and broken. And if as the census
proclaimed the closing of the frontier, American wanted absolu-
tion for the sins of its expansion, the Sioux served notice that they
would not give it freely.

▼ ▼ ▼ ▼ ▼

SEVEN

THE BLACK HILLS CLAIM

No ONE KNOWS precisely when the Sioux began agitating about the loss of the Black Hills. Major John Brennan, a longtime superintendent at Pine Ridge after 1900, dates the first organized protest to 1887. Then in 1891, he reports the establishment of the Oglala Council, a group of roughly three hundred old and non-progressive "chiefs and headmen," who began meeting almost every month "to discuss the old treaties, figure out how much money the Government owed them on account of the Black Hills . . . and make life as unpleasant as possible for the agent and other employees." The Sioux must have held nearly a hundred meetings during the 1890s to discuss their old grievances, especially the theft of the Hills. No one paid them much attention. No record of their proceedings survive; only one letter—a personal appeal from Chief Lip to the commissioner of Indian Affairs—appears in the old bureau files. No doubt the agents at the time, like Brennan later, dismissed the Black Hills meetings as "unpleasant" obstructions to the progress of the assimilation programs, the swan song of the old, recalcitrant chiefs.

But the Black Hills councils were more than that. They were an integral part of the process of survival and redefinition that encompassed Sioux life in the decades after Wounded Knee. In a world where farming and stockraising were finally taking hold, and a foreign language and foreign institutions were now commonplace, the Black Hills claim emerged as one of the few bridges to a cherished past. For a people barely sustaining themselves on meager rations and small lease payments, the prospect of reparations

for lost tribal lands kindled hopes for a better life and lent traditional Sioux leaders a sense of purpose. If memories of theft and
deception were most of what the old chiefs and headmen retained
from the buffalo days, that legacy of broken promises would be
their gift to the future. In every council, the ancient men unlocked
their memories in eloquent Lakota, passing the torch of accusation
to the next generation, and vesting in their children and grandchildren the power of their people's tragic history to inspire the com-
passion of their conquerors. Despite the pressure to assimilate and
to forget the past, despite the remoteness of success in the still alien
white world, many Sioux disciples reached for the flame.

In 1903 Red Cloud, ascendant for forty years, withdrew from
public life. On July Fourth (a holiday the Sioux borrowed annually
for their own dancing and celebration), he abdicated his chieftainship in favor of his son Jack and addressed his people about their
shared heritage and his role in it:

> My sun is set. My day is done. Darkness is stealing over me. . . . The
> Great Spirit made us, the Indians, and gave us this land we live in.
> He gave us the buffalo, the antelope, and the deer for food and
> clothing. We moved on our hunting grounds from the Minnesota
> to the Platte and from the Mississippi to the great mountains.
> No one put bounds on us. We were free as the winds and the
> eagle. . . . I was born a Lakota and I have lived as a Lakota and I shall
> die a Lakota. . . . *Taku Skanskan* (the supernatural patron of all
> moving things) is familiar with my spirit and when I die I will go
> with him. Then I will be with my forefathers. If this is not in the
> heaven of the white man, I shall be satisfied. *Wi* (the sun) is my
> father. The *Wakan Tanka* of the white man has overcome him. But
> I shall remain true to him. . . . Shadows are long and dark before
> me. I shall soon lie down to rise no more. While my spirit is with
> my body the smoke of my breath shall be towards the Sun for he
> knows all things and knows that I am still true to him.

On September 21 he appeared in tribal council one final time,
setting aside age to face down yet another emissary from the Great
Father, South Dakota Congressman E. W. Martin. The congressman had come to the Pine Ridge agency to discuss the Black Hills
treaty. He came not at Red Cloud's request, as would have been
the case in the past, but at the invitation of American Horse, who
had spoken for Crook at the 1889 treaty councils, and of George
Sword, a holy man and warrior who knew all the ancient ceremonies, had fought in many battles, but who was both a deacon in a
Christian church and a reservation policeman.

They and other younger and relatively progressive leaders had already gone so far as to coordinate their efforts with representatives from the other Sioux agencies, and even with the Cheyenne and Arapaho who had also participated in the 1876 agreement. Still, mostly blind and huddled in his wheelchair against the chill of his eighty-second autumn, Red Cloud opened the meeting, mustering his fading oratorical powers for one more explication of his most enduring complaint:

> Quite a while ago I used some words with the Great Father. It must have been twenty-six or twenty-eight years ago and I have missed most of the words. There was a man came from the Great Father who told me, "Red Cloud, the Great Father told me to come to see you because he wants the Black Hills from you." So I asked, "How much money did you bring for the Black Hills?" He answered me, "I brought six million dollars." So I answered him, "That is a little bit of a thing. . . . The Black Hills is worth to me seven generations but you give me this word of six million dollars. It is just a little spit out of my mouth." Then he said, "Let me have the Black Hills and the Big Horn mountains both together." But I told him this, "That is too small; so I won't do it." And I kept the land. "So you can go back to the Great Father and say that to me the Black Hills is worth seven generations. You can tell the Great Father that I will lend him the top of the hill, if he is satisfied that is what you can tell him. That is just the rocks above the pines." I would like to tell you this my friend [Cong. Martin]; the rations they give us only last for a day. They should give us the money from the Black Hills treaty, because we need it now.

In the last twenty-seven years, Red Cloud had forgotten much. His recitation, which was a fair rendering of his meeting with the Allison commission in 1875, entirely neglected what had happened a year later when Manypenny ordered the chief to "sell or starve." Whatever its omissions, though, this historical appeal by the most commanding chief of the treaty era reemphasized how poorly the Sioux understood the actual terms of the treaties to which they so often referred and on which they still counted to provide for them in the future. What pay exactly did Red Cloud expect if the government owed him for seven generations? Did he believe that the government had only leased the Hills? Red Cloud understood perfectly that he had been cheated, but he still did not know just how in terms that were either accurate or that the whites could comprehend.

The Black Hills would not be Red Cloud's fight. He had become,

like a great archive to a written culture, a valuable source in the
oral tradition of the Sioux. Using Red Cloud's testimony, others
had already developed a clearer and more sophisticated conception
of the Black Hills claim—a primitively legalistic conception such
as Edgar Fire Thunder advanced:

> If you [Cong. Martin] listen to the two old men [Red Cloud and Blue
> Horse] who talked to you about the Black Hills Treaty, you will
> know that they said it was no treaty. There were just some men who
> got a few signers who said they had power from all the Indians to
> sign the treaty. Now we are willing to go by the Treaty of 1876 or
> any other treaty if three-fourths of the people are willing to sign it;
> but they were not willing to sign it.

For the first time on record, the Sioux presented their claim not
as mere recollection, but as a specific indictment. Whether from
his own reading of the treaty or on the advice of some knowledge-
able adviser, Fire Thunder had latched on to the government's
violation of the 1868 treaty's Article 12 signature requirement.
And he proposed a remedy for the violation.

"We do not mean that we will take back the Black Hills and
drive the white people away. But we would like to have something
for the Black Hills treaty," Fire Thunder told Martin. "We had the
Black Hills for many years and we want something from the white
people for taking them away."

American Horse, one of the first progressive chiefs, echoed him,
calling attention to how rich the Hills had made the whites. "We
do not want to take the Black Hills back, but . . . it has been so long
since they filled so many houses with gold that we would like to
have you find a way to get some food for our children."

Congressman Martin had little sympathy for the Sioux claim.
With a response to every charge, he quickly put to rest any notion
that they had either loaned the Hills or had only sold the "rocks
above the line of the pines." He had read the treaty, Martin told
the Indians, and it said no such thing. Martin issued two rejoinders
to Fire Thunder's Article 12 argument. In the first place, he
pointed out, almost all the Sioux chiefs and headmen had signed
the 1876 Manypenny agreement terminating Sioux ownership of
the Black Hills. As representatives of their respective bands, Martin felt that their marks bound the Sioux even without a three-
quarters majority. Second, Martin read to the Sioux Section 19 of
the properly ratified 1889 agreement, a longwinded clause that
"continued in force" nonconflicting provisions of previous treaties
and agreements. Martin interpreted Section 19 as retroactively

ratifying prior agreements, including the Manypenny agreement, regardless of how many Sioux had signed it.

Finally, Martin reminded the Sioux of all the benefits, rations, clothes, and annuities the government provided for them under the very treaty that the Indians now denounced. At latest count, Martin told the council, the government had spent $35 million sustaining the Sioux under the terms of the Manypenny agreement. The food, education, and a dozen other benefits, many of which would continue until the Indians became self-supporting, more than compensated them for the loss of the Black Hills. It was a good and valid treaty, he insisted, and could not be broken.

American Horse rose in rebuttal. Though his hair fell in traditional braids far down his chest, he was clad in western attire—a stiff jacket, and dark pants with a fob watch at his waist. American Horse was a product of the expensive benefits Martin had just enumerated, but however acculturated, the chief had not turned his back on the Hills. "Of course we Indians don't write, but we have the brains and the heart to remember," he began. And American Horse did remember. He had signed Crook's treaty, and, in his mind, Section 19 had no relation to the status of the Black Hills. "Now we made that treaty, and at the time we agreed that the treaty had nothing to do with the Black Hills treaty or any of the old back treaties. That is why we signed that last treaty. This treaty will run alongside the other treaties and not be included in them."

One could almost hear in American Horse's phrasing the words of General Crook in 1889 as he strained to convince the Sioux that the new treaty would not kill the old ones. That did not mean giving away the Black Hills, American Horse was telling Martin, and after more than a decade of complaining the chief was weary of government sophistry. "You tell us that you are trying to settle up this treaty slowly, but it seems to me you are waiting until we all die, then you will take the money."

The council broke up. Martin did nothing. The Sioux kept on meeting. Thirty years after Custer's gold strike, the Black Hills resumed their place at the center of conflict between the United States and the Sioux. The land was gone, but in the minds of the Indians, the loss and the injustice were still very much alive. Experience and education had taught them that the white man's world had places to bring their grievances—and if Martin, a man of the Great Council, would give them no satisfaction, they would look elsewhere.

Charles Turning Hawk, a progressive from Pine Ridge who had

married the daughter of Chief Little Wound (son of Chief Bull Bear, whom Red Cloud had killed in 1841), was twenty years old when he attended the 1875 council session with Senator Allison and heard Red Cloud's "pay for seven generations" speech. Thirty years later, sitting in the trading store he ran at the Kyle community on Medicine Creek northeast of Pine Ridge village, Turning Hawk recalled that he "ha[d] always thought that the Government owe[d] for the Black Hills." Using his boarding school education to assert his heritage, Turning Hawk began corresponding in 1906 with R. V. Belt, an attorney in Washington, D.C.—one of a growing legion of aggressive lawyers who saw a pot of gold at the end of the Indians' claims rainbow. Turning Hawk received several reports from Belt, who clearly had some familiarity with federal Indian legal cases and had looked into the old Sioux treaties. After reviewing the most important sections of the 1868 and 1876 agreements, Belt confirmed Congressman Martin's assertion that there was no evidence to indicate that the Sioux had merely leased the Hills. In Belt's opinion, the strength of a prospective Black Hills claim would lie in the government's violation of the 1868 treaty's signature requirement, and even that, he warned Turning Hawk, was no guarantee of a favorable judgment.

Undeterred, in a September 1906 council, the Pine Ridge Sioux selected Belt "to look after their affairs with the United States Government." He never became their counsel, though. Under the law at that time, the Sioux did not have the power to hire an attorney. Ostensibly to protect Indians from the predators of the legal profession, the Indian Bureau had reserved for itself the right to pass judgment on all tribal attorney contracts. Since the bureau saw no merit in the Sioux claim, it denied the tribe the right to legal counsel, thus corrupting a well-intentioned regulation into the deprivation of a basic freedom.

Nor did the Indians have the right to sue the U.S. Government. Although in 1866 Congress waived the government's sovereign immunity against many types of lawsuits, including suits brought by Indian tribes, Congress revised the waiver of sovereign immunity in 1873 to specifically bar Indian tribes from suing the United States in court. After 1873, in order for the Sioux or any Indian tribe to bring a claim against the United States, that tribe first had to obtain from Congress a Special Jurisdictional Act granting it permission to sue and defining the scope of what claims the courts could hear. Again, the Indian Bureau would broker any application for a jurisdictional act. With no intention of advancing what it considered to be unfounded claims, the bureau placated the disgruntled Sioux by letting them hold frequent councils, but it made no effort to help these wards of the nation attain a hearing for their grievances in court.

Rather, the government's idea of discharging its trust responsibility towards the Sioux during the first decade of the twentieth century amounted to little more than hastening the assimilation process, especially land allotment, on the six separate reservations. After years of delay, the government finally completed the land surveys, parceling Sioux land into 160- and 320-acre sections. By 1910 most of the Indians had selected allotments and many were living and farming on their chosen plots, often clustered in family groups as they had camped in the old days.

At the national level, in 1906 Congress passed the Burke Act (named after South Dakota Congressman Charles Burke, a zealous advocate of opening up Indian lands to white settlement). The Burke Act modified the Dawes Act's requirement that individual Indian allotments be held in trust by the United States for twenty-five years while the Indian owner presumably adjusted to agrarian life. Because Indians lacked legal authority to sell their allotted lands during this twenty-five-year trust period, the Dawes Act substantially delayed the transfer of reservation lands into the hands of white owners. The Burke Act remedied this. It authorized the Secretary of the Interior to abbreviate the trust period and issue unrestricted fee patents (land titles) to any Indian deemed "competent and capable of managing his or her affairs."

In Sioux country, government "competency commissions," like wildcatters looking for oil, scoured the reservations in search of Indians who might be deemed sufficiently civilized to assume the responsibilities of fee patent ownership. The government elaborately feted the Indians who fit the bill. At large government-sponsored feasts, newly designated "competent" Indians would emerge one by one from a tipi, fire a last symbolic arrow from a bow, then receive a plow, purse, and American flag to commemorate their emergence from trust status. Many Indians, long impoverished and never enamored of farming, permanently dispossessed themselves by selling off their newly acquired allotments to eager whites.

While the competency commissions were getting under way, the Dakota land boomers—represented in Congress by the "Empire Builder," Senator Robert Gamble—renewed their lobbying to open up more surplus Sioux land. At their behest, from 1904 to 1912 the United States again raided Sioux country, unilaterally opening for white settlement large tracts of unallotted tribal lands on the five largest of the tribe's separate reservations. Although the act of 1889 already had reduced the eight Sioux reservations to 13 million acres (roughly 9 million acres fewer than under the 1877 act), the eight "surplus" land statutes that Congress enacted during this period eventually shrunk Sioux land holdings to about 8 million acres, less than one-third of the Great Sioux Reservation as already diminished by the loss of the Black Hills.

The United States grabbed this land entirely without tribal consent, let alone with the approval of three-quarters of the adult Sioux males required by the treaty of 1868 and confirmed in sections 12, 19, and 28 of the 1889 act. "The earth was given to mankind to support the greatest numbers of which it is capable, and no tribe or people have a right to withhold from the wants of others more than is necessary for their own support and comfort," James Monroe had admonished Congress in 1817. In a century, nothing had changed. As the guardian of Sioux welfare, including their lands, the government still considered it sound policy to make certain that the Indians kept an absolute minimum of what the whites thought they needed.

Initially, the government had sought Sioux approval for the surplus land statutes. James McGlaughlin, now bureau superintendent, who had eagerly assisted General Crook in 1889, had presented the bills to the tribal "business councils," ad hoc Indian groups that the bureau had set up on the reservations to consider leasing and financial matters. These business councils, another mechanism for circumventing what power the traditionals still had, were packed with progressives; but even they would not sell another acre of their truncated homeland.

On the Cheyenne River reservation, the business council didn't even wait for the government to ask before objecting to the land cessions. As James Crow Feather, the chairman, complained to the philanthropic Indian Rights Association, the Sioux believed the lands in question were "rich in mineral deposits and should be examined before being opened for settlement." What was more, he wrote, "the promises in the old treaties have yet to be fulfilled."

Congress passed a land statute for Cheyenne River despite the tribe's objections. Nonetheless, the Sioux were beginning to absorb some important, albeit painful, lessons in American politics. When Senator Gamble proposed an even more drastic land opening in 1910, instead of petitioning Congress, Crow Feather led an eight-man delegation to Washington, where they presented the Indian Bureau with a series of objections and counterproposals. The Sioux succeeded in delaying congressional action, pending a report from the commissioner of Indian Affairs. With Dakota land fever abating as more and more whites discovered the difficulties of homesteading in western South Dakota, this delay killed the second Gamble bill.

To say that the Sioux had mastered the white political game or that their efforts had made the crucial difference in defeating the land boomers would be an exaggeration; but with men like James Crow Feather coming to power in the business councils, the Sioux were gaining leaders who had been to Washington, had challenged the bureaucrats, and had come away with an increased understanding of the processes that controlled their collective fate.

Crow Feather epitomized this nascent class of Sioux leader, who, together with counterparts among other tribes, were dubbed the "Red Progressives." He was almost elegant in the way he affected European styles. His dark suit was well-tailored to his full frame, his black tophat shone, his wire-rimmed spectacles gave his broad face a gentle, cultured look. Only Crow Feather's lapel betrayed the Indian beneath. There, quite purposefully, he had pinned a miniature tomahawk to his suit.

When the Sioux held their annual meeting to discuss the Black Hills treaty on the Cheyenne River reservation at the end of January 1911, the first order of business was to elect James Crow Feather as chairman of the Council of Nine Agencies. All the Sioux reservations, including the Santee, had sent representatives to Cheyenne River, as had the Cheyenne and Arapaho. In all, almost a hundred Indians were listed as official delegates, among them the last of the treaty chiefs: Little Wound from Rosebud, Eagleman from Crow Creek, and John Grass from Standing Rock. A show of hands revealed that only five delegates had themselves signed the 1876 agreement. Even the young headmen of the treaty era, an American Horse or a Young-Man-Afraid, were dying off. Many of those who still lived (considered progressive by earlier standards) now generally comprised the less schooled, more conservative element on the reservations.

Red Cloud's son Jack, a notorious non-progressive, headed the Pine Ridge contingent. Judging from the fact that only two of the other sixteen Pine Ridge delegates had adopted Anglo-Saxon names, the rest shared his traditional outlook. With the exception of a few progressive like Crow Feather and Turning Hawk, principal support for the Black Hills claim had always come from the non-progressives, especially the old chiefs and headmen and their descendants, who sought to reassert the tribal power lost to the assimilation programs.

For thirty years the non-progressives had kept the Black Hills claim alive, but had never been able to move it beyond the council fire. Now, at Cheyenne River, as the Sioux conducted business in an almost comic imitation of parliamentary procedure, as James Crow Feather assumed the chair, control of the claim began to slip away from the traditionals and into the hands of the educated Sioux—the only ones with any hope of pursuing their claim in the white-controlled world.

For two days the council heard the haunting stories of the old men, of John Grass, Black Elk, Walking Hunter, and Black Spotted Elk, who remembered the terrible years of 1875 and 1876, after Custer discovered Black Hills gold and the miners flooded in. They remembered that the government had tricked them with mistranslations and had given them "intoxicating liquors" to guide their hands to the pen. They remembered the soldiers watching them, bayonets pointed; they remembered that "the Black Hills was taken by a gun." When the time came for adopting resolutions, their fragmentary and clouded recollections were summarized and submitted as supporting evidence for the councils' principal thesis: "RESOLVED: THAT THE TREATY OF THE BLACK HILLS IN 1876 WAS EXECUTED ILLEGAL"—illegal because three-fourths had not signed and because many of the chiefs who did sign had done so under duress.

One of the educated Sioux, Ed Swan, read excerpts from a copy of the Manypenny Report he somehow had obtained. This prompted the councilmen to call for an investigation of the Great Father's other books. They authorized a committee to visit the "Congressional Library" to collect more evidence for their claims. The Sioux began taking affidavits, too. However clumsily, they were at last building a case that would mean something outside their own councils.

The Indians' efforts bore fruit almost instantaneously. Having watched the Cherry Creek proceedings, Doane Robinson, the official historian of South Dakota and the author of the definitive history of the Sioux people to date, decided to adopt the Sioux cause. On February 16, the well-respected Robinson published a lengthy article in the *Pioneer Times* of Deadwood, South Dakota, smack in the middle of the Black Hills.

"The Sioux Indians have a highly interesting and equitable claim to the Black Hills which they assert they have never relinquished," he proclaimed. ". . . [the Sioux] have no thought that they can regain possession of the Hills but they think they have an equitable claim against Uncle Sam for the value of the property, and they propose to push for it until they obtain justice." The Sioux had their first white advocate.

Major Brennan at Pine Ridge, the Indian Bureau's resident expert on the Sioux, dashed off a furious response which appeared less than two weeks later, on the twenty-eighth, in the *Rapid City Daily Journal.* "The Truth About The Black Hills," the headline promised: "John R. Brennan Gives Some Facts Concerning the Treaty With the Sioux Indians, Showing the Government Acted in Good Faith and Expended About $84,000,000."

According to Brennan, "the treaty ceding the Black Hills . . . was really the best treaty for the Indians that the Sioux ever made with the Government." Brennan reckoned that "everything the Sioux have received from the Government since 1898 [his supposed expiration date of the 1868 treaty] . . . has been on account of the Black Hills treaty." By his figures, this meant that the United States had already paid $84 million in exchange for the Black Hills and would eventually pay considerably more before the Sioux finally became self-supporting. The major flatly denied that the Sioux had been coerced into signing the treaty and he reiterated Congressman Martin's refutation of the violation of Article 12 of the 1868 treaty. In conclusion, recounting an interview he had held with the deceased Red Cloud, Brennan turned the "seven generations" speech on its head. Red Cloud said "that the Black Hills treaty that he made with the Government would be the means of taking care of his people for seven generations"—a total of 700 years, Brennan said. Brennan seemed to think that the treaty had and would continue to do just that.

Despite Brennan's prompt response, the prospect of a huge Sioux claim spread quickly—especially in the legal community. By mid-March the commissioner's office was writing Brennan for more detailed information to help the bureau decide if it should let the Indians hire one of the lawyers who were already asking permission to contract with the Sioux. Congressman Martin, denouncing Robinson for having "given so serious encouragement to the claims of the Indians regarding this treaty," asked the Indian Bureau to draw up a statement of expenditures under the 1877 act. Obviously anxious to head off the claim, the bureau totaled up close to $32 million in outlays.

Not only was that figure lower than Martin's unsubstantiated $38 million as of 1903 and dramatically below Brennan's calculation, the Indian Bureau's summary was nothing more than an accumulation of all Sioux appropriations from 1878 on—a figure that was bound to be substantially higher than the actual expenditures under the 1877 act. Nevertheless, Martin and the bureau felt well-confirmed in their view that the government had generously compensated the Sioux for the Hills, and consequently they refused to sponsor the necessary legislation granting the Sioux their day in court.

Charles Burke, now chairman of the House Committee on Indian Affairs, and the congressman most vital to the passage of a Sioux jurisdictional act, also had no sympathy for the Sioux claim. "It is unfortunate," he wrote the *Sioux City Journal* in May, "that anyone is disposed to encourage the Indians to believe that there is merit in their claim as it only excites them, and as long as they are looking to the Government for a large sum of money, they will not make much progress towards civilization and self-support."

Brennan estimated "that about half the Sioux Indians devote nearly all their time to holding councils over the Black Hills treaty or some other will-o'-the-wisp proposition." All the councils were distracting the Sioux from their farming and, worse yet, rekindling a sense of identity with the past that they were supposed to be learning to forget.

Will-o'-the-wisp or not, the Sioux, greatly encouraged, continued agitating and looking around for help. In September 1911 a group of Rosebud elders calling themselves the Black Hills Council met with a young lawyer named Ralph Hoyt Case in a remote tent at the Two Strike camp, forty miles from the nearest railroad. At the end of the Civil War, Case's pioneer father, a boss carpenter at Fort Bennett (the one-time site of the Cheyenne River agency), had moved into an abandoned Sioux council room. Case had been born in that room, and though he had left Sioux country as a young boy, he liked to think there was a special affinity between the Indians and his family. A newlywed, Case had brought his bride to Sioux country to show her the land of his birth and its people. He listened intently to the stories of the old men who spoke from out of the shadows cast by a single oil lamp. They asked him to help them get justice. Case promised he would.

Another Sioux in touch with Case was Henry Standing Bear from Pine Ridge, a top graduate from Carlisle and one of the red progressives championing the Black Hills cause. While the Indian Bureau continued to obstruct Sioux efforts to retain counsel, Standing Bear pursued another avenue for bringing pressure to bear on the government. On Columbus Day 1911 (a date purposefully chosen) Standing Bear, Dr. Charles Eastman (the Santee doctor at Wounded Knee) and a small group of other prominent progressives founded the Society of American Indians, the first nationwide pan-Indian political organization.

Dedicated to full Indian participation in American society as well as to the preservation of their racial identity, the Indians of the SAI hoped to forge a new relationship between white and red America, incorporating what they saw as the best attributes of both cultures: "equality and justice." As one of its highest priorities, the SAI pressed Congress to confer jurisdiction on the United States Court of Claims to hear Indian grievances and, once and for all, balance the ledger of historic injustice. In the collective voice of the SAI, the Black Hills claim at last had a determined and reasonably well connected lobbyist in the nation's capital.

The progressive Indians out on the reservation also began touting the essentially patriotic and forward-looking nature of their claim. On stationery boasting the motto "Justice to All" over a bald eagle perched on two hands clasped in friendship, the Black Hills council published a "declaration of allegiance to the flag of the glorious Republic of the United States which stands for equality and justice." Transparently tactful, President Ed Swan and Vice-President Charles Turning Hawk reserved this request for the end: "We desire a fuller knowledge of all that [the] Government in the past has endured to do for us by treaty and legislation," they wrote, "so that we may know the relationship that have joined us to the Government as wards, obtaining this knowledge we can best and sooner . . . become independent citizens of this great United States."

In advocating a final settlement of outstanding claims within the larger framework of Indian assimilation, the red progressives struck a responsive chord with the Wilsonian Democrats who came to office in the election of 1912. No less than the Indians, Wilson and his appointee as commissioner of Indian Affairs, Texas Democrat Cato Sells, wanted to resolve outstanding tribal grievances against the government. Past injustices, the Wilsonians believed, whether real or imagined, made poor soil for good citizenship to take root.

If only to expedite the absorption of the Indian into the mainstream of American society, Sells (an ardent assimilationist) was willing to reconsider bureau policy towards the Black Hills and other claims and let courts judge the legality of America's historic treatment of the tribes. Though highly skeptical of the merits of the Black Hills claim, Sells supported a jurisdictional act for the Sioux. At his command, in early 1914 endorsement of a Sioux claims bill became established policy of the Indian Bureau.

The Sioux naturally took heart from Sells's reversal of policy. They redoubled their efforts to secure a lawyer. Arthur Tibbets, a claims leader on the Standing Rock reservation, asked S. M. Brosius, the agent for the influential Indian Rights Association, to recommend a good lawyer for the Black Hills case. Ten years before, a reform group like the IRA would have adamantly opposed a Sioux claim, but the philosophy of the philanthropists had also changed. Brosius sent Tibbets the name of Clarence C. Calhoun, a "dignified" and "competent lawyer," experienced and successful in cases against the government. The Sioux had long recognized what Calhoun now shrewdly advised Tibbets: "that great advantages will accrue to the Sioux Indians by virtue of the services that could be rendered through a capable attorney located at Washington." Calhoun knew just the man for the job, but in the absence of claims legislation, the Indian Bureau once more demurred.

Even without a lawyer, the Sioux lobbied Congress. During the summer of 1914, a Sioux delegation led by Henry Standing Bear called on their state's representatives in Washington. Not many tribesmen were eligible to vote in the 1914 elections (only allotted Indians whose lands were no longer held in trust by the U.S. enjoyed this right in 1914). Still, the Sioux made up a significant latent constituency which South Dakota politicians gladly served, at least with respect to issues such as claims legislation that might bring substantial revenues into the state. With the additional encouragement of the commissioner's office, the Dakota delegation submitted draft bills of a Sioux jurisdictional act to both houses of Congress before the end of the session. "If jurisdiction were conferred on the Court of Claims . . . it would be a wise thing and forever satisfy the Indians themselves," South Dakota Senator Thomas Sterling averred; "until there is some authoritative determination, the claims of the Indians will continue to be agitated."

Senator Sterling was right about the agitation. With the tacit sanction of the Indian Bureau, the Black Hills claim assumed an even more vital role in reservation life. The main body of progressives, many of whom had in the past held aloof from the claim for fear of offending the agents, now flocked to the Black Hills standard. Having adopted the American tradition of representative government, the Sioux now began experimenting with grassroots electioneering. Candidates for tribal office vied for the "claims" vote as the Black Hills emerged as a critical issue in the campaigns.

To raise money for council meetings, trips to Washington, and other Black Hills claim expenses, the Sioux staged "singings" at the reservation dance halls in which claims leaders would chant traditional songs of praise in return for individual donations. The Sioux considered taxing tribesmen as much as 50¢ a year to pay for the claims effort, though it is unclear whether anyone collected such a levy. The agents on the reservation prohibited the "singings" on the grounds that those least able to contribute ("some poor old woman who received $15.00 per month") often contributed the most. The Indian Bureau refused to release tribal funds for prosecuting the claim. Still, though a significant hardship, the Sioux found the money to carry on what had by now evolved into a part of tribal culture, a rallying point and rare source of hope. Every penny donated, every hour spent in council was an investment in what the Sioux hoped would be their version of a Black Hills bonanza.

More than once Commissioner Sells expressed his frustration at the Indians' insistence on "holding frequent councils and apparently wasting their time in useless discussion." Writing to Charles Turning Hawk, who was then serving as president of the Black Hills Council, Sells encouraged the progressives to take charge of the Black Hills claim on the reservation and remedy "the one great trouble" about the Sioux claims "that they are very indefinite both as to dates and facts."

Turning Hawk had been waiting for more than eight years for this sort of mandate; less than six months later Sells was already paying tribute to his accelerated efforts. "I am pleased to note that the educated and progressive members of the tribe are beginning to take an interest . . . and are making a study of the matters involved with a view to formulating the claims and getting them in such shape that they may be intelligently considered."

With the commissioner himself dangling the prospect of success, at the meeting of the Black Hills Council at Pine Ridge in June 1915 the progressives irrevocably took charge of the Black Hills claim. Under the elected leadership of Turning Hawk, Crow Feather, Standing Bear, and other educated Sioux, the June council drafted a bill for Congress to consider that would authorize the Court of Claims to hear their grievances, and would confer appellate jurisdiction on the Supreme Court of the United States. The progressives also created yet another organization to handle claims questions, the Great Council of the Dakota Nation, which (as its preamble declared) was intended "to secure to ourselves and our posterity absolute, the political and civil rights guaranteed to us by treaty and statute of the United States." Adding a note of thanks to Commissioner Sells for "his kind advice and counsel," the progressives sent their proposed legislation to Washington—confident of its imminent approval.

But the Sioux bill stalled in Congress that year, and the next year, and the year after that. The Indians' high hopes fell victim to a busy Congress increasingly preoccupied with the European war and generally unconcerned with this domestic dispute.

As had happened chronically in the past on many issues, with nothing else to do the Sioux fell to fighting among themselves. Though Sells claimed that his endorsement of the progressives was not meant "to reflect on the integrity and good intentions of the old chiefs" on the severely divided reservations, the commissioner's bias effectively undercut the traditionals' longstanding control over Sioux claims.

Once more the recipient of the short end of government policy, some of the old-timers withdrew from the generally recognized Black Hills councils and held their own meetings. On June 26, 1917, old Chief Lip held a council "consisting of old men ages (70) seventy and (75) seventy-five years, all steadly [sic] have the Treaty matters in mind, all are from different tribes of Sioux Nation." Why? he asked rhetorically: "we notice that Lawyers, Mixed bloods, and school boys had been handling this case and have everything mixed up."

But the problem was not that the progressives had everything mixed up. They understood Sioux history as well as the old chiefs, who were relying on distant and faulty memory. The problem was that the progressives controlled the claims. The wounds of assimilation would not heal. On every reservation there were two parties: those who were in with the Indian Bureau agents and those who were not. As the bureau coopted the once disfavored Black Hills claim, the outsiders were reduced to futile counciling in the hope that they might remain something more than silent and shunned partners in the Black Hills cause.

Over at Crow Creek, the progressive version of the Black Hills council was doing a fine job proving Chief Lip's charges of incompetence. No sooner had the council adjourned (having accomplished nothing) than Standing Bear was writing Sells, advising him that the meeting had been "called improperly"; in other words, without the approval of the executive committee of the Great Council of Dakota Nation—of which Standing Bear was secretary. The old chiefs were fast dying off before giving their testimony, Standing Bear observed. He implored the commissioner to let him call another meeting as soon as possible.

A noticeably exasperated Sells decided to give Standing Bear and the Sioux one more chance to organize their claims, the work he had hoped to see completed back in 1915. Sells decreed that on April 14, 1918, five representatives from each Sioux reservation (and representatives of the Cheyenne and Arapaho tribes) would convene at Crow Creek for not more than three days. There, the Indians would formulate their claims for the commissioner's use "as the basis of future action." Standing Bear objected to the commissioner's caveat. Sells had neglected to call the meeting under the auspices of the Great Council and he had reduced the number of delegates to five, from the standard ten. Sells let his orders stand.

With the meeting set, a swarm of lawyers, most persistently Calhoun, his associate Daniel Henderson, and their new-found pitchman with the Sioux, Dr. Charles Eastman, began lining up support in the upcoming council. Sells repeated his standing injunction against hiring lawyers until Congress had authorized a claim, but this time Calhoun and Henderson decided to challenge the bureau's policy. In a long letter to Standing Bear written two weeks prior to the council, Calhoun tried to goad the Sioux into defying Sells. "The principal thing the Indians are granted permission to do is pay their expenses to and from the council," he penned sarcastically, hoping to pique Standing Bear's pride. "The Indians must decide whether they are to choose their attorney or whether he is to be chosen for them by the Commissioner of Indian Affairs. . . . You know how greatly the Sioux work has been hindered for years, and you probably know how slow your progress will continue to be unless you first employ your attorneys and get them to work on the case."

It was self-serving advice, but also true. A good lawyer—and Calhoun had as many testimonials as any—could not only have helped the Sioux push a jurisdictional act through Congress, but could have drafted favorable language that would, for example, have allowed interest on any court award or limited what the government could counterclaim as an offset. As matters stood, the Indian Bureau neither permitted the Sioux counsel nor advised the tribe itself. Sells and the Wilsonians wanted to settle the Indian claims, but that did not mean they wanted them settled in favor of the Indians. No nation could serve effectively both as guardian of the claimant and as prospective defendant in the claimant's litigation. On Black Hills, the Indian Bureau was a reluctant advocate indeed.

Calhoun's plan went awry. The people of Pine Ridge rejected Standing Bear as one of their delegates and he never made it inside the Crow Creek assembly hall. Calhoun's other hope, Dr. Eastman, did get in, but only because the government had paid his way west to hawk its Liberty Loan bonds to Indians around the country—a task at which Eastman proved remarkably adept. It was no small irony that the Sioux were so patriotic, giving their money freely. In buying Liberty Bonds, Crow Creek delegates fished in near-empty pockets to help make the rest of the world safe for democracy, a form of government under which they themselves did not truly live. In a sense, the Sioux saw the Black Hills claim as their own fight for the ideals of liberty and justice they believed to be at stake in Europe; and as they gave their spare change to the government that they were then indicting for taking their most valued land, the Sioux still clung to the hope that the United States would expand its moral war to the home front in South Dakota.

Once begun, the Crow Creek council served its appointed function. After three days the Indians produced a concise text relating the history of the 1876 Manypenny Agreement and listing their allegations against the government. It contained nothing new.

Still there was anything but consensus among the Sioux. Although the council's resolutions merely restated the same complaints the old-timers had been voicing for the last decade, the traditionals who had participated at Crow Creek denounced the proceedings as unduly influenced by the five Indian Bureau agents who had attended. The traditionals objected not because of a specific quarrel with the council's formulation of their claims, but because they felt tricked and bullied by the progressives who had assumed control. They lashed out bitterly at the government that they saw behind the shift in power, once more underscoring the vast discrepancy between inalienable rights and the treatment they received.

"We request the President and Congress to stop the Indian bureau officials dealing with us as if we are their slaves," they petitioned Congressman Charles Carter, the new Chairman of the House Indian Affairs Committee. "We have proven ourselves faithful citizens, defending our common country with our white brothers with our young men and money. Surely we deserve some justice and liberty—the liberty and freedom for which we are all fighting."

The Indian Bureau filed away the old chiefs' protest—next to another one Standing Bear submitted. Meanwhile, back at Crow Creek, a group of progressives brought together twenty of the ancient men who still remembered the treaty days and took down their recollections in the form of sworn statements to preserve their testimony in the event of their death. Most had been in the

Powder River country with Sitting Bull and Crazy Horse when Allison came to buy or lease the Hills. They all remembered that Sitting Bull had promised to kill any man who would sell the Hills; they all believed that the government had only asked to lease the Hills "above the pines"; they all remembered that the Hills were "our head and heart." Eli He Dog (Crazy Horse's friend who lived to be 100), now 79, doubted whether he would see his memory vindicated. "I don't know that this will do me any good to make this statement," he concluded. "[B]ut it may do my children or grandchildren some good. I have been working on this Black Hills claim now for 25 years and we have never gotten permission even to put our proofs and evidence before the Court of Claims."

By the middle of 1919 Congress was finally prepared to give serious consideration to a Sioux jurisdictional act (and to similar legislation for many other tribes pressing claims). The House and Senate, however, differed significantly about what a just settlement of the Sioux claims—and, in particular, the Black Hills claim—would entail. According to the House bill (H.R. 400), if the Court of Claims found that the Sioux had a "legal or equitable" claim to the Black Hills, the value of that claim should be equal to the value of the land at the time it was taken, plus 3 percent simple annual interest to make amends for the long delay in restitution. The government would then have the right to subtract from the Indians' award all payments it had made to the Sioux under the 1877 act as well as any gratuitous payments Congress had authorized. The Senate, however, did not think America's conscience dictated this kind of potential drain on the federal treasury. Though allowing government offsets, the Senate's Sioux bill contained no provision for any interest on a hypothetical award.

The Sioux objected to both versions. "In view of the established custom of dealing with Indian tribes," the Sioux argued that it would be "very unjust" to let the government charge all its expenditures against their claims. They did not want to settle for the value of the land in 1877 either. The Black Hills contained less than eight million acres and the Sioux demanded compensation at prevailing (1919) land values, not the price forty years earlier, "when Custer had just kicked up a little gold with his spurs." The Sioux also objected to the section confirming the power of the Commissioner of Indian Affairs to control their attorney contracts. That "amount[ed] to having Government officials control the attorneys on both sides of the case," and the suspicious tribesmen sought completely independent counsel. Congress paid no attention.

On June 3, 1920, a Sioux Jurisdictional Act passed both houses of Congress. The House and Senate had resolved their differences in conference committee and adopted the Senate version in its entirety—authorizing government offsets with no provision for interest payment. But the legislation was by no means a cynical exercise in rigging the scales of justice against the claimant Sioux. In 1920, Congress passed jurisdictional acts for many tribes, opening the remedial process of America's democracy to the victims of its expansion. In part Congress was paying a debt to the relatives of the 10,000 Indians who had died fighting in the Great War; in part it was more thoroughly entombing the Indians' uncivilized past; and in part it was simply doing what many Americans considered right and just. The government carefully circumscribed the limits of a potential Sioux recovery, but for reasons of both conscience and self-interest, after forty-three years the opportunity for victory existed nonetheless.

From the Indians' viewpoint, if the jurisdictional act was not all that they had yearned for, it was still their ticket to court, a ticket they had sought as long as anyone could remember. Dreaming of future wealth from the Black Hills claim had become a popular pastime, and as summer browned the prairie grass and scorched the corps for another year, those dreams were more alive than ever.

Undeniably, the Sioux now needed a lawyer, and to its credit the Indian Bureau wasted no time initiating the hiring process. Hoping to avoid the spectacle of the numerous Sioux factions each contracting with its own attorneys, the bureau fixed September 30 as the date for a Sioux council to choose lawyers. Haste, though, had its price. The Rosebud Sioux, torn by internal dissension, demanded proportional rather than uniform representation from each reservation. They boycotted the council. The meeting itself, whether by bureau design or, more likely, circumstance was a sham. Several delegates (including the president of the council) were government employees, which elicited accusations that bureau agents had gerrymandered the local elections. Once begun, the proceedings were dominated by James Ryan, a mixed blood lawyer from Pine Ridge, who, whatever the value of his legal advice, alienated the conservative fullbloods, who saw him as "a white man."

The election of attorneys was accomplished by Soviet ballot: three lawyers nominated, three selected—Calhoun, former Senator Hamilton Lewis, and Charles Kappler, a noted expert on Indian law. Nobody thought the matter settled.

Protests from various Sioux cabals, from Gertrude Bonnin (an educated Sioux who was secretary of the Society of American Indians), and from Brosius, leader of the Indian Rights Association, all arrived at the Indian Bureau before November. The Rosebud Sioux, demanding proportional representation, wrote the most impassioned letter: "The question of representation is a human right dating back as far as written history can be traced," they declared, referring to the roots of western civilization for authority. "It is a question over which nations have gone to war. It is one of the fundamental basic principles upon which the Constitution of the United States was founded."

Brosius wrote the most influential letter. He, too, had questions about representation as well as about possible corruption at the September council. Both the Indians and the philanthropists routinely appealed to the government's morality and sense of fair play. Occasionally, it worked. On October 29, Secretary of the Interior John Barton Payne repudiated the September choices and called a new meeting with proportional representation for December 15.

The maneuvering out in Sioux country resumed with fresh vigor. A Sioux named Robert Two Elk convinced an Indian court judge, Noah Bad Wound, to trump up charges against Henry Standing Bear to prevent him from representing Pine Ridge at the upcoming meeting. Gertrude Bonnin contacted James H. Red Cloud, grandson of the late chief and the leader of Pine Ridge, the largest of the December delegations, to inject her two cents' worth about lawyers. She recommended Charles Evans Hughes, the former Supreme Court Justice, Republican presidential nominee in 1916, and, in Bonnin's opinion, "undoubtedly the best attorney in the United States today."

Eagleman, one of the few surviving headmen from the treaty days, did not concern himself with the problem of hiring lawyers. He and a handful of other ancients wrote the commission to protest the admission of mixed bloods into the council.

Bonnin's lobbying efforts for ex-Justice Hughes made swift headway at the three largest reservations, Pine Ridge, Rosebud, and Standing Rock. All three of these delegations received instructions from their constituents to vote for Hughes.

On December 8, however, only a week before the council, Charles Turning Hawk and others sent an emergency letter to Brosius advising him that two white men acting on behalf of Joseph Davies, a Washington lawyer, had offered bribes to the Rosebud delegates. It was too late to stop the council, too late to stop the impoverished Sioux from demonstrating that when it came to evaluating legal talent, the most important criterion was who had promised them the most, last. Davies had; and on December 15 the Sioux chose him before six other far more distinguished nominees. Hughes narrowly defeated Calhoun as runner-up.

A new round of protests followed. With letters streaming in from all interested parties, for and against Davies, in keeping with the bureau's longstanding effort to protect the Sioux from predatory lawyers, the commissioner's office began an investigation. A week later, Davies withdrew from consideration.

As the Indians' second choice, Hughes was Davies's heir apparent. Hughes was not only America's most renowned attorney, he was a man of impeccable character. Some of the old Sioux who had dealt with Calhoun for almost a decade dissented in favor of their old friend, but finally Hughes and his established Wall Street firm became the first formal advocates for the Black Hills claim. As it turned out, Hughes never worked on the case. President Warren Harding named him Secretary of State early in 1921 and the Sioux legal work fell to his son Charles Hughes, Jr., and Richard Dwight, a senior partner in Hughes's former firm, Rounds, Shurman and Dwight.

On June 22, 1921, in Omaha, Nebraska, the Sioux's Wall Street claims attorneys held their first conference with their somewhat exotic clients. They had bad news for the Sioux. Having analyzed the language of the 1920 jurisdictional act, Dwight and the younger Hughes found that they had "grave doubts" whether it empowered the Court of Claims to consider the Black Hills claim at all. The Court of Claims had an established pattern of giving jurisdictional acts their narrowest possible construction. As the lawyers interpreted recent Court of Claims decisions regarding waivers of sovereign immunity, the court would consider only those claims specifically enumerated in the jurisdictional act. Hughes and Dwight doubted that the court would interpret the vague and sweeping language of the act as authorizing it to inquire into the validity of the 1876 Manypenny Agreement or to set the agreement aside because the government had employed fraud or duress—the main premises of the Black Hills claim.

Even if the court did decide that it could consider such a claim, and even if it found in favor of the Sioux, Hughes and Dwight concluded that the size of the final award would be too small to justify the suit. By their calculation, the jurisdictional act authorized the government to offset from any judgment about $40 million in past payments of food and rations. Although Hughes and Dwight believed that deducting rations payments amounted to giving the government credit for having impoverished the Sioux, they doubted that the court, without some directive in the jurisdictional act, would accept their view. (At worst, the attorneys thought that the offsets should be charged against a claim for the taking of the Powder River hunting grounds—designated as unceded Indian territory under the 1868 treaty—because the government's seizure of these lands had made the payment of rations necessary in the first place). Furthermore, they informed the Sioux, the court probably would not permit the tribe to collect rentals for the government's use of its land in exchange for allowing the government to recover its ration payments.

What, then, was the value of the Indians' claim? The lawyers' answer was bleak. According to well-settled law, in the absence of a specific grant from the United States, an Indian tribe's rights in the land were not those of outright ownership, but rather were similar to the rights of a "tenant for life." Although the 1868 treaty recognized that the Sioux had a right to the "absolute and undisturbed use and occupancy" of the Black Hills, Hughes and Dwight concluded that the Court of Claims would not interpret the language of the treaty as granting the Sioux outright ownership of the Hills. Though the lawyers had found no case deciding the point, in the light of recent decisions generally hostile to Indian land rights, they believed that the court would treat the Sioux as life tenants in, rather than owners of, the Hills.

As life tenants, Hughes and Dwight continued, the Sioux would have no claim to the mineral or timber resources of their land—the principle resources of value in the Black Hills. Calculating the Sioux interest in the Black Hills solely according to their value as agricultural and hunting lands, the lawyers estimated that the court would award the Sioux no more than $8.75 million for the Hills. Even if the court also awarded the Sioux the value of the unceded Indian territory on the same basis (an optimistic premise), the total judgment would still amount to less than $35 million— less than the estimated total of the government's allowable offsets.

Dwight and Hughes confessed that they had not yet fully investigated the various other Sioux claims—discrepancies in annuities and education benefits and in other areas—but here too they were skeptical that the judgment would exceed the offsets. Their message was unequivocal: go back to Congress and obtain a new or amended jurisdictional act which would exclude government offsets or otherwise provide for a larger judgment and which would specifically authorize the Court of Claims to inquire into the 1876

Manypenny Agreement and adjudicate the tribe's claims of fraud and duress.

Had the Indian Bureau permitted the Sioux to retain a Charles Evans Hughes in 1906 or 1911 or 1915 or 1918 or at any of the dozens of times that the Indians had asked, perhaps new legislation would have been unnecessary. As it was, having accepted the Sioux claim on a contingency basis and with the prospect of any profit gone, the firm of Rounds, Shurman and Dwight moved to terminate its relationship with the Sioux Indians. The Sioux were once again lawyerless, and perhaps claimless as well.

The new commissioner of Indian Affairs, former South Dakota Congressman Charles Burke (sponsor of the surplus land statutes), immediately began preparation for another Sioux council to select new lawyers. Burke suggested that the Indians think about hiring a local attorney in addition to one in Washington. He recommended his old colleague in the House, E. W. Martin, who was "familiar with the nature of the claim and in sympathy with it." That was curious, since Martin had adamantly opposed the Black Hills claim; but then so had Burke. Potentially lucrative and now politically expedient, the Black Hills claim attracted all sorts of fair-weather friends. The Sioux ignored the commissioner's advice.

The Indians met on August 4 at LaPlant on the Pine Ridge reservation to chart a new course for their claims, but no sooner had the conference begun than a violent duststorm turned the dusk midnight-black, preempting the first session. The turbulent weather was an omen. With members James Red Cloud and Henry Standing Bear as chairman and secretary, respectively, the Pine Ridge delegation (again the largest) tried to run roughshod over the other representatives.

Pine Ridge wanted to pursue Rounds, Shurman and Dwight's advice and seek new legislation before filing the claims. The other reservations, most vocally Rosebud, insisted that the claims could be filed at the same time the Sioux initiated the long process of lobbying Congress. The result was a standoff. In three days of heated debate the council barely touched the subject of hiring lawyers. According to the minutes of the meeting, the Indians "voted down" Rounds, Shurman and Dwight on no fewer than three occasions, but all attempts to suggest new lawyers were frustrated by the parliamentary maneuvers of the Pine Ridge delegates, who wanted to dictate the selection. An eyewitness summarized one day's activity for Commissioner Burke:

On Saturday they voted, as I recall it, 11-9, to select new attorneys. This motion was subject to amendments. And also motions to reconsider until the Council became hopelessly involved in parliamentary tactics and finally they passed a resolution which struck out all their previous acts and they again passed a resolution to select attorneys and in the evening session on Saturday, they brought the question up again the vote standing 9-9 whereupon the Chairman after a disagreement with Mr. Ryan voted "no" and summarily adjourned the Council.

Rosebud walked out in disgust on the morning of the eighth and many others followed, abruptly ending the council. The controlling faction at Rosebud, led by Carlos Gallineaux, had already selected the lawyer it wanted: Ralph Case, who had disappeared from Sioux country to serve in World War I but had now returned to redeem his 1911 promise of help.

Aware that Congress had allotted five years for the filing of all Sioux claims, Gallineaux wanted to file the Black Hills case as swiftly as possible. He was so exasperated with Pine Ridge's dilatory tactics and the inability of the Sioux to reach a consensus that he asked Commissioner Burke to intervene and "compel us to observe the rules that govern the meetings of the white man's council." Gallineaux lamented the passing of the old days when the "bravest warriors . . . ruled the majority." He wondered whether the Sioux would ever again effectively govern themselves. He agreed to attend one last joint council, but after that the Rosebud Sioux, presumably with Case's help, intended to file separately for the Black Hills. The few remaining Sioux treaty chiefs weren't getting any younger. They deserved their Black Hills money before they died.

Commissioner Burke was also concerned about the old men and expediting the claim. He, too, had concluded that general councils were futile and directed each reservation to choose lawyers separately. For all their squabbling, the Sioux selections were remarkably consistent. Calhoun and his allies, Henderson and Victor Evans, were chosen by the Sioux of Fort Peck, Standing Rock, Cheyenne River, and, under protest, by Rosebud. Case and his local counterpart, Edward Colladay, were chosen at the Yankton and Lower Brûlé reservations. They tied with Calhoun at Cheyenne River and were selected by the other half of the factional split at Rosebud. On Pine Ridge, where the superintendent despaired of the frantic efforts of each faction to outdo the others in promoting the Black Hills claim, the people renominated Rounds, Shurman and Dwight. The only other attorney to receive any significant support was Charles Kappler, who, when approached previously, had demanded a sizable retainer in addition to the contingency fee; that excluded him.

By January 1922, Burke was supervising meetings among Henderson, Evans, Calhoun, and Case to iron out the distribution of work and fees for the Sioux claims. Bandit gangs would have had an easier time dividing up their loot than these lawyers. Each one of them had spent years, some even a decade, wooing the Sioux, yearning for a chance to reclaim some Black Hills gold for his clients—and for himself. Even as the lawyers quarreled, the Homestake Mining Company was extracting more than $10 million of ore annually from the lands in question—a sum that, depending on the court, might add to a monumental, perhaps unprecedented, legal fee.

For months the four sets of lawyers bluffed and counterbluffed. Each one of them, at one time or another, offered with feigned magnanimity to withdraw from the contract. By March, sides were clearly drawn: Case and Calhoun against Henderson and Evans. Each offered to buy out the other for a fixed 20 percent of the fee. Neither accepted. Only Case, who consented to every reasonable proposition, even mentioned the Sioux during the bickering. In a guilty moment, he chastised the others for not "considering a little more the interests of our prospective clients and your own interests a little less."

In July all sides seemed to have agreed on a formula. Case, Calhoun, and Henderson would share the legal work for 22.5 percent of the fee each; another 10 percent would go to Wilfred Hearn, Case's junior associate; and Evans, though he would do no legal work at all, would receive a 22.5 percent share plus a 6 percent bonus off the top for contributing $10,000 in expense money. For some reason, this arrangement too fell through. By mid-July both Case and Calhoun had written to Burke canceling the tentative agreement and insisting that neither one would ever work with Henderson.

"I have never before in my life wasted so much valuable time in a vain endeavor of this kind," Calhoun fumed, "and I do not think I will ever do so again."

The real victims of wasted time were not the disputatious lawyers but the destitute Sioux, who, as another summer brought no action in their claim, were growing increasingly troubled and impatient. Joseph Black Spotted Horse, an associate of the now deceased Chief Lip, having heard nothing for many months, sought the commissioner's personal guidance on what to do. Spotted Horse was one of the few left who claimed to remember the 1876 Manypenny Agreement clearly. Adding yet another twist to an ever more labyrinthine story, he told Burke that the government had promised to give the Sioux half of the gold and silver found in the Hills.

The older fullbloods at Rosebud, calling themselves the "three-fourths majority class" after the terminology of the 1868 treaty, also complained. They attacked the "self-chosen ex-students of both mixed-bloods and full-bloods" for undermining their treaty rights, but laid the principal onus for the unconscionable delay right where it belonged—on the doorstep of the United States Government and the self-proclaimed friends of the Indian. "Had there been a time when . . . the Indian Office or the Indian Rights Association representatives alike had cooperated in good faith . . . ," they noted sadly, "we would not today be lamenting over the loss of some of our good witnesses." Only twenty-one signatures adorned the petition, and a few of those were sons signing for dead fathers.

It was December 21, 1922, more than a year after selecting their attorneys, before the Sioux reached actual agreement with the lawyers and the commissioner ratified the contract. In the end, Henderson dropped out. Case became the lead attorney in partnership with Calhoun, with Evans providing the initial financing. Ensconced in a new suite of offices at the reputable District National Bank building in Washington, they erected a plaque on the front door proudly introducing themselves as "The Attorneys for the Sioux Nation." Children of the frontier, they had marched east to right the wrongs of conquest.

Born on the family homestead in Owensboro, Kentucky, strong-featured, with direct and discerning eyes, Clarence C. Calhoun had earned the rank of captain in the Kentucky National Guard while stamping out blood feuds in the mountain country. A veteran of the Spanish-American War as well, educated privately in the law, Calhoun made his name as a lawyer in 1902, when his home state sent him to Washington to settle up a $16,000 Civil War claim. He returned with $1.8 million instead, and Kentucky built a new capitol building—"Calhoun's Monument" to some.

A few years younger than Calhoun, born in Sioux country in 1879, Ralph Case had entered local politics after graduating from Yankton College in 1899. At twenty-four, after appointments as deputy sheriff, deputy auditor, and deputy clerk of the courts for Yankton County, Case won election as county auditor. Senator

Gamble, the state's most powerful politician, took notice of him. He brought Case to Washington in 1907 as his personal secretary and later named Case clerk of the Indian Affairs Committee that he chaired. Case stayed in Washington for law school and practiced some corporate law; then, when the Great War started, he earned a commission in the construction corps, returning to D.C. in 1920 as a major.

With Case doing the lion's share of the work, the Sioux lawyers started looking into the old treaties and making legal judgments about the viability of the Black Hills claim. Case dismissed the need for any amendment to the 1920 jurisdictional act. He regarded the Hughes memorandum as "weak-kneed on the law and lacking in the facts." Though he considered it "presumptuous . . . to differ with them," Case's own investigations "had convinced him that the Hughes firm was badly mistaken in its conclusion that the Government's offsets would cancel a prospective Sioux award." Case thought it "folly" to ask Congress, in a new jurisdictional act, to preclude the government's payments on the claim. In contrast to Hughes' firm's belief that under "broad principles of equity and justice" such payments should not be offset against an award for the taking of the Black Hills, Case felt that it would be "manifestly unjust" not to reduce a final judgment by the amount of the government's past expenditures.

Case found even less merit in the firm's suggestion that the Sioux bill be redrawn specifically to authorize the court to look behind the 1876 agreement. That would be "even more of a waste of time" than an offsets amendment. The jurisdictional act— thirty-five years in the seeking—was "quite as broad" as the Sioux would ever get, and broad enough for their needs. "There is nothing particularly sacred about the Treaty of 1876," Case reasoned, "and it seems to me that the claimants have the right to show that it was obtained by fraud and duress." The Hughes firm, he believed, had "devoted itself to the study of certain decisions in well known Indian cases, but had paid no attention or little attention to the facts constituting the claims of their clients." Case had no intention of making the same mistake.

On May 7, 1923, Case filed the Black Hills claim. Indeed, he filed all the Sioux claims that day: the claims for cut hay and timber, for unconstructed schools and houses, for insufficient rations and clothing, for undelivered seeds and tools, and for more than a dozen other grievances. Hand-delivered to the Court of Claims building in Washington, the one all-encompassing petition (to be amended as each separate claim took shape) finally placed Sioux history on the scales of American justice. A few years would surely pass before a verdict, but after forty-seven years of waiting, to the Sioux deliverance seemed close at hand.

In mid-June, Case traveled to the Rosebud Reservation, where an enormous council had assembled at the Two Strike camp, the same spot where eleven years earlier a cluster of old chiefs circled around a dim lamp and poured out their grievances to an eager young attorney—Ralph Case. At the podium, James McGregor, the Pine Ridge bureau superintendent, recounted Case's long-standing ties to Sioux country and South Dakota: his birth on the Cheyenne River Reservation, his education at Yankton College, his local political career, his apprenticeship with Senator Gamble (though no friend to the Sioux), and, finally, his wartime service. McGregor spared neither praise for Case nor enthusiasm over the role he was destined to play in Sioux history. Case would be the Moses of the Sioux, McGregor promised the tribe. Like Moses leading the Jews out of Egypt, Case would lead the Sioux out of the bondage of their poverty and despair and into the promised land of American prosperity.

Case, tall and lanky, with a raw-boned face and kind eyes that looked out past small round spectacles, rose to address his expectant clients. Before speaking, he paused for a moment, thinking about how Moses's trek through the wilderness had taken forty years, and how Moses died before reaching Canaan. It was a poignant moment for the lawyer, a moment of unadulterated joy for the Sioux around him. Most of them had not even been born when the Black Hills were taken, yet those acres of goldbearing land had never been more central to Sioux life. The Rosebud gathering was the largest on the reservation for many years, a bureau superintendent reported; the Indians were in "high glee" over the prospect of getting their Black Hills money. With a faith that defied their own history, the Sioux embraced their new white champion. The Rosebud inducted Case into the tribe and in unsurpassable tribute gave him the name "Young Spotted Tail" after their chief of legendary wisdom. Young Spotted Tail promised to help them until the end of his days.

From Rosebud, Case went to Pierre, the South Dakota capital, to explain the May legal petition to his clients and begin the too-long-delayed process of collecting Sioux testimony. On June 23, in the Supreme Court chambers at the State House, he met with representatives from all eight reservations to discuss the legal theories underlying the various Sioux claims. For two days, Case conducted a seminar not only on the basics of property law but on the history of U.S. treatment of the Sioux for the last half-century. Though felt history for the Indians, it took on new meaning presented in cold facts and figures which collectively indicted the government for stealing and chiseling the Sioux at every turn. According to Case's reckoning, as required by treaty, the government should have spent more than $10 million on school buildings and teachers for the reservations. It had not. According to Case's reckoning, the government should have spent more than $7 million on clothing for the Sioux. It had not. And according to Case's reckoning, the government should have paid the Sioux better than $1 million for the cutting of hay and wood on the reservation. It had not. An audit, Case explained, would reveal the size of the shortfalls.

In similar fashion, Case outlined every one of the twenty-four claims he had filed, such as those arising from the 1889 land allotments, poor government accounting, and the sale of off-reservation hunting rights. Case placed special emphasis on the Black Hills claim, which, even calculated according to articifially depressed land value estimates ("we do not want to be unfair to the United States," Case explained), still amounted to a principal sum of $156 million plus interest—roughly a total sum of $600 million. Apparently confident that he could secure a huge judgment based on the value of the gold extracted from the Black Hills after their taking, Case told the Sioux that getting interest on the principal of their prospective court award would be "our hardest fight." Still, he was "absolutely confident that we will establish this by proof even though it costs the United States a great deal of money. . . ."

In the question and answer session after lunch, the discussion returned immediately to the Black Hills claim. Case was especially anxious to impress upon the Sioux that their legal claim to the Hills merely entitled them to "just compensation"—the fair market value of the land at the time it was taken plus interest from that time forward—not to the land itself. He was worried that "most of the Sioux have hoped that they might regain the Black Hills." That was impossible, he told them. The United States "has the right to take your property or mine any time it needs it" as long as it pays just compensation, he informed the Sioux. What made the government's actions illegal, Case explained, was not that the government took the Black Hills but that it did not pay for them.

Case also instructed the Indians that the jurisdictional act that allowed them to bring their grievances before the Court of Claims did not provide for a land return. "The Court of Claims can give you judgment for one thing only and that is money," he reported.

The Sioux representatives seemed to have expected nothing different. Thomas Frosted, president of the Standing Rock Sioux, told Case that his people "d[id] not think for a minute that they could secure the Black Hills country again in the near future, but they seem to have the sentiment that the government should make it good in the way of pay. . . . We should get the price we can from the government." To be absolutely certain, Case asked for a vote on his strategy. The council was unanimous. The Sioux would seek the "best price," and the quicker the better.

A day of meetings later, Case addressed his clients one final time before returning to Washington. He seemed to understand intuitively that representing the Sioux required far more than just lawyering. As a white figure of authority, he carried about him the ghosts of the many emissaries whose bright and false promises in the name of the Great White Father resonated in Sioux memory. Through the hours of tutoring his clients in the ways of an alien legal culture, Case labored to win their trust and to infuse them with his confidence both in their cause and in the integrity of the system that would try that cause. Patriot, advocate, honorary Sioux, Case adopted the Black Hills fight as his own and promised the tribe that, however bitter their experience with the white man's ways, together they would find justice in his courts. This is "our claim," he said at the close of the council, invoking his reservation birth and his rechristening as Young Spotted Tail. "[W]e are practically one and if we just stand together and be just one for about three years and not get tired or impatient, we will win this suit."

To naïve and hopeful clients, the promise of victory, delivered with such kindness, confidence, and seeming expertise in the unfathomed world of law, must have kindled extravagant hopes. Leaving the state house, the Sioux prepared to follow their Moses. The years in the wilderness began.

EIGHT

▼ ▼ ▼ ▼ ▼

NOTHING BUT A CRUST OF BREAD

O N JUNE 2, 1924, one year after the filing of the Black Hills claim, President Warren Harding signed the Indian Citizenship Act, granting citizenship to all Indians born within the United States who had not already gained that status through treaty or allotment. A result of partisan politics and congressional gratitude for the loyal service of thousands of Indians in World War I, the act finally made all First Americans citizens of the nation to which their forefathers had ceded so much. In theory, the Indian reform program was now complete. Coming in the wake of education and allotment, citizenship had long been regarded as the last stage in the absorption of Indians into the dominant society—the emancipation of an increasingly independent and self-sufficient race. But the gap between expectation and reality was never wider.

The new Sioux-Americans hardly fit the reformers' image of the civilized and self-reliant Indian. The physical, economic, and spiritual health of the Sioux was worse than at any time since Wounded Knee—and perhaps as bad as then. With fifty years of government care behind them, the Sioux remained illiterate and malnourished and had become chronically infected with tuberculosis, trachoma, and syphilis. Thirty-five years after the Dawes Act, the Sioux were still destitute, dependent, and as aware as ever of the distinction between an Indian and a white person in the nation to which they now legally belonged.

It had not always been so. In the decade after 1900, there had been tangible signs of progress in Sioux country. On Pine Ridge the nascent stockraising industry had blossomed and by 1912 the new Sioux cowboys were herding more than 40,000 head of cattle. Every spring and fall during the twice yearly roundups, these "warriors without weapons" would ride across the open reservation rangelands, showing off their native horsemanship, steeping themselves with pleasure in the manners, dress, and familiar spirit of the cowboy life.

On every reservation more and more Sioux joined the workforce, primarily as manual laborers. On Pine Ridge, for example, the agency erected a sawmill in 1904, and it became a significant employer. Growing cash revenues and some subsistence farming for once were adequate to fend off starvation. By 1914, the Sioux required only token ration payments to sustain themselves in a life so comparatively comfortable that Frank Fools Crow, a modern-day "ceremonial chief" born around 1890, believed that "in some ways conditions were even better than in the old buffalo-hunting days."

This relative prosperity and the attendant good feeling came to an abrupt end. As cattle prices soared in 1916, inflated by wartime demand, Indian Bureau agents pressured the Sioux to sell their herds for a quick profit—advice the Indians heeded so rapidly and completely that by year's end almost all their stock was gone. White cattlemen (who also had incited Sioux enthusiasm for cashing in) moved onto the empty Indian lands, leasing huge tracts to support their continuing war boom business.

The Sioux wasted no time finding uses for their newfound cash wealth. They spent recklessly, buying up the long-coveted status symbols of white society, especially automobiles. When their dollars ran out, the Sioux began trading away their valuable horse herds, paying as much as twenty-five head for a car. Before long, the horses had vanished like the cattle and the Indians had nothing left to live on but the revenues from their leased grazing lands. With the postwar depression, that income, too, evaporated as the white renters went bankrupt and defaulted on their payments.

In the midst of this economic catastrophe, the government continued and expanded its efforts, authorized by the Burke Act, to release as many individual allotments as possible from their trust status by declaring the Indian owners "competent" to manage their own affairs. As before, many Sioux tried to sell their cattleless land at the earliest opportunity—often at bargain prices—to feed their newly acquired consumer habits as well as the old bane of alcoholism, which had become increasingly prevalent on the reservation with the return of the war veterans. They had grown accustomed to drinking in the service and now had little else to occupy their time.

The government cooperated fully with the Indians' efforts to dispossess themselves, encouraging and advertising land sales; but the Indian bureau made no effort to regulate the sales process or to insure that the business-ignorant Indians received fair value for their land. By 1922, a year of economic recovery nationwide, the whites had recouped enough money to purchase the available allotments. More land left Sioux hands forever.

The cars, iceboxes, and radios that the Sioux had bargained for were soon broken—as were the hopes of men like Fools Crow, who recorded the change:

> There were hardly any milk cows, chickens, ducks or pigs left. The once beautiful gardens were nothing but dry brush and the chicken coops were broken and falling down. Even the corrals had weeds in them, because the horses were gone. . . . The white population around the borders of the reservation was growing and expanding. They decided we owned more than we needed and they figured out a way to get it. It was easy. They encouraged the destitute Oglalas to sell or to lease their allotments to them and then move into towns, which they did, for the money, naturally!
>
> So the people left their once fine log homes and storage cellars and settled down in tents and shacks. They exchanged their freedom for money and liquor, and as it turned out there would be no end to this curse.

In 1924, the prairie rains stopped falling and drought soon turned the Dakota plains into a sun-baked, windswept wasteland—a part of the disastrous "Dust Bowl" that ruined the nation's farm economy from the late 1920s into the Great Depression. In 1929, a committee of senators visited Sioux country to investigate conditions there. They heard hours of testimony during their stay, nearly all of it in the vein of Charlie Black Horse's:

> On this reservation the conditions are in very bad shape. We are starving and most of the people here all look black; they get that way from eating too much horsemeat. . . . I am eating horses and I have only four or five left, and when I eat them up there will be no more food and I cannot go anywhere. I eat so much horsemeat I hear the horses go neigh-neigh-neigh in my sleep.

As the senators saw, after forty years of rigorous application, assimilation policy was a failure. A program intended as a means of making the Indians prosperous and free had, in fact, made them poorer and more dependent. "The Lakota are now a sad, silent, and unprogressive people suffering the fate of all oppressed," the Carlisle-educated Luther Standing Bear wrote at the time. "Today you see but a shattered specimen, a caricature . . . of the man that once was. Did a kind, wise, helpful and benevolent conqueror bring this about?"

Persistent failure—of which the Sioux were but a glaring example—gradually eroded the reformers' enduring confidence in their experiment with cultural extermination and land allotment. The intellectual foundation of these policies, the unquestioned moral superiority of western civilization, already lay broken in the trenches of Verdun, Amiens, and Ypres, a casualty of the Great War's previously unimaginable carnage. After the war, disillusioned American intellectuals turned to other cultural traditions for moral guidance; and, more specifically, a new generation of Indian policy reformers, chastened by the failure of past policy and disillusioned with what they perceived to be the atomized, Hobbesian world of twentieth-century industrial America, warmly embraced the sense of community and harmony of life that they discovered in previously spurned native societies.

Drawing upon the socioscientific rationale provided by the work of pioneer anthropologist Franz Boas, the 1920s reformers adopted "cultural pluralism" as the intellectual touchstone for another revamped Indian policy. Led by John Collier, head of the American Indian Defense Association, this new generation of critics called on the government to reverse the destructive policy of unrelenting assimilation and allotment, and instead protect the Indians' land base and foster their native cultures. In Congress, at meetings across the country, and in the muckraking press, the new liberal reformers prepared the ground for a radical reorientation of government policy.

Focusing national attention on the persistent fraud and mishandling of native resources, Collier and his followers convinced the Secretary of the Interior to commission the Institute for Government Research (later known as the Brookings Institute) to investigate the problems of Indian administration. The institute experts, under Dr. Lewis Meriam, compiled what is generally considered the most comprehensive study ever done on Indian affairs. By documenting the poverty, ill health, and illiteracy of the Indian community, by criticizing the government for inadequate funding, overcentralization, and poor planning in its management of Indian life, and by questioning the wisdom of allotment, the 1928 Meriam report showed past policy to have been a shambles.

Assimilation, while not repudiated, ceased to be the centerpiece of wise policy. If the ultimate goal of Indian administration was still to "absorb [the native] into the prevailing civilization . . . in accordance with a minimum standard of health and decency," it would now be done while nurturing the best elements of Indian life "rather than crush[ing] out all that is Indian."

The Sioux knew little if anything about the Meriam study. They spent their days watching the topsoil blow east on the prairie breeze, thinking about the next day's meal and dreaming about their Black Hills money. At rodeo time, or whenever they could, the sons and grandsons of the old chiefs—Kills Enemy, Bird Necklace, Eagle Pipe, Otto Chief Eagle, Iron Horse, Blue Horse, Flying Hawk, John Sitting Bull—would get together. In 1931, an eastern anthropologist found them passing a pipe on Pine Ridge. They were mulling over a tattered old newspaper clipping—something about the year 1874 when Custer found gold in the Hills and, in their view, the 1868 treaty became just "a little paper dirtied with a lie."

The government acknowledged the preemptive importance of tribal claims. "Until these claims are out of the way," one expert report reasoned, "not much can be expected of the Indians who are placing their faith in them." The old-timers ruminating over the Custer news story had already had their faith tested for eight bleak years, since the filing of the Black Hills claim. Every year the Sioux heard the same claims report from their agent, from the commissioner, even from their lawyers: patience. Hard advice for aged men.

While the Sioux waited, the government established (in President Coolidge's words) "a distinctly national monument" in the midst of the Black Hills. Sculptor Gutzon Borglum started carving busts of four presidents (Washington, Jefferson, Lincoln, and Teddy Roosevelt) into a stolen cleft of Mt. Rushmore, establishing the "Shrine of Democracy" in cliffs known to the Sioux as "the Six Grandfathers." At the new monument, and elsewhere in the Hills, local business men paid Indians to dress up in buckskins and pose for tourists.

Back in 1923 and 1924, before this latest indignity, it had seemed to the Sioux that all their claims would be settled by the end of the decade. Major Case and Captain Calhoun had made several trips to South Dakota with government attorney George Stormont to write down the testimony of the old men. They'd heard Marcellus Red Tomahawk tell them how "the Great Spirit created those hills for the Sioux Nation." They'd heard Joseph Black Spotted Horse explain how the whites had promised them half the Black Hills gold. They'd heard from dozens of others about Red Cloud's "seven generations" speech, about the threats of moving the Sioux to the Indian Territory, about the bribes of food and blankets for signing, about liquored-up Indians blindly touching the pen, about the white soldiers menacing the Indians with their bayonets, and about the false words of the translators. In truth, the hundreds of pages of Sioux recollections, fifty years removed from the facts, were sometimes self-contradictory, other times made of whole cloth. And to the extent that the memories of these aged Sioux recaptured the treaty conferences of 1875 and 1876, they often mistook the anguished pleas of their leaders for the actual terms of the agreement they had signed. Still, taken collectively, to the Indians and to a sympathetic advocate like Case, the stories amounted to an irrefutable indictment of the United States for deceit, coercion, and, ultimately, theft.

George Stormont was far more skeptical of the Indians' interpretation of their history. Indian claims, he believed, would not be won or lost by impassioned pleas but on points of law. He challenged every Sioux witness and highlighted every contradiction in the testimony. He moved to strike from the record every "argumentative" speech, objected to every bit of hearsay or speculation. Most dramatically, Stormont objected to all the testimony about the 1876 Manypenny commission as "incompetent, irrelevant and immaterial, for the reason that the Court of Claims is without jurisdiction to inquire into the claim growing out of the cession of the Black Hills." When the Hughes firm posed this jurisdictional issue theoretically, Case had dismissed it out of hand. Now, Stormont was posing it for real.

The government also began putting together evidence for its defense, the historical record that congressmen had frequently pointed to during the effort to head off the Sioux claims: namely, the millions of dollars the government had spent over the decades to sustain and civilize the Sioux. On January 1, 1925, a team of government auditors started to compile a comprehensive accounting of all money appropriated and spent on behalf of the Sioux people, a document that would be the basis not only for the government's offset claims but for a general defense that the government had been, if anything, generous to the Sioux.

The comptroller general's office estimated that the comprehensive audit would take two and one-half years to complete. By Case's reckoning, that timetable would bring the Black Hills claim to judgment in five years, 1930. This did not seem unreasonable for what Case informed his clients was "the largest suit ever brought against the United States Government." But Case was taking no chances with a defendant's intransigence. Before the end of 1925, he was already lobbying congressmen to supplement the original $75,000 appropriation for the Sioux accounting so that additional staff might be hired. "Justice delayed loses its quality," he wrote South Dakota Senator William McMaster. "The Sioux people have borne and forborne so many years that it seems to me simple justice requires all the expedition consistent with accuracy."

Nonetheless, the Sioux audit stretched on for seven years. It was the end of September 1932, eight years almost to the day after Case had written the attorney general to inform him that "[p]laintiff's case is practically complete," before he could report to his clients receipt of the final version. At a final cost of $177,000, reflecting consideration of 600,000 payment vouchers, the audit filled eight bound volumes totalling 4,385 pages. According to the comptroller general, the United States had spent $109 million since 1815 on matters relating to the Sioux nation.

Case cautioned his clients not to be overwhelmed by the government's figures. Much of this money—appropriations before 1876 and expenditures solely for the benefit of the government or for the execution of treaty requirements—could not be offset against the Black Hills claim. Case found "much [that was] encouraging" in the report.

Most encouraging was the simple fact that the report was done. Almost ten years had passed since the filing of the claims, over twenty years since Case first met with the Sioux. "Young Spotted Tail" was now middle-aged. Captain Calhoun was even older. Victor Evans already was dead. At one time Case had hoped the Sioux claims would make his career; instead, they had become his career. With the exception of a few other lesser Indian clients, the Sioux comprised his entire law practice; and although Case occasionally received a few dollars for probating the will of a dead Sioux friend or for obtaining treaty benefits for someone on the reservation, after a decade of work, he had yet to see a penny in fees for his labor on the claims.

Indeed, unbeknownst to his clients, Case was flat broke, and Calhoun was growing increasingly reluctant to spend the remnant of his fortune on claims he probably would not see to judgment. Facing, as their advocate told them, "one of the great moral and legal battles in the history of the United States," the Sioux were in dire need of a new legal patron. Case began the search.

On July 13, 1932, Case associated himself with the law firm of

Brewster, Ivins and Phillips, hoping, as he informed his clients, to "furnish the Sioux Nation more strength and more power in their contest with the United States." Kingman Brewster was, Case informed his clients, "a hard driver . . . with a determination to drive the case through to a conclusion." A noted tax lawyer, Brewster was also known to his partners as an entrepreneur, the sort of man to whom a one-third share of the Sioux claims fee in exchange for costs of disbursement would have sounded like a good investment. It was a satisfactory deal all around. The alliance brought Case all the financing he could want—an office, a stenographer, even a monthly stipend—as well as the respectability and services of a premier law firm.

Brewster, James Ivins, and Richard Phillips, moreover, had all served as judges on the U.S. Tax Court, and thus were presumably well acquainted with the Court of Claims judges before whom Case would argue. With these impeccable connections and the assistance of a Harvard-educated Brewster associate, Richard Barker, Case could report with confidence to his clients that together their counsel had "the resources, the spirit and the will to complete the work with which they had been entrusted."

"We have now ended the period of waiting," Case assured his clients. Once again in Sioux country, hope flourished that the old men might see their Black Hills money before they were dead.

On May 7, 1934, the eleventh anniversary of the original filing, the Sioux attorneys submitted twenty-four "Separate Amended Petitions" to the Court of Claims on behalf of the "Sioux Tribe of Indians." Bound in a single volume of more than three hundred pages, each amended petition detailed a single Sioux claim, for the first time defining in legal terms the many grievances vaguely alluded to back in 1923. The Indians brought suit for nearly $1 billion. This included $40 million plus 5 percent interest for the misappropriation of funds pursuant to the 1889 land cession, $14 million for undelivered annuities, $12 million for deficient education programs, and $8 million apiece for insufficient rations and clothing.

But these claims and all the lesser ones, even taken collectively, were dwarfed by No. C-531-(7)—the Black Hills claim—for which the Sioux gladly would have forsaken all the others.

The Black Hills petition read more like a history than a legal document. Reflecting the long litany of broken promises that the claim symbolized in Sioux minds, the Indians' formal petition recounted all the worst chapters of government-Sioux relations. Case reviewed the treaties, drawing upon events as distant as the

Louisiana Purchase and America's promise to the French Emperor Napoleon to protect "the inhabitants of the ceded territory . . . in the free enjoyment of their liberty, property and the religion they profess." In his view, these events confirmed Sioux ownership of and rights of use and occupancy in lands "knowingly and willfully misappropriate[d]" by the United States between 1874 and 1877.

Case distinguished three separate categories of land for which the Sioux deserved just compensation. The Class A lands consisted of the Black Hills proper, the 7,345,157 acres of the Great Sioux Reservation, rich in gold and timber, which the government had granted the Sioux as a permanent home in 1868 and then appropriated for itself in 1877. Case valued the Class A claim alone at over $172 million, plus interest, from the date of taking.

The Class B lands consisted of 25.8 million acres west of the Missouri River to which the Sioux obtained the right of "absolute use and occupancy" under the 1851 Laramie treaty, but which lay "outside the boundaries of the 1868 Treaty." Case appraised this allegedly abrogated right of use and occupancy at a uniform 50¢ per acre, or $13 million, plus interest. In addition, Case asked payment for more than 40 million acres north and west of the tribe's 1851 Fort Laramie treaty lands (west as far as the summits of the Big Horn Mountains and north as far as the Missouri River), over which the Sioux allegedly exercised a right to roam and hunt under the 1868 treaty. Valued at 10¢ per acre, Sioux rights in these Class C lands added another $4 million, plus interest, to the claim.

As Case had framed it, the Black Hills claim involved more than $189 million, together with interest worth several times that amount—in aggregate, approximately $750 million. A white man's court, according to white man's rules, would now decide if America's conscience as reflected in its laws required such a payment. On the floor of Congress and in the national press, the debate began whether a country in the midst of the worst depression in its history could afford such a price to redress what many viewed as bygone wrongs.

Those wrongs were present history for the Sioux. With most of the old men gone, and after so much suffering for so long, to the Indians no amount of compensation could truly render justice. Still, as they weathered the Depression, barely, through government handouts and New Deal jobs programs, most of the old Sioux, after fifty-seven years, just wanted their Black Hills "sack of beans" before they died. Victory would not restore the past, but perhaps as Red Cloud and the other old chiefs had once hoped, the

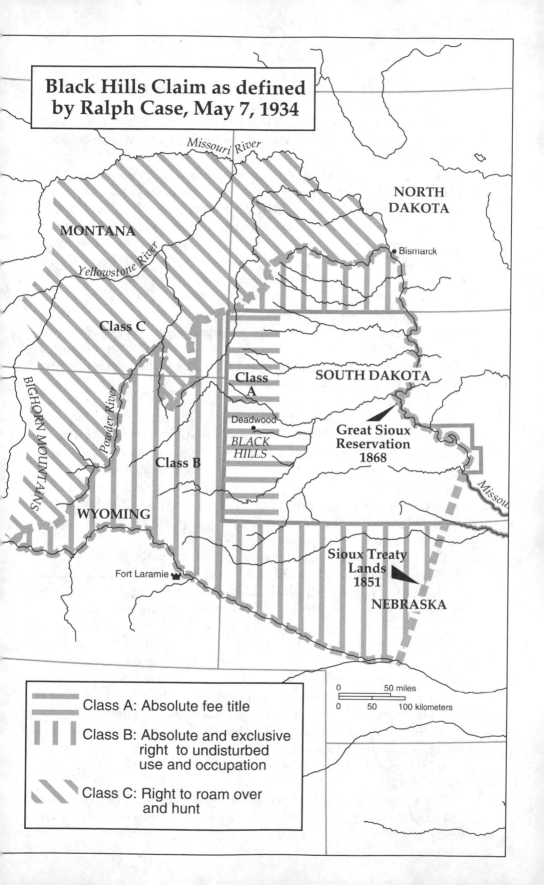

Black Hills Claim as defined by Ralph Case, May 7, 1934

NORTH DAKOTA

• Bismarck

MONTANA

Missouri River

Yellowstone River

Class C

BIGHORN MOUNTAINS

Powder River

Class A

Class B

Class A

SOUTH DAKOTA

Deadwood •

BLACK HILLS

Great Sioux Reservation 1868

WYOMING

Fort Laramie

Missou

Sioux Treaty Lands 1851

NEBRASKA

	Class A: Absolute fee title
	Class B: Absolute and exclusive right to undisturbed use and occupation
	Class C: Right to roam over and hunt

```
0          50 miles
|___|___|___|
0    50    100 kilometers
```

Black Hills might yet be a source of riches—sustenance for seven generations of Sioux yet to come.

For the moment, the Black Hills were a source only of continued political division and confrontation in Sioux country. The factionalism that had attended the inception of the claim had, if anything, grown worse during the last twenty years as the question of which Indian would be eligible to collect claims money became more pertinent. When, for administrative purposes, the government consolidated a band of Yankton Sioux with the Teton on Rosebud in the early 1930s, the western bands demanded assurances from the Indian Bureau that the merger in no way entitled their eastern kinsmen to any part of claims settlement.

Most of the disputation centered not in the claims of one band against another but in the continuing rivalry between the "sociological" mixed bloods—generally younger, more progressive, better-educated, fee patent Indians, often but not always of mixed ancestry—and the "sociological" fullbloods, who were just the opposite. Resenting the mixed bloods (the "white men and the school boys") for horning in on their historic claim, the most intractable fullbloods tried to eliminate as many mixed bloods as possible from the tribal rolls. They insisted that only Sioux of more than one-half Indian blood be eligible for membership. Compromises limiting tribal enrollment to Indians of one-eighth or one-fourth blood never progressed beyond the drafting stage, and the issue remained unresolved and divisive. Even Case, the "Little White Father," as the Sioux referred to him affectionately, could do nothing to unify his clients.

The infighting was most prevalent on Pine Ridge, where the progressive-dominated business council, the Council of 21, battled the old chiefs council, the Oglala Council, for control of the reservation. Calling themselves the Council of 100 to lend numerical superiority to their cause, the traditionals (now including first-generation progressives like Henry Standing Bear and Charles Turning Hawk, who had been superseded by even more assimilated and younger Sioux), accused the "21" of rigging the council elections and then ignoring the interests of the tribe as a whole. On February 20, 1931, the Oglala Council, presided over by Charlie Red Cloud, grandson of the chief, resolved unanimously (48-0) to establish themselves as the official council of the reservation. Self-certified, the old-timers then dissolved the progressive council.

The progressives responded with invective. "Sad to say all the old time chiefs are dead now," a group of seventeen business coun-

cilmen wrote the commissioner. "Perhaps the only object or excuse for the existence of [the Oglala Council is] to appease and
satisfy the vanity of the many vain-glorious decendants who have
deteriorated beyond recognition. . . . We Indians have a tuff [*sic*]
proposition to be ever on the guard in our affairs with the Government . . . and it's going to take younger and more enlightened
Indians. All the old fellows like to do is feast and sleep."

While the Sioux wrangled, the government was preparing a
radical departure from past policy along the lines elaborated in the
devastating Meriam report of 1928. In June 1933, newly elected
President Franklin Roosevelt named John Collier, the liberal reformer and leading force behind the Meriam report, to be his
commissioner of Indian Affairs. And, more important, Roosevelt
gave Collier a mandate to depart dramatically from past policy and
create an entirely "New Deal" for American Indians. By the beginning of 1934, Collier had submitted to Congress the corner-
stone of his program, the Indian Reorganization Act (IRA), the
statutory expression of the reform ideals of economic development, self-determination, cultural pluralism, and a revived tribalism for Indians.

Before passing the IRA, Congress modified many of Collier's
more controversial initiatives. Still, the final compromise measure
had the practical effect, among other things, of halting allotment
(which, by Collier's day, had reduced Indian land holdings to 47
million acres from 138 million in 1887) and of extending to Indian
tribes the right to organize for their common welfare under a
constitution and bylaws. The Indians' new autonomy was limited,
but it was far more than they had enjoyed at any time since the
movement onto the reservations. Tribal councils organized under
the IRA could employ legal counsel, apply for money from a
newly created revolving credit fund, consolidate and augment
tribal land holdings, prevent the disposition of lands without tribal
consent, and negotiate with federal, state, and local governments.
Instead of forcing the assimilation of individual Indians, the
United States was now authorizing the creation of Indian tribal
governments to interact with modern society while preserving a
measure of tribal independence. The nation's half-century experiment with totalitarian control of Indian life was to end, replaced,
albeit gradually, by tribal self-determination according to standard
democratic principles.

By the terms of the IRA, referendums were to be held on each
reservation to determine whether individual tribes would participate in the reorganization. Collier and several top Interior Depart-

ment officials traveled across the country "educating" Indians about the potential benefits of forging a new relationship with the United States. Shrewdly, Collier enlisted Indian employees of the bureau to help win converts within their respective tribes. And in Sioux country Collier was never without the assistance of Ben Reifel, a mixed blood born in a log cabin on the Rosebud Reservation who years later would become the first Sioux elected to the U.S. Congress.

Collier met with a large convention of Sioux at Rapid City early in March 1934, and earned the nickname Iron Man by exhausting every Lakota interpreter in the region. With the same sense of certainty as the nineteenth-century reformers, if with a radically different program, Collier admonished the Sioux that "the chance of the Indian is now and not hereafter. It is the chance of all time to get whatever you are entitled to," a chance that for their own sake the Indians must seize.

With the future of the tribe at issue, the fractious Sioux went to war over the IRA. The progressives, especially the young politicians who served on the pre-IRA bureau-sanctioned business councils, generally supported Collier's plan. They had become increasingly familiar with the principles and processes of American democracy that the IRA would graft onto what remained of Sioux culture. They were confident they would dominate the new councils as they already did the old.

The traditionals and the members of the unrecognized chiefs' councils did not know how to view a law that encouraged their once-forbidden dances and the use of their native language. But they well appreciated the new and potentially lasting obstacle to a revival of their power on the reservations. Tentatively at first, they began dancing in public, even for tourists, but they also organized a resistance to the IRA, most notably on the larger, more contentious reservations: Pine Ridge, Rosebud, and Standing Rock. "Our fathers have instructed us that we must watch our every step, every step," a fullblood, Edgar Quick Bear, reminded his followers. "There are hundreds and thousands of unscrupulous white men . . . they will deceive us." One fullblood from Pine Ridge wrote the commissioner demanding that mixed bloods— "white people, essentially . . . no more Indian than you"—should be excluded from the scope of legislation seeking to rescue native culture and return partial autonomy to Indians.

But the mixed bloods were not excluded and, at scattered meetings convened in tumbledown shacks or out on the open plains, the traditionals voiced their worst apprehensions. Many fullbloods had convinced themselves that if the mixed bloods—many of whom had sold their fee patent lands—came to power, they would contrive under the government's aegis to take fullblood land to replace their own.

Under Collier's plan, the fullbloods feared, the Sioux would "lose their treaty rights and claims," especially their rights and claims based on the 1868 treaty, which, as a symbol of Sioux ascendancy, the traditionals spoke of in sacred terms. And the fullbloods feared that they would lose their life-sustaining ration payments; they even feared that they would lose the privilege of attending church and that they would be relocated to Arizona or New Mexico.

A generation of internecine struggle and several generations of mistreatment by the bureau lent credence to these and other groundless anxieties. Frank Shorthorn and Ben American Horse, sons of chiefs and now traditional leaders, paid their own train fare to Washington to complain to Congress that Collier's New Deal would corrupt Sioux morals by fostering divorce on the reservation. "John Collier just wants to see all Indians in hell," American Horse testified. For the traditionals, change usually had brought tragedy in its wake. They resurrected all the treacheries of the past—and invented some new ones as well—to stave off the white man's latest innovation.

The "old dealers" failed. During the last months of 1934, the Cheyenne River, Lower Brûlé, Santee, Standing Rock, Rosebud, and Pine Ridge Sioux all voted to organize under the IRA. On Pine Ridge, the largest reservation, the referendum passed by only 94 votes—1,169 for, 1,075 against—out of an electorate of 4,075. Little better than 25 percent of the eligible Pine Ridge Indians voted for the IRA, a comparable number at Rosebud, where voter participation was only 49 percent. Nonetheless, overall, the referendums turned out more of the electorate than an average American election (62.5 percent in Sioux country as a whole), and the majority of Sioux chose Collier's New Deal.

Representative democracy came to Sioux country. The old ways of choosing leaders, vanished long ago, now had an official, if still essentially alien, substitute. On Pine Ridge, Rosebud, Standing Rock, and Cheyenne River, the first meaningful elections since the 1918 Black Hills council brought the mixed bloods and progressive fullbloods to power. With these elections, the Sioux embarked on the novel task of adopting constitutions and bylaws for their governance as well as the continuing and often unsuccessful process of wresting as much autonomy as possible from Indian Bureau administrators who, despite Collier, resented any loss of authority. In other words, the Sioux started to experiment again with self-rule while fighting to convert the Indian Bureau and its agencies from institutions that governed Indians to institutions that assisted Indians in governing themselves.

Many of the chiefs' descendants, though they themselves had not earned their stature according to past customs, boycotted the IRA elections, removing from consideration some of the tribes' most respected members. The traditional leaders, distinguished by the power of their Lakota oratory and the strength of their bloodtie to the glorious past, demanded a return to the treaty days, when chiefs led the tribe and met in council with the Great Father and his emissaries. They scorned the IRA tribal councils and maintained their own shadow government, just as they had ever since the bureau organized the original progressive Sioux councils more than twenty years before.

In September 1937, the IRA tribal governments organized a general Sioux council to discuss the common problems of "old age, widowed mothers, extreme rehabilitation needs, care of orphans and children [from] broken homes . . . unemployment and education." Discussion of these and other intractable problems of reservation life led nowhere, and, as would become customary, the Sioux representatives shifted the focus of their meeting to the claims issue—the elusive panacea for their predicament and the powerful symbol of the history that alone united them. The only substantive result of the weeklong conference was the establishment of a pan-Sioux claims organization—the Black Hills Sioux Nation Council—which began meeting and corresponding regularly with Case.

The old dealers quickly formed their own Black Hills Treaty and Claims Council. Its members also met with Case whenever he came to the reservation or went to see him periodically in Washington.

From time to time, a Sioux delegation of one faction or the other would ask Case for lodging during an east coast visit. More often, representatives of the competing councils would send letters requesting a "report" on the status of the Black Hills claim. New Dealer or old, Case always had something for them, a bed, a drink, or a word of encouragement. After twenty-five years, the Sioux were more than clients; they were his friends. For years the Indians called on Case whenever, in his words, "a horse stray[ed] away or somebody ha[d] an illegitimate child." In 1938, a young boy going blind with trachoma asked Case to save his sight. Case helped him raise money for medical treatment, arranging for the sale of a painted buffalo hide the boy had done.

Out on the reservations, a few more years—Depression years—slipped by. With the sale of their cattle herds in 1916 and the dissipation of their cash earnings in the 1920s, the Sioux had lost for a second time the economic foundation of their society as well as the chance to adopt the cowboy culture, the sole plains business and life that suited both their land and their heritage. Without stock for the rangelands, the Sioux returned to destitution. Many Sioux families, particularly among the fullbloods, made their homes in single-room log cabins, little more than a roof overhead sheltering bare walls, a mattress or two, and a few household items. Outside might be a wagon, two or three ponies, farming tools, and a few chickens. Others less fortunate slept in rusted-out cars. In every one of the scattered rural communities where the old bands had settled—among Crazy Horse's people around Manderson or Little Wound's band near Kyle—malnutrition was pervasive, clothing meager against the cold, plumbing and electricity scarce.

In 1931, the average annual income for a family of five on Pine Ridge was $152.80. During the mid-thirties, Sioux income swelled modestly when the Civilian Conservation Corps set up employment projects in Sioux country. Later, in the early 1940s, some Sioux would find wartime industrial work at the airfield and ammunition depot near Rapid City at the northeast tip of the Black Hills. Still, in 1942, the average per capita income on Pine Ridge was only $120, one-sixth the figure for the rest of South Dakota and less than one-third of the per capita income in Mississippi, the poorest state in the nation.

Of the paltry income the Sioux did earn, half came from government wages or relief programs, not from a self-sustaining economy. Over time, the Sioux had come to depend on the government not only for food, as in the treaty days, but also for what few decent jobs existed on their reservations. With that dependence, any real hope of escaping the stifling paternalism of the United States vanished completely.

In the absence of sufficient employment on the reservation, some among the younger generations sought wage work elsewhere. Others led an idle life, living off lease payments and public relief (which many Sioux considered their due) or moving in with more prosperous relatives, who, in keeping with the Sioux tradition of giving away surplus possessions, played obligatory host.

Neither temporary CCC projects (which ended in 1942) nor

wartime jobs offered any hope for a long-term solution to desperate Sioux poverty. In the late 1930s, the government tried to resuscitate the once-flourishing cattle industry, but intervening land sales had broken up many of the natural cattle ranges; also, credit was hard to come by. In any event, many Sioux were reluctant to trust new government initiatives. They blamed the U.S. for the loss of their original cattle herds and for the successive failure of the drought-stricken farming ventures that the Indian Bureau's "boss farmers" subsequently promoted.

With no tradition of developing their property and no memory of success, many Sioux abandoned the concept of land as a lasting resource and instead considered it principally a source of cash, either from sale or rental. This attitude (which naturally led to a continual seepage of individually held Indian lands into non-Indian hands) was substantially reinforced as older allottees started to pass away. As happened on reservations throughout the west, when Indian landowners died, their allotments (often only 160 acres) were divided among their heirs. And when the second-generation owners died, as was common by the 1930s, the land was divided again, until each inherited share amounted to just a few parched acres of grass, useless for anything but rental to white ranchers who had the capital to consolidate the splintered holdings.

The reformers who had designed allotment policy never reckoned with the possibility that tribal populations might expand. Certain that Native Americans were a vanishing species (a myth older than the Republic), early in the allotment era the reformers had stripped the tribes of "surplus" reservation lands which might have provided new allotments for future generations. As a result, instead of transforming Indians into yeoman farmers, allotment policy, though halted by the IRA, left a legacy of Indian microlandlords, each earning a few dollars a month leasing out a tiny parcel of inherited land.

Every year a few more of the original Black Hills plaintiffs died; those old men who yet survived, many still with their hair long, might sit for hours "in a semi-circle under a shade and discuss old times and the deeds of men now dead, while from mouth to mouth passe[d] the inevitable red stone pipe filled with 'red willow' tobacco." As the psychoanalyst Erik Erikson noted about them, for each of these men time was "empty except for those vivid bits of present in which he [could] be his old self, exchanging memories, gossiping, joking, or dancing, and in which he again [felt] connected with the boundless past wherein there was no one but himself, the game, and the enemy." Raised in the old ways, living on the lands where the killing and disarming had taken place, these Sioux dreamed day and night of restoration, never quite believing that the white man was in their country to stay; and they expected any moment that a bulletin at the agency would inform them that the white man's courts had made them rich.

While they dreamed, astonishingly little happened with the Black Hills claim. In 1937 a group of traditionals, descendants of Sitting Bull's band, threatened to sell the Black Hills to Canada if the government did not settle the Sioux claims. In 1938, Captain Calhoun died from a heart attack. Not a word of legal argument had yet gone before the court.

In June 1937, Case had submitted to the court a 500-page "Statement of Fact," a history of Sioux relations with the United States from their origin until February 28, 1877—the date of the act expropriating the Black Hills. Case had spent a good part of twenty-five years preparing this history of the Sioux people, having begun collecting materials as a hobby in 1912, the year after he visited Pine Ridge and Rosebud and first heard the grievances of the old chiefs. Together with Richard Barker, Case had spent two years poring over documents in the Library of Congress. The writing took over a year.

It was an impassioned work to be advanced as a statement of fact, more the creation of a crusader than a lawyer. Case derived most of his historical analysis from the sympathetic *History of the Dakotah or Sioux Indians* by Doane Robinson—the first prominent white man to take up the Black Hills claim. The rest of his interpretation Case gleaned from copiously quoted original documents carefully selected to support his central thesis that the culminating tragedy, the taking of the Black Hills, was the product of frontier gold fever dishonorably encouraged by the federal government. In conclusion, Case reaffirmed his commitment to pursue a judgment that reflected the enormous quantities of gold extracted from the Hills after they were taken.

"We restate the fact that the United States, by the Act of February 28th, 1877, took from the Sioux Tribe more than 73,000,000 acres of land and from that land there has been taken gold and other minerals in value over $400,000,000.

"We also restate the rule laid down in 1875 by Edw. P. Smith, Commissioner of Indian Affairs."

> The true equivalent to be offered the Sioux, as helpless wards of the
> Government, for the Black Hills will be found by estimating what

eight hundred square miles of gold fields are worth to us, and what three thousand square miles of timber, agricultural, and grazing lands are worth to them.

Quotations from long-dead bureaucrats, though, did not constitute legal reasoning which would determine the Sioux claim in the end. Case's Statement of Fact had promised a second volume to contain his legal brief, but another thousand days passed before he submitted a statement on the law to the court. The reasons for this delay remain unclear. Perhaps the workload in the other twenty-three Sioux claims prevented Case from completing the Black Hills filing.

More likely, the Court of Claims record in Indian cases made him hold off. The court's record on jurisdiction alone might have given Case reason to pause. Testimony before Congress in 1935 indicated that more than one-half of the special jurisdictional acts authorizing Indian claims had to be amended before the court finally agreed to hear tribal suits. That very year, the court had dismissed on jurisdictional grounds a landtaking claim brought by the Klamath and Moadoc tribes under a special jurisdictional act almost identical to the Sioux act.

In the twenty-one cases that the Court of Claims did adjudicate between July 1936 and November 1937, it ruled for the Indians only three times, awarding the plaintiff tribes less than $10 million of the $134 million that they had claimed. Among the suits rejected by the court was Case's Sioux education claim—lost forever in 1937 when the Supreme Court refused to hear an appeal.

As reflected in the Court of Claims record, the legal precedent for Indian land claims against the government was by no means clearly established. In the seminal case, *Lonewolf* v. *Hitchcock*, decided in 1903, the Supreme Court had adopted a general hands-off approach to congressional appropriations of Indian land. The Sioux could expect the government to argue for similar judicial deference with regard to Congress's appropriation of the Black Hills.

In *Lonewolf,* the Kiowa, Comanche, and Apache tribes had brought suit to enjoin the Secretary of the Interior from disposing of tribal lands under a congressional statute of 1900. This statute ratified a prior "agreement" by which the tribes allegedly had ceded to the government a portion of their joint reservation in return for allotments from the ceded lands and $2 million. As in the Black Hills case, the Indians claimed that this Act of Congress ratified an illegitimate agreement, since the government had failed to obtain the signatures of three-quarters of the adult Indian males as required, in this case, by the 1868 Medicine Lodge treaty. For the Secretary to dispose of their land in violation of a treaty, the Indians argued, would violate their right to due process of law guaranteed by the Fifth Amendment.

The government admitted that it failed to collect a sufficient number of signatures to comply with the treaty. Nonetheless, the Supreme Court refused to stop the Secretary of the Interior from carrying out his congressional mandate. "It has never been doubted," the Court concluded, "that the power to abrogate [Indian treaties] existed in Congress and that in a contingency such power might be availed of from considerations of Government policy, particularly if consistent with perfect good faith toward the Indian." Congress has always possessed a "plenary" or absolute power over Indian affairs, the Court continued, "a power that had always been deemed a political one, not subject to be controlled by the judicial department of the Government."

In other words, the justices ruled, although Congress might have a "moral obligation" to act in good faith when dealing with Indians, the courts were powerless to adjudicate how well Congress lived up to that obligation, even in the face of an admitted breach of a treaty. Invoking the time-honored constitutional doctrine of separation of powers between the three co-equal branches of government, Justice Edward White concluded for the Court's majority that justice must indeed be blind when considering the historical record of Indian policy. "We must presume," he wrote, "that Congress acted in perfect good faith in the dealings with the Indians of which complaint is made, and that the legislative branch of the Government exercised its best judgment in the premises." This judicial presumption of congressional good faith—tantamount to outright refusal to consider the constitutionality of legislative action respecting the tribes—weighed heavily against a Sioux claim based, as Case had cast it, so firmly on a history of congressional treaty breaking and bad faith.

The *Lonewolf* Court's interpretation of Indian land rights also undermined the Sioux claim. Since the earliest Indian cases in the days of Chief Justice John Marshall, the Court had held that, while ultimate title to Indian tribal lands rested in the United States, a treaty right of exclusive use and occupancy (such as the Sioux had to the Black Hills under the 1868 treaty) was "as sacred as the fee of the United States in the same lands." This compromise safeguarded the ultimate sovereignty of the United States (for example, by preventing Indian tribes from selling their land to foreign nations), but it also gave Indian tribes property rights in their territory, and thus some protection under American law against the operation of naked force in pushing them off their lands.

But in *Lonewolf* the Court opened an enormous loophole in the pattern of judicial protection of tribal ownership rights. Although it recognized that past cases safeguarded tribal property against encroachment by individual states or by private citizens, the Court found that neither case law nor the Constitution afforded the tribes any similar protection from federal appropriation of Indian lands. Previous judicial decisions, Justice White ruled, had not addressed the question of Congress's power to administer Indian land as guardian of the tribes. The Court had already determined (in *Cherokee Nation* v. *Hitchcock,* decided in the term before *Lonewolf*) that Congress possessed "full administrative power" over Indian tribal property. Now in *Lonewolf* the Court construed "full administrative power" to mean that Congress had the legal authority to convert Indian tribal lands into allotments and cash, regardless of tribal preference.

Applying this principle, the Court found in *Lonewolf* that in violating the Medicine Lodge treaty and forcing a land cession upon the Kiowa, Comanche, and Arapaho, Congress was not seizing Indian land without tribal consent, but merely performing its legitimate administrative function—"effecting a mere change in the form of investment of Indian tribal property." By the same logic, the court might easily rule that the government had not taken the Black Hills, but had merely exchanged the land for rations and other "benefits" of the 1876 Manypenny agreement.

Lonewolf transmogrified the guardian-ward concept, originally conceived for the benefit of the tribes, into a Dickensian relationship granting the guardian extraordinary power, absolving him of any wrongdoing, and leaving the ward essentially powerless. What John Marshall envisioned as a relationship binding the government to the Indians according to "moral obligations of the highest responsibility and trust," the *Lonewolf* court refashioned to suit the convenience of a conquering people imposing its will.

Throughout the opinion Justice White stressed the historical evolution from Indian self-sufficiency to Indian dependence and what the Court saw as a concurrent erosion of Indian sovereignty. White quoted at length from *Kagama* v. *United States* (1887), which ratified Congress's power to relieve tribes of their jurisdiction over major crimes committed on reservations, and ushered in a period of Indian law that recognized virtually unfettered congressional power over the tribes. "These Indian tribes *are* wards of the nation," *Lonewolf* echoed *Kagama.* "The power of the general Government over these remnants of a race once powerful, now weak and diminished in number, is necessary to their own protection, as well as the safety to those among whom they dwell." Cloaked in the judicial robes of high principle, *Lonewolf* seemed to leave Indians no legal recourse against congressionally authorized injuries.

Had Case been filing his brief back in the 1920s, *Lonewolf* would have been the Supreme Court's controlling pronouncement on the issues involved in the Black Hills claim. But fortunately for Case and the Sioux, with the advent of President Roosevelt's more progressive appointees to the bench, in the mid-1930s the Supreme Court began limiting Congress's plenary power over Indian affairs. In 1935, the high court heard *Creek Nation* v. *United States,* which concerned a surveying error by a government agent that had robbed the Creeks of roughly 5,000 acres of their reservation. The tribe was suing for relief under the "just compensation clause" of the Fifth Amendment, which provides that the government may take private property for a public purpose only on the payment of just compensation to the owner. Explicitly retreating from *Lonewolf*'s definition of Congress's administrative powers, the Court found in favor of the Creeks, and awarded them the value of their land at the time it was taken plus 5 percent simple interest.

The Court's historical analysis had not changed in the thirty years since *Lonewolf:* the Creeks remained a dependent community under the guardianship of the United States whose affairs were subject to the control and management of the government. Nonetheless, in the view of the 1930s Court, the exercise of Congress's authority to control and manage tribal affairs was not a "political question" only, beyond the appropriate consideration of the judiciary. Congress's "power to control and manage was not absolute," the Court ruled. "It did not enable the United States to give the tribal lands to others, or to appropriate them to its own purposes, without rendering or assuming an obligation to render, just compensation for them; for that would not be guardianship, but an act of confiscation."

A year later, in *Shoshone Tribe* v. *United States,* the Supreme Court affirmed its *Creek Nation* commitment to extend Fifth Amendment property rights to Indian tribes. The *Shoshone* case, in contrast to *Creek Nation,* did not arise from the simple error of a government employee but from the deliberate misappropriation of land by the U.S. Congress. Under the Medicine Lodge treaty of 1868, the

Shoshone enjoyed the right to "exclusive use and occupancy" of a large reservation in Wyoming. Despite the treaty, and specifically despite the government's explicit treaty responsibility to police the boundaries of the reservation, beginning in 1878 the United States permitted a band of Arapaho (historic enemies of the Shoshone) to settle on Shoshone land. Over time, what started as temporary shelter while the government found the Arapaho land of their own evolved into a permanent sharing of the Shoshone reservation. The Shoshone sued for compensation, claiming that the government had taken their land in violation of the 1868 treaty.

The Supreme Court agreed, ruling that this transfer of reservation land to the Arapaho constituted a congressional "taking" of private property under the Fifth Amendment. In ordering payment to the Shoshone, the Supreme Court again paid homage to the general doctrine established in *Lonewolf* that the "power to control and manage the property and affairs of Indians may be executed in many ways and at times even in derogation of the provisions of a treaty." But Justice Benjamin Cardozo, writing for the Court, significantly qualified that power. Echoing *Creek Nation*, he emphasized that "Congressional authority over Indian affairs was not exempt from either Constitutional requirements or judicial scrutiny." When Congress appropriates tribal land, compensation must be paid. "Spoilation," Cardozo concluded, in one of the most frequently cited lines in Indian law, "is not management."

In light of *Creek Nation, Shoshone,* and *Klamath and Moadoc Tribes v. United States,* a similar case decided in 1938, *Lonewolf* could reasonably be read as not controlling the Sioux claim at all. In each case, the high court had drawn a clear distinction between Congress's power to abrogate treaties and its responsibility to pay compensation when tribal lands were seized in the exercise of that power. The Indians in *Lonewolf* had argued that by alienating their lands, the United States would violate their Fifth Amendment guarantee that "No person shall be deprived of life, liberty, or property, without due process of law." They had asked the Court to *prevent* Congress from taking their property, in essence to deny Congress the right to break treaties. The tribes in the later cases were no better pleased by the government's breach of promise, but they had appealed to a wholly different Fifth Amendment protection—the just compensation clause, which prohibits the government from taking private property "for public use, without just compensation." By its very terms this clause recognized Congress's power to seize property in violation of past agreements, so long as it paid a fair price.

Ralph Case began his legal brief by placing the Sioux claim squarely in line with the Supreme Court holdings in *Shoshone* and the other just compensation cases. As Case was quick to note, the Black Hills and Shoshone claims were analogous. The two cases involved virtually identical treaties, signed in the same year, negotiated by the same commissioners, with the same hope of comprehensive peace on the plains. In both cases, the United States had violated the treaties by taking lands set aside "for the exclusive use and occupancy" of the tribe, ignoring identical provisions requiring the consent of the adult male Indian populations.

Indeed, Case was so thoroughly convinced that *Shoshone* and *Creek Nation* had to be the controlling precedents for the Sioux claim, he made no effort to anticipate and preempt the government's prospective arguments. No mention of *Lonewolf* appears in Case's brief, no attempt to distinguish this adverse and frequently cited Fifth Amendment case from the Sioux claim. Nor did Case address the critical question of the scope of the 1920 Sioux jurisdictional act (the Hughes firm's main concern), apparently relying on his unflinching belief that the plain language of the act (authorizing the judiciary to hear "all legal and equitable" Sioux claims) was proof in and of itself that Congress had authorized the Court of Claims to adjudicate the Black Hills claim.

In addition to these errors of omission, in the "Question Presented" section of his brief, Case gratuitously asked the court to determine "whether the evidence addressed in the case establishes . . . the failure of the defendant to pay over or credit to the plaintiffs monies due the plaintiff." What he could have meant by this in the absence of a scintilla of evidence in the record about payments remains a mystery. It was likewise a mystery how a lawyer twenty years on the case, assisted by a top-drawer firm, could not produce better work. The entire brief ran a thin eighteen pages (one for every year since the filing), and much of it was not law, but more history—and dubious history at that. As befit a man who ran an American Legion post from his office and who read American Legion magazine cover-to-cover every month, Case gratuitously absolved the military field commanders for their role in the Black Hills taking:

> Nothing in the record, nothing that is said here, is in derogation of the courage, the tenacity and the unqualified obedience of the men of the United States Army and Generals Sully, Terry and Gibbon, and including the heroic figure of Lieutenant Colonel George Armstrong Custer and his men.

Such a view of Custer, not shared by his clients, some of whom had developed a fear that the government would fine them $10,000 for each soldier killed at Little Big Horn, reflected the considerable romance in Case's view of frontier history. That romance seemed to carry over to his appraisal of the judicial process. Case appears never to have doubted that ultimately the courts, guardians of the high ideals of the nation that he had served proudly in the cause of liberty, would redeem broken promises and vindicate his clients' righteous cause—though he went to no great pains to establish it.

In his answer brief for the government, Stormont seized upon the failings in his adversary's work, at times to the point of sarcasm. As "Defendant's counsel" he "confessed [it] difficult to clarify plaintiff's main contention."

Stormont's own argument was straightforward and glib. Relying exclusively on *Lonewolf*, the government brief characterized the act of February 28, 1877, not as a landtaking under Congress's power of eminent domain but as "a valid exercise of the plenary power of Congress in the management and control of Indian tribes and their property." As Case had done with *Shoshone*, Stormont elaborated each of the circumstantial similarities between *Lonewolf* and *Sioux Nation*. Both involved agreements in which the government failed to collect the mandatory signatures. In both, the plaintiffs claimed that the government had used "fraud, deceit and coercion" to obtain Indian consent, that the official interpreters had lied and deceived, that Congress had amended the agreements without subsequent tribal ratification.

What relevance these ancillary similarities might have on the true legal issues in the case Stormont left to the collective imagination of the court. Stormont's real purpose in serving up these minor parallels was to make another critical and misleading analogy more palatable. In both cases, he asserted, the tribes had appealed for protection under the Fifth Amendment, a protection that the Supreme Court had denied in *Lonewolf* and ought to deny again in *Sioux Nation*.

Under *Lonewolf*, Stormont argued, the 1877 act was not a "taking," but merely "an Act to ratify an agreement" executed within the bounds of Congress's plenary power for which the Sioux were entitled to no Fifth Amendment relief. That the tribes in *Lonewolf* and the Sioux had appealed to completely different aspects of the Fifth Amendment—the former to the due process clause, the latter to the just compensation clause—Stormont obscured with silence.

Stormont also counterattacked on jurisdictional grounds, argu-

ing that it was irrelevant whether the 1877 act was validly concluded. Regardless, he claimed, *Lonewolf* required the court to
presume congressional good faith and thereby rendered the court
powerless to decide whether the United States had paid adequate
compensation for the Sioux lands. According to his interpretation
of the jurisdictional act, Congress had not granted the courts the
right to question congressional discretion in fixing payment, and,
in the absence of such a mandate, the courts could not consider the
Sioux claim.

As a third and not inconsequential defense, the government
further argued that whatever Congress's plenary powers, the
Sioux had in effect ratified the 1877 act when three-quarters of the
adult males had signed "Crooks Treaty," the agreement of 1889. As
early as 1903, claim opponents had insisted that the Sioux had
signed away their rights, and Stormont gratefully cribbed this
page from the history books. Case never bothered to discuss the
issue.

Stormont ended his brief with a short appendix denigrating
Case's "Statement of Fact" as a compilation of biased and inaccurate hearsay. After documenting a few inconsistencies, however,
Stormont decided the effort was ultimately pointless. "The court
[would] not be called upon to determine the truth of Plaintiff's
charges of double-dealing," he concluded. What the Sioux had
remembered in 1923, after sixty-four years, true or false, legal or
illegal, was just so much wasted talk.

The Court of Claims heard oral argument in the Black Hills case
in October 1941. What was said there is now lost.

Eight months later, on June 1, 1942, the court rejected the Black
Hills claim. Case's impassioned historical argument had left the
judges dry-eyed. The court's "Findings of Fact," set out at the
beginning of the opinion, rejected outright Case's central contention that the Manypenny commission had coerced the Sioux to
sign the 1876 agreement.

Nor did the court find any impropriety in the government's
inability to keep its promise to prevent miners from invading the
Hills. If an overriding theme could be discerned in the opinion's
judgment of frontier history, it was not that the government had
tricked and bullied the Sioux but rather that the government,
though it ultimately failed, had done its utmost to cushion the
collision of two incompatible cultures.

As a matter of law, Judge Benjamin Littleton's rambling seventy-six page discourse on history, legality, moral obligation, and
statutory construction was a masterpiece of judicial obfuscation.

By consensus, those who carefully read the opinion agreed that the court had dismissed for lack of jurisdiction (that is, lack of congressional authorization for the court to hear the merits of the claim), exactly as the Hughes firm had predicted. At least one Justice Department lawyer, though, thought the court had reached beyond the jurisdictional issue and addressed the claims' merits and had dismissed it, following the *Lonewolf* line, because there never had been a land "taking," only a congressional readjustment of the form of tribal investment.

Neither Case nor his associate Barker had a moment's doubt that they had lost on jurisdictional grounds. It was there on the first page of the opinion. The single pertinent legal issue, Littleton had observed, "was whether under the treaties of 1851 and 1868 and the act of February 28, 1877, the plaintiff tribe has any legal and enforceable claim within the meaning of section 1 of the Jurisdictional Act upon which the court has authority to inquire into the wisdom of the policy pursued by the Government . . . and the adequacy of consideration assumed and paid by the defendant."

A court's jurisdiction, Littleton continued, must derive from the plain language of the statute and not be enlarged by implication. It was not enough that Congress had authorized the court to hear all "legal claims" arising from the course of dealings between the government and the Sioux. In a case such as Black Hills, in which the government had paid at least some compensation, just or unjust, "in the absence of a clear grant of authority by Congress, we have no jurisdiction to go behind the acts of Congress and inquire into any moral obligation of the government or to determine what the Congress agreed to pay, and has paid, was adequate for what the Indians were required to surrender."

The critical distinction, then, which in the court's view placed the Sioux claim in line with *Lonewolf* (as opposed to *Shoshone* and *Creek Nation*) was simply that, as in *Lonewolf,* the government had promised to pay something, however inadequate or unwanted, for taking away the Hills. The extreme of this logic, it would seem, was that if the government had promised to pay just one penny in return for seven million gold-laden acres—notwithstanding whether it even delivered that one penny—in Indian cases the court had no authority to inquire into the nature of the transaction and, where appropriate, to force the United States to comply with its own Constitution and pay *just* compensation for private lands taken for public use. Thus the Indians, whose status as wards of the nation as well as citizens was intended and expected to provide them with special protection of the laws, were denied the protection ordinarily granted every other citizen.

The resurrection of the *Lonewolf* doctrine absolving Congress of its legal responsibility for past Indian policy was particularly surprising coming from Judge Littleton. Littleton had earlier written the Court of Claims opinion in *Shoshone,* which, when affirmed by the Supreme Court in 1937, had firmly established the very just compensation doctrine on which the Sioux claim was premised. There is no obvious answer to why, even for jurisdictional reasons, this judge would retreat under the *Lonewolf* umbrella. Had he wanted to find that the court had jurisdiction, the legislative history behind the 1920 act would have supported him. The central purpose of the Sioux jurisdiction act was precisely to afford the Sioux an opportunity to put the Black Hills claim before the courts.

The opening sentence of Littleton's opinion does offer one compelling explanation. There Littleton underscored the practical consequence of a judgment for the Sioux—a government liability totaling "approximately $739,116,256." No court in 1942, in the midst of a costly global war, at the end of a decade of national fiscal disaster, would award so large a sum to a single tribe of Indians. Perhaps the opinion's rambling style and confusing, even specious, analysis (which, coming from one of the court's clearest thinkers, seems premeditated) was a clever attempt to dismiss the overexpensive Sioux claim while creating as little precedent as possible.

Littleton's efforts to sow confusion or suggest compromise (at least with respect to future cases) did not soften the blow to the Sioux. For more than thirty years the Sioux had begged for a judicial determination of their rights before Congress accorded them a trial. Then, after twenty years of litigation, they were told that Congress had failed to give the courts sufficient authority to decide the very question that Congress had sent to the courts by passing the jurisdictional act in the first place. "The Sioux may, being a durable people, live out this interminable period of waiting," Case wrote his clients in summary, "but in this period of waiting, postponement delay and deferment, the plain rights of the Sioux people will be lost forever, the Sovereign Government will still be holding the Black Hills, and the Sioux will have received nothing but a crust of bread as 'just compensation' for the 'richest 100 square miles in the world.'"

Case immediately filed for a new trial, citing judicial errors in "statement, fact and law." Calculating the worth of the Black Hills claim at over $700 million dollars was both premature and inaccurate, Case argued. The size of the Sioux claim had not been an issue before the court, and publishing an estimate, he complained, "would inevitably lead to overpowering prejudice against the plaintiff in the mind of the general public and Congress." Case conveniently had forgotten for the moment that, in all likelihood, Littleton had derived his figure from Case's own calculation prominently displayed in the 1934 Amended Petition and that the press, with Case's encouragement, had ballyhooed the potential magnitude of the Sioux claim as early as 1937. Nor did Case show why the supposed attitude of the American public or Congress should determine or even affect the court's consideration of a new trial.

Case also attacked the court's historical Findings of Fact, but his argument amounted to nothing more than a three-page recapitulation of his 500-page history, which the court had already considered and rejected. On the crucial question of jurisdiction, Case made no argument at all except to quote verbatim the section of the 1920 act directing the court to hear "all claims of whatsoever nature which the Sioux tribe of Indians may have against the United States." Case reminded the court that it had already decided six other Sioux claims under the original jurisdictional act "even though not one . . . was mentioned directly in the Act of June 3, 1920." That Case and the Sioux had lost every one of these six claims—for education benefits, annuities, cows and oxen, seeds and implements, lands added to the 1868 reservation and lands ceded by the 1889 agreement—the court needed no reminder. On October 5, 1942, the court denied the motion for new trial.

The Sioux had one last recourse, an appeal to the Supreme Court; and in a matter of days Case began drafting his petition requesting a hearing before the highest tribunal in American law, the forum in which Case had always believed the Black Hills claim would be decided. "We have great confidence in the outcome," he wrote his clients at the end of October:

A great wrong was done to the Sioux people by the taking of their Black Hills lands. That wrong must be undone and the right must prevail. The Sioux people are not greedy claimants; all they ask is justice. You Sioux know that you can never be put back into the position you were in before the Hills were taken from you. No power of earth can do that. We know that the Sioux people will accept and abide by any reasonable sum as compensation for their Black Hills and we will continue to fight for that reasonable sum before the courts and before Congress until you *are* reasonably paid for the Hills.

Case's health belied his outward optimism. By mid-December, stomach ulcers, dormant for twenty-two years, returned and ruptured. Those close to him knew how gravely the Black Hills decision had poisoned Case's spirit. Despite all the warnings along the way, Case just could not fathom the loss on jurisdiction. Over and over in his office he read the plain words of the 1920 act—"all claims of whatsoever nature . . . all legal and equitable claims." What more authority did the court want?

It was the darkest winter of Case's life. His wife fell and broke her hip during an early freeze. His mother-in-law collapsed in January. Oil was short. Two small stoves—one coal, one wood— kept his two patients from freezing.

The specter of insolvency haunted Case. Brewster had soured on his Sioux investment back in 1938. Ivins still helped out with an office and a small stipend, but that hardly covered costs. The four acres of fruits and vegetables Case raised every year behind the family home in Maryland at least put good food on the table and brought in some cash. This year a late freeze followed by a drought killed off almost all the produce. Case watched helplessly as tomatoes rose to 30¢ per pound. Always something of a drinker, Case turned to a familiar source for solace—a secret his stomach ulcers now betrayed.

Just after the new year, 1943, the Supreme Court granted Case a rare sixty-day extension of time to file his appeal. With the help of his son Richard, newly admitted to the Maryland Bar, he got it done.

Late in February, Charles Ghost Bear, the secretary of the old deal Claims and Treaty Council, wrote a plaintive letter asking Case if somehow the old men could help win the claim. Case had received dozens of letters like this one over the last two decades. With every one, the number of eyewitnesses grew fewer. Ghost Bear said only seven still lived.

On April 19, the chairman of the Black Hills Sioux Nation Council, Peter Dillon, sent his longtime friend, Case, a rambling description of conditions on Pine Ridge. "Dear Sir and Friend, hello," he began. "Long time of you hear not." The council was meeting on Crow Creek soon to talk about Black Hills. "If there is to be any report by you or any suggestions now is the time; anything would be encouraging it would be like our letter to the boys in the front ranks in Europe."

As in the previous world war, the Sioux were making enormous sacrifices for the country. Over 900 Sioux from Pine Ridge alone had volunteered for service. Almost every able-bodied youth from every reservation did. For the Sioux to give freely of their children was not enough; the government confiscated thousands of acres from the northwest corner of the Pine Ridge reservation and converted it into a gunnery range. The government had been looking for "submarginal" lands and it knew where to find them. They evicted and made landless dozens of Sioux, many of them elderly and infirm.

Yet little, it would seem, could dull the Indians' patriotic fervor. At the height of Nazi power, they were already planning their "V for Victory" gardens. In August 1942, just two months after the Court of Claims decision, the Lower Brûlé Tribal Council had passed a resolution recommending that "for the best interest of justice and in the interest of National Loyal Unity," Case should suspend work on the Sioux claims until the end of the war. At Cheyenne River, a similar proposal was dropped only after long discussion, mainly for the sake of the old men.

Dillon could make no sense from the conflicting hopes and concerns of his people. They were patriots estranged from the ideals for which they were fighting, victims of broken promises placing their faith in the same nation that had taken their lands—years ago and again just yesterday. "The whole world is at the present time fighting for land and that very thing has been taken from us in the past and at the present time," Dillon mused. And, then, as if the universality of the Sioux dilemma was simply too large for him to wrestle with, he closed: "Well Ralph . . . the grass is looking good and guess the crops will be good also, wishing you a large Victory for your years of work and a permanent post-war Victory for the peoples of the World including the poor Sioux, good-bye, your friend."

As Dillon was writing, the Supreme Court declined to review the Black Hills claim. The long twilight struggle for justice was cast into darkness; the Sioux were out of court.

Dillon wrote Case again in mid-May, having seen the bad news reported in the press. "I think it best that you pay us a visit," he typed. "It will encourage the few old people who are still living and hope to see the end of the trail." Dillon, perhaps, did not realize how much had been lost. Case did. May passed, and June, and July, and August with no word from him. The rumor spread that Case had died.

Finally, in September, Case replied to Dillon's letter. "Regardless . . . Peter, we are still in the ring of full flight. My health is now o.k. and Mrs. Case is making progress. You and all my Sioux friends may feel assured that I will carry on this fight for their rights, if necessary, until hell freezes over." At month's end, Case sent out his annual report to the tribal councils. Somewhere he had found a bit of hope or at least a bit of bluster:

> This would be the place where we would stop and where you, the Sioux people, would stop, if we were the kind of people who quit when the work itself is not finished.
>
> More than twenty years ago when we undertook to do this work we assured you that we would stay with you until the work was finished. At that time what you meant and what we meant by the finish of the work was that the rights of the Sioux people should be established and just compensation paid to them for the Black Hills. This has not been done as yet. We know how you feel about this matter and we feel the same way. Nothing is ever settled until it is settled right. The decisions of the two courts do not settle the matter.
>
> The Black Hills claim must now go back to Congress for legislation which will require the courts to settle the Black Hills claims, or there must be some other action by Congress which will bring this entire controversy to an end.

For many months Case had "endeavored to develop a plan of action . . . a plan which we cannot now fully explain," requiring "the cooperation of the Congress and the Executive." It was just as well Case didn't tell them. Even the optimistic Sioux might have seen through Case's secret idea to negotiate a $75 million settlement with the government. Case probably did not believe it possible himself, at least in 1943. He had a theory about Indian–government relations. "The history of the United States shows clearly," he advised an old friend, "that our Indian tribes receive little consideration in time of war or depression. In each period of peace and prosperity we become big-hearted . . . and renew broken promises." Good times would come again; he and the Sioux would wait.

A year later, in 1944, Peter Dillon wrote again. He was still searching for some lesson in the confusion of Sioux loyalties. He thought he had found one: "All past history shows that a conquered people has to take what the conqueror gives, just or unjust, but the present will be worse if the boys who are now at the front, who are fighting for what is just and right, not only for our rights, but for the rights of this continent, fail." Peter Dillon's Sioux glimpsed something great in America and they would pursue it—in court, in Congress, or wherever the Black Hills claim would lead.

Case never responded to the letter. Before he could answer, Dillon had died.

NINE

A SECOND CHANCE

O N MARCH 2, 1945, William Hawk, an old fullblood from the remote village of Wakpala on the Standing Rock Reservation, resumed his longstanding correspondence with Ralph Case. "I would like to hear the report of the Black Hills case if there is any this year," Hawk wrote his old friend and adviser. "Among the Indians all the old people are now dead and just a few are alive, and we want our claim finished soon. You are now getting old yourself, and I am old too."

Frank Kills Enemy, the grandson of Chief Wabasha (who signed the 1868 treaty), also wrote Case a few months later wanting information. He and William Hawk both had heard rumors about an Indian Claims Commission that Congress was considering, a new place to bring the old Black Hills claim. Was Case to be one of the commissioners? Kills Enemy asked. "Was the jurisdiction broad and strong even with the government?"

On the same day that William Hawk wrote to Case, the House Indian Affairs Committee heard testimony on legislation restructuring the Indian claims process and creating the rumored commission. The old (since 1881) and continuing system by which each tribe petitioned Congress for a special jurisdictional act had proved too cumbersome during the 1930s as the number of tribal claimants multiplied. Before voting on individual bills, Congress ended up acting as a preliminary court weighing the factual basis of each claim. Even passage of a jurisdictional act did not assure tribes their day in court. The Court of Claims consistently read the jurisdictional acts narrowly, and almost universally refused on technical grounds to hear cases like the Black Hills claim based on fraud, duress, mistake of fact, or other questions of treaty validity. The court dismissed many other claims because of alleged flaws in congressional draftsmanship. The cost in time, money, and frustration argued strongly for a general and more effective tribunal for Indian cases.

Congress had considered the commission idea for years, the first bill having been introduced in 1935. By 1940, the need was so commonly admitted that both the Democratic and Republican party platforms endorsed the idea. But Pearl Harbor intervened to postpone enactment of legislation that might have resulted in large nonwar expenditures.

When debate over the commission resumed in 1945, the record of Indian wartime patriotism figured prominently. Once again the country's native minority had contributed to the nation's service far out of proportion to its numbers; once again Indians had purchased war bonds in a measure wholly disproportionate to their means; once again they had won a dazzling number of decorations for valor and sacrifice. The claims commission, like citizenship after the last great war, seemed an appropriate expression of national gratitude.

That conservatives and liberals alike found merit in the bill was reflected in the hybrid report that the House committee submitted after approving its version in December 1945. Congressional conservatives, following the intellectual tradition of the nineteenth-century reformers, supported the commission chiefly as a faster means of resolving the exaggerated but symbolically powerful tribal grievances which caused "persons of Indian blood . . . to cling to tribal associations" and resist assimilation into the mainstream of American life. To the Indian New Dealers, whose program was explicitly designed to foster that tribalism, the commission would redress a lasting discrimination and finally accord Indians the same access to America's judicial system available to other citizens. With such broad and bipartisan support, passage of the claims commission bill was certain, but when Congress enacted the enabling legislation in the summer of 1946, it remained unclear which approach to Indian policy would guide the commission's work.

On August 15, 1946, President Harry Truman, whose liberal domestic program promised a "fair deal" to all Americans, signed the Indian Claims Commission (ICC) Act. Truman's accompanying speech could just as well have commemorated many of the programs previously promoted as panaceas to the age-old Indian problem. Like the Dawes Act, the citizenship act, and the Indian Reorganization Act before it, the claims bill, in the President's words, would begin "a new era" for Indian citizens. The work of the commission would permit Indians "to take their place without special handicap or special advantage in the economic life of our nation and share fully in its programs."

However facile the President's rhetoric, no one could doubt the unprecedented scope of the new tribunal's authority, a grant of power engineered in large part by the commission's most brilliant and persistent advocate, the assistant solicitor of the Interior Department and close associate of Collier, Felix Cohen. The son of the famous philosopher Morris Raphael Cohen, Felix Cohen held a law degree from Columbia University and a doctorate in Philosophy from Harvard (both earned by the age of 24). A thinker and writer of enormous creativity and power, Cohen was the nation's foremost expert on Indian law. His *Handbook of Federal Indian Law*, published in 1942, codified for the first time the thousands of treaties, statutes, judicial decisions, and administrative regulations that governed the relationship between Indians and the United States. Cohen's blend of history, politics, morality, and law became, and has remained, the deepest reservoir of knowledge in its field and the bible of Indian rights advocates.

Cohen's vision of the claims commission transcended traditional notions about creating a new court. To provide meaningful compensation, Cohen believed, the commission would need broad extrajudicial powers to fashion creative solutions to the time-encrusted tribal claims. Drafting and redrafting the act, defending unique features against the limiting efforts of congressional conservatives, Cohen guided the lawmakers into passing a bill that at least in its terms held the prospect of extraordinary remedial power.

In addition to granting jurisdiction over customary suits in law and equity, Congress authorized the commission to hear two special categories of cases: first, "claims which would result if the treaties, contracts and agreements between the claimant and the United States were revised on the ground of fraud, duress, unconscionable consideration, mutual or unilateral mistake, whether of law or fact, or any other ground cognizable by a court of equity"; and second, "claims based upon fair and honorable dealings that are not recognized by any rule of law or equity." The claims commission act also provided for an "Investigation Division" to assist tribes in compiling evidence for their claims.

In plainer terms, Congress empowered the commission to look

at the history of American expansion not only as it had actually occurred but also as it *ought* to have occurred. The commission could reach back in history and rewrite treaties as a "fair and honorable" nation would have written them originally—and then pay in coin for the moral and legal failings of America's Indian policy. In theory, no forum had ever provided a better opportunity to recover for government wrongs. And no tribe considered itself more in need of such historical readjustment than the Sioux.

Out on the reservation, the creation of the commission set off a frenzy of hope within the rival claims organizations. The old dealer councils, who persistently maintained that the 1868 treaty (not the IRA) should govern relations between the Sioux and the United States, still considered claims matters to be their special province. Although legally powerless under the IRA (which vested all tribal authority in the elected tribal councils), the old dealer leaders demanded that the government resolve tribal claims through direct negotiations with them, just as the government had negotiated with their ancestor chiefs in the treaty days. As word spread of the new commission, the old dealers began meeting regularly again to assert their special interest in the cherished Black Hills claim.

William Fills the Pipe, chairman of the Black Hills Treaty and Claims Council—an old dealer group based on Pine Ridge—was the first to contact Case. Fills the Pipe wanted to know when the commissioners planned to visit Sioux country and fix things up as in the old treaty days. Over at Rosebud, traditional Sioux under the leadership of Daniel Thick Bread and Isaac Bear organized a new claims group, the American Sioux Treaty Claim Council, founded explicitly to oppose the more established and relatively more progressive Black Hills Sioux Nation Council. Ten years of tribal government under the auspices of the IRA had done nothing to unify Sioux politics or to quiet the sniping between old and new deal factions.

Late in October 1947, the Black Hills Sioux Nation Council, with representatives from all the reservations, met at Santee to revel in the prospect of refiling the Black Hills claim and to review the existing attorney contracts with Ralph Case. Recognizing the importance of the meeting, Case wrote an open letter to the council, recalling his long history of service to the tribe dating back to "that long night session" in 1911 when the old Black Hills Council had told him their story by lantern light. Case glossed over the fact that in the interim the Sioux had lost eighteen of the twenty-four claims he had filed for them in 1923 and that the final six were on appeal from dismissals.

Whomever or whatever the Sioux blamed for their consistent failure in court, though, it was not Case, their old comrade in the struggle. With little debate, Case's friends at Santee tendered him a vote of confidence and appreciation for his "considerable services" and recommended swift acceptance of the new attorney contracts Case had drafted for the separate tribal councils.

Twenty-five years of frustration and defeat had not dulled Case's enthusiasm for resuming the Black Hills quest, nor had it tempered the sentimentality that colored his commitment to the Sioux cause. "I here renew and restate the promise I made in September 1911," he wrote Black Hills Sioux Nation Council President James Roan Eagle, "[and also] the pledge I made in June of 1923 . . . on Rosebud Reservation. Quoting himself, he wrote:

> I will give my best endeavor to the just cause of the Sioux people against the United States arising out of their treaties and the laws of Congress. I will persevere in this work until the rights of the Sioux people are established. I will stay with you until the end of the trail.

The promise was noble, but the new route of the claims trail kept getting longer and more arduous. Despite the endorsement of the Black Hills Sioux Nation Council, collecting signed contracts from the eight often ineffectual IRA tribal councils was unexpectedly difficult and time-consuming. Case liked to joke that the Sioux were always slow when it came to the claim—something they had learned from the government. The truth was less humorous and more threatening. The creation of the claims commission, with the prospect of large legal fees, spawned renewed interest among lawyers in Indian work. Several made forays onto the reservation and found an audience among the ever-squabbling Sioux. On several reservations, anti-Case factions developed—often led by old-timers like Ben American Horse on Pine Ridge, who apparently resented the fact that Case considered the IRA tribal councils to be the only authoritative governments in Sioux country.

Somewhere on Standing Rock the rumor started that Case had been illegally charging the Sioux $6,000 a year for his services. Percy Tibbets, secretary of what he called the "Claims Council," couldn't believe it, but still wrote Case for reassurance. "I wonder if there has not been misunderstanding on both parties of the Black Hills contract," Tibbets concluded. "I wish you could answer me right away on this because it means a lot to us."

Forty thousand dollars in debt, Case no doubt wished the story were true, but with only a hint of indignation he set the record straight. He had not received a penny for filing and arguing all the claims and he would not "until and unless [he made] a recovery for the Sioux people."

Early in 1949, the Supreme Court refused to hear appeals from the last six cases filed under the original jurisdictional act, adding painful legitimacy to Case's critics and foreclosing the possibility that the lawyer's finances would improve any time soon. Having been decided on the merits (as opposed to jurisdictional grounds) in the Court of Claims, these cases, and all the other cases except for the Black Hills claim, were ineligible for resubmission to the new commission. They were lost forever, establishing as a matter of legal history that the schools and the cows and the tools and the seeds and the rations and the annuities had all been delivered in full supply; and that the childhood memories of the old men, the nightmare tales of dark days and killing winters, presumably were all false.

The Court of Claims decided in the 1889 treaty case that the government had shortchanged the Sioux by $5 million in its management of land sales arising out of "Crook's Treaty." But the court wiped out the award by setting off against it over $8 million in government "benefit payments" to the tribe—setoffs the 1920 jurisdictional act explicitly authorized.

Daniel Thick Bread did not understand how the $5 million could have vanished so easily. He assumed that the Sioux must have lent it to the government during the war—a legend that still persists among some traditionals today. "Well the war is over," Thick Bread reminded Case, "and we hear nothing more about our money."

Despite the detracting voices, Case was never in serious danger of losing the Black Hills contracts. The Oglala (Pine Ridge) Tribal Council hired Felix Cohen, who had retired from government, to do their nonclaims legal work, such as advising the tribe in its myriad dealings with the Indian Bureau. Standing Rock hired another Washington-based attorney, James Curry, for the same purpose. But the Black Hills claim and Ralph Case were virtually inseparable in the minds of the Sioux. He had heard their history of grievance from the old chiefs themselves. And the sons and the sons of sons, though shaken in faith, still looked to Young Spotted Tail for the white man's justice.

By the end of 1949, all eight tribal councils had signed the appropriate papers and sent them to Washington, where the Bureau of

Indian Affairs, which still retained the power of final approval, supposedly stood ready to protect the Sioux against unscrupulous or incompetent counsel. After cosmetic changes in the contracts, the bureau certified Case to prosecute the oldest and largest claim in American history. Unversed in the ways of the law, unable to judge for themselves the quality of their representation, unaided by the bureaucracy that supervised their choice, the Sioux once more surrendered their legal fate to the man whom, if nothing else, they knew to be their friend and impassioned champion.

Case was working alone now. James Ivins and Richard Barker, though outlasting Brewster, had returned to tax work after the last of the original claims was lost. For a while, Case cast about for a new patron to underwrite the costs of the new litigation, but he found no takers. His only apparent income came from raising jonquils in his backyard and selling them to a local florist; he must have been borrowing heavily from his son, who had become a successful lawyer in Baltimore.

Returning to work on the claim, most Sundays Case would ruminate upstairs in the study of his Maryland home, surrounded by huge bookcases filled with Indian memorabilia. For hours Case would sit at his desk, casting glances at the headdress of 100 eagle feathers that an old Sioux had given him years before, drinking himself into melancholy and dreaming about winning the claim. He was seventy years old and he would have to win it soon.

The old men on the reservation shared Case's fear of a long litigation. They also wanted to make sure Case filed every conceivable grievance that they had against the government before the commission's five-year time limit elapsed. William Hawk wrote Case again, this time asking whether he could sue the U.S. "for wounding my uncle, Mr. Gall, at the Little Big Horn." But a world of difference separated the claims that the Sioux wanted to file and those that American law might conceivably recognize. To Mr. Hawk and many others who wrote, Case dutifully replied that there were some claims even the new commission would not hear.

The sense of urgency with which the Sioux, especially the old-timers, pursued their claims was made even more poignant by the imminent threat of a new land seizure. As if to confirm the common reservation view that the history of Sioux–government relations was little more than a tale of tribal dispossession, in 1947 the Indian Bureau advised the Sioux that Congress had authorized the construction of a series of dams across the Missouri River up and down the eastern edge of Sioux country. Upon completion, this "Oahe Project" would flood over 220,000 acres on the Standing

Rock, Cheyenne River, Crow Creek, and Lower Brûlé reservations.

No one on the Sioux reservations had even heard of Oahe until three years after its passage, but once informed it took but a second to figure out not only that the dams would deprive them of another huge portion of what precious little tribal land they had left, but also that the lands to be inundated—the Missouri river bottom lands—were by far the finest in Sioux country. Those lands were vital to new cattle-raising programs on Standing Rock and Cheyenne River. They provided winter shelter for over 10,000 head of cattle—roughly 40 percent of the stock on the two reservations. The fertile soil, practically the only fertile soil the Sioux still owned, yielded almost 90 percent of the timber for the affected reservations, as well as thousands of quarts of currants, grapes, and wild chokecherries every year.

In human terms, the disruption of life would be catastrophic. Hundreds of families, whole communities, were to be uprooted and moved west. On Standing Rock and Cheyenne River the floodwaters would force 20 percent of the population to resettle. Years later, a visitor to Cheyenne River wondered why there were so few elders on the reservation. Residents explained that "the old people had died of heartache" after losing their homes.

To Case, the Oahe landtaking was Black Hills history repeating itself seventy-five years later, except that this time the Sioux would have legal representation in determining what compensation the government would pay for its acts. After almost a decade of negotiation with Case and other lawyers (Case represented only the Cheyenne River Sioux in this matter), the government would pay for the Oahe flood plain—in all a sum of roughly $12.5 million. Despite the money, to the Sioux it still seemed that little had changed from the old treaty days when the whites took their land in exchange for a paper promising them a better life.

"This time . . . we shall have full and just compensation, together with a complete plan for the re-establishment and rehabilitation of the Sioux people," Case had assured his clients when he embarked on the Oahe negotiations. The Sioux had heard such optimism all along the downward spiral of the last century, not least at the dusty convocations in the summer of 1876 when government agents deprived them of their Hills. By Sioux reckoning, the tide of adversity was already several generations late in changing direction. Still, as the cherished Black Hills claim came before a new tribunal, the extravagant hope lingered, especially among the old-timers, that Sioux fortunes might shift at last.

On August 15, 1950, seventy-four years to the day after Congress authorized the Manypenny commission to obtain the Black Hills, Case filed the Sioux claim with the Indian Claims Commission. He did not have to remind the Indians of his basic argument. His vision of Sioux history—set down over a decade before in two tomes of narrative and oral testimony—had become sacred among his clients. At old-timer claims meetings, Case's books were given the reverence of holy texts, constituting as they did the one indelible record of a history otherwise at the mercy of frail oral tradition. Even today the yellowed pages of Case's documentary have magic authority for those few who still possess them.

Once more for the commission, Case culled from these pages the historical basis of his legal claim: the treaties and the gold strikes, the invasions of Sioux country, and the failed negotiations of 1875 and 1876 for a sale or lease of the Black Hills. Case's allegations had not changed: "by force, coercion, duress and gross intimidation," the United States had tried to convince the Sioux to sign away their treaty lands. Failing that, the government had simply taken what it could not buy. The act of February 28, 1877, Case argued, gave the Indians nothing more than a promise in exchange for "the richest 100 square miles in the world. . . . That Act is a unilateral declaration in which the plaintiff Indians had no part, have never had any part and now have no part. This is not compensation, it is confiscation."

Of the thirty-five-page petition, only the last two pages set out the Indians' proposed theory of recovery. Case abandoned the Fifth Amendment theory he had advanced in the Court of Claims. Instead, echoing the charter language of the new commission, and invoking its power to rewrite history, Case demanded compensation "on the basis of fair and honorable dealings," a standard which in his view entitled the Sioux to "a reasonable portion" of the value of the minerals extracted from the Hills, a royalty on the timber stumpage, as well as payment for the farming and grazing lands and for the Indians' abrogated hunting rights.

Case refrained from even guessing what "a fair and reasonable per cent" of the gold, silver, and other minerals extracted after 1877 would amount to, or from specifying the "continuing royalty" to which he claimed his clients were entitled. He did fix $2.50 per acre plus interest as an estimated minimum payment for the timber taken from the Class A (Black Hills) lands; he also claimed "at least" 50¢ per acre for the Class B lands (25,858,594.95 acres of unceded Indian country under the 1868 treaty) and 10¢ per acre for the Class C lands (40,578,123.25 acres of hunting lands under the 1868 treaty).

Case avoided any discussion of what legal theory supported a Sioux claim for royalties, a novel formula for recovery in Indian land claims or any just compensation case. And he offered no clues about where he obtained his figures for timber payments and land values. Once again, the bulk of Case's argument was his personal view of Sioux–government relations—excerpted, abbreviated, and already once rejected by the Court of Claims. The Sioux had a history to make men weep, but Case's task was not merely to outline his clients' past, it was to mold that past to the law—with precedents and evidence. As from the beginning, Case was too much his clients' spokesman, too little their counsel.

At the Justice Department, the chief of the claims section, Ralph Barney, referred Case's Sioux petition to Maurice Cooperman, who had replaced the deceased George Stormont as lead government attorney for Indian land claims. Borrowing extensively from Stormont's filings in the Court of Claims, Cooperman flatly denied Case's charges of government fraud, duress, and misappropriation. Cooperman countered with the by-now standard recitation of governmental good faith and substantial compliance with the 1868 treaty. If miners had illegally invaded Sioux country in 1875, the cause, Cooperman asserted, was not government complicity but the utter impossibility of keeping miners out. If the army had invaded Sioux country in 1876, the cause was not Black Hills gold, but unruly Sioux bands under Crazy Horse and Sitting Bull who raided frontier settlements. If the 1876 Manypenny agreement had not been properly ratified by three-quarters of the adult Sioux males, the cause was not government impropriety but the fact that the chiefs and headmen signed as representatives of their bands. All told, the government had expended more than $50 million for the benefit of the Sioux in compliance with the 1877 act. That, Cooperman argued (turning Case's rhetoric around), was not confiscation; it was compensation.

Cooperman also reiterated the government's old defense that the agreement of 1889, properly ratified by three-fourths of the adult Sioux males, had disposed of any legal claims the tribe might have had arising out of the 1877 act. Even if the commission ruled that the U.S. had misappropriated millions of acres of Sioux land, Cooperman contended that by signing the 1889 agreement the Sioux had waived any right to compensation for the Black Hills and other past landtakings.

As a last defense, mentioned almost in passing, Cooperman argued that the Court of Claims decision in 1942 already had settled the legal and factual issues now raised before the commission and that the Sioux, having had their day in court, had no right to relitigate their moribund claims. In the technical language of law, the government argued that the Black Hills claim was *res judicata*—a matter already adjudicated and not triable again.

The validity of this *res judicata* defense rested on an interpretation of Judge Littleton's tortured and ambiguous 1942 decision. If, as the government now asserted, the Court of Claims had rejected the original Sioux claim on its merits, then the claims commission was bound by that ruling at least with respect to the issues that the 1942 court had addressed. If, on the other hand, the Court of Claims had found itself *without jurisdiction*—without the authority to decide the merits—then the commission could proceed unencumbered. Given Judge Littleton's failure to articulate a discernible rationale for the Court's decision, the *res judicata* defense offered the commission easily justifiable grounds to avoid deciding a claim that could conceivably cost the U.S. Treasury nearly $1 billion. Cooperman quietly, unobtrusively, opened this door.

The commission scheduled the Black Hills trial for March 24, 1952, over a year after the completion of Cooperman's reply brief. In the interim, the Sioux began thinking (and disputing) again about how they would divide up their judgment money. Joseph Thin Elk, chairman of one of the old-dealer councils, asked Case about drafting a "final enrollment" bill to narrow the number of eligible tribal members and cut out the mixed bloods. Case suggested diplomatically that the enrollment question should wait until the claim was won.

About the same time, the Black Hills Sioux Nation Council decided that the tribe should pursue additional avenues of possible redress. At its meeting held in October 1950, the assembled council delegates, perhaps reflecting an incipient sense of sovereignty or nationhood, resolved to send a delegation to the United Nations to present the tribe's claims. Frank Ducheneaux, the Cheyenne River chairman, skeptically reported the vote to Case: "Where they got the idea that they could hope to be heard in the U.N., or what they expect to accomplish, if by some miracle they do get a hearing, is a mystery to me." In any event, the delegation never materialized.

The trial before the ICC convened as scheduled at 10:00 A.M. on March 24 in Room 778 of the Federal Trade Commission building—a back room, in a small agency not far from the White House. To a cynic, the musty chamber symbolized the glaring contrast between the ambitious agenda and the paltry resources that marked America's Indian policy. The three commissioners, Edgar Witt, Louis O'Marr, and William Holt, presiding at the front of the room, reinforced this impression. They were patronage appointees. Witt and Holt were holdovers from the Mexican Land Commission, which had just finished settling disputes in the Southwest. O'Marr was a former grocer and small-town Wyoming lawyer, elected state attorney general in 1943. None of the new commissioners possessed any special expertise in legal theory or Indian affairs.

Dispensing with the formal trappings of a court session, Chief Commissioner Witt opened the session asking the opposing counsel which side would "bat" first. Getting no response, he summoned Case to the batter's box: "Well, I guess you're it."

Whatever Case was up to in the year preceeding the trial, it certainly did not involve the preparation of evidence. After almost thirty years, presenting an unprecedented claim that had become a desperate life's work, Case introduced only seven exhibits. Six of these were stale reprints of excerpts from the record in the Court of Claims: parts of the original government accounting, Case's Statement of Facts and the Sioux testimony from 1923. The lone new exhibit consisted of a transcript of the record accompanying Case's petition for a writ of *certiorari* filed with the Supreme Court in 1943.

The entire trial lasted barely two hours. Case filled the first forty-five minutes with his familiar recitation of broken promises and vicious threats by the government as well as the stubborn resistance of the Sioux. In the telling, Case lost most if not all of the real tragedy and grief of his clients' story. His folksy South Dakota manner had some rich feeling to it, but he rambled and wandered through the chronology, stumbling from one anecdote to another. "One of my major faults," he admitted early in his argument, "is to go into too much detail." Really Case's problem was not too much detail, but that his detail lacked a legal compass. As a consequence, the potentially vivid story of government treatybreaking got lost in a morass of facts about military maneuvers, weather conditions, topography and, not least, the history of the Black Hills claim itself.

The pressure of the moment revealed a curious division of loyalty within the Sioux attorney. Often during his presentation, he would refer to actions of the U.S. Government using the word "we": "we" did this or that. It was as though Case, an army veteran born on the frontier, shouldered a personal guilt for his nation's history that he wanted the commission to absolve.

Sheer incompetence, however, not divided loyalty, was the last-ing mark of Case's performance. The most astonishing and damag-ing error occurred as he sought to introduce an abbreviated ver-sion of his two-volume Statement of Facts resurrected from the Court of Claims record. The government asked for a clarification of issues:

MR. COOPERMAN: Your Honor, before ruling on that, may I suggest a definition of the issues so we will know to what this testimony is directed?

As you know, the petition covers three classes of lands. Class A lands are the Black Hills; Class B lands are the Fort Laramie lands outside the permanent reservations; and Class C lands are the hunting lands.

Now, as I understand it from Mr. Case, the claim is now restricted to the Black Hills and claims to the Fort Laramie and the hunting lands are no longer in there. Is that correct?

MR. CASE: Oh, I just do not know where you got that statement.

MR. COOPERMAN: You told us that back at the office, you said you had restricted it to claims to the Black Hills.

MR. CASE: I did, but that was a confidential matter and I told you that was to stay confidential. It was not to be used against me. I want to repeat what I said.

MR. COOPERMAN: I understood—

MR. CASE: Now, just a moment. The conference that Mr. Cooperman and Mr. Barney and I had was an attempt to get at the expeditious solution of this particular matter. I will be just as frank with the Commission as I was with them.

The matter of the hunting rights that were in existence on February 28, 1877, which were taken from the Sioux, themselves were self-limit-ing by the treaty of 1868. That is to say, the Sioux could use that so long as the buffalo remained in numbers sufficient to justify the chase, that therefore being a self-limited right.

It is a matter of common knowledge that the big buffalo hunting ended not later than 1882, so that we had perhaps a 5-year period where the hunting right was still going and operating.

Now, frankly, I do not consider that to be a claim of the utmost value, but for Mr. Cooperman to interject and say there were three separate claims and that I had abandoned that, is quite in error. He should not have violated a confidence, I think, of that meeting, and I think Mr. Barney will bear me out. I did not expect that the government would take advantage of my frank statement to you, that I did not think the hunting claims amounted to a great deal.

May we have a five minute recess?

As the transcript reveals, in private conference with the government's counsel, without consulting or even notifying his clients, Case revealed his intention not to press Sioux claims to hunting and other rights in over 65 million acres of land. Case's clients did not consider their interest in the Class B and C lands to be "picayune," as their advocate told the commission. But the old Sioux men who sat silent, scattered in the back row chairs—perhaps half a dozen of the 35,000 heirs to the claim—did not understand what was being surrendered. They trusted Young Spotted Tail to do right.

After his introduction of evidence, Case rested the plaintiffs' case. Confident that Sioux testimony from 1923 coupled with testimony from a few geologists about Black Hills gold production established an irrefutable record of injustice, he called no witnesses.

Cooperman immediately moved for dismissal on the ground that Case, having neglected to submit any evidence on the value of the allegedly misappropriated lands, failed to establish a basis for claiming unconscionable consideration. The United States, Cooperman asserted, had paid the Sioux the equivalent of at least $50 million under Article 5 (the food and rations provision) of the 1877 act. Without knowing what the Sioux lands were worth, how could the commission evaluate the "conscionability" of this consideration?

Witt agreed. "What is it that the Commission has before it today on which the Commission could arrive at a dollars and cents value or award to be made?" he challenged Case.

Case would not answer. To him the question of value was entirely separate from the question of whether the Sioux had a right to recover. He simply refused to recognize that a right to recover based on unconscionable consideration required a showing that the value of the land at the time of its taking was substantially greater than the value of the compensation paid.

Besides, Case argued, the Sioux claim did not rest only on grounds of unconscionable consideration. The government's unjust and unlawful treatment of the Sioux, irrespective of 1877 land values, brought their claim within the "fair and honorable dealings" clause of the ICC Act, authorizing the commission to pay compensation for claims not recognized under ordinary rules of law or equity.

Although skeptical, the commission concluded that Case might have alleged one plausible ground for the Sioux claim. It denied the government's motion to dismiss and recessed for lunch.

During the afternoon session, Case fared little better. Cooperman presented the government's case, supported by thirty-seven exhibits, including Judge Littleton's 1942 opinion, aimed at proving that the U.S. had spent tens of millions of dollars supporting the Sioux in accordance with the 1877 act.

With the government having introduced uncontroverted evidence that it paid substantial consideration for the appropriated Sioux lands, the commission returned to Case and to the issue of land value. During the lunch break, Case apparently had decided on a strategy: to argue that, notwithstanding the government's purported expenditures under the 1877 act, the government had robbed the Sioux shamelessly. To Case, the proof was obvious. It would be "a very simple matter for us to show that . . . gold production from the beginning up to now has been better than $750,000,000 in raw gold."

But if Case expected his uncorroborated estimate of Black Hills gold production to establish a case of unconscionable consideration, O'Marr abruptly disappointed him. Gross mineral values, O'Marr interjected, "even if proven . . . would not prove the value of the land." Without evidence of production costs, raw mineral values provided "no proof whatsoever of the value of the land at the time it was taken."

Although the commission did not reconsider its denial of the government's motion to dismiss the claim outright, O'Marr and Witt wondered aloud whether Case had advanced a single tenable ground for recovery. O'Marr finally suggested that Case amend his original petition to set forth a theory of the claim that did not depend on land value or, alternatively, to offer relevant evidence of value.

Case asked the commission to wait for his next brief; "then if we don't make our showing, well and good." The commission agreed and adjourned.

Almost four months later, on July 15, Case submitted a new brief including "Plaintiff's Proposed Findings of Fact"—the Sioux version of history entitling the tribe to a legal judgment. Once again Case excerpted the testimony from 1923, the voices of the daunted and deceived, conjuring up the bloody plains of Red Cloud and Crazy Horse, the threats and promises of the treaty men. Not one sentence of the brief mentioned land values. For Case the path of justice remained uncluttered with the technicalities of proof. "These people [the Sioux] are worthy of belief," he concluded. Their words were evidence enough.

The government did not bother with a formal reply. Because it contained no evidence of the 1877 value of the Black Hills, Cooperman found nothing in Case's brief for the government to answer.

Neither did the commissioners. On December 15, they summoned Case and Cooperman for a status conference. Apparently anxious to avoid throwing out the historic claim, the commission undertook to intruct Case in how he should proceed, again admonishing him to introduce evidence of 1877 land value if he wanted to establish his claim that the compensation paid to the Sioux was unconscionable. To that end, the commission permitted Case to reopen the record for the purpose of introducing additional evidence of land value.

But what Case intended to produce as evidence of land value still differed radically from what the commission expected. On February 23, 1953, Case and Cooperman met with the commission again. As recounted in his office diary, Case announced that his forthcoming brief would ask the commission "to decide the claim as though the Act [of 1877] . . . was written on the basis of fair and honorable dealings to provide for an annual royalty on gold and other minerals, a stumpage rate on timber out in the Black Hills and an annual rental for farming and grazing lands." Case's alternate plan was to propose a lump sum recovery for the Sioux "somewhere between the [Allison commission's] offer of six million and the Indians' offer of seventy millions for the right of mine in the Black Hills. . . ." According to Case's record, he not once mentioned additional evidence of 1877 land value; instead, he informed the commission that, if necessary, he would produce evidence of annual mineral and timber revenues after 1877.

In Case's view, proceeding on the commission's suggested valuation theory (based on the 1877 value of the Hills) would be fatal to the Sioux claim. As a practical matter, he believed that unless he fashioned a theory of recovery based on the value of the incredible mineral wealth extracted from the Black Hills *after* 1877, the Sioux had no chance of obtaining a sizable judgment for the seizure of the Hills. The only way to argue that the Sioux received unconscionable consideration for what the Black Hills were worth *in* 1877 was to challenge the government's $57 million of claimed expenditures under the 1877 act. But to challenge the government's figures would have entailed years of intensive legal work and delay: a scrupulous accounting to determine exactly how much money (in 1877 dollars) the government had spent under the

1877 act as well as a careful determination of 1877 Black Hills land values. This prospect held no appeal at all for a seventy-three-year-old lawyer already thirty years on the quest.

Case admitted as much in his 1952 annual report to his clients. He was seeking "a quick solution to the Black Hills claim," which in practice meant conceding all the government's claimed expenditures and ignoring the commission's demands for evidence of 1877 land values.

On June 19, 1953, Case filed an "Intermediate Brief," pinning Sioux hopes on a novel legal theory taking advantage of all the gold that whites had taken from the Black Hills. Under Case's newly minted view of the law, the Black Hills taking was not an ordinary governmental seizure of property but rather involved the violation of a "trust relationship" between the United States and the Sioux. Drawing on an analogy first suggested by Chief Justice John Marshall in the *Cherokee Cases* of the 1830s and borrowing from the political rhetoric associated with Indian policy throughout the nineteenth century, Case argued that the legal relationship between the Sioux and the United States was one of ward to guardian.

According to Case, this trust relationship imposed special responsibilities on the government and, specifically, entitled the Sioux to a wholly different type of recovery for its guardian's usurpation of tribal lands. While recovery in a run-of-the-mill land seizure case might be based on the difference between the value of the land at the time of its taking and the compensation actually paid, recovery for a guardian's misappropriation of its ward's property should be based not on outdated land values but on what the ward (the Sioux) would have earned from the land had the government lived up to its trust responsibility and held the land faithfully for the tribe.

Applying this theory, Case reasoned that the Sioux were entitled to a royalty from all mineral and timber revenues generated in the Black Hills as well as a rental fee for the Hills and the other lands. Case calculated that the Black Hills had yielded more than $600 million in gold revenues alone since 1877 (and continued to yield over $16 million annually). Adding silver, timber, and other assets, Case alleged that the government and private white owners had reaped $696,120,082 in gross revenues from the Hills.

Assuming (as he did without citing any authority) that the Sioux were entitled to the "standard" one-eighth mineral royalty, Case argued that the tribe would have received an $87 million share of the mineral wealth taken from the Hills had the government lived up to its trust responsibility. Adding to that a 5¢ per acre rental charge for the Class A lands and a 1¢ per acre charge of six years' duration for the Class B and C lands, Case reached a bottom-line figure of $118,912,809 for the consideration that the Sioux should have received under the 1877 act. Thus, even accepting as valid all $57 million in expenditures claimed by the government—which, significantly, Case now conceded on the record—the U.S. had shortchanged the Sioux by at least $62 million.

Dollar figures aside, Case also argued that the consideration the government provided for the Black Hills under the 1877 act was unconscionable because it had failed to fulfill its promise to civilize and educate the Sioux. While the government provided a "little red school house" for white children, Case declared, it provided no school house at all for the Sioux. At best, government efforts to civilize and assimilate the Sioux under the 1877 act were "like a bridge built halfway across a ravine or a dam built a halfway across a river." These halfway measures had relegated the Sioux to "near last place in the economic struggle." This was living proof that the compensation paid was unconscionable.

As a "fair and reasonable" remedy for his country's misdeeds—and for all that had happened to the Sioux since the buffalo vanished—Case called upon the commission to use its broad powers "to hear claims which would result if treaties . . . were revised." Case urged the commission to rewrite the 1877 act retroactively, as a fair and honorable nation would have written it originally. In lieu of the old Article 5 promising the Sioux rations and education, Case proposed a new Article (effective March 1, 1877) establishing a $40 million "Sioux Nation Interest Fund" by which the Sioux could support themselves. After a 100-year trust period (ending March 1, 1977), the fund would be dissolved and distributed among the Sioux people, who at long last would cease to be wards of the government.

To Case, the inherent justice (as well as convenience) of his legal theory and proposed remedy was self-evident. Calculating a Sioux award on the basis of 1877 land values—when the extent of the Black Hills gold field was still largely speculative—would deprive the tribe of the true value of what it had lost and would permit the government and white miners to reap an enormous windfall. What Case proposed instead was rough justice, a compromise between Senator Allison's $6 million offer for the Hills and the $70 million dollar counteroffer proposed by some of the Sioux chiefs.

After a fashion, Case's solution reflected one strand of Sioux oral tradition about the claim. From the earliest days of the old claims councils, the Indians had talked about getting something for all the Black Hills gold. Whatever the written terms of the 1877 act, many Sioux believed that the government had promised them half the Black Hills gold. The Homestake Mine had turned out to be one of the richest in the western world and was still producing, having already yielded a fortune to the Hearst family. Why should the Sioux lose all claim to this gold simply because the government illegally took their land before its full value was known?

Case pointed out the benefits that would accrue to both sides from his improvised solution. By settling the largest and longest-running Indian claim, and by establishing a self-sustaining economic foundation for the Sioux, the treaty revision would not only cleanse the national conscience but also save the government money in the long run. And it would redeem the United States in the eyes of the world. "Even the late unlamented Adolf Hitler," Case reminded the commission, "denounced the United States for its hypocrisy in defending minority groups abroad while we robbed the Indians at home."

Case professed that he simply lacked the vocabulary to describe Sioux feelings on the subject. He could say only that rewriting the treaty, restoring the tribe to its station as a free and independent people, would mean to the Sioux "a thousand fold what Lincoln's Emancipation Proclamation meant to the negro race."

The brief was quintessential Case, a tragic combination of passionate commitment and unlawyerly argument. It entirely disregarded the complexities of valuation—the costs of production and the risks of investment—as well as the commission's explicit instruction that unconscionable consideration could be measured *only* against the value of the property at the time of its taking. What arguments Case did advance were completely bereft of legal analysis. The brief cited no cases directly supporting its essential premise that the relationship between the U.S. and the Sioux was that of guardian to ward. (In the *Cherokee Cases*, Justice Marshall had written only that Indian tribes were "domestic dependent nations" whose relationship to the United States "resembled" that of ward to guardian).

What the brief contained instead, however ill-placed, was a zealous care for the Sioux and for justice, a quixotic stab at an instant resolution to the claim and his clients' destitution. Taken as a whole, the brief was hardly a legal argument at all; it was an appeal to conscience, an appeal to resolve the thirty years of judicial deadlock not according to legal principles and precedent, but according to basic notions of fairness.

Case never seems to have appreciated that the creation of the commission, though in part a reflection of national conscience, was not an admission of guilt by the United States. Every suggestion in Case's brief, every rationale, followed from his abiding belief that the government, even the Justice Department that had checked him at every turn since the claim began, would recognize the righteousness of his clients' cause and agree to a "fair" settlement for the sins of conquest. But the act creating the commission (which was supported by many representatives in order to dispense with what they considered to be exaggerated tribal claims) did not establish a board of arbitration before which the government would be expected to settle claims. Rather, the ICC Act had created an adversarial process to test the nation's guilt and, in some cases, to absolve it of wrongdoing.

Unwavering in its opposition to the Sioux claim, in late July the Justice Department filed its response to Case's intermediate brief. Again, Cooperman argued that the gross value of minerals extracted from the Black Hills was "a fundamentally unsound and judicially repudiated method of valuation." In contrast to Case, Cooperman cited numerous cases supporting his argument.

Cooperman's refusal to acknowledge the merit of the Sioux claim rankled Case. With a hint of betrayal, he reported to his clients that the government lawyers were not principally concerned with justice. Cooperman's effort to treat the Sioux claim "as a simple taking of land" was, Case told his clients, "simply an effort by the Attorney General to avoid paying anything at all."

Case's private writings revealed a different frustration, a sense that his time was growing short, while the prospect of victory remained hidden around blind corners. With every passing year, the memory of his defeats washed over Case in waves of reminiscence, eroding his once firm self-esteem as champion of a beleaguered people, revealing a growing concern with death and defeat. As he was preparing his intermediate brief, Case responded to a letter he had received from Nella McGregor, the widow of the bureau superintendent at Pine Ridge in the 1920s.

> Your letter to me of May 7th, 1953, was written thirty years to the day from the date I filed the Sioux Petition in the U.S. Court of Claims. It happens also to be the anniversary of the Sinking of the Lusitania in 1915, and also is VE Day 1945. Of all the anniversaries, to me the most important is the day I started the tremendous burden of work, which is still with me. . . .

I wonder if you remember the Black Hills banquet that your good husband arranged for me at Rosebud in 1923 or it may have been 1924. I remember his very complimentary remarks regarding me, in which he said I was the Moses who had come to lead the Sioux out of the wilderness into the promised land. I replied to him in a rather light mood saying that my origin was not semitic. Also that it took Moses forty years to do the job and worse than that he died on the way. Well my origin hasn't changed, but I have spent thirty years on the job and haven't gotten the boys and girls out of the wilderness yet. The prospects are fairly good at my age that if it takes forty years, I will be among those absent when the Sioux get into the promised land. It begins to look as though he was, at that time, too right for comfort.

As his seventy-fourth birthday approached, Case arranged for his lawyer-son Richard to take over the claim in the event of death or disability. "Dad. . . . I consider these assignments of academic interest only," Richard responded filially. "No one is capable of bringing the Black Hills Case to a close but yourself."

Daily, the mail brought poignant reminders that Case, the claim, and his longtime Sioux friends had grown old and frail. A typical letter came from Joseph Eagle Hawk, eighty years old and blind, who wrote to thank Case for his continued work. Eagle Hawk had found someone to translate Case's latest brief for the old people of the White Clay district on Pine Ridge. "They all departed happy in their hearts and with great encouragement to us, I assure you."

"It is a very happy day when I have so fine a letter as the one you wrote me and which I am now looking at," Case replied. He remembered when Eagle Hawk's eyes were "as bright and clear as indicated by [his] name." Another year's wait, Case promised him; just another year.

John Cadotte, a friend of the now-deceased William Hawk, ancient himself, sent a letter invoking one of Case's Sioux names, *Ohiya*. Case took pride in that cradle name—Conqueror of All Enemies. But the irony must have hurt.

James Ivins sent Case a postcard from Florida announcing his retirement:

Before the Indian Claims Commission was created, and we made our last stand in the Supreme Court, you remarked, "If we win we can quit and go fishing, if we lose we won't have anything else to do so we might as well quit and go fishing."

I am quitting and going fishing.

I see by the papers that you stand a chance of getting something respectable out of the Sioux case in the Claims Commission. If you do, come down and go fishing with me.

Case didn't think he would make it south for the fishing. He wasn't thinking about retirement. He was thinking about writing his memoirs. "When this thirty odd years of battling (maybe it will be forty years of battling) is over I have a plan to write the story of the Black Hills claim," he confessed to Bob Lee, an old friend and well-disposed journalist at the *Rapid City Journal*. "I would, of course, need someone to work with and I know of no man better fitted than you are to undertake a job of that kind and do it well. . . . That way the job might be finished before I pass on to the Happy Hunting Ground."

On April 5, 1954, the commission dismissed the Black Hills claim. Its "Findings of Fact and Opinion," the official legal version of Black Hills history, far from condemning the behavior of the government, practically commended President Grant and his advisers for doing "the best the Government could do in the circumstances." According to the commission:

> The negotiations over the years with the Indians showed a strenuously sincere effort on the part of the defendant Government to reach a fair basis of cession of the gold and silver producing lands. . . . It was a practical necessity that the lands be acquired by the defendant and made available to the white miners, and doubtless the economy of the country was taken into consideration in the need of gold and silver bullion. These considerations together with the further fact that the Indians needed protection not only against hostilities and their resulting bloodshed, but also from starvation by reason of lack of food—the wild life of the regions having at this time almost disappeared—made the acquisition of the mineral lands and the payment of a fair compensation to the Indians therefore an absolute necessity—as much in the Indians' own interest as for any other reason.

The commission especially emphasized the government's decision to feed the Sioux "gratuitously" during the years 1873–76, from the expiration of the 1868 treaty's four-year rations provision until the Manypenny commission offered the Sioux the choice to sell the Hills or starve. To the commission, Manypenny's conditional offer to feed the starving Indians was not extortion but a fair bargain for both sides—a bargain of life for land. That the whites, by annihilating the buffalo, had created the tribe's dependence commanded no attention.

The commission neatly whitewashed the government's violation of the 1868 treaty's Article 12 signature requirement on the
familiar ground that the 10 percent of the Sioux males who did
sign included many chiefs and headmen. In other words, the commission exonerated the United States for violating a treaty provision specifically intended to prevent tribal chiefs from signing
away the lands of their kinsmen, precisely because the United
States had obtained the signatures of the chiefs.

The commission sidestepped Case's guardian-ward legal theory.
Without deciding the issue, it concluded that, even if the government were guardian to the Sioux, Case had failed to demonstrate
the tribe's right to a judgment. Having introduced only evidence
of gross mineral values (taking no account of production costs or
the risk of investment), Case simply had not proved "that to have
gambled in 1877 on the prospective value of the mineral deposits
would be as safe a provision for the future subsistence of the
plaintiffs as the consideration provided for them by the Act of
Congress of 1877."

Several days passed before Case summoned the words to inform
his clients that they had lost yet again; that whatever they might
have heard from fathers and mothers, grandfathers and grand-
mothers, under the white man's law the Sioux had traded the Black
Hills for their lives, and that was fair.

Case wrote first to Frank Ducheneaux, chairman of the Cheyenne River Sioux tribal council, a savvy politician who, emulating
big-city machine politics, established a reservation dynasty
through the aggressive use of patronage and extended family ties.
Ducheneaux and Case had become close friends during negotiations over the Oahe Dam settlement. "I have a most unpleasant
duty this morning," Case began. The letter was cool and business-
like, mostly talk of forwarding copies of the opinion and deadlines
for appeal. Only towards the end did a bit of Case's usual optimism
shine through. "The decision dismissing the Black Hills Claim is
not final," he emphasized. "It is probable that the case will not be
concluded until it reaches the Supreme Court of the United
States."

Ducheneaux dutifully spread the word across Cheyenne River.
His tone, though disappointed, was not despairing. While Ducheneaux recognized the importance of the Black Hills claim to his
constituents, he himself had never wanted to win. In Ducheneaux's view, white guilt was the tribe's most powerful
weapon in new battles like his own to wrest as much autonomy as
possible from an often intransigent Indian Bureau, establish the

Sioux as a political force in South Dakota, and find an economic base for chronically impoverished reservations. He had no desire to see that weapon diminished by a successful resolution of the tribe's most compelling grievance.

Ducheneaux also knew well that for many in Sioux country, especially among the New Dealers, the prospect of winning the Black Hills claim had lost its foundation in genuine expectation. The timeworn ancient promise of future riches, though still an ever-present part of reservation life, lived on in many quarters mainly as wry Indian humor. "*Doxa* Black Hills"—"I'll pay you when I get my Black Hills money"—had become a standard reservation response to creditors.

Ducheneaux identified for his constituents the worst victim of the commission decision:

> This is indeed a sad day for us, but it is even worse for Mr. Case. He has given most of his life to the effort to win this case for us, and has served without pay of any kind for most of that time. . . .

> Most of us have grown up knowing about the Black Hills claim and after all these years it would have been nice to realize something from it, but we can be thankful that most of our older members who lived in hope of winning the case have not lived to see this day. It's hard for us to take, but it would have been much harder for them.

Those old Sioux who were still living, and other traditionals devoted to the claim, sent anxious letters to Case. Paul High Horse wrote in careful, labored script and broken English from the small Pine Ridge hamlet of Wanblee. His dead father had been a witness in the claim. High Horse knew from childhood stories that the Sioux had never sold the Black Hills. Now he had heard on the radio that the claim was dead. High Horse "still stood" for Case's last report (a description of the intermediate brief), regardless of the commission. Case had the story right.

Frank Shorthorn wrote from Gordon, Nebraska, a shack-town just off Pine Ridge named for a miner who had raided the Hills in 1875. A traditional leader, Shorthorn belonged to the old-dealer Black Hills Treaty and Claims Council, which still sought to negotiate with the United States as their ancestors had—with the Great Father himself or his agents. The council was circulating a petition on Pine Ridge addressed to "the President of the United States, Secretary of Interior, Commissioner of Indian Affairs, Senate and House Interior and Insular Affairs." Shorthorn did not tell Case what the petition requested, but his message was clear: the claim was lost again and these Sioux did not understand why.

Many Sioux attributed the commission decision to "politics," but when Case heard this talk he sent a letter to both the old deal and IRA councils insisting that politics had nothing to do with it. The commissioners were men of "high standards," Case told the Sioux, "not to be swayed in any decision by any political reason."

James Roan Eagle, an officer of the Black Hills Sioux Nation Council, tried to find another explanation. He wrote to Richard Schifter (a Felix Cohen protégé, who handled Pine Ridge's general counsel work) to obtain a copy of the commission's ruling and to suggest that Case might need the assistance of other lawyers. Schifter responded encouragingly, but Roan Eagle never followed up.

Ben American Horse and James Red Cloud, one the son of a chief, the other a grandson, traditional leaders in their own right, desperate for a way to help the cause, informed Case that they had circulated a petition requesting additional time in which to file an appeal. Case assured them that he had more than sufficient time.

Indeed, by the time he received the petition, Case already had moved for rehearing before the commission. Much as in the Court of Claims in 1942, Case's brief in support of rehearing consisted of little more than a rehash of unsuccessful contentions framed by expressions of shock and dismay at the dismissal of the claim. Once again Case recycled paragraphs from old briefs, reused stale metaphors like the "half-completed bridge," and rambled on in sentimental, but legally irrelevant, descriptions of Sioux poverty. Once again, he sounded like an American tourist in a foreign country unfamiliar with the native tongue. When the commission did not understand him the first time, he repeated himself, only louder.

He advanced one new idea which reflected his continuing faith that, someday, one branch of the government or another would arrange a just resolution to the claim. Disappointed that the Attorney General had adopted a policy against compromise settlements in Indian claims, Case asked the commission to direct the government to devise a "comprehensive plan for settlement of the matters now in issue." What prompted Case to believe that the commission possessed the extraordinary power to order "peace talks" will forever remain a mystery. The commission had no such power and Case's suggestion that it did was only further evidence that he was in no condition to continue to prosecute the claim.

Case's brief also formally admitted what had long since become evident, that he would not pursue the Class B and C land claims. In his view, "the proof requisite to establish the claims would cost plaintiff Indians more than the rights were worth." And so the Sioux, without their knowledge or consent, surrendered their claims to more than 65 million acres of land, because their lawyer, on the basis of quick guesswork and an acute sense that time was running out, thought them too much work and of too little value to pursue.

Opposing the one Sioux claim remaining, Cooperman continued his often derisive assault on Case's legal reasoning and, perhaps emboldened by the commission's favorable decision, embellished his rhetorical claims regarding the compensation that the government allegedly had paid the Sioux for the Black Hills. Cooperman now boasted that government expenditures under the 1877 Act—$57 million—actually "overpaid" the Sioux for the Black Hills.

Cooperman undoubtedly knew that his $57 million figure was wildly inflated. Even a cursory inspection of the government's accounting showed that some of the claimed offsets were payments to fulfill obligations under the 1868 treaty, not the 1877 act. These monies were not consideration for the Black Hills. Moreover, in calculating what the Sioux received as consideration, the government erroneously counted each dollar spent after 1877 as if it were the equivalent of one dollar of consideration *in* 1877. Discounting for inflation alone would seriously deflate Cooperman's $57 million figure. But that was Case's job, and he had as much as admitted that under traditional takings law (where the Black Hills would be valued as of 1877) the Sioux had received adequate compensation for the Black Hills. Cooperman encouraged that way of thinking, even if it meant distorting the truth.

On March 11, 1955, the commission, without comment, denied the motion for rehearing.

Case expected the decision, or said that he did in his correspondence with the separate tribal councils. "This is no occasion for anxiety," he wrote Black Hills Sioux Nation Council Chairman Eddie Reddoor, "but there is occasion for hope that the United States Court of Claims will and I fully expect it will reverse the Indian Claims Commission."

Case never failed to tell his clients what they wanted to hear, even when he knew better. As he had learned from experience, since the first Indian claim in 1881, the Court of Claims had compiled an extensive record of rejecting tribal grievances. Indeed, when Congress was considering creating a claims commission in the mid-1940s, Case specifically testified against establishing the Court of Claims as the appellate court for the commission. Nothing had happened in the interim to merit his newfound optimism.

Whatever his true expectations, Case immediately started to lay the groundwork for a visit to Sioux country in late July. From the publicity he arranged (through Bob Lee, who was now secretary to the governor), his trip took on the outward appearance of a victory tour, though the most likely motive for "the biggest meeting of the Sioux since the big party at Rosebud in 1923" was to help Case reaffirm Sioux loyalties strained by another defeat.

None of the tribal leaders, New Deal or old, understood Case's legal theory, or what was wrong with it. As his intermediate brief had noted, only one of the more than 30,000 Sioux had a legal education. Theirs was an attorney-client relationship based solely on long association, friendship, and trust. Despite a growing number of questioning voices, those emotional bonds remained strong enough to absorb another disappointment at the hands of a system two thousand miles to the east, from which many on the reservation no longer expected justice. In May 1955, at a special meeting of the Black Hills Sioux Nation Council, delegates from all eight reservations tendered another unanimous vote of confidence in the "Honorable Ralph H. Case." Young Spotted Tail had lived to fight another day.

That October the Black Hills claim, now thirty-two years old, returned to the Court of Claims. The briefs for both sides contained little new. Case exerpted liberally from his initial brief before the commission, interspersed a few paragraphs from his motion for rehearing, and submitted a patchwork of his guardian-ward argument. The government, not surprisingly, lavishly praised the commission's opinion, especially the section holding that even under their own theory of recovery, plaintiffs had failed to prove their case.

Out on the reservation, the Black Hills Sioux Nation Council decided that the Indians themselves should play a more active role again in the claim. Reddoor asked Case whether sixteen council members might come to Washington to testify before the Court. Case wrote back exasperated: "It seems I have been unable to convince you and the Council Members of the seven other reservations that you cannot, under any circumstances 'participate in the hearings.'" The white man's courtroom had no place for the Sioux, except the gallery, Case insisted, where they could only sit and listen in silence. In any event, Case suggested that there probably would be no open hearing, since the Court of Claims would decide the appeal on the basis of the written record only. The council's proposed trip was just a "waste of money . . . unwise and useless."

What Case hid from his curious clients, even to the point of deception, was that he already had decided to waive his right to an oral argument. Why Case refused the additional opportunity to present his argument, a highly unusual decision for the party seeking review, is not known. Most likely, however, Case was simply in no condition to appear in court. His drinking had grown progressively worse in the 1950s, to the point where common rumor in the D.C. legal community branded him an alcoholic. In Sioux country, Case's friends discounted the whisperings as the propaganda of rival lawyers or the anti-Case factions emerging on most of the reservations.

But Case's work reflected his worsening condition. In June 1956, he asked the Court of Claims to take "judicial notice" of the Supreme Court's April ruling in *Squire* v. *Capoeman,* an Indian taxation decision that Case believed confirmed his guardian-ward theory for the Sioux claim. *Capoeman* involved the question whether an Indian holding a trust patent owed taxes on timber revenues derived from the land. Although the court recognized that the Dawes Act (under which the Indian obtained his patent) created a trust relationship between the government and the individual Indian, the court's holding hinged solely on an interpretation of the Dawes Act's language establishing a twenty-five-year trust period for allotted lands. Nothing in *Capoeman* suggested the existence of a general trust relationship between the U.S. and all Indian tribes.

In short, the decision had no relevance at all to the Sioux claim, yet Case hailed it as the "most important Indian case in 50 years," and a guarantee of victory in the Black Hills claim. What logic moved Case to this conclusion, he never explained, even to the Court of Claims. He simply filed a copy of *Capoeman* with the court clerk, as if its mere presence in the court building compelled a favorable result.

Case's frailty approached infirmity; he slipped a disk at the start of summer. Bedridden, he then watched helplessly as his wife of forty-five years suddenly took sick and died.

On November 7, 1956, without reference to *Capoeman,* the Court of Claims affirmed the commission's dismissal of the Black Hills claim. Judge Laramore, writing for a unanimous seven-judge court, agreed unequivocally with the commission that the government's course of dealings with the Sioux reflected a fair and conscientious effort to compensate the Indians for their land. That the government had violated Article 12 of the 1868 treaty was legally insignificant. In *Lonewolf*, Laramore emphasized, the Supreme Court upheld Congress's authority to abrogate treaties unilaterally. "The primary consideration in negotiating with Indians," Laramore concluded, "must be the good of the country and the duty the Government owes to all its citizens, not only the obligations that arose as the result of a previous treaty with the Indians." So long as the government compensated the Sioux for the taking of their land, regardless of the breach of the 1868 treaty, the tribe had no legal claim.

The court then addressed the question whether the Sioux had received adequate compensation. Laramore made short shrift of Case's guardian-ward theory. Citing precedents as recent as the previous May, the court observed that, under well-settled law, in the absence of particular treaty or statutory language establishing a trust, the relationship between the United States and individual Indian tribes merely *resembled* that of a guardian to its ward, and did not carry with it the responsibilities of trust law. No such treaty or statute existed in this case.

It was a convenient ruling for the United States. Prior to the Indian New Deal the United States had predicated its entire Indian policy on the assumption that the tribes lacked competence to control their own affairs. Congress and the courts (as in *Lonewolf*) often had invoked the concept of Indian wardship to justify limitations on Indian rights. Regardless, according to the court, the government's treatment of the Sioux as helpless children did not make it the tribe's legal trustee.

Having dispensed with Case's trust theory, the court reiterated what had always been the law: that unconscionable compensation must be measured according to the value of the land at the time of its taking. Since Case admitted that the government (by providing $57 million in rations) had compensated the Sioux in excess of the 1877 value of the Black Hills, the court found absolutely no basis for a Sioux recovery.

Local newspapers and the attorneys in the Indian Claims Section of the Justice Department agreed that the great Sioux case had "finally reached the end of its long, long trail." The day after the decision, confident that the Supreme Court would decline review of a claim so conclusively decided, the chief of the claims section, Ralph Barney, dictated a closing memo summarizing the government's victory. "This could have been a dangerous case," he concluded, "if the attorney for the plaintiff had proceeded on a proper valuation theory."

Case, meanwhile, wrote his clients to notify them of another temporary setback and to remind them that ultimately justice would prevail. "I expected an adverse decision from the Court of Claims," he now told them. He would appeal to the Supreme Court and ask the justices to reverse the Court of Claims on the basis of their decision in *Squire* v. *Capoeman*, the irrelevant taxation case. "I sincerely trust and believe that the Supreme Court will follow its own decision."

Case neglected to mention that the Supreme Court might decline to review the Court of Claims decision, just as it declined review of the vast majority of cases from which appeals were sought, and just as it had declined review of the original 1942 Court of Claims decision in the Black Hills case. Indeed, in 1956 the Supreme Court had yet to review any Indian claims cases brought under the ICC Act.

Despite Case's convenient omissions and upbeat tone ("Justice, decency, and history are all on our side," he was fond of telling the press), this time his assurances did little to quell Sioux fears. A number of old-timers wrote their elected representatives to complain about the decision. James White Dress and a few others sent angry and bewildered letters to the Court of Claims.

"Chief" James Red Cloud, much as his distinguished grandfather might have done, wrote directly to President Eisenhower suggesting a personal conference to set right the misjudgments of the judicial branch. "The judge in Court of Claims won't pay us for the Black Hills and we sure are sorry and we don't like it," Red Cloud told the Great Father. "God created us Indians on this land and so we were the first ones to win this land of riches and here you white people came across the ocean and made Presidents and Congressmen and Senators and took over our country and the things you promised us are nothing now and we have no place to go." Red Cloud expected payment for the Black Hills. He was "depending" on the President to arrange it.

Among the IRA tribal councils (the only tribal entity with legal authority to oversee the claims), doubts and suspicions about Case reemerged with unprecedented intensity. Aroused by the prospect of losing the possibility of a Black Hills judgment, finally and irrevocably, Rosebud and Standing Rock sent delegations to Washington both to meet with Case and to sound out other Indian law attorneys about the quality of Case's work. Only one lawyer they met encouraged their inquiries. That was Marvin Sonosky, a former Justice Department lawyer, now in private practice, who handled general counsel and claims work for a number of tribes.

The Oglala Sioux (Pine Ridge) Tribal Council appointed Helen Peterson, a tribal member and executive director of the National Congress of American Indians, to be their Washington representative for claims matters. Peterson immediately consulted Richard Schifter, general counsel for Pine Ridge, whom James Roan Eagle had contacted after the commission's original decision in 1954.

Both Schifter and Sonosky essentially confirmed what the tribal councils must have strongly suspected: the first step in resuscitating the Black Hills claim, if it could be done at all, was to get rid of the man who had bungled the job for thirty-five years. If Case proceeded to the Supreme Court, especially seeking review on the basis of *Capoeman,* the Sioux would lose forever. The tribe's only chance, the lawyers reported, was to convince the Court of Claims to let it start over again in the Indian Claims Commission with a radically different legal theory and competent counsel.

Although the Indians could request review in the Supreme Court up to ninety days after the Court of Claims decision, if they wanted the Court of Claims to retain jurisdiction, they had to file papers within thirty days, before December 6. Fractious and indecisive in the past, the Sioux moved swiftly now.

Peterson, Robert Burnette, the chairman of the Rosebud Sioux Tribal Council, and J. Dan Howard, James McLean, and Isaac Hawk from the Standing Rock Sioux Tribal Council arranged to meet Case on the morning of November 30. They arrived well primed. In long discussions with Schifter and Sonosky, the Sioux had relearned several decades of claims history without Case's familiar, ever-reassuring voice obscuring the real reasons for the tribe's unrelenting defeats in court. The Sioux now knew that Case had surrendered without a fight the tribe's claims to the Powder River hunting grounds and more than 25 million acres of land outside the Great Sioux Reservation reserved to the Sioux in the 1851 Fort Laramie treaty. They now knew that he had needlessly conceded government payments of $57 million in offsets, vitiating any argument based on the 1877 value of the Hills. They now knew that the evidentiary record, impregnable according to Case, was hopelessly incomplete. They now knew that an appeal on the basis of *Capoeman* would be a farce.

Case started the meeting by telling the Sioux that he had prepared an appeal to the Supreme Court, though he could not find it when Burnette asked to see it. The Sioux challenged Case about the *Capoeman* decision as a basis for appeal, his failure to pursue valuable claims, and his numerous concessions and omissions. They suggested that in light of his ill-health Case might want to assign the claim to new attorneys. Case resisted. He was fine now, he said. He would be happy to consider "associate counsel," but only after meeting with all the candidates and arranging to preserve his interest in and control over the claim.

The Sioux left, agreeing to reconvene on Monday, December 3.

On Sunday, the Indians met to ratify officially the foregone decision to file some kind of motion for reconsideration in the Court of Claims. As authorized representatives of their respective reservations, Peterson, Burnette, and Howard signed a "Motion to Vacate the [Court of Claims] Judgment of Affirmance . . . In Order to Preserve Appellants' Rights Pending the Selection . . . of New Counsel Who May Take Appropriate Action on Behalf of the Tribes." Drafted by Sonosky in the Indians' voice, the motion stated succinctly the Sioux dilemma: "We know that the Indian Claims Commission Act was intended to give Indian tribes their day in court where full presentation of all the facts on all their claims could be made for a just determination of their cause. This right has been denied to these Tribes because of the lack of competent or adequate representation."

Less comfortable with her mandate than the others, Peterson called around Pine Ridge in search of elected council members and Henry Black Elk, Jr., a respected traditional leader. She wanted to explain in person why, despite all the years of service and friendship, Case simply had to be fired. She knew that many back home, especially among the traditional Sioux, would be hard pressed to understand why the Little White Father must be let go—that loyalty and shared hopes alone could not transform losing arguments into winners.

The Sioux met with Case again on Monday. Informing him about the motion for an extension of time, they instructed him not to jeopardize their strategy by petitioning the Supreme Court for review. The Indians had agreed beforehand to ask directly for Case's resignation, but none of the elected Sioux could bring himself to do it. After awkward pauses, the chore fell to Peterson. Unelected, a Cheyenne by birth (though an enrolled member of the Oglala Sioux tribe of Pine Ridge), she would pay no political price for cutting loose an old ally.

Peterson asked Case plainly whether he would resign. Case sat in silence; they all sat in silence. Perhaps too stunned to realize that the request for his resignation was just a gracious alternative to dismissal, Case asked to think about it overnight.

In the evening, Peterson drafted a written report for the Oglala Sioux, urging them to fire Case unilaterally. For the first time, someone put to paper for Sioux eyes the long record of Case's incompetence. More than that, Peterson tried to strip myths from Sioux images of *Ohiya*:

> You have all heard that Mr. Case possesses much information that is of value and is irreplaceable in the case. If he had information that was pertinent to the case, he should have made it a part of the record, and if he did make it a part of the record it is there for any future use. If he had valuable information and did not make it a part of the record he neglected his clients. . . .

> I urge you to keep in mind that when you decide whether to terminate Mr. Case's contract you are deciding out of sentimental concern for only one man, if you keep him—I feel sure now that there are no good reasons from a legal standpoint why you should. If you decide to terminate his contract, you are taking the first and essential step, I believe, toward saving the only chance the Tribe has—and it is a very slim one, indeed—to salvage something out of the Black Hills claim. Out of concern for the Tribe, I urge this course of action.

Three weeks later, Case tendered his resignation to each of the eight tribal councils. Proud to the end, Case explained his resignation as the product of old age, ill-health, and his lifelong commitment to "the right of the American Indian to choose his own attorney."

By this time, Pine Ridge had already replaced Case with the late Felix Cohen's law firm, Strasser, Spielberg, Fried and Frank, at which Schifter was an associate. Standing Rock and Rosebud had selected Sonosky, who had represented Santee for some years. Crow Creek and Lower Brûlé soon followed suit, naming both Sonosky and Strasser, Spiegelberg as counsel.

Old ties held more firmly at Cheyenne River, still controlled by Case's closest friend among the Sioux political leadership, Frank Ducheneaux. Under Ducheneaux's direction, the Cheyenne River tribal council refused to accept Case's resignation and asked him to continue work on the claim. Case also still represented the Sioux of the Fort Peck Reservation (mainly descendants of Sitting Bull's band who had ended up settling near Poplar, Montana, after returning from exile in Canada). There, Eddie Reddoor convinced the council not to switch lawyers.

For the next few months, the new lawyers and Case worked at cross purposes. Case sought to sever the Cheyenne River Sioux from the other tribes prosecuting the claim. The Court of Claims refused. Sonosky, Schifter, and Arthur Lazarus, Jr. (another Cohen protégé at Strasser, Spiegelberg) started work on a motion to vacate the Court of Claims decision. Meanwhile, opposed by the other lawyers, Case filed for rehearing.

Early in June 1957, as he crossed the street in front of his home in College Park, Maryland, Case was struck by a car speeding through a red light. The impact broke virtually every bone in his body.

On June 27, Ralph Hoyt Case died, age 77 years. At Cheyenne River, the Sioux named a new community building in his honor. Throughout Sioux country, even today, old-timers recall in hushed tones his passionate devotion to their cause and his friendship to an abandoned people. They recall that he won many victories, though they cannot name one. Generous memories have forgotten or never wanted to accept: the Sioux Moses never made it to the promised land, nor even to Sinai.

In thirty-five years, two courts in three decisions had dismissed or rejected the Black Hills claim. On the merits, both the commission and the Court of Claims had ruled not only that Case had proceeded on an untenable theory of valuation, but that the government's treatment of the Sioux had been reasonable under the circumstances, and even generous.

Still lost in the wilderness, now despairing of the promised land, the Sioux did not need another Moses; they needed a conjurer to raise their claim from the dead.

NEW COUNSEL, OLD PROBLEMS

ARTHUR LAZARUS, JR., came to the practice of Indian law by chance. When he finished law school in 1949, a good position in a law firm was difficult to find, even for Yale graduates, especially those who were Jewish. Had it been otherwise, Lazarus almost certainly would not have interviewed for a job working on Indian law and immigration cases with Felix Cohen at the Washington, D.C., office of Riegelman, Strasser, Schwarz & Spiegelberg (an established New York-based firm). Indian law by and large was a professional backwater—mainly the bailiwick of local attorneys who either possessed mediocre talents or (despite obvious conflicts of interest) considered Indian work a useful sideline to a more lucrative practice representing oil companies or ranchers seeking access to tribal resources.

Still, the prospect of working for Cohen was attractive. Lazarus knew him from the jurisprudence course Cohen taught at Yale, a course reknowned for the professor's rare combination of idealism and exacting logic. Lazarus also appreciated Cohen's reputation as a superb practitioner committed to representing the underrepresented. Besides, Lazarus was young and unemployed. An apprenticeship with Cohen, for a year or two, even in Washington—then a drab Jim Crow town—was too good a chance to pass up. In January 1950, Lazarus left his native New York to become an associate in the Washington office of Riegelman, Strasser. He would never leave.

Cohen's practice flowed naturally from his government work as well as from his personal idealism. In his capacity as general counsel for numerous tribes and as an advocate for Indian interests before Congress (he was counsel to the Association on American Indian Affairs, a liberal philanthropic group), Cohen labored at every turn to preserve and nourish the mandate for Indian self-rule that he had helped to frame and implement during his fifteen years of government service.

Cohen also served as a manager and intellectual resource for the prosecution of tribal claims under his brainchild, the Indian Claims Commission Act. He acted as consultant to the Joint Efforts Group, a consortium of more than a dozen law firms, some quite prominent, that had agreed to pool their resources to explore legal questions common to tribal claims across the country.

As counsel to Indians and aliens, Cohen faced a Congress and Executive Branch increasingly hostile to the New Deal policies he had helped to shape. By 1950, the most aggressive reformers among the New Dealers, like John Collier and Cohen himself, had resigned from government service. The formerly Democratic Congress, receptive to Roosevelt's liberal initiatives, was now controlled by a conservative coalition of Republicans and southern Democrats, who checked President Truman's efforts at domestic reform. In the wake of the communist takeover in China, the Alger Hiss case, and the Rosenberg spy scandal, Senator Joseph McCarthy was soon to establish himself as the nation's grand inquisitor for political thought. And as anticommunism ripened into a national obsession, so too a white American nativist campaign to create a more homogeneous society also reemerged in great strength. With fear of communism animating some, hostility toward otherness animating others, a broad spectrum of the nation closed ranks against ideas, individuals, and institutions that deviated from the mainstream.

With regard to immigration, the new national urge for conformity and consensus spawned tight restrictions on the rights of aliens, most notoriously the 1952 McCarran-Walter Act. The act provided for the exclusion of aliens who espoused unpopular political beliefs, notably Socialists, Communists, and anarchists. With his new associate, Lazarus, Cohen lobbied hard against McCarran-Walter, drafting statements for sympathetic congressmen and publishing articles attacking the bill as unworthy of a nation that cherished political liberty. These activities along with Cohen's other work prompted inquiries into his own loyalty.

In Indian affairs, rising nativism and the infectious fear of Communism produced a resurgent drive towards the forced assimilation of individual Indians, yet another about-face in the nation's ambivalent policy towards its native population. Nativists and anti-Communists shared a powerful antipathy towards the communal, noncapitalist structure of Indian society. Together, they rejuvenated and broadened longstanding conservative opposition to Roosevelt's commitment to tribal sovereignty and ethnic pluralism.

A number of liberals, too, repudiated the goals of the Indian New Deal. As President Truman integrated the armed forces and legal reformers launched a coordinated assault on segregation in the South, some in the vanguard of the struggle for racial equality regarded Indian reservations not as havens for preserving tribal authority and ethnic identity but as unacceptable bastions of segregation and separatism. These reformers' vision of a colorblind America, free from racial distinctions of any kind, reserved no place where Indians might choose segregation and pursue their own cultural destiny.

Traditional, less political enemies of tribal sovereignty also weighed in against Roosevelt's Indian policy. Spurred by the booming postwar economy, western land developers again directed their attention towards opening up reservation lands, this time for use as commercial farms, mines, resorts, shopping centers, and suburban housing.

As in the nineteenth century, ideology and the prospect of economic gain combined to produce a policy intended to dissolve Indians completely into the American melting pot. The nineteenth-century assimilationists sought to "free" the Indians through allotment, education, and citizenship. Their mid-twentieth-century counterparts, borrowing their predecessors' rhetoric, proposed to "emancipate" Indians by terminating federal responsibility for Indian groups and individuals. In theory, the end of trusteeship, coupled with a plan for the ultimate dissolution of tribes as political entities, would free Indians from oppressive governmental paternalism and the allegedly debilitating bonds of tribalism.

Truman's commissioner of Indian Affairs, Dillon Myer, aggressively championed the new assimilationist cause. A high-handed administrator whose previous government service included the directorship of the War Relocation Authority (the euphemistically named government department that oversaw Japanese internment camps during World War II), Myer awakened the government's dormant effort to eradicate Indian cultures and sever ties between Indians and their tribal lands. Ultimately, Myer and his fellow "terminationists," as they became known, proposed to dismantle the Indian Bureau entirely and transfer its responsibilities—such as education and health services—to state and local governments. In the short term, they planned to disestablish the most acculturated tribes by liquidating tribal trust funds, selling off or distributing tribal lands, and subjecting the detribalized Indians to state (as opposed to federal or tribal) law in all civil and criminal matters.

In Congress, Arthur Watkins, a conservative Utah senator who was chairman of the Subcommittee on Indian Affairs and a special friend of western developers, worked closely with Myer. Under Watkins's stewardship, on August 1, 1953, Congress adopted House Concurrent Resolution 108, which declared termination to be the government's official policy. In deceptively benevolent terms, Congress resolved "as rapidly as possible, to make Indians . . . subject to the same laws and entitled to the same privileges and responsibilities as are applicable to other citizens of the United States, to end their status as wards of the United States and to grant them all of the rights and prerogatives pertaining to American citizenship."

Congress also decided that a number of tribes were already sufficiently acculturated to handle termination. Resolution 108 proposed to end immediately federal recognition of and responsibility for all tribes in California, Florida, New York, and Texas as well as the Flathead, Klamath, Menominee, one Potowatami, and The Chippewa of Turtle Mountain, North Dakota.

Two weeks later, while awaiting the bureau's detailed plan for implementing this termination mandate, Congress enacted Public Law 280, providing that for all Indian lands (excluding three named reservations) in California, Minnesota, Nebraska, Oregon, and Wisconsin, jurisdiction over criminal offenses and many civil matters would rest solely with each individual state rather than, as previously, with the federal government or the affected tribes themselves. Public Law 280 further provided that every other state could assume similar jurisdictional control over Indian reservations through its own legislative action. Although such state action would subject tribes to the political control of historically hostile local governments, Congress required neither the consent of nor even consultation with affected tribes.

Even prior to this congressional action, Myer had instituted his own programs to hasten Indian assimilation. In addition to reinstituting old efforts at curbing the use of native languages and encouraging off-reservation schooling, he started a new program of actively "relocating" individual Indians away from what he called reservation "prison camps" and into large metropolitan areas. Like the allotment policy that Collier had jettisoned in the 1930s, relocation was intended to isolate individual Indians from their traditional cultures and transform them into productive and integrated members of American society.

To entice impoverished reservation Indians into leaving their ancestral homes, the government mounted a far-reaching public relations campaign. Throughout Indian country, the bureau posted advertisements depicting former reservation Indians who had "made it" in the white world. Well-groomed and smiling, they posed beside new televisions and other appliances or were shown working in factories at apparently high-paying jobs.

During the 1950s, the bureau induced 35,000 Indians to relocate to Denver, Phoenix, Albuquerque, San Francisco, Dallas, Los Angeles, Tulsa, Cleveland, and Chicago, draining the reservations of their workforce. "The relocation program wants Indians from 18 to 35," remarked a Sioux relocated from Pine Ridge to Cleveland. "The old people can die on the reservation, but they want the young ones to move to the city, intermarry, forget their traditions, and disappear."

City life rarely lived up to its billing. For Indians rooted in rural folk cultures, reared in open country, and accustomed to life in small communities, adjusting to the routines of urban American society proved traumatic. "The simplest facts of life in the city were new to them: gearing your entire day by a clock, when to go to work, when to eat lunch," observed Richard McKenzie, a young Sioux who became a leader at the Indian Center in San Francisco. "They don't even understand where you board a bus, how to pay, and how to open and close the doors." Amid the crowds and narrow streets, disoriented Indians discovered the fear and loneliness of strangers in big cities.

Some fled back to the comparative shelter of reservations; many who stayed fell quickly into poverty. Generally unskilled and poorly educated, with histories of virtually continuous unemployment, most Indians who relocated found jobs in seasonal work, if at all. Only three thousand, less than 10 percent of those who came to the cities, joined the permanent labor force, usually as factory workers in defense-related industries. Few were equipped to manage their new lives. Born to cultures that knew little or nothing of capitalist ways, the new urban Indians lacked even a rudimentary understanding of budgeting or saving. On the reservations, their health care had been free, rents and other costs low. Overwhelmed by unforeseen expenses, thousands drifted into city boweries. For them, the white man's road led straight from homeland to ghetto.

Indians on the terminated reservations met with comparable disaster. The experience of the Menominees of Wisconsin was typical. In 1951, the Menominees won an $8.5 million judgment in the Court of Claims to settle their historic grievances, but Senator Watkins blocked congressional appropriation of the judgment money until the Indians agreed to expedite their own termination as a tribe. In 1954, after the Menominees finally acquiesced, Congress enacted a statute providing for per capita distribution of their claims money and termination of all federal services and tribal recognition by 1958.

Signing the bill, President Eisenhower congratulated the Menominees for inaugurating "a new era in Indian affairs." What followed instead was but a new chapter in an old story of tribal ruin. The Menominees labored desperately to develop a termination plan that would preserve valuable tribal assets (including $34 million in tribal property), meanwhile begging Congress to delay termination by at least ten years. When Congress refused to extend the deadline beyond 1961, the Menominees (with bureau guidance) decided to organize Menominee Enterprises, Incorporated (MEI), a private company that would assume ownership of tribal lands and forests as well as the tribal lumber mill. As part of the privatization of tribal assets, each Menominee would receive a 4 percent negotiable bond worth $3,000 and 100 shares of MEI stock. The tribe also decided to organize as a separate Wisconsin county.

In 1961, as planned, the bureau officially terminated the Menominees. In the bureau's view, Menominee County and its people, supported by a profitable MEI, would become self-sustaining within a few years.

The bureau's prediction was fantasy. At the time of its incorporation, Menominee County ranked last among Wisconsin's seventy-two counties in total population, family income, employment, adequate housing, high school graduates, and farmland. Saddled with $380,000 in expenses for welfare, health services, and transportation (previously underwritten by the federal government), the county had no choice but to levy heavy taxes on its sole property owner, MEI, which in turn was suffering from the loss of guaranteed federal lumber contracts for its mill.

To raise money to pay its taxes, MEI required Menominee homeowners to purchase their properties. For most, this meant trading in their only cash holding, the $3,000 negotiable bond. Having used all their money to buy their homes, many Menominees defaulted on their debts. An epidemic of home and farm auctions followed. As the undercapitalized county economy faltered, unemployment rose to 25 percent and welfare payments doubled. Lacking sufficient funds for staff and facilities to comply with state licensing requirements, the county closed its only hospital. By 1965, nearly one-third of the Menominees tested positive for tuberculosis. Less than a decade after termination, a relatively prosperous Indian community collapsed into poverty and ill-health.

To Indians of the 1950s these consequences of termination were predictable. With the help of skilled advocates like Cohen, and employing their own increasingly sophisticated understanding of political tactics, the tribes organized to fight termination policy and its supporters. Every year representatives from dozens of tribes across the country converged on Washington to protest what they perceived to be the government's renewed disregard for longstanding treaty obligations, for the right of tribal self-government, even for Indian life itself. After generations of acquired reliance on the protective arm of the Great Father, with many tribes still dependent on the federal government for basic subsistence, the termination bills conjured up old nightmares of extermination. Earl Old Person, chairman of the Blackfeet in the late 1950s, remembered the feeling of his people. "In our Indian language," he wrote, "the only translation for termination is 'to wipe out' or 'kill off.' We have no Indian words for termination."

For Old Person, as for all Indian leaders, the 389 treaties, 5,000 statutes, and many hundreds of court decisions and executive orders that defined the relationship between the tribes and the United States conferred upon those tribes the right (in Old Person's words) "to develop our reservations and to develop as a people free from interference." On battlefields and treaty grounds Indian ancestors had fought for their people's future and exacted promises from their conquerors. While these promises may have held little meaning during the decades of complete bureau control of Indian life, for tribal leaders in the post-IRA era, they were etched in stone and inviolate. Testifying against termination policy, John Wooden Legs, a Cheyenne, described what his ancestors had reserved for him through their struggles: "To us, to be Cheyenne means being one tribe—living in our own land—in America, where we are citizens. Our land is everything to us. . . . It is the only place where Cheyenne remember same things together. I will tell you one of the things we remember on our land. We remember that our grandfathers paid for it—with their lives."

While Indian voices were raised against new betrayals, Felix Cohen published numerous broadsides attacking the false promise of freedom and prosperity in which the government cloaked its new policy. For all the talk of freeing Indians from warship and conferring upon them the rights and opportunities of citizenship, termination granted Indians nothing that was not theirs already. By law, all Indians were citizens and had been since 1924. Certainly, every Indian possessed the right to abandon his heritage voluntarily and jump with both feet into the mainstream of American society. What termination offered was not greater freedom but the loss for all Indians of rights that even conquest had not destroyed: their rights to remain Indian and to govern themselves as Indians. Cohen remarked on the irony. "If a government repudiates its obligations to a white man we speak of 'governmental bankruptcy'. . . . [I]f a government repudiates its obligations to an Indian, this is commonly referred to as 'emancipating the Indian.'"

In a 1953 *Yale Law Journal* article, "The Erosion of Indian Rights," Cohen also noted that, except for those reservations facing immediate termination, the government's renewed efforts at "emancipation" actually had resulted in a sharp increase in governmental control over reservation life—a throwback to pre-IRA days. For example, to ensure acquiescence in Myer's policies, the Indian bureau used government money and employees to influence tribal elections in favor of bureau-approved candidates; to silence Indian critics who won election anyway, the bureau impounded the bank accounts of their tribes. Myer also transferred or fired bureau employees who were seen as overly sympathetic to Indian interests and restructured the bureau, closing many local offices, to make it less responsive to tribal needs.

To the delight of western developers, Myer consistently opposed tribal control of their own resources. During his tenure, for example, the Indian bureau resumed the pre-Collier practice of leasing Indian property without tribal consent, almost always to non-Indians. And although Myer and the other terminationists claimed to seek full equality for all Indians, they opposed legislation that would have repealed discriminatory laws such as those prohibiting Indians from buying guns, liquor, or ammunition— laws that perpetuated the status of Indians as second-class citizens. In practice, the "emancipation" the terminationists conducted promoted neither equality nor independence.

To protect his initiatives from informed opposition, Myer proposed new regulations reviving the old practice of strict bureau control over tribal attorney contracts. Although his advertised motive was to protect Indians from shyster lawyers, Myer's obvious ploy (which included pressuring tribes to hire local counsel—the very attorneys most likely to be unscrupulous in looking after Indian interests) was to put Cohen and other uncooperative practitioners out of the Indian business.

As Cohen remarked, with characteristic legal precision, "for Indians, as for other underprivileged groups, denial of the right to independent counsel means undermining all the rights which require independent counsel for enforcement." This lesson was not lost on Indians. "We believe that we need an attorney to protect us," the Standing Rock Sioux Tribal Council complained about the proposed new regulations. "if we had an attorney during the last century we would not have lost the Black Hills."

The collective outrage of the tribes (mainly orchestrated by Helen Peterson and her cadre of lobbyists at the National Congress of American Indians) and the persuasive opposition of Cohen forced the Interior Department to hold a public hearing on Myer's proposed regulations. Eventually, in a rare victory for the Indians, the Secretary of the Interior, Myer's boss Oscar Chapman, squelched the regulations.

In 1953, President-elect Eisenhower, under pressure from Indian groups across the country, replaced Myer with Glenn Emmons, an affable New Mexico banker. As was expected of an appointee with close ties to the western business community, Emmons continued his predecessor's termination policies, albeit less confrontationally.

That year, too, Felix Cohen, 46, died of lung cancer. The legal profession lost prematurely one of its most intelligent and creative voices. Indians lost their "Double-Runner," as the Blackfeet called him, their most tireless and effective advocate. As Supreme Court Justice William Douglas later observed, "No mind that ever delved into Indian affairs was keener, more discerning, more enlightened."

Arthur Lazarus lost his mentor, the man who had drawn him to Washington, trained him meticulously in the craft of lawyering, and bequeathed to him a vision of equal justice under law. In three years, Lazarus had developed a commitment to Cohen's practice, especially his representation of Indians. Tribal clients presented a unique intellectual challenge, the opportunity to shape policy and law on behalf of people who every day wrestled with their partially restored powers of self-government and tried to redefine their relationship with the dominant society. The work called for all the skills in a lawyer's intellectual arsenal—the abilities to draft legislation, negotiate with businessmen and bureaucracies, and litigate in a field with few established precedents and principles. In short, representing Indians was a perfect specialty for Lazarus, an ambitious young lawyer with a highly analytic and precise turn of mind.

Indian law also suited Lazarus's personal political views. As the son of a leading pacifist (his mother was active in the War Resisters' League) and a conscientious objector himself, liberal by upbringing and inclination, Lazarus was predisposed to share Cohen's enthusiasm for representing the underprivileged as well as his contempt for the racism that often informed government Indian policy. Long before Cohen's death, Lazarus had adopted his professional credo, the belief inscribed in his *Handbook of Federal Indian Law*, "that the protection of minority rights and the substitution of reason and argument for force and dictation represent a contribution to civilization." At 27, four years out of law school, he and Richard Schifter, another Yale Law graduate who had joined Riegelman, Strasser in 1951, assumed Cohen's practice—and the spirit with which it was imbued.

Ironically, Cohen's death opened the door to new kinds of legal work, specifically in the claims field. Because of his government experience, Cohen had consistently refused to represent individual tribes in their claims before the Indian Claims Commission. As the principal draftsman and proponent of the ICC Act, he had wanted to avoid even the appearance of having benefited in private practice from legislation with which he had been involved as a government official.

Lazarus and Schifter, however, had no reason to refuse claims work, and in 1954, when James Roan Eagle of the Black Hills Sioux Nation Council first approached Riegelman, Strasser about assisting Ralph Case with the Sioux claims, Schifter expressed interest. Having heard that the Indian Claims Commission had dismissed the Black Hills claim, but not knowing why, Roan Eagle asked Schifter whether the Sioux should hire additional attorneys—Riegelman, Strasser in particular—to help Case with the appeal. Although constrained in his response by another Cohen policy—not interfering in the relationship between a tribe and its counsel—Schifter assured Roan Eagle that he would be happy to collaborate. While avoiding any comment on Case's competence, Schifter tactfully reminded Roan Eagle that clients have the right to choose any counsel they wish at any time they wish.

But Roan Eagle never followed through. More than two years

passed before the Sioux became sufficiently unsettled about Case's work to contact Helen Peterson and begin in earnest the process of replacing Case with Riegelman, Strasser (now renamed Strasser, Spiegelberg, Fried & Frank) and Marvin Sonosky. By that time, Case already had lost the claim on appeal, making the job of new counsel infinitely more difficult.

Indeed, Case had so bungled the Black Hills claim that the Sioux had trouble finding new lawyers to take their business. When the delegation from Rosebud and Standing Rock came around to see Sonosky, Bob Burnette told him that thirteen lawyers previously recommended by the Indian Bureau had turned them away. Sonosky was less hasty. After meeting with the Sioux, he arranged with Lazarus and Schifter to do some preliminary research. Like them, he readily agreed to tackle the job of reviving a potentially rich, if badly weakened, claim.

It was a reunion for the lawyers. Sonosky, too, had been associated with Cohen. Born and bred in Duluth, Minnesota, a college and law school graduate of the state university, Sonosky had entered a small hometown law practice after passing the bar in 1932. Then, as it had for Cohen, the New Deal provided Sonosky with a ticket to Washington. He had raised money for Roosevelt in the 1936 campaign and, in exchange, received a letter of introduction to help him find a job in D.C. In 1937, Sonosky started as a junior attorney in the Lands Division of the Justice Department.

Although he had no special interest in Indians—Sonosky's Minnesota education included not one reference to the state's rich Indian history—he was soon handling a slew of Indian cases. In fulfillment of the federal government's trusteeship over Indians and Indian tribes, Sonosky defended Indian interests against third parties such as mineral companies and land developers. Eventually, he rose to assistant chief of the Indian section.

From time to time, Sonosky worked with Cohen (then assistant solicitor in the Interior Department), who drafted lawyers from the Lands Division to help advance the cause of Indian self-government in the courts. And when Sonosky decided to leave government in 1951, he opted to work with Cohen at Riegelman, Strasser. He stayed there for a year, often working with Lazarus, before leaving to start a small firm of his own. By the time the Sioux came to call, Sonosky had developed a sizable roster of Indian clients, including the Shoshone, Chippewa, and Fort Peck tribes, for whom he was doing general counsel and some claims work.

Together, Sonosky, Schifter, and Lazarus pitched into the mammoth process of investigating the Sioux land claims, reviewing the existing record, and identifying the flaws in Case's legal arguments. At the same time, the new team faced the additional problems of winning the confidence of lawyer-shy clients and combating old allegiances to Case, such as those of the Fort Peck and Cheyenne River Sioux, who stood by *Ohiya* until his death.

In February 1957, Sonosky received a letter from Bob Burnette reflecting the confusion and ignorance that often clouded Sioux perceptions of their legal claims. Burnette reported that John Little Cloud (the "claims committee" chairman at Cheyenne River) had met with Case and learned from him that the Sioux stood "to lose more by winning the [Black Hills] case than by losing it." Apparently Case had told Little Cloud that winning the claim would cancel the government's continuing treaty obligations to the Sioux and, thereby, more than offset a Black Hills judgment.

Sonosky wrote back, pointing out the obvious: first, Case was dead wrong; second, if Case had been right, he never should have filed the claim in 1923. Sonosky suggested that Burnette might want to remind Little Cloud that his valued consultant had failed to file claims for millions of acres of Sioux treaty lands and, in the Black Hills claim, had conceded that the government paid the Sioux the value of the taken land as of 1877. Once Case did that, Sonosky closed emphatically, "you never had a chance."

On October 4, 1957, four months after Case's death, Sonosky, Schifter, and Lazarus filed with the Court of Claims a motion seeking a new lease on life for the Sioux claims. Specifically, Sioux counsel asked the court to vacate its November 1956 decision and remand the Sioux claims to the ICC for a full and complete hearing on their merits. The crux of their argument was simple. Ralph Case's representation of the Sioux was so "grossly incompetent," the record he established so "distorted and empty," his arguments so "erroneous and untenable," his briefs so "inaccurate and wholly misleading," that "for all practical purposes, these Indians were without legal representation."

Writing at a time when lawyers rarely criticized each other publicly, the new Sioux counsel worried that their catalogue of Case's errors would offend the court or appear exaggerated. But the risk of understating Case's bungling was enormous. Convincing the Court of Claims to vacate its 1956 decision was the only conceivable way to revive the Sioux claims, and incompetence of counsel was by far the most compelling grounds to support such a rare, even unprecedented, exercise of judicial power.

Even this ground was shaky. Sonosky, Schifter, and Lazarus did not cite, nor does there appear to have been, a single case prior to the filing of this motion in which a court had vacated a final appellate decision in a civil case because of incompetent representation, much less a case where a court had so done after six years of litigation. In the absence of supporting case law, the lawyers could do no more than call upon the Court of Claims to exercise its power to do "as justice requires" and to breath life into Congress's apparent intention in enacting the ICC Act that Indian claims receive full and fair hearings before the courts.

Recognizing that their attempt to revive the Black Hills claim depended entirely on the success of this motion, Sonosky, Schifter, and Lazarus fired round after round into the corpus of Case's legal work. Although they commenced with a nodding reference to the ancient adage *de mortuis nil nisi bonum* (ironically, one of Case's favorites), their argument, twenty-six scathing pages, was unrelenting. "The just demands of over 32,000 destitute Sioux Indians requires a frank discussion of unpleasant facts," the new lawyers told the court:

> Unknown to the Tribes, their legal representative apparently volunteered concessions—based upon guesses and contrary to fact—which could be destructive to their claims. In addition, counsel wholly failed to introduce into evidence even the most elementary data necessary to show liability and stubbornly urged legal theories which were clearly untenable in the light of established precedent. . . .

> No attorney conscious of his responsibilities to his clients and to the courts, or cognizant of the facts in this case, or with any understanding of the law, would persistently advance as the sole and exclusive ground for recovery so weak a legal theory [Case's guardian-ward theory entitling the Sioux to mineral royalties], particularly in the face of uniform judicial holdings that the standard value to be employed is the market value at the time of the loss of the land. . . .

And so the motion continued, paragraph after paragraph. Next it excoriated Case for his failure to investigate the government's claimed offsets or to show that many could not possibly be charged to the Sioux as consideration under the 1877 act. Later the attorneys reminded the court of its first-hand experience with Case's ineptitude.

> This Court undoubtedly remembers counsel's performance on appeal, including the glaring inadequacies of his briefs, his waiver of oral argument although he was seeking reversal, and his submission

of an opinion of the United States Supreme Court [*Capoeman*] on motion. His conduct obviously did not constitute adequate legal representation for any litigant, much less dependent Indian tribes.

In addition to lambasting Case, Sonosky, Schifter, and Lazarus also argued that the commission itself deserved a share of the blame for their clients' predicament. When creating the Indian Claims Commission, they noted, Congress had specifically provided for a Division of Investigation to ensure (as the Court of Claims had itself recognized in previous cases) that final claims determinations would be made "on the basis of *all* available facts." Congress did not intend for the commission to rest on legal ceremony in adjudicating outstanding tribal grievances, rushing cases to judgment once the procedural trappings of justice had been applied. Congress intended for the commission to go beyond the standard procedures of courts and guarantee that Indian claims received full and fair hearings.

In this case, Sonosky, Schifter, and Lazarus argued, "the Commission knew that appellants' counsel was making disastrous concessions, was omitting basic evidence and was advocating untenable legal theories. Under such circumstances . . . the Commission was under a duty to conduct an independent investigation, to build up a full and complete record concerning all ascertainable facts." This failure of the commission to carry out its congressionally authorized mission, the lawyers asserted, warranted a reopening of the original proceedings.

Tough and technically precise, the motion to vacate reflected an unmistakable contrast between the tribe's old and new counsel. Gone was Case's essentially romantic view of the legal process and his sentimental confidence that the government's overriding sense of fairness would lead it to a just settlement with the Sioux. Instead, Sonosky, Schifter, and Lazarus brought to the Sioux claims a hard-nosed view of the law and a degree of skepticism about the federal government. To them, the law was a two-edged sword to be wielded boldly and carefully in the service of clients. The legal system was a battlefield where the better cause did not always prevail. And the federal government was sometimes an ally, sometimes an adversary, but rarely the impartial purveyor of justice.

The lawyers differed in their attitude towards their clients as well. To Case—the frontiersman's son inspired by the melting pot image of America—the Sioux were warriors to the last man who, nonetheless, wanted to assume their rightful place as members of an integrated national family. Sonosky, Schifter, and Lazarus, by contrast, heirs to a Jewish sensitivity about issues of ethnicity and discrimination, believed deeply in the New Deal's promise of cultural pluralism and Indian self-rule. They thought Indian law generally, and the claims process specifically, should be directed not towards ultimate assimilation but towards obtaining for Indians every penny to which they were entitled under law and guaranteeing to them a degree of independence in the direction of their own destinies.

The aggressive tactics of their new opponents rankled the lawyers in the Justice Department, who considered the Sioux claims all but buried. Ralph Barney, chief of the Indian Claims section, who eleven months earlier had written a departmental memo gloating over the government's Black Hills victory in the Court of Claims, was especially indignant. Although, as noted earlier, he had remarked that the Sioux claims could have been "dangerous" had Case pursued a "proper valuation theory," Barney characterized his successors' argument as "one of the nastiest I have ever seen," as though Sonosky, Schifter, and Lazarus had overstepped the bounds of professional propriety in exposing Case as the incompetent Barney knew him to be. Maurice Cooperman, six years Case's adversary, seconded Barney's opinion. "This is a stinker," he wrote.

While they waited for the government to respond, Sonosky, Schifter, and Lazarus fretted about the disarray within their own camp. Even after Case's death, the Sioux remained divided in their choice of legal counsel. While Sonosky, Schifter, and Lazarus represented Pine Ridge, Rosebud, Standing Rock, and three smaller Sioux tribes (Crow Creek, Lower Brûlé, and Santee), both the Cheyenne River Sioux and the Sioux at Fort Peck, who had stuck with Case until the bitter end, refused to hire the lawyers who had undermined and ultimately supplanted their old friend *Ohiya*.

Immediately after Case's death, Frank Ducheneaux approached Sonosky about taking over the Cheyenne River tribe's claims work on the condition that he also undertake a personal tax case that Ducheneaux had brought to avoid paying taxes on his family's ranch. When Sonosky declined the tax case as a dead certain loser, Ducheneaux took his business—and Cheyenne River's share of the Black Hills claim—to a lawyer named William Howard Payne. Fort Peck, apparently following Cheyenne River's lead, also hired Payne.

William Howard, as colleagues called him, bore a remarkable similarity to Ralph Case. In addition to sharing Case's western charm and affability, like Case, Payne was born in Indian country

(Oklahoma) and maintained strong home ties. Both had started their careers at the Indian Affairs Committee and obtained their law degrees while working for Congress. Like Case, Payne developed his first Indian clients (the Cheyenne-Arapaho) among the tribes of his home state. Payne also shared a few of Case's least desirable attributes as a lawyer. He was lazy, not terribly exacting, and fond of drink.

Payne's first act as partial Sioux counsel did nothing to endear him to his potential future collaborators. He got his clients to throw a big wet blanket on whatever fire Sonosky, Schifter, and Lazarus might have sparked with their October motion: Cheyenne River and Fort Peck asked for a ninety-day delay in the court's consideration of the Sioux claims while the tribes obtained formal bureau approval of Payne's attorney contracts. Sonosky, Schifter, and Lazarus responded vigorously, but to no avail. Granting delays in Indian cases was virtually a way of life both in the Court of Claims and in the commission.

The delay inevitably led to a new round of infighting, both among the various tribes now working at cross-purposes and between the longstanding Black Hills Sioux Nation Council and the leadership of the separate tribal councils who had retained Sonosky and Strasser, Spiegelberg. The BHSNC, of which Eddie Reddoor was the secretary and dominant member, met on the Fort Peck Reservation shortly after the hiring of Payne. Not wanting to be shunted aside, the BHSNC passed a resolution requesting that the Sioux tribal councils (which held complete legal control over claims matters) recognize the BHSNC as the official claims organization for the entire Sioux nation. The BHSNC also passed a resolution calling for cooperation among the different tribal attorneys and voted to reconvene in Washington in January 1958 for a meeting with all three.

By the time Sonosky responded to these resolutions, Bob Burnette, the outspoken Rosebud chairman, already had tipped him off that the so-called annual meeting of the BHSNC had amounted to little more than a gab session between Fort Peck and Cheyenne River delegates, including John Little Cloud, Case's crony, with whom Burnette had been sparring a few months before. In particular, Burnette informed Sonosky that the BHSNC meeting had not met the organization's own standards for a quorum (representation from at least five of the eight Sioux reservations) and that, therefore, the resolutions were invalid. Forewarned, Sonosky responded coolly to the BHSNC, inquiring about its quorum rules and the attendance at the last meeting.

The Black Hills of South Dakota *Richard Erdoes*

Treaty conference at Fort Laramie, April 1868
The Bettman Archive

Spotted Tail, Chief of the Brûlé *Smithsonian Institution*

The Manypenny Commission's 1876 visit to Sioux country, as depicted by Oglala Sioux artist Amos Bad Heart Bull around the turn of the century. *From A Pictographic History of the Oglala Sioux, by Amos Bad Heart Bull, text by Helen H. Blish. Copyright © 1967 by the University of Nebraska Press. University of Nebraska Press*

Red Cloud with his son and grand-
daughter *Smithsonian Institution*

Sioux delegation to Washington, D.C., 1888 *Smithsonian Institution*

Beef ration allotment at Standing Rock Reservation *Smithsonian Institution*

Pine Ridge Agency Office, 1936 *Charlotte Lloyd (Westwood) Walkup*

Pine Ridge Tribal Council, 1936 *Charlotte Lloyd (Westwood) Walkup*

Sioux reservation life, 1936 *Charlotte Lloyd (Westwood) Walkup*

Cheyenne River Sioux debate the Indian Reorganization Act, ca. 1936 *Charlotte Lloyd (Westwood) Walkup*

Ralph Case on the Cheyenne
Agency, 1951 *South Dakota
State Historical Society*

Russell Means at the occupation of the BIA
building in Washington, D.C., November
1972 *Richard Erdoes*

Dennis Banks at the BIA
occupation, 1972 *Richard
Erdoes*

The occupation of Wounded Knee, 1973 *Owen C. Luck*

Russell Means and Leonard Crow Dog inside the occupied church at Wounded Knee, 1973 *Richard Erdoes*

Arthur Lazarus, Marvin Sonosky, and William Payne (seated), 1981 *NYT Pictures*

The Black Hills today *Richard Erdoes*

Burnette dispensed with such diplomacy. One of the generation of World War II veterans who were bringing to Sioux politics greater assertiveness and a broader understanding of the off-reservation world, Burnette had no patience with what he perceived to be the "meet and eat" variety of Sioux claims politician—the kind that had stood by contentedly during the Case years. In a letter to the BHSNC officers, Burnette scoffed at the council's proposed trip to Washington:

> It is my opinion that you are coming to Washington a year too late. . . . Almost a year ago, Standing Rock, Pine Ridge and Rosebud sent delegates to Washington and saved the case from being thrown out of court altogether by the very poor job done by Mr. Case . . . now that the case has been saved, you people have all of a sudden become concerned about getting the attorneys together.

Burnette blamed the BHSNC (and the staunch Case defenders who were its officers) for the retention of Payne, "who knows nothing about the case." He warned the BHSNC that at least on Rosebud there would be no "meddling" by outsiders in their choice of attorney or any other aspect of claims business. As head of a legally recognized tribal council, Burnette intended to keep the old pan-Sioux treaty council as powerless, indeed as irrelevant, as possible.

On November 15 the government filed its response to the motion to vacate. Faced with the prospect of reopening the largest Indian claim ever, Barney and Cooperman were taking no chances. They refused to acknowledge even a single shortcoming in Case's representation of the Sioux. Instead, they characterized him as an "able" and "conscientious" advocate.

The government's primary tactic, though, was to distract the court from the specifics of Case's representation by arguing that the Sioux claims were worthless on their merits. Case's omissions and concessions, the government suggested, reflected wise tactical maneuvering from a position of legal hopelessness.

The government contended, for example, that Case shrewdly recognized that the Sioux held only a worthless hunting right to the 40 million acres of Powder River country designated as Class C lands. Pursuing this claim would have cost more than it was worth. And the government proposed a similar theory to explain why Case abandoned the claim to the Class B lands (over 25.8 million acres of land recognized as Sioux in the 1851 treaty of Fort Laramie).

Finally, with respect to the Black Hills taking, the government reiterated its well-rehearsed argument that the offsets to which the government was entitled far outweighed the possible value of the Hills as of 1877. Again the government transformed error into strategy. In neglecting to collect and produce proof of value, Case had shrewdly saved his client a lot of time and money.

These legal arguments, however, had a self-defeating component to them. The government's own careful estimate of the value of Sioux rights in the Class B and C lands, and its comparison of Black Hills land value with estimated government offsets (accurate or not), unintentionally underscored Case's failure to litigate these issues. The government's argument, by its very nature, implicitly acknowledged that the Court of Claims had nothing before it with which to evaluate the government's estimation of the merits of the Sioux claims—except the government's own self-serving assertions.

So Sonosky and Lazarus pointed out in their reply to the government's response (by this time, Schifter and Lazarus had agreed that Lazarus would handle all the Sioux claims work at Strasser, Spiegelberg). Because Case abandoned the claims without a trial, no one knew whether the Sioux interest in the Class B and C lands was a hunting right, an aboriginal title (title based on use and occupancy unconfirmed by treaty), or a treaty-recognized title. And because Case had introduced no evidence on the subject, no one knew how plausible the government's estimated value of the Black Hills was or what proportion of its claimed offsets were legitimate.

Like a car salesman telling a customer to dispense with a test drive and inspection in exchange for a personal guarantee of quality, the government's "trust us, we're sure the Sioux claims are worthless" assurances raised more suspicions than they allayed. The adversarial system of American justice was not premised on trust. The system was premised on test drives and inspections, trials and evidence, the critical processes that Case had foregone.

On November 5, 1958, thirteen months after the filing of Sonosky and Lazarus's Motion to Vacate, in the impersonal way courts may change forever the lives of the parties that appear before them, the Court of Claims lifted the sentence of death that it had pronounced on the Sioux claims. In a one-page order containing not a single word of explanation, the court vacated its November 1956 decision and returned the Sioux claims to the ICC for a determination of whether the record should be reopened. The court further authorized the commission to receive additional proof and reconsider its prior decision should it deem such action appropriate.

On November 19, two weeks after the Court of Claims order remanding the Black Hills to the ICC, the commission announced that it was reopening consideration of the Sioux claims. For the first time in thirty-five years of claims litigation, the Sioux had won something—if not a victory, at least a reprieve. Sonosky would remember years later that he thought the biggest hurdle had been cleared. The Sioux had survived the legacy of Casc. Now, with a little luck, Sonosky and Lazarus could try the claims as they should have been tried long before.

The preliminary victory prompted a new round of statements and resolutions from the self-promoting BHSNC. In December Eddie Reddoor distributed a memorandum to the tribe's three attorneys, staking out the organization's historic claim to represent all of the Sioux tribes in claims matters. The council also called for a prompt determination of enrollment in the eight separate Sioux tribes, hoping to limit persons eligible for claims money to "descendants of those chiefs and headmen who signed the Sioux Treaty at Fort Laramie on April 29, 1868." Not everyone with Sioux blood deserved a Black Hills sack of beans.

In the hope of resolving the question of the BHSNC's status, Sonosky polled the tribal councils of his five Sioux clients about their participation in Reddoor's outfit. Rosebud, Standing Rock, and Crow Creek all concurred with Lower Brûlé, whose chairman, J. W. Thompson, replied: "I personally attended the last two meetings of the Black Hills Sioux Nation Council and could not see that they have any substantial evidence to offer for the Black Hills claim. . . . I do not believe there is enough real interest in this organization so that it can be of much assistance. . . ."

"My personal views coincide with yours precisely," Sonosky wrote back. With only the tiny Santee tribe among his clients opting to participate in the BHSNC, Sonosky regarded the issue of who spoke for the Sioux on claims matters as now settled—the elected tribal councils, and they alone.

This had been Lazarus's view from the outset. He had little interest in internal Sioux politics. As the elected representatives of the Pine Ridge Sioux and the only Pine Ridge government recognized by the United States, the Oglala Tribal Council had employed him. Accordingly, he reported to the council. Lazarus's sole concern was fashioning a legal strategy to bring the Sioux claims to successful judgment, and with this task his untutored clients (only one attorney among them) could not help him. As had been true even before Ralph Case filed the tribe's twenty-four original claims in 1923, for the Sioux, for virtually all American Indians, the basic truths behind their claims consisted of broken promises remembered and rued across generations. The power to translate this defining history into legal strategies, however, lay beyond their ken. In seeking redress from a judicial system barely understood even in general terms, according to rules often obscure to trained practitioners, the Sioux were blind and mute, entirely dependent on the white experts with whom they had deposited their faith to guide them successfully through the labyrinth of law.

For all the squabbling among the Sioux over who would represent the tribe on claims matters, the fight was mainly over symbolic possession. The Sioux were not divided by competing visions of their people's claims or over different legal theories. They were divided over the question of which groups were associated most closely with the claims, the one strand of their lives that at once linked the Sioux to their glorious past and explained the desolation of their contemporary existence. For as long as the Black Hills claim had existed, rival Sioux had competed to embrace this symbol of their history. For as long as the claim continued to exist, that struggle would endure.

Among the lawyers at least there was now harmony. By 1959, Payne apparently realized that Sonosky and Lazarus were actively pursuing every avenue for resuscitating the Sioux claims. He was content to piggyback on their efforts, which satisfied Sonosky and Lazarus's main concern that Payne not disrupt their legal work by pursuing separate strategies. In June the lawyers signed a formal agreement under which Sonosky and Lazarus became parties to Payne's two Sioux contracts and would receive a 60 percent share of whatever portion of the final legal fees might be finally attributable to Cheyenne River and Fort Peck. The agreement also provided that none of the parties would file legal papers without the consent of the others, which they all understood to mean that Sonosky and Lazarus would do all the Sioux legal work without interference from Payne. In essence, Sonosky and Lazarus paid Payne 40 percent of his potential fee in exchange for his giving them a free hand. He was "the smartest damn lawyer in Washington," Sonosky kidded. "Got paid for doing nothing."

In any event, Sonosky and Lazarus were already hard at work reformulating the Sioux claims for their second go-round at the commission. They worked smoothly on the job and were close friends as well. For Lazarus, a displaced New Yorker, Sonosky, his wife Shirley, and their three daughters provided a home away

from home. Years later, Sonosky would joke that Lazarus used to
bring girlfriends by his house for approval. In 1956 Lazarus married the only one Sonosky claims to have liked, an actress from
New York. Eighteen months later Lazarus asked Sonosky to be
godfather to his first child, Andrew.

In close collaboration, Sonosky and Lazarus started in earnest
the extensive historical and legal research necessary to retry the
Black Hills claim and also began searching for expert witnesses to
help build the record of Sioux land rights and values that Case had
neglected. They also decided to file amended petitions with the
commission, reasserting and clarifying the claims never pressed
for what Case had called the Class B and C lands.

In the meantime, in December 1959, as part of his firm's thriving
Indian practice, Lazarus argued his first case before the United
States Supreme Court, *Federal Power Commission* v. *Tuscarora Indian
Nation.* The argument and decision turned out to be a disillusion-
ing lesson in the elastic nature of legal rules when national priori-
ties or large sums of money are at issue.

In *Tuscarora,* the tribe sought to block Robert Moses and the
New York Power Authority's efforts to build a pump station dam
that would inundate over one-fifth of the Tuscarora's ten-square-
mile homeland. The federal statute under which New York was
proceding authorized the condemnation of reservation lands *except*
where that condemnation would "interfere or be inconsistent with
the purpose for which such reservation was created." Although
the taking of so great a proportion of Tuscarora land undoubtedly
interfered and was inconsistent with the intended use of the reservation, the Supreme Court (reversing the Court of Appeals) nonetheless held that the taking complied with the statute. Faced with
the prospect of ordering a costly halt to New York's program to
cure an electric power shortage in the Niagara valley, the Court
chose instead to pretend that the Tuscarora's tribal lands did not
constitute a "reservation" for the purposes of the statutory exception because (by an irrelevant historical quirk) the lands were not
held in trust for the tribe by the United States (as was usual) but
rather were owned outright by the tribe itself.

As Justice Hugo Black lamented in an historic dissent, the Court
had seized on a meaningless distinction to avoid the clear mandate
of a federal statute. As a result, the Tuscaroras lost lands that they
had occupied for 180 years—ever since losing an earlier New York
homeland as a result of tribal support for American revolutionar-
ies. The young republic had recognized that debt in solemn treaty,
acknowledging the tribe's ownership of its small corner of New

York, and Congress had done nothing to disturb those rights. "I regret that this Court is to be the governmental agency that breaks faith with this dependent people," Black wrote in conclusion. "Great nations, like great men, should keep their word."

However stirring, Black's words were cold comfort to Lazarus and his clients. For the lawyer—now poised to prosecute the biggest claim ever brought against the United States—*Tuscarora* became a cautionary tale. In court, even the Supreme Court, money and power sometimes determined the law, even if precedent and reason were on the other side.

By the time of the *Tuscarora* argument, Sonosky and Lazarus had virtually completed two amended petitions, sharpening, reformulating, and even expanding Case's original allegations. The purpose, they informed the commission frankly, was to free the Sioux claims of "the heritage of dross left by petitioner's former counsel."

Case's original petition had focused exclusively on those lands and rights that he alleged to have been "extinguished" through the process of negotiation and conquest culminating in the 1877 act that took the Black Hills. According to Case, during the years 1874–77, the U.S. unilaterally appropriated three categories of Sioux rights: the tribe's treaty-recognized title to the Black Hills lands (Class A); the tribe's absolute right to use and occupy (as distinct from title to) those lands recognized as Sioux in the 1851 Fort Laramie treaty but not included in the permanent Sioux reservation as defined in the 1868 treaty (Class B); and the tribe's right to roam and hunt in the Powder River country (Class C).

By contrast, in the amended petitions, Sonosky and Lazarus divided the claims into two separate cases, reflecting what they perceived to be two distinct historical events by which the United States obtained lands and rights from the Sioux. In the first amended petition (designated Docket 74A), Sonosky and Lazarus demanded fair compensation for Sioux land rights and ceded to the United States under the 1868 treaty. The second petition (Docket 74B) demanded compensation for tribal rights obtained by the United States through the act of February 1877 which removed the Black Hills from the Great Sioux Reservation and abrogated Articles 11 and 16 of the 1868 treaty.

This restructuring added substantially to the sum total of Sioux claims. As Sonosky and Lazarus now emphasized in the petition dealing with the 1868 treaty, under Articles 2 and 11 of that treaty, the Sioux "relinquish[ed] all rights to occupy permanently the territory outside" the Great Sioux Reservation. Under this provision, Sonosky and Lazarus charged, the Sioux relinquished to the U.S. their rights of *ownership* to both Case's Class B and Class C lands. Case, by contrast, sought compensation for only a lost right of use of and occupancy in the Class B lands, and only a lost hunting right in the Class C lands. In addition, they asserted that the Sioux relinquished title to 15 million acres east of the Missouri River and more than 10 million acres between the two forks of the Platte River; for this land, Case had made no claim at all. Although Sonosky and Lazarus recognized that the cession of these rights occurred under a legally ratified treaty, they argued that the compensation provided by that treaty was unconscionable—grossly disproportionate to the fair value of the land. Under the ICC Act, if Sonosky and Lazarus could prove such a disproportion, the Sioux were entitled to recover the difference between the true value of what they had relinquished and the compensation that the United States actually had paid.

In the petition asserting Sioux claims based on the 1877 act, Sonosky and Lazarus restated the all-important Black Hills claim. They also alleged that under the 1877 act the U.S. appropriated Sioux rights in the entire "unceded Indian territory" defined in Article 16 of the 1868 treaty (the Powder River country and Nebraska land above the North Platte river), abrogated Sioux Article 11 hunting rights along the Platte and Smoky Hill rivers, and acquired three new rights-of-way across the Great Sioux Reservation. According to the lawyers, the tribe had never received adequate compensation for any of these expropriations.

To some extent, Sonosky and Lazarus decided to take a "kitchen sink" approach to the Sioux claims—to throw in every plausible allegation in both cases, although some appeared in both petitions and even potentially conflicted. Legal research or strategic considerations later would dictate which allegations should be revised or discarded in order to attain the largest total award. Indeed, at this stage, Sonosky and Lazarus had little alternative. At the outset, they had to find some way to circumvent Case's abandonment of the Class B and C claims and to manufacture a recovery in the Black Hills claim despite Case's concession of $57 million in allowable government offsets. With no way to ascertain beforehand which claim—the 1868 treaty case or the Black Hills claim—was the more promising, they decided to include in the amended petitions every reasonable allegation and keep open as many options as possible.

Filing the amended petitions proved unexpectedly difficult. Sonosky and Lazarus had delayed filing pending bureau and tribal approval of their contractual deal with Payne. Now Cheyenne River and Fort Peck were balking. At a BHSNC meeting in February 1960, Eddie Reddoor and Alex Chasing Hawk (Cheyenne River's delegate) embraced the idea that the Sioux needed undivided counsel, but they insisted that Payne was the only "logical" choice. The other Sioux tribes, most vocally the Oglala of Pine Ridge, wanted no part of that arrangement. When the stalemate dragged on until June, Sonosky and Lazarus decided that they could not wait any longer without prejudicing the claims through unwarranted delay. Cheyenne River jumped aboard at the last minute. Fort Peck, assuming Reddoor finally acquiesced, would have to be added later.

At the Justice Department, the amended petitions provoked outrage to match the already strong sense of disbelief with which the claims section received the judicial order reopening the Sioux claim. Reflecting the scarcely concealed fury of its authors, the government in its response objected to the filing of the amended petitions, employing the patently false argument that "the Court of Claims refused the Sioux request to vacate its [November 1956] judgment of affirmance." From this premise, the government argued that the court's 1957 order remanding the Sioux claims to the commission provided solely for the submission of additional proof, not amendments to the original petition.

The government also objected, with reason, that the amended petitions, in addition to restructuring old claims, improperly added entirely new claims. Under the ICC Act, tribes were required to file all claims by 1951. Allowing new counsel not only to revamp existing claims but also to append new claims clearly violated this deadline. The behavior of Sioux counsel, the government charged, was "akin to that of some itinerant salesmen. They have gotten their foot into the doorway and are now abusing the hospitality of the householder by attempting to exploit the intrusion."

If so, the commission decided that it at least wanted to see what sort of goods Sonosky and Lazarus were selling. On November 4, 1960, it granted the Sioux (now including Fort Peck) leave to file the amended petitions.

The Justice Department, though, refused to give up the fight. Whether out of a sense of wounded pride or a commitment to pursue what it perceived to be procedural (if not substantive) justice, the claims section decided to employ every imaginable legal maneuver to avoid or at least to delay a meaningful trial on the merits. Rather than answer the amended petitions—the natural next step in moving the cases towards judgment—the government sought from the Court of Claims a writ of *mandamus* (an extraordinary request for an appellate court to interfere with a lower tribunal's handling of an ongoing proceeding). The proposed writ would order the commission to rescind its allowance of the amended Sioux pleadings.

This dilatory, never-concede-an-inch strategy typified more than twenty-five years of Justice Department policy towards Indian claims. Certainly, as the government's lawyers against the tribes, the Indian Claims section bore the responsibility of defending the government's interest vigorously. It was the Justice Department's job both to ensure that the United States defeated unjustified claims and to protect the national treasury from excessive judgments in those claims that were justified. But in the fulfillment of these responsibilities the Justice Department often seemed overzealous, to the detriment of national policy.

From the days of the Wilson administration, Congress had repeatedly expressed its desire to resolve tribal claims fairly and expeditiously—first through special jurisdictional acts and later through the ICC Act. Nonetheless, the Justice Department had done its utmost to delay and avoid substantive claims determinations as well as limit in every possible way the size of claims judgments.

In the 1920s and 1930s, as observed earlier, Justice Department officials repeatedly lobbied Congress to adopt the broadest possible legislative definition of allowable government offsets against claims awards. In court, department lawyers sought to deduct from awards every imaginable expense, including many undertaken to serve governmental, not tribal interests, such as salary payments to the government's own reservation employees. In an attempt to avoid claims awards altogether, the Justice Department consistently urged the Court of Claims to adopt the narrowest plausible readings of jurisdictional acts, and thereby derail substantive judicial decisions, often after many years of costly litigation. Later, under the ICC Act, the Justice Department adopted a strict policy of refusing to settle tribal claims, even meritorious ones, without a full-blown trial. This phobia of pretrial negotiation ultimately cost the government money and imposed an especially heavy burden on indigent tribes.

Determined and effective advocacy in the service of the national interest demands strategies and tactics more enlightened than circumvention and absolute denial of wrongdoing. President Truman's attorney general, Tom Clark, once remarked that "the Government does not lose any case if by its results justice was done." This principle applied with special force to Indian cases, where the government, as a matter of declared policy, should have sought not merely victory but actual substantive justice for the tribes. To vindicate this policy, as well as to defend the government's position in each individual case, attorneys in the claims section needed to demonstrate a sense of fair play and an appreciation of the merits of tribal grievances where appropriate. These qualities the Justice Department rarely displayed.

On February 6, 1961, the Court of Claims denied the government's petition for a writ of *mandamus*. Having vacated one of its own decisions because of the incompetence of prior Sioux counsel, the court was not prepared to hamstring the tribe's new lawyers in their efforts to repair the past.

Trial before the commission was now set for April 9, 1962, and Sonosky and Lazarus sought to refine further the Sioux claims and to guide the commission in structuring its deliberations. In a motion filed March 24, 1961, Sonosky and Lazarus restated precisely the Sioux claims, winnowing out some that now appeared untenable. In the 1868 treaty case (Docket 74A) they reduced the Sioux claims from those set forth in the amended petition. They no longer alleged that the Sioux had relinquished actual ownership rights to the Powder River country or to the lands lying between the forks of the Platte River. (Docket 74B still included claims for lesser rights in these lands, but Sonosky and Lazarus concluded that proving Sioux title to lands recognized as belonging to other tribes in the 1851 Fort Laramie treaty would be impossible). Sonosky and Lazarus now claimed that under the 1868 treaty the U.S. paid unconscionable consideration for two tracts of lands: 1) Sioux lands recognized in the 1851 Fort Laramie treaty but not included in the 1868 permanent reservation (Case's Class B lands) and 2) 15 million acres of aboriginal (nontreaty) Sioux lands lying east of the Missouri River.

To resolve Sioux claims based on the 1868 treaty, Sonosky and Lazarus proposed three issues for the 1962 trial date: What lands and interests were ceded under the 1868 treaty? Did the Sioux have title to these lands and interests at the time? And, what was the value of the consideration promised in the treaty for the interests ceded?

In Docket 74B (the Black Hills claim), where the tribe's allegations remained unchanged from those contained in the Amended Petition, Sonosky and Lazarus proposed three additional questions for trial: What lands and interests did the government acquire under the 1877 act? Did the Sioux have title to these lands and interests? And, what was the value of the consideration promised by the United States in acquiring these lands and interests?

Consistent with its strategy of delay, the government refused to respond to the motion. Having waited a month, Lazarus wrote Chief Commissioner Arthur Watkins, the former senator and architect of termination policy whose 1960 appointment to the ICC attested to the continuing power of western conservatives in Indian affairs and thoroughly dismayed the Indian claims bar. Lazarus requested that the commission grant the tribe's motion for a definition of issues as unopposed. The letter was answered with silence.

Three weeks later, on May 17, the government asked for a thirty-day extension of time in which to respond to the amended petitions and subsequent motion. Before even permitting the Sioux to object, the commission granted the extension.

On June 16, the government finally filed papers with the commission, but not one responded to the amended petitions. Instead, the Justice Department continued its guerrilla war against the two-and-a-half-year-old decision reopening the Sioux claims. In a single multipurpose motion, the government sought to dismiss the amended Sioux petition in Docket 74A as vague and contradictory. Alternatively, the government requested that the commission order the Sioux to rewrite the petition to separate and clarify each allegation.

In a separate motion, the government moved to dismiss the Black Hills claim (Docket 74B). According to the government, the Sioux had "failed to state a claim upon which relief can be granted." In the view of the claims section, the Sioux could not maintain an unconscionable consideration claim for the taking of the Black Hills because the U.S. was still paying consideration to the Sioux under the terms of the 1877 act. Since the ultimate value of the consideration paid for the Hills was continuing to increase (and was therefore indeterminate), the commission would have no basis for determining whether the consideration paid for the Black Hills would ultimately prove to be unconscionable.

As yet another dilatory tactic, the government moved to consolidate the Sioux claims with the pending claims of six other tribes. Without specifying precisely, the government asserted that the claims overlapped.

With respect to the Sioux motion for clarification of issues, after twelve years of litigation, the government described it as "premature."

Sonosky and Lazarus replied with invective. Contemptuously, they recounted the government's studious efforts to delay trial and derided government arguments as, by turns, "frivolous," "utterly lacking in merit," and "patently ridiculous." Only the government's attempt to dismiss the Black Hills claim received a serious reply. Sonosky and Lazarus pointed out that the government's argument about the incalculability of the compensation paid for the Black Hills ignored well-settled claims law stating that the value of consideration (like the value of the land taken) must be determined as of the date of the taking, not contemporaneously. After all, what the Sioux received in 1877 for their land was a promise of rations of unknown quantity and duration; and it was the value of that promise, not the value of the rations the government ultimately delivered, that constituted consideration under the 1877 act.

Most of Sonosky and Lazarus's response was not legal argument at all, but rather a calculated effort to belittle the government's motions and thereby expose them as transparent efforts at delay. On this point they also prodded the commission, which, in their view, had acted indifferently, if not complicitously, towards the government's failure to answer the amended petitions. "The Commission once again has an opportunity to move [the Sioux claims] forward in an orderly fashion to trial and a final decision," they closed. "At some point there must be an end to defendant's procrastination and evasive tactics, and that time has long since arrived."

The commission apparently did not agree; nor did it take such a dismissive view of the government's filings. Between January and March 1961 the commission issued a series of rulings on the pending motions, summarily denying the government's motion to dismiss the Black Hills claim. On the other hand, it did "strike" (throw out) Sonosky and Lazarus' amended petition in the 1868 treaty claim (apparently for lack of clarity), offering Sioux counsel the alternative of either proceeding under Case's original petition or drafting a new amended petition. (Sonosky and Lazarus opted for the latter). In addition, the Commission consolidated the 1868 treaty case, but not the Black Hills claim, with five other pending cases.

Last, the commission agreed with the government that the Sioux motion for definition of issues was "premature since the parties are not yet at issue" under the amended pleadings. That was true, of course, only because the government refused to answer the amended petitions. Still, the commission did not impose a deadline for the government's answer. And, without this compulsion, no answer was forthcoming.

In March the commission delayed the scheduled April trial until June 25. It also struck (as still not clear enough) Sonosky and Lazarus's second version of an amended petition in Docket 74A. Despite the resulting absence of a satisfactory petition delineating Sioux claims under the 1868 treaty, the commission announced the issues to be tried in June.

The commission had established a standard practice of dividing major claims into three distinct trial phases. In the initial "title" phase, it would determine the scope and nature of the lands and rights at issue in a claim. Next, in the "valuation" phase, it would determine the value of the lands and rights at issue as well as the nature and amount of any compensation paid by the government. Finally, if the results of the valuation phase established that the government was liable, it would determine allowable government offsets and render a final judgment.

Following this pattern, the commission limited the June 1962 hearing in the Sioux claims to the "title" questions basic to the 1868 treaty claims: what lands and interests were ceded under the 1868 Treaty and whether, at the time, the Sioux held title to those lands and interests. Apparently the commission had decided that the Black Hills claim could wait.

Such halting progress was normal in litigation before the commission. In its first ten years (1947–57, the complete run of its original mandate), the Commission decided only 102 of 852 separate claims on its docket. This snail's pace particularly distressed those (like the terminationists) who supported the ICC Act primarily as another mechanism for accelerating assimilation through the rapid resolution of old grievances.

At the same time, the commission thoroughly disappointed those who, like Cohen, had conceived of it as a grand expression of America's legal conscience and others who had hoped that it would provide meaningful expiation for the sins of conquest. Of the 102 cases that the Commission decided in its first ten years, the Indians prevailed in only 21. Of the nearly $1 billion claimed by the tribes, it awarded judgments totaling only $13 million, less than 2 percent.

Several of the ICC Act's most innovative provisions went unrealized. As Sonosky and Lazarus noted in their attempts to reopen the Sioux claims, the commission's investigative section never materialized; Congress had failed to allocate the necessary funds and the commission had made no request. Though not for lack of

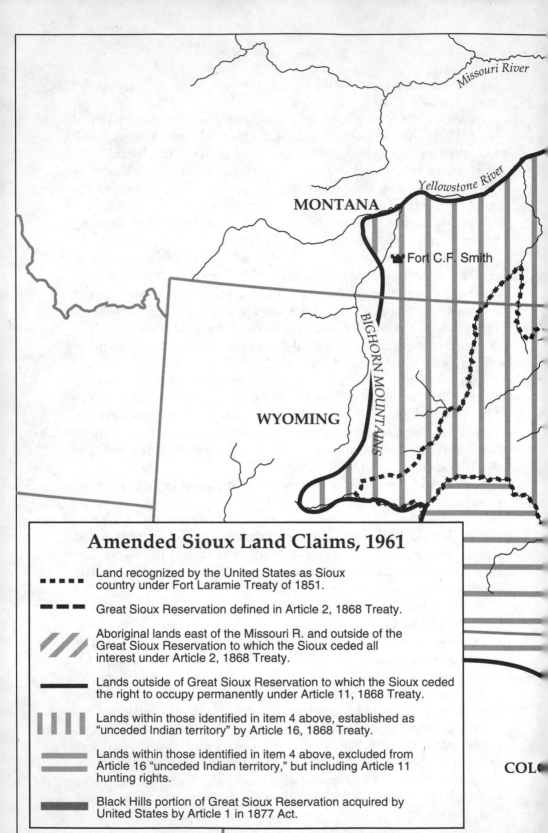

Amended Sioux Land Claims, 1961

Land recognized by the United States as Sioux country under Fort Laramie Treaty of 1851.

Great Sioux Reservation defined in Article 2, 1868 Treaty.

Aboriginal lands east of the Missouri R. and outside of the Great Sioux Reservation to which the Sioux ceded all interest under Article 2, 1868 Treaty.

Lands outside of Great Sioux Reservation to which the Sioux ceded the right to occupy permanently under Article 11, 1868 Treaty.

Lands within those identified in item 4 above, established as "unceded Indian territory" by Article 16, 1868 Treaty.

Lands within those identified in item 4 above, excluded from Article 16 "unceded Indian territory," but including Article 11 hunting rights.

Black Hills portion of Great Sioux Reservation acquired by United States by Article 1 in 1877 Act.

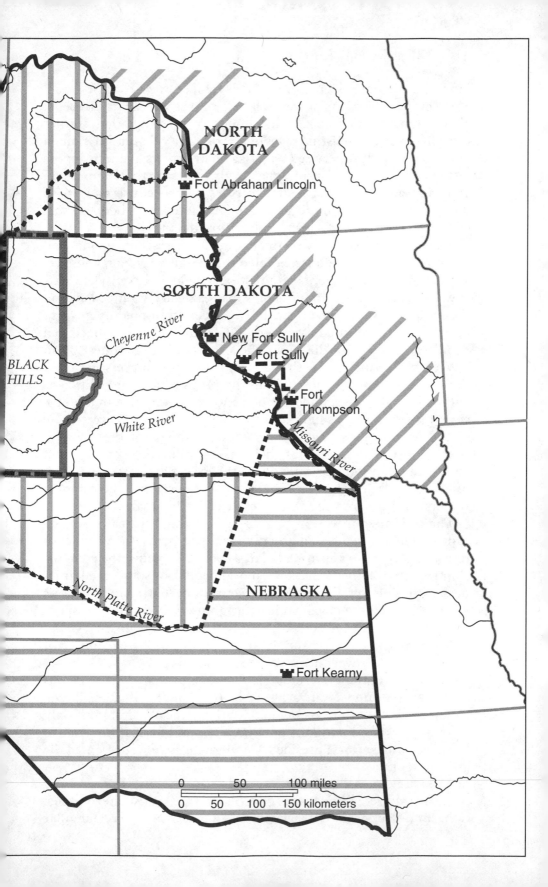

NORTH
DAKOTA

Fort Abraham Lincoln

SOUTH DAKOTA

Cheyenne River

New Fort Sully

Fort Sully

BLACK
HILLS

Fort
Thompson

White River

Missouri River

NEBRASKA

North Platte River

Fort Kearny

| 0 | 50 | 100 miles |

| 0 | 50 | 100 | 150 kilometers |

money, the commission also never developed the broadest aspect of its legal mandate, its power to hear moral as well as strictly legal claims, those "based on fair and honorable dealings that are not recognized by any existing rules of law or equity." Nor did it much experiment with supervised negotiation or arbitration to promote settlements and avoid protracted trials. Instead, the commission generally adopted strict courtlike rules of procedure and, in so doing, converted itself into a traditional adjudicatory body—a sort of substitute Court of Claims solely for Indians.

The commission followed the path of least resistance, one well marked by previous efforts to solve the claims problem, and irresistible to commissioners ill-suited to their jobs. Even when narrowly conceived, the commission's mandate surely ranked among the most ambitious legal undertakings ever attempted by government: to hear and adjudicate every outstanding claim of aboriginal peoples arising from the rapid and often violent conquest of an entire subcontinent. To this enormous task Congress assigned three commissioners chosen from the ranks of former politicians and politicians' aides, undertrained and unimaginative in the process of judging. It was ludicrous to expect such men to create new categories of claims or to pioneer new methods for their resolution. The bare minimum of their task—evaluating complex and conflicting ethnohistorical and anthropological testimony, adjudicating billions of dollars in claims—far overtaxed the commissioners' abilities and the resources at their disposal.

The commission was, in this sense, a characteristically American creation. Conceived in grandly idealistic terms, the product of the nation's can-do approach to large social problems, the commission reflected both the nation's moral aspirations and the stinginess with which it allocated the resources necessary to realize its vision. What emerged was an institution fearful of its own responsibilities, one that welcomed delay and, especially in the eyes of tribal counsel, leaned strongly towards the cost-free option of finding for the government whenever possible.

Before this tribunal the first trial in the rejuvenated Sioux claims convened on June 25 in a hearing room in the Federal Trade Commission building, a stone monolith by the Washington Mall. Arthur Watkins, among the greatest enemies of tribal interests in the twentieth century, presided. Cooperman again represented the government.

At Sioux counsel table sat Sonosky, Lazarus, and Payne. They made an odd set. With his craggy, Slavic face, midwestern inflection, and thick-framed black-rimmed glasses in the rectangular style of the day, the middle-aged Sonosky projected a mixed image of down-home country lawyer and east coast sharpie. The younger Lazarus presented no such contradictions. In his conservative dark suit—neatly trimmed dark hair carefully brushed back, clever hazel eyes scanning the courtroom—he looked every bit the rising big-firm lawyer. The round-faced, white-haired Payne quietly advertised his western roots. He sat by quietly, a "silent Sam" with a penchant for ribbon bowties, keeping up appearances for his clients in the audience.

Sonosky handled most of the four-day trial. Belatedly starting the process of building a record that Case had so egregiously disregarded, Sioux counsel introduced 535 exhibits, totaling over 10,000 pages, to prove Sioux title to the Fort Laramie lands and the lands east of the Missouri. Sonosky also presented the written report and oral testimony of their expert historian, Harry Anderson, a college professor from Pierre, South Dakota.

The government naturally countered with its own expert, as well as 150 additional exhibits. Cooperman disputed Sioux title to the lands east of the Missouri and argued that the Fort Laramie lands recognized as Sioux in 1851 were much smaller than the at least 25 million acres claimed by the tribe. The commission took both issues under advisement and adjourned.

Throughout the four days, a host of Sioux sat quietly in the wooden pews of the commission room gallery. William Fills the Pipe, 84, was the oldest, lean and long-boned under his loose-fitting suit. Edward Iron Cloud, 80, an aged cowboy in the white man's court, clutched a ten-gallon hat that rested on his ample lap. Eddie Reddoor attended, of course, as did Moses Two Bulls, William Whirlwind Horse, Chester Red Kettle, Charlie Under Baggage, Isaac Hawk, and others. Their long-featured mahogany faces, crested and ridged like the prairies they called home, betrayed little of their thoughts or of how much they understood.

At one remarkable point during the brief trial Chief Commissioner Watkins had called on these Sioux delegates to ratify one of the legal decisions that Sonosky and Lazarus had made on their behalf. Sonosky had announced to the commission that he did not intend to present any evidence of "use and occupancy" to prove Sioux ownership of the tribe's 1851 Fort Laramie lands. He and Lazarus would rely solely on the language of the 1851 treaty itself as legally sufficient proof of Sioux title.

Watkins insisted that Sonosky had no authority from his clients to "waive" their arguments based on use and occupancy. Over Sonosky's objection, he demanded that Sonosky immediately confer with those Sioux present in the courtroom and obtain their approval for his legal strategy. After a fifteen-minute recess, Eddie Reddoor, chosen to be the impromptu Sioux spokesman, put an end to the charade. "Sonosky is our mouthpiece," he informed Watkins. "Whatever Sonosky says goes."

The trial had commenced on the eighty-sixth anniversary of the Little Big Horn. Some of the old-timers thought this a good omen. But the courtroom battle would yield no swift and decisive victories. Having heard only a few of the many issues in the 1868 treaty case, the commission had not yet even addressed the Black Hills claim and the hard questions of what the Hills had been worth when they were taken and how much the government had paid.

Some of the more cynical tribal councilmen kidded Sonosky that for three bucks cash they would sell him their interest in the claims. But they never would have. Cynical or not, dozens of Sioux had traveled 2,000 miles to Washington to see their hired counsel retell the history of the old chiefs and the treaties and how the Great Father broke his word. Two generations had made the same journey before them and, if necessary, their children would follow, too.

▼ ▼ ▼ ▼ ▼

ELEVEN

TRIALS AND TRIBALISM

THE POLICY OF termination backfired completely on those who believed that it would hasten the demise of tribalism and Indian self-identity. Unified by the perceived threat to their survival as independent peoples, tribes across the nation—many with little in common except their treatment by the government—joined in a singleminded and unprecedented opposition to congressional and bureau policy. Coordinated Indian voices, angry, fearful, and ever more conversant in the language of American politics, pricked at the delicate national conscience with compelling accusations of contemporary faithbreaking.

Responding to the threat of termination, a new generation of Indian leaders stepped forward to reexamine the government's legal and moral obligations to the tribes. Frustrated by persistent bureau interference with native self-government, these leaders promised to reclaim the power of Indians to set their own course according to their own compass. Since the time of Chief Justice John Marshall, near to the founding of the Republic, U.S. courts had recognized the sovereign power of these "domestic dependent nations" to govern their internal affairs. John Collier and the IRA reaffirmed and reinvigorated that right of sovereignty. As the 1950s drew to a close, an increasingly aroused Indian community resolved to assert as much tribal authority as the dominant society legally accorded them—and to agitate for more.

By 1958, the National Congress of American Indians (NCAI) and an expanding list of followers and well-wishers convinced the Eisenhower administration to suspend efforts to force termination on relatively acculturated tribes. Although the policy remained in force, and although Congress occasionally tried to link appropriations for specific tribes with acquiesence in termination, as a general matter tribal consent became a prerequisite to termination.

Presidential candidate John Kennedy promised this and more. Under his administration, "there would be no change in treaty or contractual relationships without the consent of the tribes concerned. No steps would be taken by the Federal Government to impair the cultural heritage of any group." Upon election, Kennedy appointed Stewart Udall, an Arizonan keenly interested in Indians, to be Secretary of the Interior. "Maximum development," not termination, was the catchphrase of his approach to the tribes.

In June 1961, 420 Indians from 67 tribes—leaders from reservations and cities alike—assembled at the University of Chicago to hammer out a Declaration of Indian Purpose, an affirmative program for asserting and developing Indian identity in the post-termination era. Organized by Helen Peterson at NCAI and Sol Tax, a University of Chicago anthropologist, the conference heralded a new pan-Indian resolve to safeguard and nurture Indianness in America. Part lamentation, part rallying cry, their declaration promised a sustained and stronger tribalism in America:

> When Indians speak of the continent they yielded, they are not referring only to the loss of some millions of acres in real estate. They have in mind that the land supported a universe of things they knew, valued, and loved. With that continent gone, except for the few parcels they still retain, the basis of life is precariously held, but they mean to hold the scraps and parcels as earnestly as any small nation or ethnic group was ever determined to hold to identity and survival.

Younger Indian leaders were even more assertive. Organizing their own conference, a group of mainly college-educated Indian youth—the sort who in a previous era actively campaigned for assimilation—derided the "Uncle Tom-a-hawks" (including the elder statesmen of NCAI) whose cautious and cooperative exercise of tribal power had hardly diminished bureau domination of the reservations.

While critical of what they considered craven tribal leadership, the assembled Indian youth placed the burden of blame for the desperate situation of Indians directly on the shoulders of the white man. Forming their own National Indian Youth Council (NIYC), they issued a bitter manifesto on Indians in America.

"Our viewpoint," the NIYC Statement of Policy announced, "based in a tribal perspective, realizes, literally, that the Indian problem is the white man, and, further, realizes that poverty, educational drop-out, unemployment, etc., reflect only symptoms of a social-contact situation that is directed at unilateral cultural extinction."

Nor was the new Indian assertiveness limited to conferences and written declarations. Having watched the black civil rights movement successfully employ the tactic of civil disobedience, some Indians decided to stage their own versions of the Nashville lunchcounter sit-ins or the Montgomery bus boycott. In the far northwest, members of the Muckleshoot, Puyallup, and Nisqually tribes conceived an Indian strategy of planned confrontation directed at reasserting their tribal sovereignty and reclaiming much-trammeled treaty rights. In violation of state laws regulating salmon fishing, members of these small tribes defiantly exercised their treaty-recognized right (dating to 1854) to "fish at all usual and accustomed grounds and stations . . . in common with all citizens of the Territory." Although state regulations proscribed the gill nets that the Indians were using and prohibited salmon fishing altogether in some seasons, the Indian fishermen believed that their treaty rights superseded the state's regulatory authority.

In one ugly and violent clash after another, local game wardens (often aided by vigilante white fishermen jealous of fishing rights they did not share) ambushed, roughed up, and arrested Indian fishermen, confiscating the boats and nets upon which their livelihood depended. State and federal courts began the glacial process of determining the boundary between Indian treaty rights and legitimate state regulation. (Over the next decade, the judiciary generally held that state officials possessed little authority to regulate treaty-recognized tribal fishing rights). In the meantime, the "Great Northwest Fishing War," actively joined by NIYC, and featuring staged "fish-ins" by celebrities such as Marlon Brando and Dick Gregory, emerged as a national symbol of a new Indian militancy in the pursuit of their legal rights.

In the same spirit, though accompanied by far less fanfare, the Sioux ventured into their own critical battle against encroaching state power. After the 1953 passage of Public Law 280 (authorizing individual states to assume criminal and civil jurisdiction over Indian reservations), non-Indians living in and around Sioux country convinced sympathetic state politicians to draft legislation assuming jurisdiction over South Dakota's Sioux reservations. White residents and reservation landowners had no doubt that South

Dakota courts and law enforcement officers would better secure their interests than either the federal government or the tribes. The least scrupulous of this group also hoped that state jurisdiction would eventually lead to the taxation of Indian lands and, in turn, to increased white ownership as tax-delinquent Sioux sold off their property, or had it confiscated.

The South Dakota legislature passed the first jurisdiction bill in 1957, but made implementation contingent on both tribal approval and reimbursement from the federal government for the costs of extending jurisdiction. In referendums on Pine Ridge and Rosebud the Sioux opposed state jurisdiction 5 to 1. Also, despite efforts by the South Dakota congressional delegation in Washington, no promise of federal funds was forthcoming.

The South Dakota legislature tried again in 1961. This time it passed legislation assuming jurisdiction solely over the highways on the Sioux reservations. Although the new bill required neither federal money nor tribal consent, a South Dakota court held the law unenforceable on the ground that the state could not assume only partial jurisdiction over the reservations.

Agitation for a jurisdiction bill continued in 1962, especially after a legislative committee report concluded that assumption of jurisdiction would advance the state's interest in domestic relations, juvenile affairs, and institutional commitments. In other words, the South Dakota legislature preferred not to have Sioux judges making important decisions about divorce, adoptions, and guardianship for non-Indians who happened to appear before them.

As a new comprehensive jurisdiction bill (again requiring neither federal funding nor tribal consent) circulated in the legislature, Sioux leaders lodged concerted and sometimes strident protests. At a meeting of the state Commission on Indian Affairs, Oglala Sioux Tribal Judge John Richards accused the legislature of "trying to shove [the jurisdiction bill] down their throat."

The new chairman at Rosebud, Cato Valandra, reported that his people lived in "dread fear" of state jurisdiction. "I believe that equal treatment to Indians and whites would make a big difference in whether or not Indian people accept civil jurisdiction," he continued. "They are not being treated equally. I think every person in this room knows that."

What every person in the room, especially the Sioux, knew was that South Dakota Indians regularly suffered discrimination, humiliation, and brutality at the hands of both the white citizenry and state officials. In the western part of the state (in the Black

Hills and around Rapid City) signs reading "No Indians or Dogs Allowed"—the plains equivalent of the South's "White Only" signs—were commonplace. The police chief of Martin (a town surrounded by the Rosebud Reservation) made the analogy to the South explicit. "As near as I can figure out, it's about like the Negroes down South. You can't let them get the upper hand."

With like-minded officers in charge of incarcerated Indians, the results were tragically predictable. Sioux witnesses testifying before the Senate subcommittee on Constitutional Rights in Washington told of vicious jailhouse beatings, of rapes, of Indian prisoners being kicked and dragged about the streets, then chained to their cell bunks.

For Indian defendants, the constitutional guarantee to a trial by one's peers meant in practice trial by an all-white jury. Because few Indians paid state property taxes (they were exempt under law), their names never appeared on the rolls from which the state selected prospective jurors. And when South Dakota courts meted out justice, Indian life was valued at a heavy discount. As Robert Burnette recounted, "[a] white man, 'Nig' Ryan, killed an Indian and was sentenced to a one hundred dollar fine and thirty days in jail. Another white man shot an Indian in the back seven times, killing him, and received two years in the penitentiary, of which he served six months. A white man who stole a saddle was sentenced to five years."

The jurisdiction bill threatened to bring this cruel and demeaning regime onto the reservations themselves. Joining together to form United Sioux Tribes, Sioux leaders vowed to fight what Valandra dubbed the "Wounded Knee of 1963."

Impervious to Sioux concerns, the South Dakota legislature passed a third jurisdiction bill in March. The sponsors claimed that they supported the law for the good of the Indians—"to afford Indians and whites alike the protection of South Dakota laws." They declined, however, to make that protection a matter of choice.

The United Sioux Tribes staged a last-ditch effort to convince Governor Archie Gubbrud to veto the legislation, but under heavy pressure from "West River" cattlemen he signed the bill. Still, the Sioux did not give up. Instead, they turned to the state's referendum procedure. Under state law, if the Sioux gathered signatures from 5 percent of the number of voters participating in the last gubernatorial election, they could suspend implementation of the jurisdiction bill and have the issue placed on the ballot for the next general election—November 1964.

Gathering 13,000 valid signatures was a daunting task with broad implications for the political status of Indians generally. As Lazarus's partner Dick Schifter wrote in a letter seeking financial support for the petition drive, "[i]f the petition effort is successful . . . it will show Indians throughout the West that they can be a potent political force, that if they stand on their feet and exercise their rights as citizens they can have an impact."

The Sioux accepted the challenge. With help from Strasser, Spiegelberg, Sonosky, a local law firm, and other well-wishers, Sioux volunteers spread out across the reservations and the rest of the state in a carefully organized signature campaign. Before the referendum deadline, they collected over 18,000 signatures, thousands more than necessary to place the issue on the 1964 ballot and to stave off state jurisdiction for at least eighteen months.

For the referendum campaign itself, the Sioux hired a politically experienced public relations firm. After extensive polling revealed a large number of uninformed and undecided voters, the firm advised the tribe to base its campaign on two basic themes: first, that forcing jurisdiction on the tribe was fundamentally undemocratic and unfair; and, second, that state jurisdiction would result in higher taxes statewide to pay for the increased services. In addition, the firm advised the Sioux to present an affirmative alternative to the current jurisdiction bill by agreeing to work with state officials in the future to draft a new bill that would be satisfactory to both the state and the Indians.

In a series of pamphlets and speeches, through radio, television, and newspaper ads, and even a campaign film widely distributed across the state, the Sioux hammered home their central theme, "Keep Faith with Our Indians." The jurisdiction bill, the Sioux material declared, would "cripple the tribal councils" and deprive the Indians of "the incentive and opportunity to advance from within." While the tribe ostensibly supported gradual extension of state jurisdiction, it wanted a bill that provided for Indian consent and preservation of its right to self-government. Of course, all of the tribe's public information also stressed the hundreds of thousands of dollars that the jurisdiction bill would cost.

The tribe's fair play approach immediately won over several large church groups. The Veterans of Foreign Wars, with a significant Indian membership, also joined the Sioux cause. By feeding white guilt over the historical treatment of Indians and by emphasizing South Dakotans' financial self-interest, the Sioux succeeded in having non-Indian South Dakotans carry the jurisdiction fight for them. And having forged a strong coalition of Indians, philanthropic groups, and fair-minded South Dakotans (mainly those who lived east of the Missouri, away from the reservations), the Sioux defeated the jurisdiction bill 4 to 1.

Like the termination movement generally, South Dakota's legislative effort to reduce the sovereign authority of the Sioux served mainly to instruct the tribe in how to use those sovereign powers more effectively. In South Dakota, in the far northwest, and elsewhere, the days of Indian complacency and compliance were coming to a close.

Yet while Indian attitudes were changing, the tragic circumstances of their daily lives were not. Tribes across the nation, the Sioux in particular, continued to suffer unrelenting and grinding poverty. By every standard, the Sioux were desperately poor, sick, undereducated, and unproductive. In South Dakota, 60 percent more Sioux were dying from tuberculosis than were their white neighbors. Rare diseases causing deafness, blindness, and the gradual wasting away of the body—ailments virtually unknown in other parts of the country—afflicted them in shocking numbers. Gastritis, enteritis, and other forms of diarrhea, inevitable in communities without running water or modern sanitation, raced through families again and again, killing children and the infirm. The infant mortality rate for Indians generally ran 30 percent above the national average. It was much higher still among the Sioux.

For those who survived infancy, life was short. In the mid-1960s, reservation Indians enjoyed a life expectancy of a mere 43.5 years, a full twenty years less than the national average. The sickness was an old story, as old as the poverty that had haunted the Sioux ever since the buffalo culture died, when a vigorous life and healthy diet gave way to empty days and chronic malnutrition. Four of every five Sioux families fell below the poverty line. Among fullblood families on Pine Ridge, 40 percent lived on an annual income of less than $1,000. The Sioux were as poor as any community in America, as poor as the country folk in Appalachia, as poor as the sharecroppers in the deep South and the migrants in the west. Maybe poorer.

In 1969, fewer than one in five Sioux adults possessed a high school education. More than half had dropped out before completing eighth grade. For those who remained in the bureau-sponsored schools, the quality of education was by all accounts substandard and often still tinged with the rigid and even brutal anti-Indian caste of the strict assimilationist days.

Perhaps one Sioux in three held a permanent job, almost always with the tribe or the bureau or the Indian Health Service. Perhaps another third found work for a season or two, picking potatoes, or at some odd job. The rest did nothing, scraping by on government handouts and minor lease payments, whiling away time in the lean-tos and tarpaper shacks that still made do for home. Over time, with the help of relocation grants, many able-bodied Sioux started to drift away, leaving behind those too young, too old, or too infirm to try a different life.

What all the studies and statistics (and there were many) could not really capture was the ceaseless pain that almost a century of this life had visited upon a people. Hundreds of Sioux families knew the grief of a son or daughter lost to suicide. It happened all the time. Every Sioux family knew what it was like to drink and drink, everyday, without end—a habit dating to the earliest days of the fur trade. Thousands did it, starting at nine or ten or whenever. One Sioux woman, Mary Crow Dog, who grew up on Rosebud in the 1950s and 1960s remembers:

> The little settlements we lived in—He-Dog, Upper Cut Meat, Parmelee, St. Francis, Belvidere—were places without hope where the bodies and souls were being destroyed bit by bit. Schools left many of us almost illiterate. . . . Jobs were almost nonexistent on the reservation, and outside the res whites did not hire Indians if they could help it. There was nothing for the men to do in those days but hit the bottle. . . .
>
> On weekends the lease money and ADC [Aid to Dependent Children] checks were drunk up with white lightning, muscatel-mustn't tell, purple Jesus, lemon vodka, Jim Beam, car varnish, paint remover—anything that would go down and stay down for five minutes. . . . There was hardly a weekend when somebody did not have an eye gouged out or a skull cracked. "Them's eyeballs, not grapes you're seeing on the floor," was a standing joke.

Such social decay made Indian tribes prime targets for the social programs of Kennedy's "New Frontier" and Johnson's "Great Society." Under the Kennedy administration's Area Redevelopment Agency (which issued grants to develop industries and construct municipal buildings) tribes replaced dilapidated New Deal-era community facilities. Later, during the Johnson administration, federal authorities enlisted tribal governments as front-line posts for conducting the War on Poverty. The government set up a special Indian Desk at the Office of Economic Opportunity to assist tribes in obtaining grants and organizing community action programs on reservations.

Generally, these programs had a significant and beneficial impact in Indian country. Suddenly tribal governments found themselves with enough funding to implement real programs for self-development. Tribal councils obtained large grants to develop Head Start and neighborhood youth corps. With sufficient money to pay decent salaries, tribal jobs started to attract college-educated Indians back to the reservation as administrators. They returned with new ideas and new devotion to communities that in past years they probably would have abandoned.

On the Sioux reservations, government social programs gave birth to tribal efforts at developing tourism and manufacturing. On Pine Ridge, in 1961, the tribe used government funding to attract a fishhook snelling firm to the reservation. Lightweight and easily transported to distant commercial centers, fishhooks were one of the few commodities suitable for production in such an isolated community. During 1965, the Wright & McGill company employed as many as 200 Sioux at three different plants and contributed more than $600,000 to the reservation economy. The fishhook business came to an abrupt end, however, when Congress eliminated trade restrictions on fishhooks manufactured in the Far East. Wright & McGill moved to Florida. Eventually a moccasin factory, employing up to 80 Indians, took over the fishhook plant.

The Rosebud Sioux experimented with similar ventures. They started a furniture manufacturing business and a company to manufacture electrical equipment. They promoted the production and sale of Indian arts and crafts. The tribe also operated a 40,000-acre ranch.

But along with these modest successes, there were notable failures. In 1962, for example, the Rosebud tribe created the Rosebud Housing Authority, which (among other projects) oversaw the construction of 400 desperately needed government funded prefab houses on the reservation. As a result of poor coordination among the relevant government agencies, the construction firm completed the houses and stocked them with appliances before another contractor had completed the sanitation and drainage facilities. As a result, the houses suffered severe water damage before Sioux families could take possession. Vandals made off with the appliances.

Even when completed, the houses were grossly substandard. They lacked adequate heating and insulation to fend off the severe plains weather. Doors and windows did not fit or work. Roofs leaked. Chagrined government officials eventually gave the houses to the tribe for a dollar apiece, but Sioux residents ended up paying a comparative fortune for repairs and maintenance.

The fundamental inadequacy of the Great Society social programs, though, was not the unavoidable failure of individual reservation projects. It was the failure of the programs to provide even a semipermanent economic foundation for many reservations.

The Sioux reservations were classic examples. Millions of dollars of well-intentioned government money flowed into Sioux country. The government's largesse created new jobs. It gave additional purpose and direction to the tribal governments. It supported a sizeable class of reservation bureaucrats. And it attended to some basic needs. Still, however earnest the War on Poverty, however generous the Great Society, these government programs could not change the fact that the government had pushed the Sioux off all of their land that was useful for anything but running cattle, then had broken up the cattle ranges by allotting and checkerboarding what remained.

In the wake of government policy the Sioux were left with virtually no natural resources to develop except lands that for the most part were too scattered and fractionated for profitable use. The reservations were too remote to attract much industry, even with government subsidies. Moreover, after generations of idleness accompanied by widespread alcoholism, in a community where one person in five graduated from high school, the potential Sioux workforce was untrained and unreliable.

The Sioux needed more nourishing medicine than even the Great Society had to offer. They needed a new economy to replace the nomadic life that had vanished long ago. They needed a new sense of purpose to resurrect spirits buried deep in the rubble of cultural ruin. One hundred years of poisoned existence could not be cured in a few years, if it could be cured at all.

In the meantime, the almost mythical prospect of a monumental claims windfall as the miracle antidote to Sioux woes languished before the commission. During the eighteen months following the June 1962 trial, Sioux counsel and the government exchanged legal briefs supporting their respective positions about the boundaries of the tribe's 1851 Fort Laramie lands and the scope and validity of its claim to 15 million acres of aboriginal lands east of the Missouri River. Although all papers were filed by February 1964, in September the commission still had issued no opinion on Sioux land titles and had yet to indicate when a trial on valuation might take place. It also had done nothing to prompt a government answer to the amended Sioux petition in the Black Hills claim.

As the months wore on, Sonosky and Lazarus tried to goad the commission into action without jeopardizing their clients' legal interests. Late in 1964, Lazarus wrote to the commission requesting oral argument on the title issues in the 1868 treaty case—not so much because he thought it was necessary as because he hoped that the request would spur some action. Instead, Watkins wrote back informing Lazarus that decision in Docket 74A would have to wait for the trial of overlapping cases brought by the Three Affiliated Tribes of the Fort Berthold Reservation, and that this trial was delayed by the withdrawal of the Indians' original counsel. Faced with the possibility of indefinite delay, Lazarus asked Watkins to reconsider. As Lazarus pointedly reminded the chief commissioner, the Fort Berthold overlap covered only 3 million of the 39 million acres involved in Docket 74A.

Watkins would hear none of it. His decision stood. Another six months passed. Utterly frustrated, in March 1965 Sonosky and Lazarus even risked filing a motion with the commission asking it to decide immediately Sioux title to the 1851 Fort Laramie lands (over which no conflict existed). They also asked the commission to hold a hearing within 90 days on the alleged Fort Berthold overlap (reduced in the interim to 2 million acres). Inviting trouble, they concluded the motion sarcastically. "How much longer can the claim of 45,000 Indians to 14 million acres [east of the Missouri] be held up because of a possible claim of 2500 Indians to 2 million acres? The answer is, of course, 'Indefinitely', unless this Commission, as it has in so many other cases, orders the claimant in an overlapping case to speak or hold its peace."

The commission declined Sioux counsel's suggestion that it hold an expedited hearing on the Fort Berthold problem, but at the end of August, it did render an opinion defining the boundaries of the 1851 Sioux Fort Laramie lands. The decision left Sonosky and Lazarus shaking their heads.

The basic dispute between the government and the Sioux concerned whether the 1851 Fort Laramie treaty's Sioux country boundary line "along the range of mountains known as the Black Hills" referred to the modern-day Black Hills on the South Dakota-Wyoming border (the government's position) or (as the Sioux contended) to a different mountain range in western Wyoming that was also known as the Black Hills in the mid-1800s. Instead of drawing the boundary along one of the two Black Hills ranges, the commission marked the boundary along a watershed bearing no relation to either set of mountains. This decision not only ignored the plain language of the Fort Laramie treaty, it completely disregarded its scheme to apportion the entire great plains among its competing tribal inhabitants. When viewed in conjunction with its other opinions interpreting the treaty, the commission's decision in the Sioux claim created a 5 million-acre no-man's-land in the middle of the plains map. As Sonosky and Lazarus thought they had demonstrated beyond serious doubt, those 5 million acres properly belonged to the Sioux.

Because the commission's opinion was an intermediary decision (an interlocutory order only partially deciding a case, as opposed to a final judgment), under the rules of procedure Sonosky and Lazarus could not appeal to the Court of Claims until the commission resolved the remaining title issues in the claim. They did have the option of asking the commission to reconsider its decision, but Sonosky and Lazarus considered this futile. Watkins was an autocrat, and always had been. Lazarus angrily recalled his experience in the *Hualapai* case, where he had sought to prove (for the purpose of establishing aboriginal title) that his client tribe used a certain waterway to the middle of the stream. All the evidence and expert testimony supported Lazarus's thesis, but Watkins didn't care. "I know that country and they didn't use to the middle of the river," Watkins announced from the bench. "An opinionated and vicious man," Lazarus remembers. Watkins's word was law and there was no turning him around.

Sonosky and Lazarus had other plans for remedying the commission's mistakes. They and others in the Indian claims bar had long cultivated congressional dissatisfaction with the commission's performance—both among those who considered its progress too slow and those who also faulted its conservative rulings and niggardly claims awards. With the commission's legislative mandate due to expire at the end of 1966, Sonosky and Lazarus hoped that Congress would terminate the commission altogether and transfer its responsibilities to the Court of Claims. Alternatively, Congress might reconstitute the commission, enlarging it and replacing Watkins as chairman.

The idea of returning Indian claims to the Court of Claims was ironic. Congress had created the commission precisely because the claims court, through uncharitable interpretation of special jurisdictional acts, had frustrated efforts to resolve tribal grievances on their merits. Despite this congressional intent, the commission had, if anything, exacerbated the problem. Though originally animated by Felix Cohen's idealism about justice for Indians, the commission matured in the era of termination and was dominated by Arthur Watkins. The practical result was a tribunal even stingier in its legal rulings than the court whose conservatism it had been designed to circumvent.

In yet a further twist, after the 1946 creation of the commission, the Court of Claims had developed an increasingly sympathetic attitude towards tribal claims. In its role as appellate court for the commission, the Court of Claims frequently reversed uncharitable commission decisions or rulings that failed to implement its broad congressional mandate. In the 1950s, for example, the Court of Claims upbraided the commission for its failure to develop and employ its congressionally authorized investigative division. The claims court also rebuked the commission for failing to invoke its unique powers to redress moral as well as legal grievances. Time and again, the court reversed commission decisions that undervalued Indian lands, improperly trimmed reservation boundaries, or in some other fashion gave a crabbed interpretation of Indian rights.

In its own rulings, the Court of Claims turned back government efforts to circumscribe the types of claims that tribes might assert under the ICC Act. In *Otoe and Missouria Tribe of Indians* v. *United States,* the Court of Claims rejected the Justice Department's argument that the ICC Act did not recognize claims based on aboriginal Indian land title—claims where the tribe's interest in the lands in question was based not on a treaty but on longstanding use and occupancy. While the commission waffled, the Court of Claims emphatically upheld the right of tribes to bring suits based on aboriginal Indian title. And, in so doing, the court vindicated one of Felix Cohen's most fiercely held beliefs, that federal law should recognize that tribes held property rights in the lands under their control simply as a consequence of their prior occupancy, regardless of any governmental recognition.

With the more recent Court of Claims record in mind, Lazarus and Sonosky hoped that the commission's expiration in 1966 might open the door to a more favorable forum for the Sioux claims. Accordingly, they swallowed the commission's erroneous title decision and waited for better times.

While Sonosky and Lazarus bided their time, a new government lawyer, Walter Rochow, assumed responsibility for the Sioux cases. After five years of silence, he finally raised the subject of the Black Hills claim. In a March 1966 motion for clarification of the record, Rochow tried to make sense of the confused Sioux pleadings. He understood that the commission had stricken Sonosky and Lazarus's amended petition in the 1868 treaty case, but he had no idea whether, as a result, the claim was proceeding under Case's original petition or if Sioux counsel intended further amendments. He also wondered about the status of the amended petition in the Black Hills claim. While the commission had not stricken this petition, what was its validity if Case's original petition (which combined all of the Sioux claims) was still in effect?

Sonosky and Lazarus welcomed the government's motion. They, too, wanted to clear up the muddled pleadings. Responding, they reiterated their position that the 1868 and 1877 Sioux claims involved wholly distinct legal issues and ought to be tried separately. Sonosky and Lazarus urged the commission to reinstate the stricken amended petition in the 1868 treaty case. As an alternative, they argued that the commission should recognize the two cases as distinct and designate them as separate dockets. With respect to the Black Hills claim, they suggested that the government file its five-year overdue answer to the amended petition and that the commission then define the issues for trial in the claim.

Late in May the commission adopted Sonosky and Lazarus's alternate proposal. Without reinstating the amended petition in the 1868 treaty case, it ordered the two Sioux claims to be tried separately, under separate docket numbers (74 for the 1868 treaty case and 74B for the Black Hills claim). The commission also ordered the government to answer the tribe's amended petition in the Black Hills claim. This sleeping giant was to be awakened.

From Sonosky and Lazarus's perspective, the timing was nearly perfect. In the hearings on terminating or extending the life of the commission, Senator McGovern and others had rebuked the commission for dilly-dallying with the Sioux claims. More important, although Congress did not transfer the commission's cases to the Court of Claims, effective in 1967 it did expand the commission to five members. Most important, even before the commission was to expand, and in anticipation that he might not be reappointed, Watkins stepped aside.

In reconstituting the commission, however, Congress did little to upgrade its overall quality. Commissioners Holt and Scott stayed on from the Watkins regime. As for the new commission, the principal qualification continued to be good political connections, not judicial imagination or legal expertise. John Vance, slated to be the new chairman, was a Montana lawyer and counsel to the Montana Trade Commission. Prominent in Montana veterans' affairs, Vance owed his appointment to his friend and homestate Senator Lee Metcalf, a powerful member of the Interior Committee.

Jerome Kuykendall, a lawyer in D.C. private practice and former chairman of the Federal Power Commission, filled another vacancy. He promoted himself as an expert on overcoming administrative delay, the bane of the claims commission.

President Johnson nominated Richard Yarborough, son of the senior senator from his native Texas, to fill the final open seat. A victim of crippling arthritis, the younger Yarborough had served on his father's Senate staff. It was generally assumed that he received the commission appointment as a sinecure.

Though hardly impressed with the new commissioners, Sonosky and Lazarus expected them to be a substantial improvement. Watkins's absence alone accomplished that much. In any event, Sonosky and Lazarus immediately prepared to educate the new commissioners about the Black Hills claim and to guide them towards a trial on its merits. Even these preliminary steps, though, were fraught with difficult strategic decisions and delicate maneuvering. After a decade of swimming against the tide of Ralph Case's blunders, Sonosky and Lazarus remained in deep and murky legal waters, far from certain about the best direction for maximizing the potential for a Sioux recovery in either docket, much less both.

This much they now knew: Ralph Case not only had mistried the Black Hills claim but, even more fundamentally, had argued the claim under a wholly inappropriate provision of the ICC Act. Case had based his claim for compensation primarily on that section of the ICC Act providing for recovery in cases where the United States paid "unconscionable consideration" for acquired lands. Such unconscionable consideration claims arose from circumstances where an Indian tribe had contractually agreed to cede land to the United States, albeit for consideration (a price) grossly disproportionate to the fair market value of the land.

But as Sonosky and Lazarus parsed Sioux history, the Sioux and the United States never entered into a contractual agreement regarding the Black Hills. In the lawyers' view, the 1876 "sell or starve" agreement purportedly ceding the Hills to the government was null and void (as the Sioux always had maintained). The government had failed to obtain the consent of three-fourths of the adult Sioux males as required by the 1868 treaty. As a legal matter, Sonosky and Lazarus believed, the government obtained the Black Hills not through agreement, but through Congress's unilateral appropriation of the land, the act of February 28, 1877. In other words, the Black Hills claim was not an unconscionable consideration claim at all; it was a *no* consideration claim, an outright abrogation of Sioux rights.

Accordingly, Ralph Case should have brought the Black Hills claim under one of the provisions of the ICC Act dealing with nonconsensual governmental takings of Indian lands and, specifically, under the provision permitting claims that the government had violated its obligation under the Fifth Amendment to the Constitution not to take private property without payment of just compensation. (Case had asserted this Fifth Amendment argument in the original litigation before the Court of Claims, but changed his theory to unconscionable consideration when arguing before the commission. Presumably, he thought that unconscionable consideration would be easy to prove given his theory that the Sioux were entitled to an enormous royalty for the minerals taken out of the Hills.)

By grounding the Sioux claim in a violation of the Fifth Amendment, Sonosky and Lazarus hoped both to reflect accurately the historical facts and to alleviate yet another residual headache from the Case era, his concession of $57 million in government payments under Article V of the 1877 act. Under "takings" law, if the Sioux prevailed, the tribe would be entitled not only to the 1877 value of the Black Hills land but also to interest on that value from the time of the taking. (Awards in unconscionable consideration cases did not yield interest.) Between the value of the land and the much larger amount of accumulated interest, a successful takings argument might secure some recovery for the Sioux even if Sonosky and Lazarus could not wriggle out of Case's $57 million concession.

As a strategic matter, though, Sonosky and Lazarus felt constrained from declaring forthrightly their change of legal theory. They had expended considerable effort over the last ten years slipping away from Case's original allegations, claiming compensation for lands and interests not mentioned in Case's original petition. The government had opposed vigorously all of these reworkings, with some success. By keeping the precise basis for their claim as vague as possible for as long as possible, Sonosky and Lazarus wanted to prod the commission into resolving the legal issues underlying a Fifth Amendment taking claim without provoking Justice Department objections to their Fifth Amendment theory. (The deception was possible because many of these underlying issues, such as whether the 1877 act provided any consideration or payment for the Black Hills, were almost identical to the issues underlying an unconscionable consideration claim.) On the other hand, Sonosky and Lazarus did not want their takings argument to be a complete surprise. Caught off guard, the commission might resent their strategy or panic when faced with a legal theory that would compound a judgment with interest.

In mid-1967, Lazarus started drafting a motion for definition of issues intended to shape the commission's thinking about how to proceed. The final version, filed in February 1968, suggested three questions for prompt determination, all necessary to the prosecution of a Fifth Amendment claim, but none directly raising the Fifth Amendment issue. First, what lands and rights did the United States acquire under the 1877 act? Second, was there any consideration for the acquisition by the United States of these lands and rights, and, if so, what constituted that consideration? Third, if there was no consideration (an agreed-upon price), was there any payment (compensation for a unilateral appropriation) for the acquisition? (This third question was essential, because even if Sonosky and Lazarus proved a taking they would also have to show that the government did not pay just compensation.)

The government objected to Sonosky and Lazarus's proposed issues for determination. The Justice Department saw no reason to separate the issue of whether there was consideration for the relinquishment of Sioux rights from the issue of what payments, if any, were made for those rights. Far from recognizing a legal difference between consideration and payment, and far from acknowledging that this difference might reflect alternative legal theories for the Sioux claim, the government used the terms "consideration," "payment," and "compensation" interchangeably and tacitly assumed that its payments under the 1877 act were consideration for the rights obtained.

In October the commission set down for determination precisely the three questions that Sonosky and Lazarus had suggested, and it established a briefing schedule for each. For the next eighteen months, the claim proceeded along two separate tracks. On the first track, the Sioux and the government submitted opposing briefs on the critical legal issues in the claim, namely the scope of Sioux rights obtained under the 1877 act and what consideration or payment, if any, was received for those rights. On the second track, both sides prepared for trial on the value of the Black Hills— the 7.3 million acres of land that the United States indisputably acquired under the 1877 act.

On March 16, 1969, Sonosky and Lazarus filed two briefs. The first defined Sioux lands and rights that they deemed to have been lost under the 1877 act, specifically the Black Hills lands, the tribe's

Article 11 and 16 rights under the 1868 treaty, three rights-of-way across the reservation, and a navigational right on the Missouri River.

In the second and much more substantial brief, Sonosky and Lazarus put forward their view of the scope and meaning of Articles 11 and 16 of the 1868 treaty. The definition of these two treaty provisions was absolutely critical to the litigation of both the Black Hills and 1868 treaty cases.

Under Article 2 of the 1868 treaty, the Sioux "relinquished all claims or rights in and to any portion of the United States" except for the Great Sioux Reservation and "as hereinafter provided." The exceptions "hereinafter provided" were contained in Articles 11 and 16. Under Article 11, the Sioux reserved the right to hunt on the lands "north of the North Platte, and on the Republican Fork of the Smoky Hill River for as long as the buffalo may range thereon in such numbers as to justify the chase."

Under Article 16, the United States recognized a vast area north of the North Platte River and east of the summits of the Big Horn Mountains as unceded Indian territory. This country appeared to include all the tribe's 1851 Fort Laramie lands outside the Great Sioux Reservation (33 million acres) and perhaps 25 million additional acres that the Fort Laramie treaty designated as belonging to other tribes.* The government agreed that no white person would be allowed to settle or even enter the region without the consent of the Indians.

For the purposes of the 1868 treaty case (in which the Sioux claimed unconscionable consideration for the rights they relinquished), the commission's definition of the scope of Articles 11 and 16 would, in turn, define what lands and interests the Sioux ceded under Article 2 of the treaty. In addition, since Article 16 recognized Sioux rights in lands not previously recognized as belonging to the tribe, the commission's definition of this article would also partially determine what consideration the United States provided for the lands and rights it obtained through the treaty. In other words, the commission's ruling on the scope of

---

*These acreage figures for what Ralph Case had designated the Class B and Class C lands do not correspond with Case's own figures. Case estimated the size of the Sioux 1851 Fort Laramie lands lying outside the boundaries of the Great Sioux Reservation (his Class B lands) at 25.8 million acres. Although I have used Case's figure when discussing his legal arguments, these Sioux lands actually measured 33 million acres, and from this point on I use the correct figure. Case estimated the size of the Sioux Article 16 lands *outside* the tribe's 1851 Fort Laramie lands (Class C) at 40 million acres. Sonosky and Lazarus estimated these lands to include 25 million acres.

Articles 11 and 16 would go a long way towards deciding whether the Sioux claim for unconscionable consideration—a gross disparity between what they relinquished and what they received—could prevail.

The commission's definition would also profoundly affect Sioux prospects in the Black Hills claim. Sonosky and Lazarus were asserting that the 1877 act abrogated both Articles 11 and 16. (Indeed, the act itself said as much.) Obviously, how the commission defined these articles would determine the scope of the Sioux claim. Given Sonosky and Lazarus's long-range plan to convert the Black Hills claim into an interest-bearing Fifth Amendment takings case, a favorable definition of Articles 11 and 16—especially Article 16, which involved an estimated 58 million acres—might vastly increase the size of a potential Sioux judgment.

To complicate matters further, at least with respect to Article 16, the two Sioux cases were potentially in conflict. A commission decision that Article 16 granted the Sioux substantial compensable rights would significantly increase the potential recovery in the Black Hills claim. Under the 1877 act, the United States appropriated the tribe's Article 16 rights no less than the Black Hills themselves, and it would have to pay compensation for the taking.

But that same decision (giving an expansive definition to Sioux rights under Article 16) would probably render the 1868 treaty case worthless. If Article 16 recognized substantial Sioux rights in all the tribe's Fort Laramie lands as well as in lands not previously owned by the Sioux, then the Sioux relinquished very little under the 1868 treaty and received substantial benefits in return. The chance of showing unconscionable consideration under these circumstances was essentially nil. Of course, if the commission decided that the Sioux possessed few compensable rights in Article 16's unceded Indian territory, then the effect on the two claims would be precisely the reverse.

Because it was impossible to know in advance what definition of Articles 11 and 16 would ultimately prove to be most beneficial to the Sioux, Sonosky and Lazarus decided to let history and not strategic considerations guide their interpretation of the 1868 treaty. Accordingly, they steeped themselves in the history of relations between the Sioux and the government, especially the peace conferences that preceded the signing of the 1868 treaty. What the lawyers found was very much what their clients had been telling their children for 100 years: that the 1868 treaty marked a glorious Sioux triumph over an invading white army and recognized the tribe's right to be left alone to roam and hunt over all the lands in their enormous domain. The lawyers' job was to translate that understanding into a legally compelling interpretation of the language of the treaty, setting that language against the history that surrounded its drafting, and translating this historical interpretation into the lexicon of law.

In a lengthy brief overflowing with historical citations, Sonosky and Lazarus argued to the commission that Article 16, read in context, clearly guaranteed to the Sioux virtual ownership over the lands within its purview. Over vociferous Sioux protests, the lawyers recalled for the commission, the 1851 Fort Laramie treaty (the first treaty formally to apportion the plains) had divided the Article 16 lands among the Sioux, the Crow, and, to a lesser extent, the Mandan, Gros Ventres, and Arikara. By the late 1850s, however, even the government's own agents recognized that the Sioux, having defeated the other tribes in battle, absolutely controlled all of the lands east of the Big Horn mountains and north of the North Platte River. The United States implicitly confirmed this Sioux dominion when, in 1865 and 1866, its representatives Newton Edmonds and Nathaniel Taylor entered into negotiations with the Sioux for a right-of-way (the Bozeman Trail) through this country to the Montana mining districts.

These negotiations failed when the military arrived to secure the Bozeman trail by armed force. Red Cloud led the Sioux into war, promising to banish whites from the Powder River country. The impetuous Colonel Fettermen, vowing to destroy the whole Sioux nation, rode directly into ambush. And the nation, faced with a stark choice between a protracted war and negotiating for peace, chose to abandon the Bozeman forts and acquiesce in Sioux demands that whites stay out of the tribe's last inviolate hunting ground.

Article 16, Sonosky and Lazarus argued, embodied this understanding between the parties. It acceded to the unwavering determination of the Sioux to continue the buffalo life in the Powder River and Big Horn regions and acknowledged the tribe's successful defense of the land that it considered home. At the same time, the article reflected the nation's conviction both to make peace and to provide for the eventual civilization of the Sioux.

Accordingly, Sonosky and Lazarus asserted, under Article 16 the United States conceded Sioux ownership rights, except for the right of "permanent occupancy," in all the lands north of the North Platte River and east of the Big Horn Mountains not already recognized as Sioux in the 1951 Fort Laramie treaty. As for the Article 16 lands already recognized as Sioux in 1851, the Sioux surrendered solely the right of permanent occupancy.

For the Indians, many of whom never envisioned making a home within the permanent reservation and who had won a promise of absolute freedom in their hunting grounds, this concession was essentially meaningless. Sioux hunters and warriors like Red Cloud and Crazy Horse and Man-Afraid-of-his-Horses did not think in terms of "permanent occupancy"; what they cared about was the right to roam and hunt undisturbed. The treaty guaranteed them precisely these rights in all the lands to which they lay claim. If the whites hoped that someday they would settle down on the reservation, that was no business of theirs.

In sum, for all practical purposes, Sonosky and Lazarus interpreted Article 16 as confirming Sioux ownership to an estimated 25 millions of acres north and west of the tribe's 1851 Fort Laramie lands and reducing the Sioux interest in the 33 million acres of Sioux Fort Laramie lands outside the "permanent" Great Sioux Reservation by only a virtually meaningless right of permanent occupancy. Put differently, if property rights are like a bundle of sticks, and a full bundle is equal to fee title (complete ownership), then, in Sonosky and Lazarus's view, Article 16 had guaranteed to the Sioux every stick in roughly 58 million acres of land except the inconsequential twig of permanent occupancy.

The history of Article 11, Sonosky and Lazarus observed, was very different. Under the 1851 Fort Laramie treaty, the lands in Article 11 were allocated to the Pawnee, Cheyenne, and Arapaho tribes. Although technically tribes signing the 1851 treaty did not "abandon or prejudice" their claims to lands outside their designated territories, and although the Sioux frequently hunted on the Article 11 lands after 1851, Sonosky and Lazarus conceded that the United States consistently resisted any further recognition of Sioux rights in the Article 11 area.

Crucial to the United States, the much-traveled California Trail lay across these lands and the Union Pacific Railroad would shortly follow suit. In negotiating the 1868 treaty, the government had determined that the Sioux must be moved away from the oncoming white settlements and major transportation routes as expeditiously as possible. Accordingly, although the peace commission reluctantly agreed to a self-limiting Sioux hunting right south of the North Platte and along the Republican, it insisted (in Article 2 of the 1868 treaty) that the Sioux give up all other claims to this area and that the tribe not oppose the onrushing white migration. Sonosky and Lazarus believed that in signing the 1868 treaty the Sioux agreed to these terms. Accordingly, they now claimed no more than a self-limiting Sioux hunting right in the Article 11 lands.

The potential import of this historical interpretation of the 1868 treaty was enormous. If the treaty confirmed Sioux ownership of roughly 58 million acres of Article 16 lands, then the 1877 act deprived the Sioux not only of the 7.3 million acres of goldbearing Black Hills lands but also of this many times larger, though less valuable, territory. If, in turn, Sonosky and Lazarus could prove that the 1877 act was an unconstitutional taking, the value of the Article 16 lands (plus interest) might add several hundred million dollars to a final judgment in the claim. Even if they had to settle for an unconscionable consideration claim, the value of the Article 16 lands would help considerably to make up for Case's $57 million offsets concession.

On the other hand, Sonosky and Lazarus's interpretation of Articles 11 and 16, if accepted by the commission, would kill the 1868 treaty case. Under their interpretation, by the 1868 treaty the Sioux gave up only a right of permanent occupancy in the Fort Laramie lands outside the Great Sioux Reservation, in addition to aboriginal title to 14 million acres of land east of the Missouri. For these interests, the Sioux received virtual ownership of as much as 25 million acres previosly allocated to the Crow, Gros Ventres, Arikara, and Mandan, as well as extensive promises of food, education, clothing and other benefits. Proving unconscionable consideration would be impossible.

The government, not surprisingly, responded with a very different interpretation of the 1868 treaty, and especially Article 16. The Justice Department argued that under the 1877 act the United States acquired *no* compensable rights other than the Black Hills themselves. Under the government's reading of the 1868 Treaty, the Sioux ceded to the United States all of their 1851 Fort Laramie lands outside the Great Sioux Reservation. Article 11 did reserve for the tribe a temporary and exclusive hunting right to the south of the permanent reservation, but this self-limiting right (to expire with the buffalo) was noncompensable.

The government asserted that Article 16 granted the Sioux even fewer rights than Article 11. The Sioux interest in the so-called unceded Indian territory amounted merely to "temporary permissive use," and even this limited interest was held not exclusively but rather in conjunction with other tribes. This minor tribal interest, the government urged the commission, was also noncompensable. Thus, according to the government's construction of the 1868 treaty, the Sioux fought "Red Cloud's War" and forced the government to abandon its forts in the Powder River country in order to preserve for themselves no meaningful rights in lands under their exclusive control and which they considered at the time absolutely indispensable to their survival.

Six months later, in September 1969, Sonosky and Lazarus filed yet another brief, this one presenting their argument that the government obtained the Black Hills and other Sioux rights without either consideration or payment. They noted that the Court of Claims, both in 1942 and 1956, had recognized that the "purported" agreement of 1876, lacking the proper number of Sioux signatures, was null and void. Accordingly, the government's acquisitions were made through unilateral action, not contract. Since "consideration" is the price that induces a party into a contract, the lawyers asserted that no consideration could exist in this case.

Sonosky and Lazarus further argued that the government made no "payment" for the lands and rights acquired under the 1877 Act. Under Article 5, the government had promised "schools and instruction in mechanical and agricultural arts, as provided for by the treaty of 1868" and rations "as may be necessary . . . until the Indians can support themselves." But the education provision, by its own terms, merely continued one of the government's outstanding obligations. That was not payment.

The promise of rations, moreover, "was so conditional as to be illusory." It depended on full Sioux compliance "with each and every obligation" contained in the act; it terminated whenever the Indians could support themselves; it could be suspended for those parents holding their children out of school. These conditions were "absolutely inconsistent with any theory that such rations reflected the purchase price for real property." According to Sonosky and Lazarus, the rations and other material provided by the government under Article 5 of the 1877 act constituted not consideration or payment but a gratuity, much like the rations the government had provided between 1874 and 1876, after the rations provision of the 1868 treaty had expired.

As a fallback position, Sonosky and Lazarus argued that if the commission concluded that the Article 5 benefits did constitute consideration or payment, at most the value of that consideration or payment was the 1877 value of the government's promised subsistence less the 1877 value of outstanding government commitments under the 1868 treaty. In either case, Sonosky and Lazarus concluded, the 1877 act effected "a taking of Sioux lands without the payment for such lands of compensation agreed to by the petitioners."

The Sioux brief on consideration provoked a sharp response from the new government attorney on the case, Craig Decker, a large, lumbering, red-faced man with an "aw shucks" country style—the fourth government attorney to take on the Black Hills claim. The Justice Department suddenly woke up to Sonosky and Lazarus's quiet effort to maneuver the claim away from unconscionable consideration into a Fifth Amendment case. Decker prefaced his consideration argument with an emphatic section announcing in bold type that "THE COURT OF CLAIMS HAS ALREADY DECIDED THAT THERE WAS NO FIFTH AMENDMENT TAKING UNDER THE 1877 ACT." According to Decker, the Court of Claims had decided the Fifth Amendment issue on its merits in 1942, and under the principle of *res judicata*, (an issue once conclusively adjudicated may not be relitigated), the Sioux were not now free to raise it.

With respect to the issue of what consideration, if any, was provided for the Sioux lands and interests obtained under the 1877 act, the government's answer was straightforward. Quoting directly from the 1942 Court of Claims decision, Decker asserted that the 1877 act required the Sioux to sell the Black Hills and their off-reservation rights " 'in return for a *consideration* of 900,000 acres of additional land and approximately one million dollars a year until such time as the Indians become self-supporting. . . .' " By Decker's reckoning, based on two enormous General Accounting Office reports on government expenditures for the Sioux, in addition to the value of the 900,000 acres added to the Great Sioux Reservation, the government had expended $52 million in consideration under the 1877 act prior to 1951. Post-1951 disbursements had not yet been calculated.

The government did not directly address Sonosky and Lazarus's argument that without a voluntary agreement there could be no consideration for the lands and interests that the Sioux lost. In a footnote, Decker declined to distinguish between consideration and payment. The government's expenditures were, in Decker's words, "payments on the claim" for which the government deserved credit regardless of their technical designation.

In their reply, Sonosky and Lazarus tried to steer the commission away from deciding anything about their long-range plan to convert the claim into a Fifth Amendment taking or from reaching the government's *res judicata* argument. The question of whether the United States acquired the Black Hills under the 1877 act in violation of the Fifth Amendment, they asserted, was "not now before the Commission for decision."

Sonosky and Lazarus reminded the commission that the ICC Act contained two separate provisions for recovery in cases where the United States had appropriated land without tribal agreement: first, cases where the United States had violated the Fifth Amendment by failing to pay just compensation for lands taken under its sovereign power of eminent domain; and, second, cases where no constitutional violation had occurred, but where, nonetheless, the United States had appropriated tribal land "without the payment for such lands of compensation agreed to by the claimant." (According to Sonosky and Lazarus, this second cause of action—never actually defined by the commission—did not provide interest on any award granted the claimant tribe.) The commission, they submitted, must first decide the "threshold question of the Government's liability," or whether the government could be held legally accountable under either relevant provision of the ICC. Only if liability were established would the commission have cause to decide whether the Fifth Amendment issue was *res judicata* and, if not, whether a constitutional violation had occurred.

While the commission pondered the numerous briefs, the parties accelerated their preparation for a trial on the 1877 value of the Black Hills. Knowing that a valuation trial was inevitable (no one disputed that the 1877 act appropriated the Black Hills lands), both sides had, as early as 1966, engaged expert witnesses to appraise the surface and mineral value of the Black Hills lands as of the time of the taking.

Assessing fair market value ninety years after the valuation date was largely an exercise in imagination. As was true in most Indian land claims, there was no fair market for the Black Hills lands in 1877. Indeed, there was no market at all. The Hills were Indian country. The resident miners were trespassers. There were no clear titles to be bought and sold, and little reliable Black Hills sales data from which overall values might be extrapolated.

The Court of Claims in several recent cases had established a legal definition of fair market value for Indian claims: the price that a "well-informed buyer" and "well-informed seller" would agree to in an "arm's length" negotiation. But in practice these buyers and sellers were hypothetical, and what they would have known if "well-informed" was highly conjectural. The job of the expert appraisers was to amass as much relevant market data as they could find and, using approved appraisal techniques, to weave that data into a compelling tale about what price the imaginary buyer and seller would have agreed upon in a market that simply didn't exist.

The job of the lawyers was to guide the appraisers in this speculative endeavor, to inform them of what appraisal methods had impressed the commission or the Court of Claims in other cases, to coax their own experts towards favorable subjective judgments, and to evaluate draft reports for thoroughness, consistency, and accuracy. At trial, the combined efforts of appraiser and counsel would be tested in the crucible of the adversary process, as each side subjected the other to the inquisition known as cross-examination.

For this job, Sonosky and Lazarus selected Don Myers of the huge real estate firm Coldwell, Banker to assess the surface value of the Hills. Lazarus had worked with Myers to great success in the *Hualapai* claim several years earlier. In that case, Myers had invented a unique method for valuing grazing lands that largely alleviated the major problem for determining surface value in Indian claims: the lack of *comparable* land sales at or near the valuation date from which the value of a subject tract might be rationally estimated.

Myers had developed a calculation called the "cattle-carrying capacity multiplier," an objectively defensible standard for comparing grazing land sales even where the lands themselves were significantly different. In so doing, Myers could manufacture a hypothetical market even where historically none had existed. He would reduce every land sale to a common denominator, the price for each head of cattle that the land could carry.

For example, grazing land selling in the 1870s for $5 per acre with a carrying capacity of 50 head of cattle had a value of 10¢ for every head of cattle it could carry. By accumulating large amounts of data on grazing land sales roughly near the valuation date, Myers could then arrive at an average per-head price for all of the land sales combined. In appraising grazing lands taken by the government, he then needed only to estimate the lands' cattle-carrying capacity and multiply it by the average per-head cattle price to determine fair market value. In the *Hualapai* case, the commission had been favorably impressed with Myers's invention, and Lazarus hoped to take advantage of it a second time.

To appraise the mineral value of the Black Hills, Sonosky and Lazarus hired Roy Full, who ran his own firm, Shenon and Full. As he had done in expert testimony on behalf of several other Indian tribes, Roy Full used an "estimated future profits" method—a standard appraisal technique approved by the Court of Claims in several cases—for assessing the mineral value of the Black Hills. The future profit formula calls upon the appraiser to determine the amount that a well-informed prudent buyer would pay for a mine in order to receive the return *of* his investment and a reasonable return *on* his investment. This, in turn, requires a consideration of such factors as the market price of the mineral, the costs of converting raw ore into finished minerals and of marketing those minerals, the estimated size and productive life of the mineral deposit, and a determination of a reasonable rate of return on investment, given the risk involved.

From Sonosky and Lazarus's perspective, the future profits formula had the important advantage of allowing the appraiser to take some cognizance of the vast mineral wealth extracted from the Black Hills *after* the taking date. Although information available only after the taking date was theoretically unusable as proof of value, in considering what a *well-informed* buyer would have known about the Hills—for example, someone like George Hearst, who brought in his own geologist to assess the mineral deposits— the appraiser would have ample opportunity to infuse post-1877 data into his calculations. Such data, including Hearst's 1878 report that "from present appearances [Homestake] will make perhaps the largest and best gold mine in the world" would inevitably raise the value of the Hills.

The government's mineral appraiser, Ernest Oberbillig, had anticipated a strategy of this sort. In his contract proposal to the Justice Department, he warned the government that "the Indian attorneys have hired Shenon and Full . . . to dream up some . . . plan to pull the $500 million total Homestake production back to the valuation date. How they plan to do this is the big problem we face here."

Oberbillig intended to use a comparable sales approach, even though the commission had announced in several cases that "prices realized in the trafficking in mineral claims . . . are not a sound basis for valuing the mineral content of the land." As the commission recognized, because each mine was unique in richness, accessibility, and other critical factors, appraisers could not rationally establish fair market value by analyzing comparable mine sales elsewhere. There simply was no such thing as a comparable mine.

Nonetheless, the comparable sales approach remained very attractive to the government. Using that approach "would result in a mineral value figure about $1.5 to $2 million at the most generous interpretation based on my preliminary study," Oberbillig had assured the Justice Department when he applied to do the Sioux appraisal. Presumably this low prediction had overcome what must have been some misgivings in the Department about hiring an appraiser who proposed to use a disfavored methodology.

To conduct the surface appraisal, the government hired Harry Fenton, head of his own Seattle-based consulting firm; the Justice Department had found his work competent in other claims cases. Nonetheless, Walter Rochow, the attorney who made the selection warned him in advance that the Black Hills job would require particular care. Rochow advised "that counsel for the Indians were excellent trial lawyers; and that no stone should be left unturned to make this appraisal 'stand up' under severe cross-examination." Two years later, in November 1968, Rochow expanded the admonition, writing Fenton that his opposing expert, Don Myers, was "quite smart and handles himself well on the witness stand."

By the time of this letter, both Myers and Full were well along in completing preliminary reports. Once received, they fell far short of Sonosky and Lazarus's hopes. After reviewing Full's preliminary draft, Sonosky questioned his data, methodology, and overall organization. The lawyers suggested significant changes, urging the appraisers to heed more closely the standards that courts had established in other cases. Asking Full to reexamine his entire appraisal, Sonosky firmly reminded him that, above all else, the appraisal must present a *legally* sound valuation theory. After several redrafts, the Sioux appraisers produced reports satisfactory to the attorneys.

Full, whom Lazarus would later praise as "a good bullshitter about mineral value," estimated the mineral worth of the Black Hills on February 28, 1877 to be $13,558,449. Don Myers's report set the surface value of the Black Hills, including 200,000 acres of agricultural land, 750,000 acres of forest land, 6,369,000 acres of grazing land, and 1,500 acres of townsites, at $12,780,000. Myers estimated that the trespassing whites had made $625,000 worth of improvements on the land. In sum, the two appraisers concluded that the total value of the Hills in 1877, including improvements, was $26,963,489. In addition, Full estimated that by 1877 trespassing miners already had removed from the Hills gold with a net value of $1,075,000.

Oberbillig wrote Ralph Barney (head of the claims section) in late 1968 to report that after initial difficulties his mineral appraisal suddenly "fell into place like a jigsaw puzzle." Oberbillig valued the Black Hills minerals at $2.1 million, less than one-sixth of the

Sioux appraisal, but close to his original projection.

Harry Fenton appraised the surface value of the Hills at $2.6 million, roughly one-fifth of Myers's figure. After completing his report in early 1969, Fenton asked Rochow, who was about to retire, whether the appraisal was convincing. He admitted that the evidence permitted a "wide swing" in value "depending upon one's judgment." Fenton had been "all the way up and down the scale from 20¢ an acre to the 35¢ [he] finally put on it." Since he could not be definitive, Fenton decided to "give the Indians the benefit of all the doubts."

Together, Oberbillig and Fenton opined that the fair market value of the Black Hills in February 1877 was $4.7 million. That figure was $1.3 million (or almost 25 percent) less than the Allison commission had offered the Sioux for the land in 1875.

Sonosky and Lazarus were not surprised by the low government appraisal. Forwarding Fenton's report to Myers, Lazarus noted that he and Sonosky "had estimated that the Government would come in at 32 cents per acre, and we were not off by much." From experience, they knew that the commission had generally awarded about 50¢ an acre for grazing lands acquired by the government in the 1870s. Undoubtedly, the government had argued in those cases, and would again argue, for even lower land values on the well-founded assumption that such commission judgments were often rough compromises between the competing appraisals supplied by the parties.

The trial on mineral value, a so-called battle of the experts, commenced on November 10, 1969. Under commission rules, the reports of the experts constituted their direct testimony and the parties proceeded immediately to cross-examination, with petitioner's witness Roy Full taking the stand first. Commissioner Vance presided alone.

The government lawyer, Craig Decker, and Sonosky (who handled the mineral value trial for the Sioux) took significantly different approaches to cross-examination. In a plodding style that matched the slight slouch of his big-boned frame, Decker walked Roy Full through the data that he had used to generate figures for the future profits formula on which his appraisal was based. Decker probed Full's assessment of what an informed buyer and seller would have known about individual mines in 1877; he tried to discredit Full's use of post-1877 assessments as evidence of 1877 value; and he disputed Full's assessment of such factors as ore depth and the productive life of each mine. But Decker mounted only a cursory challenge to Full's basic methodology, and thus his cross-examination amounted almost exclusively to quibbling over isolated numbers.

Sonosky, by contrast, objected not only to the evidentiary basis of Oberbillig's appraisal but to his entire "comparative sales" approach to mineral valuation. In the course of his questioning Sonosky repeatedly reminded the commission it had rejected this method in several previous cases. (Where sales records had been destroyed, Oberbillig employed a royalty method for determining fair market value. As Sonosky also emphasized, the commission and Court of Claims had rejected this method as well.) While never straying too far from this theme, Sonosky challenged virtually every sale upon which Oberbillig relied, forcing the witness to admit over and over again that he had missed relevant sales data, or had relied on unsubstantiated hearsay about sales prices, or had relied on evidence of sales that on close inspection turned out not to be full sales at all but rather leases or sales of fractional interests.

Though he tried to put a decent face on it, Decker apparently recognized that after trial Oberbillig's "jigsaw puzzle" lay in a thousand pieces. In a trial summary prepared for his boss Ralph Barney, Decker dutifully reported that "Mr. Oberbillig . . . relying primarily on a sales approach appraised the minerals at $2.1 million. The sales used were mostly those that occurred in the two or three year period after the valuation date and were incomplete, requiring interpolations and roll backs in arriving at the appraisal figure of $2.1 million. There were some weaknesses, of course, in such an approach but, all things considered, I think it was the best approach that could be used for this particular case." What Decker almost certainly meant was that a more legally sound approach would have resulted in a much higher price tag for the Hills.

The parties crossed swords over surface values in May 1970. Decker spent less than three hours disputing Don Myers's estimates of cattle-carrying capacity, his valuation of improvements that miners had made in their Black Hills townsites, and his estimation of timber stumpage that would be yielded by Black Hills ponderosa pine. Myers proved every bit as good a witness as Walter Rochow had feared, sidestepping trick questions, demonstrating complete command of his report and unflappable confidence in its conclusions. Decker gave up before the noon break.

Lazarus kept the government appraiser, Fenton, on the stand for more than two full days. Cross-examining expert witnesses was Lazarus's favorite part of litigation. He loved immersing himself in an expert's written report, then plotting question sequences designed to unsettle the expert on the witness stand, trap him in contradictions, and force admissions of error. He did not merely question expert witnesses, he chided, and mocked, and baited them in a nasal, sarcastic, and penetrating voice. Small and slight, ordinarily reserved, in court Lazarus transformed himself into a assassin of professional credibility.

Forewarned by Rochow about the ordeal he would face, confident that he had given the Sioux "the benefit of all the doubts," Harry Fenton took the stand. Lazarus started by examining Fenton's methodology, specifically his decision to value the Hills as "virgin" land (unimproved and unsettled) despite the presence of thousands of trespassing white settlers in 1877.

Q: That means, does it not, that you are not valuing the subject tract as of the valuation?

A: No.

Q: You have assumed away the existence of at least 12,500 people [the trespassing miners], have you not?

A: No.

Q: When you say, "no," what did you do with those people?

A: I have assumed they were trespassers at that time.

Q: They were, in fact, on the land?

A: Oh, yes.

Q: And they did, in fact, create value in the land?

A: Yes.

Q: So your valuation is not a valuation of the subject tract as it existed on the valuation date, correct?

A: My valuation is in relation to that assumption.

Q: Which is not the way the subject tract was on the valuation date?

A: Yes, it was the subject tract. It did not include the things that had been added to it though.

Q: But the things that were added to it were a fact?

A: Oh, yes.

Q: So, getting back to the question, your valuation was of a hypothetical situation, not the actual situation?

A: No, I don't think that is—that is not the fact. It was the valuation of a certain portion of what was there.

Q: So you took the subject tract as of the valuation date and subtracted something from it?

A: No.

Q: You said you had valued only a portion. How did you arrive at your valuation of a portion?

A: I arrived at it by comparing it with other virgin land.

Q: This land was not virgin land on the valuation date, isn't that correct?

A: That would be true.

A few minutes later, Lazarus switched to a different methodological issue, Fenton's caveat that "No part of this appraisal is to be used out of context and by itself alone. No part of this appraisal is necessarily correct as being only part of the evidence upon which the final judgment as to value is based."

Q: Mr. Fenton, that is not an appraisal premise, is it? That is just a defense mechanism in case we find mistakes in your report. . . . And how many errors do we have to find before we can assume your final value judgment is incorrect?

A: As far as I'm concerned, enough to make me change my mind.

Q: I see, is that one or two?

A: I wouldn't know.

Q: Ten—fifty facts wrong?

A: I wouldn't commit myself.

Q: Suppose we found that every fact was wrong, would you then be willing to change your mind?

A: If every fact was wrong?

Q: Yes.

A: I think maybe I might modify my judgment a little bit. . . .

Q: Suppose you said in your report that there were no farms in the subject tract, and we proved that 100,000 acres were under cultivation on the valuation date. Would that be a figure significant enough to lead you to change your conclusion?

A: It would certainly be something to reconsider.

Q: Yes, and suppose we could show that you didn't even know what land you were appraising. Would that indicate your value conclusion might be wrong?

A: It might.

Q: It might very well, wouldn't it?

A: Yes.

Fenton must have known that Lazarus was setting him up, and, after a five-minute recess, he learned for what. In his appraisal he had relied heavily on the Gordon Report, a 1880 census document about the Dakota and Wyoming territories. The trouble was that the section of the report that Fenton had relied on for information comparing eastern Dakota to the Black Hills actually described the Wyoming territory and had nothing to do with Dakota, much less the Black Hills.

Q: And where do we find ourselves, Mr. Fenton?

A: It looks like that is an error.

Q: We find ourselves in Wyoming, don't we?

A: Yes we do.

Q: Do you think that is a significant error, Mr. Fenton? That you don't know the land that you are appraising?

A minute later, Lazarus was boring down on Fenton again, dissecting one of the ninety-six so-called comparable sales from which he had arrived at his Black Hills valuation figure. In his written report, Fenton had placed great weight on an alleged sale of land by the Cherokee tribe: "The Cherokee sale of thirty million acres of land at 40¢ an acre is certainly significant for, if this better land sold for only 40¢ per acre in the late sixties, the [Black Hills] in the depressed seventies must have had a lower value . . . about 30¢ per acre seems indicated."

Thirty questions later, Lazarus had pressured Fenton into admitting that the quoted sentence contained five separate errors. The tribe involved was the Crow, not the Cherokee. The transaction was not a sale, but an Indian Claims Commission decision. The so-called Cherokee land lay far west of the Black Hills, not east where Fenton had placed it. The so-called Cherokee land was not better than the Black Hills land, but far worse; it was located in the Great American Desert, in which the Black Hills were an oasis. The Black Hills were not economically depressed in 1877, as Fenton had suggested. They were in the midst of a boom.

A few moments later, Lazarus turned to Fenton's decision to give no agricultural value to the Hills. Within minutes, Fenton was admitting that his own sources recognized at least 200,000 acres of Black Hills land to be ideally suited for farming.

And so it went, hour after hour. Some of Fenton's purportedly comparable sales proved not to be sales at all, but rather leases or the exchange of other lesser interests. In many cases, Fenton's prices turned out to be wrong or his sources suspect.

One of the most damaging moments came at the start of the second day, when Lazarus starting probing Fenton's selection of ninety-six sales as representative of western land values around the valuation date. Conspicuously absent were any sales where land had sold for more than $1 per acre; indeed, despite his professed desire to resolve "all the doubts in favor of the Indians," Fenton admitted in his report to having excluded such sales.

Q: On page 23 . . . you say that you use large Government to Government sales as a floor, as the low range of value, and sales of railroad land in small tracts to homesteaders as the upper range of value in your report. Is that a correct description of your appraisal process?

A: Yes, with one other factor added. I think there was a chronological increase in price also. . . .

Q: But that is not, in fact, what you did. You didn't use the railroad sales as the high end of your range, did you?

A: I didn't?

Q: Did you?

A: I thought I did.

Q: How much per acre did those railroad sales come to? In general, what was the range of the railroad sales? . . .

A: Four to six dollars in small tracts and less in large tracts. . . .

Q: Yes, but in fact you eliminated every sale over one dollar an acre, didn't you?

A: Not in my compilation. . . .

Q: On page 31 of your report you say . . . "with so much evidence indicating that logically the value of the subject property was below a dollar per acre, it seemed reasonable to eliminate sales in this light that were made for over one dollar." But is your statement correct?

A: Yes. . . .

Q: In effect you didn't use all your comparable sales, but only those of less than a dollar?

A: Well, in the early stages of my thinking, I used them, but I omitted them in my final stages of arriving at a decision.

Q: In the later stages of arriving at a final conclusion, did it occur to you that it was inconceivable the land could be worth less than ten cents per acre?

A: I hadn't thought of that.

Q: No, you didn't think of that. You had a reported Cherokee, but, in fact, Crow sale for forty cents an acre immediately in the vicinity of the subject tract and nine years earlier as a guide to what values would be, didn't you?

A: Yes, I did.

Q: But, nonetheless, you did not come to the conclusion that it was out of the range of possibility that sales below ten cents an acre were not comparable either.

A: I don't recall using any sales below ten cents an acre.

Q: You don't recall using any sales under ten cents an acre?

A: Not seriously.

Q: But am I safe in saying that you eliminated sales over one dollar an acre, but to the extent we may find sales in your appraisal of less than ten cents, you did not eliminate those sales?

A: Yes, I don't think I used those. I may not have said, factually, I eliminated them, but I don't even recall any. I suppose there are some in here.

Q: Look at sale number one.

A: Well, yes. . . .

Q: Yes.

A: Louisiana Purchase.

Q: How much was that sale price?

A: Slightly under three cents an acre.

Q: And look at Sale 3.

A: 5.4 cents.

Q: And look at sale 8.

A: Yes, just under two cents.

Q: Do you say anywhere in your report that you eliminated these sales from your consideration?

A year later, when he briefed the issue of value, Craig Decker made only a single passing reference to his own expert's surface value appraisal. Fenton, Lazarus wrote in a brief of his own, became the government's "little man who wasn't there."

Oberbillig's report survived with not much greater standing. Indeed, the Sioux cause had emerged from trial as well as could possibly have been expected. But however favorable the testimony about the fair market value of the Hills, the issue still resided with a tribunal notorious for its low valuations of Indian lands. And even a favorable judgment on value, even a valuation near to the Sioux figure of $26 million, might be rendered inconsequential if the commission ruled against the Sioux on critical issues of law.

Less than two months after the surface value trial, on June 8,

1970, the commission ruled on the scope and meaning of Articles 11 and 16 of the 1868 treaty. It agreed with Sonosky and Lazarus that Article 11 reserved for the Sioux a self-limiting hunting right, although it did not recognize any antecedent Sioux rights in these lands.

Far more important, the commission rejected Sonosky and Lazarus's argument that Article 16 recognized virtually full Sioux title to all of the tribe's Fort Laramie lands outside its permanent reservation (33 million acres) and an additional 25 million acres of Powder River and Big Horn country that the 1851 treaty had designated as belonging to the Crow and other tribes. Instead, the commission ruled that Article 16 granted the Sioux an exclusive hunting right (and not a more substantial ownership right) in a substantially smaller area, only 15.7 million acres of the Fort Laramie lands and a mere 9.3 million acres of land formerly belong to the Crow and other tribes (in total an astonishing 33 million acres less than Sonosky and Lazarus had estimated).

Moreover, while the commission ruled that these hunting rights (abrogated by the 1877 act) were compensable, it also ruled that the government was entitled "to credit their 1868 value against plaintiff's recovery." To the extent that Article 16 recognized Sioux hunting rights in former Crow land, the value of those rights constituted consideration for other rights the Sioux relinquished under the 1868 treaty. To the extent that Article 16 reserved for the Sioux a hunting right in their previously owned Fort Laramie lands, the value of those reserved rights would correspondingly diminish the value of what the Sioux ceded to the United States under the 1868 treaty.

As a quick way of sorting out the various additions and subtractions required by it legal ruling, the commission decided that for the purposes of the 1868 treaty case it would value the Sioux lands ceded to the government (33 million acres of Fort Laramie land outside the Great Sioux reservation) without deducting for any Sioux Article 16 rights reserved in this territory. The commission also would not count as consideration under the 1868 treaty the value of the tribe's Article 16 hunting rights in formerly non-Sioux lands. To balance out this artificial reading, the commission ruled that it would not permit the Sioux to recover for the taking of their Article 11 and 16 rights in 1877 (as part of the Black Hills claim) unless the tribe could prove that the Article 11 and 16 rights were worth more in 1877, when they were lost, than in 1868, when they were granted. (Given the continuing disappearance of the buffalo, such a showing was impossible.)

According to the commission, this artificial arrangement would have the net effect of compensating the Sioux for their lost hunting rights. In the 1868 treaty case, the commission would pretend that the rights granted the tribe under Articles 11 and 16 did not constitute consideration for the lands that the Sioux relinquished under the treaty. On the other hand, the commission would also pretend that the 1877 act did not abrogate those Article 11 and 16 rights. Thus, the Commission would not "charge" the Sioux for the value they received when the government first recognized Sioux rights in the Article 11 and 16 lands in 1868, but neither would it "charge" the government for taking those same rights away in 1877.

To Lazarus, the commission's convenient "wash out" of the Article 11 and 16 rights from both cases was "dumb as a matter of history, dumb as a matter of logic, and dumb as a matter of law." The 1868 treaty was the 1868 treaty and the 1877 act was the 1877 act. Each had to be evaluated on its own terms. The commission had no business cutting and pasting the two transactions together, in essence pretending that the 1868 treaty did not contain Articles 11 and 16 and that the 1877 act did not abrogate them.

Its merits aside, the commission's decision presented Sonosky and Lazarus with an agonizing and crucial strategic choice. By a quirk of circumstance, if they appealed the irrational ruling and *won*, the result might well be that the Sioux would lose entirely both the 1868 treaty case and the Black Hills claim.

The lawyers saw their dilemma this way: Suppose the appeals court (as Sonosky and Lazarus thought likely) reversed the commission's decision that the 1868 treaty and 1877 act neutralized each other with respect to Articles 11 and 16 but upheld its decision that those articles granted only hunting rights to the Sioux.

To obtain a recovery in the 1868 treaty case, Sonosky and Lazarus would have to show that the value of what the Sioux relinquished under the 1868 treaty was grossly disproportionate to the consideration the tribe received from the government. If they won the appeal, the commission would then be required in the 1868 treaty case, either to subtract the value of the tribe's Article 11 and 16 hunting rights from the value of the land ceded or to add the value of the hunting rights to the treaty consideration promised by the government. The ledger would look roughly as follows, assuming that the commission found the land to be worth 50¢ per acre and a hunting right worth half of that: The Sioux ceded to the government the value of 15 million acres of aboriginal land east of the Missouri River and about 33 million acres of Fort Laramie land outside the Great Sioux Reservation, *minus* the value of the tribe's Article 16 hunting right in the Fort Laramie lands. Sonosky and Lazarus could reasonably expect the commission to value the total package of the tribe's ceded rights at approximately $16 million.

On the other side of the ledger, the Sioux received consideration in the form of an Article 16 hunting right in 9.3 million acres of land previously owned by other tribes and at least $9 million in government payments for food, education, clothing, and other benefits provided by the treaty. Even assuming that they could defeat the government's claim to many millions of dollars more in offsets, Sonosky and Lazarus could reasonably estimate that the Sioux received consideration worth over $11 million. The difference between perhaps $16 million of interests ceded and $11 million of consideration received was not the stuff of an unconscionable consideration claim. The 1868 treaty case would be a loser.

Turning to the Black Hills claim, the commission would be required to value the Article 11 and 16 hunting rights among those rights appropriated by the government under the 1877 act. The Sioux would be claiming the loss of the Black Hills land, the Article 11 and 16 hunting rights, and a few other minor interests. At best, Sonosky and Lazarus could expect a valuation of these interests at $30 million. On the other side, the government was claiming, and Ralph Case had conceded, $57 million in offsets. Although Sonosky and Lazarus thought that they probably could wriggle out from under Case's concession and that the government's figures were substantially inflated, they also knew that their Fifth Amendment taking argument (to get interest) very well might fail, and that certainly the government would succeed in setting off against any judgment a fair portion of its claimed expenditures. Faced with what they considered a hostile commission that in Lazarus's words "would do them in if it could," the lawyers saw a clear path to losing the Black Hills claim, too.

Given these calculations, Sonosky and Lazarus decided not to appeal the commission's decision, however much it galled them, and even though it meant not recovering any award for the taking of the tribe's Article 11 and 16 rights. They believed strongly that the commission had erred in denying Sioux ownership to the Article 11 and 16 lands—the richest Sioux hunting grounds—and they thought the commission's logic absurd, but to risk everything would be a foolish gamble.

In optimistic moments, Sonosky and Lazarus took comfort in the fact that while the commission had denied them their fondest hope of making a takings claim for both the Black Hills and the vast Article 16 lands, in its own illogical and unintended way the commission had opened the door to a Sioux victory in both dockets. In the past, Sonosky and Lazarus had always thought that Articles 11 and 16 put the two Sioux claims in competition with each other. A high valuation of the rights contained in those articles would benefit the Black Hills claim but diminish the 1868 treaty case, and vice versa. Now the commission had washed out consideration of these articles entirely. In the 1868 treaty case (hopelessly bogged down in litigation over overlapping claims by other tribes), Sonosky and Lazarus could now argue that under the 1868 treaty the Sioux lost a complete ownership interest in 48 million acres of land (33 million acres of Sioux land recognized in the 1851 Fort Laramie treaty lying outside the Great Sioux Reservation and 15 million acres of aboriginal Sioux land east of the Missouri), perhaps $25 million in value. With luck, they could keep the government's consideration to $9 million in food, education, and the like. That probably would be enough of a disparity to win an unconscionable consideration claim.

In the Black Hills claim, although deprived of their claim for lost rights in the Article 11 and 16 lands, Sonosky and Lazarus still lay in wait with their Fifth Amendment argument for the Black Hills themselves. If they could escape Case's concession and eliminate a fair number of the government's offsets, this claim too might yield a substantial judgment.

For a decade, the Sioux legal team had been like a wilderness rider with two horses, switching back and forth between mounts, assuming that eventually one would break down and have to be abandoned. Although the distances were uncertain, thanks to the commission decision, both horses remained sound, if a bit winded. On the other hand, after forty-seven years of litigation and a dozen years of repairing Case's work, despite hundreds of pages of legal argument and thousands of pages of exhibits, Sonosky and Lazarus could only guess at their prospect of obtaining compensation for what seemed to be a clear case of theft. For all the planning, calculation, and effort of two fine lawyers, they could offer their clients little more than a familiar refrain: Time will tell.

For more than ninety years the clock had been running. And time remained the enemy of justice.

TWELVE

▼ ▼ ▼ ▼ ▼

THE GHOST DANCE RETURNS

WHILE SONOSKY and Lazarus were presenting a Sioux legal interpretation of the 1868 treaty of the commission, individuals and factions among the Sioux were developing their own interpretations of the treaty and reassessing its continued application to their lives. In 1964 a small band of Sioux, relocatees in San Francisco, landed on and claimed possession of Alcatraz Island, an abandoned rock in the shadow of the Golden Gate Bridge that until 1963 had served as a federal penitentiary. When U.S. marshals ousted them a day later, the Indians brought suit in federal court asserting their right to settle on the island. Article 6 of the 1868 treaty, the Sioux argued, guaranteed them the right to occupy and seek eventual ownership of any parcel of federal land "which is not mineral land, nor reserved by the United States for special purposes other than Indian occupation. . . ."

A federal court dismissed the Indians' suit. Still, their brief occupation, and their invocation of long-dormant treaty rights, placed these Sioux at the core of a burgeoning militancy among urban Indians, who by 1970 numbered roughly half the entire native population. Despite the aspirations of terminationists, the children of relocation never abandoned their cultural roots. On the contrary, amid poverty and petty criminality, coping with alcoholism and cold-shouldering neighbors, city Indians found their shared ethnic identity—regardless of tribal affiliation—to be a rare source of strength and community. Around the Indian centers that cropped up in every city with a native population, in the jails and bars and pool halls where many urban Indians spent their time, young natives steeped themselves in their common histories of grievance and celebrated a resurgent sense of cultural identity.

Urban Indians joined readily in the culture of social upheaval that was transforming the nation's campuses and major cities. Having witnessed the black civil rights movement and the fishing rights protests of reservation Indians in the Northwest, hearing now the angry and powerful rhetoric of a Stokely Carmichael or Malcolm X, watching the rising tide of the movement against the Vietnam War, many city Indians embraced the politics of militancy and united under the banner of Red Power. Almost overnight, American Indians became Native Americans, who vowed in strident terms to reclaim their rights and heritages.

In Minneapolis, with a native population of 10,000, a handful of activist Indians, most notably Dennis Banks, George Mitchell, and Clyde Bellecourt, founded in 1968 the American Indian Movement, "a coalition of Indian people willing to fight for Indians." With a constituency of young, mainly Chippewa Indians, many of them ex-convicts (Banks and Bellecourt, both Chippewa, had served time on burglary charges), AIM organized an Indian Patrol to monitor police activities in predominantly Indian sections of the city. Vigilant against what they considered the discriminatory arrest practices of the Minneapolis police, determined to prevent the violence that seemed selectively to accompany Indian detentions, AIM members shadowed the police in their sweeps through the Indian ghettoes. Under AIM observation, Indian arrests and harassment diminished significantly and AIM expanded its program to cities throughout the Midwest.

In fall 1969 Indians returned to Alcatraz. A group of seventy-eight west coast native students, inspired by black and third world activism at Berkeley, claimed possession of the island "in the name of all American Indians." With a crowd of news reporters in attendance, they issued a PROCLAMATION: TO THE GREAT WHITE FATHER AND ALL HIS PEOPLE, which read in part:

> We feel that this so-called Alcatraz Island is more than suitable for an Indian Reservation, as determined by the white man's own standard. By this we mean that this place resembles most Indian reservations in that:
>
> 1.   It is isolated from modern facilities, and without adequate means of transportation.
> 2.   It has no fresh running water.
> 3.   It has inadequate sanitation facilities.
> 4.   There are no oil or mineral rights.

5. There is no industry, and so unemployment is very great.
6. There are no health care facilities.
7. The soil is rocky and unproductive; and the land does not support game.
8. There are no educational facilities.
9. The population has always exceeded the land base.
10. The population has always been held as prisoners and kept dependent on others.

Further, it would be fitting and symbolic that ships from all over the world, entering the Golden Gate, would first see Indian land, and thus be reminded of the true history of this nation. This tiny island would be a symbol of the great lands once ruled by free and noble Indians.

The occupation of Alcatraz lasted from November 1969 until June 1971, when federal marshals escorted away the fifteen remaining Indians. Over time, a lack of food and electricity weakened the occupiers; factionalism and intertribal rivalries reduced their numbers. But if Indians of All Tribes (as they called themselves) failed to convert Alcatraz into an Indian oasis, they succeeded in electrifying the imaginations of countless Indians. From all over the country, natives came west to sample the power of the Alcatraz experiment and share in the act of rebellion. A former prison became the symbol of a renewed Indian quest for freedom, a declaration of independence from the strangling embrace of white society and compliant Indian leaders who enjoyed this affection.

Alcatraz also demonstrated to Indians that, like activists in the civil rights and antiwar movements, they could effectively adopt the tactic of civil disobedience to attract national attention to their cause and marshall support in liberal America. Church groups and sympathetic philanthropists arranged for shipments of food and medical supplies. Hundreds of reporters and thousands of well-wishers sailed out to visit Alcatraz during the Indian occupation. "We had no wish to become tourist attractions or public curiosities," one of the occupiers later said. Nonetheless, as the militants themselves made certain, every one of the visitors to Alcatraz, most vitally the reporters, sailed back to the mainland with stories about the Indians' search for true self-determination and the desperate conditions that these people endured everywhere, everyday.

The Indian experience had regained its power to inspire the guilt of sympathetic Americans. A year before Alcatraz, a Standing Rock Sioux named Vine Deloria, Jr., published *Custer Died for*

Your Sins: An Indian Manifesto, a scathing indictment of white attitudes towards Native Americans and a bold assertion of the supremacy of native values. Shortly after Alcatraz, Dee Brown published *Bury My Heart at Wounded Knee,* a history of the conquest of the west told with excruciating poignancy from the perspective of the Indians. Both books became national bestsellers; *Bury My Heart at Wounded Knee* became one of the most popular books of the decade. As liberal Americans protested what they saw as the new U.S. imperialism of the Vietnam War, they reindicted themselves for the nation's old imperialism, its often brutal conquest of the Indians. Millions read of the poetry and beauty of the old Indian way, reproached themselves for what their ancestors had destroyed, and warmly embraced the new Indians, the Indians of Alcatraz, who defiantly promised a rebirth of native heritages that many whites had feared extinct. In the wake of Alcatraz, as both reflected in and compelled by popular culture, the cause of Native Americans found a place again on the American political agenda.

After Alcatraz, Indian occupations and takeovers became the hallmarks of a widespread campaign demanding, in essence, a return to the days centuries earlier when, in the militants' view, Indian tribes enjoyed full independence and dealt with the United States as equal sovereigns. At reservation powwows, in soapbox speeches on city corners, the militants, particularly the spokesmen of AIM, preached the gospel of Indian nationalism: a tale of genocide and resurrection in the form of absolute tribal sovereignty.

The incendiary message of Indian rejuvenation sparked brushfire rebellions in tinder-dry Indian communities. In Littleton, Colorado, and Alameda, California; in Chicago, Minneapolis, Cleveland, Los Angeles, Albuquerque, and Philadelphia, Indians staged protests and sit-ins at the offices of the "neo-colonial" BIA. The Indians assailed the bureau for plundering tribal resources while promoting cultural extinction. They called for the eradication of bureau-sponsored tribal governments and for strict U.S. compliance with the old treaties. Meanwhile, the militants dared their oppressors to drag them away in chains. "If the government doesn't start living up to its obligations," a Chippewa remarked at one protest, "armed resistance and occupation will have to become a regular thing."

In spring 1971, AIM, still the most radical of the new Indian activist groups, organized an occupation of Mt. Rushmore in the heart of the Black Hills. On June 6, twenty Indians set up camp above the huge granite busts of Washington, Jefferson, Lincoln, and Theodore Roosevelt. They demanded that the United States honor the 1868 treaty, which, if carried out, would mean at a minimum the return of Mt. Rushmore and all of South Dakota west of the Missouri River to the Sioux. After twelve hours, park rangers carried the Indians down the mountain, charging them with trespass.

Leading the Mt. Rushmore occupation was Russell Means, an Oglala Sioux born at the small community of Porcupine on the Pine Ridge Reservation in 1940. Means's early background resembled that of thousands of urban Indians. Mostly raised in Oakland, California, he spent a year drinking on skid row in Los Angeles. He tried college—five of them—but never graduated. He worked as a rodeo hand and as an Indian dancer. Eventually, after a stint in the offices of the Rosebud tribal council, Means moved to Cleveland and became head of its Indian Center.

Tall, powerfully built, handsome, Means projected the perfect image of the proud Sioux warrior transported into the modern age. His long braids, bone neck-choker, red windband, black shirt with embroidered vest, beaded belt, turquoise jewelry, jeans, and boots became a virtual uniform for the young men of AIM, though few could wear it with Means's panache.

As Bob Burnette (the Rosebud Sioux activist) described him, Means possessed a "bizarre knack for staging demonstrations. . . . [a] genius for public relations." This flair for the dramatic led him, for instance, to stage a Thanksgiving Day takeover of the ship *Mayflower II* in 1970. Eloquent and charismatic, fullblood in appearance (unlike many AIM leaders), and yet to be convicted of a felony, Means joined Dennis Banks (the movement's brooding intellectual) as AIM's leading spokesman and the nation's most visible Indian leader.

While the militants, especially the AIM leaders, set fire to angry Indian hearts, their meteoric rise to prominence exposed severe divisions among Indian leaders. In addition to unrelenting criticism of "genocidal" U.S. policy, the militants attacked IRA tribal governments as pawns—usually corrupt pawns—of the Indian Bureau. To AIM, Indian self-government under the IRA was not self-government at all, but rather proxy rule by the Indian Bureau through selected Indian puppet politicians. As one follower recalled, AIM was tired of "tribal leaders kissing ass—white man's ass," and they meant to do something about it.

Many of AIM's criticisms of the IRA governments and the Indian bureau were borne out in the daily life of the reservation. IRA tribal governments were often poorly, and sometimes dishonorably, run. Frequently, lazy or venal tribal leaders surrendered effective control of their reservations to the Indian bureau or permitted outside interests, white-owned, to exploit tribal resources. And, even thirty-five years after the Indian New Deal's restoration of tribal self-government, in many places the bureau still meddled excessively in tribal affairs and resisted its own conversion from an omnipotent administrator of reservation life to a vital resource in tribal regeneration.

In addition, for some tribes that chose to organize under the IRA, representative democracy remained an alien method for selecting leaders, an unnatural, foreign-born replacement for indigenous systems disrupted or destroyed by the advancing white frontier. In these fledgling democracies, the most respected Indians did not always run for office. Rampant factionalism, fights over patronage, and greed sometimes immobilized tribes, as a newly minted class of professional politicians—rough equivalents of small-time machine politicians—vied for control of reservations.

But, in a larger sense, AIM's criticisms were wide of the mark. On most reservations, even those with poor leadership, tribal self-rule was real, not a sham; leadership was elected, not imposed. The shortcomings of many IRA tribal governments resulted not, as AIM charged, from catering to the white imperialists in Washington, but from the very novelty of modern Indian self-government. Prior to the IRA, the government had completely controlled reservation life. As a result, Indians elected to run IRA tribal governments possessed no experience with self-rule. A legacy of some degree of incompetence and corruption was inevitable.

Indeed, far from doing the Indian bureau's bidding, most tribal governments were engaged in a constant struggle with the bureau to exercise the full measure of the IRA's substantial (though not complete) grant of sovereign authority. Especially after the advent of the Great Society, tribal governments oversaw large budgets and controlled an impressive array of programs. Every day tribal governments, on their own terms, wrestled with the intractable problems of inadequate economic development, substandard reservation schools, and splintered Indian land holdings, as well as the burden of enforcing civil and criminal laws. Though angry about their relationship with the Indian bureau and frustrated with assistance programs that provided sufficient resources to survive but never enough to prosper, reservation leaders scorned the militants' attack on their IRA government as a self-wounding repudiation of the only true self-determination that Indians had known in the last century.

Many tribal leaders also objected to the militants' tactics, partic-

ularly the brandishing of weapons and their tough talk about violent confrontation. Fearing a backlash among white supporters,
the National Congress of American Indians and even the more
activist National Indian Youth Council condemned the Alcatraz
occupation. In April 1972, an armed contingent of AIM showed up
in Cass Lake, Minnesota, to support Chippewa efforts to enforce
their power to require white fishermen to purchase licenses from
the tribe. Guns bared and roadblocks established, AIM demanded
that the Chippewa tribal council take a stronger stand against the
whites. When the council responded by asking AIM to leave, various Indian factions nearly turned their guns on each other.

Other reservation critics, like Luther Clearwater, a respected
elder on Rosebud, simply didn't have much patience with a bunch
of city Indians talking about the old ways as though they knew
something about them.

> [T]he indi'n militants keep wantin' to put things way back a hun-
> dred years ago. We're gettin' pushed back enough without help! Get
> ever'body killed or dyin' off, runnin' around crazy and shootin'—
> that's white man. So many of these nationsists get militant and go
> away and say they talk for their people. They stay out too long,
> away from home. They don't know how to *be* Indi'n, so busy *actin'*
> Indi'n.

What generally seemed to distinguish many reservation leaders,
including those committed to expanding tribal self-determination,
from militant groups such as AIM was their concept of the relationship between Indian tribes and the United States. Tribal leaders sought self-determination as pragmatists coping with military
impotence, political weakness, and almost total economic dependence on the federal government. They accepted, or at least accommodated themselves to, the overarching jurisdiction of the United
States; they searched for autonomy or justice in its institutions,
according to its legal rules. And they accepted, or at least accommodated themselves to, the historical process by which individual
Indians had become full citizens of the United States, fought in its
wars, and partly shared its destiny.

As Bob Burnette admonished Indian nationalists, "If Indians
had an army as big as the Soviet Union, they might be sovereign.
But they do not have an army. We are part of the United States
of America . . . subject to the plenary powers of Congress. . . . We
have to do those things that are practical in government." What
many reservation leaders sought was not an unattainable separatism but rather the best alternative under the circumstances, as

independent an identity as they could establish in the midst of, and as part of, the nation as a whole.

During the late 1960s, Indian tribes had made tangible progress towards this goal. As landmark Supreme Court decisions and unprecedented federal legislation (such as the Voting Rights Act and Fair Housing Act) broke down old barriers to racial equality, so too the nation codified as law a renewed commitment to ethnic pluralism. At the urging of tribal attorneys such as Sonosky and Lazarus, in 1968 Congress passed the Indian Civil Rights Act, which essentially repealed Public Law 280, the termination-era legislation permitting states to assume civil and criminal jurisdiction over reservations. The act required tribal consent for any such state action, finally laying to rest the greatest residual fear from the termination days.

In 1969 President Nixon placed additional locks on the door back to termination. He proposed, and Congress in large part enacted, legislation explicitly affirming "the integrity and right to continued existence of all Indian tribes . . . recognizing that cultural pluralism is a source of national strength." He pursued a policy of empowering Indian communities on their own initiative to take over the administration of federally funded programs. He successfully promoted the return of the sacred Blue Lake to the Taos Pueblo. He named an Indian, Robert Bruce (part Sioux, part Mohawk) to be commissioner of Indian Affairs, the second Indian to hold the post after Ely S. Parker (his Johnson administration predecessor, Robert Bennett, being the first).

Although militant Indians correctly identified some of these actions as fig leaves to cover the shame of the nation's treatment of its native peoples, they also repudiated substantive efforts to find a secure place for Indian tribes to coexist within the larger framework of American society. Indian nationalists, for example, denigrated the Indian Civil Rights Act, even though it repealed dreaded P.L. 280, because it extended many constitutional protections to individual Indians at the expense of the absolute sovereign authority of tribes.

In response to several well-publicized horror stories about tribal abuses against individual civil liberties—such as the jailing of tribal judges for making unpopular rulings—Title II of the Indian Civil Rights Act imposed on tribal governments most of the limitations contained in the Constitution's Bill of Rights. (The act did not extend all civil rights to Indians. For example, in deference to the theocratic nature of some tribes, the act exempted them from compliance with the First Amendment's required separation of church and state.) Tribal attorneys who promoted the act thought of the extension of constitutional prohibitions to tribal governments as "an idea whose time had come," an acceptable accommodation of tribal sovereignty with the status of individual Indians as U.S. citizens entitled to the civil liberties guaranteed by American law. Most tribal governments and their umbrella group, NCAI, agreed.

But in AIM's view, the United States Congress had no more business telling Indian tribes to conform their actions to American constitutional norms than it did telling France to do so. Every tribe was its own independent nation, with its own norms to be administered in its own manner. In the AIM future, the glorious Indian past would be created anew, political relationships returned to the status quo prior to conquest. "They call us the New Indians. Hell, we are the Old Indians," Dennis Banks corrected, "the landlords of this continent, coming to collect the rent."

AIM's appeal was almost religious. "The American Indian Movement hit our reservation like a tornado," writes Mary Crow Dog, a Rosebud Sioux who married Leonard Crow Dog, AIM's spiritual leader and great-grandson of the Crow Dog who murdered Chief Spotted Tail. "It was almost like the Ghost Dance fever that had hit the tribes in 1890 . . . spreading like a prairie fire."

Wovoka's Ghost Dancers had believed that the whites would be miraculously swept away and all the Indians who ever lived resurrected from the dead. AIM's dream was not of literal resurrection but of resurrected sovereignty, of a time warp throwing back the relationship between Indians and the United States a century or more. They preached of a world where Indians governed themselves not by permission of the whites but by natural right. And as happened in the days of the old Ghost Dance, the fervor of belief charged the air with a threat of desperate confrontation.

On a Saturday night in January 1972, in Gordon, Nebraska— one of the string of whiskey towns that lie due south of the Rosebud and Pine Ridge reservations—five drunken whites (four men and a woman) kidnapped Raymond Yellow Thunder, an unassuming fifty-one-year-old Sioux cowboy. The abductors stripped Yellow Thunder of his pants, then tossed him butt-naked into the middle of a dance at Gordon's American Legion hall. Afterwards, two of the kidnappers, brothers named Hare, stuffed Yellow Thunder into a car trunk, where he died from the beating he had received in the interim.

Local police picked up the Hare boys, then released them without bail pending trial on second-degree manslaughter charges. Ru-

mors started to circulate that the police were preparing to exoner-
ate the Hares and blame Yellow Thunder's death on a nasty fall.
Yellow Thunder's family turned to AIM for help. Means and
Banks organized a 200-car caravan from Pine Ridge to Gordon.
Red flags waving, drums beating, the 1,300 Indians marched the
streets of Gordon until they exacted promises from local officials
that the Hares' trial would proceed. AIM also succeeded in forcing
the dismissal of the Gordon police chief.

Means returned home to Pine Ridge a conquering hero and
received a commensurate reception. "It was one big weekend
orgy," one Sioux woman remembered, "dancing and drinking 'til
four in the morning." The homecoming got out of hand when
Means tried unsuccessfully to get himself appointed reservation
police commissioner and some AIM people roughed up the owner
of the Wounded Knee trading post. Still, he and his people had
faced down the white system and won. The Hares were ultimately
convicted of manslaughter.

Among a people who had experienced little except defeat and
humiliation at the hands of their white neighbors, AIM's exploits
in Gordon won many converts. "It was flint striking flint," recalls
Mary Crow Dog, "lighting a spark which grew into a flame at
which we could warm ourselves after a long, long winter." Lloyd
Eaglebull, an elder statesman on Pine Ridge, used a different meta-
phor. "They came in and kicked over the rock," he said. "We will
never get over it."

In late summer 1972, at the instigation of Bob Burnette (now
NCAI Executive Director), AIM and activist groups joined together to plan an election-season caravan to Washington, the Trail
of Broken Treaties, a transnational march to dramatize Indian
problems and generate support for expanded Indian self-determination. In cars, buses, and vans—almost any sort of vehicle that
would move—Native Americans from the west coast set out from
various posts for Washington early in October, stopping at reservations on route to supplement their numbers.

In Minneapolis, where one AIM-directed contingent picked up
Chippewa supporters, the caravan paused to sit-in at the Indian
Bureau area office and, in the name of the "Trail of Broken Treaties," to issue a twenty-point demand for full restoration of Indian
sovereignty. Point number one demanded the repeal of the 1871
statute terminating the government's practice of entering into
treaties with individual tribes, which the activists interpreted as
repudiating the status of Indian tribes as independent sovereign
nations. Other points, on the same theme, called for a review of all

past treaty violations, complete restitution for those violations, and an admission of the tribal right to interpret all past treaties.

Actually, the United States never had accorded the tribes independent sovereign status. As Chief Justice John Marshall carefully articulated in the *Cherokee Cases* of the 1820s and 1830s, United States law recognized tribes as "domestic dependent nations," under the protection of the United States, endowed with only limited rights of sovereignty. The 1871 statute altered the form of U.S. negotiation with individual tribes, mainly to provide the House of Representatives with a greater say in Indian policy (under the Constitution only the Senate ratifies treaties). But the law at most formally codified the longstanding legal position of the government that Indian tribes were not fully independent nations.

When the Trail of Broken Treaties arrived in Washington, the participants discovered that their advance team had failed to secure adequate housing—indeed, any housing at all except for a rat-infested church. (The Nixon administration had instructed the bureau not to provide assistance.) Angry AIM leaders organized an abortive march on the White House, then headed towards the BIA building, headquarters for the racism and corruption they had come to protest. After a brief scuffle with federal officers at the back door (the precise sequence of events is much debated), dozens of Indians—ranging from infants and their mothers to young toughs and old traditionals—swarmed into the building, determined to hold it until the bureaucracy furnished decent accommodations.

In the late afternoon, the police apparently tried to evict the protesters and the relatively peaceful sit-in turned into a full-scale occupation tinged with the threat of violence. The Indians ousted the police and secured the building, barricading the windows and doors with filing cabinets, Xerox machines, and office furniture. Talk about housing turned to talk about martyrdom as Indians armed themselves with chair legs, scissors, and a few pistols. Young militants started chanting Crazy Horse's battle cry, "It's a good day to die." Floyd Young Horse, a Sioux from the Cherry Creek community on the Cheyenne River Reservation, donned war paint. Many others, Means among them, followed suit. "Those of us who have painted our faces have taken a vow to die for what we believe in," he explained.

No soldiers stormed the building. No shots were ever fired. No one was killed. Church groups arranged to supply the Indians with food and water. Russell Means and other AIM spokesmen gave regular news conferences as riot police and U.S. marshals, in full gear, ringed the building. The National Tribal Chairmen's Association, a relatively conservative group backed by the Nixon administration and headed by Webster Two Hawk, the chairman of the Rosebud Sioux, denounced the occupiers. The commissioner of Indian Affairs, Robert Bruce, spent a night with the protesters as a sign of sympathy.

The Nixon administration (at the behest of presidential aide John Ehrlichman) planned, but ultimately decided against, storming the building and risking a public relations nightmare on the eve of the presidential election. After six days of negotiation, the White House agreed to set up an interagency task force to respond to the caravan's twenty points in exchange for the Indians' evacuation of the building. The administration also agreed to provide $66,650 to cover the costs of getting the Indians back home.

As a final gesture of defiance (and as a publicity stunt), AIM carted off dozens of cartons of BIA documents claimed to be evidence of BIA corruption and anti-Indian activity. In their wake, the militants left the BIA building thoroughly looted and defaced, a testament to rage and the desire to exact a small measure of revenge on the bureau. For its part, the bureau used the loss of the stolen documents as an excuse for its usual tardiness and ineptitude in helping the tribes.

In the end, the Trail of Broken Treaties changed nothing and perhaps deepened further the divisions within Indian country and between militant Indians and the reelected Nixon administration, which considered them subversives. The White House informed "Trail" leaders that they would not respond to the twenty points until the stolen documents were returned. Despite this threat, the interagency task force did respond in January 1973. It rejected all the Indian demands.

By this time, the nation had all but forgotten the dramatic pictures of modern Indian warriors, makeshift clubs in hand, standing guard outside the BIA, or of the gutted building they left behind. In the interim, AIM moved its operation to Sioux country, where the incumbent tribal president on Pine Ridge, Dick Wilson, had openly denounced AIM after the Trail of Broken Treaties. AIM now had, in Wilson, a new target in its campaign against the bureau and bureau-recognized tribal governments. And the Sioux people, one hundred years divided, moved towards the brink of civil war.

The 12,000 Oglala Sioux of the Pine Ridge reservation had elected Wilson—a mixed-blood with a reputation for heavy drinking—in late 1971. A corpulent man whose pudgy face, crew cut, and omnipresent dark glasses called to mind the bullying sheriffs of the deep South, Wilson owed his election to strong support among the more assimilated mixed bloods of Pine Ridge town itself and to the failure of fullblood leaders in the outlying districts to endorse a candidate of their own. Gerald One Feather, the fullblood incumbent, apparently alienated his natural constituency because he had been insufficiently generous in handing out tribal jobs on the basis of kinship and blood quantum. "[A] chairman cannot do that," one traditional observed, "without paying a heavy price for it."

Wilson displayed no such reticence. With a tribal budget in excess of $3 million (due to federal grant programs), and patronage jobs aplenty, Wilson freely doled out high-paying positions to friends and relatives. Neither nepotism nor the spoils system was foreign to Sioux politics—far from it. As one Sioux politician explained, "Jobs are so scarce that a janitorial job becomes a political appointment."

Wilson's election, however, upset the customary allocation of jobs. In the past, the fullbloods generally had controlled Pine Ridge's political offices while mixed bloods filled most of the reservation's administrative jobs. With the advent of Wilson's presidency, mixed bloods—many of them actively hostile to the fullbloods' more traditional way of life—came to control virtually everything of value on the reservation.

Old wounds between "loafers" and "hostiles," assimilationists and traditionals, old dealers and New Dealers, mixed bloods and fullbloods, had not healed. Under the Wilson administration, the bleeding started anew.

Wilson ruled Pine Ridge like a petty tyrant. Using federal highway funds, he augmented the tribal police with a "goon squad" of young hardcases, who intimidated and sometimes beat up his opponents. Gunshots in the dark, mysterious home burnings, cars run off narrow reservation roads—"accidents" of all kinds—befell Wilson's critics. The critics got the message. "You have to carry a gun on this reservation now," remarked Ellen Moves Camp, "ever since he's been in there."

Wilson ignored the tribal council as much as possible, governing mainly by fiat or through action of a loyal five-man executive committee. Opponents initiated impeachment proceedings, but like every one of his predecessors, each of whom had suffered attempted impeachment, Wilson weathered the storm unscathed and undaunted.

Into this fracas strode Russell Means and AIM. Ever since its triumph in the Yellow Thunder episode, AIM had been recruiting heavily on Pine Ridge, seeking a grassroots reservation base for its urban-born movement. At meetings across the reservation, AIM members spoke about the corrupt BIA, the destruction of Sioux heritage, racism, and treaty violations. The AIM message struck home not only with disaffected Sioux youth, especially those who had served time in either the armed forces or jail, but also among the traditionals for whom the treaties and the old ways remained a living legacy of the past.

In contrast to Wilson, who scorned the fullbloods and their traditions (he charged admission to the tribal-sponsored Sun Dance), the city-born AIMers looked to them for guidance in rediscovering lost roots. AIM youth brought new vigor to the sun dance, sought new visions at Bear Butte. They yearned to hear the echo of the old ways.

And in contrast to Wilson, who embodied the traditionals' worst nightmare about the consequences of the Indian New Deal, AIM had no truck with the IRA tribal governments. These city youth (often of mixed heritage) and the old dealer reservation fullbloods were natural allies in the undeclared civil war against Wilson.

Wilson detested AIM, and Means in particular. After the Trail of Broken Treaties, when Means announced his intention to return to Pine Ridge, Wilson threatened that "if Russell Means sets foot on this reservation, I, Dick Wilson, will personally cut his braids off." Means came anyway and started to address the Sioux Landowners Association (a fullblood group) about what had happened in Washington, only to find himself arrested by BIA police. They were enforcing a tribal court order Wilson had obtained banning AIM spokesmen from addressing public gatherings. Means was released the next day.

On January 21, 1973, at a bar in Buffalo Gap, South Dakota, a white service station attendant stabbed to death a Sioux named Wesley Bad Heart Bull. Like the Hare brothers who stuffed a dying Raymond Yellow Thunder in a trunk, Bad Heart Bull's killer, Darold Schmidt, was charged with second-degree (involuntary) manslaughter. He walked away from the Custer, South Dakota, jail on $5,000 bail.

Bad Heart Bull's mother, Sarah, called in AIM, which rapidly assembled 200 angry Indians for a caravan to Custer, a town in the heart of the Black Hills where relations between Indians and whites had never lost the frontier antagonism that its namesake had done so much to foster. The Indians assembled at the courthouse while Means, Banks, and a Choctaw named Tom Hill negotiated with the jittery state's attorney, Hobart Gates, over the light charge and low bail.

Gates had tried to head off this confrontation. While AIM was assembling its forces, he had called Ramon Roubideaux, the first Sioux ever to attain a law degree, and had asked him if he would accept a temporary appointment to prosecute the Bad Heart Bull case.

Roubideaux's was an extraordinary story. In the mid-1940s, while a second lieutenant in the air force, he had returned on home leave to Edgemont, South Dakota, where his mother (like a number of Sioux) worked at the local ordinance depot. The Roubideaux family ventured into town to enjoy an evening at an Edgemont dance hall, but the management kicked them out because they were Indians. Roubideaux returned to pick a fight and, before long, the manager was holed up in a back room, having summoned the MPs.

A first lieutenant finally talked Roubideaux out of the bar and into contacting a lawyer to file a complaint about the treatment of his family. No local lawyer, however, would touch the case. As Roubideaux recalls with some perspective, these lawyers simply didn't want to waste their energy on a sure loser. No western South Dakota jury would sanction a bar owner for discriminating against Indians. At the time, Roubideaux complained to the press about the overabundance of "gutless" attorneys in South Dakota.

Shortly thereafter Roubideaux received a letter from South Dakota Senator Francis Case, who suggested that Roubideaux improve the quality of South Dakota's legal community by attending law school himself. Accepting Case's offer of a job in his Washington office to help defray expenses, Roubideaux moved east and enrolled at George Washington University law school.

Roubideaux returned to South Dakota after graduation in 1950. He decided to set up shop in Pierre, not least because he considered it "the toughest place in the state for an Indian to earn a living." His first night in business, some locals dumped a tub full of cow guts on his front stoop ("guteaters" is a common anti-Indian slur). Roubideaux persevered, then prospered in a largely criminal practice. In 1970 he ran for state attorney general and lost by less than one vote per precinct.

Roubideaux had a simple response for Gates. He would prosecute the Bad Heart Bull case if the state would indict Schmidt for murder—just as it would if the victim had been white. As Gates knew well, after trial the jury could always acquit on the murder charge and convict on the lesser manslaughter offense if the evidence so warranted. Still, he refused to agree to a murder charge. Roubideaux said good-bye.

When the AIM representative arrived at his office, Gates promised a vigorous prosecution of the manslaughter charge but again refused to indict for murder. The AIM people grew furious. These Indians, indeed all South Dakota Indians, had suffered enough of what they considered the state's threadbare, hand-me-down version of justice when it came to the killing of their people. Means starting shouting; some say Sarah Bad Heart Bull got pushed by the police; others say that the Indians rushed the building. In any case, as Bob Burnette put it, "All hell broke loose."

Police and Indians went at each other wildly, generations of hate unleashed in fistfighting, clubbings, tear gas, and makeshift firebombs. Before the riot ended, the Indians had set fire to a pair of patrol cars and an abandoned Chamber of Commerce building designed as an imitation log cabin. Outside, the town's welcoming banner went up in flames. "WELCOME TO CUSTER," it had read, "THE TOWN WITH THE GUNSMOKE FLAVOR." Both sides suffered numerous injuries, though miraculously no one died. The police arrested twenty-seven Indians, including Means and Hill.

Freed on bail, the AIMers marched on Rapid City at the northeastern tip of the Black Hills, a city many Indians considered the most racist in America. Another riot ensued that night after a scuffle in a bar. Dozens more people were injured, dozens more AIMers arrested. The frontier days of fighting Indians returned to Dakota, as did all the fear, anger, and prejudice that a century of unhappy proximity could generate.

To the south in Pine Ridge town—a cluster of government buildings, churches, and house trailers complemented by a few dilapidated cafés and stores, two gas stations, and a hair salon— Wilson and federal authorities braced for an anticipated militant demonstration. To protect the local BIA building, the Nixon administration dispatched to Pine Ridge sixty-five heavily armed federal marshals, who set up a command post in town. "Fort Wilson," some Indians called it. The scene echoed the old days, when agents called in the army whenever the hostiles caused trouble.

The arrival of federal reinforcements on the reservation coincided with a second attempt to impeach Dick Wilson. When Wilson succeeded in delaying his trial, 300 angry Sioux, now organized as the Oglala Sioux Civil Rights Organization (OSCRO), marched on the BIA building, demanding the president's ouster.

The impeachment trial eventually took place on February 22 and 23, presided over by a Wilson-appointed tribal judge. To the dismay of both reservation militants and traditionalists, the council voted unanimously (14–0) in Wilson's favor.

Convinced that Wilson and his goon squad had cowed the council into supporting him regardless of the tribe's best interests, OSCRO adjourned to the community hall at Calico, a log house a few miles west of Pine Ridge town. Having failed to topple Wilson constitutionally, OSCRO enlisted the help of the one organization that had demonstrated a capability for success using extralegal methods—what one anti-Wilson tribal councilman called the "warrior troops of this century." OSCRO invited AIM leaders to Calico and asked Means and Banks for their supporters to help in overthrowing Wilson and his corrupt BIA-supported government.

Traditional leaders like Frank Fools Crow, nephew to Iron Cloud (a chief in the treaty days), fifty years a medicine man, spoke of the outrages of the Wilson government. He and other traditional leaders asked AIM to restore them to their rightful place at the head of Sioux government. "Go ahead and do it, go to Wounded Knee," Ellen Moves Camp, an OSCRO leader, recalled the elders as saying to Means and Banks. "You can't get in the BIA Office and the Tribal office, so take your brothers from the American Indian Movement and go to Wounded Knee and make your stand there."

In directing AIM to Wounded Knee, to *Cankpe Opi*, OSCRO and the traditionals had selected the most symbolically rich location in Indian America. There in 1890, Custer's onetime outfit, the 7th Cavalry, had closed the Indian wars in a burst of runaway savagery. There, 300 Sioux men, women, and children lie buried in a mass grave, marking the spot—indelible in Sioux memory—where Black Elk's "beautiful dream" perished in pools of blood frozen on the plains tundra.

On the hamlet's highest rise, presiding over the mass grave of Big Foot's band, the Sacred Heart Church, its rectangular white steeple commanding the plain, reminded every resident and visitor of the long Sioux walk along the "black road" of the whites. Catholic missionaries had worked among the Sioux since Father De Smet joined the tribe at the height of its power. Now the Holy Rosary Church was the Pine Ridge Reservation's largest single landowner. "It has been said of the missionaries," observed Vine Deloria, Jr., the nationally prominent Sioux author, "that when they arrived they had only the Book and we had the land. Now we have the Book and they have the land."

Below the church, about 200 yards, stood a large trading post, a central fixture in reservation life, home to the *icazopi* economy, "the making of a mark" as illiterate Sioux bought on credit. There, for generations, the Sioux had come to buy or trade for those things the government did not supply. Prices were high and many Indians felt cheated. To many, the post was a potent and inescapable reminder of an exploitation that dated to the trapping days when the mountain men would trade a stack of pelts for a shot of whiskey.

The AIM caravan of 54 cars and 250 Indians arrived at Wounded Knee early in the evening of February 27. They shot out the hamlet's few street lights, seized the trading post, ransacked it for guns and ammunition, and took its white owner and some others hostage. The young men, eagle feathers tied to their braids, started digging trenches and making bunkers along a line surrounding the white church. The occupiers named Leonard Crow Dog spiritual leader. Eighty three years earlier, his great-grandfather, a Ghost Dance leader who had taken refuge in the Badlands with his followers, had surrendered to federal troops rather than see his people die. Now, with the great-grandson, the Ghost Dancers returned.

Federal marshals, FBI agents, and BIA police blocked the roads into Wounded Knee and started a siege. A makeshift army soon gathered on the reservation, complete with armored personnel carriers and heavy automatic weapons. South Dakota's Senators George McGovern and James Abourezk, staunch Indian sympathizers, met briefly with the occupiers, satisfied themselves about the safety of the hostages, but refused AIM demands including immediate congressional review of all Indian treaties and suspension of the Pine Ridge Constitution. On March 4, Justice Department officials opened negotiations, but the talks quickly broke down. The siege wore on, punctuated by daily firefights; two Indians were wounded.

On March 11, the occupiers, together with a delegation of Sioux traditionals who had entered Wounded Knee during a truce, proclaimed the new Independent Oglala Nation, a revival of the Great Sioux Nation established by the 1868 treaty. The founding principles of the Independent Oglala Nation called for the abolition of the BIA-sponsored tribal government and the return of traditional Sioux government, the restoration of tribal treatymaking status, and the recognition of Sioux rights guaranteed by the 1868 treaty. The ION announced its intention to send a delegation to the United Nations. According to an AIM press release, on March 16, 349 people were sworn in as citizens, including 189 Oglalas and 160

"Indians and chicanos of other tribes and seven whites and blacks."

The siege lasted seventy-one days. At one point, no fewer than five separate roadblocks, each manned by a different entity (AIM, the FBI, Wilson people, anti-Wilson people, displaced residents), surrounded Wounded Knee. Through all these checkpoints, AIM sympathizers smuggled food and supplies.

At times, a full-scale assault appeared imminent, as heavily armed federal troops readied for action and Means and others vowed to die for their treaty rights. Gunfire, often intense, claimed victims both inside and outside the Independent Oglala Nation.

Other times, the parties appeared near settlement. In early April, a Wounded Knee delegation traveled to Washington to conclude an agreement ending the occupation in exchange for the creation of a special commission to reexamine treaty rights and a promise that the federal government would actively investigate alleged abuses by the Wilson regime. The Washington trip proved futile, however. AIM blamed government intransigence. Sioux lawyer Ramon Roubideaux, whom both sides had asked to participate in negotiations, blamed AIM. The AIM leadership, he decided, "was more intent on keeping the pot boiling than on getting anything settled."

And the pot was boiling away. On the front page of every newspaper in America, on every edition of the nightly television news, Indians could see themselves taking a dramatic stand. Members of sixty-four separate tribes spent at least some time at Wounded Knee, as did white, black, and chicano supporters. Sioux children scratched "AIM" on their skin, clothes, and possessions, and flashed AIM's "V for Victory" salutes at passersby.

Outside of Indian country, the Wounded Knee occupation cast a bright spotlight on the desperate situation of reservation Indians, exposing once more the raw nerve of white racial guilt, the prime source of Indian political power in the dominant society. Every family in America was reminded that their own prosperity derived in part from the suffering and subjugation of Indian peoples. Every family was reminded that this original sin, like the sin of slavery, had known no expiation.

Church and philanthropic groups across the country expressed their solidarity with the occupiers. The National Council of Churches even announced that it would post members between the firing lines in case of government attack.

But appeals to guilt, however much they might marshal support in some quarters, could not break the deadlock at Wounded Knee.

AIM demands exceeded what even liberal Americans could provide. At one point Means declared with his usual flair that if the
U.S. did not recognize the 1868 treaty, "then you might as well kill
me, because I have no reason for living." No U.S. government,
though, would return western South Dakota to the Sioux, declare
five western states to be unceded Indian territory, and recognize
each and every tribe as an independent sovereign nation. As
Roubideaux observed, Means was just "keeping the pot boiling,"
knowing that for one of the few times in the century the nation
was focused on the problems of Indians—and that a nation so
focused would not unleash its army against the women and children manning the bunkers under the eaves of the Wounded Knee
church.

The occupation drew sharp criticism. Many Indians and Indian
sympathizers perceived in AIM's Wounded Knee mission a wealth
of contradictions. Although one anti-Wilson tribal councilman
admiringly referred to AIM as the "shock troops of Indian Sovereignty," AIM's demand that the United States oust Wilson and
recognize a "traditional" Sioux government was poorly grounded
in notions of tribal self-rule. Whatever his faults, Wilson was
democratically elected, and therefore susceptible to ouster by the
Sioux themselves at the end of his term. (Indeed, the Pine Ridge
Sioux had never reelected a president to a second term.)

The Wounded Knee occupiers, on the other hand, many (if not
most) of whom were not Sioux, were in essence asking for an
outside power (the U.S.) to intervene in Sioux internal affairs and
install a government of "traditional chiefs." Jealous of the powers
of the tribal governments, these "chiefs" had come to that title not
through the old process of winning authority in the hunt and in
battle but rather by heredity or self-selection. Moreover, their
notion of tribal governance did not exalt self-determination but
rather presumed a return to the treaty era when a bureau superintendent controlled reservation affairs while paying token respect
to the prerogatives of the tribal elders.

From their opponents' perspective, what AIM actually sought
was the disenfranchisement of all Sioux who did not recognize
Red Cloud's grandson or grandnephew as entitled to leadership,
or the right of mainly Chippewa agitators to occupy a part of their
reservation and impose change through force. Many Sioux, even
among those who opposed Wilson, resented AIM's presence on the
reservation. They agreed with the three Native American law
students from Harvard who concluded from their visit to
Wounded Knee that the occupiers, "parad[ing] around in their

beads and feathers," had caused "tremendous disruption" on the reservation and "undermined" the tribal structure of the Sioux. In any case, the civil war at Wounded Knee failed to address the employment, housing, and medical needs of the people on whose behalf it was supposedly being fought.

The sporadic firefights wore on through April. The Holy Rosary Church burned to the ground. Both sides suffered more casualties.

The siege ended May 8. The previous week, Kent Frizzell, Nixon's newly appointed Interior Department solicitor, had met with a group of Sioux traditionals at Frank Fools Crow's place in Kyle. Frizzell announced that the White House would appoint representatives to discuss the 1868 treaty if the occupation ended. After some negotiation, the occupiers agreed to leave Wounded Knee. Those subject to outstanding arrest warrants agreed to surrender themselves. In return, the government consented to a meeting with the traditionals to discuss treaty rights, protection for the traditionals and AIM supporters against Wilson-instigated retribution, and an investigation into civil and criminal violations allegedly committed by the Wilson regime. On the eighth, when federal marshals finally entered Wounded Knee village, only 129 Sioux and AIM people remained. Many others had vanished in the night.

On May 17 a White House delegation led by Brad Patterson, the President's Indian affairs troubleshooter, returned to Fools Crow's home in Kyle, where they listened to the traditionals. Frank Kills Enemy, over 80, an old friend of Ralph Case, captured the elders' sentiments. "The treaty law of 1868 . . . stands firm like the Black Hills," he said. "This law cannot be moved, like the Black Hills."

Patterson promised to return two weeks later with a formal response to the traditionals' treaty-based demands, but instead a courier delivered a letter from Leonard Garment, the President's counsel. "The days of treaty making with the American Indians ended in 1871, 102 years ago," Garment wrote. "Only Congress can rescind or change in any way statutes enacted since 1871, such as the Indian Reorganization Act. . . ." Under American law, Congress enjoyed "plenary power" over Indian affairs. As the Supreme Court ruled in its 1903 *Lonewolf* decision, that plenary power included even the power to break treaties. However much Kills Enemy wished it otherwise, Congress could "move" the law of 1868—and by the act of 1877 (and others) it already had.

Wounded Knee II was over. Dick Wilson stayed in office. The Independent Oglala Nation disappeared. Buddy Lamont, the first

Indian fatality at Wounded Knee II, was laid to rest in a martyr's grave behind the charred foundation of the Holy Rosary Church next to the remains of Big Foot's band. On the surface, little seemed changed, except that a cold war between Sioux factions had given way to violence.

Something profound had changed, though. At the first Wounded Knee, the Ghost Dance vision of an all-Indian paradise on earth died with Big Foot's band in a storm of bullets. At Wounded Knee II, where Leonard Crow Dog had conducted the old Ghost Dance for the occupiers, a new Ghost Dance vision, the dream of old sovereignty restored, survived the siege to inflame the imaginations of a people woozy from misery. Like the prophet Wovoka, the militants preached that a new Indian golden age lay just around the corner, that the people's sacred hoop—the hoop Black Elk thought broken—was whole again. For many Sioux, the dream of returning to the glory days of 1868, once the stuff of bedtime stories and idle musing, took root as a tenet of political and even religious orthodoxy. They would live by the treaty and demand that the United States do the same.

There were naysayers—for one, Toby Eaglebull, a councilman. "Are we going to get the Black Hills back?" he asked rhetorically. "Are we going to get back the hunting grounds in Nebraska, in North Dakota, in Wyoming and in Montana? . . . You and I know that we can't turn back the clock. . . ." But in many shanties on the Pine Ridge Reservation, and elsewhere, people started to hope and believe that old promises of freedom might be redeemed, that old dreams of resurrection might yet come true.

THIRTEEN

▼ ▼ ▼ ▼ ▼

GOOD FAITH EFFORT

LAZARUS AND SONOSKY had little contact with the Indian militants. Lazarus's partner, Dick Schifter, served as general counsel to the Oglala Sioux tribe and, in that capacity, he publicly defended Dick Wilson's administration as the recognized, elected, and therefore legitimate tribal government on the Pine Ridge reservation. Neither Lazarus nor Sonosky thought that AIM's takeover strategy accomplished much that was constructive, but it posed no apparent hindrance to their work. Through Alcatraz, the Trail of Broken Treaties, the BIA takeover, and finally Wounded Knee II, as the militants rebelled against the government, defied its laws, and denigrated its "neo-colonialist" treatment of aboriginal peoples, Sonosky and Lazarus continued to prosecute the Sioux claims to the full extent of the law, in the sole forum that Congress had provided, on behalf of the tribal councils that had hired them.

Over the years, Lazarus had settled into a comfortable, if strictly professional relationship with his Pine Ridge Sioux client. He was not a Ralph Case. Although he wrote forcefully about the tragedy of Sioux history in his court papers, he did not write personal letters to Indians on the reservation exchanging reminiscences or musing about the nature of things. Lazarus rarely visited Sioux country. As the Oglala's general counsel, Dick Schifter made the necessary periodic trips to South Dakota, where he helped the tribe set up vital reservation projects such as the Felix Cohen Old Age Home and the Pine Ridge Housing Authority. From Washington, Lazarus submitted cordial but formal reports to the tribal

312

council, recounting progress in the claims and frankly assessing their future prospects.

Lazarus's persona permitted no greater intimacy. Though kind and personable, he was not an affable man, not someone who joked, kidded, or shared his feelings easily with others. In contrast to Case, sharing a drink and a laugh with Indian clients did not come naturally, and he counted few of them among his friends. Lazarus was a lawyer's lawyer, "the very best I've ever met," one of his partners freely declared. He did his job at arm's length from his clients, even natives who were inclined to want a personal connection with their advocate in Congress and the federal courts.

Sonosky was more inclined to a personal involvement. As general counsel as well as claims counsel to four Sioux tribes, his work brought him in virtually daily contact with his clients and gave full rein to his midwestern yarn-spinning charm. Like Case, Sonosky received many letters from Sioux old-timers. "Dear Friend," many began.

Partly as a result of his friendships in Indian country (and because of his considerable legal skills), Sonosky's law practice thrived. In addition to his four Sioux tribal clients, he represented the Shoshone, Chippewa, and several smaller tribes. Besides this general counsel work, Sonosky handled several potentially lucrative land claims. In one, a claim of the Mississippi River Sioux bands to aboriginal land lying mainly in Minnesota, Sonosky already had obtained a $12.2 million settlement, which made the claim one of the largest on record.

Lazarus also worked on several large Indian claims, but as a member of the Strasser, Spiegelberg (changed to Fried, Frank, Harris, Shriver and Jacobson) "joint efforts" team, not as lead counsel. Most of his practice consisted of general counsel work for the Senecas, Tuscaroras, Miccosukee, and San Carlos Apache. On their behalf, and as general counsel to the Association on American Indian Affairs, Lazarus filed *amicus curiae* (friend of the court) briefs in almost every Indian litigation heard by the Supreme Court during the 1960s and 1970s. Many of these cases involved questions of tribal sovereignty, such as the extent of tribal civil and criminal jurisdiction, tribal taxing power, and water or treaty rights. In brief after brief, Lazarus devised legal theories to support the exercise of tribal power and confirm in American law that Indian tribes were sovereign over their own people and all others who entered their lands.

Lazarus also engaged in substantial lobbying on behalf of Indian causes. He and Sonosky worked closely with Senator Sam Ervin's

staff to ensure that the Indian Civil Rights Act adequately safeguarded tribal autonomy and, most important, provided for suspension of Public Law 280. Lazarus also drafted the "native version" of what became, in somewhat diluted form, the landmark
Alaska Native Claims Settlement Act of 1971, undoubtedly the
most generous settlement ever achieved between a conquering
sovereign and its aboriginal peoples. Finally resolving all outstanding aboriginal claims in Alaska, the act permitted the state's natives to organize into corporations and awarded the natives more
than 40 million acres of land and $962 million.

For both lawyers, though, regardless of their other notable successes, the Black Hills claim held a unique and enduring appeal.
The sheer length of the litigation and the dramatic frontier history
from which it arose practically guaranteed as much. The huge
sums of money involved and the enormous potential fee (if they
won) clinched it.

But progress in the claim itself remained agonizingly slow. By
May 1971, a full year after the surface valuation trial, Lazarus and
Sonosky still had not completed their written brief and proposed
Findings of Fact on value. This particular delay was strategic.
Lazarus and Sonosky deliberately dragged their feet during the
valuation phase of the claim in the hope that the commission
would first decide the long-since argued issue of what consideration, if any, the Sioux had received for the Hills. The commission's
resolution of the consideration issue, Lazarus believed, was the key
factor in whether the Sioux would obtain a substantial recovery in
the claim. He and Sonosky wanted the commission to decide what
consideration the Sioux had received before committing themselves to a valuation figure for the Black Hills.

Although Lazarus and Sonosky obtained an embarrassing six
extensions of time for filing their brief and findings of fact on
value, the commission remained silent on the issue of consideration. Their plan foiled, the lawyers finally submitted their valuation arguments, concluding (as their experts had testified) that the
Hills were worth more than $26 million in 1877.

Over the course of the next ten months, the government presented its own findings of fact and brief on the issue of value and
registered its objections to Lazarus and Sonosky's submissions.
They, in turn, filed their objections to the government's proposed
valuation of $4.9 million.

Yet another year of legal skirmishing followed as the government again tried unsuccessfully to have portions of the Black Hills
claim dismissed on jurisdictional grounds. Also, the parties traded

motions and memorandums about the compensability of gold removed from the Black Hills by trespassing miners (prior to the 1877 act) and whether the Sioux could recover for rights-of-way through Sioux country that the U.S. obtained under the 1877 act. Still, the commission issued no decisions on the previously briefed legal issues, some of which had been pending for almost four years.

Instead, on December 7, 1973 (seven months after the end of Wounded Knee II), the commission scheduled oral argument on the major outstanding issues in the claim, including whether the Court of Claims 1942 decision barred Sonosky and Lazarus's Fifth Amendment taking argument on the ground of *res judicata;* if *res judicata* did not apply, had a Fifth Amendment taking occurred, and what consideration or payments had the government provided in exchange for the Black Hills.

The argument commenced at 10:00 on December 18 in a nondescript hearing room on the eighth floor of the downtown office building that served as the commission's fourth home since its inception. John Vance presided. He was joined by Richard Yarborough and two new appointees, Margaret Pierce and Brantley Blue, who had replaced Holt and Scott, the holdovers from the Watkins era. Pierce had served for many years as a staff attorney for the Court of Claims, and many considered her the commission's most qualified member.

Blue was a Lumbee Indian from rural North Carolina. A cobbler's son, one of nine children, he had put himself through law school, settled as an attorney in Kingsport, Tennessee, and became president of the local bar association. Yet another symbol of how far the process of assimilation had progressed, Blue would now sit in judgment on the claims of distant cousins against the nation that had conquered their ancestors.

Roughly half the three-hour oral argument focused on the single question of whether Judge Littleton's rambling and abstruse 1942 Court of Claims opinion had dismissed the Sioux tribe's Fifth Amendment claim to just compensation for the taking of the Black Hills because the claim lay outside the court's jurisdiction (as defined in the 1920 jurisdictional act), or whether the court had considered and rejected the tribe's Fifth Amendment claim on its merits. In the latter case, Sonosky and Lazarus's Fifth Amendment argument would be barred under the doctrine of *res judicata.*

For more than an hour, in his slightly folksy but closely reasoned style, Sonosky walked the commissioners through his reading of the 1942 ruling, trying to convince them (as Ralph Case had never doubted at the time) that the Court of Claims decision was jurisdictional. As Sonosky explained the 1942 opinion, the court held only that the 1920 jurisdictional act did not give it authority to "go behind . . . the 1877 Act to see whether, in fact . . . consideration was adequate, or whether it was paid at all, or what the circumstances of it were, or what motivated Congress—that was none of the Court's business." At least thirteen times, by Sonosky's count, the 1942 court had reiterated its lack of authority to question "the policy, wisdom, or authority of Congress."

However odd this extreme judicial deference might sound in 1973, Sonosky explained, it reflected consistent practice by the Court of Claims thirty years earlier of both narrowly construing jurisdictional statutes and also invoking the Supreme Court's 1903 decision in *Lonewolf* to accord extraordinary latitude to Congress in its control of Indian affairs. Under *Lonewolf* (especially as interpreted in 1942), Sonosky reminded the commission Congress possessed plenary authority over Indian affairs, including unfettered power to change the form of Indian investment (i.e., to turn land into rations), even in violation of a treaty. As interpreted by the 1942 Court of Claims, the 1920 jurisdictional act simply did not give the court permission to examine or second-guess Congress's legal exercise of this plenary authority. Accordingly, the court had dismissed the Sioux claim for lack of jurisdiction, without reaching the merits of the tribe's Fifth Amendment argument.

Sonosky acknowledged that other Supreme Court cases, specifically *Shoshone* and *Creek Nation* (decided in the mid-1930s), established the principle that under the Fifth Amendment, regardless of its plenary powers, Congress must pay just compensation for the taking of Indian lands. Nonetheless, Sonosky argued that Judge Littleton had distinguished those cases on the ground that in both *Shoshone* and *Creek Nation* Congress had made *no* effort to pay *any* compensation. In taking the Black Hills, by contrast, Congress had at least purported to give the Indians something, such as rations, in return for their lands.

The distinction, Sonosky asserted, was critical. As the Court of Claims viewed the law in 1942, for an Indian tribe to recover under the Fifth Amendment, it needed to show not only that the United States took its land, but also that the consideration the tribe received for the land was unfair or inadequate. In *Shoshone* and *Creek Nation* the inadequacy of consideration was apparent; there had been no consideration. But in the case of the Black Hills taking, Congress had authorized *some* payment in return for the land, and the 1920 jurisdictional act, Sonosky argued, left the court powerless to examine the fairness or morality of the deal that Congress had fashioned for the Indians.

If all this seemed rather tortured, Sonosky had a ready explanation. What the court really was trying to do, he frankly suggested, was to duck a vexing case. The court knew that the government had taken valuable Sioux land in return for almost nothing. "But when you [the Court] are confronted with a claim for $789 million, you are not searching for a way to render a judgment. The search here was for a way to get rid of that case. . . . And it wasn't hard to do in those days because of the special jurisdictional act giving them the opening. And that's the opening they took."

Sonosky did not see how the commission could read the 1942 opinion as anything other than an elaborate coverup for a nifty bit of judicial abdication. After all, Judge Littleton had still been on the Court of Claims in 1956 when the Black Hills claim came back up after Ralph Case refiled it under the Indian Claims Commission Act. If the judge's 1942 decision had decided the Fifth Amendment issue on its merits, surely the court of which he was a member would have said so in its 1956 opinion. But it did not.

When Sonosky finished his *res judicata* argument, the commission asked for the government's response. Craig Decker virtually declined. "I hate to go on all day on this," he complained. In Decker's opinion, "Much of [the argument] lends itself better to written briefs than it does to oral arguments. . . ."

Sonosky exploded. "We want to avoid written briefs. My god, we've been here too long, Mr. Decker."

As appeared from a later exchange, Decker had made afternoon travel plans that were being endangered by Sonosky's deliberate parsing of the 1942 opinion. "I can see that this can go on forever the way they're moving here," he groused.

Decker kept his presentation brief. He asserted that the 1942 court had "very definitely" decided the Fifth Amendment issue. In his view, the Court of Claims looked at the Fifth Amendment issue, saw that the United States had expended over $40 million in rations to feed the Sioux, and therefore correctly concluded that the Sioux had already received just compensation for their land— precisely as the Constitution required. Indeed, Decker asserted, the court not only had decided against the Sioux on the Fifth Amendment issue; "in the eyes of the court" the issue "wasn't a close [call]."

Commissioners Yarborough, Pierce, and Blue were skeptical. Blue wanted to know why the government had waited until now, twenty-three years into the litigation under the ICC Act, before pleading the defense of *res judicata*. Decker explained that this was the first time the Sioux had argued the *res judicata* issue, completely missing Commissioner Blue's point (underscored by Sonosky in his rebuttal) that under the rules of procedure, the defendant (not the plaintiff) bears the burden of raising this defense.

Pierce and Yarborough also wanted to know how Decker explained Judge Littleton's lengthy discussion of the jurisdictional act if the point of his decision had been to decide the Fifth Amendment claim on its merits. Decker responded that Littleton's discussion of the jurisdictional act had nothing to do with the tribe's untenable Fifth Amendment claim. Rather, in this section of the opinion, Littleton had been considering whether (under the jurisdictional act) the Sioux might challenge Congress's exercise of plenary powers as unfair or immoral. According to Decker, the 1942 court decided that the tribe could not so challenge.

Commissioner Blue threw up his hands in confusion. He could not believe that Judge Littleton could so effectively have hidden the legal basis for his opinion. "It is amazing," Blue interjected with a hint of disgust, "that a Court can talk for 70 pages, and we don't know which way they decided the basic question."

Judge Littleton might well have considered Blue's reaction a tribute to his talent for obfuscation. After all, if Littleton had written the opinion more clearly, he would have had to choose to award the Sioux over $700 million, to deny the Sioux any recovery for the taking of one of the most valuable goldfields in the western world, or to admit to an act of colossal judicial cowardice. Best, he must have thought, to hide behind a dense bank of legal pettifoggery and let later generations argue over the opinion's meaning.

After a brief adjournment, the commission turned to the other issues in the claim, principally the question of what consideration or payment, if any, the government had given the Sioux for the Black Hills. Presenting the Sioux position, Lazarus reiterated the arguments previously presented in the Sioux briefs. Decker responded in kind.

Neither Lazarus nor Sonosky asserted directly exactly how, in their view, the United States had violated its Fifth Amendment obligation to pay just compensation for lands that Congress appropriates in the public interest. As Lazarus remarked at one point during the hearing, "the facts speak for themselves."

At 1:10 P.M. the commission adjourned, with ample time for Decker to make his plane. Fifty years after its birth, sixteen years after its resuscitation, the Black Hills claim was ready for decision again.

Two months later, on February 15, 1974, the commission handed down its ruling. As Sonosky and Lazarus described the mammoth 213-page opinion, it gave the Sioux a great victory on the one hand and then took almost all of it away with the other.

The "great victory" consisted of two principal holdings: first, that the United States had taken the Black Hills in violation of the Fifth Amendment; and, second, that the 7,345,157 acres that the government appropriated under the 1877 act were worth $17.1 million.

Writing for all of the commissioners except Yarborough (who dissented), Commissioner Vance rejected the government's *res judicata* argument. Vance observed that when the government responded to Sonosky and Lazarus's amended petition in Docket 74B in 1966, it had conceded that the Court of Claims had dismissed the Black Hills claim in 1942 solely for lack of jurisdiction. This concession, the commission ruled, precluded the government from raising the defense of *res judicata* by now asserting that the Court of Claims 1942 decision had actually reached the merits of the Black Hills claim.

Holding the government to its 1966 concession, the commission further observed, caused no injustice. A "close examination of the . . . 1942 decision reveals that the court did dismiss the plaintiffs' claim solely on jurisdictional grounds, and did not rule on the merits of the Fifth Amendment taking claim." In other words, even if the commission had not held the government to its 1966 concession, it would have rejected the government's *res judicata* defense.

The commission reached this judgment through very much the interpretive process Sonosky had followed at oral argument. Through eighteen pages of close reading interspersed with long excerpts from Judge Littleton's 1942 opinion, the commission traced the Court of Claim's pervasive concern with the scope of the 1920 Sioux jurisdictional act. According to the commission, the 1942 court had interpreted the jurisdictional act as conferring authority to decide only "legal claims," those "based on violations of legal rights possessed by the Sioux under treaties or laws of Congress." The Black Hills claim, the 1942 court had decided, did not fall in this category. Under *Lonewolf,* Congress possessed the "legal right" to break the 1868 treaty. Accordingly, the Black Hills claim (based on a violation of the 1868 treaty) did not allege a violation of any "legal right" possessed by the Sioux. In other words, the tribe's Black Hills claim was "moral, rather than legal," and therefore outside the scope of the 1920 jurisdictional act.

Having decided that the Court of Claims's decision was no bar to consideration of the Sioux Fifth Amendment claim, the commission itself now had to face the question whether, in fact, the 1877 act effected a Fifth Amendment taking of the Black Hills. To provide an answer, the commission invoked the *"Fort Berthold* test" (which the Court of Claims first enunciated in the 1968 takings case *The Three Affiliated Tribes of the Fort Berthold Reservation* v. *United States*), and established as its formula for determining whether a taking of Indian land has occurred.

The *Fort Berthold* test reflected the Court of Claims's attempt to "resolve a seeming conflict" between two well-established lines of Supreme Court cases. The first, the plenary power cases culminating in *Lonewolf,* recognized the "paramount power [of Congress] over the property of the Indians by reason of its exercise of guardianship over their interests," a power (so *Lonewolf* states) "not subject to be controlled by the judicial department of the government." The second line of cases, most notably Justice Cardozo's majority opinions in *Shoshone* and *Creek Nation,* held that when Congress exercises its constitutional power of eminent domain (its "takings" power) to appropriate tribal land, it must pay just compensation to the tribe.

To the Court of Claims in *Fort Berthold,* it was "obvious" that Congress could not simultaneously exercise its plenary power to manage Indian property and its power of eminent domain to take Indian lands. As the court put it, "Congress can own two hats, but it cannot wear them both at the same time."

How then, the Court of Claims asked itself, could it determine which hat Congress was wearing when in a given instance it disposed of Indian lands? Was it the plenary powers hat which conferred on the Congress immunity from judicial scrutiny? Or was it the eminent domain hat which permitted the judiciary to adjudicate just compensation claims?

To answer this question, the Court of Claims invented the "good faith effort" standard to distinguish between governmental acts pursuant to its trusteeship over the tribes and governmental acts, independent of that trust responsibility, such as the taking of tribal land through the sovereign power of eminent domain. The court ruled that where Congress has made a good faith effort to give tribes full value for their taken lands, the government shall be deemed to have invoked its plenary powers as trustee for the tribes. In other words, where Congress has made a good faith effort to pay full value to the tribes, the Court of Claims would consider the decision to take tribal lands basically an investment decision undertaken by the trustee, or (quoting *Lonewolf*) "a mere change in the form of investment of Indian tribal property." By contrast, where Congress has not acted in good faith to give a tribe fair value, the Court of Claims ruled that the government shall be deemed to have exercised its eminent domain power and to have triggered its constitutional obligation to pay just compensation (fair market value at the time of the taking plus interest) for the taken lands.

While the Court of Claims opinion bears the earmarks of a judicious reconciliation of conflicting Supreme Court precedents, the *Fort Berthold* test is blatant and needless discrimination masquerading as compromise. The Fifth Amendment just compensation rule for white property owners is clear as air. If a white man owns a house with a fair market value of $100,000 and the government takes it, the government must pay the owner $100,000 (plus interest from the time of the taking). Under the *Fort Berthold* approach, if an Indian tribe owns that same house and the government takes it but in "good faith" pays the tribe only $50,000 (mistakenly thinking that this was all the house was worth), the tribe may not collect the $50,000 difference between the government's payment and the actual fair market value of the property. The Court of Claims would deem the government to have acted in its plenary capacity, thereby placing its actions beyond judicial scrutiny.

In addition to being patently unfair, the *Fort Berthold* rule makes a mockery of the concept of trusteeship—the supposed legal relationship between the United States government and the tribes. Ordinarily, courts hold trustees strictly accountable for the disposition of trust property. Yet in *Fort Berthold* the Court of Claims used the government's trusteeship over Indian property as an excuse for holding it less accountable for its disposition of trust property (Indian property) than for its disposition of nontrust (white-owned) property. In sum, the *Fort Berthold* test not only inadequately and unequally protects Indian property rights, it does so in a circumstance where Indians should have been able to expect especially fair treatment under the law.

All this the Court of Claims engineered in order to resolve an alleged conflict between two sets of prior Supreme Court decisions. But, in point of logic, it is not at all evident that the *Lonewolf* and *Shoshone* lines of cases do conflict, and even to the extent that they might, the various precedents could easily have been reconciled without entrenching the status of Indians as poor stepchildren before the law.

A wiser Court of Claims, or one less concerned with the financial implications of permitting Indian tribes to pursue Fifth Amendment takings claims under the traditional just compensation doctrine, would have ruled that the *Shoshone* line of cases, which postdated *Lonewolf* by thirty years, simply limited the *Lonewolf* cases: To the extent that the *Lonewolf* cases placed congressional disposition of Indian property, even in violation of the Constitution, outside the purview of the courts, they were no longer good law. Put differently, the Court of Claims should have read the *Lonewolf* cases *in light of* the *Shoshone* cases to stand for the proposition that Congress enjoys plenary power over Indian property *but* must exercise that power in conformity with the Constitution— including the Constitution's Fifth Amendment requirement that the United States pay just compensation for lands it takes.

This reconciliation of the cases, one which preserves tribal equality under the law, does no violence to *Lonewolf* itself. In that case, individual Indians sought to prevent Congress from disposing of certain tribal lands. The Supreme Court denied the requested injunction. *Shoshone* and its legal progeny in no way suggest that the courts may stop Congress from taking or otherwise administering tribal lands. These cases merely say that *when* Congress takes land, the Constitution requires the payment of just compensation. Thus, the actual rulings in *Lonewolf* and *Shoshone* do not conflict at all.

The sad lesson of *Fort Berthold* was that Americans and American law remained unwilling to recognize fully the rights of Indian tribes to own and control land. For centuries, Europeans, colonists, frontiersmen, Protestant reformers, land developers nurtured and acted on the "menagerie" theory of Indian property rights. To them, Indians were not meaningfully different from wild animals in their use of the land and therefore enjoyed no greater rights of ownership. Neither animals nor Indians adhered to the European practice of individual ownership, putting lands to their "highest and best use," and establishing land titles and fixed boundaries. In the minds of the immigrants, the natives roaming wild through forests or across prairies did not constitute the sort of use or control over land that merited legal recognition of ownership.

Naturally, such a rationale for denying property rights to Indians salved the conscience of a nation bent on tribal dispossession through either outright conquest or allegedly humanitarian measures—for example, allotment policy, which reduced tribal land holdings while it coerced Indians into adopting approved forms of land use. Once the nation's land hunger abated, stale rationales for devaluing Indian property rights resurfaced as reasons for limiting the rights of tribes to recover for lands taken in the conquest. In 1955 the Supreme Court ruled (in the case of *Tee-Hit-Ton Indians v. United States*) that tribes had no inherent compensable rights in their aboriginal lands. Such rights arose only when the United States confirmed tribal ownership of aboriginal lands in treaties or when Congress (as in the ICC Act) gratuitously permitted tribes to seek compensation for lost aboriginal lands. *Fort Berthold* fit neatly into this time-honored reluctance to grant Indians their due.

Whatever *Fort Berthold*'s shortcomings, the commission (as a lower court) had no choice but to apply it to the Black Hills claim. Doing so, it found (with little ado) that the United States had made "no effort to give the Sioux the full value of their land," and, therefore, that the United States had to pay just compensation for the Black Hills.

To determine just compensation, the commission—for the first time in fifty years of Black Hills litigation—fixed a dollar value for the Hills. As might have been expected in light of Lazarus's and Sonosky's cross-examinations, it explicitly rejected the government's surface and mineral appraisals. In the commission's view, Oberbillig's and Fenton's reports were so thoroughly ill-founded and inaccurate as to be practically worthless.

Instead the commission almost uniformly adopted the methodologies of the Sioux appraisers. To be sure, like a butcher cleaving away fat, it frequently rejected the valuation assumptions of the Sioux appraisers, such as the estimated average depth of ore deposits or the number of days a mine might be worked in a given year, thereby reducing the ultimate value of the land. Still, as Sonosky and Lazarus had hoped, at least the commission's valuation was conducted in the framework provided by their own experts and not according to whatever methodology the commission saw fit to use.

By the time the commission finished whittling away at the "over optimistic" valuation assumptions of the Sioux appraisers, it had reduced the value of the Black Hills from the Sioux estimate of over $26 million dollars to $17.1 million. Given the government's $4.7 million appraisal, the commission's record of much lower per acre valuation figures, and the magnitude of the potential judgment that might eventually result from the $17.1 million figure, Sonosky and Lazarus felt pleased and relieved. At least on the issue of value, they had done as well as they had hoped and better than they had expected. (The commission also held the government liable for gold removed by trespassing miners in the amount of $450,000 and for three rights-of-way across the reservation, which the commission did not yet value.)

The commission's opinion, though, was by no means all good news. Although its valuation figure, when compounded by 5 percent simple interest from the time of the taking (the legal formula for just compensation generally used by courts in Indian cases), opened the door to a Sioux recovery in the neighborhood of $100 million, its decision on allowable government offsets endangered virtually the entire potential award. The commission ruled that the government was entitled to credit against the Sioux award "the value of all property transferred to plaintiffs under the [1877] act, and . . . all expenditures on behalf of the Sioux made by the United States in fulfillment of the new obligations under the act." These allowable "payments on the claim," the commission further ruled, would be credited as of the time of payment.

To account for the fact that the government's expenditures under the act occurred over many years, the commission fashioned a complicated formula by which it permitted the government, on a year-by-year basis, to deduct most of its allowable offsets from the interest-bearing principal (the $17.1 million) rather than from the noninterest-bearing accumulating interest. As a result, if the government succeeded (in later proceedings) in proving significant legitimate expenditures under the 1877 act, the principal would be rapidly eaten away, resulting in far less accrued interest and a drastically reduced final judgment.

How small this final judgment would be depended on what expenditures the commission eventually found to be actual payments on the claim. As Lazarus reported to his clients, however, "a real possibility exists that the Commission's formula . . . will wipe out almost all the potential recovery." Specifically, Lazarus estimated that the commission formula would reduce the Sioux award for the Black Hills to between four and six million dollars. And from sources at the commission, he and Sonosky learned that the commissioners had made the same estimate themselves in designing their complicated and atypical offset formula. Apparently, four to six million dollars was all they intended the Black Hills claim to be worth.

Because of anticipated delays as the government prepared its offset claims, Sonosky and Lazarus also estimated that getting a final decision on the offsets issue would entail as much as another six years of litigation unless the Congress or the Executive Branch could be persuaded to intervene. Accordingly, they promptly began hatching plans for an appeal to Congress to change the provisions of the ICC Act defining allowable offsets and, in effect, reverse the offsets portion of the commission's decision. That was a long shot, but perhaps the only way still open to secure anything approaching a meaningful recovery.

Although Lazarus forwarded a copy of the commission's decision to the Oglala Sioux Tribal Council, he received no response. After so many years of waiting, with the prospect of several more years yet to come, the mixed blessing of the commission's opinion may not have made much of an impression on the battle-scarred Wilson administration.

The militants, however, took notice. At the time of the commission decision, Means, Banks, and some other AIMers were preparing to defend themselves against federal criminal charges stemming from the takeover at Wounded Knee. As a first line of defense, they planned to argue that the 1868 treaty did not recognize United States criminal jurisdiction over the Sioux nation, and that the federal government had no authority to prosecute citizens of that independent state.

Some months earlier, in June 1973, an AIM attorney had contacted Sonosky to ask his advice regarding this defense. Sonosky replied that he saw "no prospect that the jurisdiction of the United States will be denied upon the basis of a parallel between the Sioux nation and a foreign nation, or the basis of a parallel between treaties with the Sioux and treaties with foreign countries, or on a premise that the Sioux Indians are citizens of independent nations at war with the United States." (Although few Wounded Knee participants would be convicted of offenses arising from the occupation, Sonosky accurately predicted the fate of the defendants' jurisdictional argument.)

In any event, the commission's 1974 decision alerted the militants to an irreconcilable conflict between their strict adherence to the terms of the 1868 treaty and the Sioux nation's half-century old effort to attain compensation for the Black Hills. If the relationship between the United States and the Sioux nation was to be governed strictly by the 1868 treaty, then the Black Hills were still Sioux land. Seeking compensation for the taking of the Black Hills was not only logically absurd, it represented a capitulation to U.S. treaty breaking, a sellout to white and capitalist notions that land and money were interchangeable, or, more crassly, that the Sioux and their lands could be bought.

On March 18, 1974, Ramon Roubideaux issued a press release

reporting that the Black Hills Sioux Nation Council had rejected "the recent award of 17.1 million plus $450,000 for gold removed prior to 1875" as "totally inadequate to pay for this valuable land."

"The Sacred Black Hills rightfully belong to the Sioux," Roubideaux continued. They were "not for sale."

He "congratulated the council for insisting on return of the land rather than acceptance of a woefully inadequate compensation as determined by the Claims Commission." (Roubideaux declined to mention that, depending on its offsets determination, the commission might award the Sioux as much as $85 million dollars of interest in addition to the value of the land and gold in 1877. This omission by a savvy attorney could not have been accidental.) The Black Hills Sioux Nation Council, Roubideaux reported, was asking the commission and the Court of Claims to hold the Black Hills case in abeyance until it could secure passage of legislation returning "the entire Black Hills area to the Sioux Nation."

On March 22, Sonosky forwarded a copy of Roubideaux's statement to Lazarus with a note asking Lazarus if there were anything they should do. Lazarus's response was undoubtedly: Do nothing. The Black Hills Sioux Nation Council has no authority to speak.

The elected tribal councils still stood firmly behind the claim. Besides, it was difficult to take very seriously the BHSNC's change of heart. For years, mainly through Eddie Reddoor, it had clamored for a greater role in prosecuting the Sioux compensation claims. Since Sonosky and Lazarus took on the Sioux cases, the BHSNC had passed dozens of resolutions calling for speedier action by the commission and written numerous letters offering the lawyers advice about how to secure the largest possible claims award.

In light of the BHSNC's past history, Roubideaux's press release appeared to be nothing more than another gambit in the seventy-year-old struggle among various Sioux factions to control the tribal claims. The release itself suggested as much. Promoting the BHSNC as the Sioux organization "primarily authorized under law to conduct [claims] negotiations," the release professed "shock" that the tribal chairmen should "circumvent the Treaty organizations and the Sioux Indian people" in handling claims matters. "Such tyrannical and despotic moves were one of the causes of the Wounded Knee confrontation," Roubideaux warned, " . . . and the Indian people will not stand for dictatorships on the reservations any longer."

Sonosky and Lazarus continued with their work on behalf of the elected Sioux governments. What the Wounded Knee alliance of disgruntled traditionals and angry young radicals had to say about the claim was of little or no practical consequence.

But whether the lawyers either noticed or cared, after Wounded Knee, the terms of the internal Sioux debate changed with respect to the tribe's land claims. Where once rival factions fought to control the claim, now the militants rejected the claims process entirely. Theirs was the religion of absolute sovereignty, exalting the 1868 treaty as scripture. It was heresy to acknowledge that the United States or white citizens owned their treaty lands or to seek money in exchange for them—even as the best that could be done in an unjust world.

All the old men now long dead—Red Cloud and American Horse, Henry Standing Bear and Peter Dillon—all the Sioux who for three generations had carried the Black Hills claim in their hearts, hoping vainly someday to see their "Black Hills bag of beans," they had all sold out, according to the militants, or been duped by fee-seeking white attorneys. These Sioux had never imagined that they might reclaim the Hills themselves or that an independent Sioux nation might still exist. They had never imagined that the Ghost Dance—the messaianic vision of restored Indian supremacy born of despair and buried in tragedy at the first Wounded Knee—would return. But it had.

FOURTEEN

Skinning a Cat

In 1974 russell means challenged Dick Wilson for the presidency of Pine Ridge. Means won the primary, beating Wilson and former president Gerald One Feather, who finished a close third. In the runoff election, though, Wilson narrowly defeated Means. And while Means charged Wilson with vote-buying and intimidation, Wilson assumed the presidency for an unprecedented second two-year term.

Both before and after the election, Wilson's goon squad and AIM toughguys traded threats, beatings, and even shootings. Along the dark and narrow roads of rural Pine Ridge, cars were forced into gullies or chased into the night. Out on the prairies, political rivals strafed opponents' homes with bullets or tried to burn them out. During Wilson's second administration, Pine Ridge's undeclared civil war resulted in an estimated sixty "unexplained" deaths on the reservation.

The FBI and BIA police remained in force on Pine Ridge while as part of the Nixon administration's COINTELPRO penetration of "subversive" groups, FBI agents covertly infiltrated AIM and started hounding its leaders. On June 25, 1975, a BIA policeman killed a young Coeur d'Alene Indian named Joe Stuntz, who had been living at an AIM camp on the Jumping Bull property fifteen miles west of Pine Ridge village. The next morning, in a shootout at the Jumping Bull compound, two FBI agents were slain, shot point-blank after having been wounded. In the aftermath, the government stepped up its investigation, harassment, and prosecution of AIM members. (One, Leonard Peltier, in a controversial case, was eventually convicted of murdering the FBI agents. Two other AIM members were acquitted of the crime.)

Even without FBI assistance, AIM was starting to unravel. At Wounded Knee, AIM had played to its strengths: its ability to inspire a renewed ethnic commitment among Indians and to rivet national attention on the terrible conditions that Indians everywhere endured. But once the occupation ended, once the opportunities for dramatic speechmaking disappeared, AIM possessed no program for effecting change in reservation life.

Out of the spotlight, AIM's penchant for internal dissention and what Ramon Roubideaux called its "preference for publicity over policy" crippled the movement. Not long after Wounded Knee, in a quarrel unusual only for its level of violence, Carter Camp (an occupation leader) shot Clyde Bellecourt (one of AIM's founders) in the stomach. AIM also started to lose part of its Sioux following, even among those who remained loyal to the movement's overarching goal of reclaiming tribal heritages. "AIM overstayed their welcome," one disaffected AIM sympathizer recalls. "At some point they should have left. They had a lot of people who were not really sincere. They'd preach nonalcoholism, yet you'd see them drunk as hell."

Only after Al Trimble defeated Wilson in the 1976 presidential election did a modicum of peace return to Pine Ridge. A mixed blood and longtime BIA bureaucrat, Trimble won by convincing the traditional fullblood communities that he would serve their interests as well as those of the mixed bloods in Pine Ridge village. Once in office, Trimble broke up the goon squad and worked hard to fulfill the promise of his campaign.

In Washington, meanwhile, the claims process churned along, in low gear as usual. At every step, the Justice Department tried to limit the financial cost of its congressionally imposed accounting with history. Meanwhile, tribal lawyers labored to exact as much as they could on behalf of clients—great-grandchildren of the original victims—for whom no amount of compensation could truly remedy the past.

In the Black Hills claim, the lawyers for both sides met with the commission more than once to discuss how the government should attempt to prove its claimed offsets—that is, how it could distinguish between government expenditures actually made in fulfillment of the 1877 act (legitimate offsets) and those made gratuitously or in fulfillment of other obligations. A government accountant estimated that the General Accounting Office would need three to five years to complete a new Sioux audit.

After eighteen years of work on a claim now more than a half-century old, Sonosky and Lazarus could not imagine idling for five years while the government scoured its books for ways to reduce the Sioux judgment. Nor did they intend to leave unchallenged the commission's claim-defeating offset formula. Figuring that there are more ways than one of skinning a cat, Sonosky and Lazarus had decided that the best way to stop the commission from perpetuating an unfavorable decision was to change the underlying law.

What Sonosky and Lazarus had in mind was an amendment to the ICC Act of 1946 that would exclude "food, rations, or provisions" from the category of allowable legal offsets against claim awards. Though couched in general terms, the amendment's principal effect would be to eliminate almost all the government's offsets in the Black Hills claim and secure (subject to appeal) a $100 million judgment for the Sioux.

In Sonosky and Lazarus's view, this strategy was equitable as well as expedient. When Congress imposed the 1877 act on the Sioux, the tribe neither negotiated for nor accepted the government's food and rations as payment for its land. On the contrary, the food and rations were made necessary by the government's unilateral seizure of the tribe's hunting grounds and its long-term assault on the Indians' buffalo-hunting way of life. As Lazarus argued in the written statement he circulated as part of his congressional lobbying campaign:

> The facts are, as the Commission has found, that the United States disarmed the Sioux and denied them their traditional hunting areas in an effort to force the sale of the Black Hills. Having violated the 1868 Treaty and having reduced the Indians to starvation, the United States should not now be in the position of saying that the rations it furnished constituted payment for the land which it took. In short, the government committed two wrongs: first, it deprived the Sioux of their livelihood; secondly, it deprived the Sioux of their land. What the United States gave back in rations should not be stretched to cover both wrongs.

To sponsor the food, rations, and provisions amendment, Sonosky and Lazarus selected South Dakota Senator James Abourezk, who represented most of the 60,000 Sioux who would benefit from the amendment. Abourezk had been born and raised in Wood, South Dakota, a town of no more than 100 located on the Rosebud Reservation. His father ran Wood's general store. An Indian-baiting racist youth by his own admission, Abourezk "never understood the damage [his] own racism was doing" until he left the reservation to attend college. In the Senate, Abourezk had proven a faithful ally of Indians generally and the Sioux in particular. Significantly, he served on the Senate Committee on Interior and Insular Affairs, which oversaw Indian-related legislation.

Lazarus met with the senator in April 1974 and Abourezk readily agreed to champion the amendment. He asked Lazarus to prepare specific statutory language for attachment as a "rider" to the annual authorization bill for the commission. The authorization bill (S. 3007) was already pending before the Subcommittee on Indian Affairs, which Abourezk chaired. Under his stewardship, the Sioux amendment sailed through the Senate. The Republican staffperson on the Interior Committee was so impressed with the merits of the Sioux claim that he circulated his own endorsement of the amendment to every GOP member. All the Democrats followed Abourezk's lead, and the committee voted unanimously to attach the food, rations, and provisions amendment to S. 3007. Moreover, through the good offices of Forrest Gerard, a Native American member of Abourezk's staff, the committee adopted word-for-word as its official report Lazarus's memorandum summarizing the history behind the Black Hills claim and presenting the moral case for excluding food, rations, and provisions as offsets. On May 28, the Senate passed the amended version of S. 3007 by unanimous consent.

Meanwhile, Lazarus was marshaling support for the Sioux amendment at the White House and the Indian Bureau. Early in June, he met with LaFollette Butler, the deputy BIA commissioner, who responded sympathetically, especially after Lazarus convinced him that of the cases still pending before the commission, only the Black Hills claim involved a meaningful amount of food, rations, or provisions that the government might claim as offsets. Statutes (such as the 1877 act) that purported to substitute rations for land were as rare as they were unjust.

Lazarus also enlisted the help of Brad Patterson, Nixon's Indian affairs troubleshooter. They had worked together often and Lazarus, knowing that Patterson would respond favorably to the Sioux amendment, asked him to quell any opposition that might arise in the powerful Office of Management and Budget. Presumably, someone in OMB—the bureaucratic lion guarding the federal purse—would object to S. 3007's probable cost of over $85 million. Patterson agreed to do what he could to "keep OMB quiet."

Meanwhile, on Capitol Hill, Lazarus shifted his amendment campaign to the House of Representatives. There, even before the

Senate passed S. 3007, the House Interior and Insular Affairs Committee already had completed its hearings on a companion bill (H.R. 12356) identical to S. 3007 except that it did *not* include the food, rations, and provisions amendment. More discouraging still, neither the Democratic chairman of the House Subcommittee on Indian Affairs, Lloyd Meeds (from Washington) nor Ralph Regula, the subcommittee's ranking Republican (from Ohio), favored the Sioux amendment. Although Meeds saw merit in the idea of excluding food, rations, and provisions as allowable offsets, he balked at changing the commission's rules of decision in the middle of a case.

In mid-June, with the encouragement of Meeds and Regula, the full House passed H.R. 12356 without the Sioux amendment.

Lazarus immediately encouraged his Senate allies to call for a Conference Committee, a meeting of key committee members from both chambers to resolve the conflict between the House and Senate. But he was skeptical of the outcome. In a memo to Dick Schifter, Lazarus predicted that "if [a conference] is called . . . the Senate conferees will stand by their initial position at the beginning, but will give way if the House puts up a strong fight for its version. What we must do, therefore, is work on the House members for them to recede."

Before the end of June, the Senate did call for a conference and named Abourezk as one of the conferees. The House delegation was led by Meeds, whom Lazarus continued to try to turn around. In this endeavor he could count on influential help from Meeds's chief staff assistant for Indian affairs, Franklin Ducheneaux, son of the Frank Ducheneaux who had run the Cheyenne River Reservation for the better part of two decades. Naturally, Ducheneaux strongly supported the Sioux amendment.

Lazarus spared no effort. At his instigation, South Dakota Congressman James Abdnor contacted each of the House conferees, educating them about the merits of the Sioux amendment and asking them not to insist on the House version of the commission authorization bill. Lazarus also enlisted the assistance of Ben Reifel, the only Sioux ever to serve in Congress (and who, as a young man, had helped John Collier sell the IRA to the Sioux). Formerly a Republican member of the House Interior and Insular Affairs Committee, Reifel vigorously lobbied his one-time House colleagues in favor of the Sioux amendment.

As a final precaution, Lazarus prepared compromise amendments that Abourezk might bring forward if the conference proceeded badly. For example, Lazarus drafted alternative language that would give the commission the *discretion* (rather than a binding obligation) to disallow food, rations, and provisions as offsets.

Abourezk did not need to compromise. The Senate conferees stood firmly behind the Sioux amendment and, in the end, worked out a satisfactory settlement with Meeds and the House delegation. The House conferees agreed to introduce a bill in the House containing the Sioux amendment, to hold hearings on that bill (before Meeds's subcommittee), and to report to the House Committee on Interior and Insular Affairs. In the interim, the conference would stand in recess.

As promised, Meeds, Regula, Abdnor, Lujan (of New Mexico), and Thone (of Nebraska) introduced a bill (H.R. 16170) identical to S. 3007 *with* the Sioux amendment. In the meantime, Lazarus, aided by Sonosky, continued to work on behind-the-scenes strategy with Ducheneaux and his GOP staff counterpart, Mike Jackson. Lazarus also consulted with the chief counsel for the commission, who, in response to Meeds's inquiry, was preparing a memorandum showing that the Sioux amendment would not be a significant factor in pending cases other than the Black Hills claim. Lazarus prepared a similar memorandum of his own, which he used in a persistent effort to convince representatives of the Interior Department to endorse the Sioux amendment.

The subcommittee hearing on the Sioux bill commenced on August 8, 1974. From Sonosky and Lazarus's perspective, the hearing could hardly have proceeded more favorably. Meeds's opening remarks suggested that he had grown more receptive to the Sioux amendment. His statement consisted mainly of a highly sympathetic historical account of the government's seizure of the Black Hills, including Custer's illegal invasion in 1874, President Grant's precipitous decision to provoke a war with the Sioux, and the Manypenny commission's sell or starve proposition to the disarmed and dismounted Indians. Meeds borrowed the material for his remarks from the summary of Sioux history that Lazarus had prepared to inform individual Congressmen about the merits of his clients' grievance.

As Lazarus had hoped (but not expected), the first witness, Assistant Secretary of the Interior John Kyl, endorsed the Sioux amendment, albeit a bit tepidly. In a line of argument that Meeds received warmly, Kyl echoed Lazarus's central point that the government, having deprived the Sioux of both their livelihood and their land, committed two wrongs, and that the rations should not be stretched to cover both. In Kyl's words, "for the United States both to have disrupted Indians' means of obtaining food and now to charge them for having given them the food necessary for their very survival does not comport with the role of the Indian Claims Commission as a court of conscience. . . ."

The Justice Department, whose spokesman, Donald Mileur, testified second, predictably did not find the argument nearly so compelling. While the Interior Department spoke from its perspective as the arm of government charged with administering the nation's guardianship over Indian tribes, the Justice Department evaluated the merits of the Sioux amendment as the arm of government charged with defending the United States against tribal claims. In that capacity, and in keeping with the department's fifty-year tradition of opposing any proposal that would increase claim awards, Mileur questioned the long-run wisdom of the amendment.

Although he did not dispute the inherent fairness of excluding food, rations, and provisions as offsets, and although he did not oppose the Sioux amendment outright, Mileur worried that this amendment to the original ICC Act would open the floodgates to a host of special bills designed to expedite and augment one tribal claim or another. Mileur's was what lawyers commonly call the "slippery slope" argument. If Congress started down the slope of excluding certain government expenditures as offsets, it would inevitably slip into excluding more and more expenditures, and not just in future cases (as provided in the Sioux amendment) but in past cases as well.

Meeds thought Congress more surefooted than that. "Do you seriously think," he asked Mileur, "that the members of Congress are so naïve that they are going to take the same step that you have taken [in your testimony]?"

Lazarus followed Mileur to the witness table. Having submitted for the record a detailed account of the history behind the Black Hills claim, Lazarus used his live testimony to emphasize the uniqueness of the claim itself. In no other claim, he explained, did the government assert a substantial amount of food, rations, and provisions as offsets. In no other claim had the government created decades of delay (with more threatened) and so thoroughly denied the possibility of justice.

The theme of Lazarus's presentation, both written and oral, was simple: The Sioux were not asking for preferential treatment. They were asking no more than that Congress shortcircuit the lengthy and inherently unjust audit and trial process necessary to resolve the offsets issue and provide instead a fair and expeditious resolution of a century-old injustice. "[I]f Congress takes no action," Lazarus concluded his formal statement, "the Sioux clearly will be forced to wait another generation before the litigation comes to an end. . . . [I]f Congress takes no action . . . the Black Hills claim will turn to ashes—an award so small and so meaningless as to leave in Sioux mouths a taste even more bitter than the original taking."

Meeds adjourned the hearing after receiving a neutral report from the commission itself. As he gavelled his subcommittee into recess, the man who once had believed that the Sioux amendment improperly adjusted the claims process in midcourse walked from the hearing room a firm convert to the Sioux cause. "The more I heard about it," Meeds recalled years later, "the more I became convinced that a grave injustice had been done." Meeds became the Sioux amendment's stauchest supporter, and under his leadership, the subcommittee favorably reported H.R. 16170, including the exclusion of food, rations, and provisions as allowable offsets, to the full House Committee on Interior and Insular Affairs.

The fight over the Sioux amendment, however, was far from over. When the full committee took up the bill on September 25, Congressman Regula (the ranking minority member of the subcommittee) offered an unfavorable amendment. Instead of disallowing food, rations, and provisions as offsets, Regula proposed to give the commission discretion to allow or disallow such offsets as it deemed appropriate. If passed, the amendment (similar to the compromise that Lazarus had suggested to Abourezk as a last resort) would force the Sioux to litigate the offsets issue before the commission and necessitate precisely the time-consuming government audit that the Sioux amendment was, in part, meant to avoid. In any case, if the theory of the Sioux amendment was correct— that food was not a proper way to pay for land whose taking had created near-famine—then giving the commission discretion to allow it as an offset made no sense. The main accomplishment of the reasonable-sounding Regula amendment would be again to place the Black Hills claim at the commission's mercy.

It took some sharp nose-counting and fast thinking for Meeds and the other supporters of the Sioux amendment to defeat Regula's last-minute surprise. The committee's first vote on Regula's "let-the-commission-decide" provision resulted in a 15–15 tie. Apparently, the Regula amendment would have succeeded on a second ballot, but Congressman John Melcher (Democrat from Montana), a Sioux supporter, cleverly absented himself from the committee room, thereby depriving the committee of a "live quorum"—enough members present to conduct business. Stymied, the committee put off a final decision until the next week.

In the interim, Lazarus orchestrated a crash campaign. Schifter wrote committee members with whom he was friendly. Congressman Abdnor and former Congressman Ben Reifel paid joint visits to most of their colleagues; they were especially effective in turning around committee Republicans who would be inclined to follow Regula. Sympathetic congressional staffers lobbied their bosses.

The campaign worked beyond the attorneys' most optimistic expectations. Before the next session, Regula withdrew his amendment. The committee approved H.R. 16170 with the Sioux amendment 31–3. The House-Senate conference reconvened and accepted the Sioux amendment as part of S. 3007. On October 15, the House approved the conference's action. The following day, the Senate did the same, and forwarded the Sioux amendment to the President for signature.

At the White House, Brad Patterson had done his part. Despite the likelihood that the Sioux amendment would cost the United States $85 million, OMB did not recommend a veto. On October 27, President Ford signed the Sioux bill, praising it as a "just and fair" measure to "heal . . . wounds from the past." The Sioux amendment was law.

Lazarus had engineered an unprecedented legislative triumph. Prior to the Sioux amendment, Congress had not once substantively altered the original ICC Act. Now, not only had Congress amended the act, it had done so on behalf of a single tribe at potentially enormous cost. For the Sioux, and for the lawyers now eighteen years at the chase, final victory had never seemed so close.

The fate of the Black Hills case now rested with the Court of Claims. While Lazarus was pushing the Sioux amendment through Congress, the government had appealed two critical aspects of the commission's 1974 ruling: first, that *res judicata* did not preclude consideration of the tribe's Fifth Amendment takings claim; and, second, that the 1877 act effected a Fifth Amendment taking—for which just compensation must be paid. If the government prevailed on either point, the Sioux would lose at the least their right to interest on the value of the Black Hills in 1877, and the award in the Black Hills claim could shrink from roughly $103 million dollars to $17.5 million—the bare value of the Hills when they were taken—or nothing at all.

On August 27, 1974, Craig Decker filed with the Court of Claims a sixty-page brief attacking the commission's decision. Its indignant tone perhaps stemmed from embarrassment over the commission's ruling that the government had waived the defense of *res judicata* by conceding (in its 1966 answer to the amended Sioux petition) that the 1942 Court of Claims decision had dismissed the Sioux claim for lack of jurisdiction. Losing because of a concession smacked of carelessness.

Decker's brief echoed his oral argument before the commission. He again asserted that in 1942 the Sioux had presented two separate claims to the court, a moral claim to compensation and a "legal" claim based on an alleged violation of the Fifth Amendment. The government's 1966 concession, Decker claimed, referred only to the 1942 court's dismissal (for lack of jurisdiction) of the tribe's moral claims, not to its Fifth Amendment claim—which, according to Decker, the court rejected on its merits.

In any event, Decker continued, the commission had wrenched the government's supposed concession completely out of context. Read as a whole, Decker alleged, the government's 1966 answer to the amended Sioux petition clearly indicated that the government did not intend to waive its *res judicata* defense. Other government's pleadings both before and after 1966 confirmed the point. These pleadings, Decker argued, "clearly show that . . . the Government had no intention of waiving or admitting itself out of court with respect to its *res judicata* defense. . . ." The government had raised the *res judicata* defense in its 1951 answer to Ralph Case's original petition in the Black Hills claim and again in 1969 when responding to Sonosky and Lazarus's arguments about what consideration or payment the government offered for the Hills under the 1877 act. By focusing exclusively on one paragraph of the government's 1966 answer to the amended petition (rather than on the entire course of litigation), the commission had found a waiver where none fairly could be inferred.

Reading between the lines of Decker's brief, it is clear that he thought, with reason, that Sonosky and Lazarus had lulled the government into its 1966 concession by obscuring for as long as possible their intent to pursue a Fifth Amendment claim. That concession had occurred at a time when the Sioux were prosecuting the Black Hills claim under a theory that the tribe received unconscionable consideration for the Hills. The government could raise no *res judicata* defense to this claim because the 1942 Court of Claims opinion had nothing to say about unconscionable consideration. This basis of recovery did not exist prior to the 1946 ICC Act.

As soon as Sonosky and Lazarus hinted at a possible Fifth Amendment claim in 1969, the government reiterated its *res judicata* defense. Thus, while the technical rules of pleading might support the commission's waiver ruling, the underlying purpose of those pleading rules—to provide adequate notice to the opposing party of all intended claims and defenses—did not demand such a strict application. Sonosky and Lazarus always knew that the government might counter their Fifth Amendment claim with the defense of *res judicata*. And, notably, they had not pressed a waiver theory on the commission. That was its own invention.

All this no doubt contributed to Decker's main charge against the commission, its "lack of evenhandedness." On the one hand, the commission interpreted an isolated government concession as constituting a binding waiver of "a primary defense"; on the other hand, it "totally ignored" Ralph Case's "unequivocal admission" of $57 million in legitimate government offsets. "The two rulings . . . are most arbitrary and capricious."

Of course, even if Decker convinced the Court of Claims that the government had not waived *res judicata,* he still would have to show that Judge Littleton's 1942 opinion decided the merits of the Sioux Fifth Amendment claim—thereby barring its relitigation. To this end, Decker repeated for the Court of Claims the government's argument, amplified in Commissioner Kuykendall's dissent, that the plain language of the 1920 jurisdictional act vested the Court of Claims with jurisdiction to decide the Sioux Fifth Amendment claim and that the 1942 court had carried out this mandate.

As for the government's second issue on appeal—whether the 1877 act's appropriation of the Black Hills constituted a Fifth Amendment taking (assuming that *res judicata* did not bar this claim)—Decker asserted that no constitutional violation had occurred. Applying the *Fort Berthold* good faith effort test to determine whether the 1877 act constituted a Fifth Amendment taking as opposed to an exercise of the government's "plenary power" to control tribal assets, Decker argued that "there was a good faith effort to give the Indians fair compensation for the land transferred." Accordingly, the 1877 act did not constitute a taking under the Fifth Amendment for which just compensation must be paid. Thus, while Decker admitted that the United States might be liable for the 1877 value of the Black Hills ($17.5 million), under no circumstances were the Sioux entitled to interest on that amount, because no constitutional violation had occurred.

According to Decker, under the *Lonewolf* plenary powers doctrine, the commission was obligated to presume "that Congress acts in good faith" and to accord Congress "substantial discretion" in its handling of Indian assets. The commission, he complained, had failed in these obligations and "without any basis of merit, arbitrarily conclude[d] that Congress wrongfully confiscated the Sioux land despite the fact that over $57 million has been paid to the Sioux . . . for the lands now valued at $17.1 million."

Sonosky and Lazarus's response started where the government left off, with the issue of whether the 1877 act effected a Fifth Amendment taking of the Black Hills. They harbored no doubts themselves that even under the *Fort Berthold* test, if fairly applied, the government had taken the Hills in violation of the Fifth Amendment's obligation to pay just compensation for taken lands. Still, given the complete subjectivity of the *Fort Berthold* standard ("good faith" is whatever a court says it is), with $85 million at stake, Sonosky and Lazarus worried that the court would find congressional good faith in spite of the historical evidence to the contrary.

With this concern in mind, Sonosky and Lazarus inundated the court with details of the government's effort to dispossess their clients of the lands they cherished most. This historical approach reflected Lazarus's conviction that cases are "won on their facts." As he frequently instructed the young associates he trained at Fried, Frank, when properly presented, the facts of a case should drive the court towards ruling for your client as if any other result would be wholly unfair or unrealistic.

In the Sioux case, Sonosky and Lazarus benefited from a long history of dishonorable government conduct towards their client, and they worked those sordid facts hard. For sixteen pages, they recounted one broken government promise after another: Custer's unlawful 1874 goldseeking incursion into the Hills, the Allison commission's unsuccessful attempt to buy or lease the Hills, Grant's decision to allow miners into the Hills regardless of his responsibility under the 1868 treaty to keep them out, his decision to provoke a war by ordering all Sioux bands to return from their hunting grounds to the permanent reservation in the dead of winter, and, finally, the Manypenny commission's failure to secure the consent of 75 percent of the adult Sioux males for a cession of the Black Hills. Sonosky and Lazarus believed that the appeal would hinge on the application by the Court of Claims of the *Fort Berthold* good faith effort test. And they hoped that their recitation of the facts would, as Lazarus put it, "pay off" in that application.

In the legal section of their brief, Sonosky and Lazarus defended and embellished the commission's 1974 ruling. On the Fifth Amendment issue, the lawyers argued that the 1877 act was a "classic example" of a Fifth Amendment taking, precisely the kind of transfer of ownership that the Supreme Court had recognized as a taking in *Shoshone, Creek Nation,* and *Klamath and Moadoc.* In *Shoshone,* Sonosky and Lazarus reminded the Court of Claims, Justice Cardozo had observed that plenary power "does not extend so far as to enable the Government to give the tribal lands to others, or to appropriate them to its own purposes, without rendering, or assuming an obligation to render, just compensation."

As the commission rightly held, the lawyers argued, according to the principles of *Shoshone,* the 1877 act clearly constituted not an act of guardianship but an exercise of the eminent domain power for which just compensation must be paid. Congress did not make a good faith effort to pay the Sioux the full value for the Black Hills; rather, as the commission recognized, "there is no indication in the record that Congress attempted to relate [its obligations under the Act] to the value of plaintiff's land." The government's claim to the contrary, Sonosky and Lazarus concluded, "is simply an assertion without regard to the controlling facts."

As for the issue of *res judicata,* Sonosky and Lazarus virtually scoffed at the government's arguments. They ridiculed Decker's contention that the government's 1966 concession (interpreting the 1942 Court of Claims decision as jurisdictional) referred only to the Sioux tribe's moral claim (not its Fifth Amendment claim). "What the Government overlooks is a basic rule of pleading: since its answer did not deny the allegation of the amended petition that . . . [the] 1942 dismissal was for lack of jurisdiction, that allegation stands admitted."

Nor, Sonosky and Lazarus alleged, could the government remedy its omission by reference to its original 1951 answer. "The government forgets," Sonosky and Lazarus chided (while citing numerous cases), "that the original petition and the answer to the original petition are dead." In general, they observed, "the government permitted the entire case to proceed, through a myriad of motions, briefings, arguments, decisions and orders, to an expensive trial on value . . . and finally to judgment . . . without once raising the defense. . . . " For this neglect, as the commission properly held, there could be no valid excuse. "To permit the Government to assert the defense for the first time on appeal . . . would be in wholesale conflict with the established law governing affirmative defenses."

In case the Court of Claims somehow reversed the commission's decision that the government had waived the *res judicata* defense, Sonosky and Lazarus also presented their own interpretation of

Judge Littleton's 1942 decision. Much as they had in oral argument before the commission, they culled Littleton's opinion for its frequent passages discussing the scope of the 1920 jurisdictional act. These cumulatively suggested that "in 1942 the Court dismissed the [Black Hills] claim because it was not a 'legal' claim within the meaning of the jurisdictional act, and thus lay outside the power vested in the court." Such a jurisdictional ruling, of course, did not render the tribe's current Fifth Amendment claim *res judicata*.

Sonosky and Lazarus insisted that no other interpretation was possible. "From beginning to end," they wrote, "the opinion turned on jurisdictional considerations." Actually, though, it was very difficult to tell what Judge Littleton's opaque opinion turned on; and Sonosky and Lazarus's zealous efforts to see clear paths in Littleton's judicial fog occasionally tested credulity. "Judge Littleton wrote with clarity," they declared without a hint of sarcasm. "If the intent were to take jurisdiction and dispose of the case on the merits, surely plain words signifying that would have found their way into the opinion." The government might have argued with equal validity that such a "clear" author would not have written a seventy-six-page opinion which ventured all sorts of remarks about the strengths and weaknesses of the Sioux claim merely in order to rule that the court was without authority to decide the case.

Sonosky and Lazarus's best argument, stressed several times, was simply that at this stage of the proceedings, given the highly technical nature of the *res judicata* defense and the drastic remedy that would follow its successful invocation (dismissal of the Fifth Amendment claim), any doubt about Judge Littleton's opinion should be resolved against the defense and in favor of hearing the Black Hills claim on its merits. After fifty-two years of litigation, no other rule of thumb made sense.

In his reply brief, Decker made no effort to cloak his outrage at what he must have considered the peremptory and professorial tone of Sonosky and Lazarus's submission. It was evidently his view—no doubt shared by his colleagues at the Justice Department—that Sonosky and Lazarus had been getting away with murder in the Sioux claims for nearly twenty years. First, the Court of Claims had vacated its own decision and remanded the claim to the commission; then, the commission had reopened the record and allowed the Sioux to sneak in new claims while liberally amending Ralph Case's original petitions. Next, the commission had overvalued the Black Hills and denied the government its *res judicata* defense against the Fifth Amendment claim that Sonosky and Lazarus raised at the eleventh hour. And as if that was not enough, these pesky lawyers had convinced Congress to wipe out food and rations as offsets. Now, they had written a brief pretending that Sitting Bull, Crazy Horse, and the other hostiles were a band of angels, meanwhile lecturing the Justice Department about the proper way to plead a defense only made necessary by Sonosky and Lazarus's own devious effort to hide their Fifth Amendment claim until the last possible moment.

The Justice Department countered with its own view of Black Hills history. "We believe that [Sonosky and Lazarus's] account is calculated to generate sympathy for the Sioux rather than to present an objective portrayal of the events. . . . " Actually, "the United States conducted itself with moral concern and a continuing desire to help effectuate the eventual welfare of the Sioux Indians. The hostile Sioux, on the other hand, were lawless, demanding and indifferent to the welfare of the other Indians and non-Indians of the region." According to the Justice Department, the United States attempted diligently to keep the miners out of the Hills, but the task proved impossible. And the United States made repeated good faith efforts to buy the Hills, including the Manypenny commission of 1876. The Sioux were "judiciously treated throughout. . . . no apology is due, no sense of guilt appropriate, with respect to the way the United States conducted itself. . . . "

Decker also returned to the central theme of his previous brief: excoriating the commission for its bias in favor of the Sioux. The commission's ruling "represents an intolerable lack of even-handedness and abuse of procedural due process," he charged. "The Commission first permitted plaintiffs to add on claims based on an earlier 1868 Treaty. . . . [then] the Commission permitted the Sioux . . . to enlarge by several million acres the previously determined land award. . . . [and] after plaintiffs . . . waived any compensable claim under Article 11 of the 1868 Treaty . . . [they] were permitted to reinstate the claim. . . . Moreover, the Sioux were permitted to add a claim for the gold the trespassing miners took out of the land." In sum, its own claims tribunal had given the United States a raw deal.

While they waited for the Court of Claims to schedule oral argument, Sonosky and Lazarus tried to shore up a potential weak point in their historical account of the Black Hills taking. Sonosky and Lazarus had always contended, on the basis of only secondary sources, that in November 1875 President Grant had "directed the Army to withdraw from the Black Hills, thus leaving that country open to invasion by non-Indians." By this decision, the United States reneged on its obligation to keep miners out of the Hills and left itself no alternative but to obtain the Hills from the Sioux virtually immediately, by whatever means necessary. For the purposes of the Black Hills claim, Grant's alleged decision to withdraw federal troops from the Hills formed an integral part of Sonosky and Lazarus's efforts to characterize the 1877 act not as a good faith effort by the government to pay the Sioux full value for the Hills, but rather as the culmination of a dishonorable policy of "precipitating" a war with the Sioux as a pretext for taking their goldbearing treaty lands.

To further document their account, Sonosky and Lazarus hired a research specialist, Fred Nicklason. After less than a day in the Library of Congress, he not only found primary evidence to support their thesis, he found a proverbial "smoking gun" to prove their case—three letters from top military officers confirming a November 3, 1875 meeting at which Grant decided to issue secret orders for the army to cease its efforts to keep miners out of the Black Hills. As General Sheridan, commander, Division of the Missouri, wrote to General Terry, commander, Division of Dakota, "the President decided that while the orders heretofore issued forbidding the occupation of the Black Hills country, by miners, should not be rescinded, still no further resistance by the military should be made to the miners going in."

Sheridan forwarded a copy to his superior General Sherman, Commanding General of the Army. In reply, the United States' highest-ranking field officer approved of and amplified Grant's new policy. "My own idea of the [1868] Treaty is that settlements may now be made all along the Western Boundary. And if some go over the Boundary into the Black Hills, I understand that the President and Interior Department will wink at it for the present."

Sonosky and Lazarus prepared this evidentiary surprise for introduction at oral argument, set for April 1, 1975.

When oral argument commenced, however, it was Sonosky and Lazarus who were caught off-guard. Although no transcript of the proceedings survives, Lazarus remembers how the Court of Claims, sitting *en banc* (all seven members in attendance instead of the usual panel of three), ambushed Sonosky when he tried to defend the commission's ruling that the government waived its *res judicata* defense. "Marvin just kept pressing the point," but the Court was having none of it. As Sonosky's time for arguing the *res judicata* issue dwindled, Lazarus passed him a note pleading with him to move on from the waiver question to their interpretation of Judge Littleton's 1942 decision. But that interpretation was complicated. Explaining it to the commission would consume the better part of an hour and Sonosky had no more than a few minutes left before Lazarus was scheduled to argue the other issues in the claim. It was too late.

After argument, Sonosky and Lazarus prepared a supplemental memorandum containing the analysis of Judge Littleton's 1942 opinion that Sonosky had failed to present in court. Generally, the memo simply amplified their previously stated interpretation, but it also gave them a chance to set forth ten passages in which Judge Littleton seemed to focus his inquiry on the scope of the jurisdictional act. That Sonosky and Lazarus felt compelled to file the memo at all, having had ample opportunity to brief the point prior to oral argument, reflected their fear that the Court of Claims had come to oral argument favorably disposed towards the government's *res judicata* argument, and that they had failed in their oral presentation to change the court's collective mind. Sonosky and Lazarus thought they were in trouble, regardless of their new historical evidence.

On June 25, 1975, the ninety-ninth anniversary of Custer's defeat at the Little Big Horn, the Court of Claims confirmed Sonosky and Lazarus's worst apprehensions. With only one of seven judges dissenting, the court ruled that its own decision in 1942 had dismissed the original Sioux Fifth Amendment claim on its merits and that the Fifth Amendment issue, being *res judicata*, could not now be relitigated.

The commission, the Court ruled, had improperly "strained to find an abandonment" of the *res judicata* defense. The commission "should have accepted the Government's explanation of its pleadings, as we do." As for Judge Littleton's 1942 opinion, the court observed that it would be "a rare thing for a court to write findings and an opinion totalling 76 pages in length, all just to say it has no jurisdiction." And Judge Littleton had not done so. Instead, he had reached the merits of the Sioux Fifth Amendment claim and held that, under *Lonewolf,* the tribe's claim failed.

The court emphasized that it did not necessarily agree with its own 1942 decision. As an historical matter, the court observed that "a more ripe and rank case of dishonorable dealings [than the government's conduct in obtaining the Black Hills] will never, in all probability, be found in our history. . . . " But that historical evaluation could not change the technical requirements of the law. Whether "rightly or wrongly," the 1942 court had decided the Fifth Amendment issue once and for all.

As a consequence, the Sioux could seek compensation for the loss of the Black Hills only on "the ground of dishonorable dealings." That ground would support an award of $17.5 million—the 1877 value of the Hills plus the value of the gold removed illegally by trespassing miners—but not the $85 million of interest to which the Sioux would have been entitled had the court affirmed the commission's 1974 ruling. "The Congress which wiped out the rations offset could correct this situation also," the court advised the Sioux, "but we are without the power to do so."

The ghost of Ralph Case, held at bay eighteen years, haunted every word of the calamitous Court of Claims ruling. Sonosky and Lazarus had erased his defeats before the commission in 1954 and the Court of Claims in 1956; they had found a way around his $57 million offsets concession; yet they could not escape his original mismanaged effort under the old jurisdictional act. Blaming Case, though, however appropriate, was cold comfort. Whatever the cause, the Sioux and their lawyers had suffered a terribly expensive defeat.

Sonosky and Lazarus informed the Sioux tribal councils that they would appeal to the Supreme Court. But they knew better than to expect that the court was likely to grant review, even of such a famous claim. Each year the Supreme Court is asked to hear thousands of appeals. Of these cases, the justices agree to hear and decide only about 150. In making this narrow selection, they care little whether the lower court has decided a case correctly. As a general rule, the Supreme Court reviews only cases that present legal issues of paramount importance, issues that transcend the individual case under review, and apply to whole categories of cases pending in lower courts. An erroneous decision, no matter how glaring, does not qualify a case for Supreme Court consideration.

Search as they did, Sonosky and Lazarus could find no question of broad import buried in the Black Hills claim. The best they could argue was that the *res judicata* decision was "wrong," that "allowing the decision to stand will perpetuate a grave miscarriage of justice." Judge Oscar Davis, the lone dissenter from the Court of Claims and an old friend, offered Lazarus a bit of encouragement. "One should never forecast what the Sup. Ct. will do with respect to a cert. application, but you have certainly put your best foot forward." But Lazarus was too much the realist to be cheered.

On December 4, the Supreme Court denied Sonosky and Lazarus's petition for *certiorari*. The maximum recovery in the Black Hills claim, therefore, apparently would be limited to $17.5 million the Court of Claims had authorized on the ground of dishonorable dealings, less allowable offsets.

Gone were the dreams of riches, both for lawyer and client. Gone was the hope of any true measure of justice, however belated. In their place stood a highly technical ruling based on a questionable reading of an impenetrable opinion thirty-three years old. For a century the Sioux had pleaded for a fair day in court. Now the Court of Claims had ruled that this day had come and gone, unnoticed, in the past.

Lazarus still harbored one last faint hope for a fair hearing. It was the alternative suggested by the Court of Claims itself. Congress alone possessed the authority to waive the defense of *res judicata* on the government's behalf and thereby reopen consideration of the tribe's Fifth Amendment claim. Lazarus could not think of a single instance where Congress had exercised this alleged power to waive *res judicata* in a pending case, but he intended to prepare a bill to that effect nonetheless. This legal magician was looking deep into his bag of tricks, and it looked distressingly empty. Still, he would see what could be done.

FIFTEEN

▼ ▼ ▼ ▼ ▼

DEAD, BUT NOT DEAD, DEAD

On December 8, 1975, four days after the Supreme Court declined to review the Black Hills claim, Senator Abourezk introduced a second Sioux amendment to the original 1946 ICC Act. Drafted by Sonosky and Lazarus, the amendment instructed the Court of Claims to consider the Black Hills claim on its merits, without regard to the defense of *res judicata*. Put simply, the amendment would grant the Sioux another chance—another chance to prove their Fifth Amendment taking claim, another chance to obtain interest on their potential $17.5 million Black Hills award, another chance to attain a reasonable reckoning with their conquerors and make at least a partial peace with their past.

Once again Lazarus found himself walking the halls of Capitol Hill, reiterating to congressmen and their staffs the story of how many times the United States had broken its word to his Sioux clients, and with what unfathomably tragic results. What Lazarus asked of Congress was extraordinary: to waive a scrupulously honored legal defense, *res judicata*, so that a single tribe might reassert a legal claim already fifty-three years in litigation, and at a potential cost to the United States of more than $85 million.

In support of this virtually unprecedented request, Lazarus told Congress that his clients would never believe or accept that the Court of Claims had decided their Black Hills Fifth Amendment claim in 1942, or that on the basis of a "legal technicality" the government would pay them what seemed only a paltry sum for the treasure chest it had stolen. Unless Congress provided for another hearing in the Black Hills claim, Sioux resentments—the feelings of anger and betrayal that had led to Wounded Knee—would continue to fester and inflame.

Enacting the Sioux amendment, Lazarus admonished Congress in a memo prepared for Senator Abourezk's use, "is the litmus test for whether Indians ever can get justice in the white man's courts," the test of the country's oft-claimed devotion to the rule of law. In waiving the defense of *res judicata,* Congress would "redress an ancient wrong . . . and bring new hope to the Sioux people." If, on the other hand, Congress failed to act, it would end forever "the largest, the most historically and socially significant and . . . oldest land claim on record."

As chairman of the Subcommittee on Indian Affairs, Abourezk scheduled a hearing on the *res judicata* waiver for May 4, 1976. In the interim, both the Justice and Interior departments submitted written statements opposing the Sioux bill. Although the Interior Department acknowledged that the government's treatment of the Sioux constituted "a tragic chapter in our history," it concluded that enactment of the Sioux bill would "create an inequitable result with regard to all those tribes" whose claims had failed on *res judicata* grounds. "We see no reason," Commissioner of Indian Affairs Morris Thompson informed the subcommittee, "to so uniquely benefit one group when other groups . . . have been precluded from such relief."

The Justice Department agreed that enacting the Sioux bill would set a bad precedent, although for different reasons. According to Donald Mileur (who had presented the Justice Department position on the "food, rations, or provisions" amendment), waiving the defense of *res judicata* in the Sioux claim would do a "disservice" to Indian peoples. When Congress passed the original ICC Act, Mileur contended, it meant to bring Indian claims litigation to a quick end and to encourage tribes "to look not to the past, but to the present and future." Raising the bar of *res judicata* and permitting the Sioux to relitigate the merits of the Black Hills claim—already decided in 1942—would encourage dozens of other tribes to seek similar relief. The result, Mileur contended, would be to undermine the central purpose of the claims process to the ultimate detriment of the Indians themselves.

Abourezk, who enjoyed his reputation as a liberal populist at war with an impersonal federal bureaucracy, did not think much of either department's position. At the May 4 hearing, the senator freely took advantage of his power as chairman to berate both Thompson and Mileur for their passionless invocation of technical legal arguments and to lecture them about the impoverished conditions in which his Sioux constituents lived. Particularly galling to Abourezk was Mileur's argument that the doctrine of *res judicata* has a "salutary effect" on Indians by refocusing their attention from the past to the present. "It just doesn't seem right; it doesn't ring right," Abourezk lashed out, "even though it is a wonderful legal theory. It sounds beautiful coming from a Justice Department attorney who is well paid and very comfortable. . . . I just want to say that I think it stinks."

After completing his critique, Abourezk encouraged Lazarus to fire his own broadsides at Thompson and Mileur. Lazarus found baffling the Interior Department's view that Congress should not remedy one injustice simply because it might not remedy other possible injustices involving Indian claims. Such logic left Lazarus "cold"—and prompted speculation that the real basis of the Interior Department objections was the potential $85 million cost of the waiver.

Lazarus found the Justice Department's position—that waiving *res judicata* in the Sioux case would invite piecemeal waivers in dozens of similar cases—more logically coherent, but factually unfounded. Lazarus knew that demonstrating the uniqueness of the Black Hills claim was crucial to passage of the waiver. Congress would never open the door to the relitigation of a substantial number of claims long since thought resolved. Addressing this point directly, Lazarus accused the Justice Department of "grossly exaggerating" the number of cases comparable to the Black Hills claim. And in the weeks after the hearing, he supplied Abourezk with lengthy memos distinguishing from the Black Hills claim every case suggested by the Justice Department as comparable.

Before adjourning the hearing, Abourezk agreed to hear statements from various Sioux elders who had come east to speak directly to the Great Council about their claims. Matthew King, a traditional from Pine Ridge, nearing eighty, spoke first. King was friend of and interpreter for Fools Crow, the ceremonial chief who had negotiated with the government to resolve the standoff at Wounded Knee and ever since had agitated for full recognition of Sioux rights as defined in the 1868 treaty. The previous June 1, Fools Crow and Charlie Red Cloud (the ninety-year-old grandson of the great chief) had signed a formal "resolution of sovereignty" based on the 1868 treaty. The document also repudiated all subsequent congressional legislation affecting the Sioux, "especially the Indian Reorganization Act of 1934 and the Citizenship Act of 1924."

In keeping with such declarations of full independence and sovereignty, speaking for the eighty-seven-year-old Fools Crow, who sat at his side, King made clear the revised position of many Sioux traditionals: "The Black Hills is not for sale for no amount of money. We will never sell it. If the Government wants to lease the Black Hills, we would be willing to talk or negotiate. But first we want the Government to pay one-half of everything he took from the Black Hills."

Frank Kills Enemy, whose grandfather signed the 1868 treaty, himself over eighty, echoed King. "The Black Hills and all the claims," he concluded, "legally and morally belong to the Sioux Nation, the Oglala Nation."

In one sense, King and Kills Enemy did no more than voice what Sioux elders had claimed from the earliest days of the Black Hills councils, from before Ralph Case, from before Congress let the tribe into court. Under the 1868 treaty the Black Hills were Sioux land and could not be sold without the consent of three-fourths of the tribe's adult males. Even in 1876, when they had faced the choice to sell or starve, three-fourths had not signed; nor even close. As Sioux leaders had claimed sixty years earlier, the 1876 Manypenny agreement was "executed illegal"; it was "null and void." The United States may have seized the Hills, but as Kills Enemy put it, as many Sioux would swear, "legally and morally," the Hills still belonged to the Sioux.

For 100 years the Sioux had neither acknowledged nor even comprehended the *Lonewolf* doctrine granting Congress "plenary power" over Indian lands or the sovereign power of eminent domain by which the government could take private property, including tribal property, for its own use so long as it paid just compensation. Four generations of Sioux had accommodated themselves to the loss of the Hills, but not because they recognized the legal right of the United States to take them.

Rather, in the past, the Sioux had resigned themselves to the loss of the Hills and had fixed anxious eyes on the prospect of a huge money recovery because they believed, as Peter Dillon had once written Ralph Case, that "all past history shows that a conquered people has to take what a conqueror gives, just or unjust." So it was that American Horse and James Roan Eagle and Henry Standing Bear and many others asked no more than that the United States make good the Black Hills taking "by way of pay." And so it was that Ralph Case explained to them that, however much every Sioux might desire to have the Black Hills back, the U.S. courts would give them only money.

But after Wounded Knee, the old Sioux traditionals, the men of

the treaty, looked with new eyes past the pot of g
claims rainbow to the Black Hills themselves. Rej*
governments the whites had foisted upon them, r*
ship in what they now regarded as a foreign nation, r**
Kills Enemy, and their political companions were no longer co**
tent "to take what a conqueror gives, just or unjust." And the
militants told them they did not have to.

"The land belongs to us," King informed the Senate, "and we
haven't said much in the past, but we are getting fed up . . . and
[now] we are talking."

Neither Sonosky and Lazarus nor the Senate subcommittee paid
King, Fools Crow, or Kills Enemy much heed. In testifying before
the subcommittee, they represented only themselves. Their abso-
lutist view did not hold sway in the elected tribal councils. These
councils, through their duly named attorneys, wanted a waiver of
res judicata. And Abourezk intended to deliver precisely that.

Under Abourezk's firm hand, and despite the objections of both
the Justice and Interior departments, the subcommittee favorably
reported the *res judicata* waiver amendment to the full Committee
on Interior and Insular Affairs. On June 21, 1976, that committee,
in turn, favorably reported the bill to the entire Senate. Nine days
later, the Senate voted unanimously to direct the Court of Claims
to review the Indian Claims Commission's 1974 ruling on the Fifth
Amendment issue without regard to the defense of *res judicata*.

Lazarus immediately moved his campaign to the House of Representatives, where he suspected that passage of a similar waiver
far less likely. Still, the Sioux could count on strong support from
Lloyd Meeds, who still chaired the House Subcommittee on Indian Affairs, as well as his subcommittee staffers Franklin Ducheneaux, Rebecca Shapiro, and Mike Jackson.

Jackson, the Republican staff assistant for the subcommittee,
read Judge Littleton's incomprehensible 1942 opinion for himself.
He recalls the experience as being like "a walk in the thickets."
Jackson knew that he'd "been in the woods, but wasn't sure if I'd
seen any trees." On the basis of his own reading, Jackson had no
doubt that the "squirrelly" decisions of the Court of Claims had
denied the Sioux a meaningful opportunity to present their Fifth
Amendment claim.

Shapiro, as she wrote in a private memo to Meeds, evidently was
so convinced "the Sioux got screwed" that she believed, erroneously, that unless Congress enacted the *res judicata* amendment the
Sioux would receive nothing whatsoever in the Black Hills claim
(rather than as much as $17.5 million). This kind of sympathetic

response, engineered in no small part by Lazarus's compelling presentation of Sioux history, helped the lawyer gloss over a significant logical weakness in his case for the amendment.

Lazarus's basic pitch was that unless Congress waived the "technical" defense of *res judicata*, the Sioux Fifth Amendment claim would never receive a hearing on its merits. Simple fairness, he emphasized, dictated that Congress should set aside legal hairsplitting and permit the Sioux their day in court. But the Court of Claims' 1975 *res judicata* decision, if correct, did not reject the Sioux Fifth Amendment claim on a technicality, without reaching its merits. Rather, the court had refused to consider the Sioux Fifth Amendment claim precisely because in its view the claim already had received a hearing on its merits—in 1942—and had been rejected.

As a logical matter, then, Lazarus could not argue to Congress that the Sioux Fifth Amendment claim had never received a hearing on its merits, without also arguing that the 1975 decision was flat wrong. Although Lazarus certainly believed this to be the case, he generally shied away from a direct assault on the court's *res judicata* ruling. Asking Congress directly to overturn a court decision smacked of congressional interference in judicial business and did not make for successful lobbying.

What did make for successful lobbying was to foster the misimpression that the Sioux had lost their legal battle on "technical" grounds, meanwhile riveting congressional and public attention on the tragic story behind the Black Hills claim. Sioux history, more than that of any other tribe, had the power to inspire the conscience of America. Especially after the 1970 publication of *Bury My Heart at Wounded Knee*, hardly a person in America did not know the story of the proud warriors who had killed Custer to save their culture, only to have the government steal their lands anyway and destroy their way of life. Hardly a person in America did not know the picture of Chief Big Foot's corpse lying frozen on the snow at Wounded Knee, his band massacred around him, while, in Black Elk's words, the Sioux "dream died." As Lazarus emphasized in to a Congress increasingly sensitive to Indian grievances, for the nation that had subjugated these people in pursuit of its "manifest destiny," there could be no redemption, no return to grace, without a true reckoning for the "most ripe and rank" case of dishonorable dealings in frontier history.

On September 10, 1976, Meeds's subcommittee conducted hearings on the *res judicata* amendment. As on the Senate side, and for the same reasons, the Interior and Justice Departments testified in opposition. As on the Senate side, Lazarus presented his by now well-polished recitation of Sioux history as well as his case for why the application of *res judicata* in the Black Hills claim perpetuated a unique injustice.

Speaking to those congressmen who might vote against the Sioux amendment because of its potential $85 million price tag, Lazarus emphasized that the *res judicata* amendment merely permitted the Sioux to reassert their Fifth Amendment claim. The bill did not decide that the Sioux claim was valid. "If the government is right," Lazarus testified, "and if the Court of Claims in 1942 correctly decided that this was not a fifth amendment taking, then our legislation does not cost Uncle Sam a nickel. If, however, there was a fifth amendment taking and the Sioux have not been paid, then a gross injustice has been done and . . . the national conscience demands that we correct it."

As they had before the Senate subcommittee, Fools Crow and Kills Enemy followed Lazarus with testimony demanding far more than simply another day in court. This time, though, the aged Sioux did not speak in their own untutored English, but through a carefully drafted, lengthy written statement evidently prepared on their behalf by Larry Leventhal, an AIM lawyer. In the angry rhetoric of AIM, Fools Crow and Kills Enemy poured forth the political agenda that they shared with their young militant partners. In the name of the "Traditional Lakota Treaty Council" (newly established for the occasion), they denounced the IRA "puppet governments" and accused those who supported the Black Hills claim as having been "brainwashed . . . by the white man."

Fools Crow and Kills Enemy (who forty years earlier had asked hopefully of Ralph Case whether the Black Hills claim could be filed with the new claims commission) were "not fooled" by the ICC Act. By paying off the tribes for their lands, the government intended to "clear their own conscience, then terminate us." Fools Crow and Kills Enemy "wonder[ed] where the white man ever got the idea that these wrongs had to be settled in his courts by his rules. Anyone can win a ball game if he makes up his own rules," they observed.

Fools Crow and Kills Enemy now declined to play. "The Black Hills are sacred to the Lakota people. . . . Whatever the rules are, and whatever the Claims Commission awards for the Black Hills, please remember that we will never sell." Instead, the two Sioux elders announced their own set of rules based on their own view of history. "There never has been any conquest of the Sioux Nation by the United States," they told Congress. Rather, the Sioux "have lived in peace with the United States in accordance with the treaty as equals." As a matter of law, "the United States government [does not have] the power of eminent domain over us, anymore than we have the power of eminent domain over them." The whites and the Lakota inhabit "equal nations living side by side."

In this world, under these rules, Fools Crow and Kills Enemy concluded, "There can only be one settlement for the Black Hills. The Black Hills must be immediately returned to the rightful owners, the Lakota people. After that we can talk about compensation for damages done to . . . the land."

Fools Crow and Kills Enemy wondered how whites could "expect us to sell our church and our cemeteries for a few token white man dollars." In this regard, they specially indicted their white lawyers. According to Fools Crow and Kills Enemy, Sonosky and Lazarus supported the *res judicata* waiver solely because of the potential increase in their contingency fee, because "they would rather get 10 percent of $102 million than 10 percent of $17.5 million." As Jews, Fools Crow and Kills Enemy continued, Sonosky and Lazarus should "hold their heads in shame for what they are trying to talk us into doing here. They lost their lands for almost 2,000 years and have just got them returned. . . . We wonder if they will be willing to sell Israel to the Arabs for $17.5 million plus interest."

In the past, traditional leaders on the reservation had vied with the recognized IRA councils merely for control of the Black Hills claim. Many, like Kills Enemy, followed and supported the money compensation claims for decades (Kills Enemy even addressed Congress supporting the claims in 1971). Regardless, they now declared that accepting money was a betrayal of the very notion of Indianness, a treason to Crazy Horse's defiant admonition "one does not sell the land the people walk on," a total surrender to the alien and corrosive values of the whites. "I do not want our people . . . to think that we have sold out," Fools Crow explained.

Not surprisingly under the circumstances, Eddie Reddoor, chairman of the Black Hills Sioux Nation Council, forty years in active pursuit of a money judgment, a permanent fixture on Sioux delegations to Washington, prudently did not attend the hearing. Reddoor was a consummate reservation politician. He knew that in Sioux country no political charge carried as much destructive power as the charge of having sold out, especially of having sold out the past.

For 120 years, the Sioux had been divided between the friendlies

and the hostiles, the Hangers-Around-the-Fort and the free bands
in the Powder River country, the assimilationists and the traditionals. No one on the reservation wanted to bear the stigma of
having assimilated or even cooperated—of having played by the
white man's rules. Together with AIM, the traditionals sought to
ensure that those Sioux who did not repudiate the money claim
would suffer exactly that fate.

Borrowing a phrase from Richard Nixon, Fools Crow and Kills
Enemy claimed to represent a "silent majority." And who was to
say that they were wrong? What Sioux, in the abstract, wouldn't
prefer the Hills themselves to money compensation if that were
the choice? Reddoor wrote the House Interior and Insular Affairs
Committee an equivocal letter promising that "[a]dditional reports
and information" would be submitted later.

Fools Crow and Kills Enemy's strident message generated no
appreciable interest in the subcommittee. The elders lacked both
endorsement from the elected Sioux governments and grounding
in political reality. Crazy Horse's message of uncompromising
defiance lost much of its power when delivered not by a legendary
warrior from hunting grounds still rich in buffalo, but by old men,
quaint in the eyes of congressmen, who spoke for a people wholly
dependent on the government that they professed to repudiate.
Meeds accorded them the courtesy of testifying, but their demand
for a return to the 1868 treaty earned them no more attention than
that.

Three days after the hearing, Becky Shapiro wrote a long memo
to Meeds addressing his one concern about the Sioux bill—the
Justice Department's insistence that a *res judicata* waiver in the
Black Hills claim would open the floodgates for similar legislation
on behalf of other unsuccessful tribal claimants. Borrowing extensively from material supplied by Lazarus, Shapiro put the lie to the
Justice Department's scare tactics. The Black Hills claim, she explained to Meeds, was basically the only Fifth Amendment claim
still pending in which the government had prevailed on *res judicata*
grounds.

Meeds was convinced. "I would like to try to pass this," he
responded in a note to Shapiro. "We'll have a Subcomm. meeting
and mark [it] up and see if we can get [it] thru the Comm. and thru
the House on suspension of the rules."

True to his note, Meeds scheduled a "mark-up" (a subcommittee
session where legislation is considered and voted on prior to refer-
ral to full committee) for September 22. The scheduling of a mark
up, especially by the subcommittee chairman, usually indicates

that the foundation for subcommittee approval is complete. Certainly, Lazarus considered a favorable subcommittee report to be imminent.

Then, as Lazarus later recalled, "a disaster occurr██ In a primary held on September 21, Meeds, who ordinaril██ed only token opposition, won renomination by a hair's-bre██ver a challenger who campaigned on the theme that Meeds ███ll his time looking after Indian affairs and none looking af██is constituents. The charge had scored big points in Washington state, where Indians and local fisherman continued a decade of ugly confrontation over tribal fishing rights.

With his political survival in jeopardy, Meeds canceled the mark-up on the Sioux bill and announced that his Indian Affairs Subcommittee would hold no further meetings that year. Privately, Meeds assured Lazarus that if he won reelection he would make the Sioux bill a priority for the next year. Lazarus knew better than to place much faith in such promises. And, as it turned out, after winning reelection in November Meeds gave up his chairmanship of the Indian Affairs Subcommittee. Once at the brink of victory, Lazarus would have to start over from scratch.

Even before they could seek reintroduction of the *res judicata* waiver in the next Congress, Sonosky and Lazarus had to fend off government efforts to subvert their impending lobbying campaign. During 1975 and early 1976, the government and the Sioux had continued to fight before the commission over unsettled minor issues in the Black Hills claim, specifically the value of three rights-of-way across Sioux country and the value of any legal offsets (except for food, rations, and provisions) that the government might claim. In May 1976 the commission issued a preliminary report valuing the rights-of-way (as of 1877) at $3,484 and declaring that the government was entitled to *no* legal offsets on the claim.

Although it had until November 15, 1976, to object to the commission's report, on October 15 the government suddenly announced that it had "decided not to press its setoff claims any further." More important, the government moved the commission to enter a final award in favor of the Sioux in the total amount of $17,553,484—the sum of the 1877 value of the land, the gold extracted, and the rights-of-ways, without interest.

In so moving, the government offered the Sioux a poisoned apple. Although the government had surrendered on the offsets issue and was actually encouraging the commission to enter a very large judgment against it, the government's motion, if granted, would kill whatever chance the Sioux still possessed of securing a *res judicata* waiver. As Sonosky and Lazarus explained to the commission in their opposition to the government's motion, "if final judgment is entered now, [the Black Hills claim] will fall in the same category as the other cases that have been finally determined by the Commission. . . . The government is aware . . . that so long as this is an open case the Congress feels free to waive the technical defense of *res judicata*. But, if the Government can close this case, then [it] can argue to Congress that to waive the defense in this case would set a dangerous precedent in other closed cases."

Behind the government's rush to judgment, Sonosky and Lazarus concluded, lurked a calculated attempt to prevent another hearing on the Fifth Amendment issue, a strategic decision to accept a $17.5 million loss immediately rather than risk a $103 million loss down the line. Though it placed them in the peculiar position of delaying a $17.5 million award, Sonosky and Lazarus practically begged the commission to defer entry of final judgment until after the new Congress could consider a *res judicata* waiver. On November 10, the commission granted their wish.

Having escaped the government's trap, Sonosky and Lazarus requested Senator Abourezk to reintroduce the *res judicata* waiver. Under his stewardship, the Sioux bill again sailed through the Senate, passing by unanimous consent and without debate on May 3, 1977.

Meanwhile, in the House, Sonosky and Lazarus assessed the damage resulting from the November election and Meeds's resignation from the Indian Affairs Subcommittee. They were pleasantly surprised. Succeeding Meeds as chairman was Tino Roncalio, a Wyoming Democrat well known to Sonosky through his longtime representation of the Wind River tribes in Roncalio's home state. Roncalio proved almost as enthusiastic about the Sioux bill as Meeds—who continued his still-influential support from the wings.

Sonosky and Lazarus also hoped that the election of Jimmy Carter might result in a change of executive branch policy. They immediately set up meetings with the new political appointees in the Interior and Justice Departments to persuade them to rethink their predecessors' opposition to the *res judicata* waiver.

These efforts bore fruit almost instantaneously. After meeting with Sonosky and Lazarus on March 24, 1977, the Interior Department completely reversed its position on the waiver. Where the previous year it had seen "no reason to change the law to so uniquely benefit" the Sioux, now the department informed Congress "that the unique facts and history" surrounding the Black

Hills claim warranted special treatment by Congress. Accordingly, although the Interior Department spoke solely in its capacity as "trustee" for the tribes and did not present the official administration position, it recommended enactment of the *res judicata* waiver.

Speaking officially for the administration, the Justice Department (representing OMB as well) also retreated from its prior opposition to the Sioux bill. The Justice Department now conceded that the waiver might represent an "appropriate correction of past wrongs," but "strongly recommend[ed] that Congress defer action" until the administration "had the opportunity either to develop its overall policies on Indian affairs or to complete the review of all unresolved Indian claims. . . ." Alternatively, the department recommended that the Sioux bill be amended to provide for a new trial on the Sioux Fifth Amendment claim rather than (as drafted) for appellate review by the Court of Claims of the commission's 1974 decision.

Chairman Roncalio convened a subcommittee hearing on May 10 where the Interior and Justice Departments presented their revised positions. Lazarus again testified—almost word for word as he had before—in favor of the Sioux bill.

Eddie Reddoor filed a statement for the record on behalf of the Black Hills Sioux Nation Council, the oldest of the pan-Sioux claims organizations. Reddoor and the BHSNC evidently had decided which way the wind was blowing in Sioux country. Over the past several months, the BHSNC had passed resolutions condemning the current $17.5 million Black Hills award as "totally inadequate." The BHSNC further resolved that "the best interests of the Sioux Nation would best be served by immediate return of the Black Hills . . . and that negotiations must begin immediately for such return."

Reddoor, who had once stood before the commission and formally endorsed Sonosky as the definitive "mouthpiece" of the Sioux people, now joined Fools Crow and Kills Enemy in blaming him and Lazarus for pursuing a money judgment for the Black Hills. Reddoor assailed the lawyers for "putting their own financial interest above the interest of the Sioux Nation" and for failing to explain to "the Sioux people that by accepting the award of the Indian Claims Commission. . . . the Sioux Nation forever gives up its legal right to get the Black Hills back."

Sonosky and Lazarus's failure to so advise the Sioux was deliberate. They did not believe that the Sioux relinquished their "right to get the Black Hills back" by pursuing monetary compensation for their seizure. On the contrary, as Lazarus had publicly advised the Sioux as early as mid-1973, in enacting the ICC Act, Congress had not authorized the judicial branch to return land to the tribes; accordingly, no U.S. court would entertain a suit for a return of the Black Hills.

On the other hand, Congress had the power to return all federally held Black Hills land to the Sioux, regardless of whether they accepted money compensation for the 1877 taking of the Hills. Sonosky and Lazarus saw no inherent incompatibility in accepting money and seeking land. Lazarus even thought that the Sioux should identify those particular Black Hills lands with special religious or cultural significance, which then might become the nucleus of a land restoration bill.

What the lawyers considered unwise was the idea of abandoning the just compensation claim in order to file a legally hopeless land return claim or replacing constitutional arguments for just compensation with political rhetoric about the inviolability of the 1868 treaty and how the Hills still belonged to the Sioux. However much the Sioux might wish it otherwise, the 1868 treaty was no different from any other treaty signed by the United States, whether with Indian tribes or foreign sovereigns. The United States retained the power to abrogate these treaties, unilaterally. The only relevant legal question was whether the Constitution, specifically the just compensation clause, required the government to pay for that abrogation.

With the help of an unknown lawyer, on July 23 the Black Hills Sioux Nation Council filed a Special Appearance and Notice before the commission to challenge Sonosky and Lazarus's legal representation of the Sioux. Signed by Eddie Reddoor, the document notified the commission that the BHSNC constituted "the traditional and lawful governmental entity of the Sioux Nation authorized to deal with the United States Government in any matter dealing with the Black Hills and aboriginal territory."

The BHSNC then proceeded to disassociate itself from the money claim. "The land in question has never been lawfully ceded . . . and it remains the property of the Sioux Nation," the Council announced.

> This Council is not and does not wish to become a party to these proceedings, for the reason that the Indian Claims Commission provides only money awards and this Council expressly renounces any claim for money as compensation for our sacred

Black Hills. . . . Any judgment or award of the Commission in this matter will be null and void.

For the moment, Sonosky and Lazarus ignored the Special Appearance. Despite its claim to the contrary, the BHSNC still had no authority to speak for any individual Sioux tribe or for the Sioux nation (the original Teton and Yanktonai bands who had owned the Great Sioux Reservation) as a whole. The Special Appearance, therefore, carried no legal weight.

Instead, Sonosky and Lazarus continued to seek a *res judicata* waiver on behalf of the eight elected Sioux tribal governments. And the House continued to appear sympathetic to the idea. After receiving a favorable report from Roncalio's subcommittee, the influential and highly respected chairman of the Committee on Interior and Insular Affairs, Morris Udall (Democrat from Arizona), pushed the Sioux bill through the full committee by voice vote on June 16, 1977.

In the written committee report, issued six weeks later, only one congressman, North Carolinian Lamar Gudger, dissented. A courtly southern lawyer who (like his home state's senior senator, Sam Ervin) fancied himself a constitutional scholar, Gudger believed that the Sioux bill "contravene[d] . . . the separation of powers doctrine." In Gudger's view, the Sioux bill called upon Congress to review and reverse a properly arrived-at judicial decision, thereby improperly overstepping its "exclusively legislative role" in the constitutional scheme.

Neither Sonosky and Lazarus nor Roncalio and Udall thought that Gudger's idiosyncratic constitutional concerns would carry much weight. Indeed, given the virtual unanimity of support in his committee, Udall was so certain that the Sioux bill would pass that he decided to bring it before the full House under "suspension of the rules," a procedure for expediting noncontroversial legislation that requires a two-thirds majority for passage. As a final precaution, Udall, Roncalio, Meeds, and the Interior Committee's ranking Republican, Jim Johnson, jointly distributed a "Dear Colleague" letter in which they "strongly urge[d]" each individual member to vote in favor of the Sioux bill.

The bill reached the House floor on September 27, 1977. With Sonosky watching from the gallery (Lazarus was at Yale teaching a seminar in Indian law), Roncalio read the bill into the record and exhorted his colleagues not to "hide behind the technical defense of res judicata and deny the Sioux their day in court. . . ." Congressmen Johnson and Meeds echoed his remarks.

Congressman William Cohen of Maine, though, rose in opposition. Cohen was enmeshed in his own Indian claims problem, and not one that fostered sympathy for aggrieved tribes. Since 1971, the Passamaquoddy and Penobscot Indians of Maine had been engaged in a complex legal battle with Cohen's home state over the ownership of millions of acres of rich timber lands. The two tribes acknowledged that they had sold their aboriginal lands to Maine in a series of agreements between 1794 and 1833, but they now argued that these agreements violated the Nonintercourse Act of 1790, a federal statute specifically designed to protect Indian tribes from unauthorized land grabs. Under the Nonintercourse Act, the tribes contended, individual states such as Maine had no authority to buy Indian lands without prior express approval from Congress.

For the last six years, a resourceful young lawyer named Tom Tureen had argued on behalf of the Passamaquoddys and Penobscots that the violation of the Nonintercourse Act completely nullified the original sales from the tribes to the state. Because the original sales were illegal, title never passed from the tribes to the state and, accordingly, the thousands of current white residents were trespassers on tribal land. Although Tureen's theory at first seemed farfetched, several important preliminary successes in federal district court had prompted one prominent New England law firm to withhold unqualified endorsement of municipal bonds within the disputed area. Rumors soon started to circulate that people living on these lands might find it impossible to transfer real estate or obtain mortgages.

Naturally, the widespread clouding of land titles and the possibility of returning large portions of Maine to Indian ownership did not please Congressman Cohen's non-Indian constituents. While Tureen offered to negotiate a settlement (albeit an expensive one), Maine's congressional delegation, with Cohen at the forefront, introduced legislation to eliminate the legal underpinnings of the Passamaquoddy and Penobscot claims. In March 1977, they put forward a bill to extinguish all aboriginal title that might be held by the Passamaquoddy and Penobscott and to limit any possible monetary damages that their claims might generate. Senator Abourezk (chief Senate sponsor of the Sioux bill) denounced the Maine bill as "a very one-sided attempt to obviate and preclude any just claim on the part of the tribes."

The Passamaquoddy and Penobscot claims were still dominating Maine politics (and the extinguishment bill still pending) when the Sioux *res judicata* waiver reached the House floor in

September. The Maine situation, moreover, had unnerved state delegations throughout the east. Tureen's Nonintercourse Act theory applied with equal force to large tribal land sales in Massachusetts, New York, and North Carolina. Tribes in each of these state had initiated litigation parroting Tureen's efforts in Maine.

Thus, when Cohen took the House floor to oppose the Sioux bill, he addressed an audience already jittery on the subject of Indian claims and ill-informed about the crucial differences between the Nonintercourse Act claims (which were directed at *states* for *violation* of federal law) and the vast majority of Indian claims, including the Black Hills claim (in which tribes sued the *United States* over the *effect* of federal statutes). In the latter situation, the doctrine of sovereign immunity protected the United States against suits like the Nonintercourse Act claims, seeking return of tribal lands.

Most congressmen at the time, however, undoubtedly did not understand that promoting the Sioux claim would in no way encourage the unrelated Nonintercourse Act claims. Cohen, for his part, played to their ignorance and fear, reminding his colleagues, for example, of "an item in the paper that certain tribes in Nevada and Montana are going to be seeking the return of large amounts of land or $30 billion in lieu of land."

Having captured his colleagues' attention, Cohen did not address the bill's merits directly. Instead, he amplified and endorsed the Justice Department's request that Congress defer action on the bill until the Carter administration developed a comprehensive Indian claims policy. He also echoed the department's complaint that the bill ought to provide for *de novo* consideration of the Black Hills claim (thereby opening the door to an entirely new trial), instead of instructing the Court of Claims to conduct appellate review of the commission's 1974 decision without regard to the defense of *res judicata*. By directing his attack at alleged "procedural flaws" in the bill, Cohen colored his own position with the patina of fairness that the Sioux had worked so hard to appropriate exclusively for themselves.

Roncalio, Meeds, and Udall, caught off-guard, all took the floor to refute Cohen's critique, but when the speaker called the yeas and neas the Sioux bill not only failed to command the necessary two-thirds majority, it lost decisively—173 in favor to 239 opposed. Hearing the news in New Haven, Lazarus felt like he'd "been hit by a truck coming out of nowhere."

Meeds, too, had been blindsided. "We thought we had all our ducks in a row and they just clobbered us," he told one reporter.

In Meeds's view, and in the view of a number of Hill watchers, the Sioux bill had run headlong into an "anti-Indian backlash" newly in evidence in Congress. "There's no question that a very substantial shift in feeling is under way, particularly where these [land] claims are being felt," Meeds lamented. As Massachusetts Congressman Gerry Studds summed up the situation, between the Nonintercourse Act claims threatening to cloud land titles in the east and the continued fishing rights wars in the Northwest, "some people in Congress . . . have just had it with Indians."

Sonosky and Lazarus's own post-mortem was more complicated. In addition to the backlash problem, they also had stumbled inadvertently into a growing resentment among some congressmen that too many big and potentially controversial bills were being railroaded through the House under "suspension of the rules." The lawyers could attribute at least some negative votes solely to efforts at curbing this abuse. Other members apparently voted against the Sioux bill as a matter of principle because they believed that it should have been routed through the Judiciary Committee, rather than the Interior and Insular Affairs Committee. Most important, a number of members seemed genuinely concerned that the Sioux bill did not accommodate the Justice Department's request for a new trial.

In early October, Sonosky and Lazarus agreed on a last-ditch, two-prong strategy for reviving the bill. First, they would attempt to negotiate a compromise with Congressman Cohen on the new trial issue. Second, independent of that compromise, they would redouble their efforts to convince individual congressmen of the merits of the bill. With luck they hoped to maneuver themselves back to a position from which Congressman Udall might fruitfully seek a rule under which the *res judicata* waiver would be reconsidered by the House needing only a simple majority for passage.

William Howard Payne—Sonosky and Lazarus's ostensible co-counsel, who also attended the meeting—was pessimistic. The Sioux bill was "dead," he told Sonosky. Sonosky did not entirely agree. "It may be dead," he replied, "but it isn't dead, dead." He and Lazarus would press on.

Starting in mid-October, and from time to time thereafter, Lazarus tried to set up meetings with Cohen or otherwise engage him and his staff in substantive negotiations. Lazarus got nowhere. Cohen, who was preparing a campaign for the Senate in which he would run television ads suggesting that his opponent was willing to give half of Maine back to the Indians, wouldn't even meet with Lazarus. (The Passamaquoddy and Penobscot eventually settled for $27 million plus a land acquisition fund of $54.5 million).

Nonetheless, Lazarus and Sonosky passed the word that they were willing to compromise. They would not object to an amendment providing for a new trial of the Fifth Amendment issue. What they could not swallow was an amendment that would provide for a new trial covering *every* issue in the claim (including title, liability, value, and consideration), which would likely result in another decade of litigation. Unfortunately, as finally reported by his staff, Cohen was insisting on a new trial for all issues on the ground that the Justice Department had requested and justified this approach.

Cohen's intransigence left Sonosky and Lazarus only one alternative: to convince the Justice Department to change its position that Congress should either defer action on the Sioux bill pending administration review of claims policy or amend the bill to provide for a new trial. (In fact, despite Cohen's protestations to the contrary, the Justice Department itself had never demanded a new trial of every issue).

In a five-page single-spaced letter addressed to Assistant Attorney General James Moorman, Sonosky and Lazarus pointed out that, as far as they were aware, the Justice Department had never undertaken a study of what it called "ancient" tribal claims, much less a study requiring deferral of the Sioux bill. As for the new trial issue, Sonosky and Lazarus admitted their willingness to accept a new trial of the Fifth Amendment issue, though they knew of no "material that is not now in the record that could be placed in the record." In other words, they questioned what possible function a new trial might serve.

On January 25, 1978, the Justice Department responded. In a letter to Interior Committee Chairman Udall, Assistant Attorney General Pat Wald wrote that "the focus of our general study of ancient claims now centers on the so-called 'Eastern Claims' . . . [and thus] is no longer a reason for deferring consideration of [the Sioux bill]." And although Wald's letter reiterated the department's "request that the bill be amended to allow the Fifth Amendment taking issue to be tried *de novo,*" it did not insist on a trial *de novo* on all issues in the claim.

With the Justice Department having now adopted an acceptable position, Udall and Roncalio pressed Cohen to compromise. At the same time, Lazarus stepped up his lobbying campaign targeting individual members. With Udall and Roncalio aiming for a House vote in early February, in the last ten days of January, Lazarus (and every lawyer at his firm with congressional connections) blanketed

Capitol Hill with letters explaining the merits of the Sioux bill. Again, Lazarus enlisted Ben Reifel to importune his former House colleagues, especially the Republicans. On the Democratic side, former vice-presidential candidate and Kennedy in-law Sargent Shriver, one of Lazarus's partners, persuaded the party leadership to list the *res judicata* waiver as a bill on which Democratic members should vote favorably. In one effective bit of arm-twisting, Senator Abourezk turned around the entire North Carolina delegation, which to a person had followed Congressman Gudger in opposing the Sioux bill. Abourezk made clear to the North Carolinians that legislation of vital interest to their state would remain stalled in his Senate committee unless they experienced a change of heart regarding his Sioux constituents.

After several false starts, Udall and Roncalio finally prevailed upon Cohen to compromise. As Lazarus recalls, they caught up with Cohen one final time just as he was leaving for a campaign swing in Maine. Whether because he was growing tired of the fight, or because he sensed that the mood of the House was shifting against him—or because compromise seemed appropriate after all—Cohen agreed to limit *de novo* review solely to the Fifth Amendment issue.

By the time the Sioux bill reached the House floor on February 9, 1978, the fight was won. Cohen introduced an amendment, drafted by Sonosky and Lazarus, authorizing the Court of Claims to "receive and consider any additional evidence . . . on the issue of a fifth amendment taking and shall determine that issue de novo." (Sonosky and Lazarus doubted that there would be any such additional evidence.) The House voted overwhelmingly in favor of the Sioux bill as now revised and, in due course, the Senate adopted the House version. For only the second time in thirty-two years, Congress amended the original ICC Act. Both times it did so to further a single case, the Black Hills claim.

On March 13, President Carter signed the *res judicata* waiver into law. That afternoon, William Howard Payne wrote to Sonosky asking a favor: "when you hear I am dead please issue orders not to bury me until I am *dead dead.*" The phoenix of the Black Hills claim had risen once more from the ashes: the Sioux were back in court.

Sonosky (writing on behalf of his partners as well) immediately informed his Sioux clients of their remarkable victory, expressing confidence that they would "join us in our delight with the action of Congress and the President. . . ."

Lazarus wrote his clients on Pine Ridge, too, but doubted they would celebrate. Lazarus understood at this point that no news about the money claim, regardless of how positive, was welcome among his clients on Pine Ridge, where, at least on issues of land and spirituality, the powerful alliance of militants and traditionals now held sway in the elected tribal council. On a reservation in the midst of a cultural renaissance, all the talk about getting the sacred Black Hills back, of regaining the land they called The Heart of Everything That Is, wildly inflated the expectations and demands of a people who for the most part did not understand that practically, and as a matter of American law, they did not possess this choice.

As Lazarus prepared to relitigate the Fifth Amendment issue before the Court of Claims, he tried on numerous occasions to "explain the limits of the white man's justice system" to questioning Sioux. In June 1978, Moses Two Bulls wrote to ask about a land return. Two Bulls had been chairman of the Oglalas in the mid-1950s when the tribe first hired Fried, Frank to handle the claim. No longer in tribal office, but now vice-chairman of the Black Hills Sioux Nation Council, he told Lazarus that "some of the Sioux would like to have the land back." Two Bulls wanted to know "What would happen if the Tribes insisted on land recovery?"

"I am afraid that the Sioux Tribes simply are not in a position to 'insist' upon a land recovery," Lazarus replied (sending copies of his letter to the elected Pine Ridge leadership). "Only Congress can return the land and the Tribes have no way to force Congress to do so. Moreover, if the Tribes, in an effort to get their property back, insist that the claims be dropped, I can see you ending up with neither land nor money."

Lazarus's slightly impatient tone may have reflected the fact that the burgeoning land return movement was starting to impede litigation of the claim. On November 5, 1977 (while the *res judicata* bill was still pending), the Lakota Treaty Council, represented by Fools Crow, Kills Enemy, King, and one other elder, Lewis Bad Wound, had followed Reddoor's lead and filed a Special Appearance and Notice with the Commission. This second special appearance was identical to the first, except that the Lakota Treaty Council identified itself, rather than the BHSNC, as "the traditional and lawful government of the Lakota People or Sioux Nation."

In all likelihood, Sonosky and Lazarus would have ignored the second special appearance too, but to the lawyers' surprise, the Justice Department moved the commission to give both the BHSNC and the Lakota Treaty Council "full opportunity to present their adverse claims. . . ." Although the government doubted the validity of their claims to be the true representatives of the Sioux nation, it asked the commission to hear their views in order that "the Black Hills case may be unequivocally decided 'once and for all. . . .' "

Sonosky and Lazarus fired off a response, calling the government's motion "frivolous and . . . also deliberately mischievous." As they saw it, the government's "let's hear what they have to say" attitude, if taken seriously, would put the Justice Department in the bizarre position of questioning the United States's own title to the Black Hills as well as undermining the IRA tribal governments to which the United States historically accorded exclusive recognition. Rather than responding to the motion directly, Sonosky and Lazarus suggested that the commission ask the government a series of questions designed to highlight these apparent self-contradictions. Did the government intend to take the position that "the government-recognized tribal councils, as opposed to the BHSNC and Lakota Treaty Council, are not the proper parties to the claim?" Did the government intend to endorse the BHSNC and Lakota Treaty Council position that the Black Hills "remains the property of the Sioux Nation?"

The commission did not bother with the questions. On December 29, 1977, it denied the government's motion, finding "inappropriate" the attempt to introduce new Indian parties into the claim.

Sonosky and Lazarus plunged ahead. After the President signed the *res judicata* waiver, they immediately sought review of the Fifth Amendment taking issue in the Court of Claims. In a memorandum submitted April 10, 1978, they argued that the commission's 1974 decision awarding the Sioux interest on the value of the Black Hills was correct and that the Court of Claims should review that decision on the basis of the existing record. By late April, the parties and the court agreed to treat the latest Sonosky and Lazarus memorandum as the opening Sioux brief. Despite congressional provision for a trial *de novo,* both sides decided to rely basically on the existing record.

On September 6, 1978, the government filed a 127-page answer brief. Six weeks later, on October 18, the Sioux filed a 42-page reply. Like two old fighters who had squared off many times before, the parties resorted to a familiar pattern of punches and parries, approaching occasionally from a different angle or in a different rhythm, but mainly reenacting past encounters.

As a matter of law, both sides sought to distance themselves from the Court of Claims *Fort Berthold* test (its attempted compromise between the *Lonewolf* plenary powers doctrine and *Shoshone* line of takings cases), albeit in diametrically opposite directions. The government argued, quite simply, that "*Lonewolf* controls."

As the government interpreted *Lonewolf* (Decker wrote the brief), Congress retained the authority to take tribal property without tribal consent using its plenary power "without it being a Fifth Amendment taking." *Lonewolf* imposed no requirement that Congress "determine the market value of the land transferred or the adequacy of the consideration paid prior to effecting the transfer." Instead, *Lonewolf* mandated only that "Congress act in good faith in light of the circumstances that were then prevailing." As long as Congress met this standard of conduct, "if injury was occasioned . . . relief must be sought by an appeal to Congress and not to the courts."

The government dismissed as essentially irrelevant *Shoshone* and the related cases requiring the U.S. to pay just compensation for the taking of tribal lands. In these cases, Decker contended, Congress had demonstrated "an arbitrary disregard of the Indians' rights in the land or an arbitrary indifference to trying to insure a fair exchange to the Indians for their land." No such arbitrariness, however, was present in the United States's dealings with the Sioux.

On the contrary, in the Justice Department's view, the course of dealings between the government and the Sioux in the years 1874–77 showed that Congress had been "sincere in its desire to act in the Sioux's best interests as well as those of the country as a whole" and that Congress "made bona fide attempts to protect and advance . . . Sioux interests. . . ." From the Allison commission's attempt to negotiate a sale of the Black Hills through the many provisions of the 1877 act providing for the education, health, and welfare of the Sioux, the government had made a reasonable and well-intentioned effort to cushion the tribe's inevitable loss of the Black Hills.

Indeed, given the government's humanitarian policy of civilizing the Sioux coupled with the incessant marauding of hostile Sioux bands (frustrating this policy), the 1877 act was "the best the government could do under the circumstances." Rather than simply starve the Sioux into relinquishing the Black Hills, the government had provided the tribe with both 900,000 additional acres of land and rations that, by as early as 1926, had cost the government more than $39 million. In sum, "factually and legally, there is no basis for holding that Congress did not act in good faith . . . within its [*Lonewolf*] plenary powers over Indian affairs."

In typically aggressive fashion, Sonosky and Lazarus opened

their reply brief by describing the government's argument as "wholly without merit." They proposed a legal standard directly opposite to *Lonewolf.* Citing the Court of Claims own 1971 decision in *Klamath and Moadoc Tribes* v. *United States,* Sonosky and Lazarus argued that the *Fort Berthold* good faith effort test did not apply where the government has obtained tribal land without consent for its own account (as opposed to for third parties). Where the government has taken Indian land for itself, as it did when taking the Black Hills, it must pay just compensation under the Fifth Amendment regardless of congressional good faith.

As for *Lonewolf,* a seventy-five-year-old case decided years before Congress even granted courts jurisdiction to hear tribal claims, Sonosky and Lazarus asserted that it had no bearing on the just compensation issue presently before the court. *Lonewolf* was a suit seeking to prevent the Secretary of the Interior from disposing of tribal lands in accordance with a 1900 statute that apparently violated the Medicine Lodge Treaty. While the Supreme Court upheld Congress's authority to abrogate Indian treaties as a constitutional exercise of its plenary powers, the court had no occasion to consider, much less decide, whether such an abrogation might give rise to a Fifth Amendment obligation to pay just compensation. Far from controlling, *Lonewolf* was beside the point.

Finally, Sonosky and Lazarus argued that if the court saw fit to apply its *Fort Berthold* test, it had no choice but to find that the 1877 act was a Fifth Amendment taking, not an exercise of Congress's plenary power. Notwithstanding the government's "distortion and excision" of the historical record, notwithstanding its assertion, on the basis of hindsight, that the government's rations payments amounted to more than the 1877 value of the Hills, *Fort Berthold* states that to escape the payment of just compensation Congress must have made a good faith "attempt to pay the full present value of the land." From the record, Sonosky and Lazarus summarized, "the conclusion is inescapable that Congress in the 1877 Act was not making any effort, in good faith or otherwise, to pay [the Sioux] the then full present market value of the land."

Sonosky and Lazarus thought their arguments would carry the day. Even when it ruled against them in 1975, the court had acknowledged the duplicity of the government's policy towards the Sioux and even hinted that its own 1942 decision might have been wrong. If governmental good faith became the issue, Sonosky and Lazarus expected to prevail.

Moreover, Sonosky and Lazarus felt that the government had failed to put forward its most convincing defense, or at least the defense for which they had no ready reply. For twenty years, they had waited for the government to argue that the 1889 act—based on an agreement which three-quarters of the adult male Sioux apparently had signed—retroactively ratified the 1876 sell or starve agreement ceding the Black Hills to the United States. South Dakota Congressman E. W. Martin had raised this defense against the Sioux claim as early as 1903. George Stormont, the first Justice Department lawyer in the claim, raised it before the Court of Claims in the 1930s. But somewhere along the claim's tortured path through the courts, as responsibility for the claim passed from one lawyer to another to yet another still, the government's institutional memory failed. With the briefs submitted, Sonosky and Lazarus figured thankfully that the 1889 statutory argument was one punch they would not have to slip.

Early in November, a few weeks after filing the Sioux brief, Lazarus received a letter from Elijah Whirlwind Horse, the new president at Pine Ridge. "First, I want to congratulate you for the excellent job you did in preparing the Reply Brief in the Court of Claims case," Whirlwind Horse began. "Your responses to the government's various positions were very well done."

Lazarus must have laughed to himself as he read. During his entire tenure as claims counsel for Pine Ridge, Lazarus had received few if any substantive letters from his client. Lazarus's own reports to the tribe, often many letters a year, simply "disappeared into a black hole." He hardly ever heard a word—one way or another—from the tribal council or tribal officers about his work.

In any event, Whirlwind Horse's comment was transparently disingenuous. Far from approving of Lazarus's handling of the Black Hills claim, Whirlwind Horse was a leading member of the chorus denouncing the money claim and accusing Lazarus personally of grubbing for a big fee. Indeed, because of his opposition to Lazarus's legal efforts and the controversy that these efforts sparked on Pine Ridge, the tribe had let Lazarus's attorney contract expire five months earlier, in May 1977. Despite requests for a renewal (and assurances that the council would consider the matter), the tribe had taken no action.

Instead, Whirlwind Horse had hired a new lawyer to advise the tribe about the Black Hills claim—a Sioux lawyer to provide a Sioux perspective on how the tribe should present its historical grievances to the white man's courts. At Whirlwind Horse's shoulder, drafting his letters to Lazarus, now stood Mario Gonzalez, the first Pine Ridge Sioux ever licensed to practice law.

A thirty-five-year-old of mixed blood, tall, broad, and congenial, descended on his mother's side from Chief Lip (one of the first Sioux agitators in the Black Hills claim), Gonzalez never expected to become a lawyer. He grew up as a "country boy" on his grandfather's ranch in the eastern part of Pine Ridge, doing "lots of riding and fixing fence."

After his grandfather's death, Gonzalez transferred to an off-reservation high school near Ellsworth Air Force Base east of Rapid City. There, for the first time, he sat in integrated classrooms and listened to his classmates talk about going to college.

That ambition was contagious. After graduation, Gonzalez enrolled at Black Hills State College, where he traded his love of basketball for a passionate interest in the Indian history he previously spurned. Immersing himself in the lore of the tribes, Gonzalez became especially fascinated with the treaties that bound his people to the nation at large.

After graduation, at his grandmother's urging, Gonzalez followed up a local newspaper ad describing a prelaw training course for Indians at the University of New Mexico, which had initiated an intensive program to recruit Indians to the law. He arrived just in time for the birth of the American Indian Law Center, which, in addition to training lawyers, tribal judges, and clerks (on government-funded scholarships), filed *amicus* briefs in selected cases, and distributed a newsletter dealing with Indian legal matters.

At the American Indian Law Center, Gonzalez found it "hard to adjust" to legal reasoning, but he liked the program. When a professor at the center offered to arrange his admission to the University of North Dakota law school, Gonzalez figured he'd give it a try.

Gonzalez stuck at it. His first summer he returned to Pine Ridge as a legal intern for Oglala Legal Services, a legal aid group. His second summer, 1971, Gonzalez arranged an internship with his tribe's Washington attorneys, Schifter and Lazarus. Gonzalez remembers that it "seemed like law was very easy."

On receiving his degree, Gonzalez carried his legal training back to the reservation. After a stint at Oglala Legal Services (interrupted by the Wounded Knee takeover), he went to Rosebud to become chief tribal judge. In that capacity, Gonzalez earned a degree of fame when he granted AIM leader Dennis Banks's petition to have South Dakota Attorney General William Janklow disbarred from practice in tribal court. Banks's petition had charged that Janklow sexually assaulted a teenage Indian girl, Jancita Eagle Deer. Janklow (who would later win the governorship by running an anti-AIM campaign) had ignored Gonzalez's summons to answer the charge.

Gonzalez left the bench in 1976, gained some litigation experience in private practice in Martin, South Dakota, then in 1978 returned to Pine Ridge, where he began giving legal advice to the tribe.

Gonzalez believed as a matter of law that the Sioux still owned the Black Hills, and so advised the tribal council. In his view, the 1877 act taking the Hills was unconstitutional. The Fifth Amendment to the Constitution states that private property shall not "be taken for public use without just compensation." According to Gonzalez, the United States had not taken the Black Hills for a public use but rather for the private use of turning it over to homesteaders and miners. Gonzalez contended that this failure to pursue a public use rendered the 1877 act null and void. Consequently, the United States never obtained legal title to the Hills. "Personally," Gonzalez told the Pine Ridge council, "I want the land back." And he wanted to bring suit in federal court to achieve that result.

Lazarus considered Gonzalez's legal theory completely untenable. To anyone's knowledge, no federal court ever had prevented, much less rescinded, a governmental taking on the ground that it was not for a public use. And regardless of the merits of Gonzalez's public use argument, Lazarus was certain that no federal court would even listen to his theory. Congress simply had not authorized courts to return to Indian tribes lands taken under federal statutes. Instead, Congress had created the Indian Claims Commission to award monetary compensation. Without congressional authorization, Lazarus believed that a suit like the one Gonzalez proposed would be "dismissed on day one for lack of jurisdiction."

The Oglalas of Pine Ridge had no expertise with which to choose between Gonzalez's legal advice and continued prosecution of the Black Hills claim. On the one hand, a native son told the council that the Sioux would get the land back if they followed him; and loud voices in the community demanded no less. On the other hand, a little known white man who had won for them great victories in both Congress and the courts told them that to pursue the land in court would get them nothing and cost them a likely $105 million judgment. For the poorest people in the United States that risk was enormous.

Faced with this perilous choice, the tribal council resorted to expedience and inaction. It passed an innocuous resolution declaring, "The Black Hills are not for sale." About Lazarus's expired contract, the council did nothing.

For his part, Lazarus continued to represent Pine Ridge as he always had, contract or no contract. Pine Ridge's equivocal status as a client did not affect his prosecution of the Black Hills claim. The claim belonged to all the Teton and Yanktonai bands that had historically constituted the Sioux nation, not just to the Oglalas of Pine Ridge. Whether or not Pine Ridge participated, Lazarus and Sonosky would pursue the Black Hills claim on behalf of the other seven modern-day Sioux tribes. At the same time, until Pine Ridge stated definitively that it wanted out of the claim, Lazarus considered it his ethical duty to continue representing the tribe. Given the choice of leaving his client of twenty years unrepresented in the final stages of a fifty-five-year-old $100 million claim or of carrying on as before without a contract, Lazarus chose the latter. Unless he received orders to the contrary, or was replaced officially by another attorney, he resolved to file papers on behalf of Pine Ridge (along with the other Sioux tribes) and report the claims' progress to the tribal government.

On November 27, 1978, the Black Hills claim was argued to the Court of Claims for the fourth time. In light of the historic significance of the case and the amount of money at stake, the court once again sat *en banc*, all seven judges presiding instead of the usual three. They looked out at a sea of Sioux faces, variously skeptical, hopeful, and disdainful. Decker presented the government's case. Lazarus spoke for the Sioux. There were no surprises.

Sonosky and Lazarus both thought that the oral argument had gone well. They felt confident of three judges, Chief Judge Friedman, Senior Judge Cowen, and Judge Davis, the lone dissenter from the court's adverse 1975 opinion (and Lazarus's favorite). To prevail, the Sioux needed only one other vote.

Early in the spring of 1979, at the request of Gonzalez, Lazarus traveled to Pine Ridge to explain at an open meeting the status of the Black Hills claim and in particular his continued pursuit of a money judgment. Confronting a boisterous and hostile crowd, Lazarus tried again to explain what was possible under the white man's system and urged the Sioux to pursue the best possible result that this system would provide. He tried again to explain that while "The Black Hills are not for sale" might be an attractive political slogan, it had no real meaning in the legal world. The United States had seized title to the Black Hills in 1877. The Sioux could not "sell" the Black Hills even if they wanted to—and certainly the Black Hills claim, though it involved money, did not involve a modern-day sale of the land.

Lazarus could sympathize with the many Sioux who shouted at him in anger that the United States had no right to break Indian treaties unilaterally. Were the year 1879 instead of 1979 he would have agreed with them. But a hundred years had passed. And that hundred years, he told the Sioux, had changed everything. In the interim, the Supreme Court had handed down an unbroken line of decisions, including most notoriously *Lonewolf*, establishing as the Court wrote quite flatly in the 1870 case *Cherokee Nation* v. *Cherokee Tobacco Co.* that under the Constitution "an act of Congress may supercede a prior treaty." That Congress possessed authority to break treaties was the rule governing relations with foreign nations, the Court had noted; and it was the rule with respect to Indian treaties as well. As Lazarus consistently had informed every Sioux who would listen, to argue in any American court for the contrary proposition would be pointless.

Because the courts had no power to restore the Black Hills to tribal ownership, Lazarus advised that the best *judicial* resolution of the claim was to pursue the greatest possible monetary award. If, at the same time, the Sioux wished to pursue a land return in Congress (the one institution with power to return land), the money judgment would be no obstacle. Lazarus pointed out that the Havasupai tribe and two Pueblo tribes recently had persuaded Congress to return culturally significant lands even though all three tribes already had obtained money judgments from the commission for the loss of these lands. What might ultimately convince Congress to return part of the Black Hills, Lazarus suggested, was the power of Sioux history and the depth of their present needs, not an untenable Sioux claim to present-day ownership of the land.

The Pine Ridge audience announced in reply that it had had "enough of the white man's nonsense."

At a tribal council meeting in April, Gonzalez among others tried to get the council to pass a resolution firing Lazarus if he refused to pursue a land return in court. "It's been two years [since Lazarus's contract expired]," Gonzalez declared, "and Eagle Nest District wants something done before it's too late." But others were afraid to do anything definitive. "I am concerned about 12 people of the Tribe voting on this issue," a councilman named Wayne Tapio said. "It should be taken back to the people." Tapio's motion to table the Black Hills issue passed easily.

On June 13, 1979, the Court of Claims handed down its final

decision in the Black Hills claim. By a 5–2 majority, it affirmed the commission's 1974 decision that the 1877 act had taken the Hills in violation of the Fifth Amendment. Distinguishing *Lonewolf* as suggested by Sonosky and Lazarus, and applying the *Fort Berthold* test, the court rejected the government's argument that the 1877 act was a good faith exercise of Congress' plenary power. After a detailed review of the history behind the act, the court concluded that "there is no indication that Congress believed that, or even considered whether, the obligations it assumed to furnish the Sioux with rations until they could support themselves, con-stituted the fair equivalent of the value of the lands the United States was acquiring from them."

On the contrary,

> The terms upon which Congress acquired the Black Hills were not the product of any meaningful negotiation or arm's-length bargain-ing, and did not reflect or show any considered judgment by Con-gress that it was paying a fair price. In the "negotiations" the United States gave the Indians the Hobson's choice of ceding the Black Hills or starving. Not surprisingly, the Sioux chiefs and head men chose the former rather than the latter.

In accordance with its July 13 opinion, on July 31, 1979, the court entered a final judgment for the Sioux nation in the amount of $17,553.484, with interest at 5 percent from February 28, 1877—a total of roughly $105 million. After fifty-six years, the Sioux had won by far the largest monetary judgment ever entered against the United States in an Indian land claim, indeed the largest judgment anyone could remember in any type of claim against the government. And although $105 million might seem inadequate compensation in the light of all the Sioux had suffered and all the gold that whites had taken from the Hills, it was at least the same measure of justice (the value of the land at the time of its taking plus interest) that American courts applied when a white owner sought compensation for property that the government had taken.

While Sonosky and Lazarus were thrilled with the courts' deci-sion, out on the reservation, the huge legal victory generated mixed feelings and a great deal of confusion. "Everybody's talking about it here but we don't know what to do about it," Isadore White Hat, a fullblood from Rosebud, explained. "Right now it's awful hard to decide. A lot of people might think that we're happy that we're getting a settlement, but we're scared."

Dick Schifter tried to allay some of those fears in a personal letter to an old Sioux friend, Enos Poor Bear, a former Pine Ridge president and current council member. If the Sioux wanted land, Schifter suggested, they should use the judgment money to *buy* it. "There is enough money there to buy back all the alienated land in Shannon County," Schifter estimated, "and to make quite a number of purchases in Bennett county as well."

In many Sioux minds, however, there could be no substitute for the Black Hills themselves. Those Hills and the claim arising for their theft had come to symbolize all things Sioux, especially the tribe's sustaining myth that they had never given in to the white man's deceits. Whether described as "selling the Hills" or merely agreeing to "settle" the claim for their taking, to accept the Court of Claims verdict would be to end forever their century-old grievance against the United States and diminish their status as still defiant victims of its expansion. The Sioux defined themselves in no small part by that status and they trembled at the possibility of change.

"What will happen to us if we sell the Black Hills?" White Hat wondered. "If we accept [the judgment], the Black Hills are gone. After the Black Hills, are the reservations next? We have to think of our kids. If we sell them out, where will they go? Our culture, our tradition, our customs will just evaporate."

In early September, Lazarus returned to Sioux country to present the tribe with a settlement offer from the government in its other major claim against the United States, the 1868 treaty case. In the last decade of complex litigation, Sonosky and Lazarus had convinced the commission to correct its own erroneous boundary determination of the Sioux 1851 Fort Laramie lands, largely defeated an overlapping claim of the Yankton Sioux, and obtained a favorable $44 million valuation of the lands and interests acquired by the United States under the 1868 treaty. By the summer of 1979, the lawyers had convinced the Justice Department to reduce its $57 million in claimed offsets to a mere $4.2 million.

To litigate further, Sonosky and Lazarus calculated, would be counterproductive. Until the entry of final judgment the Sioux would receive no interest on their potential award (this was a noninterest-bearing unconscionable consideration claim). Since litigating the offsets issue would probably take several years, the tribe would lose money even if it succeeded in eliminating all the government's claimed expenditures. Pure logic dictated that the Sioux should agree to the $39,949,700 settlement figure that the government was now offering.

But neither the political leadership nor the militants in Sioux country had any interest in a monetary settlement of tribal claims, regardless of the context. Unlike the Black Hills claim, the 1868 treaty case did not involve even a potential conflict between land and money. In the 1868 treaty case, Sonosky and Lazarus had merely proven that under the 1868 treaty, which the Sioux agreed was valid, the government had undercompensated the Sioux for the lands and rights it had acquired. The $39.9 million settlement offer was for all practical purposes found money for the Sioux—an extra payment to make amends for a 110-year-old unconscionable deal.

In Sioux country, however, the distinctions between the Black Hills claim and the 1868 treaty case disappeared under an avalanche of angry rhetoric. Money was a sellout. Land was sacred— and none of it was "for sale." On Pine Ridge, no quorum even assembled to consider the settlement proposal. At Rosebud, Sonosky confronted a hostile crowd of perhaps 500 Sioux who cursed him, slashed his car's tires, and threatened to beat him up. Both he and Lazarus left the reservations under police escort. More than half the Sioux tribes rejected the settlement. Sonosky and Lazarus returned to Washington to litigate the offsets issue and watch their clients deprive themselves of roughly $100,000 per week in interest.

While the settlement talks soured, Sonosky and Lazarus waited to see whether the Justice Department would seek Supreme Court review of the Court of Claims Black Hills ruling. The decision whether to appeal rested with Solictor General Wade McCree, whose office represents the United States in the Supreme Court. The solicitor's office determines which cases the United States will appeal to the Court and also what legal positions the United States will take in those cases and any others before the Court in which the United States has an interest. By long tradition, the solicitor's office has served as a so-called Tenth Justice, not merely evaluating what legal positions might win cases for the United States, but also advocating to the Court in a less adversarial sense what the law ought to be, regardless of U.S. interest in a particular litigation.

Appealing to this aspect of the solicitor's function, in mid-August Sonosky and Lazarus wrote McCree urging him to forego an appeal in the Black Hills claim. The government's case, they observed, rested on a sweeping view of *Lonewolf* that seventy-six years of intervening history had rendered obsolete. The solicitor's office, Sonosky and Lazarus suggested, should not adopt the unseemly position of asking the Supreme Court to reverse the Court of Claims based on an ancient decision that reflected discredited racial attitudes and a long-since abandoned judicial deference to Congress. Putting to rest a fifty-six-year-old claim would serve justice with no shame. "The Department of Justice has presented a skilled and vigorous defense to the claim at all stages of these proceedings," Sonosky and Lazarus assured McCree. "We suggest, though, that the time now has come to let the matter rest."

On October 17, 1979, Sonosky and Lazarus received their answer. The solicitor general filed at the Supreme Court a petition for a writ of *certiorari* asking the Court to overturn the 1979 Court of Claims decision. In an effort to convince the Supreme Court that the Black Hills claim warranted its attention, the solicitor alleged the Court of Claims decision was "inconsistent with *Lonewolf*," which (in his view) held that "whenever the operative statute 'purport[s] to give an adequate consideration' for the lands appropriated, the courts 'must presume that Congress had acted in perfect good faith. . . .' " Here, the government claimed, the court had not only given *Lonewolf* an excessively narrow reading, but had even reversed *Lonewolf*'s presumption of good faith and "attributed bad faith to Congress simply because it failed expressly to say that it was giving fair value for the lands appropriated."

The Sioux, the government argued, had received unwarranted special treatment by the court. "It may not seem like equal justice," the solicitor suggested, "if the present claimants, who received benefits far exceeding the value of the lands involved but were exceptionally excused from offsets, are allowed to recover by way of interest many times the value of what they lost." And this special treatment came at an extraordinary price. "[T]he present decision creates a precedent that may well embarrass future litigation, at very substantial cost to the national treasury. It ought not stand unreviewed."

Sonosky and Lazarus were nonplused by the government's petition and found it unpersuasive. For all the reasons stated many times before over the last decade, they considered the government's reliance on *Lonewolf* misplaced—and so told the Supreme Court in their response to the petition. Although the government justified its petition as furthering "equal justice," Sonosky and Lazarus countered that the rule of law proposed by the government would deny Indian tribes precisely that. They reminded the Supreme Court that the "standard rule in just compensation cases is . . . that the owner of acquired property has a right to receive its fair market value as of the date of the taking, plus interest as a measure of just compensation. . . . [The United States] proposes a new rule saying, in effect, that the United States owes a significantly lesser constitutional duty to Indians, for whom it acts as trustee, then it owes to other citizens, for whom it has no special obligations."

The Court of Claims ruling, Sonosky and Lazarus asserted, was nothing other than a highly fact-specific application of the *Fort Berthold* test, a ruling with virtually no reach beyond the unique circumstances from which it arose. The United States, they continued, should not be permitted to vest the case "with a significance it does not possess," by alleging that the Sioux judgment " 'represents a substantial and unwarranted charge against the public fisc and invites like awards in other pending cases'. . . . The lesson to be learned from such a situation is that the United States should pay its debts on time, not that the victims of delay should be denied their Fifth Amendment rights."

With the filing of Sonosky and Lazarus's response, the waiting started while for a third time the Supreme Court considered a petition for *certiorari* in the Black Hills claim. On November 21, the clerk of the Supreme Court scheduled the claim (*United States v. Sioux Nation of Indians*, No. 79-639) for consideration at the justices' regular Friday decisionmaking conference set for December 7. His office then circulated to the chambers of each of the nine justices the solicitor general's petition together with the Sioux response.

Each justice (usually in consultation with a law clerk assistant) individually evaluates the merits of a petition for *certiorari*. Nonetheless, given the enormous task of selecting about 150 cases for full consideration from approximately 5000 applications that the Court receives every term, a majority of the justices pool their resources to expedite the process of evaluating whether to grant review in an individual case. Rather than having each justice consider every case completely independently, a clerk for one justice in the "cert. pool" circulates an advisory memorandum to all the justices in the pool. This pool memo summarizes a case and assesses whether it is "certworthy"—that is, whether it raises a sufficiently important and controversial issue to merit Supreme Court review. Although the justices in the cert. pool do not follow pool memo recommendations slavishly, in practice the memos carry great weight. (At the time of *Sioux Nation*, Chief Justice Warren Burger and Associate Justices Byron White, Potter Stewart, Lewis Powell, Harry Blackmun, and William Rehnquist belonged to the pool. Associate Justices William Brennan, Thurgood Marshall, and John Paul Stevens did not).

The pool memo assignment in the Black Hills claim fell to one of the clerks of the Chief Justice. In his one-paragraph discussion section, the Chief's clerk agreed with the solicitor general that the Supreme Court's previous decisions requiring the payment of just compensation for the taking of tribal lands (such as *Shoshone*) dealt solely with instances "in which no payment was made or inadequate payment after the fact was made." Accordingly, the clerk concluded that the Black Hills claim presented a novel issue, "whether acquisition of Indian land for present but inadequate compensation constitutes a taking." And, in his opinion, the case also presented the Court with a useful opportunity to revisit *Lonewolf* and reach a more contemporary understanding of Congress's plenary power over Indian affairs. The clerk cautioned that the Court might want to pass on the case if the justices were inclined merely to adopt the same *Fort Berthold*-type standard applied by the Court of Claims. Overall, however, he advised that "the case seems certworthy."

At their December 7 conference (a closed-door session where the justices exchange views and vote on cases) at least four (the number required to grant a petition) either agreed with Schechtman or for other reasons considered the Black Hills claim to be certworthy. On December 10, the Court announced that it was granting the solicitor general's petition. As is its unvarying custom, the Court did not announce why.

For Sonosky and Lazarus, the Court's action was extremely disheartening. The Sioux had no place to go but down. And as Sonosky and Lazarus knew, as they were no doubt celebrating over in the solicitor general's office, the Supreme Court rarely grants a petition for *certiorari* merely to affirm the decision of the court below. Several Justices must have disapproved (at least preliminarily) of the Court of Claims disposition of the Black Hills claim. Lazarus worried that the justices had balked at the size of the Sioux judgment—that the Black Hills claim would mimic the *Tuscarora* case and the Indians would lose, regardless of the law, because of money.

Ralph Case always had insisted that the Supreme Court would ultimately decide the Black Hills claim and that the Sioux would prevail. Sonosky and Lazarus prayed that, for once, he would prove right.

▼ ▼ ▼ ▼ ▼

SIXTEEN

THE HIGHEST COURT
IN THE LAND

"ON THE WHOLE," wrote Vine Deloria, Jr., lawyer, best-selling author, and caustic critic of American society, "the [Supreme] Court has been a friend, not a foe, and the last bastion of sympathetic understanding in the American political system available to the tribes."

The origins of this sympathetic understanding date to the seminal decisions of the 1820s and 1830s: *Johnson* v. *McIntosh, Cherokee Nation* v. *Georgia,* and *Worcester* v. *Georgia.* In these cases, Chief Justice John Marshall established the foundation for what would become the defining principle of tribal sovereignty, that Indian tribes constitute self-governing "domestic dependent nations," retaining all sovereign powers not necessarily incompatible with their subordinate status or expressly divested by Congress. Indian tribes, Marshall declared, possess largely autonomous governments subject to overriding federal authority but generally free from the control of individual states.

Marshall's pronouncements about Indian self-government, though, lay mostly dormant for more than a century. Although the Court never repudiated his landmark opinions, their larger promise of significant tribal autonomy yielded first to the exigencies of military conquest, then to the national drive for Indian assimilation and total federal control of Indian life.

During this dormancy the Court developed competing doctrines far less solicitous of tribal governments, subverting tribal sovereignty whenever federal policy demanded. At the height of the movement to eradicate Indian life, the Court (always having recognized federal responsibility for Indians) put its imprimatur on the sweeping power of the federal government to manipulate tribal property and eliminate tribal sovereignty. In cases like *Lonewolf* and *United States* v. *Kagama* (1886), the Court recognized Congress's seemingly limitless power to break consensual treaties through unilateral federal legislation and to substitute federal authority for tribal authority whenever it deemed it wise. "These Indian tribes *are* wards of the nation," the Court stressed in *Kagama.* "They are communities *dependent* on the United States," and therefore subject to its power.

Thus, while the Court sometimes upheld tribal interests against competing claims of state and local governments (most notably in water and fishing rights decisions), and even ruled against the federal government on a rare occasion like the *Shoshone* case of the mid-1930s, the Court's "sympathetic understanding" of tribal rights did not significantly reassert itself until the twilight of termination policy in the early 1960s. Only after Congress reinvigorated tribal governments, and only after tribal governments themselves sought to reexert their sovereignty, did the Court (itself having become more assertive in establishing and protecting the rights of minorities) seriously address the task of defining the scope of those powers possessed by Chief Justice Marshall's "domestic dependent nations."

In the 1960s, as tribes laid claim to fishing and water rights and as they resisted state regulation of various sorts, federal courts became the battleground for determining the reach of tribal governments and the right of tribes to resist the competing power of individual states. And in the 1970s, the legal tug-of-war between Indian tribes and state governments intensified as tribes more boldly experimented with their powers of taxation and sought to exercise civil and criminal jurisdiction over all persons within their reservations.

Similarly, the resurgence of tribal governments and new federal programs promoting self-determination set the stage for a judicial reexamination of the relationship between Indians and the federal government. In the late 60s and 70s, Congress passed the Indian Civil Rights Act, effectively ending termination; the Indian Self-Determination and Educational Assistance Act, fostering Indian control of their children's schooling; and the Indian Child Welfare Act, which promoted "the stability and security of Indian Tribes and families." By 1980, Congress was appropriating as much as $2 billion annually for tribal programs, while a new congressional commission (the American Indian Policy Review Commission) recommended even larger contributions to tribal welfare and even broader recognition of tribal sovereignty. In keeping with these political changes in Indian policy, legal advocates for the tribes laid siege to timeworn doctrines based on (and perpetuating) notions of Indian wardship and impotence.

On most of the newly emerging Indian law issues the Supreme Court acted as final arbiter. Despite its reputed dislike of Indian law cases—forays into an often arcane and hermetic field—the Supreme Court decided thirty-five such cases in the 1970s. The Indians, as Deloria's assessment reflects, fared well. In case after case, the Court struck down state efforts to tax reservation property or the income of reservation Indians and businesses. On three separate occasions, it blocked discriminatory state regulations that impinged on tribal fishing rights. In numerous other cases, the Court upheld either inherent tribal authority to govern Indians on the reservation or federal statutes delegating to tribes on-reservation authority over civil matters such as the regulation of alcoholic beverages.

The tribes did not always prevail. In a major 1978 decision, *Oliphant* v. *Suquamish Indian Tribe,* the Court denied tribes any criminal jurisdiction over non-Indians, a ruling that indicated its reluctance to allow Indians to govern whites even within reservations. Still, the tribes won so often that Court clerks joked that two things were certain about Indian cases: the Indians would win and either Justice Marshall or Justice Blackmun, their two most sympathetic arbiters, would write the opinion.

The Black Hills claim was the seventh Indian case that the Court had agreed to hear before June 1980, the end of its 1979 term. In February, the government and the Sioux both filed their briefs, restaging yet again old debates over case law and history.

Once more the government rested its case principally on *Lonewolf*'s command that the judicial branch "must presume that Congress acted in perfect good faith in [its] dealings with the Indians." The lesson of *Lonewolf* and other similar early twentieth-century cases, the government alleged, was that "Congress must be assumed to be acting within its plenary power to manage tribal assets [as opposed to exercising its eminent domain power] if it reasonably can be concluded that the legislation was intended to promote the welfare of the tribe." In enacting the 1877 act, the government urged, Congress clearly had acted within the scope of this plenary power. No Fifth Amendment violation had occurred and, consequently, the Sioux were not entitled to interest on their $17.5 million Black Hills award. (For reasons left unexplained in its brief the government challenged only the interest portion of the Court of Claims award. Apparently the solicitor was conceding the validity of the 1975 Court of Claims ruling that awarded the Sioux $17.5 million, without interest, on the ground of "dishonorable dealings.")

Lazarus (who had taken over primary responsibility for prosecuting the claim) and Sonosky countered that *Lonewolf* provided no guidance at all on the Fifth Amendment question at issue in the Black Hills claim. As before, they relied on *Shoshone* and its legal progeny as establishing that "the Fifth Amendment applies on exactly the same basis to a treaty-recognized Indian reservation as any other lands and property in the United States." When Congress takes such property, it must pay just compensation, regardless of good faith.

In applying their respective legal principles, the government lawyers and Sonosky and Lazarus also reenacted their debate over the history behind and intent of the 1877 act. According to the government, in exchanging the Black Hills for a promise of rations and additional grazing land, "the United States was sensitive to the need to give the Sioux a just equivalent for the Hills."

Moreover, even if the rations were not an exact *quid pro quo* for the Hills, the 1877 act was still a legitimate exercise of Congress's plenary power to manage tribal affairs. In administering the Sioux estate, the government argued, "Congress need not [have] insist-[ed] on prior proof of precise economic equivalence before responding on behalf of the tribe to meet [an] emergency." Rather, "Congress was entitled to conclude that [the crisis] facing the Sioux would best be solved and the welfare of the Sioux best promoted by the cession of the Black Hills to the United States in exchange for a long-term commitment to supply food and a plan calculated to lead them to independence." The 1877 act, the government concluded, effected precisely this mutually beneficial exchange—an exchange according to which the government supplied the Sioux with $43 million or more worth of rations, an amount far greater than the value of the Hills.

Sonosky and Lazarus, in turn, took direct aim at the government's we-did-it-for-their-own-good defense of the 1877 act. Their counterhistory attempted to show not only that Congress had made no effort to pay the Sioux full value for the Black Hills in 1877, but also that, as the Court of Claims had twice concluded, the government's conduct towards the Sioux constituted in all probability " 'the most ripe and rank case of dishonorable dealings' " in U.S. history. The so-called consideration provided under the 1877 act, specifically the rations, were neither payment for land nor a reasonable emergency measure to save the Sioux from starvation. On the contrary, having pursued a "western settlement policy which was destroying the buffalo herds upon which [the tribe's] very existence depended," the government used the promise of rations as a very big stick in its "attempt to coerce the Sioux into capitulating to congressional demands." To argue otherwise, Sonosky and Lazarus wrote, was unconscionable.

Despite the familiarity of these disputes to the parties, from the Court's perspective the Black Hills claim was anything but stale. Underlying the competing views of history and precedent presented in the briefs lay legal questions of broad and enduring significance. To decide the Black Hills claim, the Court necessarily would have to determine the contemporary validity of cases such as *Lonewolf* or *Kagama*, predicated on the status of Indians as (in *Kagama*'s words) "remnants of a race once powerful, now weak." A full generation into the era of racial equality under the law that the Court itself had ushered in with its 1954 decision in *Brown* v. *Board of Education*, it would have to decide whether Indian lands should be subject to a different degree of Fifth Amendment protection than that afforded the property of every other landowner in America. And, forty-five years into the era of Indian self-determination, the Court would have to declare whether Congress could play by special (and uniquely lenient) rules in its treatment of tribes for whom it remained trustee.

Oral argument in *United States* v. *Sioux Nation of Indians* commenced at 11:02 A.M. on Monday, March 24, 1980. At the front of the velvet-draped chamber, on a raised dais behind an imposing, dark mahogany bench, sat the nine black-robed high priests of American law: Chief Justice Burger, and in order of seniority, Brennan, Stewart, White, Marshall, Powell, Blackmun, Rehnquist, and Stevens. They looked out on a full courtroom, clerks posted between the marble columns on the left, journalists in the pews to the right, lawyers straight before them at gleaming mahogany tables flanking a small lectern.

In the public gallery toward the rear, behind a polished brass rail, the usual mix of tourists, students, friends, and family members of the advocates listened intently as Chief Justice Burger announced the case. Among them were many Sioux faces, none friendly to Sonosky and Lazarus, or at least none that they remember. High above their heads, directly in the justices' view, a large frieze depicted a mythological battle between the forces of "Good" and "Evil."

At the solicitor general's customary position immediately to the right of the lectern, Deputy Solicitor Louis Claiborne rose to argue on behalf of the United States. Claiborne was a living legend in the solicitor's office, great-great-great-grandson of the first non-French governor of Louisiana, educated in Europe, a man of enormous offhand charm, with a reputation for absolute dedication to arguing solely for what he thought right and proper in the law.

Claiborne had come to the solicitor's office by an odd route. In his first appearance before the Supreme Court in 1959 (a few months prior to Lazarus's debut), as a young private practitioner from Louisiana, he had caught the eye of Justice Felix Frankfurter, who appointed himself guardian angel of Claiborne's career. Frankfurter arranged a clerkship with a respected federal district court judge in New Orleans; later, in 1962, the justice practically ordered Solicitor General Archibald Cox to hire Claiborne as an assistant. Claiborne remained in the solicitor's office into the Nixon administration, an unusually long stint. Then, for both personal and political reasons, he departed for his wife's native England, where he became a full-fledged barrister.

Claiborne's expatriation was short-lived. By the mid-70s, he began summering in the solicitor's office, filling in for vacationing attorneys. In 1978 he returned fulltime. British manner and accent tempering his southern roots, Claiborne assumed primary responsibility for Indian cases.

As the government's Supreme Court lawyer on Indian matters, Claiborne almost always found himself arrayed on the Indians' side, counsel to the trustee arguing in favor of tribal sovereignty or other tribal rights. In that sense, his participation in the Black Hills claim was a notable departure, especially because as a senior lawyer in the solicitor's office, he easily could have ducked the Sioux claim had he so desired. But Claiborne was quite comfortable with the government's legal position. Despite his consistent sympathy for Indian rights, he felt strongly that the Court of Claims had treated the Sioux with unique and unwarranted preference.

As Claiborne parsed the cases, the Court of Claims had blatantly reversed *Lonewolf*'s required presumption of congressional good faith in its handling of Indian property, erroneously placing the burden on the United States to prove congressional beneficence in passing the 1877 act. The result, Claiborne believed, was an inequitable ruling that permitted the Sioux, for the first time ever in an Indian case, to recover just compensation under the Fifth Amendment, in a circumstance where (unlike the *Shoshone* line of cases)

Congress had provided substantial consideration for appropriated lands.

In Claiborne's view, moreover, the 1877 act had saved the Sioux from certain starvation at the sole expense of Black Hills lands that armed parties of miners and settlers surely would have taken from the tribe regardless. In other words, had Congress done nothing in 1877—instead of providing the Sioux with rations and grazing land—the Indians would have lost the Black Hills anyway and received no consideration at all. Claiborne did not understand how Congress's basically humanitarian intervention could give rise to a just compensation claim.

Confident that the United States "had an overwhelming case on the law," Claiborne stepped to the lectern and in resonant voice started his argument with the universal catechism of Supreme Court advocates: "Mr. Chief Justice and may it please the Court."

Claiborne proceeded only two full sentences before Justices Stewart and Stevens barraged him with questions from an unanticipated direction. They could not fathom why the government had challenged only the interest portion of the Court of Claims Sioux award (roughly $85 million that stemmed from the court's finding of a Fifth Amendment violation), meanwhile conceding the validity of the Court of Claims ruling that the United States owed the Sioux $17.5 million for "dishonorable dealings" in appropriating the Black Hills. If, as the government argued in its brief, the 1877 act overpaid the Sioux for their land, why should the government accept liability for dishonorable dealings in taking the land? And, conversely, if the government accepted liability for dishonorable dealings, how could it assert congressional good faith as a defense against the tribe's Fifth Amendment claim?

Claiborne blamed the apparent inconsistency on "the peculiar circumstances" of Congress's 1975 food, rations, and provisions amendment to the ICC. Had Congress not eliminated rations as legal offsets, the government would have wiped out the $17.5 million dishonorable dealings award, the government would have no outstanding judgment against it, and no inconsistency would arise.

As Justice Stewart in particular seemed to feel, Claiborne's explanation rang hollow. Although Congress prohibited the deduction of rations from the Sioux award, it did not prohibit the Court of Claims from taking account of the promised rations when assessing whether the government was guilty of "dishonorable dealings" with the Sioux. In awarding the Sioux $17.5 million for dishonorable dealings, the court evidently concluded that the government's conduct towards the Sioux was reprehensible regardless of the ration payments. Thus, the government's acquiescence to that ruling did conflict with Claiborne's argument that the 1877 act was not only honorable but generous.

Unfortunately for Claiborne, his initial exchange with Stewart and Stevens consumed more than five minutes of his allotted half-hour and threw the deputy solicitor off stride. Like a race horse jostled at the starting gate, Claiborne took a while to settle himself and never recovered the lost ground.

Even when he found his rhythm, he encountered surprising hostility from the bench. Justice Blackmun scoffed at Claiborne's discussion of the government's allegedly substantial efforts to keep miners out of the Black Hills. With faintly veiled sarcasm, Blackmun found the exchange of letters between Generals Sherman and Sheridan discussing Grant's secret decision to end such efforts "of profound interest as to how serious the government's attempt to prevent the miners' influx was."

Here and there, Claiborne made his points, stressing especially the Court of Claims misreading of *Lonewolf* and its mischaracterization of Black Hills history. Whenever possible, Claiborne emphasized what he evidently considered the government's strongest argument: its overpayment for the Hills in the form of rations. Thus, when Chief Justice Burger asked how much money the rations amounted to over time, Claiborne responded at length.

> There is the figure of $57 million which is based upon General Accounting Office reports once upon a time conceded by former counsel for the Sioux. . . . There is a finding by the Court of Claims itself in 1942 when this case first reached that court that as of 1942 the total amount had reached $42 million. Even allowing for discount, considering that the payments in the first twenty years exceeded or averaged something over $1 million it is evident that the U.S. not only paid interest but repaid the principal [on the Black Hills] long before 1942.

In light of these payments, Claiborne contended, the Court could not possibly fit the Black Hills claim within the category of cases in which it previously had found a Fifth Amendment taking to have occurred—cases where "the government made . . . no payment whatever, or the most derisory one."

At 11:30, Claiborne reserved the remaining few minutes of his time for rebuttal and sat down.

Lazarus rose to address the Court. No less than Claiborne, he believed that the law was irrefutably on his side. He also agreed with Sonosky's preargument assessment that "the Sioux simply had too many good facts going for them to lose."

Despite Lazarus and Sonosky's shared confidence about their case, the strain of appearing before the Court had injected a rare discordant note in their relationship. After Lazarus had submitted the Sioux brief to the Court, Sonosky's two partners, Reid Chambers and Harry Sachse (undoubtedly speaking for Sonosky as well), had approached Lazarus about the possibility of hiring a Supreme Court expert to handle oral argument in the claim. They proposed Archibald Cox, the former solicitor general and Watergate special prosecutor fired by President Nixon in the so-called Saturday Night Massacre. Cox personified the legal conscience of the nation. Who better to charge the government with betraying its trust to the Sioux?

Lazarus hid his anger. Waiting a few days, he called Sonosky's office to let Chambers and Sachse know that, having succeeded in the litigation to this point, he would see the claim to the end.

In any event, Lazarus prepared for this oral argument like no other in his life. For the first time in his career, he developed an outline in advance and distributed typed copies to other lawyers, Sonosky and his partners, for comment.

As he approached the lectern to address the Supreme Court for the first time since *Tuscarora*, Lazarus stood at the height of his professional career. In 1974, Fried, Frank (now one of the nation's leading law firms) had named him managing partner of its rapidly expanding Washington office. As the head (together with Dick Schifter) of the nation's premier Indian law practice, Lazarus took special pride in having trained a roster of successful young attorneys, including an increasing number of Native Americans. In 1979, his protégé Richard West, a member of the Cheyenne tribe, was elected to the Fried, Frank partnership, becoming the first Indian partner at a major firm. As for Lazarus's legal prowess, a long-time partner recalls how colleagues beheld him with "something approaching awe" for the "singularly organized, all-encompassing, and creative intelligence" that he brought to bear on legal problems.

Facing the Court, Lazarus presented a sharp contrast to Claiborne. Where the tall and implacable deputy solicitor argued coolly, the much smaller and more expressive Lazarus responded to the justices' questions in a voice tense with conviction, abandoning his usual reserve. Through dozens of exchanges, he never strayed far from his central theme, that Congress had taken the Black Hills in exchange for only promises, not payment; and that for Indian tribes and white people alike promises do not constitute just compensation under the law. "[A] kewpie in war paint," one journalist reported, Lazarus "mounted his rhetorical horse and rode loudly and menacingly through Claiborne's argument."

Justice Rehnquist, the Court's most conservative member, took up the government's cause, challenging Lazarus with a series of hypothetical situations—a law professor leading an unwitting student into a deep legal thicket. But Lazarus had scouted this territory for twenty-three years. He knew where the brambles lay and the clear paths.

Q: Well, what if Congress had simply said instead of trying to take back the 800 square miles consisting of the Black Hills, "We have a lot of demands on our resources and our Army can't protect you Sioux tribes, but we concede it is your property and you fight off the individual white citizens that come in looking for gold as best you can"?

A: Well, that would have been—that would have been allowable self-help, except under the 1868 Treaty the Sioux had promised to maintain peace and the Sioux did maintain peace and it was the United States that broke the peace. It was the United States that sent Custer on the reservation to publicize that there was gold. As soon as the gold was publicized the whites invaded the reservation. That was a violation of Article 2 of the—

Q: But now what if the invasion had been simply by white citizens having no connection with the government?

A: The Government had a treaty commitment to keep them out. Under the 1868 Treaty the United States promised to keep whites out of the Great Sioux Reservation and it had a military obligation to do so. . . .

Q: You stated that the construction of the treaty made it an absolute obligation to keep the whites out no matter what the demands on the Federal Treasury and no matter what Congress would have appropriated?

A: Yes, until the United States changed that treaty, that was its obligation. And I would point out to Your Honor that the United States always found enough troops to round up Indians. Its only trouble was finding enough troops to round up white people.

Q: Well, take the situation of say something completely divorced from Indians, a local county or city government. And if it were to devote 90 percent of its tax dollars to increasing the police force it could prevent any burglaries. It instead has any number of demands on those resources so it only appropriates 20 percent. Therefore, there are burglaries in the area which depreciate the value of the property and put pressure on people to sell, perhaps.

Now, does that amount to a "taking"?

A: Your Honor, let us assume your hypothetical.

First, the United States created this crisis; it wasn't the Indians who created it, it was the United States that created it. The United States took the bulk of the Sioux land under the 1868 Treaty and . . . paid them $40 million less than the land was worth. As a result of that they started impoverished; that was the fault of the United States. And the United States kept them from their hunting grounds, so they became dependent on the United States for food.

Then, the United States first encouraged the miners to come in and then withdrew the troops. Then, the United States rounded up the Sioux and put them on the reservation and took their guns and horses so they couldn't hunt. And there we had this crisis that the United States created.

Now, let us assume the United States didn't have enough money to handle that crisis other than to take the Black Hills away from the Sioux, which is exactly what it did. All we say is, "O.K., pay us." And that is what the United States did not do.

Moments later, Chief Justice Burger merely wanted to know "how many Sioux are there now?" Lazarus responded with what he had intended as his peroration.

Your honor, there are 60,000 or more Sioux now. They are at the very bottom of the economic ladder even compared to other Indians. The Sioux are among the most depressed people in the entire United States and they are so depressed, not in least part, because the United States in 1877 took their most valuable asset, the Black Hills, and hasn't paid for it yet.

As his time expired, Lazarus improvised a new closing. Twenty-six years earlier, as lead attorney for the NAACP, future Justice Thurgood Marshall had argued to the Court in *Brown* v. *Board of Education* that "the Constitution is color blind." Lazarus, fixing his gaze directly on Marshall, invented a new twist to the Justice's famous appeal.

I suggest to you, Your Honors, that you should not think of the amount of money involved. The Constitution is not only color blind, it is dollar blind; and we are entitled to just compensation under every single ruling of this Court and the Court of Claims should be affirmed.

But Justice Stevens would not let Lazarus retire. Lazarus had argued that, under the *Shoshone* line of cases, the Sioux, like every other property owner, were entitled to just compensation regardless of congressional good faith. He had not once mentioned the *Fort Berthold* good faith test that the Court of Claims had applied. Justice Stevens wanted to know why.

"Your Honor," Lazarus responded, "our basic position is that you do not have to reach the rationale of the Court of Claims, because the good faith test, in our opinion, is not a valid test. If you applied the good faith test . . . we win anyway, because as [the Court of Claims] said there was no good faith."

The Court broke for lunch, postponing Claiborne's rebuttal for one hour. During the recess, the deputy solicitor mustered some of the fire that had seemed deliberately absent from his morning presentation. He opened the afternoon session with an angry rejoinder: "It ill behooves the Sioux Nation—who at least since 1920 have been very much the special favorites of the law—to put themselves in the shoes of a white claimant who would not be here having been barred by limitations, *res judicata*, estoppel by the admission of counsel, setoffs. . . ."

In the lawyers' section of the gallery, Sonosky's partner, Reid Chambers gnashed his teeth as the Court permitted a rejuvenated Claiborne to restate his case for governmental good faith and reemphasize the tens of millions of dollars of ration payments that the government allegedly had made to the Sioux. Chambers wished that Lazarus had shortened his argument in order to force Claiborne to issue his rebuttal before lunch. In the heat of argument, that strategy had never even crossed Lazarus's mind.

At 1:10 P.M., the Chief Justice called the argument to a close.

On the next Wednesday, March 26, the Justices convened to decide the Black Hills claim. Chief Justice Burger, obviously discomfited by the case, opened the discussion. Burger reminded his colleagues that he had voted against reviewing the Court of Claims decision to begin with. Having been denied that option, he leaned towards affirming the Court of Claims, albeit tentatively. The Chief Justice thought that the lower court's ruling might be erroneous, but not so clearly erroneous as to warrant reversal.

Justice Brennan, the next senior Justice, followed the Chief with roughly similar sentiments. He thought the factual record sufficient to support the Court of Claims decision. He, too, therefore, voted to affirm—though not adamantly.

Justice Stewart was more certain. Notwithstanding *Lonewolf,* in his view the 1877 act constituted a Fifth Amendment taking which, in turn, entitled the Sioux to interest on their $17.5 million award.

Justice White voted to affirm as well. He did not think that the same legal test necessarily applied to the taking of tribal property as to the taking of white-owned property. Still, because Congress had made no effort to pay a fair price for the Black Hills, the 1877 act did constitute a Fifth Amendment taking. White, too, reached this conclusion reluctantly. He invited the other Justices to talk him out of his vote.

Justice Marshall voted to affirm and declined to comment further.

Justice Powell, the Court's soft-spoken Virginia patrician, was also brief. He considered the whole Black Hills business to be a series of U.S. bungles, including a violation of Congress's Fifth Amendment duty to provide just compensation for taken lands. Powell voted to affirm.

Justice Blackmun injected a new theme into the discussion, returning to a point he had raised at oral argument. Blackmun had asked Claiborne whether Congress's 1978 *res judicata* waiver, which appeared to overrule the 1942 Court of Claims decision in the Black Hills claim, violated the separation of powers doctrine. (North Carolina Congressman Gudger had opposed the bill on precisely this ground.) Responding to Blackmun, Claiborne had conceded Congress's power to waive the *res judicata* defense. "Congress," Claiborne ventured, "is entitled to say, 'You may have another opportunity to litigate your lawsuit.' " Blackmun was inclined to agree, but he found the issue troubling.

The Justice did not, however, find the Fifth Amendment issue such a close call. He found unconvincing Claiborne's contention that the United States acted in the tribe's best interest. And he thought that intervening cases had cut back substantially on *Lonewolf*'s continuing validity. Blackmun saw no reason to presume congressional good faith. He voted to affirm.

Justice Rehnquist raised the first dissenting voice. Amplifying Justice Blackmun's separation of powers concerns, Rehnquist agreed with Congressman Gudger that in enacting the *res judicata* waiver Congress had crossed the boundary of its legislative function and unconstitutionally usurped judicial power. He voted to vacate or reverse the Court of Claims on separation of powers grounds.

Justice Stevens, the junior Justice and last to speak, observed that the government had failed to argue for reversal on separation of powers grounds. He wanted to consider the issue further. Regarding the Fifth Amendment question, Stevens found the controlling precedent to be Justice Cardozo's opinion in *Shoshone*. The 1877 act was a plain taking. Stevens voted to affirm.

With the preliminary vote standing at 8–1 in favor of affirmance, the prerogative of assigning the opinion fell to Chief Justice Burger as the senior Justice in the majority. He asked Justice Blackmun to assume the unenviable job of holding together a coalition of eight Justices that included at least three (and perhaps more) doubting Thomases and which had come to no agreement about what legal theory to apply to the case.

On April 7, Justice Rehnquist circulated a memo calculated to exacerbate Blackmun's difficulties. Rehnquist reported that he had done some further looking into the separation of powers question and that these investigations had confirmed his earlier view that Congress had improperly tampered with the workings of the judicial branch. Rehnquist announced his intention to circulate a written dissent on this point in due course.

To those Justices uncomfortable with the $105 million Sioux award who, nonetheless, believed that the 1877 act constituted a taking, Rehnquist's memo pointed to a graceful exit from their legal predicament. If Congress had violated the separation of powers doctrine in enacting the *res judicata* waiver, then the Court could overturn the Court of Claims judgment without damaging the fabric of Fifth Amendment takings law.

Justice Powell quickly signaled his willingness to walk that path. "Quite apart from the large sum of money involved in this particular case," he wrote on April 10,

> I have wondered whether our decisions will establish a precedent that will give rise to similar claims from Indian tribes that—over the past century or more—may have been persuaded or coerced to surrender lands under circumstances that now would be viewed as a taking.
>
> In sum, if Bill Rehnquist's further study indicates that there is indeed a substantial constitutional question as to congressional power, I could vote for a reargument on this issue.

Justice Blackmun had been doing some further study of his own. The next day, April 11, he circulated a response to both the Rehnquist and Powell memorandums, addressing the merits of the separation of powers issue.

According to Blackmun's research, whether Congress had exceeded its constitutional authority depended mainly on an interpretation of the Court's decision in *United States* v. *Klein*, a 108-year-old case arising out of the social and political turmoil following the Civil War. The *Klein* case started as a suit by the heirs of V. F. Wilson, a southerner whose cotton crop (664 bales) had been seized as "captured and abandoned property" and sold by U.S. Treasury agents in the summer of 1863. The heirs sued the United States in the Court of Claims for recovery of the cotton proceeds ($125,300). They argued that the Abandoned and Captured Property Act of 1863 provided for such a recovery upon proof that the owner had "never given any aid or comfort to the present rebellion." As proof of this required loyalty, the heirs introduced into evidence a presidential pardon which, in return for an oath of loyalty to the Union, promised "unconditionally and without reservation" to restore all "rights of property as before." In light of Wilson's pardon, the Court of Claims held that the heirs were entitled to recover the $125,300.

The United States, however, moved the Supreme Court to dismiss the claim in accordance with a 1871 statute amending the rules for ex-Confederates seeking property restoration in the Court of Claims. In effect, this new statute (a proviso to the act appropriating money for the payment of Court of Claims judgments) declared that no pardon or loyalty oath shall be admissible as evidence in support of any suit against the United States in the Court of Claims. Moreover, the proviso required that the Supreme Court dismiss for want of jurisdiction any suit involving an appeal from a judgment of the Court of Claims in favor of a claimant who had established his loyalty through a pardon.

The Supreme Court denied the United States's motion and ruled the new statute unconstitutional. Although the *Klein* Court acknowledged that Congress possessed explicit constitutional authorization "to make 'such exceptions from the appellate jurisdiction' [of the Supreme Court] as should seem to it expedient," the Court nonetheless held that this particular jurisdictional exception violated the separation of powers doctrine. Notwithstanding Congress's power to limit court jurisdiction, the legislature could not constitutionally use that power to impair the effect of a presidential pardon. Nor could Congress use its jurisdictional power to dictate "rules of decision to the judicial department of government. . . ." In either case, Congress would be unconstitutionally interfering with the functions of a coequal branch of government. Accordingly, the proviso, which committed both sins, could not stand.

In the Black Hills claim, the question before the Court was

whether the *res judicata* waiver, like Congress's 1871 proviso, unconstitutionally dictated a rule of decision to the judiciary. Justice Blackmun thought not. He viewed *Klein* as distinguishable from the Black Hills claim on two grounds. First, in *Klein*, Congress had "attempted to render the President's pardon power a nullity," itself an apparent violation of the separation of powers doctrine. The *res judicata* waiver had no such unconstitutional goal. Second, in *Klein*, the congressional proviso "had the effect of retroactively closing the doors of the Court of Claims to a party who already had been adjudged to have a legitimate claim against the United States." The waiver, of course, had the opposite effect; it gave a claimant against the government a second chance. "Arguably," Justice Blackmun suggested to his colleagues, "legislative action by which Congress waives its right to a judgment in its favor does not present the same kind of equitable concerns that were present in *Klein.*"

Blackmun also directed his colleagues' attention to *Cherokee Nation* v. *United States*, a 1923 decision upholding a *res judicata* waiver as within Congress's constitutional power. "[S]ince our prior cases establish the authority of Congress to waive the res judicata effects of a prior judgment in the Government's favor," Blackmun saw no need for reargument on the point.

Blackmun's memo won immediate agreement from Chief Justice Burger.

Justice Rehnquist, though, stuck by his guns. Only a few hours after Blackmun's memo circulated, Rehnquist sent around a polite but firm refutation. He read *Klein* as standing for the general principle that Congress "may not interfere with the exercise of judicial power by stripping a judgment of its finality." In Rehnquist's view, Congress had not merely waived the *res judicata* defense in the Black Hills claim, it had granted "a new trial on an issue which has been finally decided." Rehnquist was "not ready to conclude that simply on the authority of *Cherokee Nation* there is no invasion of judicial powers when Congress declines to respect the finality of this Court's decisions, sets aside a valid judgment, and orders a new trial on an issue previously decided in an Article III Court." Hinting at reargument, Rehnquist wanted to give this issue "the consideration it deserves."

After a weekend's contemplation, Blackmun asked for a head count. He had no desire to start a major opinion "until the dust settles."

Powell responded with a "join 4" vote, an indication that he would vote for rebriefing or reargument on the separation of powers issue if four other Justices were so inclined. Otherwise, Powell said that he would adhere to his conference vote to affirm the Court of Claims.

Rehnquist and Powell waited for other expressions of interest. Potter Stewart disappointed them. He expressed ":more than a little concern about the impact of a decision that there was a 'taking' " in the Black Hills claim, but he decided against hearing argument on an issue that the parties themselves had not raised.

At conference, Justice White had seemed willing to be talked out of affirming the Court of Claims, but Rehnquist's separation of powers argument would have no appeal for him. White was the Court's foremost defender of congressional acts against separation of powers challenges.

The silence of the other Justices killed the prospect of reargument and the possibility that the Black Hills claim would be decided on an issue unrelated to its merits (and uncontroversial in the eyes of the lawyers for both sides). In late April, Justice Blackmun (and his clerk Bill Murphy, who did the initial drafting) started work on an opinion affirming the Court of Claims. Rehnquist reiterated his intention to dissent.

On June 10, Justice Blackmun circulated a first draft of his proposed opinion. Fifty pages long, elaborate in historical detail, it clearly reflected the interests and inclinations of its author. Seventy-one years old, born in Illinois but raised in Minnesota, Harry A. Blackmun had a passion for history. Behind his desk hung the sword of a grandfather who had fought for the Union in the Civil War. On another wall, the Justice had arranged a virtual shrine to Abraham Lincoln: framed quotations, a silhouette, and documents bearing the signature of the former country lawyer who had freed the slaves and saved the Union. Blackmun's was the office of a man who believed deeply, almost romantically, in the *idea* of the United States, especially its commitment to live by a Constitution embodying broad principles of moral governance. In *Sioux Nation,* the Justice evidently meant to give some small measure of content to that uniquely American commitment as well as register his own unabashed sympathy for Indians.

For eleven pages, the length of some full opinions, Blackmun traced the history of relations between the United States and the Sioux from the signing of the 1868 treaty to Custer's Black Hills expedition, the Allison commission, Grant's secret decision to open the Hills to miners, the Manypenny sell or starve commission, and finally Congress's unilateral expropriation of the Hills. Guided by the Indian Claims Commission's 1974 factual findings

in the claim, but embellishing liberally with details culled from a
wide variety of historical sources outside the evidentiary record of
the case (including the 1904 history of Duone Robinson, the first
white advocate for the Sioux claim), Blackmun painted a vivid
picture of government perfidy.

Blackmun then traced the long history of the Black Hills litigation itself, which, in turn, led naturally into his discussion (anticipating Rehnquist's dissent) of the constitutionality of Congress's 1978 *res judicata* waiver. Again, this time for public
explanation (and at greater length), Blackmun distinguished Congress's unconstitutional actions in *Klein* from its waiver of *res
judicata* in the Black Hills claim. And, again, he relied mainly on
Cherokee Nation as establishing that "Congress may recognize its
obligation to pay a moral debt not only by direct appropriation,
but also by waiving an otherwise valid defense to a legal claim
against the United States. . . ."

Blackmun did not even reach the merits of the Sioux claim itself
until page 35. There, and throughout the final third of his opinion,
he explicitly rejected the government's *Lonewolf*-based appeal and
wholeheartedly embraced the Court of Claims ruling. After noting
that *Lonewolf* was distinguishable from the Black Hills claim on a
number of factual grounds, Blackmun emphasized that the *Lonewolf* Court's abdication to Congress of exclusive control over Indian affairs embodied a view of judicial and legislative power "long
since . . . discredited in takings cases, and . . . expressly laid to rest
in *Delaware Tribal Business Comm.* v. *Weeks*" (a 1977 case also undermining *Lonewolf*).

Indeed, Blackmun concluded, in light of the *Shoshone* line of
cases, *Lonewolf* had "limited relevance" to the Black Hills claim.
Furthermore, its virtually conclusive presumption of congressional good faith had "little to commend it as an enduring principle
for deciding questions of the kind presented here." Rather, Congress's power to manage tribal affairs was " 'subject to pertinent
constitutional restriction' " (quoting *Creek Nation* v. *United States*),
and courts would only deem congressional action to be within that
managerial capacity after engaging in "a thoroughgoing and impartial examination" of the historical record. "A presumption of
congressional good faith," Blackmun admonished, "cannot serve
to advance such an inquiry."

Though he both limited and disparaged *Lonewolf,* Blackmun
nonetheless endorsed the *Fort Berthold* good faith test as the "appropriate" legal standard for determining whether Congress has
exercised its power to manage tribal property or its sovereign

power of eminent domain. The Court of Claims, moreover, having conducted an "exhaustive review of the historical record," had applied that good faith test properly. "In sum," Blackmun wrote,

> we conclude that the legal analysis and factual findings of the Court of Claims fully support its conclusion that the terms of the 1877 Act did not effect "a mere change in the form of investment of Indian tribal property." *Lonewolf* v. *Hitchcock*, 187 U.S., at 568. Rather, the 1877 Act effected a taking of tribal property, property which had been set aside for the exclusive occupation of the Sioux by the Fort Laramie Treaty of 1868. That taking implied an obligation on the part of the Government to make just compensation to the Sioux Nation, and that obligation, including an award of interest, must now, at last, be paid.

Within twenty-four hours after Blackmun circulated his draft, Justices Brennan, Stewart, Marshall, and Stevens circulated memos joining the opinion. These votes ensured Blackmun of a Court majority for his opinion and relieved any worries about what arguments Rehnquist might advance in his dissent. While awaiting Rehnquist's writing, Blackmun fined-tuned his opinion.

Justice White, meanwhile, decided not to join either Blackmun's historical discussion or his analysis of the good faith effort test. White found it a "much closer" case on the merits than Blackmun's opinion indicated. And White disapproved of "the atmosphere of [Blackmun's] draft that often casts the conduct of the government in such an unfavorable light." To White's pointed displeasure, Blackmun had strayed outside the record for his historical reconstruction, improperly relying "on accounts by historians and other writers whose accuracy and objectivity have not been put to the test." Thus, while White agreed that the Court of Claims should be affirmed, he announced his intention to write a short separate concurrence.

Rehnquist distributed a draft dissent on June 19. At length, he argued that in enacting the 1978 *res judicata* waiver Congress had improperly exercised judicial as opposed to legislative power. "It is . . . apparent," Rehnquist wrote in summary of his argument, "that Congress has accomplished more than a private litigant's attempted waiver. . . . What Congress has done is uniquely judicial. It has reviewed a prior decision of an Article III Court, eviscerated the finality of that judgment, and ordered a new trial in a pending case."

But Rehnquist did not challenge Blackmun's opinion merely on legal grounds. In strident terms, he chastised the Court majority for rejecting the 1942 Court of Claims interpretation of Black Hills history and specifically its assessment that the 1877 act had taken the Hills in exchange for rations and grazing land "in the best interests of the Sioux and the nation." What Blackmun had substituted instead was the work of "revisionist" historians who ignored the Indians' "share of villainy," creating a "stereotyped and one-sided impression both of the settlement regarding the Black Hills portion of the Great Sioux Reservation and of the gradual expansion of the national government from the Proclamation Line of George III in 1763 to the Pacific Ocean."

Rehnquist advanced his own version of frontier history as well as a very different view of what role the Court should play in that history's assessment.

> That there was tragedy, deception, barbarity, and virtually every other vice known to man in the three hundred year history of the expansion of the original thirteen colonies into a nation which now embraces more than three million square miles and fifty states cannot be denied. But in a Court opinion, as a historical and not a legal matter, both settler and Indian are entitled to the benefit of the Biblical adjuration: "Judge not, that ye be not judged."

Justices Powell and Burger, whose final votes remained outstanding, may not have shared Blackmun clerk Bill Murphy's view that Rehnquist's dissent was "singularly unpersuasive," but they did join Blackmun's proposed opinion in short order. In all likelihood, they found wanting Rehnquist's overblown separation of powers argument. With respect to the *res judicata* waiver, Rehnquist accused Congress of improperly performing a "uniquely judicial" function, even though the executive branch (through the Justice Department) unquestionably could have performed the very same function by declining to plead *res judicata* in the first place. In other words, according to Rehnquist, Congress had usurped an exclusively judicial function by reviewing the 1942 Court of Claims opinion, setting it aside, and ordering a new trial. Yet, without any conceivable constitutional objection, Craig Decker (an employee of the executive branch) could have undertaken precisely the same tasks and achieved precisely the same result by deciding not to interpose a *res judicata* defense in the first place.

Blackmun did not even bother responding to Rehnquist's separation of powers argument. And he added only a single footnote to refute the dissent's charge of historical revisionism. "The dissenting opinion," Blackmun countered in part, "does not identify a single author, non-revisionist, neo-revisionist, or otherwise, who takes the view of the history of the cession of the Black Hills that the dissent prefers to adopt."

As for Rehnquist's plea for judicial restraint in assessing history, Blackmun maintained a critical silence. What could he say, after all, to a Supreme Court Justice who responded to an Indian tribe's claim of constitutional deprivation by invoking the biblical admonition "Judge not, that ye be not judged"? As an editorial in New Jersey's *Paterson News* later remarked, "Whatever else is the Supreme Court for?"

With its internal debate at an end, on June 30, 1980, fifty-seven years after Ralph Case first filed the Black Hills claim, the Supreme Court decided it once and for all, voting 8–1 to affirm the Court of Claims award of $17.5 million plus interest, a total of slightly more than $106 million. The longest-running claim in U.S. history—the *Jarndyce* v. *Jarndyce* of American jurisprudence—was finally over.

From the Indian perspective, even leaving aside the question of land restoration, several flaws marred the victory. In endorsing the *Fort Berthold* good faith effort test, the Court rejected Sonosky and Lazarus's plea that it apply the same Fifth Amendment standard to Indian tribes as it applied to every other property owner—and had done so without public explanation. The Court, moreover, had adopted a wholly subjective legal standard, one that required judges to decide tribal takings claims not by reference to familiar legal principles but rather through detailed historical examination, an endeavor for which even the best judges are often ill-suited. Such an historical approach invited the very charges of revisionism or bad history to which Blackmun's opinion was itself already subject.

In the larger scheme of things, though, these complaints were trivial. After 100 years, the Sioux people had forced a legal and moral reckoning with their conquerors—and had vindicated their abiding sense of grievance. The Sioux nation had achieved the best possible legal result available under the law, by far the largest judgment ever in an Indian land claim. The poorest people in America had won $106 million that they might use to improve their schools, provide jobs and better health care, or however they saw fit. And the highest Court in the land had severely limited and openly disparaged the single most dreaded case in Indian law, essentially extinguishing the notion that Indian tribes were at the legal mercy of Congress.

Lazarus was at his office when the call came from the Court that after 23 years, after thousands of hours of work and thousands of pages of briefs, after two special acts of Congress, he had won a claim thrice lost—and by a landslide.

Lazarus did not pretend that the Supreme Court's decision in the Black Hills claim could either reverse history or truly compensate the Sioux for their loss of land, livelihood, culture, and self-esteem. Still, he took enormous satisfaction in having gained for the Sioux a $106 million inheritance upon which the tribe might build, a long overdue first step towards self-sufficiency.

At the same time, Lazarus feared for the tribe's future. In February, before the Supreme Court argument, he had received a letter from Walter Lakota, a seventy-two-year-old Pine Ridge fullblood, descended from Man-Afraid-of-His-Horse's band. Describing himself as a member of the "claim payment group," Lakota complained about the "young punks" and "constitution violators" currently running the tribal council. He demanded a 50 percent Sioux blood quantum test for tribal membership—and its accompanying qualification for claims money. "Maybe it is time to prove who is an INDIAN," Lakota closed.

As Lakota's letter sharply reminded, a large Black Hills judgment was certain to reopen many of the issues that had divided Sioux from Sioux for generations. And now those ancient divisions about who controlled the tribe's claims and who should benefit from them were compounded with new arguments about whether to use claims money at all. As Lazarus hinted in his response to Lakota, he thought it would be at least several painful years before the Sioux managed to agree on a plan for apportioning and using their Black Hills judgment.

Sipping champagne with his wife on the afternoon of the judgment, Lazarus had no idea how much pain would follow.

SEVENTEEN

THE BLACK HILLS ARE NOT FOR SALE

O N JULY 1, 1980, the day after the Supreme Court decision, a former tribal council member from Pine Ridge, C. Hobart Keith, filed a complaint in the United States District Court for the District of Columbia, belatedly seeking an injunction to prohibit Arthur Lazarus "from pursuing a monetary award in the Black Hills case on behalf of the Oglala Sioux Tribe contrary to the desires and best interests of the Oglala Sioux people." Keith claimed that, because the Oglalas had permitted Lazarus's contract to expire, his representation of them was "illegal and contrary to law." Unless the court stopped Lazarus's representation, Keith further alleged, the Oglala Sioux would "lose the possibility of having their sacred lands in the Black Hills returned to them, since acceptance of the monetary award by the Oglala Sioux people fully discharges the United States of all claims and demands touching any matter involved in the Black Hills controversy."

On July 9, at a public meeting held at the Porcupine community on Pine Ridge, Oglala attorney Mario Gonzalez announced that he would ask the Supreme Court to declare a mistrial in the Black Hills claim on the ground that Lazarus had represented the Oglala Sioux without a valid contract. Gonzalez also declared his intention to seek an injunction barring the Secretary of the Interior from developing any plan to distribute the judgment money to the various Sioux tribes without their prior consent.

Two days later, on July 11, the Black Hills Sioux Nation Council reiterated its recent position repudiating monetary compensation for the Black Hills. "We've got a treaty and that's it," Reginald

Bird Horse, a delegate from Standing Rock, told the press. "We are not going along with the sale of the land in the original boundaries of the 1868 Treaty." In the view of Simon Broken Leg, a Rosebud Sioux delegate, the Black Hills judgment would yield only $300 to each Sioux claimant (the actual amount would have been closer to $1,500 if the judgment were distributed per capita). After spending the money, Broken Leg asked, "then what you got tomorrow? You got no land; you got no future; you got no nothing."

At the time of the judgment, Sonosky had doubted that the land return movement would hold much sway in the elected tribal councils. He described the Sioux politicians who spurned the Black Hills judgment and demanded a land return as "a minute dissident group that is loud and articulate." Sonosky predicted that "the leaders of the tribal councils [would] accept the money."

But this was the view from Washington. Closer to the reservation, Vine Deloria, Jr., observed that "in the last five years so many people have moved to a hard-line position that any kind of solution that doesn't include land just won't be accepted. You'd be taking your life into your own hands if you went out on one of those reservations and preached just a cash settlement."

Deloria proved to be the better analyst. On July 9, having kept its silence until after the Supreme Court issued its decision, the Oglala Sioux tribal council unanimously adopted a resolution disavowing any participation in the Black Hills just compensation claim and declaring that the Supreme Court decision should be vacated "on the grounds that the Tribe was not represented by counsel in those proceedings." In addition, the Oglalas authorized Gonzalez to initiate new "legal proceedings . . . for trespass and a return of land. . . ."

In August, the Cheyenne River Sioux tribal council joined the Oglalas in repudiating the Black Hills award. "The welfare of ourselves and our descendants will not be promoted by accepting an award of money for our claim to the Black Hills of South Dakota," the council members unanimously resolved. "We hereby reject any award of money for the Black Hills . . . and do not abandon our claim to the lands taken by the Act of 1877."

Over time, all the Sioux tribal governments turned their backs on a court award of $106 million that everyone agreed was desperately needed for housing, food, health care, education, alcohol treatment, and a host of other basic necessities. Some Sioux leaders, like Cheyenne River Treasurer Mona Cudmore, regretted the decision. She wanted "to accept the settlement and get on with the business of planning some development and at least get some of the money for those of us who will use [it]." Any other choice, Cudmore thought, was simply unrealistic. "With the world situation being what it is today, it would be futile to think we would ever get the Black Hills back."

In the tribal councils, though, different priorities and different logic prevailed. At the council meetings and all over the reservations old traditionals and angry young Sioux, still partners in the revival of tribal traditions, successfully portrayed "acceptance" of the Black Hills award as a betrayal of everything Indian and everything Sioux. Invoking the treaty, invoking the belief that the Great Spirit had given the Black Hills to the Sioux as a permanent gift, passionate voices demanded that the councils fight for the land. "I cannot accept money for the Black Hills," Severt Young Bear, a young activist, explained, "because land is sacred to me. . . . [The whites] are trying to change our value system. To be a traditional person is to believe in our own culture, is to believe in yourself as a Lakota person; then you cannot sell the land."

Sioux leaders faced a choice that was really no choice at all. On the one hand, if they voted to use the Black Hills money, they faced certain accusation of having repudiated their heritage and having accepted as justly resolved the tribe's grievances against the United States that for a century had served to explain and excuse four generations of shattered lives.

On the other hand, if Sioux leaders voted to reject the Black Hills money, they could don the mantle of traditionalism (some sincerely, others not) while in fact sacrificing nothing. Regardless of what the tribal councils might say about "rejecting" the Supreme Court's just compensation award (which they also erroneously referred to as a "settlement"), after the Court's decision, the Black Hills judgment funds belonged irrevocably to the modern Sioux tribes. Even if the tribal councils never decided to use their $106 million, the money would remain in the Treasury invested on their behalf at interest rates varying between 8.75 and 10.25 percent. In other words, the tribal councils could always change their minds about using the money at no penalty.

By refusing to touch the Black Hills money, Sioux leaders also avoided the potentially disastrous results of distributing the judgment funds to their impoverished constituents. The eldest Sioux still remembered with bitterness and disappointment what happened after the last large cash infusion into Sioux country when Indian stockmen had sold their cattle herds during World War I. As Fools Crow recalled, the Sioux had "exchanged their freedom for money and liquor."

Vine Deloria, Jr., foresaw history repeating itself if the various Sioux tribes divided most of the Black Hills award into per capita payments. "With the distribution of funds," Deloria prophesied, "will come the drug dealers, bootleggers, used car dealers, and appliance salesmen who would ordinarily cross the street to avoid saying hello to an Indian. One great spasm of spending will occur and then the people, as poor as they ever were, will return to normal lives."

Nor were most Sioux any more sanguine about what would happen if the tribal governments somehow resisted the pressure to distribute the Black Hills money per capita and, instead, channeled the award into new or existing tribal programs. For a dozen years the U.S. government had poured tens of millions of dollars into Sioux tribal governments and the people had little to show for it except their bare survival. Tribal leaders, common sentiment held, specialized mainly in nepotism, petty graft, and "business" trips. By dint of hard experience, the Sioux had grown almost boundlessly cynical about the ability of their tribal leaders to improve their lives. Many shared the view of Ramon Roubideaux that if the Black Hills money bypassed the liquor stores and used car salesmen, it would be "squandered by our bureaucratic tribal officials."

Given the widespread belief that the Black Hills award could be of no long-term benefit, the notion of holding out for a better deal—a return of the Black Hills themselves and perhaps a lot more money in damages—was enormously attractive, especially to a people ignorant of Washington and unable to assess independently their chances for success. Thus, amid much talk of sovereignty, sacredness, and ultimate triumph, the Sioux renewed the Black Hills fight, now more than a century old.

For sixty years, the direction and strategies for pursuing the Black Hills claim had emanated from white attorneys whom the Sioux had hired to navigate it through legal waters that they themselves could not fathom. But *that* Black Hills claims voyage was now safely over. The Indians could jettison their old pilots and follow their own hearts in setting new courses for their claim. The Sioux now had lawyers of their own to take the helm and attempt to steer the tribe through the perils of the white system. And Gonzalez stepped forward to take a turn at the wheel, a novice on a rough sea.

On July 18, Gonzalez filed suit against the United States asking for a return of the Black Hills lands and $11 billion in damages—$1 billion for "hunger, malnutrition, disease and death" and another

$10 billion for the removal of nonrenewable resources from the Hills. Gonzalez based the Oglalas' complaint on his long-espoused legal theory that the United States seizure of the Black Hills violated the Fifth Amendment's requirement that governmental takings be for a "public" purpose and was, therefore, null and void. "We are arguing . . . that Congress cannot take Indian land and give it out to private homesteaders, mining interests, and other individuals," Gonzalez explained. "That is not a taking for public purposes." Accordingly, he argued, the Sioux had remained "the rightful owners [of the Black Hills] from 1877 to the present time."

Gonzalez believed that the $10 billion in damages for trespass and illegal use of the Black Hills was "quite conservative in view of the fortunes and property values claimed by the present illegal occupants of our Black Hills land." Gonzalez described the $1 billion for personal damages as a "pittance" compared to the suffering the Sioux had endured in the last century.

Like another lawyer who had represented the Sioux, Gonzalez assured his clients of success. "We feel our case has a lot of merit," he proclaimed. "We will win this case." And as the Sioux had placed their faith in Ralph Case's extravagant promises, so the Oglalas trusted Gonzalez when he told them that under the white man's law, in the white man's courts, they could recover the Black Hills and a previously undreamed-of fortune, too.

After filing his land return suit, Gonzalez spent the balance of July and August seeking to prevent the Secretary of the Interior from actually paying out to the Oglalas any part of the $106 million Sioux judgment fund—thereby allegedly endangering the tribe's new lawsuit. On behalf of the Oglalas, Gonzalez also filed a Motion to Change Attorney with the Court of Claims, which had retained jurisdiction over the original Black Hills claim for the purpose of determining Sonosky and Lazarus's attorneys' fees. Charging Lazarus with "fraud of counsel" and "conduct which may conceivably result in an action for malpractice," Gonzalez told the court that "it is inappropriate for Mr. Lazarus to collect a fee for misconduct." Instead, Gonzalez argued, the court should oust Lazarus as the Oglalas' counsel.

Lazarus responded testily. "The case is over," he pointed out. "With the exception of applications for allowance of attorneys' fees . . . no further action remains to be taken in this litigation. The Tribe's request for permission to change attorneys, therefore, is moot." Lazarus also argued that the Oglalas' motion was inappropriate. "To allow a stranger at this late date in the proceedings to appear as attorney of record for any plaintiff would do a positive disservice to the lawyers involved and to the Court." If the Oglalas wished to contest his fee, Lazarus added, they would have ample opportunity to do so after his fee application was actually filed.

Although Lazarus seriously doubted that the Court of Claims would grant Gonzalez's motion, he nonetheless resented its contents as well as Gonzalez's frequent allegations in Sioux country, amplified in the press, that his handling of the Black Hills claim had been incompetent and deceitful. In response to Gonzalez's charges, Lazarus asked the trial judge in the still-pending 1868 treaty case to permit him to withdraw as counsel for the Oglalas. But the judge refused on the ground that his withdrawal would leave the tribe unrepresented. And although the judge invited the Oglalas to replace Lazarus, they did not do so, leaving him no choice but to continue to represent them even as they smeared his name.

Hobart Keith withdrew his lawsuit against Lazarus before any response was required. The Court of Claims rejected Gonzalez's motion to change attorneys.

The federal district court in Rapid City also dismissed Gonzalez's land return and damages suit against the United States (*Oglala Sioux Tribe* v. *United States*). As Lazarus had predicted, the court ruled that it was without jurisdiction to consider the Oglalas' land return claim because the United States had not waived its sovereign immunity to such a suit. Gonzalez vowed to appeal.

On October 6, Lazarus filed a motion for attorneys' fees (for himself, Sonosky, and Payne) in the Court of Claims, which, under the ICC Act, had authority to award fees in any amount not exceeding 10 percent of the claims judgment. After a sixty-one-page history of services rendered for the tribe, Lazarus argued that the maximum fee was more than justified. "From any perspective," he asserted in the necessarily immodest application, "the results we achieved in this case are nothing short of sensational. Viewed from the 1956 affirmance of the Commission's dismissal . . . the ultimate award of almost $106 million borders on the miraculous. That accomplishment, unique and without precedent in the annals of American jurisprudence, fully justifies [the requested] fee. . . ."

Russell Means filed an opposition to the fee application, repeating the familiar accusation that the attorneys had prosecuted a "claim for money without proper authorization and without the understanding and consent of the Dakota people. . . ." A group of old dealer traditional leaders from the Standing Rock Reservation (designating themselves the Yanktonai Bands of the Dakotah Nation, Inc.) expressed similar dissatisfaction with Sonosky and Lazarus's authorization. "IRA and modern day tribal council have hired these lawyers without involvement of the people," they complained. "[The attorneys'] claim must *not* be allowed in any amount."

Gonzalez did not oppose the fee application on behalf of the Oglalas, evidently believing that he had blocked payment to Lazarus through other channels. In *Oglala Sioux Tribe* v. *United States*, the Oglalas' land return suit, Gonzalez and the United States attorney had stipulated that no officer of the United States would "tender payment" of any part of the Black Hills award or take any other action to disturb the status quo between the parties pending the outcome of the tribe's appeal. Gonzalez interpreted the agreement as barring the United States from paying Lazarus attorneys' fees out of the Black Hills judgment fund. He was wrong.

On May 20, 1981, in a unanimous *en banc* opinion, the Court of Claims awarded Lazarus, Sonosky, and Payne $10,595,943 in attorneys' fees, the maximum 10 percent. "The result the attorneys have obtained for their clients has been extraordinary," Chief Judge Friedman wrote in summary of the court's view.

> Starting with a case that appeared doomed, they obtained an award of more that $100 million—which is more than twice as large as any other made in an Indian claims case. Both the attaining of any award and the magnitude of the award made were attributable solely to the endeavors of the attorneys. Considering all the circumstances—the nature of the case, the obstacles the attorneys had to overcome, the low initial prospect of success, and the great skill and dedication with which the attorneys did their work—we conclude that attorneys' fees of 10% of the award, or $10,595,943, are appropriate.

The fee decision, not surprisingly, made front-page news, as in the *New York Times*, which ran a long story and a photograph of Lazarus, Sonosky, and Payne under the banner headline "Big Wampum for a Legal Tribe." According to Stephen Glasser, publisher of the Federal Attorneys' Fee Awards Reporter, the $10.6 million Sioux fee ranked as one of the largest, if not the largest, fee ever awarded by a court.

The response in Sioux country was predictable. Having argued for years that Sonosky and Lazarus represented the Sioux solely out of financial self-interest, AIM leader Russel Means denounced the lawyers as "parasites" and called the fee "the largest rip-off of Indian claims money in the history of this country." To Gonzalez the whole fee proceeding was a "sham." Other commentators concurred in the judgment of prize-winning author Peter Matthiessen, who wrote in his book *In the Spirit of Crazy Horse* (a Sioux history focused on the 1975 Pine Ridge murder of two FBI agents) that the Black Hills claim "had been won by the wealthy lawyer [Lazarus] and lost by his poverty-stricken clients. . . ."

Sonosky shrugged off the criticism, most of which (because of the Oglala contract expiration issue) was directed at Lazarus. In 1956, Sonosky had gambled that he could win the Black Hills claim and that gamble had paid off handsomely. The Court of Claims fee decision made Sonosky a rich man overnight. His personal share amounted to more than $4.8 million.

Like a grandfather recounting the hardships of his youth, Sonosky was fond of recalling the old days when he "had to support two practices, one to keep my family alive and the other to keep this [Black Hills] case going." Sonosky remembered working "terrible hours" researching the Black Hills claim, "then doing my paying oil, gas, and mineral cases on the side." He even went through the archives by himself, too poor to afford a researcher. Those days were now gone forever, of course, and Sonosky, over seventy, could easily have retired. But he loved his work and his image as a wily old Indian hand. He kept at his practice full-time at the small firm he had built over the years.

William Howard Payne, who had done no legal work on the Black Hills claim, received a fee of almost $700,000. Richard Case, Ralph Case's son and a successful Baltimore attorney, also received $25,000 pursuant to an old agreement that Sonosky had negotiated to settle his father's interest in the case.

The remaining $5 million belonged to Lazarus's firm, which rewarded him with a one-time year-end bonus of $150,000. From Sonosky, Lazarus also received a case of very expensive champagne. In July, as the now unrelenting attacks on his professional conduct reached a crescendo, after a year of heavy traveling and insufficient attention to diet, he entered a hospital suffering from a bleeding ulcer.

Shortly after the fee award, the United States Court of Appeals for the Eighth Circuit (the federal appellate court for South Dakota) affirmed the dismissal of the Oglalas' land return and damage action against the United States. Echoing the district court, the Eighth Circuit ruled that "Congress has deprived the district court of subject matter jurisdiction by expressly providing an exclusive remedy for the alleged wrongful taking [of the Black Hills] through the enactment of the Indian Claims Commission Act."

Gonzalez promised to take the Oglalas' case to the Supreme

Court and did so, fruitlessly. In January 1982, the Court declined to review the Eighth Circuit's decision.

Even before Gonzalez's latest setback, the Dakota chapter of AIM had grown impatient and disillusioned with the prospect of achieving a return of the Black Hills through the judicial process. "If Indian people think we can get the Black Hills back only by going to Court, then we must not remember our history," observed Bill Means, Russell's brother and the head of Dakota AIM.

On April 4, 1981, an AIM caravan of twenty cars left the Porcupine community on Pine Ridge, entered the Black Hills, and established a camp in Victoria Creek Canyon, a well-watered site surrounded by lush ponderosa pine about a dozen miles southwest of Rapid City. Dakota AIM justified the Black Hills occupation as the Indians' legal right under the 1868 treaty, the American Indian Freedom of Religion Act of 1978, and a federal statute dating to 1897 that permitted the use of wilderness sites for educational and religious purposes. AIM named the camp after Raymond Yellow Thunder, the Sioux from Porcupine whom the Hare brothers had killed in Gordon, Nebraska in 1972.

By noon, the Indian occupiers had started building tipis and settling in. Chief Frank Fools Crow came to bless the camp the next day. "Remain strong in your commitment," he told the Indians, "and you will win." Ron Two Bulls, a security guard at Yellow Thunder, took Fools Crow's words to heart. "I've been waiting for this for many years," he said of the occupation. "There's going to be a lot of us that will probably die here."

Despite the "last stand" rhetoric, no one perished at Yellow Thunder. And despite AIM's high hopes that its occupation would mark a meaningful first step towards the reacquisition of the Black Hills, the Yellow Thunder occupation soon became a footnote in that struggle.

Leaders of the Oglala, Cheyenne River, and Rosebud Sioux tribes denounced the occupation as counter-productive. The Black Hills Sioux Nation Council withdrew its support for the Yellow Thunder Camp after less than a week.

Having been granted a camping permit by the government, AIM applied to the U.S. Forest Service for permission to build eighty-three permanent structures at the Yellow Thunder Camp. Expecting rejection, Bill Means talked about defending his new home with his blood, but when the government denied AIM's permit application he merely filed suit in federal court to contest the rejection. The permit litigation dragged on for years as did Yellow Thunder Camp, without major incident. The courts ultimately upheld the government's denial of AIM's permit request and Yellow Thunder Camp eventually disbanded.

Not to be eclipsed by AIM, on June 25, 1981 (the 105th anniversary of the Little Big Horn), the Oglalas instigated a tribally-sponsored occupation of the Black Hills. Led by Stanley Looking Elk, who was then president of the Oglalas, and Robert Fast Horse, a sharp young traditional with a law degree from the University of New Mexico, the Oglalas set up camp in the Wind Cave National Park, a place of rolling grassy knolls and even free-running buffalo.

Fast Horse explained the Oglalas' goals. "The basic theme we're trying to establish is a symbol of protest that the Black Hills are not for sale," he said. "What we'd like to do is keep the symbol of protest going until we get some kind of negotiation going." Nellie Red Owl, an eighty-year-old traditional, promised to stay as long as necessary. "I'm home now," she said upon arriving at Wind Cave, "and I am free."

The Wind Cave occupation failed disastrously. By September, the camp was vacant except for a veritable landfill of garbage, tools, toys, auto parts, clothing, and animal carcasses which gave rise to public mocking at the Indian's professed devotion to the sacredness of Mother Earth.

In January 1982, immediately after the Court of Appeals dismissed the Oglalas' land return suit against the United States, Gonzalez renewed his effort to force a judicial consideration of the validity of the 1877 act extinguishing Sioux title to the Black Hills. On the Oglalas' behalf, Gonzalez now sued the Homestake Mining Company for title to its five-acre mine and $6 billion in damages for trespassing and the illegal extraction of more than $1 billion dollars in gold.

Homestake called the suit "frivolous" and, in short order, the courts agreed. The federal district court, later affirmed on appeal, threw out Gonzalez's suit on the same grounds as his prior suit against the United States: lack of subject matter jurisdiction. As in the Oglalas' litigation against the United States, the courts in the Homestake case ruled that the Indian Claims Commission was the only forum Congress had provided in which the Sioux could contest the constitutionality of the 1877 act. Because Gonzalez's suit against Homestake turned on that issue, the courts dismissed it.

Gonzalez denounced the Homestake decision as "political" and criticized the courts for "rul[ing] against us every time, despite our legal rights." But Gonzalez's legal defeats did not result because the courts skewed existing law to defeat Sioux claims. Those defeats resulted because the American legal system simply did not recognize either the rights or the remedies that Gonzalez and his Indian clients sought.

What Gonzalez demanded as his clients' "legal rights" was something no nation ever had required of itself. Since the dawn of history, militarily stronger peoples had conquered weaker ones and seized their land. So it was when the Sioux built their plains empire, dispossessing the Crow, Kiowa, Pawnee, and other tribes. And for all that time, the conquerors hardly thought to compensate their enemies for what they had wrought, much less return their lands.

In this regard, the United States held itself to a higher level of accountability. Through its laws and Constitution, it vested aboriginal peoples with property rights in their lands and established a forum where they could assert those rights. That the United States authorized this legal forum to provide only monetary compensation (and not land restoration) did not, as Gonzalez charged, violate Native Americans' "legal rights." Those rights existed, to their admittedly limited extent, only because for all the deceit, greed, and brutality that accompanied the government's subjugation of the Indians, American legal culture, almost uniquely, at least recognized some legal limits on its conduct toward aboriginal peoples. And thus while the United States can be justly criticized for the cruelties that it visited on its native population and for often failing to live up to its own legal and moral promises, Gonzalez could not fault the courts for refusing to vindicate "legal rights" that no people, even his own, ever had recognized.

Indeed, while Gonzalez charged the courts with handing down "political" decisions, it was actually Gonzalez and the Oglalas who filed "political" lawsuits, ones not based on a realistic assessment of the law but rather designed to advance an unrealistic ideological agenda. As a result, for two years Gonzalez had tilted at legal windmills, gaining nothing for his clients but deeper disillusion.

The Sioux fared no better in the international legal community where, since 1977, they had asked for assistance in reclaiming the Black Hills. AIM's international arm, the International Indian Treaty Council, presented Sioux grievances to numerous United Nations-sponsored meetings in Geneva, Rotterdam, and elsewhere. The Oglalas (wary of AIM's ties to the communist block and the PLO) separately filed grievances with the U.N. Subcommission on Prevention of Discrimination and Protection of Minorities. A few traditional Sioux leaders, sometimes accompanied by Gonzalez, made numerous trips abroad to muster sympathy from foreign governments. But Sioux efforts to convince the world community to pressure the United States to return the Black Hills petered out by 1983. As activist Sioux lawyer Robert Fast Horse observed, all the conferences and presentations accomplished nothing except to give "Indian people a chance to put on eagle feathers and buckskin outfits and say rhetorical things in Europe."

Beginning in 1982, the Sioux gradually started to direct their efforts at the one political institution that realistically might return some Black Hills land to the various tribes—the Congress of the United States. During the spring and summer of 1982, Sioux leaders discussed asking Congress to return all the Black Hills taking area or, at a minimum, all the federal Black Hills lands. In September, at the instigation of the Oglalas, representatives from Pine Ridge, Standing Rock, Rosebud, and Crow Creek agreed to create a Black Hills Steering Committee (consisting of one representative from each Sioux tribe) that would draft land return legislation and undertake a lobbying campaign to secure its passage.

Lazarus's partner Richard West (who until recently had handled general counsel work for Pine Ridge and still did so for Cheyenne River) volunteered advice about legislative strategy in a meeting with Robert Fast Horse. To secure a significant land return, West suggested, the Sioux would have to identify provable sites of religious significance, mount a national and even international public relations campaign, and secure the support of the South Dakota congressional delegation. With a little luck, West believed, the Sioux stood a chance of recovering all federally held public lands outside of existing national forests and parks.*

West's moderate program, though, found no advocates within the Steering Committee, where practical political strategy took a backseat to Sioux claims of contemporary title to the Black Hills and demands that the United States revive the terms of the 1868 treaty. In January 1983, the Steering Committee debated what lands to include in its land return legislation: all the 1868 treaty lands (including the Article 11 and 16 lands), the Black Hills taking area, the federal lands in the Black Hills, or the federal lands exclusive of national parks. The Steering Committee voted unani-

---

*West also relayed to the Sioux Lazarus's belief that the tribe should seek a new jurisdictional act permitting it to bring the numerous claims that Ralph Case had failed to file under either the 1920 Sioux jurisdictional act or the ICC act. Lazarus estimated that these claims would likely yield a combined judgment in excess of $100 million. To this day, however, the Sioux have never approached Congress to obtain such an act.

mously to seek a return of all the Black Hills lands—federal, state, and private—an area that included hundreds of thousands, if not millions, of acres owned by non-Indian South Dakotans.

The Steering Committee also selected Gerald Clifford, 43, a highly educated, deeply religious mixed blood from Pine Ridge, as coordinator of their legislative effort. Much like Gonzalez, Clifford had grown up in Sioux country, then left the reservation for education and employment, ultimately to return home as a tribal adviser working at the intersection of the Indian and white worlds.

As a child Clifford had attended the Red Cloud School on Pine Ridge, a Catholic parochial school where his father coached sports. Despite his mother's urging him to become a priest, Clifford attended college in the Black Hills at the South Dakota School of Mines and, in 1959, earned a degree in engineering. After a stint with North American Aviation, he went to work in a smaller Los Angeles firm, applying his engineering skills to the manufacture of exit cones for Minutemen missiles.

Military contract work disgusted Clifford, as did much of urban life. In 1962, he entered a monastery, where he remained as a monk for six years until he decided that his quest for spirituality was leading him home to Pine Ridge.

Like many off-reservation Indians who returned to Indian country to rediscover their identities, Clifford devoted himself to the restoration of traditional Indian ways and values in everyday tribal life. On a personal level, he applied his training in Christian self-denial to the self-sacrificing rituals of Lakota religion: sundancing, fasting, and vision-questing. In public life, he coordinated a national tribal coalition that helped convince Congress to give control of Indian education back to Indians themselves. Later, in the mid-1970s, he worked to heal Pine Ridge after the occupation of Wounded Knee, overseeing the dismantling of Dick Wilson's goon squad and the restructuring of the Pine Ridge police.

To his new job as coordinator of the Black Hills Steering Committee, Clifford brought a passing familiarity with Washington and an uncompromising devotion to the return of the Black Hills. With his wife, Charlotte Black Elk, he saw the Black Hills restoration in almost apocalyptic terms. At a sun dance held in 1929 despite a government ban, Black Elk's great-grandfather, the presiding medicine man Hollow Horn, had issued a terrible prophesy. "A day will come in your lifetime," Hollow Horn had said, "when the earth, your mother, will beg you, with tears running to save her. Ho, if you fail to help her, you [the Lakota] and all people will die like dogs. Remember this."

In Clifford's eyes, the day of Hollow Horn's vision had arrived. Animating the fight for the Black Hills was the earth herself, crying for help. "Our first priority must be to keep faith with our sacred traditions," Clifford preached. "The Lakota were placed around the Black Hills for a purpose by God. . . . [and] it is a moral imperative that we reject the idea of selling the land."

Once chosen as Steering Committee coordinator, Clifford, with Gonzalez and others, immediately started the formidable process of drafting legislation that would be acceptable to all the different factions in Sioux country. That meant predicating the bill on the fundamental precepts of the 1868 treaty, both its geographical definition of the Great Sioux Reservation and what the Sioux perceived to be the treaty's recognition of their status as an independent sovereign people. At the same time, the Steering Committee had to translate those Sioux premises and demands into terms that the American political system would not immediately reject.

To achieve this goal, Clifford had to contend with the different Sioux leaders who professed an interest in the Black Hills claim, most notably Oliver Red Cloud, the great-grandson of the old chief. Red Cloud was a traditional (and old dealer) who had taken over the chairmanship of the Black Hills Sioux Nation Council after Eddie Reddoor's death in the late 1970s. He enjoyed a large following, especially on Pine Ridge, and (like his famous ancestor) aspired to be chief of all the Oglalas. Red Cloud detested Clifford, whom he derided as "a white man" who had no business acting as caretaker for the tribal claims. That role, Red Cloud believed, belonged to no one but himself.

In practical terms, the conflict between Clifford and Red Cloud emerged in disputes over the composition of the Steering Committee, the number of Black Hills acres to be returned to the tribe, and what pan-Sioux governing body would oversee the new Black Hills reservation that land return legislation would create. Red Cloud wanted proportional representation on the Steering Committee (which would benefit the Oglalas) instead of the committee's current one-tribe, one-vote structure. Red Cloud sought the return of 5.5 million acres in the Black Hills while the Committee gradually reduced its demands to 1.3 million acres. And Red Cloud wanted the BHSNC, which he chaired, to control the returned lands.

The split between Red Cloud and Clifford, moreover, ran even deeper than these substantial differences in policy. The two men were unbridgeably divided by history. Red Cloud traced his heritage to the Oglala chief who had forced the United States to sue

for peace in 1868 and then settled on the Great Sioux Reservation
to continue the process of negotiating with the whites over the
future of his people. For Red Cloud, as for his great-grandfather,
the 1868 treaty formed the basis for the entire legal and political
relationship between the Sioux and the United States. His reverence for the Black Hills and his demand for their return stemmed
from this document and from his great-grandfather's plea that the
Hills must support the Sioux for seven generations to come.

Clifford, by contrast, associated himself through marriage and
religious belief not with Chief Red Cloud but with Crazy Horse
and his followers, those whom Clifford viewed as the true keepers
of the Lakota spirit. Charlotte Black Elk descended directly from
Little Big Man, Crazy Horse's close friend who in 1875 had threatened to kill any Sioux who spoke for selling the Black Hills. Crazy
Horse's people had signed no treaties, not even the treaty of 1868.
Their attachment to the land came not from the white man's legal
papers but from the Lakota tradition that had inspired Crazy
Horse's famous admonition, "You do not sell the land the people
walk on." And just as Crazy Horse's band had scorned Chief Red
Cloud in his later days as a patsy of the whites, so Clifford scorned
Oliver Red Cloud as a man with a "fixation on being Chief of all
the Sioux," but an apostate to the purest principles of the tribe.

Red Cloud and Clifford even differed about the origins and the
early history of the Sioux. As old Chief Red Cloud had related
many times, as followers of Oliver Red Cloud enjoyed elaborating
in detail, in the seventeenth and eighteenth centuries the Sioux
had moved to the Dakota plains from their former homes in Minnesota and Wisconsin, gradually expanding west to the Black Hills
and beyond.

Clifford and Black Elk, though, espoused what anthropologist
Raymond DeMallie, Jr., a leading expert on the Sioux, calls "a new
tradition" about the genesis of the tribe. They rejected the old
belief in eastern Sioux origins (well-supported by historical evidence) and claimed instead that the Lakota were born in the caves
of the Black Hills themselves, in a place called *Wamaka Og'naka
Icante,* the "heart of everything that is." And like a "creationist"
interpreting Genesis as the literal story of man's beginnings, Clifford insisted as a matter of historical fact that far from migrating
from Minnesota, the Sioux had lived in the Hills for at least 10,000
years and had spread out from there.

Because of these and other divisions among the Sioux, Clifford
and the Steering Committee consumed two years of discussion,
negotiation, cajoling, and compromise before they settled on a

Black Hills land return bill that, notwithstanding some disagreement about acreage, seemed acceptable to all the Sioux tribal councils, if not Red Cloud himself.

In the end, the Steering Committee drafted legislation that would create a new Sioux nation reservation in the entire area of the original Great Sioux Reservation appropriated by the United States under the 1877 act (7.3 million acres). Within this "reestablished area," the Sioux would receive actual title to all federal lands other than Mount Rushmore (approximately 1.2 million acres). On the other hand, the proposed bill permitted the State of South Dakota and private citizens to retain their land titles on the condition that the tribe would have the "right of first refusal" to purchase any privately held lands within the reestablished area. The draft bill also granted the Sioux extensive water rights throughout the entire region.

The Steering Committee also provided monetary compensation for the tribe. Under the proposed bill, the Sioux would keep their Black Hills claim money (now at $160 million with accrued interest), though to avoid any implication that the tribe had ever lost title to the Black Hills, the bill carefully characterized the money as damages for lost use of the land rather than just compensation for its expropriation. As protection against their own desperate need for money, the legislation established a permanent trust account for the compensation funds and prohibited the tribe from depleting the principal. Finally, on the issue of compensation, the Steering Committee bill ordered the federal government to give the Sioux title to an additional 50,000 acres of land outside the Black Hills area, but within the lands described in Articles 11 and 16 of the 1868 treaty.

In addition to compensation, the draft bill insured substantial revenues for the tribe as it gradually took over the administration of grazing permits and timber leases in the Black Hills. At the same time, the bill curtailed future mineral leases on the lands reconveyed to the Sioux and included significant provisions applying the Lakota principle of "respect for the earth" to the new Sioux reservation. Specifically, the bill established both a Sioux Park and a Black Hills Sioux Forest to protect Indian religious sites and the quality of existing wilderness areas.

The Steering Committee shrewdly avoided the divisive question of who would govern the new pan-Sioux reservation. The bill created a Sioux National Council to govern the reestablished area but deliberately did not address how that government would be constituted.

In a significant coup, Clifford succeeded in convincing New Jersey Senator Bill Bradley to sponsor the Sioux bill in Congress. During his basketball-playing days with the New York Knicks, Bradley had run a series of summer sports clinics for the children of Pine Ridge. There, he had heard for the first time about the theft of the Black Hills and the tribe's century-old struggle for justice. He had long ago pledged to help the Sioux if he could, and he redeemed that promise now. .

On July 17, 1985, Bradley introduced the Sioux Nation Black Hills Act in the Senate with an impassioned plea to his colleagues. "History and other nations judge us by our deeds," he told the Senate after reviewing the government's deceitful treatment of the Sioux. "We now have the opportunity to write a new chapter in the history of the deeds dealing with the Sioux people. This chapter could describe a nation of honor, a nation of understanding, and a nation that affirms its great principles with great deeds. Let us write that chapter."

A realist by nature, Bradley undoubtedly knew that Congress would decline his east coast appeal to return 1.2 million acres of western land to the Sioux. The South Dakota delegation, whose support was essential to passage of any Black Hills act, aggressively opposed the Bradley bill. Their non-Indian constituents, never friendly to the Indians beforehand, grew virtually apoplectic at the prospect of giving the Sioux substantial civil jurisdiction over Black Hills lands that produced $600 million in annual revenue from tourism, mining, and timber harvesting. South Dakota Senator Larry Pressler suggested that he might introduce legislation returning New Jersey to the Indians.

Notwithstanding political reality, out in Sioux country, Clifford exuded confidence. He predicted that "Reagan would sign the [Bradley] bill before the year was out." But the Sioux Nation Black Hills Act died quietly in the 99th Congress, without so much as a subcommittee vote.

While Clifford had managed to put together a bill on which the Indians could basically agree, even that bare minimum of what would satisfy the Sioux had absolutely no chance of becoming law. Franklin Ducheneaux, still the chief staffer for Indian affairs in the House, thought a bill returning between 10,000 and 70,000 (as opposed to 1.2 million) acres of land might stand a chance of passage. Mike Jackson, the Republican staffer who had worked on the two previous Sioux bills, thought the Indians would have to trade money for land (and a lot less land at that) if they wanted to get a bill through. In short, although Clifford and the Sioux claimed to be taking a pragmatic approach to the Black Hills issue, their demands and practical politics were miles apart.

The Steering Committee promised better results in the next Congress. Meanwhile, life on the Sioux reservations continued much as it had for a hundred years. Once again in 1985 the government reported that the nation's two poorest counties were located in Sioux country. Many Sioux still lived in crumbling shacks or junked cars. Of those Sioux who did have homes, many still lacked running water and working electricity. Amid the rusting house trailers of the larger villages, around the one-room cabins that dotted the plains, stray dogs and ill-clad children roamed.

Eight of every ten Sioux adults still spent the year without a job, getting by on government handouts that shrunk substantially with the advent of the Reagan presidency. Nonetheless, between the BIA's General Assistance program, VA benefits, and other federal programs, such as Aid to Families with Dependent Children, many Sioux idled from cradle to early grave, transfixed in a welfare culture that had killed the spirit of generations. Dependence on the government had broken the Sioux in the 1870s; it was crippling them still.

For many Sioux, the downward pull of reservation life was irresistible Along the gullied dirt roads of rural Sioux villages, drunks wandered like aimless phantoms. Many had taken to drinking the household cleanser Lysol, which was cheap, densely alcoholic, and "a real quick high." On Standing Rock, federal officials estimated that as many as one-half of the adults were alcoholics. Drink-related child neglect and domestic violence of all sorts were endemic. On Pine Ridge, the alcohol abuse of pregnant mothers caused permanent prenatal brain damage in perhaps as many as 25 percent of all Oglala babies.

Health care remained abysmal. In a three-year period on Rosebud, 200 temporary doctors rotated in and out of the reservation, coming and going so fast that the hospital administrator suggested that his title should be changed to transit authority chief. Of those doctors who arrived, several turned out to be drunks or drug addicts, one an exhibitionist, one a phony, others in trouble with the law. The hospital operating room shut down when the last surgical resident left in 1978. Given the horror stories of what had happened in that room, some Indians considered the closing a blessing. In one recent year, 40 percent of the Indians who died on Rosebud were under the age of forty-five—the life expectancy of a century before.

In 1984, the federal judge presiding over the 1868 treaty case (the

Sioux tribe's still unresolved unconscionable consideration claim), hoping to avoid a trial to determine government offsets, ordered Sonosky and Lazarus to resubmit the government's previously rejected $39.7 million settlement offer to the Sioux. All the Sioux tribes except tiny Crow Creek and Santee again refused to settle. The leaders of the land return movement, dominant in most of the tribal councils, now claimed Sioux ownership not only of the Black Hills but also of the lands contained in Articles 11 and 16 of the 1868 treaty (large sections of Nebraska, Wyoming, Montana, and North Dakota). As with the Black Hills, they believed that accepting money would extinguish Sioux claims to these lands and preclude their restoration to the tribe. And more broadly, they reflected a growing feeling in Indian country that the entire claims commission process—the substitution of money for lost lands— was directed not at justice but at the old goal of eradicating the separate identity of Indians in America.

At the same time, even the Sioux tribes most vociferously opposing settlement declined to withdraw their suit. For example, although Lazarus repeatedly requested to be relieved of his duties as Oglala counsel, and although Oglala leaders continued to accuse him of misrepresenting them and of seeking only his fee, they would not replace him. Sioux politicians were loath to vote affirmatively to accept a monetary settlement for any claim that they considered to involve land, but they also refused to take any affirmative action to stop their claims.

Over the next three years, impatient to resolve what had become the oldest pending claim on record and extricate himself from his frustrating relationship with the Sioux, Lazarus steered the 1868 treaty case to conclusion. With the active encouragement of the trial judge, Robert Yock, Lazarus and the Justice Department resolved through stipulation all outstanding factual issues in the case, thereby permitting the court to decide the remaining legal questions and render final judgment without trial. In July 1987, the Court of Claims awarded the Sioux $40,245,807.02 in additional consideration for the interests they had relinquished under the 1868 treaty.

As in the Black Hills claim, after judgment the Sioux tribal councils "rejected" the money judgment. And like the Black Hills money, the $40 million 1868 treaty case judgment still resides in the Treasury, gaining interest for the tribes. By Lazarus's estimate, had the Sioux accepted the government's virtually identical settlement offer in 1979, by 1989 they already would have received an additional $37 million in interest.

The 1868 treaty case was the last significant Indian litigation that Lazarus handled. In the early 1980s, a sea change occurred in the legal profession as a new generation of lawyers, specialists in the booming and supremely lucrative practice of corporate mergers and acquisitions, rose to the fore. At Fried, Frank, these corporate attorneys had little interest in preserving the firm's longstanding commitment to the practice of Indian law, particularly at the reduced fees the tribes always had been charged.

Accordingly, in 1985, Fried, Frank decided to give up the Indian law practice that since the days of Felix Cohen had been the soul of the firm's Washington business. One by one Lazarus divested himself of his Indian clients, some of which he had served since he joined the firm in 1950. With the Indian practice dwindling, the two Native American associates whom Lazarus was then training, Kevin Gover and Susan Williams, left Fried, Frank to start their own firm in Albuquerque. At the same time, Fried, Frank suggested to Rick West that he retrain himself as a banking lawyer. He did, but his heart wasn't in it. In July 1988, West left Fried, Frank to join Gover and Williams at their new firm.

Lazarus mourned his departure and all that it symbolized. For West's going-away party, Lazarus penned a farewell that was also a eulogy for the firm's efforts to secure justice for Indians.

> Rick's leaving brings formally to its end a unique part of the firm's history—the 40-year period when Fried, Frank was pre-eminent in the practice of Indian law. With Rick's joining Gover, Stetson & Williams, that mantle will now pass to Fried, Frank graduates. In a very real sense, the good work the firm started goes on.
>
> Those of us who have practiced Indian law learned at the feet of Felix Cohen: Dick Schifter and I directly; Rick, Kevin Gover, Leroy Wilder and others learned from him through us. The high standards he set and the dedication to excellence in service to Indians which the firm carried forward are traditions of which we all can be proud.

On March 10, 1987, at Gerald Clifford's behest, Senator Bradley reintroduced the Black Hills Sioux Nation Act in the Senate, having gained Interior Committee chairman Daniel Inouye (Democrat from Hawaii) as a cosponsor. New Jersey Congressman James Howard agreed to introduce the Sioux bill in the House, and Interior Committee chairman Morris Udall lent his name to the legislation to help insure fuller consideration this time around.

In the opinion of Lloyd Meeds, the former congressman who had volunteered his services to the renewed Bradley bill campaign, the prospect of the Bradley bill's passage remained "very poor." Meeds figured that even with the addition of Inouye and Udall as cosponsors, the Sioux needed at a minimum to convince the South Dakota delegation to support a land return. And fulfilling this prerequisite undoubtedly would entail considerable compromise in the Sioux position as well as an extensive and expensive national publicity campaign to generate sympathy. Still, Meeds expected that, with the House and Senate committee chairmen on board, the Sioux probably would receive a full hearing, from which some "movement" might result.

Sioux politics, however, soon erased whatever small progress Clifford had started to make in Washington. One week after Bradley reintroduced the Sioux bill, the Black Hills Sioux Nation Council and the Grey Eagle Society (an organization of Sioux elders), both of which Red Cloud controlled, announced their opposition to the present version of the Bradley land return bill. Without elaborating on his substantive objections, Red Cloud called for Clifford's ouster as Steering Committee coordinator and for his replacement by "one that can be trusted with [the people's] support."

Red Cloud proposed a new candidate to lead the Sioux legislative campaign, a California businessman named Phil Stevens who claimed to be the great-grandson of the Oglala chief Standing Bear. Since the summer of 1986, Stevens had been trying to convince Red Cloud and others that the Sioux should appoint him their chief negotiator with Congress. A self-described streetwise son of a boilermaker and welder, Stevens claimed to have hustled his way from an east Los Angeles slum to the top of his own engineering firm that specialized in obtaining lucrative government defense contracts. Along the way, Stevens assured the Sioux, he had obtained precisely the political experience and connections in Washington that they needed to secure passage of a Black Hills land return.

Touting his expertise in the world of finance, Stevens also told the Sioux that the Bradley bill did not sufficiently compensate them for their loss of the Black Hills. As Stevens calculated Sioux damages from the 1877 act, the government owed the Sioux 110 years of rent on the Hills at 11¢ per acre (with interest compounded) plus $310 million in mineral royalties, a total of $3.1 billion. If the Sioux would give him proper authority, Stevens promised, within a year he would convince Congress not only to return the federal lands asked for in the Bradley bill but also to enact his $3.1 billion additional compensation package.

Armed with a winning smile and an unflappable can-do manner, Stevens won rapid converts among the Sioux. Red Cloud and Gonzalez (who disliked Clifford and had allied himself with Red Cloud) endorsed the new Stevens plan, especially after they attended a Stevens-run California fundraiser for the Red Cloud School that garnered $34,000 in a single star-studded, head-turning night. "I'm pretty positive that Phil can pull this off," said Reginald Cedarface, secretary of the BHSNC, appraising the Sioux Horatio Alger who had appeared in their midst. For generations, the Sioux had proven unable to resist extravagant promises and they did not do so now. Except within the Steering Committee, support for Stevens spread like prairie fire.

Clifford viewed the emergence of Stevens's program as an unmitigated disaster, the work not of a savior but of a "manipulator and salesman," a gloryhound whose ties to the tribe were at best attenuated, at worst fictitious. (Clifford doubted Stevens's story about his relationship to Standing Bear.) As a practical matter, Stevens's intervention drastically undercut the central premise of Clifford's land return efforts, the religious significance of the Black Hills to the Sioux. "The unfortunate part of Mr. Stevens coming here," Clifford rued, "is that he's turned the focus to money."

Despite Clifford's resistance, Stevens's widespread support made him impossible to ignore. Under pressure from Red Cloud, the BHSNC, and the Oglala tribal council, Clifford agreed to accompany Stevens to Washington and let him present his plan to Sioux congressional sponsors and relevant staff people on Capitol Hill. As Clifford (supported by Lloyd Meeds) recalls the meetings, Bradley's staff as well as Ducheneaux and others all told Stevens that his proposal was totally unrealistic and counterproductive. Stevens's much ballyhooed Washington connections proved basically nonexistent.

The baleful consequences of Stevens's Washington tour soon became evident. Bradley had no intention of amending his bill to include Stevens's $3.1 billion dollar compensation package or of getting caught in the crossfire between competing Sioux factions. With Clifford's reluctant concurrence, Bradley decided to hold his bill in abeyance until the Sioux settled their internal dispute. "The relevance of what we're trying to do is, on one hand, to right a wrong, and on the other to focus on the restorative quality of the land," the senator said. "It seems to me that's lost if the focus is on money."

Opponents of a Black Hills land return, meanwhile, seized on Stevens's appearance to rally against any attempt to augment the

Supreme Court's just compensation award—either with land or more money. South Dakota Senator Tom Daschle, describing Stevens's plan as adding insult to injury, exacted a promise from Interior Committee Chairman Inouye that no hearings, mark ups, or other action would be taken on Black Hills legislation without Daschle's prior agreement. Daschle also set up the Open Hills Committee, a South Dakota citizens group designed to counter what Daschle foresaw as a "long-term nationwide campaign" by "those who seek to replace the 1980 Supreme Court settlement with a massive land and an even more massive money transfer."

Daschle asked David Miller, a friend and historian at Black Hills State College, to chair the committee. Miller opposed both the Bradley and Stevens land return proposals because, in his view, they failed to safeguard either the region's natural resources or the interests of non-Indians who would fall under the civil jurisdiction of the reconstituted Sioux nation, even though they would have no vote in its government.

The Open Hills Committee, though, spent little time talking to the Sioux about these reasonable concerns. Mainly, it riled up what Miller himself described as South Dakota's considerable redneck population, people who would "just as soon load up the shotguns" as return any portion of the Hills to the Sioux. In a part of the country where many people thought of Indians as either dirty drunks or crazed militants, the Open Hills Committee had no difficulty with recruiting. "If you put dead pigs in a well it ruins the water," Miller observed about relations between Indians and whites in South Dakota. "The Black Hills bill was a big dead pig."

For his part in scuttling Sioux land return efforts, Senator Larry Pressler drafted a bill requiring an election on each reservation to decide whether to distribute the Supreme Court's just compensation award. Like Sioux leaders who since 1980 had assiduously blocked such referendums, Pressler no doubt figured that impoverished Sioux voters would lack the strength to resist an immediate cash payout of several thousand dollars. Pressler's bill never passed, but its introduction alone scared all the Sioux land return politicians who knew that plebiscites on the Black Hills issue could only discredit their claim that the Sioux would never accept the Black Hills award.

Despite his rebuff in Washington, throughout October and November, Stevens renewed his promises to the Sioux and continued to win converts. Three weeks after Stevens alienated every Sioux advocate in Congress, the Oglala tribal council officially repudiated the Bradley bill in favor of the Stevens plan, which also enjoyed strong support on Rosebud and Cheyenne River.

After a relatively quiet winter, in the spring Stevens launched an intensive publicity campaign for himself, the Black Hills claim, and his proposed solution. In late March, as a group of elders prepared to name him *Itancankel* (special chief), the debate in Sioux country erupted anew. Many Sioux resented the notion of bestowing such a special honor on a man who had yet to accomplish anything on their behalf and had not even legally enrolled as a member of one of the tribes. Others resented Stevens's false claim, picked up widely by the press, that the Sioux were about to name him their first "war chief" in 100 years.

The self-described master salesman had misjudged his audience, which began to grow restive and skeptical as his promises of quick success proved illusory. A Black Hills parade for which Stevens predicted 2,000 participants drew scarcely 200. Months dragged by with nothing but bad news from Washington. Although the Grey Eagles formally adopted Stevens into their group, and although Red Cloud and Gonzalez defended him, in light of his unfulfilled boasts Stevens's support melted like ice in the plains sun. "We are just a little sick and tired of. . . . Stevens in his war bonnet, Stevens in his fur cap, Stevens in his leather, fur-lined jacket and Stevens as spokesman for the Lakota Nation," Tim Giago, editor of the *Lakota Times*, commented in an editorial.

In August, the Oglala tribal council voted to rescind its endorsement of Stevens. Two months later, Cheyenne River did the same. Red Cloud, speaking for the Grey Eagles, asked Stevens to step back into a more private advisory role.

Stevens's $3.1 billion compensation plan, though, did not follow its author into the wings. On the contrary, among the Grey Eagles, the idea of attaining billions of dollars in damages for white trespass in the Hills had taken firm hold. Picking up where Stevens left off, in 1989 Red Cloud and his Grey Eagle followers asked Gonzalez and Jim Wilson (Dick Wilson's brother) to draft a bill for a return of the Black Hills and additional compensation.

Like the Bradley bill (though with some modifications), the Grey Eagle bill provided for the return of all federal lands in the Black Hills. The bill would establish a blue ribbon panel to provide "fair and just" compensation for the 113-year illegal occupation of the Black Hills. To guide the panel in its work, the Grey Eagle bill admonished that "the loss to the Sioux Nation must be measured in terms of the actual adjusted value of the resources extracted from the Black Hills which exceeds $18,000,000,000. . . ." Stevens had calculated his $3.1 billion compensation figure by using exactly this benchmark.

In the final section of their bill, the Grey Eagles also proposed to revise the entire political relationship between the Sioux Nation and the United States. Essentially, they asked Congress to grant the Sioux complete civil and criminal jurisdiction over all persons (including non-Indians) on all lands within the various Sioux reservations, even lands owned in fee patent by non-Indians. In effect, the Grey Eagles asked Congress to exempt the Sioux from literally dozens of federal laws and Supreme Court decisions that strictly limited the power of Indian tribes to criminally prosecute, tax, zone, or license non-Indians and their property. Almost incidentally, the Grey Eagles also demanded complete immunity from state taxation and the refunding of federal taxes paid by the Sioux.

On September 19, 1990, as a favor to his constituent Phil Stevens, Congressman Matthew Martinez introduced the Grey Eagle bill in the House. It received no action in Washington, though on the reservations the Sioux tribal councils split over whether to support the new initiative. Citing this dissension among the Sioux, Congressman Martinez declined to reintroduce the Grey Eagle bill in the 1991 Congress. As the Grey Eagle bill joined the Bradley bill in the Congressional dustbin, the combined value of the untouched Sioux judgment funds from the Black Hills claim and the 1868 treaty case topped $300 million.

More than 100 years ago, the veteran Indian fighter General George Crook admonished the Sioux that "instead of complaining of the past, they had better think of the future." And for almost that long, it has been the policy of the United States to resolve tribal grievances in the hope that, with past accounts settled, Indians would take their place as productive and forward-looking members of American society while the nation itself would be absolved of the great sin of its expansion. During that same hundred years, the Sioux, for their part, have many times expected that their tribal claims would deliver them miraculously from the poverty and despair that followed unremittingly upon their conquest.

The story of the Black Hills claim is the story of these false hopes. There has been no cleansing of guilt on the one side, neither adjustment nor deliverance on the other.

In 1875, Chief Red Cloud announced to the whites and to his own people that the Black Hills must support the Sioux for seven generations to come. Both sides have failed him. The whites exchanged the Black Hills for a $106 million court award, sixty years in the making, a sum too little and too late even to begin the process of healing wounds that they had allowed to fester for a century.

As for the Sioux, the claims process has encouraged them to evade any real responsibility for repairing the tragic condition of their lives. They have come to believe that their status as victims, their sense of grievance, is their greatest source of strength and only hope for unity. And in this belief the Sioux have abandoned any meaningful attempt to control their own destiny in favor of rhetorical claims to sovereignty and independence.

A few lonely Sioux voices have harkened back to Red Cloud's plea—to the basic truth that without economic self-sufficiency, without a larger land base of their own, the Sioux will never again know political or spiritual freedom. In 1980, after the Supreme Court's decision in the Black Hills claim, Vine Deloria, Jr., suggested that the Sioux use their judgment money to buy land either in the Black Hills or on the existing reservations to start the process of rebuilding the tribe's economic foundation. Ramon Roubideaux has suggested that the Sioux trade their Black Hills money for federal lands in the Black Hills. Others have advised the Sioux to use their $300 million claims legacy not only to purchase land, but also to finance a massive lobbying campaign to turn around the South Dakota congressional delegation and actually secure passage of Black Hills legislation.

But these have been lonely cries in the plains wilderness. And, in the meantime, of Red Cloud's seven generations, four already have died. The fifth is dying now.

▼ ▼ ▼ ▼ ▼

CHRONOLOGY

1775 Standing Bull and his band of Teton Sioux reach the Black Hills.

1787 Congress passes Northwest Ordinance declaring that the "land and property [of Indian tribes] shall never be taken from them without their consent."

1804 Lewis and Clark meet with Sioux.

1825 Atkinson-O'Fallon mission signs peace treaties with Teton Sioux.

1842 First wagons cross Sioux country on Oregon Trail.

1851 Fort Laramie treaty between the United States and plains tribes recognizes Sioux ownership of 60 million acres of land, but allocates Powder River and Big Horn country to other tribes.

1862 Sioux wars begin with Santee uprising in Minnesota.

1865 United States negotiates treaty with "friendly" Sioux bands.

1866 United States enters negotiations with hostile Sioux over travel routes to Montana. Red Cloud declares war when United States moves to fortify Bozeman Trail. Sioux annihilate Colonel William Fetterman and his troops.

1868 Treaty of 1868 establishes Great Sioux Reservation as permanent home of the Sioux Nation and preserves Powder River and Big Horn country as "unceded Indian territory."

1874   Custer Expedition explores Black Hills and discovers gold.

1875   Allison Commission attempts to purchase or lease Black Hills, but fails.

1876   United States declares war on Sioux. After Sioux defeat Custer at the Little Big Horn, Manypenny Commission demands that Sioux relinquish Black Hills or starve.

1877   Congressional Act of February 28, 1877 ratifies Manypenny Agreement, taking the Black Hills and extinguishing all Sioux rights outside Great Sioux Reservation.

1889   United States and Sioux sign agreement breaking up Great Sioux Reservation into six separate reservations and substantially reducing Sioux land holdings.

1890   Massacre at Wounded Knee ends era of armed confrontation between Sioux and United States.

1903   Supreme Court confirms in *Lonewolf* v. *Hitchcock* that Congress has authority to break Indian treaties. Court also broadly defines Congress's plenary power over Indian affairs.

1920   Sioux Jurisdictional Act authorizes Court of Claims to adjudicate tribes' legal and equitable claims against United States.

1922   Ralph Case and associates hired as counsel by eight Sioux tribes.

1923   Ralph Case files 24 separate Sioux compensation claims in Court of Claims.

1934   Indian Reorganization Act reverses U.S. policy of forced Indian assimilation and provides for increased tribal sovereignty. Sioux tribes vote to organize tribal governments under its auspices.

1937   Supreme Court rules in *Shoshone* v. *United States* that the Fifth Amendment requires Congress to pay just compensation for takings of tribal land.

1942   Court of Claims dismisses Black Hills claim.

1946   Congress passes Indian Claims Commission Act.

1950   Ralph Case refiles Black Hills claim in the Indian Claims Commission.

1953   Congress passes major legislation aimed at terminating federal responsibility over Indians.

1954   Indian Claims Commission rejects Black Hills claim.

1956   Court of Claims affirms Indian Claims Commission deci-
        sion.

        Oglala (Pine Ridge), Rosebud, and Standing Rock Sioux
        tribes replace Ralph Case with Arthur Lazarus, Jr., and
        Richard Schifter (of Riegelman, Strasser, Schwarz & Spie-
        gelberg) and Marvin Sonosky.

1957   On motion of new Sioux counsel, Court of Claims vacates
        prior proceedings in Black Hills claim.

1961   Sioux counsel file amended petitions dividing Sioux claims
        into the Black Hills claim and the 1868 Treaty case.

1964   Sioux Indians occupy Alcatraz Island under auspices of
        1868 treaty.

1968   Court of Claims decides *Three Affiliated Tribes of the Fort
        Berthold Reservation* v. *United States*, establishing good faith
        effort test for Fifth Amendment taking claims.

        Congress passes Indian Civil Rights Act suspending termi-
        nation policy and extending many constitutional rights to
        individual Indians living on reservations.

        American Indian Movement founded.

1970   Valuation trials in Black Hills claim.

1972   Trail of Broken Treaties. Indian occupation of Bureau of
        Indian Affairs.

1973   Occupation of Wounded Knee.

1974   Indian Claims Commission awards Sioux $17.5 million
        plus interest for taking of the Black Hills pending determi-
        nation of government offsets.

1975   Congress amends Indian Claims Commission Act of 1946
        to eliminate food, rations, and provisions as allowable off-
        sets.

        Court of Claims rules that Sioux Fifth Amendment taking
        claim is barred by *res judicata*, thereby reversing Indian
        Claims Commission decision.

1978   Congress waives defense of *res judicata* in Black Hills claim
        and provides for new trial on Fifth Amendment taking
        issue.

1979   Court of Claims awards Sioux $17.5 million plus interest
        for taking of Black Hills.

1980   Supreme Court affirms Court of Claims ruling in Black
        Hills claim and awards Sioux $106 million.

1982 Federal appeals court dismisses Oglala Sioux claims against United States and Homestake Mining Company.

1985 Senator Bill Bradley introduces first Black Hills land return legislation.

1989 Court of Claims awards Sioux $40 million in 1868 treaty case.

Appendix A:
The Treaty of 1868

TREATY WITH THE SIOUX—BRULÉ, OGLALA, MINICONJOU, YANKTONAI, HUNKPAPA, BLACKFEET, CUTHEAD, TWO KETTLE, SANS ARCS, AND SANTEE—AND ARAPAHO, 1868.

Apr. 29, 1868

15 Stats., 635
Ratified, Feb. 16, 1869.
Proclaimed, Feb. 24, 1869.

Articles of a treaty made and concluded by and between Lieutenant-General William T. Sherman, General William S. Harney, General Alfred H. Terry, General C. C. Augur, J. B. Henderson, Nathaniel G. Taylor, John B. Sanborn, and Samuel F. Tappan, duly appointed commissioners on the part of the United States, and the different bands of the Sioux Nation of Indians, by their chiefs and head-men, whose names are hereto subscribed, they being duly authorized to act in the premises.

War to cease and peace to be kept.

ARTICLE 1. From this day forward all war between the parties to this agreement shall forever cease. The Government of the United States desires peace, and its honor is hereby pledged to keep it. The Indians desire peace, and they now pledge their honor to maintain it.

Offenders against the Indians to be arrested, etc.

If bad men among the whites, or among other people subject to the authority of the United States, shall commit any wrong upon the person or property of the Indians, the United States will, upon proof made to the agent and forwarded to the Commissioner of Indian Affairs at Washington City, proceed at once to cause the offender to be arrested and punished according to the laws of the United States, and also re-imburse the injured person for the loss sustained.

Wrongdoers
against the whites
to be punished.

If bad men among the Indians shall commit a wrong or depredation upon the person or property of any one, white, black, or Indian, subject to the authority of the United States, and at peace therewith, the Indians herein named solemnly agree that they will, upon proof made to their agent and notice by him, deliver up the wrong-doer to the United States, to be tried and

Damages.

punished according to its laws; and in case they wilfully refuse so to do, the person injured shall be reimbursed for his loss from the annuities or other moneys due or to become due to them under this or other treaties made with the United States. And the President, on advising with the Commissioner of Indian Affairs, shall prescribe such rules and regulations for ascertaining damages under the provisions of this article as in his judgment may be proper. But no one sustaining loss while violating the provisions of this treaty or the laws of the United States shall be reimbursed therefor.

Reservation
boundaries.

ARTICLE 2. The United States agrees that the following district of country, to wit, viz: commencing on the east bank of the Missouri River where the forty-sixth parallel of north latitude crosses the same, thence along low-water mark down said east bank to a point opposite where the northern line of the State of Nebraska strikes the river, thence west across said river, and along the northern line of Nebraska to the one hundred and fourth degree of longitude west from Greenwich, thence north on said meridian to a point where the forty-sixth parallel of north latitude intercepts the same, thence due east along said parallel to the place of beginning; and in addition thereto, all existing reservations on the east bank of said river shall be, and the same is, set apart for the absolute and undisturbed use and occupation of the Indians herein named, and for such other friendly tribes or individual Indians as from time to time they may be willing, with the consent of the United States, to admit

Certain persons
not to enter or
reside thereon.

amongst them; and the United States now solemnly agrees that no persons except those herein designated and authorized so to do, and except such officers, agents, and employés of the Government as may be authorized to enter upon Indian reservations in discharge of duties enjoined by law, shall ever be permitted to pass over, settle upon, or reside in the territory described in this article, or in such territory as may be added to this reservation for the use of said Indians, and henceforth they will and do hereby relinquish all claims or right in and to any portion of the United States or Territories, except such as is embraced within the limits aforesaid, and except as hereinafter provided.

Additional arable land to be added, if, etc.

ARTICLE 3. If it should appear from actual survey or other satisfactory examination of said tract of land that it contains less than one hundred and sixty acres of tillable land for each person who, at the time, may be authorized to reside on it under the provisions of this treaty, and a very considerable number of such persons shall be disposed to commence cultivating the soil as farmers, the United States agrees to set apart, for the use of said Indians, as herein provided, such additional quantity of arable land, adjoining to said reservation, or as near to the same as it can be obtained, as may be required to provide the necessary amount.

Buildings on reservation.

ARTICLE 4. The United States agrees, at its own proper expense, to construct at some place on the Missouri River, near the center of said reservation, where timber and water may be convenient, the following buildings, to wit: a warehouse, a store-room for the use of the agent in storing goods belonging to the Indians, to cost not less than twenty-five hundred dollars; an agency-building for the residence of the agent, to cost not exceeding three thousand dollars; a residence for the physician, to cost not more than three thousand dollars; and five other buildings, for a carpenter, farmer, blacksmith, miller, and engineer, each to cost not exceeding two thousand dollars; also a school-house or mission-building, so soon as a sufficient number of children can be induced by the agent to attend school, which shall not cost exceeding five thousand dollars.

The United States agrees further to cause to be erected on said reservation, near the other buildings herein authorized, a good steam circular-saw mill, with a grist-mill and shingle-machine attached to the same, to cost not exceeding eight thousand dollars.

Agent's residence, office, and duties

ARTICLE 5. The United States agrees that the agent for said Indians shall in the future make his home at the agency-building; that he shall reside among them, and keep an office open at all times for the purpose of prompt and diligent inquiry into such matters of complaint by and against the Indians as may be presented for investigation under the provisions of their treaty stipulations, as also for the faithful discharge of other duties enjoined on him by law. In all cases of depredation on person or property he shall cause the evidence to be taken in writing and forwarded, together with his findings, to the Commissioner of Indian Affairs, whose decision, subject to the revision of the Secretary of the Interior, shall be binding on the parties to this treaty.

Heads of families may select lands for farming.

ARTICLE 6. If any individual belonging to said tribes of Indians, or legally incorporated with them, being the head of a family, shall desire to commence farming, he shall have the privilege to select, in the presence and with the assistance of the agent then in charge, a tract of land within said reservation, not exceeding three hundred and twenty acres in extent, which tract, when so selected, certified, and recorded in the "land-book," as herein directed, shall cease to be held in common, but the same may be occupied and held in the exclusive possession of the person selecting it, and of his family, so long as he or they may continue to cultivate it.

Others may select land for cultivation.

Any person over eighteen years of age, not being the head of a family, may in like manner select and cause to be certified to him or her, for purposes of cultivation, a quantity of land not exceeding eighty acres in extent, and thereupon be entitled to the exclusive possession of the same as above directed.

Certificates

For each tract of land so selected a certificate, containing a description thereof and the name of the person selecting it, with a certificate endorsed thereon that the same has been recorded, shall be delivered to the party entitled to it, by the agent, after the same shall have been recorded by him in a book to be kept in his office, subject to inspection, which said book shall be known as the "Sioux Land Book."

Surveys.

The President may, at any time, order a survey of the reservation, and, when so surveyed, Congress shall provide for protecting the rights of said settlers in their improvements, and may fix the character of the title held by each. The United States may pass such laws on the subject of alienation and descent of prop-

Alienation and descent of property.

erty between the Indians and their descendants as may be thought proper. And it is further stipulated that any male Indian, over eighteen years of age, of any band or tribe that is or shall hereafter become a party to this treaty, who now is or who shall hereafter become a resident or occupant of any reservation or Territory not included in the tract of country designated and described in this treaty for the permanent home of the Indians, which is not mineral land, nor reserved by the United States for special purposes other than Indian occupation, and who shall have made improvements thereon of the value of two hundred dollars or more, and continuously occupied the same as a homestead for the term of three years, shall be entitled to receive from the United States a patent for one hundred and sixty acres of land including his said improvements, the same to be in the form of the legal subdivisions of the surveys of the public lands. Upon application in writing, sustained by the proof of two disinterested witnesses, made to the register of the local land-office when the land sought to be entered is within a land district, and when the tract sought to be entered is not in any land district, then upon said application and proof being made to the Commissioner of the General Land-Office, and the right of such Indian or Indians to enter such tract or tracts of land shall accrue and be perfect from the date of his first improvements thereon, and shall continue as long as he continues his residence and improvements, and no longer. And any Indian or Indians receiving a patent for land under the foregoing provisions, shall thereby and from thenceforth become and be a citizen of the United States, and be entitled to all the privileges and immunities of such citizens, and shall, at the same time, retain all his rights to benefits accruing to Indians under this treaty.

Certain Indians may receive patents for 160 acres of land.

Such Indians receiving patents to become citizens of the United States.

Education.

ARTICLE 7. In order to insure the civilization of the Indians entering into this treaty, the necessity of education is admitted, especially of such of them as are or may be settled on said agricultural reservations, and they therefore pledge themselves to compel their children, male and female, between the ages of six and sixteen years, to attend school; and it is hereby made the duty of the agent for said Indians to see that this stipulation is strictly complied with; and the United States agrees that for every thirty children between

Children to attend school.

said ages who can be induced or compelled to attend school, a house shall be provided and a teacher competent to teach the elementary branches of an English education shall be furnished, who will reside among said Indians, and faithfully discharge his or her duties as a teacher. The provisions of this article to continue for not less than twenty years.

ARTICLE 8. When the head of a family or lodge shall have selected lands and received his certificate as above directed, and the agent shall be satisfied that he intends in good faith to commence cultivating the soil for a living, he shall be entitled to receive seeds and agricultural implements for the first year, not exceeding in value one hundred dollars, and for each succeeding year he shall continue to farm, for a period of three years more, he shall be entitled to receive seeds and implements as aforesaid, not exceeding in value twenty-five dollars

And it is further stipulated that such persons as commence farming shall receive instruction from the farmer herein provided for, and whenever more than one hundred persons shall enter upon the cultivation of the soil, a second blacksmith shall be provided, with such iron, steel, and other material as may be needed.

ARTICLE 9. At any time after ten years from the making of this treaty, the United States shall have the privilege of withdrawing the physician, farmer, blacksmith, carpenter, engineer, and miller herein provided for, but in case of such withdrawal, an additional sum thereafter of ten thousand dollars per annum shall be devoted to the education of said Indians, and the Commissioner of Indian Affairs shall, upon careful inquiry into their condition, make such rules and regulations for the expenditure of said sum as will best promote the educational and moral improvement of said tribes.

ARTICLE 10. In lieu of all sums of money or other annuities provided to be paid to the Indians herein named, under any treaty or treaties heretofore made, the United States agrees to deliver at the agency-house on the reservation herein named on or before the first day of August of each year, for thirty years, the following articles, to wit:

For each male person over fourteen years of age, a suit of good substantial woolen clothing, consisting of

---

Marginal notes (left column):

Schoolhouses and teachers.

Seeds and agricultural implements.

Instructions in farming.

Second blacksmith.

Physician, farmer, etc., may be withdrawn.

Additional appropriation in such cases.

Delivery of goods in lieu of money or other annuities.

Clothing.

coat, pantaloons, flannel shirt, hat, and a pair of home-made socks.

For each female over twelve years of age, a flannel skirt, or the goods necessary to make it, a pair of woolen hose, twelve yards of calico, and twelve yards of cotton domestics.

For the boys and girls under the ages named, such flannel and cotton goods as may be needed to make each a suit as aforesaid together with a pair of woolen hose for each.

Census.

And in order that the Commissioner of Indian Affairs may be able to estimate properly for the articles herein named, it shall be the duty of the agent each year to forward to him a full and exact census of the Indians, on which the estimate from year to year can be based.

Other necessary articles.

And in addition to the clothing herein named, the sum of ten dollars for each person entitled to the beneficial effects of this treaty shall be annually appropriated for a period of thirty years, while such persons roam and hunt, and twenty dollars for each person who engages in farming, to be used by the Secretary of the Interior in the purchase of such articles as from time to time the condition and necessities of the Indians may indicate to be proper. And if within the thirty years, at any time, it shall appear that the amount of money needed for clothing under this article can be appropriated to better uses for the Indians named herein, Congress may, by law, change the appropriation to other purposes; but in no event shall the amount of this appropriation be withdrawn or discontinued for the period named. And the President shall annually detail an officer of the Army to be present and attest the delivery of all the goods herein named to the Indians, and he shall inspect and report on the quantity and quality of the goods and the manner of their delivery. And it is hereby expressly stipulated that each Indian over the age of four years, who shall have removed to and settled permanently upon said reservation and complied with the stipulations of this treaty, shall be entitled to receive from the United States, for the period of four years after he shall have settled upon said reservation, one pound of meat and one pound of flour per day, provided the Indians cannot furnish their own subsistence at an earlier date. And it is further stipulated that the United States will

Appropriation to continue for thirty years.

Army officer to attend the delivery.

Meat and flour.

furnish and deliver to each lodge of Indians or family of persons legally incorporated with them, who shall remove to the reservation herein described and commence farming, one good American cow, and one good well-broken pair of American oxen within sixty days after such lodge or family shall have so settled upon said reservation.

Cows and oxen.

ARTICLE 11. In consideration of the advantages and benefits conferred by this treaty, and the many pledges of friendship by the United States, the tribes who are parties to this agreement hereby stipulate that they will relinquish all right to occupy permanently the territory outside their reservation as herein defined, but yet reserve the right to hunt on any lands north of North Platte, and on the Republican Fork of the Smoky Hill River, so long as the buffalo may range thereon in such numbers as to justify the chase. And they, the said Indians, further expressly agree:

Right to occupy territory outside of the reservation surrendered.

Right to hunt reserved.

1st. That they will withdraw all opposition to the construction of the railroads now being built on the plains.

Agreements as to railroad.

2d. That they will permit the peaceful construction of any railroad not passing over their reservation as herein defined.

3d. That they will not attack any persons at home, or travelling, nor molest or disturb any wagon-trains, coaches, mules, or cattle belonging to the people of the United States, or to persons friendly therewith.

Emigrants, etc.

4th. They will never capture, or carry off from the settlements, white women or children.

Women and children.

5th. They will never kill or scalp white men, nor attempt to do them harm.

White men.

6th. They withdraw all pretence of opposition to the construction of the railroad now being built along the Platte River and westward to the Pacific Ocean, and they will not in future object to the construction of railroads, wagon-roads, mail-stations, or other works of utility or necessity, which may be ordered or permitted by the laws of the United States. But should such roads or other works be constructed on the lands of their reservation, the Government will pay the tribe whatever amount of damage may be assessed by three disinterested commissioners to be appointed by the President for that purpose, one of said commissioners to be a chief or head-man of the tribe.

Pacific Railroad, wagon roads, etc.

Damages for crossing their reservation.

7th. They agree to withdraw all opposition to the

Military posts and roads.

military posts or roads now established south of the North Platte River, or that may be established, not in violation of treaties heretofore made or hereafter to be made with any of the Indian tribes.

No treaty for cession of reservation to be valid unless, etc.

ARTICLE 12. No treaty for the cession of any portion or part of the reservation herein described which may be held in common shall be of any validity or force as against the said Indians, unless executed and signed by at least three-fourths of all the adult male Indians, occupying or interested in the same; and no cession by the tribe shall be understood or construed in such manner as to deprive, without his consent, any individual member of the tribe of his rights to any tract of land selected by him, as provided in article 6 of this treaty.

United States to furnish physician, teachers, etc.

ARTICLE 13. The United States hereby agrees to furnish annually to the Indians the physician, teachers, carpenter, miller, engineer, farmer, and blacksmiths as herein contemplated, and that such appropriations shall be made from time to time, on the estimates of the Secretary of the Interior, as will be sufficient to employ such persons.

Presents for crops.

ARTICLE 14. It is agreed that the sum of five hundred dollars annually, for three years from date, shall be expended in presents to the ten persons of said tribe who in the judgment of the agent may grow the most valuable crops for the respective year.

Reservation to be permanent home of tribes.

ARTICLE 15. The Indians herein named agree that when the agency-house or other buildings shall be constructed on the reservation named, they will regard said reservation their permanent home, and they will make no permanent settlement elsewhere; but they shall have the right, subject to the conditions and modifications of this treaty, to hunt, as stipulated in Article 11 hereof.

Unceded Indian territory.

ARTICLE 16. The United States hereby agrees and stipulates that the country north of the North Platte River and east of the summits of the Big Horn Mountains shall be held and considered to be unceded Indian territory, and also stipulates and agrees that no

Not to be occupied by whites, etc,.

white person or persons shall be permitted to settle upon or occupy any portion of the same; or without the consent of the Indians first had and obtained, to pass through the same; and it is further agreed by the United States that within ninety days after the conclusion of peace with all the bands of the Sioux Nation, the military posts now established in the territory in this article named shall be abandoned, and that the road leading to them and by them to the settlements in the Territory of Montana shall be closed.

Effect of this treaty upon former treaties.

ARTICLE 17. It is hereby expressly understood and agreed by and between the respective parties to this treaty that the execution of this treaty and its ratification by the United States Senate shall have the effect, and shall be construed as abrogating and annulling all treaties and agreements heretofore entered into between the respective parties hereto, so far as such treaties and agreements obligate the United States to furnish and provide money, clothing, or other articles of property to such Indians and bands of Indians as become parties to this treaty, but no further.

In testimony of all which, we, the said commissioners, and we, the chiefs and headsmen of the Brulé band of the Sioux nation, have hereunto set our hands and seals at Fort Laramie, Dakota Territory, this twenty-ninth day of April, in the year one thousand eight hundred and sixty-eight.

> N. G. Taylor,   [SEAL.]
> W. T. Sherman,   [SEAL.]
> Lieutenant-General.
> Wm. S. Harney,   [SEAL.]
> Brevet Major-General U. S. Army.
> John B. Sanborn,   [SEAL.]
> S. F. Tappan,   [SEAL.]
> C. C. Augur,   [SEAL.]
> Brevet Major-General.
> Alfred H. Terry,   [SEAL.]
> Brevet Major-General U. S. Army.

Attest:
A. S. H. White, Secretary.

Executed on the part of the Brulé band of Sioux by the chiefs and headmen whose names are hereto annexed, they being thereunto duly authorized, at Fort Laramie, D. T., the twenty-ninth day of April, in the year A.D. 1868.

Ma-za-pon-kaska, his x mark, Iron Shell. [SEAL.]	Zin-tah-gah-lat-skah, his x mark, Spotted Tail. [SEAL.]
Wah-pat-shah, his x mark, Red Leaf. [SEAL.]	Zin-tah-skah, his x mark, White Tail. [SEAL.]
Hah-sah-pah, his x mark, Black Horn. [SEAL.]	Me-wah-tah-ne-ho-skah, his x mark, Tall Mandas. [SEAL.]

She-cha-chat-kah, his x
  mark, Bad Left Hand. [SEAL.]
No-mah-no-pah, his x
  mark, Two and Two. [SEAL.]
Tah-tonka-skah, his x mark,
  White Bull. [SEAL.]
Con-ra-washta, his x mark,
  Pretty Coon. [SEAL.]
Ha-cah-cah-she-chah, his x
  mark, Bad Elk. [SEAL.]
Wa-ha-ka-zah-ish-tah, his x
  mark, Eye Lance. [SEAL.]
Ma-to-ha-ke-tah, his x
  mark, Bear that looks
  behind. [SEAL.]
Bella-tonka-tonka, his x
  mark, Big Partisan. [SEAL.]
Mah-to-ho-honka, his x
  mark, Swift Bear. [SEAL.]
To-wis-ne, his x mark,

Cold Place. [SEAL.]
Ish-tah-skah, his x mark,
  White Eyes. [SEAL.]
Ma-ta-loo-zah, his x mark,
  Fast Bear. [SEAL.]
As-hah-kah-nah-zhe, his x
  mark, Standing Elk. [SEAL.]
Can-te-te-ki-ya, his x mark,
  The Brave Heart. [SEAL.]
Shunka-shaton, his x mark,
  Day Hawk. [SEAL.]
Tatanka-wakon, his x mark,
  Sacred Bull. [SEAL.]
Mapia shaton, his x mark,
  Hawk Cloud. [SEAL.]
Ma-sha-a-ow, his x mark,
  Stands and Comes. [SEAL.]
Shon-ka-ton-ka, his x
  mark, Big Dog. [SEAL.]

Attest:

Ashton S. H. White, secretary
  of commission
George B. Withs,
  phonographer to
  commission.
Geo. H. Holtzman.

John D. Howland.
James C. O'Connor.
Chas. E. Guern, interpreter.
Leon F. Pallardy, interpreter.
Nicholas Janis, interpreter.

Execution by the Ogallalah band.

Executed on the part of the Ogallalah band of Sioux by the chiefs and headmen whose names are hereto subscribed, they being thereunto duly authorized, at Fort Laramie, the twenty-fifth day of May, in the year A.D. 1868.

Tah-shun-ka-co-qui-pah, his
  x mark, Man-afraid-
  of-his-horses [SEAL.]
Sha-ton-skah, his x mark,
  White Hawk. [SEAL.]
Sha-ton-sapah, his x mark,
  Black Hawk. [SEAL.]
E-ga-mon-ton-ka-sapah, his
  x mark, Black Tiger. [SEAL.]
Oh-wah-she-cha, his x
  mark, Bad Wound. [SEAL.]
Pah-gee, his x mark,
  Grass. [SEAL.]
Wah-non-reh-che-geh, his
  x mark, Ghost Heart. [SEAL.]
Con-reeh, his x mark,
  Crow. [SEAL.]
Oh-he-te-kah, his x mark,
  The Brave. [SEAL.]
Tah-ton-kah-he-vo-ta-kah,
  his x mark, Sitting
  Bull. [SEAL.]
Shon-ka-oh-wah-mon-ye,
  his x mark,

Whirlwind Dog. [SEAL.]
Ha-hah-kah-tah-miech, his
  x mark, Poor Elk. [SEAL.]
Wam-bu-lee-wah-kon, his x
  mark, Medicine Eagle. [SEAL.]
Chon-gah-ma-he-to-hans-ka,
  his x mark, High
  Wolf. [SEAL.]
Wah-se-chun-ta-shun-kah,
  his x mark,
  American Horse. [SEAL.]
Mah-hah-mah-ha-mak-near,
  his x mark, Man
  that walks under the
  ground. [SEAL.]
Mah-to-tow-pah, his x
  mark, Four Bears. [SEAL.]
Ma-to-wee-sha-kta, his
  x mark, One that kills
  the bear. [SEAL.]
Oh-tah-kee-toka-wee-chakta,
  his x mark, One that
  kills in a hard place. [SEAL.]
Tah-ton-kah-ta-miech, his x

mark, The poor Bull. [SEAL.]
Oh-huns-ee-ga-non-sken,
his x mark, Mad
Shade. [SEAL.]
Shah-ton-oh-nah-om-
minne-ne-oh-minne,
his x mark, Whirling
Hawk. [SEAL.]
Mah-to-chun-ka-oh, his x
mark, Bear's Back. [SEAL.]
Che-ton-wee-koh, his x
mark, Fool Hawk. [SEAL.]
Wah-hoh-ke-za-ah-hah, his x
mark, One that has the
lance. [SEAL.]
Shon-gah-manni-toh-tan-
ka-seh, his x mark,
Big Wolf Foot. [SEAL.]
Eh-ton-kah, his x mark,
Big Mouth. [SEAL.]
Ma-pah-che-tah, his x
mark, Bad Hand. [SEAL.]
Wah-ke-yun-shah, his x
mark, Red Thunder. [SEAL.]

Wak-sah, his x mark, One
that Cuts Off. [SEAL.]
Cham-nom-qui-yah, his x
mark, One that Presents
the Pipe. [SEAL.]
Wah-ke-ke-yan-puh-tah,
his x mark, Fire
Thunder. [SEAL.]
Mah-to-nonk-pah-ze, his x
mark, Bear with Yellow
Ears. [SEAL.]
Con-ree-teh-ka, his x mark,
The Little Crow. [SEAL.]
He-hup-pah-toh, his x mark,
The Blue War Club. [SEAL.]
Shon-kee-toh, his x mark,
The Blue Horse. [SEAL.]
Wam-Balla-oh-con-quo, his
x mark, Quick Eagle. [SEAL.]
Ta-tonka-suppa, his x mark,
Black Bull. [SEAL.]
Moh-to-ha-she-na, his x
mark, The Bear Hide. [SEAL.]

Attest:

S. E. Ward.
Jas. C. O'Connor.
J. M. Sherwood.
W. C. Slicer.
Sam Deon.

H. M. Matthews.
Joseph Bissonette, interpreter.
Nicholas Janis, interpreter.
Lefroy Jott, interpreter.
Antoine Janis, interpreter.

Execution by the
Minneconjon band.

Executed on the part of the Minneconjon band of
Sioux by the chiefs and headmen whose names are
hereto subscribed, they being thereunto duly authorized.

At Fort Laramie, D. T., May 26, '68, 13 names.

Heh-won-ge-chat, [SEAL.]
his x mark, One Horn.

Oh-pon-ah-tah-e-manne. [SEAL.]
his x mark, The Elk that bellows Walking.

At Fort Laramie, D. T., May 25, '68, 2 names.

Heh-ho-lah-reh-cha-skah.
his x mark, Young White Bull. [SEAL.]

Wah-chah-chum-kah-coh-
kee-pah, his x mark,
One that is afraid
of Shield. [SEAL.]
He-hon-ne-shakta, his x
mark, The Old Owl. [SEAL.]
Moc-pe-a-toh, his x mark,
Blue Cloud. [SEAL.]

Oh-pong-ge-le-skah, his x
mark, Spotted Elk. [SEAL.]
Tah-tonk-ka-hon-ke-schne,
his x mark, Slow
Bull. [SEAL.]
Shonk-a-nee-shah-shah-
a-tah-pe, his x mark,
The Dog Chief. [SEAL.]

Ma-to-tah-ta-tonk-ka, his x
mark, Bull Bear. [SEAL.]
Wom-beh-le-ton-kah, his x
mark, The Big Eagle. [SEAL.]
Ma-toh-eh-schne-lah, his x
mark, The Lone Bear. [SEAL.]
Mah-toh-ke-su-yah, his x
mark, The One Who
Remembers the Bear. [SEAL.]

Ma-toh-oh-he-to-keh, his
x mark, The Brave
Bear. [SEAL.]
Eh-che-ma-heh, his x mark,
The Runner. [SEAL.]
Ti-ki-ya, his x mark, The
Hard. [SEAL.]
He-ma-za, his x mark, Iron
Horn. [SEAL.]

Attest:

Jas. C. O'Connor.
Wm. H. Brown.

Nicholas Janis, interpreter.
Antoine Janis, interpreter.

Execution by the
Yanctonais band.

Executed on the part of the Yanctonais band of
Sioux by the chiefs and headmen whose names are
hereto subscribed, they being thereunto duly authorized.

Mah-to-non-pah, his x
mark, Two Bears. [SEAL.]
Ma-to-hna skin-ya, his x
mark, Mad Bear. [SEAL.]
He-o-pu-za, his x mark,
Louzy. [SEAL.]
Ah-ke-che-tah-che-ca-dan,
his x mark, Little
Soldier. [SEAL.]
Mah-to-e-tan-chan, his x
mark, Chief Bear. [SEAL.]
Cu-wi-h-win, his x mark,
Rotten Stomach. [SEAL.]
Skun-ka-we-tko, his x mark,
Fool Dog. [SEAL.]
Ish-ta-sap-pah, his x mark,
Black Eye. [SEAL.]
Ih-tan-chan, his x mark,
The Chief. [SEAL.]
I-a-wi-ca-ka, his x mark,
The one who Tells
the Truth. [SEAL.]
Ah-ke-che-tah, his x mark,
The Soldier. [SEAL.]
Ta-shi-na-gi, his x mark,
Yellow Robe. [SEAL.]
Nah-pe-ton-ka, his x mark,
Big Hand. [SEAL.]
Chan-tee-we-kto, his x mark,
Fool Heart. [SEAL.]
Hoh-gan-sah-pa, his x mark,
Black Catfish. [SEAL.]
Mah-to-wah-kan, his x mark,
Medicine Bear. [SEAL.]
Shun-ka-kan-sha, his x mark,
Red Horse. [SEAL.]
Wan-rode, his x mark, The
Eagle. [SEAL.]
Can-hpi-sa-pa, his x mark,
Black Tomahawk. [SEAL.]

War-he-le-re, his x mark,
Yellow Eagle. [SEAL.]
Cha-ton-che-ca, his x mark,
Small Hawk, or
Long Fare. [SEAL.]
Shu-ger-mon-e-too-ha-ska,
his x mark,
Tall Wolf. [SEAL.]
Ma-to-u-tah-kah, his x mark,
Sitting Bear. [SEAL.]
Hi-ha-cah-ge-na-skene, his x
mark, Mad Elk. [SEAL.]
Arapahoes:
Little Chief, his x mark. [SEAL.]
Tall Bear, his x mark. [SEAL.]
Top Man, his x mark. [SEAL.]
Neva, his x mark. [SEAL.]
The Wounded Bear, his x
mark. [SEAL.]
Thirlwind, his x mark. [SEAL.]
The Fox, his x mark. [SEAL.]
The Dog Big Mouth, his x
mark. [SEAL.]
Spotted Wolf, his x
mark. [SEAL.]
Sorrel Horse, his x
mark. [SEAL.]
Black Coal, his x mark. [SEAL.]
Big Wolf, his x mark. [SEAL.]
Knock-knee, his x mark. [SEAL.]
Black Crow, his x mark. [SEAL.]
The Lone Old Man, his x
mark. [SEAL.]
Paul, his x mark. [SEAL.]
Black Bull, his x mark. [SEAL.]
Big Track, his x mark. [SEAL.]
The Foot, his x mark. [SEAL.]
Black White, his x mark. [SEAL.]
Yellow Hair, his x mark. [SEAL.]
Little Shield, his x mark. [SEAL.]

Black Bear, his x mark. [SEAL.]   Big Robe, his x mark.   [SEAL.]
Wolf Mocassin, his x   Wolf Chief, his x mark. [SEAL.]
mark.   [SEAL.]

Witnesses:

Robt. P. McKibbin, captain,   Fourth Infantry.
Fourth Infantry, brevet   Theo. E. True, second
lieutenant-colonel, U.S.   lieutenant, Fourth Infantry.
Army, commanding Fort   W. G. Bullock.
Laramie.   Chas. E. Guern, special Indian
Wm. H. Powell, brevet major,   interpreter for the peace
captain, Fourth Infantry.   commission.
Henry W. Patterson, captain,

                     Fort Laramie. Wg. T. *Novr. 6, 1868.*
Makh-pi-ah-lu-tah, his x   tuyah, his x mark,
mark, Red Cloud.   [SEAL.]   High Eagle.   [SEAL.]
Wa-ki-ah-we-cha-shah, his   Ko-ke-pah, his x mark, Man
x mark, Thunder   Afraid.   [SEAL.]
Man.   [SEAL.]   Wa-ki-ah-wa-kou-ah, his x
Ma-zah-zah-geh, his x   mark, Thunder Flying
mark, Iron Cane.   [SEAL.]   Running   [SEAL.]
Wa-umble-why-wa-ka-

Witnesses:

W. McE. Dye, brevet colonel,   G. L. Luhn, first lieutenant,
U.S. Army, commanding.   Fourth Infantry, brevet
A. B. Cain, captain, Fourth   captain, U. S. Army.
Infantry, brevet major, U.S.   H. C. Sloan, second lieutenant,
Army.   Fourth Infantry.
Robt. P. McKibbin, captain,   Whittingham Cox, first
Fourth Infantry, brevet   lieutenant, Fourth Infantry.
lieutenant-colonel, U. S.   A. W. Vogdes, first lieutenant,
Army.   Fourth Infantry.
Jno. Miller, captain, Fourth   Butler D. Price, second
Infantry.   lieutenant, Fourth Infantry.

Headqrs., Fort Laramie, *Novr. 6, '68.*

Executed by the above on this date.

All of the Indians are Ogallalahs excepting Thunder Man and Thunder Flying Running, who are Brulés.

Wm. McE. Dye,
Major Fourth Infantry, and Brevet-Colonel
U.S. Army, Commanding.

Attest:

Jas. C. O'Connor.   missionary among the
Nicholas Janis, interpreter.   Indians.
Franc. La Framboise,   Saml. D. Hinman, B. D.,
interpreter.   missionary.
P. J. De Smet, S. J.,

Execution by the   Executed on the part of the Uncpapa band of Sioux,
Uncpapa band.   by the chiefs and headmen whose names are hereto

subscribed, they being thereunto duly authorized.

Co-kam-i-ya-ya, his x mark,
The Man that Goes in
the Middle. [SEAL.]
Ma-to-ca-wa-weksa, his x
mark, Bear Rib. [SEAL.]
Ta-to-ka-in-yan-ke, his
x mark, Running
Antelope. [SEAL.]
Kan-gi-wa-ki-ta, his x mark,
Looking Crow. [SEAL.]
A-ki-ci-ta-han-ska, his x
mark, Long Soldier. [SEAL.]
Wa-ku-te-ma-ni, his x mark,
The One who Shoots
Walking. [SEAL.]
Un-kca-ki-ka, his x mark,
The Magpie. [SEAL.]
Kan-gi-o-ta, his x mark,
Plenty Crow. [SEAL.]
He-ma-za, his x mark,

Iron Horn. [SEAL.]
Shun-ka-i-na-pin, his x mark,
Wolf Necklace. [SEAL.]
I-we-hi-yu, his x mark,
The Man who Bleeds
from the Mouth. [SEAL.]
He-ha-ka-pa, his x mark,
Elk Head. [SEAL.]
I-zu-za, his x mark, Grind
Stone. [SEAL.]
Shun-ka-wi-tko, his x mark,
Fool Dog. [SEAL.]
Ma-kpi-ya-po, his x mark,
Blue Cloud. [SEAL.]
Wa-mln-pi-lu-ta, his x
mark, Red Eagle. [SEAL.]
Ma-to-can-te, his x mark,
Bear's Heart. [SEAL.]
A-ki-ci-ta-i-tau-can, his x
mark, Chief Soldier. [SEAL.]

Attest:

Jas. C. O'Connor.
Nicholas Janis, interpreter.
Franc. La. Frambois[e],
interpreter.

P. J. De Smet, S. J.,
missionary among the
Indians.
Saml. D. Hinman, missionary.

By the Blackfeet
band

Executed on the part of the Blackfeet band of Sioux
by the chiefs and headmen whose names are hereto
subscribed, they being thereunto duly authorized.

Can-te-pe-ta, his x mark, Fire Heart. [SEAL.]

Wan-mdi-kte, his x mark, The One who Kills Eagle. [SEAL.]

Sho-ta, his x mark, Smoke. [SEAL.]

Wan-mdi-ma-ni, his x mark, Walking Eagle. [SEAL.]

Wa-shi-cun-ya-ta-pi, his x mark, Chief White Man. [SEAL.]

Kan-gi-i-yo-tan-ke, his x mark, Sitting Crow. [SEAL.]

Pe-ji, his x mark, The Grass. [SEAL.]

Kda-ma-ni, his x mark,
The One that Rattles as he Walks. [SEAL.]

Wah-han-ka-sa-pa, his x mark, Black Shield. [SEAL.]

Can-te-non-pa, his x mark, Two Hearts. [SEAL.]

Attest:

Jas. C. O'Connor.
Nicholas Janis, interpreter.
Franc. La Framboise,
interpreter.

P. J. de Smet, S. J., missionary
among the Indians.
Saml. D. Hinman, missionary.

Execution by the
Cutheads band.

Executed on the part of the Cutheads band of Sioux
by the chiefs, and headmen whose names are hereto

subscribed, they being thereunto duly authorized.

To-ka-in-yan-ka, his x mark,
The One who Goes Ahead Running.   [SEAL.]

Ta-tan-ka-wa-kin-yan, his x mark, Thunder Bull.   [SEAL.]

Sin-to-min-sa-pa, his x mark, All over Black.   [SEAL.]

Can-i-ca, his x mark, The One who Took the Stick.   [SEAL.]

Pa-tan-ka, his x mark, Big Head.   [SEAL.]

Attest:

Jas. C. O'Connor.
Nicholas Janis, interpreter.
Franc. La Frambois[e],
    interpreter.

P. J. De Smet, S. J.,
    missionary among the
    Indians.
Saml. D. Hinman, missionary.

By the Two Kettle band.

Executed on the part of the Two Kettle band of Sioux by the chiefs and headmen whose names are hereto subscribed, they being thereunto duly authorized.

Ma-wa-tan-ni-han-ska, his x mark, Long Mandan.   [SEAL.]

Can-kpe-du-ta, his x mark, Red War Club.   [SEAL.]

Can-ka-ga, his x mark, The Log.   [SEAL.]

Attest:

Jas. C. O'Connor.
Nicholas Janis, interpreter.
Franc. La Framboise,
    interpreter.
P. J. De Smet, S. J.,

missionary among the
    Indians.
Saml. D. Hinman, missionary
    to the Dakotas.

By the Sans Arch band.

Executed on the part of the Sans Arch band of Sioux by the chiefs and headmen whose names are hereto annexed, they being thereunto duly authorized.

He-na-pin-wa-ni-ca, his x mark,
The One that has Neither Horn.   [SEAL.]

Wa-inlu-pi-lu-ta, his x mark, Red Plume.   [SEAL.]

Ci-tan-gi, his x mark, Yellow Hawk.   [SEAL.]

He-na-pin-wa-ni-ca, his x mark, No Horn.   [SEAL.]

Attest:

Jas. C. O'Connor.
Nicholas Janis, interpreter.
Franc. La Frambois[e],
    interpreter.

P. J. De Smet, S. J.,
    missionary among the
    Indians.
Saml. D. Hinman, missionary.

Execution by the Santee band.

Executed on the part of the Santee band of Sioux by the chiefs and headmen whose names are hereto subscribed, they being thereunto duly authorized.

Wa-pah-shaw, his x mark, Red Ensign. [SEAL.]

Wah-koo-tay, his x mark, Shooter. [SEAL.]

Hoo-sha-sha, his x mark, Red Legs. [SEAL.]

O-wan-cha-du-ta, his x mark, Scarlet all over. [SEAL.]

Wau-mace-tan-ka, his x mark, Big Eagle. [SEAL.]

Cho-tan-ka-e-na-pe, his x mark, Flute-player. [SEAL.]

Ta-shun-ke-mo-za, his x mark, His Iron Dog. [SEAL.]

Attest:

Saml. D. Hinman, B. D.,
  missionary.
J. N. Chickering, Second
  lieutenant, Twenty-second
  Infantry, brevet captain,

U.S. Army.
P. J. De Smet, S. J.
Nicholas Janis, interpreter.
Franc. La Framboise,
  interpreter.

▼ ▼ ▼ ▼ ▼

APPENDIX B:
ACT OF FEBRUARY 28, 1877

Agreement with
Sioux Indians and
Northern Arapaho
and Cheyenne
Indians confirmed,
except, etc.

See note to 1876,
ch. 289, ante, p.
166.
109 U.S., 555; 121
U.S., 89.
Sioux not to be
removed.

Part of agreement
not confirmed.

Articles of
agreement.

Be it enacted by the Senate and House of Representatives of the United States of America in Congress assembled, That a certain agreement made by George W. Manypenny, Henry B. Whipple, Jared W. Daniels, Albert G. Boone, Henry C. Bulis, Newton Edmunds, and Augustine S. Gaylord, commissioners on the part of the United States, with the different bands of the Sioux Nation of Indians, and also the Northern Arapaho and Cheyenne Indians, be, and the same is hereby, ratified and confirmed: *Provided,* That nothing in this act shall be construed to authorize the removal of the Sioux Indians to the Indian Territory and the President of the United States is hereby directed to prohibit the removal of any portion of the Sioux Indians to the Indian Territory until the same shall be authorized by an act of Congress hereafter enacted, except article four, except also the following portion of article six: "And if said Indians shall remove to said Indian Territory as hereinbefore provided, the Government shall erect for each of the principal chiefs a good and comfortable dwelling-house" said article not having been agreed to by the Sioux Nation: said agreement is in words and figures following, namely: "Articles of agreement made pursuant to the provisions of an act of Congress entitled "An act making appropriations for the current and contingent expenses of the Indian Department, and for fulfilling treaty stipulations with various Indian tribes, for the year ending

June thirtieth, eighteen hundred and seventy-seven, and for other purposes," approved August 15, 1876, by and between George W. Manypenny, Henry B. Whipple, Jared W. Daniels, Albert G. Boone, Henry C. Bulis, Newton Edmunds, and Augustine S. Gaylord, commissioners on the part of the United States, and the different bands of the Sioux Nation of Indians, and also the Northern Arapahoes and Cheyennes, by their chiefs and headmen, whose names are hereto subscribed, they being duly authorized to act in the premises.

Boundaries of reduced reservation.

Vol. 2, p. 998.

"ARTICLE 1. The said parties hereby agree that the northern and western boundaries of the reservation defined by article 2 of the treaty between the United States and different tribes of Sioux Indians, concluded April 29, 1868, and proclaimed February 24, 1869, shall be as follows: The western boundaries shall commence at the intersection of the one hundred and third meridian of longitude with the northern boundary of the State of Nebraska: thence north along said meridian to its intersection with the South Fork of the Cheyenne River; thence down said stream to its junction with the North Fork; thence up the North Fork of said Cheyenne River to the said one hundred and third meridian; thence north along said meridian to the South Branch of Cannon Ball River or Cedar Creek; and the northern boundary of their said reservation shall follow the said South Branch to its intersection with the main Cannon Ball River, and thence down the said main Cannon Ball River to the Missouri River; and the said Indians do hereby relinquish and cede to the United States all the territory lying outside the said reservation, as herein modified and described, including all privileges of hunting; and article 16 of said treaty is hereby abrogated.

Roads, etc., through reservation.

"ARTICLE 2. The said Indians also agree and consent that wagon and other roads, not exceeding three in number, may be constructed and maintained, from convenient and accessible points on the Missouri River, through said reservation, to the country lying immediately west thereof, upon such routes as shall be designated by the President of the United States; and they also consent and agree to the free navigation of the Missouri River.

Annuities, where received.

"ARTICLE 3. The said Indians also agree that they will hereafter receive all annuities provided by the said treaty of 1868, and all subsistence and supplies which may be provided for them under the present or any future act of Congress, at such points and places on the said reservation, and in the vicinity of the Missouri River, as the President of the United States shall designate.

Vol. 2, p. 998.

"ARTICLE 4. [The Government of the United States and the said Indians, being mutually desirous that the latter shall be located in a country where they may eventually become self-supporting and acquire the arts of civilized life, it is therefore agreed that the said Indians shall select a delegation of five or more chiefs and principal men from each band, who shall, without delay, visit the Indian Territory under the guidance and protection of suitable persons, to be appointed for that purpose by the Department of the Interior, with a view to selecting therein a permanent home for the said Indians. If such delegation shall make a selection which shall be satisfactory to themselves, the people whom they represent, and to the United States, then the said Indians agree that they will remove to the country so selected within one year from this date. And the said Indians do further agree in all things to submit themselves to such beneficent plans as the Government may provide for them in the selection of a country suitable for a permanent home, where they may live like white men.]

Delegation to select home in Indian Territory Article 4 Lot confirmed. [See act above.]

Removal within one year.

"ARTICLE 5. In consideration of the foregoing cession of territory and rights, and upon full compliance with each and every obligation assumed by the said Indians, the United States does agree to provide all necessary aid to assist the said Indians in the work of civilization: to furnish to them schools and instruction in mechanical and agricultural arts, as provided for by the treaty of 1868. Also to provide the said Indians with subsistence consisting of a ration for each individual of a pound and a half of beef, (or in lieu thereof, one half pound of bacon.) one-half pound of flour, and one-half pound of corn: and for every one hundred rations, four pounds of coffee, eight pounds of sugar, and three pounds of beans, or in lieu of said articles the equivalent thereof, in the discretion of the Commissioner of Indian Affairs. Such rations, or so much thereof as may be necessary, shall be continued until the Indians are able to support themselves. Rations shall, in all cases, be issued to the head of each separate

Assistance, schools, rations, purchase of surplus, employment.

Sioux rations.

How issued.

family; and whenever schools shall have been provided by the Government for said Indians, no rations shall be issued for children between the ages of six and fourteen years (the sick and infirm excepted) unless such children shall regularly attend school. Whenever the said Indians shall be located upon lands which are suitable for cultivation, rations shall be issued only to the persons and families of those persons who labor, (the aged, sick, and infirm excepted:) and as an incentive to industrious habits the Commissioner of Indian Affairs may provide that such persons be furnished in payment for their labor such other necessary articles as are requisite for civilized life. The Government will aid said Indians as far as possible in finding a market for their surplus productions, and in finding employment, and will purchase such surplus, as far as may be required, for supplying food to those Indians, parties to this agreement, who are unable to sustain themselves; and will also employ Indians, so far as practicable, in the performance of Government work upon their reservation.

Government will purchase surplus production.

"ARTICLE 6. Whenever the head of a family shall, in good faith, select an allotment of said land upon such reservation and engage in the cultivation therof, the Government shall, with his aid, erect a comfortable house on such allotment; [and if said Indians shall remove to said Indian Territory as hereinbefore provided, the Government shall erect for each of the principal chiefs a good and comfortable dwelling-house.]

Erection of houses on allotments.

So much of articles as is embraced in the brackets is not confirmed. [See act above.]

"ARTICLE 7. To improve the morals and industrious habits of said Indians, it is agreed that the agent, trader, farmer, carpenter, blacksmith, and other artisans employed or permitted to reside within the reservation belonging to the Indians, parties to this agreement, shall be lawfully married and living with their respective families on the reservation; and no person other than an Indian of full blood, whose fitness, morally or otherwise, is not, in the opinion of the Commissioner of Indian Affairs, conducive to the welfare of said Indians, shall receive any benefit from this agreement or former treaties, and may be expelled from the reservation.

Artisans and other employees to be married, etc.

Unfit persons to receive no benefits.

"ARTICLE 8. The provisions of the said treaty of 1868, except as herein modified, shall continue in full force, and, with the provisions of this agreement, shall apply to any country which may hereafter be occu-

Vol. 2, p. 998. In force.

pied by the said Indians as a home; and Congress shall, by appropriate legislation, secure to them an orderly

Indians subject to laws of United States.

government; they shall be subject to the laws of the United States, and each individual shall be protected in his rights of property, person, and life.

Indians pledged to this agreement.

"ARTICLE 9. The Indians, parties to this agreement, do hereby solemnly pledge themselves, individually and collectively, to observe each and all of the stipulations herein contained, to select allotments of land as soon as possible after their removal to their permanent home, and to use their best efforts to learn to cultivate the same. And they do solemnly pledge themselves that they will at all times maintain peace with the citizens and Government of the United States; that they will observe the laws thereof and loyally endeavor to fulfill all the obligations assumed by them under the treaty of 1868 and the present agreement, and to this end will, whenever requested by the Presi-

Police force.

dent of the United States, select so many suitable men from each band to co-operate with him in maintaining order and peace on the reservation as the President may deem necessary, who shall receive such compensation for their services as Congress may provide.

Annual census to be taken in December.

"ARTICLE 10. In order that the Government may faithfully fulfill the stipulations contained in this agreement, it is mutually agreed that a census of all Indians affected hereby shall be taken in the month of December of each year, and the names of each head of family and adult person registered; said census to be taken in such manner as the Commissioner of Indian Affairs may provide.

Term "reservation."

"ARTICLE 11. It is understood that the term reservation herein contained shall be held to apply to any country which shall be selected under the authority of the United States as the future home of said Indians.

Agreement subject to approval.

"This agreement shall not be binding upon either party until it shall have received the approval of the President and Congress of the United States.

Signatures.

"Dated and signed at Red Cloud agency, Nebraska, September 26, 1876.

"GEORGE W. MANYPENNY. [SEAL.]

"HENRY B. WHIPPLE.   [SEAL.]

"J. W. DANIELS.   [SEAL.]

"ALBERT G. BOONE.   [SEAL.]

"H. C. BULIS.   [SEAL.]

"NEWTON EDMUNDS.   [SEAL.]
"A. S. GAYLORD.   [SEAL.]

Attest:
    "CHARLES M. HENDLEY,
        "*Secretary.*

[Here follows the signature of Marpuja-luta, and others of the Oglala Sioux, Arapaho, and Cheyenne.]

"Dated and signed at Spotted Tail agency, Nebraska, September 23, 1876.

[Here follows the signature of Sinta-gleska, and others of the Brule Sioux.]

Consent of Sioux at Cheyenne River.

"The foregoing articles of agreement having been fully explained to us in open council, we, the chiefs and headmen of the various bands of Sioux Indians, receiving rations and annuities at the Cheyenne River agency, in the Territory of Dakota, do hereby consent and agree to all the stipulations therein contained, with the exception of so much of article 4 of said agreement as relates to our visit and removal to the Indian Territory; in all other respects the said article remaining in full force and effect.

"Witness our hands and seals at Cheyenne River agency, Territory of Dakota, this 16th day of October, A. D. 1876.

[Here follows the signature of Kangi-wiyaka, and others.]

Consent of Sioux at Standing Rock

"The foregoing articles of agreement having been fully explained to us in open council, we, the undersigned chiefs and headmen of the various bands of Sioux Indians receiving rations and annuities at the Standing Rock agency, in the Territory of Dakota, do hereby consent and agree to all the stipulations therein contained, with the exception of so much of article four of said agreement as relates to our visit and removal to the Indian Territory: in all other respects the said article remaining in full force and effect.

"Witness our hands and seals at Standing Rock agency, Territory of Dakota, this 11th day of October, A. D. 1876.

[Here follows the signature of Mato-nonpa, and others.]

Consent of Sioux at Crow Creek.

"The foregoing articles of agreement having been fully explained to us in open council, we, the undersigned chiefs and headmen of the Sioux Indians, receiving rations and annuities at Crow Creek agency, in the Territory of Dakota, do hereby consent and agree to all the stipulations therein contained, with the exception of so much of article 4 of said agreement as relates to our visit and removal to the Indian Territory; in all other respects the said article remaining in full force and effect.

"Witness our hands and seals at Crow Creek agency, Territory of Dakota, this 21st day of October, A. D. 1876.

[Here follows the signature of Wanigi-ska, and others.]

Consent of Sioux at Lower Brule.

"The foregoing articles of agreement having been fully explained to us in open council, we, the undersigned chiefs and headmen of the Sioux Indians, receiving rations and annuities at Lower Brule agency, in the Territory of Dakota, do hereby consent and agree to all the stipulations therein contained, with the exception of so much of article 4 of said agreement as relates to our visit and removal to the Indian Territory: in all other respects the said article remaining in full force and effect.

Witness our hands and seals at Lower Brule agency, Territory of Dakota, this 24th day of October, A. D. 1876.

[Here follows signature of Maza-oyate, and others.]

Consent of Sioux at Santee Reservation.

"The foregoing articles of agreement having been fully explained to us in open council, we, the undersigned chiefs and headmen of the Sioux Indians, receiving rations and annuities at the Santee reservation, in Knox County, in the State of Nebraska, do hereby consent and agree to all the stipulations therein contained, saving, reserving, and excepting all our rights, both collective and individual, in and to the said Santee reservation, in said Knox County and State of Nebraska, upon which we, the undersigned, and our people are now residing.

"Witness our hands and seals at Santee agency, county of Knox, State of Nebraska, this 27th day of October, A. D. 1876.

[Here follows signature of Joseph Wabashaw, and others.]

Approved, February 28, 1877.

Note.—See report of Sioux Commission, in Annual Report for 1876, page 330. See Senate Executive Document No. 9, Forth-fourth Congress, second session. See also relinquishment of hunting privileges by Sioux, Annual Report, 1875, page 179.

▼ ▼ ▼ ▼ ▼

NOTE ON SOURCES

THE HISTORIES OF THE SIOUX Indians, of white attitudes and government policy towards Indian tribes, and of the military
confrontations between the plains tribes and the U.S. army have
all given rise to enormous literatures. What follows below is not
a comprehensive bibliography of every source that I scoured in the
composition of this book, but rather a guide to those sources on
which I particularly relied and which might prove especially useful to a reader interested in pursuing additional research.

WORKS OF GENERAL INTEREST

The history of the Sioux Indians, of course, is part of the larger
story of the Indian experience in America. For general background about the relationship between Indian tribes and the European settlers generally, I found especially informative: Angie
Debo, *A History of the Indians of the United States*, Norman: University of Oklahoma Press, 1977; Peter Farb, *Man's Rise to Civilization:
The Cultural Ascent of the Indians of North America*, New York: Dut-
ton, 1978; Alvin M. Josephy, Jr., *The Indian Heritage of America*,
New York: Alfred A. Knopf, 1970; Ruth M. Underhill, *Red Man's
America: A History of Indians in the United States*, Chicago: Univer-
sity of Chicago Press, 1971; Wilcomb E. Washburn, *The Indian in
America*, New York: Harper & Row, 1975.

On the subject of American Indian policy, white attitudes towards Native Americans, and the interplay between those attitudes and government policy, I relied particularly on: Robert F.
Berkhofer, *The White Man's Indian: Images of the American Indian from*

Columbus to the Present, New York: Vintage Books, 1978; Brian W. Dippie, *The Vanishing American: White Attitudes and U.S. Indian Policy,* Middleton, CT: Wesleyan University Press, 1982; and Bernard W. Sheehan, *Seeds of Extinction: Jeffersonian Philanthropy and the American Indian,* Chapel Hill: University of North Carolina Press, 1973. Also of significant interest are: Richard Drinnon, *Facing West: The Metaphysics of Indian-Hating and Empire Building,* Minneapolis: University of Minnesota Press, 1980; and Roy Harvey Pearce, *The Savages of America: A Study of the Indian and the Idea of Civilization,* Baltimore: Johns Hopkins Press, 1965.

The best general survey of U.S. Indian policy, in my view, is Francis Paul Prucha, *The Great Father: The United States Government and the American Indian,* Lincoln: University of Nebraska Press, 1984. Another standard survey is Lyman S. Tyler, *A History of Indian Policy,* Washington, D.C.: U.S. Government Printing Office, 1973. For a good work on the legal and practical ramifications of government policy, see Wilcomb E. Washburn, *Red Man's Land/ White Man's Law: A Study of the Past and Present Status of the American Indian,* New York: Charles Scribner's Sons, 1971. Also, for excellent short biographies of the Commissioners of Indian Affairs, see Robert M. Kvasnicka and Herman J. Viola, (Eds.), *The Commissioners of Indian Affairs, 1824–1977,* Lincoln: University of Nebraska Press, 1979.

Of the numerous sympathetic and deeply moving general accounts of U.S. treaty breaking, military conquest, and tribal dispossession, I favor Ralph K. Andrist, *The Long Death: The Last Days of the Plains Indians,* New York: MacMillan, 1964. Better known and also noteworthy is Dee Brown, *Bury My Heart at Wounded Knee,* New York: Holt, Rinehart and Winston, 1970. A less passionate yet extremely informative account of political and military confrontation along the frontier is: Robert M. Utley, *The Indian Frontier of the American West 1846–1890,* Albuquerque: University of New Mexico Press, 1984.

CHAPTERS 1–6: 1775–1890

My history of the relationship between the Sioux and the United States in the eighteenth and nineteenth centuries is derived in large part from primary source material. Particularly important are The Annual Reports of the Commissioner of Indian Affairs. These reports reveal the policies advanced and pursued by Federal officials and contain invaluable accounts by the bureau agents in Sioux country informing Washington about the progress of and problems with government programs at the Sioux agencies. The reports also contain useful statistical data about the Sioux and, in some years, transcripts of crucial negotiations with the Sioux. The annual report for 1875, for example, includes a transcript of the Allison Commission's negotiations in 1875 for a sale or lease of the Black Hills.

The Annual Reports of the Secretary of War contain voluminous letters and recommendations from the military field officers in Sioux country. Taken together, the annual reports of the Commissioner of Indian Affairs and of the Secretary of War create an indispensable record of the divisions in U.S. policy and the history of the government's relationship with the Sioux.

Because of my special focus on the legal relationship between the Sioux and the United States, I paid particularly close attention to the treaty conferences between the Sioux and the United States and to the texts of the treaties and agreements between them. A definitive version of all treaties and agreements between the Sioux and the United States, as well as the 1877 act expropriating the Black Hills, can be found in Charles J. Kappler (Comp. and Ed.), *Indian Affairs, Laws and Treaties.* For the most important documents relating to the 1868 treaty, see *Papers Relating to Talks and Councils Held with the Indians in Dakota and Montana Territories in the Years 1866–1869,* Washington, D.C.: U.S. Government Printing Office, 1910. A transcript of the negotiations conducted by the Manypenny Commission are collected in Senate Executive Document No. 9, 44th Congress, 2nd Session. A transcript of the councils relating to the Sioux Agreement of 1889 appears in Senate Executive Document No. 51, 51st Congress, 1st Session.

A crucial primary source for understanding Sioux perspectives on their treaties with the United States, and on the taking of the Black Hills in particular, is the testimony of Sioux participants in the Manypenny agreement that Ralph Case collected in 1923. This testimony became part of the Court of Claims' record in the Black Hills claim and is now housed in Record Group 75 at the National Archives in Washington, D.C.

The journals, autobiographies, and other writings of explorers, settlers, military officers, and Indians also provide much valuable information. Francis Parkman's *The Oregon Trail* (New York: New American Library, 1956) is essential reading. Also important is George Catlin's travelogue, *North American Indians* (Philadelphia: Leary, Stuart and Company, 1913).

Several participants in the Black Hills exploration and gold rush published works informative either for the facts they reveal or the attitudes they betray. William Ludlow, the chief engineer of Custer's 1874 expedition into the Hills published *Report of a Reconnaissance of the Black Hills of Dakota 1874* (Washington, 1875). Similarly, Colonel Richard I. Dodge, who led the military escort for the 1875 Jenney expedition into the Hills, published *The Black Hills: A Minute Description of the Routes, Scenery, Soil, Climate, Timber, Gold, Geology, Zoology, Etc.* (New York: James Miller, 1876). A first-hand account of illegal Black Hills mining appears in Annie Tallent, *The Black Hills or the Last Hunting Grounds of the Dakotahs*, St. Louis: Nixon-Jones, 1899.

Several eastern-educated Sioux wrote reminiscences about the end of the buffalo hunting days. Charles Eastman, the Santee Sioux doctor who became the agency physician at Pine Ridge in the late 1880s, wrote several books about traditional Sioux values and about his own life as perhaps the best educated member of the tribe. I found most interesting *From the Deep Woods to Civilization, Chapters in the Autobiography of an Indian* (Boston: Little, Brown, 1916) and *The Soul of an Indian* (Boston: Houghton, 1911). Two books by Carlyle graduate Luther Standing Bear also provide insight into traditional Sioux life and the experience of Sioux Indians coping with forced assimilation into white society. See *Land of Spotted Eagle* (Boston: Houghton Mifflin, 1932) and *My People the Sioux* (Boston: Houghton Mifflin, 1932).

By contrast, *Black Elk Speaks*, the astonishingly poetic memoir of the Lakota holy man Black Elk as recorded by John G. Niehardt (New York: William Morrow, 1932), presents the recollections and teachings of the Sioux leader who, though a convert to Christianity, remained committed to his enduring vision of the old Sioux way. Additional teachings of Black Elk are collected in *The Sixth Grandfather*, edited by Raymond J. DeMallie, Lincoln: University of Nebraska Press, 1984.

In addition to these primary sources, several comprehensive secondary works about the Sioux are indispensable to understanding the tribe's eighteenth and nineteenth century history. The pioneering history of the Sioux is Duone Robinson, *A History of the Dakota or Sioux Indians*, South Dakota Historical Collections, vol. 2. Pierre, SD, 1904. Although now dated, Robinson's work contains many interesting details not found elsewhere. The standard history of the Sioux is George Hyde's excessively cynical, but very informative trilogy: *Red Cloud's Folk: A History of the Oglala Sioux Indians*, Norman: University of Oklahoma Press, 1937; 2nd ed., 1957; *A Sioux Chronicle*, Norman: University of Oklahoma Press, 1956; *Spotted Tail's Folk: A History of the Brule Sioux*, Norman: University of Oklahoma Press, 1961.

These works recount in detail all of the major episodes in the Sioux tribe's relations with the United States, for example, the 1851 Fort Laramie Treaty Conference, the Grattan fight, the abortive peace treaties of 1865–66, Red Cloud's war, the 1868 Treaty, Custer's Black Hills exploration, and the Sioux war of 1876. They also describe internal divisions within the tribe, the history of various Sioux agencies, and the vagaries of government Indian policy as played out in Sioux country.

These incidents are also well-treated in a number of biographies of important Sioux leaders and American military officers. James C. Olson, *Red Cloud and the Sioux Problem*, Lincoln: University of Nebraska Press, 1965, is an excellent guide to U.S. policy towards the Sioux in the mid to late 1800s and to the response of a leading Sioux chief to white encroachment on his people's land. I found a wealth of fascinating anecdotal material in several books on Crazy Horse, Custer, Sherman, and Sitting Bull. Of special note are Stephen E. Ambrose, *Crazy Horse and Custer: The Parallel Lives of Two American Warriors*, Garden City, NY, 1975; Robert G. Athearn, *William Tecumseh Sherman and the Settlement of the West*, Norman: University of Oklahoma Press, 1956; Evan S. Connell, *Son of the Morning Star*, San Francisco: North Point Press, 1984; Mari Sandoz, *Crazy Horse: The Strange Man of the Oglalas*, New York: Alfred E. Knopf, 1942; Edgar I. Stewart, *Custer Luck*, Norman: University of Oklahoma Press, 1955; Stanley Vestal, *Sitting Bull: Champion of the Sioux*, Boston: Houghton Mifflin, 1932.

Many sources informed my interpretation of the Indian reform movement. Of the works specializing in this subject, I relied most heavily on: Henry E. Fritz, *The Movement for Indian Assimilation, 1860–1890*, Philadelphia: University of Pennsylvania Press, 1963; William T. Hagan, *Indian Police and Judges: Experiments in Acculturation and Control*, New Haven: Yale University Press, 1966; Robert W. Mardock, *The Reformers and the American Indian*, Columbia: University of Missouri Press, 1971; and D. S. Otis, *The Dawes Act and the Allotment of Indian Lands*, Norman: University of Oklahoma Press, 1973. In seeking to understand the reformers, however, there is no substitute for their own writings. One good collection is: Francis Paul Prucha, (Ed.), *Americanizing the American Indians: Writings by the "Friends of the Indian," 1880–1890*, Cambridge: Harvard University Press, 1973. Helen Hunt Jackson's influential polemic *A Century of Dishonor* (1881, reprint ed., Minneapolis: Ross & Haines, 1964) also merits attention.

My treatment of the Sioux life between the taking of the Black Hills in 1877 and the Wounded Knee massacre of 1890 draws heavily on Robert M. Utley's excellent *The Last Days of the Sioux Nation* (New Haven: Yale University Press, 1963). Other important sources for Sioux history leading up to the Ghost Dance craze are James Mooney, *The Ghost-Dance Religion and the Sioux Outbreak of 1890*, Smithsonian Institution, Bureau of American Ethnology, Annual Report 14 pt. 2, Washington, D.C., 1896; and Elaine Goodale Eastman, "The Ghost Dance War and Wounded Knee Massacre of 1890–91," *Nebraska History* 26 (1945), pp. 26–42. In evaluating government policy toward the Sioux after 1877, I also used Helen H. Tanner, *A Review of Federal Government Dealings with the Sioux*—an unpublished expert witness report prepared for use in the Sioux claims against the United States.

As my guide to Sioux society and religion, I relied mainly on Joseph Epes Brown (Recorder and Ed.), *The Sacred Pipe: Black Elk's Account of the Seven Rites of the Oglala Sioux*, Norman: University of Oklahoma Press, 1963; Royal B. Hassrick, *The Sioux: Life and Customs of a Warrior Society*, Norman: University of Oklahoma Press, 1964; William K. Powers, *Oglala Religion*, Lincoln: University of Nebraska Press, 1977; and three books by James R. Walker—*Lakota Belief and Ritual*, edited by Raymond J. DeMallie and Elaine A. Jahner, Lincoln: University of Nebraska Press, 1980; *Lakota Society*, edited by Raymond J. DeMallie, Lincoln: University of Nebraska Press, 1982; *Lakota Myth*, edited by Elaine A. Jahner, Lincoln: University of Nebraska Press, 1983.

For information regarding the founding and early history of the Dakota Territory, I relied on two standard works. Herbert S. Schell, *A History of South Dakota*, Lincoln: University of Nebraska Press, 1961; and Howard R. Lamar, *Dakota Territory 1861–1889: A Study of Frontier Politics*, New Haven: Yale University Press, 1956. For information about the Black Hills gold rush, I also used Watson Parker, *Gold in the Black Hills*, Norman: University of Oklahoma Press, 1966. And I also referred to Ian Frazier's *Great Plains* (New York: Farrar, Straus, & Giroux, 1989) which includes many interesting anecdotes from Sioux history.

CHAPTERS 7–9: 1890–1956

Most of my information about the early history of the Black Hills claim—descriptions of tribal gatherings, activities of various claims organizations, letters to government officials and their replies, contacts with attorneys—comes from Record Group 75 at the National Archives in Washington, D.C. Record Group 75 also contains a wealth of material about disputes between Progressive and Non-progressive Sioux over control of the Black Hills claim

and other reservations matters. In addition, the Eli S. Ricker manuscript collection at the Nebraska State Historical Society contains handwritten minutes of a 1903 meeting between Sioux leaders and Congressman E. W. Martin to discuss the Black Hills
claim.

Ralph Case's personal papers, located at the Archives of the I.
D. Weeks library at the University of South Dakota in Vermillion,
South Dakota, contain Case's voluminous correspondence with
the Sioux as well as various congressmen, government officials,
and other lawyers. His papers also include many important legal
documents related to his representation of the tribe. All the legal
papers that Case submitted on behalf of the Sioux—both in the
Court of Claims and in the Indian Claims Commission—can be
found in Record Group 75 of the National Archives.

In addition to the histories of U.S. Indian policy to which I made
reference earlier, I used numerous studies of assimilation policy in
the early twentieth century and of the origins and implementation
of the Indian New Deal. On the subject of assimilation policy, I
found of particular interest: Fredrick E. Hoxie, "Beyond Savagery: The Campaign to Assimilate the American Indians, 1880–
1920," Ph.D. diss., Brandeis University, 1977; and Janet McDon-
nell, "Competency Commissions and Indian Land Policy,
1913–1920," *South Dakota History* 11 (Winter 1980). Of course, the
Meriam Report—Lewis Meriam et al., *The Problem of Indian Administration*, Baltimore: Johns Hopkins Press, 1928—contains a comprehensive critique of assimilation policy. Also informative on this
subject is the general survey of U.S. Indian policy during the
twentieth century: James S. Olson and Raymond Wilson, *Native
Americans in the Twentieth Century*, Urbana: University of Illinois
Press, 1984. And on the subject of the pan-Indian movements that
developed during the early twentieth century, the definitive work
is: Hazel W. Hertzberg, *The Search for an American Indian Identity:
Modern Pan-Indian Movements*. Syracuse, NY: Syracuse University
Press, 1971.

Several scholarly works describe and analyze the affect of assimilation policy and reservation life on the Sioux. Vitally important
are: Ethel Nurge (Ed.), *The Modern Sioux*, Lincoln: University of
Nebraska Press, 1970; Gordon MacGregor, *Warriors Without Weapons: A Study of the Society and Personality Development of the Pine Ridge
Sioux*, Chicago: University of Chicago Press, 1946; and Erik H.
Erikson, "Observations on Sioux Education," *Journal of Psychology*,
VII (1939), pp. 101–56. I also found extremely informative: Richmond L. Clow, "The Rosebud Sioux: The Federal Government

and the Reservation Years, 1878–1940," Ph.D. diss., University of New Mexico, 1977; Fredrick E. Hoxie, "From Prison to Homeland: The Cheyenne River Indian Reservation before World War I," *South Dakota History* 10 (Winter 1979); Skudder Mekeel, *The Economy of a Modern Teton-Dakota Community*, "Yale Publications in Anthropology," No. 6. New Haven: Yale University Press, 1936 and "A Short History of the Teton-Dakota," *North Dakota Historical Quarterly*, X (1943), pp. 137–205; and John Useem, Gordon MacGregor, and Ruth Useem, "Wartime Employment and Cultural Adjustments of the Rosebud Sioux," *Applied Anthropology*, II (1943), pp. 1–9.

Vivid descriptions of conditions in Sioux country also appear in Thomas E. Mails, *Fools Crow*, Garden City, NY: Doubleday, 1979; and the government's 1929 *Survey of Conditions of the Indians of the United States. Hearings Before a Subcommittee of the United States Senate . . . South Dakota*, part 7. Also, the Sioux experience with the Oahe Dam project is well described in Michael I. Lawson, *Damned Indians: The Pick-Sloan Plan and the Missouri River Sioux, 1944–80*, Norman: University of Oklahoma Press, 1982.

In evaluating the origins and impact of the Indian New Deal, I paid especially close attention to: Harold E. Fey and D'Arcy McNickle, *Indians and Other Americans: Two Ways of Life Meet*, New York: Harper & Row, 1970; D'Arcy McNickle, *Native American Tribalism: Indian Survivals and Renewals*, New York: Oxford University Press, 1973; Kenneth Philp (Ed.), *Indian Self-Rule: First-Hand Accounts of Indian-White Relations from Roosevelt to Reagan*, Salt Lake City: Howe Brothers, 1986; Graham D. Taylor, *The New Deal and American Indian Tribalism: The Administration of the Indian Reorganization Act, 1934–1945*, Lincoln: University of Nebraska Press, 1980; and Wilcomb E. Washburn, "A Fifty-Year Perspective on the Indian Reorganization Act," *American Anthropologist* 86 (June 1984).

Several scholars have written specifically about the Indian Claims Commission Act of 1946. Although I did not find these studies especially insightful, a few are worth nothing: Robert W. Barker, "The Indian Claims Commission—the Conscience of the Nation in Its Dealings with the Original Americans," *Federal Bar Journal* 20 (Summer 1960); Sandra C. Danforth, "Repaying Historical Debts: The Indian Claims Commission," *North Dakota Law Review* 49 (Winter 1973); Nancy O. Lurie, "The Indian Claims Commission," *Annals of the American Academy of Political and Social Science* 436 (March 1978); John T. Vance, "The Congressional Mandate and the Indian Claims Commission," *North Dakota Law Review* 45 (Spring 1969).

My discussion of government policy, Sioux life and politics, Ralph Case, and the Black Hills litigation is shaped in significant part by personal interviews that I conducted over the last nine years. Reginald Cedarface (a longtime member of the Black Hills Sioux Nation Council), Alex Chasing Hawk (a now-deceased leader on the Cheyenne River Reservation), Wayne Ducheneaux (a former chairman of the Cheyenne River Sioux Tribe), Leo Vacu (a Pine Ridge businessman and one-time officer of the Oglala Sioux tribe), Cato Valandra (a former chairman of the Rosebud Sioux Tribe), Steven Feraca (a former Indian bureau expert on the Sioux), Helen Peterson, Richard Schifter, and Billy Werber (Ralph Case's nephew), all contributed significantly to my understanding of these matters.

Chapters 10–17: 1956–1991

My history of the Black Hills litigation after 1956 and of the legislative activity that accompanied that litigation is derived almost exclusively from unpublished sources. Principal among these are the voluminous court papers filed by the lawyers for both sides as well as the transcripts of various judicial proceedings relating to the Black Hills claim and the published record of congressional proceedings having to do with the claim. Through the Freedom of Information Act, I was able to gain access to a number of internal Justice Department documents relating to the claim. I also obtained access to congressional files relevant to the 1975 amendment to the Indian Claims Commission Act eliminating food, rations, and provisions as an allowable offset and to the 1978 *res judicata* waiver. In addition, I had access to the files of the Sioux lawyers in the claim. My account of the Supreme Court's deliberations in the Black Hills claim owes much to the assistance of Justice Harry A. Blackmun and his former law clerk William Murphy.

My account of the Black Hills claim, Sioux land return efforts, and modern Sioux politics also reflects numerous personal interviews. Discussions with Marvin Sonosky, Mario Gonzalez, Gerald Clifford, Ramon Roubideaux, and my father, Arthur Lazarus, Jr., all contributed enormously to my understanding. I also benefited from conversations with Charlotte Black Elk, Royal Bull Bear, Pete Catches, Reid Chambers, Richmond Clow, Raymond DeMallie, Franklin Ducheneaux, Robert Fast Horse, Kevin Gover, Mike Jackson, former Congressman Lloyd Meeds, David Miller, Oliver Red Cloud, John Steele, W. Richard West, and Dr. Jim Wilson.

U.S. Indian policy and changing attitudes among Indians over the last forty years have generated a great deal of polemical writing, but few scholarly assessments. In other words, the secondary sources must be handled with care—and a degree of skepticism.

Several sources, in addition to the histories of U.S. Indian policy already mentioned, are important for understanding the termination era. Essential are Felix S. Cohen, "The Erosion of Indian Rights, 1950–53: A Case Study in Bureaucracy," *Yale Law Journal* 62 (February 1953), pp. 348–90; and, from the opposite viewpoint, Arthur Watkins, "Termination of Federal Supervision: The Removal of Restriction Over Indian Property and Person," *Annals of the American Academy of Political and Social Science* 311 (May 1957), pp. 47–55. Excessively strident, but also informative is Richard Drinnon, *Keeper of the Concentration Camps: Dillon S. Myer and American Racism*, Berkeley: University of California Press, 1987. Two standard critiques of Indian policy during this period are William A. Brophy and Sophie E. Aberle (Comps.), *The Indian: America's Unfinished Business: Report of the Commission on the Rights, Liberties and Responsibilities of the American Indian*, Norman: University of Oklahoma, 1966; and Edgar S. Cahn (Ed.), *Our Brother's Keeper: The Indian in White America*, New York: World Publishing Co., 1969. On the application of termination policy in Sioux country, see Richmond L. Clow, "State Jurisdiction on Sioux Reservations: Indian and Non-Indian Responses, 1952–64," *South Dakota History* 11 (Summer 1981).

The writings of Indians themselves are the best sources on the rise of Indian activism. Of particular note for assessing Indian attitudes towards white society and the root causes of Indian activism are the books of Vine Deloria, Jr.: *Behind the Trail of Broken Treaties: An Indian Declaration of Independence*, New York: Delacorte Press, 1974; *Custer Died For Your Sins: An Indian Manifesto*, New York: Macmillan Company, 1969; *God is Red*, New York: Grosset and Dunlap, 1973. Also enlightening are two books written by Robert Burnette, his memoir, *The Tortured Americans*, Englewood Cliffs, NJ: Prentice-Hall Inc., 1971; and his analysis of the occupation of Wounded Knee (co-authored with John Koster), *The Road to Wounded Knee*, New York: Bantam Books, 1974. A useful anthology of Indian writings is: Shirley Hill Witt and Stan Steiner (Eds.), *The Way: An Anthology of American Indian Literature*, New York: Alfred A. Knopf, 1972.

No study of Native American militancy would be complete without reference to two publications of the Mohawk Nation press, *Akwesasne Notes: B.I.A., I'm Not Your Indian Any More*, Mohawk Nation via Roosevelttown, New York, 1973; and *Voices from Wounded Knee, 1973*, Mohawk Nation via Roosevelttown, New York, 1974. Also critical to assessing the Wounded Knee occupation is the testimony about Sioux history introduced in federal court at the "Sioux Treaty Hearing" held in connection with the Wounded Knee trials and collected in Roxanne Dunbar Ortiz (Ed.), *The Great Sioux Nation: Sitting in Judgment on America*, New York: American Indian Treaty Council, 1977; and *Lakota Woman* (New York: Grove Weidenfeld, 1990), the recent memoir of Mary Crow Dog (with Richard Erdoes) of a Sioux woman who joined AIM, married its medicine man, Leonard Crow Dog, and gave birth to a child while under siege at Wounded Knee.

Of the secondary sources dealing with the Northwest fish-ins, the occupation of Alcatraz, the rise of AIM, the Trail of Broken Treaties, Wounded Knee, and their aftermath, I found most comprehensive Alvin M. Josephy, Jr., *Now That the Buffalo's Gone: A Study of Today's American Indians*, New York: Alfred A. Knopf, 1982. A useful but tendentious history of AIM appears in Peter Matthiesen, *In the Spirit of Crazy Horse*, New York: The Viking Press, 1983. (Matthiessen's book also deals briefly and inaccurately with the Black Hills claim itself.)

In my own evaluation of the events leading up to and during the Wounded Knee occupation I also drew on articles published in *The New York Times*, *The Washington Post*, *The New Republic*, the *Harvard Law Record*, as well as material contained in congressional hearings held after the occupation ended and in Kenneth Lincoln with Al Logan Slagle, *The Good Red Road: Passages into Native America*, New York: Harper & Row, 1987.

Other works worthy of attention are: William T. Hagan, "Tribalism Rejuvenated: The Native American Since the Era of Termination," *Western Historical Quarterly* 12 (January 1981), pp. 6–16; Alvin M. Josephy, Jr. (Ed.), *Red Power: The American Indians' Fight for Freedom*, New York: American Heritage Press, 1971; and Stan Steiner, *The New Indians*, New York: Delta, 1968; and Jack A. Waddell and Michael O. Watson (Eds.), *The American Indian in Urban Society*, Boston: Little, Brown, and Company, 1971.

For my assessment of the legal status of Indian tribes I am indebted to Felix Cohen's *Handbook of Federal Indian Law* (Washington, D.C.: U.S. Government Printing Office, 1942; reprint ed., Albuquerque: University of New Mexico Press, 1976). Also important is Charles F. Wilkinson, *American Indians, Time, and the Law*, New Haven: Yale University, 1987. For an Indian view of the legal status of Indians, see Vine Deloria, Jr. and Clifford M. Lytle,

American Indians, American Justice, Austin: University of Texas Press, 1983.

My treatment of events since the Supreme Court's 1980 decision in the Black Hills claim—the repudiation of the monetary award, the Oglala land return lawsuits, the Yellow Thunder and Wind Cave occupations of the Black Hills, Sioux efforts to promote a Black Hills land return in the international community, the Bradley bill, the rifts between various Sioux leaders over the Black Hills issue, the Grey Eagle bill, and the continuing economic depression on the Sioux reservations—is derived from personal interviews (noted above), published judicial decisions, the minutes of various tribal council meetings, as well as magazine and newspaper articles (noted below).

Sioux reaction to the Supreme Court's 1980 decision in the Black Hills claim, the Oglala's land return lawsuits against the United States and the Homestake Mining Company, and the two separate Indian occupations of the Black Hills were all extensively covered in the *Sioux Falls Argus Leader.* Significant articles also appeared in *The New York Times, The Washington Post, The American Lawyer, The Nation, The Guardian,* and the *Rapid City Journal.* In addition, the views of a number of Sioux leaders on the Black Hills issue are collected in *A View from Sacred Mountain,* a publication of the Oglala Lakota Legal Rights Fund.

Essential to following the tribe's more recent legislative efforts to secure a Black Hills land return are the many articles that have appeared in the *Lakota Times. Rolling Stone* and *The National Law Journal* each published an extensive article on the Sioux land return movement (focusing on Gerald Clifford and Mario Gonzalez respectively), while *The Washington Post* and *The Los Angeles Times* have run elaborate profiles of Phil Stevens and his pledge to win a Black Hills land return. *The Washington Post* also has published periodic articles on social and economic problems on the Sioux reservation. Also, *The Philadelphia Inquirer* ran an insightful multi-part series describing life and politics on the Standing Rock Reservation.

INDEX

Abdnor, James, 332, 333, 336
Abourezk, James, 307, 330–33, 335, 347,
    348–49, 351, 357, 365
Act of 1877
  and Court of Claims [1942], 129–30, 137,
      158, 167–68, 174–75, 176, 274, 337
  and Court of Claims [1957], 233–34
  and Court of Claims [1974], 337, 338–40,
      343
  and Court of Claims [1979], 369, 372,
      374–75
  and education, 103
  and Indian Claims Commission [1954],
      191, 192, 197, 198–99, 200, 201, 205,
      208
  and Indian Claims Commission [1974],
      238, 239, 242–45, 250, 260–61,
      263–69, 272, 273–85, 287, 288–89,
      315, 319, 320–21, 324, 330, 336
  and the land return movement, 372,
      373–74, 404, 412, 418
  passage of the, 93
  and the public use argument, 372
  and Supreme Court [1980], 383, 384–85,
      386–88, 391, 392–93, 394–401
  See also Treaty of 1876
Activism
  and Alcatraz Island, 290–92, 312
  and the Bad Heart Bull murder,
      303–5
  and the BIA takeover, 300–301, 312
  and civil rights, 297–311
  and Indian Claims Commission [1974],
      312, 325–27
  and social programs, 295, 297, 302
  and sovereignty, 251, 253, 291–311,
      325–27
  and the Trail of Broken Treaties,
      299–301, 312

and the Treaty of 1868, 293–94, 307,
    308–9, 310, 325
and the United Nations, 307
and the Wilson administration, 301–11
and the Wounded Knee protest, 306–9
and the Yellow Thunder murder,
    298–99
See also AIM [American Indian
    Movement]
Agencies, Indian, 65–66, 68, 69, 97. See also
    name of specific agency/reservation
Agents, Indian, 57, 66, 114, 136, 138. See
    also name of specific agent
Agreement of 1889 [Crook Commission],
    110–13, 116, 122–23, 126, 157, 175,
    178, 188, 192, 369–70
AIM [American Indian Movement]
  and the Bad Heart Bull murder, 303–5
  and the BIA sit-in, 300–301, 312
  and the FBI, 328–29
  founding of, 291
  and Indian Claims Commission [1974],
      312
  internal dissension in, 329
  and the Mt. Rushmore protest, 293–94
  and the Second Sioux Amendment, 353
  and Sioux factionalism, 294–311
  and sovereignty, 295–311
  and the Trail of Broken Treaties,
      299–301
  and the Wilson administration, 301–11
  and the Wounded Knee protest, 306–9
  and the Yellow Thunder Camp protest,
      411–12
  and the Yellow Thunder murder,
      298–99
  See also Banks, Dennis; Means, Russell
Alaska Native Claims Settlement Act
    [1971], 314

471

▼ ▼ ▼ ▼ ▼

ABOUT THE AUTHOR

A graduate of Yale College and Yale Law School, Edward Lazarus
served as a law clerk to Judge William A. Norris on the United
States Court of Appeals for the Ninth Circuit and Justice Harry
A. Blackmun on the United States Supreme Court. He has taught
constitutional law at the Cardoza School of Law and received a
research fellowship from Yale Law School to complete this book.
Born and raised in Washington, D.C., he currently lives in Los
Angeles. This is his first book.